MARINE AND COASTAL LAW

MARINE
AND
COASTAL
LAW

Cases and Materials

Dennis W. Nixon

PRAEGER

Westport, Connecticut
London

Library of Congress Cataloging-in-Publication Data

Nixon, Dennis W.
      Marine and coastal law : cases and materials / Dennis W. Nixon.
         p.   cm.
      Includes index.
      ISBN 0–275–93763–1 (alk. paper)
      1. Coastal zone management—Law and legislation—United States—
   Cases.   2. Marine mineral resources—Law and legislation—United
   States—Cases.   3. Maritime law—United States—Cases.   I. Title.
   KF5627.A7N59   1994
   346.7304'6917—dc20
   [347.30646917]   93–30986

British Library Cataloguing in Publication Data is available.

Library of Congress Catalog Card Number: 93–30986
ISBN: 0–275–93763–1

First published in 1994

Praeger Publishers, 88 Post Road West, Westport, CT 06881
An imprint of Greenwood Publishing Group, Inc.

Printed in the United States of America

∞™

The paper used in this book complies with the
Permanent Paper Standard issued by the National
Information Standards Organization (Z39.48–1984).

10 9 8 7 6 5 4 3 2 1

To my parents,
Jack and Rita Nixon

CONTENTS

PREFACE

The study of marine and coastal law has grown enormously in the past twenty years. Increased coastal development, struggles over fishing stocks, and a deepening concern over our coastal environment has created a new specialty in the practice of law. That, in turn, has spawned an interest in studying the historical development of the law both for its own sake and for the ability to predict future directions.

After teaching the subjects of admiralty, fisheries, and coastal law for the past sixteen years, I have found that some clear patterns in the law have emerged; this book is an effort to explore those themes through the progressive development of case law. As an instructional tool, the book is designed to serve both the law school audience and the growing number of graduate marine affairs programs around the country. Earlier drafts of this text have been "tested" at the University of Rhode Island's Marine Affairs Program for the past several years, where graduate students have studied the law as part of an interdisciplinary program designed to prepare them for careers in coastal and ocean management. For those already involved in those fields,

either in governance or the practice of law, this text should provide a compact reference tool.

I make no claim that this is a comprehensive list of all the topics and cases that could be included in the title *Marine and Coastal Law*. Practitioners in each area are certainly aware of many more issues, statutes, and cases which could have been considered. However, the clarity of presentation would almost certainly have suffered—a fatal flaw in a text intended for instructional use.

I must also acknowledge two earlier works in the field which served as major contributions to the literature. Hildreth and Johnson's *Ocean and Coastal Law* (1983) was the first casebook that attempted to integrate issues of marine affairs and law. Kalo's more recent *Coastal and Ocean Law* (1990) builds on that earlier work but places a much greater emphasis on statutory and regulatory material. My approach differs from that of Kalo in that I have reverted to a pure casebook approach, with limited statutory material.

Because this is primarily an instructional text, cases have been edited for brevity and clarity, and only those citations considered significant remain. Unlike many more recent casebooks, however, my experience as a teacher has shown me that editing a large number of cases down to a few key paragraphs detracts from the learning process in the traditional "casebook experience." As a result, fewer opinions, but closer to their natural length, are included.

I would like to thank the fine group of research assistants who helped me with these materials: Pam Barrick Baker, Chris Beal, Sean Bercaw, Steve Williamson, and Jane Wright. Finally, the patience and skill of Susan Myette, whose untiring hands typed this manuscript, is gratefully acknowledged.

INTRODUCTION

One of the reasons law can be a confusing area of study is that there is a variety of sources which are always in the midst of creating and interpreting "the law." The United States Supreme Court makes the news when a new ruling is handed down; congressional debate on new laws is followed closely, particularly when the president has indicated interest in the issue. However, these two highly visible sources of law are the proverbial "tip of the iceberg" when discussing the broader structure responsible for creating, interpreting, and enforcing the law. Before the subject of marine law can be discussed in detail, it is important to understand how these sources of law operate.

What is "law"? A rough definition is a rule of conduct, adopted by a legislative body or court with the authority to do so, enforced by the appropriate governmental authority. It can be as simple as a no parking ordinance for the town wharf or as complex as the Oil Pollution Act of 1990 adopted by Congress. Although some critics of the legal system might argue that we have laws only to keep lawyers employed, there are a number of important functions to remember.

First, laws serve as a guide for what is "acceptable behavior" in our society. The fact that sanctions (like prison) await those who violate those standards is an incentive to help people make the right decision. Second, we turn to law to resolve disputes, both public (criminal) and private (civil). If a set of facts indicates that a rule of conduct has been violated, the appropriate sanction can be selected and applied.

The United States Constitution establishes the system of governance in our country and the methods for adopting and enforcing the law. The three branches of government (legislative, executive, judicial) all play an important role in the legal system. Congress, best known for passing new laws, also performs a less glamorous, but critical function: through the complex committee system, it uses its "oversight" authority to review the effectiveness of existing legislation. Hearings on specific issues are scheduled by committees of Congress either because of new developments in an area of law that merit attention or because a law has a so-called "sunset" provision and will expire unless it is specifically reauthorized by Congress. Issues of governance reserved for the individual states are considered in a similar manner by the state legislatures.

The executive branch of government is charged with enforcing the law. From the FBI to the IRS, the executive branch carries out the will of Congress as expressed in the United States Code. In marine law, we see the Coast Guard enforcing customs regulations, the National Marine Fisheries Service enforcing fisheries laws, and the Army Corps of Engineers regulating the dredging and filling of the shoreline. At the state level, coastal zone management agencies regulate the development of the shore and fisheries agencies regulate the harvest of fisheries found in state waters.

The judicial branch exists to balance the power of the other two sources of law. Courts make the final decision on whether the executive branch has gone too far in enforcing an ordinance or whether the legislative branch has exceeded its constitutional authority. At the federal level (and in most states), there are three layers in the judicial system. The first is the trial court, whose principal task is to "find the facts" and apply the law as interpreted by higher courts. The primary tool used by the trial court in determining the facts is the jury. Jurors are instructed as to the applicable law by the trial court judge, but only they can determine the veracity of witnesses and other critical issues of fact. The next level in the judicial system, the appeals court, does not reexamine the facts found by the jury; rather, it determines if the trial court judge correctly applied the law to the particular facts found by the jury. If the appeals court disagrees with the trial court's determination of the law, it reverses that decision. If more facts must be considered to apply the law

correctly, the appeals court will reverse and remand (hand back) the case to the trial court. The U.S. and the various state supreme courts have a similar appellate function. However, their principal function is to guide the uniformity of the law. Without a "supreme" court to settle an issue finally, different circuit courts within the same jurisdiction could reach different conclusions of law based upon the same set of facts. That lack of uniformity would destroy the predictability so critical in the legal system.

Our study will examine the interaction of those three sources of law, but will primarily focus on the judicial branch with a selection of cases which demonstrate the progressive development of the important concepts in marine and coastal law. Five areas of law will be studied in detail: the traditional law of the shore as it has developed in the United States, the contemporary law of coastal management, state and federal fisheries law, and selected issues in admiralty law, with a particular emphasis on vessel-source marine pollution.

Such a list is by no means comprehensive, but it represents my view of which areas are of the greatest interest and utility for a "first look" at the wide range of issues in the general category. Each area selected also has a strong legacy of case law.

Conceptually, we will move from the shore to the high seas, with a logical progression of issues. However, just as a small boat is constantly in motion at sea, so is the state of marine and coastal law. It is a body of law that subtly changes with the frequency of the tides—always evolving, moving forward in the continuing struggle to balance the interests of man and the oceans.

MARINE AND COASTAL LAW

Chapter 1

OWNERSHIP AND BOUNDARIES OF SUBMERGED LANDS

Martin v. Lessee of Waddell, 41 U.S. 367 (1842)

The questions before us arise upon an action to recover one hundred acres of land, covered with water, situated in the township of Perth Amboy, in the State of New Jersey. At the trial in the Circuit Court, the jury found a special verdict, setting forth, among other things, that the land claimed lies beneath the navigable water of the Raritan River and Bay, where the tide ebbs and flows. And it appears that the principal matter in dispute is the right to the oyster fishery in the public rivers and bays of East New Jersey.

The plaintiff makes title under the charters granted by Charles II to his brother the Duke of York, in 1664 and 1674, for the purpose of enabling him to plant a colony on this continent.

The boundaries in the two charters are the same, and they embrace the territory which now forms the state of New Jersey. The part of this territory, known as East New Jersey, afterward, by sundry deeds and conveyances, which it is not necessary to enumerate, was transferred to twenty-four persons, who were called the proprietors of East New Jersey; who by the terms of the grants were invested, within the portion of the territory conveyed to them, with all the rights of property and government which had been originally conferred on the Duke of York by the letters patent of the king. Some serious difficulties, however, took place in a short time between these proprietors and the British authorities; and after some negotiations upon the subject, they, in 1702, surrendered to the crown all the powers of government, retaining their rights of private property.

The defendant in error claims the land covered with water, mentioned in the declaration, by virtue of a survey made in 1834, under the authority of the proprietors, and duly recorded in the proper office. And, if they were authorized to make this grant, he is entitled to the premises as owner of the soil, and has an exclusive right to the fishery in question. The plaintiff in error also claims an exclusive right to take oysters in the same place; and derives his title under the law of the state of New Jersey, passed in 1824, and a supplement thereto, passed in the same year.

The point in dispute between the parties,

therefore, depends upon the construction and legal effect of the letters patent to the Duke of York, and of the deed of surrender subsequently made by the proprietors.

The letters patent to the duke included a very large territory, extending along the Atlantic coast from the River St. Croix to the Delaware Bay, and containing within it many navigable rivers, bays, and arms of the sea; and after granting the tract of country and islands therein described,

together with all the lands, islands, soils, rivers, harbours, mines, minerals, quarries, woods, marshes, waters, lakes, fishings, hawkings, huntings, and fowlings, and all other royalties, profits, commodities, and hereditaments to the said several islands, lands, and premises belonging and appertaining with their and every of their appurtenances, and all the estate, right, title, interest, benefit, and advantage, claim, and demand of the king, in the said land and premises;

the letters patent proceed to confer upon him, his heirs, deputies, agents, commissioners, and assigns the powers of government with a proviso that the statutes, ordinances, and proceedings, established by his authority should

not be contrary to, but as nearly as might be, agreeable to the laws, statutes, and government of the realm of England; saving also an appeal to the king, in all cases, from any judgment or sentence which might be given in the colony, and authorizing the duke, his heirs and assigns, to lead and transport out of any of the realms of the king to the country granted, all such and so many of his subjects or strangers not prohibited who would become the "loving subjects" of the king.

The right of the king to make this grant, with all of its prerogatives and powers of government, cannot at this day be questioned. In order to enable us to determine the nature and extent of the interest which it conveyed to the duke, it is proper to inquire into the character of the right claimed by the British crown in the country discovered by its subjects, on this continent; and the principles upon which it was parceled out and granted.

The English possessions in America were not claimed by right of conquest but by right of discovery. For according to the principles of international law, as then understood by the civilized powers of Europe, the Indian tribes in the New World were regarded as mere temporary occupants of the soil, and the absolute rights of property and dominion were held to belong to the European nation by which any particular portion of the country was first discovered. Whatever forbearance may have been sometimes practiced toward the unfortunate aborigines, either from humanity or policy, the territory they occupied was disposed of by the governments of Europe at their pleasure, as if it had been found without inhabitants. The grant to the Duke of York, therefore, was not of lands won by the sword; nor were the government or laws he was authorized to establish intended for a conquered people.

The country mentioned in the letters patent was held by the king in his public and regal character as the representative of the nation, and in trust for them. According to the theory of the British constitution all vacant lands are vested in the crown as representing the nation, and the exclusive power to grant them is admitted to reside in the crown, as a branch of the royal prerogative. It has been already shown that this principle was as fully recognized in America as in the island of Great Britain.

This being the principle upon which the charter in question was founded, by what rules ought it to be construed?

We do not propose to meddle with the point which was very much discussed at the bar, as to the power of the king since the Magna Carta to grant to a subject a portion of the soil covered by the navigable waters of the kingdom, so as to give him an immediate and exclusive right of fishery either for shellfish or floating fish within the limits of his grant. The question is not free from doubt. But from the opinions expressed by the justices of the court of King's Bench, the question must be regarded as settled in England against the right of the king since the

Magna Carta to make such a grant. The point does not, however, arise in this case unless it shall first be decided that in the grant to the Duke of York the king intended to sever the bottoms of the navigable waters from the prerogative powers of government conferred by the same charter; and to convert them into mere franchises in the hands of a subject, to be held and used as his private property. This subject has ceased to be a matter of much interest in the United States. For when the Revolution took place, the people of each state became themselves sovereign; and in that character hold the absolute right to all their navigable waters and the soils under them for their own common use, subject only to the rights since surrendered by the Constitution to the general government. A grant made by their authority must therefore manifestly be tried and determined by different principles from those which apply to grants of the British crown when the title is held by a single individual in trust for the whole nation.

Neither is it necessary to examine the many cases which have been cited in the argument on both sides, to show the degree of strictness with which grants of the king are to be construed. The decisions and authorities referred to apply more properly to a grant of some prerogative right to an individual to be held by him as a franchise, and which is intended to become private property in his hands. The dominion and property in navigable waters, and in the lands under them, being held by the king as a public trust, the grant to an individual of an exclusive fishery in any portion of it is so much taken from the common fund intrusted to his care for the common benefit. In such cases, whatever does not pass by the grant still remains in the crown for the benefit and advantage of the whole community. Grants of that description are therefore construed strictly— and it will not be presumed that he intended to part from any portion of the public domain, unless clear and especial words are used to denote it. But in the case before us, the rivers, bays,

and arms of the sea, and all prerogative rights within the limits of the charter, undoubtedly passed to the Duke of York, and were intended to pass, except those saved in the letters patent. The words used evidently show this intention; and there is no room, therefore, for the application of the rule above mentioned.

The questions upon this charter are: whether the dominion and propriety in the navigable waters, and in the soils under them, passed as a part of the prerogative rights annexed to the political powers conferred on the duke; and whether in his hands they were intended to be a trust for the common use of the new community about to be established, or private property to be parceled out and sold to individuals, for his own benefit. And in deciding a question like this, we must not look merely to the strict technical meaning of the words of the letters patent. The laws and institutions of England, the history of the times, the object of the charter, the contemporaneous construction given to it, and the usages under it, for the century and more which has since elapsed, are all entitled to consideration and weight. It is not a deed conveying private property to be interpreted by the rules applicable to cases of that description. It was an instrument upon which was to be founded the institutions of a great political community; and in that light it should be regarded and construed.

Taking this rule for our guide, we can entertain no doubt as to the true construction of these letters patent. The object in view appears upon the face of them. They were made for the purpose of enabling the Duke of York to establish a colony upon the newly discovered continent, to be governed, as nearly as circumstances would permit, according to the laws and usages of England; and in which the duke, his heirs, and assigns were to stand in the place of the king, and administer the government according to the principles of the British constitution. And the people who were to plant this colony, and to form the political body over which he was to rule, were subjects of Great Britain, accustomed to be governed according to its usages and laws.

It is said by Hale in his treatise *De Jure Maris*, when speaking of the navigable waters, and the sea on the coasts within the jurisdiction of the British crown, "that although the king is the owner of this great coast, and, as a consequent of his propriety, hath the primary right of fishing in the sea and creeks, and arms thereof, yet the common people of England have regularly a liberty of fishing in the sea, or creeks, or arms thereof, as a public common of piscary, and may not, without injury to their right, be restrained of it, unless in such places, creeks, or navigable rivers, where either the king or some particular subject hath gained a propriety exclusive of that common liberty."

The principle here stated by Hale, as to "the public common of piscary" belonging to the common people of England, is not questioned by any English writer upon that subject. The point upon which different opinions have been expressed is whether since the Magna Carta "either the king or any particular subject can gain a propriety exclusive of the common liberty." For, undoubtedly, rights of fishery, exclusive of the common liberty, are at this day held and enjoyed by private individuals under ancient grants. But the existence of a doubt as to the right of the king to make such a grant after the Magna Carta, would of itself show how fixed has been the policy of that government on this subject for the last six hundred years; and how carefully it has preserved this common right for the benefit of the public. And there is nothing in the charter before us indicating that a different and opposite line of policy was designed to be adopted in that colony. On the contrary, after enumerating in the clause herein before quoted, some of the prerogative rights annexed to the crown, but not all of them, general words are used, conveying "all the estate, right, title, interest, benefit, advantage, claim, and demand" of the king in the lands and premises before granted. The estate and rights of the king passed to the duke in the same condition in

which they had been held by the crown, and upon the same trusts. Whatever was held by the king as a prerogative right passed to the duke in the same character. And if the word "soils" be an appropriate word to pass lands covered with navigable water, as contended on the part of the defendant in error, it is associated in the letters patent with "other royalties," and conveyed as such. No words are used for the purpose of separating them from the royal rights, and converting them into private property, to be held and enjoyed by the duke, apart from and independent of the political character with which he was clothed by the same instrument. Upon a different construction, it would have been impossible for him to have complied with the conditions of the grant. For it was expressly enjoined upon him, as a duty in the government he was about to establish, to make it as near as might be agreeable in their new circumstances, to the laws and statutes of England; and how could this be done if, in the charter itself, this high prerogative trust was severed from the regal authority? If the shores, and rivers, and bays, and arms of the sea, and the land under them, instead of being held as a public trust for the benefit of the whole community, to be freely used by all for navigation and fishery, as well for shellfish as floating fish, had been converted by the charter itself into private property, to be parceled out and sold by the duke for his own individual emolument? There is nothing we think in the terms of the letters patent, or in the purposes for which it was granted, that would justify this construction. And in the judgment of the Court, the land under the navigable waters passed to the grantee as one of the royalties incident to the powers of government; and were to be held by him in the same manner, and for the same purposes that the navigable waters of England, and the soil under them, are held by the crown.

This opinion is confirmed by referring to similar grants for other tracts of country upon this continent, made about the same period of time. Various other charters for large territories on the Atlantic coast were granted by different monarchs of the Stuart dynasty to different persons, for the purposes of settlement and colonization, in which the powers of government were united with the grant of territory. Some of these charters very nearly resembled in every respect the one now in controversy; and none of them, it is believed, differed materially from it in the terms in which the bays, rivers, and arms of the sea, and the soil under them were conveyed to the grantees. Yet, in no one of these colonies has the soil under its navigable waters, and the rights of fishery for shellfish or floating fish, been severed by the letters patent from the powers of government. In all of them, from the time of the settlement to the present day, the previous habits and usages of the colonists have been respected, and they have been accustomed to enjoy in common the benefits and advantages of the navigable waters for the same purposes, and to the same extent, that they have been used and enjoyed for centuries in England. Indeed, it could not well have been otherwise; for the men who first formed the English settlements could not have been expected to encounter the many hardships that unavoidably attended their emigration to the New World, and to people the banks of its bays and rivers if the land under the water at their very doors was liable to immediate appropriation by another as private property; and the settler upon the fast land thereby excluded from its enjoyment, and unable to take a shellfish from its bottom, or fasten there a stake, or even bathe in its waters without becoming a trespasser upon the rights of another. The usage in New Jersey has, in this respect, from its original settlement conformed to the practice of the other chartered colonies. And it would require very plain language in these letters patent to persuade us that the public and common right of fishery in navigable waters, which has been so long and so carefully guarded in England, and which was preserved in every other colony founded on the Atlantic borders, was intended in this one instance to be taken away. But we

see nothing in the charter to require this conclusion.

The same principles upon which the Court decided upon the construction of the letters patent to the Duke of York apply with equal force to the surrender afterward made by the twenty-four proprietors. It appears by the special verdict that all the interests of the duke in East New Jersey, including the royalties and powers of government, were conveyed to these proprietors, as fully and amply and in the same condition as they had been granted to him; and they had the same dominion and propriety in the bays, and rivers, and arms of the sea, and the soil under them, and in the rights of fishery, that had belonged to him under the original charter. In their hands, therefore, as well as in those of the duke, this dominion and propriety was an incident to the regal authority, and was held by them as a prerogative right, associated with the powers of government. And being thus entitled, they, in 1702, surrendered and yielded up to Anne, queen of England, and to her heirs and successors, "all the powers and authorities in the said letters patent granted."

. . .

We give the words of the surrender as found by the special verdict, and they are broad enough to cover all the royal rights which belonged to the proprietors. They yield up "all the powers, authorities and privileges of and concerning the government of the province"; and the right in dispute was one of these authorities and privileges. No words are used for the purpose of withholding from the crown any of its ordinary and well-known prerogatives. The surrender, according to its evident object and meaning, restored them in the same plight and condition in which they originally came to the hands of the Duke of York. Whatever he held as a royal or prerogative right was restored, with the political power to which it was incident. And if the great right of dominion and ownership in the rivers, bays, and arms of the sea, and soils under them, were to have been severed from the sovereignty, and withheld from the crown; if the right of common fishery for the common people, stated by Hale in the passage before quoted, was intended to be withdrawn, the design to make this important change in this particular territory would have been clearly indicated by appropriate terms; and would not have been left for inference from ambiguous language.

The negotiations previous to the surrender have been referred to in order to influence the construction of the deed. But whatever propositions may have been made, or opinions expressed before the execution of that instrument, the deed itself must be regarded as the final agreement between the parties; and that deed, by its plain words, reestablished the authority of the crown, with all of its customary powers and privileges. And when the people of New Jersey took possession of the reins of government, and took into their own hands the powers of sovereignty, the prerogatives and regalities which before belonged either to the crown or the parliament became immediately and rightfully vested in the state.

This construction of the surrender is evidently the same with that which it received from all the parties interested at the time it was executed. For it appears by the history of New Jersey, as gathered from the acts, documents, and proceedings of the public authorities, that the crown and the provincial government established by its authority always afterward in this territory exercised the same prerogative powers that the king was accustomed to exercise in his English dominions. And, as concerns the particular dominion and the property now in question, the colonial government from time to time authorized the construction of bridges with abutments on the soil covered by navigable waters; established posts; authorized the erection of wharves; and, as early as 1719, passed a law for the preservation of the oyster fishery in its waters. The public usages, also, in relation to the fisheries, continued to be the same. And from 1702, when the surrender was made, until a very recent date,

the people of New Jersey have exercised and enjoyed the rights of fishery, for shellfish and floating fish, as a common and undoubted right, without opposition or remonstrance from the proprietors. The few unimportant grants made by them at different times running into the navigable waters, which were produced in the argument, do not appear to have been recognized as valid by the provincial or state authorities, nor to have been sanctioned by the Courts. And the right now claimed was not seriously asserted on their part before the case of *Arnold v. Mundy*, reported in 1 Halsted, 1; and which suit was not instituted until the year 1818; and, upon that occasion, the Supreme Court of the state held that the claim made by the proprietors was without foundation.

The effects of this decision by the State Court has been a good deal discussed at the bar. It is insisted by the plaintiffs in error that, as the matter in dispute is local in its character, and the controversy concerns only fixed property within the limits of New Jersey, the decision of her tribunals ought to settle the construction of the charter; and that the Courts of the United States are bound to follow it. It may, however, be doubted whether this case falls within the rule, in relation to the judgments of State Courts when expounding their own constitutions and laws.

The question here depends not upon the meaning of instruments framed by the people of New Jersey, or by their authority, but upon charters granted by the British crown, under which certain rights are claimed by the state, on the one hand, and by private individuals, on the other. And if this Court had been of opinion that, upon the face of these letters patent, the question was clearly against the state, and that the proprietors had been deprived of their just rights by the erroneous judgment of the State court, it would, perhaps, be difficult to maintain that this decision of itself bound the conscience of this Court. It is, however, unquestionably entitled to great weight. It confirms the construction uniformly placed on these charters and instruments, by the other public authorities; and in which the proprietors had so long acquiesced. Public acts and laws, both of the colonial and state governments, have been founded upon this interpretation; and extensive and valuable improvements made under it. In the case referred to, the sanction of the judicial authority of the state is given to it. And if the words of the letters patent had been far more doubtful than they are, this decision, made upon such a question, with deliberation and research, ought, in our judgment, to be regarded as conclusive.

Independently, however, of this decision of the Supreme Court of New Jersey, we are of opinion that the proprietors are not entitled to the rights in question; and the judgment of the Circuit Court must, therefore, be reversed.

Questions

1. According to the Supreme Court, how does the State of New Jersey's ownership of submerged lands differ from a citizen's right to own private property ashore?

2. What responsibility does the state have in managing its commonly held fishery resources?

3. What legal basis did the U.S. Supreme Court have for overruling the Circuit Court?

4. Why, after the American Revolution severed all legal ties, did our Supreme Court devote so much attention to English common law?

Shively v. Bowlby, 152 U.S. 1 (1894)

In the case at bar, the lands in controversy are below high water mark of the Columbia River where the tide ebbs and flows; and the plaintiff in error claims them by a deed from John M. Shively, who, while Oregon was a Territory, obtained from the United States a donation claim, bounded by the Columbia River, at the place in question.

The defendants in error claim title to the

lands in controversy by deeds executed in behalf of the State of Oregon, by a board of commissioners, pursuant to a statute of the State of 1872, as amended by a statute of 1874, which recited that the annual encroachments of the sea upon the land, washing away the shores and shoaling harbors, could be prevented only at great expense by occupying and placing improvements upon the tide and overflowed lands belonging to the State, and that it was desirable to offer facilities and encouragement to the owners of the soil abutting on such harbors to make such improvements; and therefore enacted that the owner of any land abutting or fronting upon, or bounded by the shore of any tide waters, should have the right to purchase the lands belonging to the State in front thereof; and that, if he should not do so within three years from the date of the act, they should be open to purchase by any other person who was a citizen and resident of Oregon, after giving notice and opportunity to the owner of the adjoining upland to purchase; and made provisions for securing to persons who had actually made improvements upon tide lands a priority of right so to purchase them.

Neither the plaintiff in error nor his grantor appears to have ever built a wharf or made any other improvement upon the lands in controversy, or to have applied to the State to purchase them. But the defendants in error, after their purchase from the State, built and maintained a wharf upon the part of these lands nearest the channel, which extended several hundred feet into the Columbia River, and at which ocean and river craft were wont to receive and discharge freight.

The theory and effect of these statutes were stated by the Supreme Court of the State, in this case, as follows: Upon the admission of the State into the Union, the tide lands became the property of the State, and subject to its jurisdiction and disposal. In pursuance of this power, the State provided for the sale and disposal of its tide lands by the act of 1872 and the amendments of 1874 and 1876. By virtue of these acts, the owner or owners of any land abutting or fronting upon or bounded by the shore of the Pacific Ocean, or of any bay, harbor, or inlet of the same, and rivers and their bays in which the tide ebbs and flows, within this State, were given the right to purchase all the tide lands belonging to the State, in front of the lands so owned, within a certain time and upon conditions prescribed; and providing further that in case such owner or owners did not apply for the purchase of such tide lands, or, having applied, failed to prosecute the same as provided by law, then that such tide lands shall be open to purchase by any other person who is a resident and citizen of the State of Oregon; but in consideration of the fact that prior to 1872, as it would seem, these lands had been dealt with as private property, and sometimes improved by expensive structures, the acts further provided, in such cases, that where the bank owners had actually sold the tide lands, then the purchaser of the tide land from the bank owner, or a previous bank owner, should have the right to purchase from the State. These statutes are based on the idea that the State is the owner of the tide lands, and has the right to dispose of them; that there are no rights of upland ownership to interfere with this power to dispose of them and convey private interests therein, except such as the State saw fit to give the adjacent owners.

. . .

I. By the common law, both the title and the dominion of the sea, and of rivers and arms of the sea, where the tide ebbs and flows, and of all the lands below high water mark, within the jurisdiction of the Crown of England, are in the king. Such waters, and the lands which they cover, either at all times, or at least when the tide is in, are incapable of ordinary and private occupation, cultivation, and improvement; and their natural and primary uses are public in their nature, for highways of navigation and commerce, domestic and foreign, and for the purpose of fishing by all the king's subjects. Therefore the title jus privatum, in such lands,

as of waste and unoccupied lands, belongs to the king as the sovereign; and the dominion thereof, jus publicum, is vested in him as the representative of the nation and for the public benefit.

. . .

In England, from the time of Lord Hale, it has been treated as settled that the title in the soil of the sea, or of arms of the sea, below ordinary high water mark, is in the king, except so far as an individual or a corporation has acquired rights in it by express grant, or by prescription of usage; and that this title, jus privatum, whether in the king or in a subject, is held subject to the public right, jus publicum, of navigation and fishing. The same law has been declared by the House of Lords to prevail in Scotland.

It is equally well settled that a grant from the sovereign of land bounded by the sea, or by any navigable tide water, does not pass any title below high water mark, unless either the language of the grant, or long usage under it, clearly indicates that such was the intention.

By the law of England, also, every building or wharf erected, without license, below high water mark, where the soil is the king's, is a purpresture, and may, at the suit of the king, either be demolished, or be seized and rented for his benefit, if it is not a nuisance to navigation.

By recent judgments of the House of Lords, after conflicting decisions in the courts below, it has been established in England that the owner of land fronting on a navigable river in which the tide ebbs and flows has a right of access from his land to the river; and may recover compensation for the cutting off of that access by the construction of public works authorized by an act of Parliament which provides for compensation for "injuries affecting lands, including easements, interests, rights and privileges in, over or affecting lands." The right thus recognized, however, is not a title in the soil below high water mark, nor a right to build thereon, but a right of access only, analogous to that of an abutter upon a highway. *Buccleuch v. Metropolitan Board of Works*, L.R. 3 H.L. 418. "That decision," said Lord Selborne, "must be applicable to every country in which the same general law of riparian rights prevails, unless excluded by some positive rule or binding authority of the *lex loci*." *North Shore Railway v. Pion*, 14 App. Cas. 612, 620, affirming 14 Canada Sup. Ct. 677.

II. The common law of England upon this subject, at the time of the emigration of our ancestors, is the law of this country, except so far as it has been modified by the charters, constitutions, statutes, or usages of the several Colonies and States, or by the Constitution and laws of the United States.

The leading case in this court, as to the title and dominion of tide waters and of the lands under them, is *Martin v. Lessee of Waddell* 41 U.S. 367, (1842).

. . .

III. The governments of the several Colonies, with a view to induce persons to erect wharves for the benefit of navigation and commerce, early allowed to the owners of lands bounding on tide waters greater rights and privileges in the shore below high water mark than they had in England. But the nature and degree of such rights and privileges differed in the different Colonies, and in some were created by statute, while in others they rested upon usage only.

In Massachusetts, by virtue of an ancient colonial enactment, commonly called the Ordinance of 1641, but really passed in 1647, and remaining in force to this day, the title of the owner of land bounded by tide water extends from high water mark over the shore or flats to low water mark, if not beyond one hundred rods. The private right thus created in the flats is not a mere easement, but a title in fee, which will support a real action or an action of trespass, and which may be conveyed by its owner with or without the upland; and which he may build upon or enclose, provided he does not impede the public right of way over it for boats and vessels. But his title is subject to the public

rights of navigation and fishery; and therefore, so long as the flats have not been built upon or enclosed, those public rights are not restricted or abridged; and the State, in the exercise of its sovereign power of police for the protection of harbors and the promotion of commerce, may, without making compensation to the owners of the flats, establish harbor lines over those flats, beyond which wharves shall not thereafter be built, even when they would be no actual injury to navigation. Mass. Colony Laws, (ed. 1660) 50. It is because of the ordinance vesting the title in fee of the flats in the owner of the upland that a conveyance of his land bounding on the tide water, by whatever name, whether "sea," "bay," "harbor," or "river," has been held to include the land below high water mark as far as the grantor owns. *Boston v. Richardson*, 13 Allen, 146, 155 and 105 Mass. 351, 355, and cases cited. As declared by Chief Justice Shaw, grants by the Colony of Massachusetts, before the ordinance, of lands bounded by tide water did not include any land below high water mark. *Commonwealth v. Alger*, 7 Cush. 53, 66. The decision in *Manchester v. Massachusetts*, 130 U.S. 240, affirming 152 Mass. 230, upheld the jurisdiction of the State, and its authority to regulate fisheries, within a marine league from the coast.

The rule or principle of the Massachusetts ordinance has been adopted and practiced on in Plymouth, Maine, Nantucket, and Martha's Vineyard since their union with the Massachusetts Colony under the Massachusetts Province Charter of 1692. *Commonwealth v. Alger*, 7 Cush. 53, 76, and other authorities collected in 9 Gray, 523.

In New Hampshire, a right in the shore has been recognized to belong to the owner of the adjoining upland, either by reason of its having once been under the jurisdiction of Massachusetts, or by early and continued usage.

In Rhode Island, the owners of land on tide water have no title below high water mark; but by long usage, apparently sanctioned by a colonial statute of 1707, they have been accorded the right to build wharves or other structures upon the flats in front of their lands, provided they do not impede navigation, and have not been prohibited by the legislature; and they may recover damages against one who, without authority from the legislature, fills up such flats so as to impair that right. Angell on Tide Waters (2d ed.), 236, 237; *Folsom v. Freeborn*, 13 R.I. 200, 204, 210. It would seem, however, that the owner of the upland has no right of action against any one filling up the flats by authority of the State for any public purpose. *Gerhard v. Seekonk Commissioners*, 15 R.I. 334.

In Connecticut, also, the title in the land below high water mark is in the State. By an ancient usage, without any early legislation, the proprietor of the upland has the sole right, in the nature of a franchise, to wharf out and occupy the flats, even below low water mark, provided he does not interfere with navigation; and this right may be conveyed separately from the upland; and the fee in flats so reclaimed vests in him. *Ladies' Seamen's Friend Society v. Ilalstead*, 58 Conn. 144, 150–52. The exercise of this right is subject to all regulations the State may see fit to impose, by authorizing commissioners to establish harbor lines, or otherwise. *State v. Sargent*, 45 Conn. 358. But it has been intimated that it cannot be appropriated by the State to a different public use, without compensation. *Farist Col. v. Bridgeport*, 60 Conn. 278.

In New York, it was long considered as settled law that the State succeeded to all the rights of the crown and Parliament of England in lands under tide waters, and that the owner of land bounded by a navigable river within the ebb and flow of the tide had no private title or right in the shore below high water mark, and was entitled to no compensation for the construction, under a grant from the legislature of the State, of a railroad along the shore between high and low water mark, cutting off all access from his land to the river, except across the railroad. *Lansing v. Smith*, 4 Wend 9, 21. The owner of the upland has no right to wharf out without legislative authority; and titles granted in lands under tide water are subject to the right of the State to establish harbor lines.

· · ·

The foregoing summary of the laws of the original States shows that there is no universal and uniform law upon the subject; but that each State has dealt with the lands under the tide waters within its borders according to its own views of justice and policy, reserving its own control over such lands, or granting rights therein to individuals or corporations, whether owners of the adjoining upland or not, as it considered for the best interests of the public. Great caution, therefore, is necessary in applying precedents in one State to cases arising in another.

IV. The new States admitted into the Union since the adoption of the Constitution have the same rights as the original states in the tide waters, and in the lands below the high water mark, within their respective jurisdictions.

· · ·

VIII. Notwithstanding the dicta contained in some of the opinions of this court, already quoted, to the effect that Congress has no power to grant any land below high water mark of navigable waters in a Territory of the United States, it is evident that this is not strictly true.

By the Constitution, as is now well settled, the United States, having rightfully acquired the Territories, and being the only government which can impose laws upon them, have the entire dominion and sovereignty, national and municipal, Federal and state, over all the Territories, so long as they remain in a territorial condition. *American Ins. Co. v. Canter*, 1 Pet. 511, 542.

We cannot doubt, therefore, that Congress has the power to make grants of lands below high water mark of navigable waters in any Territory of the United States, whenever it becomes necessary to do so in order to perform international obligations, or to effect the improvement of such lands for the promotion and convenience of commerce with foreign nations and among the several States, or to carry out other public purposes appropriate to the objects for which the United States hold the Territory.

IX. But Congress has never undertaken by general laws to dispose of such lands. And the reasons are not far to seek.

As has been seen, by the law of England, the title in fee, or jus privatum, of the king or his grantee was, in the phrase of Lord Hale, "charged with and subject to that jus publicum which belongs to the King's subjects," or, as he elsewhere puts it, "is clothed and superinduced with jus publicum, wherein both natives and foreigners in peace with this kingdom are interested by reason of common commerce, trade and intercourse." As observed by Mr. Justice Curtis, "This soil is held by the State, not only subject to, but in some sense in trust for, the enjoyment of certain public rights." *Smith v. Maryland*, 18 How. 71, 74. The title to the shore and lands under tide water, said Mr. Justice Bradley, "is regarded as incidental to the sovereignty of the State—a portion of the royalties belonging thereto, and held in trust for the public purposes of navigation and fishery." *Hardin v. Jordan*, 140 U.S. 371, 381. And the Territories acquired by Congress, whether by deed of cession from the original States, or by treaty with a foreign country, are held with the object, as soon as their population and condition justify it, of being admitted into the Union as States, upon an equal footing with the original States in all respects; and the title and dominion of the tide water and the lands under them are held by the United States for the benefit of the whole people, and, as this court has often said, in cases above cited, "in trust for the future States." *Pollard v. Hagan*, 3 How. 212, 221, 222.

The Congress of the United States, in disposing of the public lands, has constantly acted upon the theory that those lands, whether in the interior or on the coast, above high water mark, may be taken up by actual occupants, in order to encourage the settlement of the country; but that the navigable waters and the soil under them, whether within or above the ebb and flow of the tide, shall be and remain public high-

ways; and, being chiefly valuable for the public purposes of commerce, navigation, and fishery, and for the improvements necessary to secure and promote those purposes, shall not be granted away during the period of territorial government; but, unless in case of some international duty or public exigency, shall be held by the United States in trust for the future States, and shall vest in the several States, when organized and admitted into the Union, with all the powers and prerogatives appertaining to the older States in regard to such waters and soils within their respective jurisdictions; in short, shall not be disposed of piecemeal to individuals as private property, but shall be held as a whole for the purpose of being ultimately administered and dealt with for the public benefit by the State, after it shall have become a completely organized community.

. . .

By the law of the State of Oregon, therefore, as enacted by its legislature and declared by its highest court, the title in the lands in controversy is in the defendants in error; and, upon the principles recognized and affirmed by a uniform series of recent decisions of this court, above referred to, the law of Oregon governs the case.

The conclusions from the considerations and authorities above stated may be summed up as follows:

Lands under tide waters are incapable of cultivation or improvement in the manner of lands above high water mark. They are of great value to the public for the purposes of commerce, navigation, and fishery. Their improvement by individuals, when permitted, is incidental or subordinate to the public use and right. Therefore the title and the control of them are vested in the sovereign for the benefit of the whole people.

At common law, the title and the dominion in lands flowed by the tide were in the king for the benefit of the nation. Upon the settlement of the Colonies, like rights passed to the grantees in the royal charters, in trust for the communities to be established. Upon the American Revolution, these rights, charged with a like trust, were vested in the original States within their respective borders, subject to the rights surrendered by the Constitution to the United States.

Upon the acquisition of a Territory by the United States, whether by cession from one of the States, or by treaty with a foreign country, or by discovery and settlement, the same title and dominion passed to the United States, for the benefit of the whole people, and in trust for the several States to be ultimately created out of the Territory.

The new States admitted into the Union since the adoption of the constitution have the same rights as the original States in the tide waters, and in the lands under them, within their respective jurisdictions. The title and rights of riparian or littoral proprietors in the soil below high water mark, therefore, are governed by the laws of the several States, subject to the rights granted to the United States by the Constitution.

The United States, while they hold the country as a Territory, having all the powers both of national and of municipal government, may grant, for appropriate purposes, titles or rights in the soil below high water mark of tide waters. But they have never done so by general laws; and, unless in some case of international duty or public exigency, have acted upon the policy, as most in accordance with the interest of the people and with the object for which the Territories were acquired, of leaving the administration and disposition of the sovereign rights in navigable waters, and in the soil under them, to the control of the States, respectively, when organized and admitted into the Union.

Grants by Congress of portions of the public lands within a Territory to settlers thereon, though bordering on or bounded by navigable waters, convey, of their own force, no title or right below high water mark, and do not impair the title and dominion of the future State when created; but leave the question of the use of the shores by the owners of uplands to the sovereign control of each State, subject only to the rights vested by the Constitution in the United States.

The donation land claim, bounded by the Columbia River, upon which the plaintiff in error relies, includes no title or right in the land below high water mark; and the statutes of Oregon, under which the defendants in error hold, are a constitutional and legal exercise by the State of Oregon of its dominion over the lands under navigable waters.

Judgment affirmed.

Questions _____

1. Why did the court review the law from the original states in reaching its decision?

2. What principle in federal-state relations can be deduced from the court's holding?

3. Does the Oregon statute of 1874 represent current thinking about shoreline erosion and protection?

_____

Brusco Towboat v. State of Oregon, 589 P.2d 712, (Oreg. 1978)

HOWELL, JUSTICE

At issue in these three consolidated cases is the validity of the State Land Board's (hereinafter Board) requirement that, with some exceptions, anyone who maintains a permanent structure on or over state-owned submerged and submersible lands under navigable waters enter into a lease and pay rent. Upon petitions from all parties, we granted review of the decision of the Court of Appeals to consider primarily the following issues:

1. Whether the state has the power to lease its submerged and submersible lands in this manner, and whether the authority to do so has been given to the State Land Board.

2. Whether the Board, if it has the authority to impose this leasing program, is calculating its rental on an improper basis.

3. Whether the leasing program impairs, or is con-

stitutionally limited by, the rights of riparian owners.

4. Whether the lease program, if otherwise valid,
   may be applied to the port districts.

The status of these cases and the details of
the Board's leasing program were well described in the Court of Appeals's opinion:

The first case, an action in ejectment, was commenced by the Board against the Fort Vancouver
Plywood Company to compel it either to enter into
a lease for or to vacate submerged lands which it
used for a log boom. It was treated below as a suit
for declaratory judgment and it will be so treated
here. The other two cases are suits for declaratory
judgment commenced by various tugboat companies
and by several port districts seeking to have the
Board's leasing program declared invalid. Judgments
in all three cases upheld the lease program and this
appeal followed. For convenience, all parties challenging the leasing program will be referred to herein
as plaintiffs.

I. The Rules

The rules in issue establish a program for
leasing state-owned submerged and submersible lands: " 'Any person engaged in a permanent or long-term use of state-owned submerged or submersible lands not exempted
from leasing by statute or these regulations
must obtain a lease from the Division.' " OAR
141-82-015(1)

Under the program, leases are required for
most long-term uses of submerged and submersible lands which effectively preclude any
other use and enjoyment of such lands and the
overlying waters. Thus, leases are required for
most industrial and commercial uses including
log booms, aquatic cultivation facilities, and ma-
rinas, as well as for private uses such as houseboat moorages and private docks.

The rules exempt from the resale program
uses which are essentially navigational or in aid
of navigation, such as vessels which are temporarily anchored or hove to and temporary log
tie-ups. Buoys, channel markers, and beacons
authorized by state or federal authorities are

also exempt. In addition, (1) the owner of any
land lying upon any navigable stream or other
like water, and within the corporate limits of
any incorporated town or within the boundaries
of any port, may construct a wharf upon the
same, and extend the wharf into the stream or
other like water beyond low water mark so far
as may be necessary for the use and accommodation of any ships, boats, or vessels engaged
exclusively in the receipt and discharge of
goods or merchandise or in the performance of
governmental functions upon the stream or
other like water. (2) As used in this section,
"wharf" does not include new lands created
upon submersible or submerged lands by artificial fill or deposit.

Under the rules, the leasing process is initiated by filing an application with the Board,
which then establishes a minimum annual rental
for the parcel sought. Owners of land abutting
the parcel are then notified that they have fourteen days in which to exercise their statutory
right to lease the land at the minimum rental. If
abutting landowners fail to exercise this right,
the parcel is opened to competitive bidding. The
Board may reject lease applications which it
deems to be contrary to the public interest. The
Board is authorized, but not required, to conduct
public hearings on the question of whether to issue a particular lease. Leases may be for a period
of up to twenty years.

The construction of permanent facilities such
as those subject to the Board's lease program
requires a permit from the United States Army
Corps of Engineers. Issuance of such a federal
permit is without prejudice to rights of the state
regarding construction. Conversely, the Board's
rules provide that a lease from the state does
not obviate the need for compliance with the
Corps of Engineers' permit requirement. All of
the plaintiffs, in connection with the ordinary
conduct of their business, maintain permanent
facilities overlying submerged and submersible
lands which are not exempted from the Board's
leasing program. With minor exceptions, these
facilities preclude the public's use and enjoy-

ment of the lands and waters which overlie them. At least some of the plaintiffs are riparian landowners.

The Board's Authority to Require Leases

The Court of Appeals correctly concluded that the Board has the authority to require users of these lands to enter into leases and to pay rental for their use. Plaintiffs do not contest the state's title to the lands in question. The legislature has specifically authorized the Division of State Lands to lease state-owned submerged and submersible land. ORS 274.915 provides: "Except as otherwise provided in ORS 274.905 to 274.940, the division may sell, lease or trade submersible or submerged lands owned by the state." Plaintiffs argue that this authority was not intended to extend to requiring rental for uses related to navigation, such as moorage facilities, log booms, and other permanent installations maintained by the plaintiffs. They rely on the legislative history of this provision. That history evidences an urgent concern with providing a mechanism for facilitating waterfront commercial and industrial development. However, we do not find, either in the language of the statute or in the legislative history, any suggestion that the leasing authority was to be limited to lands used for purposes unrelated to navigation.

The power of the legislature is plenary, except as it may be limited by the federal or state constitution. Plaintiff's federal constitutional challenges to the leasing program are addressed later in this opinion. They have not suggested any state constitutional limitations on the legislature's power to authorize the collection of revenue for the use of state-owned lands. In fact, general authority for such legislation is found in article VIII, 5(2) of the state constitution, which provides: "The [State Land] board shall manage lands under its jurisdiction with the object of obtaining the greatest benefit for the people of this state, consistent with the conservation of this resource under sound techniques of land management."

Subsection (2) was part of an initiative measure adopted in 1968. Material concerning that measure in the voters' pamphlet shows that the amendment was presented to the voters primarily as a vehicle for enhancing the revenue produced by state lands. Although those materials do not indicate that the measure was intended to provide any new authority for the legislature to authorize the leasing of state-owned lands, there was no suggestion that any limitation on the legislature's plenary power was intended. We find no provision in the state constitution which denies to the legislature (or to the Board) the power to require occupiers of state-owned submerged and submersible lands to enter into leases and compensate the state for their use.

The Court of Appeals's opinion discusses at some length the distinction between the state's proprietary interest in these lands—the jus privatum—and its interest or obligation as trustee for the benefit of the public—the jus publicum. The accuracy of that summary of the traditional view of the nature of the state's ownership of lands under navigable waters has not been challenged here, and we see no need to reexamine it now. We did, at oral argument, raise questions about the constitutional or other predicate for any concept of the jus publicum as a special limitation on any attempt by the legislature to abdicate its power to protect the rights of the people of the state. Counsel were unable to enlighten us. There is, however, no need to consider that question in this case because the Board has not attempted to give up that power on the State's behalf. The leasing rules provide:

82-025 Reservation of Rights

(1) The Division reserves the right to reject any application for lease which would not be in the best interests of the State of Oregon or contrary to State or Federal law. No lease may be issued if it would result in an unreasonable interference with the public rights of navigation, fishing, recreation, or environmental reasons.

(2) The Division reserves the right to reject any

and all bids received for lease of publicly owned lands.

(3) A lease granted under these rules does not authorize any injury to private property or invasion of private rights, or any infringement of Federal, State, or local laws or regulations, nor does it obviate the necessity of obtaining other Federal, State, or local government's assent required by law for the structure or work proposed.

Thus it is clear from the rules themselves that the lease program does not purport to divest the legislature or the Board of the state's power to protect the rights of the public in the state's navigable waters or to pursue other governmental objectives.

Propriety of the Rental Formula

Plaintiffs' petition for review suggests that some confusion has resulted from the Court of Appeals's statement that the state "is the owner of both the navigable waters and the underlying land." Ownership of the water was apparently considered material because the Board, in calculating the amount of rental required for a particular structure, bases its calculation in part on the total amount of water surface area which is occupied rather than on the amount of bed area occupied by pilings, dolphins, or other structural features which actually touch the bed. It also appears from the record that at least some of plaintiffs' structures do not rest on the bed at all, but are anchored only to the adjoining privately owned riparian land.

Plaintiffs insist that it is the public, not the state in its proprietary capacity, which is the owner of the waters of the state. We need not reach that question. We conclude, rather, that the parties' concern about the ownership of the water itself is misplaced, and that the Court of Appeals's ruling on that issue was not necessary. The state's ownership of the submerged and submersible lands alone is sufficient to justify the rental which the Board proposes to charge for occupation of the surface of the water.

We are aware of no general principle which requires a lessor, whether public or private, to

calculate rentals on any particular basis such as the amount of surface area physically in contact with structures. Assuming, although plaintiffs have not submitted any authority to this effect, that when the state is the lessor it must calculate its rentals on a reasonable basis, there is nothing unreasonable about basing that calculation on the amount of the state's land which is effectively occupied and thus unavailable for lease to others or for use by the public, whether or not that occupation is accomplished by physical contact with the land.

. . .

We hold, then, that the state, by virtue of its ownership of the submerged and submersible land under navigable waters, has the power to require leases and the payment of rent for the occupation of those lands, and has delegated that power to the Board. We further hold that the basis upon which the Board calculates the rentals has not been shown to be improper.

Riparian Rights to Build Structures in Aid of Navigation

The next question is whether riparian owners have a right, which may not be taken without compensation, to place permanent structures on the state's submerged and submersible land adjacent to their riparian property. It is clear that, as to riparian owners who have not yet done so, the Board's leasing program does not interfere with any vested rights. The Court of Appeals correctly so held.

Even when considering the legislature's express grant of a riparian privilege to build wharves on state-owned land, this court has consistently described that privilege as one which may be withdrawn at any time before it is exercised. For example, in *Montgomery v. Shaver*, 40 Or. 244, 248, 66 P. 923, 924 (1901), the opinion describes the wharfing statute as "a permissive statute, which alludes to certain things that may be done, but does not vest any right until exercised. It constitutes a license revocable at the pleasure of the legislature until acted upon." The court spoke at greater length in *Bowlby v. Shively*, 22 Or. 410, 420–21, 30 P. 154, 157 (1892), *aff'd*, *Shively v. Bowlby*, 152 U.S. 1 (1894):

an upland owner on tidal waters has no rights as against the state or its grantees to extend wharves in front of his land, or to any private or exclusive rights whatever in the tide lands, except as he has derived them from the statute.... But this act is not a grant: It simply authorizes upland owners on navigable rivers within the corporate limits of any incorporated town to construct wharves in front of their land; it does not vest any right until exercised; it is a license, revocable at the pleasure of the legislature, until acted upon or availed of.

Although *Bowlby* involved tidelands, the state's title to other land underlying navigable waters stands on the same footing, and the same principles are applicable.

In circumstances where the legislature has not expressly granted permission to occupy the submerged and submersible land, we have held that the riparian owner had, as a matter of custom, been accorded the privilege of doing so, subject to the power of the legislature to regulate or prohibit such occupation. In *Coquille M. & M. Co. v. Johnson*, 52 Or. 547, 551–52, 98 P. 132, 134 (1908), we held that a riparian owner on navigable water had, in the absence of any statute regulating or prohibiting such activity, the "right" to construct a log boom adjacent to his property. That right, which we termed a "mere franchise," was described in the following quotation:

Riparian owners upon navigable fresh waters and lakes may construct, in the shoal water in front of their land, wharves, piers, landings, and booms, in aid of and not obstructing navigation. This is a riparian right, being dependent upon title to the bank, and not upon title to the bed of the river. Its exercise may be regulated or prohibited by the State; but, *so long as not prohibited*, it is a private right, derived from a passive or implied license by the public. 2 Gould, Waters (2d ed.) 179.

That quotation is also made a part of the opinion in *Lewis v. City of Portland*, 25 Or., *supra*, at 163–64, 35 P. 256. Neither statutes nor the decisions of this court have recognized any irrevocable riparian right to construct structures, even in aid of navigation, on state-owned land.

One case cited by plaintiffs in support of their claim of riparian rights requires additional comment. In *Pacific Elevator Co. v. Portland*, 65 Or. 349, 133 P. 72 (1913), plaintiff owned a tract, within the city limits, consisting of both upland and the adjoining submersible land. It had never exercised its statutory wharfing privilege. The city proposed to build a wharf on plaintiff's submersible land and on out past the original low water line onto the state-owned land. The decision holds that the city was not entitled to do so. It does not, however, as plaintiffs claim, stand for the proposition that wharfing privileges, even though not yet exercised, cannot be taken by the state. It holds only that the legislature, when it authorized the city, in its charter, to provide for the construction of wharves and docks, had not impliedly repealed the wharfing statute and thus revoked private wharfing privileges within the city, and that the city did not have the power to build wharves on either private or state-owned land without taking the proper steps to acquire the land it proposed to use.

Admittedly, the opinion contains language which might be read as supporting plaintiff's position in this case. At page 401, 133 P. at page 82, the opinion describes the wharfing privilege: "The act of 1862 grants the right of wharfage across the state's land out to the harbor line fixed by state authority to the riparian owner. This license has never been revoked by the state but has been reaffirmed by the lawmakers and upheld by the courts." Then, it describes the plaintiff's title to the submersible land over which the city proposed to build: "Plaintiff has succeeded to the title which the state formerly had in the lots described. Its title is subject to the paramount right of navigation existing in the public and subject to such reasonable regulation as the state through its municipality may prescribe." The opinion then continues: "To allow this property to be taken for public use without just compensation would work a great injustice and do violence to the Constitution of Oregon."

The sentence last quoted refers to the land owned by the plaintiff in fee, not to its unexercised wharfing privilege to occupy state-owned land. As to that privilege, the court had concluded earlier in its opinion that the city did not stand in the state's shoes. There was, then, no need to determine whether the state could revoke the privilege before it was exercised without compensating the riparian owner. Earlier cases had, as we have shown, indicated that the state could do so. The decision in *Pacific Elevator* is consistent with those cases. It does not aid plaintiffs here.

We find, then, no authority for plaintiffs' position that riparian owners on navigable waters have a right to build navigational structures on the state-owned beds adjacent to their property which may not be revoked without compensation prior to its exercise. They have cited a series of New York cases, some of which appear to hold that riparian owners do have such a right. We are not convinced that these cases stand for everything that plaintiffs claim for them. Assuming that they do, however, only means that New York has recognized a proprietary riparian right which Oregon has not. That choice is within the power of each state. *Oregon ex rel. State Land Board v. Corvallis Sand & Gravel Co.*, 429 U.S. 363 (1977).

Structures Existing Prior to the Leasing Program

A more difficult question concerns those structures for which the Board proposes to require leases and which were constructed prior to the institution of the state's leasing program. We are not concerned, in this case, with wharves which the legislature has expressly authorized by ORS 780.040 and its predecessor, and for which the Board does not require leases.

. . .

In view of our repeated description of the riparian privilege to construct navigational structures on state-owned submerged or submersible land as a passive or implied license, the Court of Appeals turned to the private law of licenses to determine the rights of those riparian owners who exercised the privilege before the institution of the leasing program. Between private parties, the general rule is that when expenditures have been made to construct permanent improvements on another's land in reliance on an express license to do so, the license cannot thereafter be revoked, at least without payment of compensation. This rule is, however, limited to expenditures made in reliance on an express license or agreement, and does not apply where the landowner has not given express permission, but has merely silently acquiesced or failed to object to the improvements. The Oregon cases are collected, and their rationale examined, in Comment, 31 Or. L. Rev. 242 (1952). These cases suggest that when a license becomes "irrevocable" under the general rule, the rights acquired by the licensee are perpetual. However in *Rouse v. Roy L. Houch Sons*, 249 Or. 655, 660, 439 P.2d 856, 858 (1968), in which the purported license was for a five-year term, we said:

A licensee under such a license who has made expenditures of capital or labor in the exercise of his license in reasonable reliance upon representations by the licensor as to the duration of the license is privileged to continue the use permitted by the license to the extent reasonably necessary to realize upon his expenditures. Restatement of Property 519(4).

In that case we did not find the necessary expenditures in reliance on the licensor's representations, and so did not have occasion to apply the Restatement rule.

The Court of Appeals held the rule applicable in this case, however, concluding that riparian owners who had built structures on state-owned submerged and submersible land prior to the Board's institution of its leasing program had done so in reasonable reliance on the continuing availability of their license to occupy that land and were therefore entitled to maintain those structures rent-free for whatever period of time was necessary to permit them to recoup their investments.

The difficulty with applying the general rule in this case is that, as pointed out above, it has been held applicable only where the license to use the land was express. We have consistently described the riparian owner's license under consideration here as a "passive" or "implied" license. The Court of Appeals, mindful of this problem, found the necessary affirmative license or representation in the decisions of this court which recognized the riparian privilege to construct navigational structures on the state's land. That recognition, however, was of a revocable privilege or license, not of a perpetual license or one of any particular duration. We cannot agree with the Court of Appeals that the legislature is estopped to revoke the privilege by the decisions of this court which declare that only a revocable privilege exists. While application or pronouncement by this court of a rule of property law may create vested rights, our recognition that a privilege exists until prohibited by the legislature does not entitle those who choose to exercise that privilege to assume that the legislature will not act to limit or prohibit it in the future.

In short, we find that the Board's requirement that riparian owners who have taken advantage of the legislature's past failure to prohibit their exclusive occupation of the state's submerged and submersible land pay rental for the privilege of continuing to do so in the future does not violate any right of property. Leases may, therefore, be required of those parties who claim riparian status and who have exercised in the past the privileges accompanying that status.

Constitutional Claims

Plaintiffs have renewed in this court the federal constitutional challenges to the validity of the leasing program which they raised in the Court of Appeals. Although we did not, when we granted plaintiffs' petition for review, request additional argument on those challenges, we have considered them and find them to be unpersuasive. We approve the Court of Appeals's disposition of the arguments based on the Commerce Clause, the Equal Protection Clause of the Fourteenth Amendment, the supremacy of the Transportation Act of 1940 (19 U.S.C. 902–923), and the Oregon Admission Act. As to the last, we add some further observations. Section 2 of the Oregon Admission Act provides: "All the navigable waters of said State, shall be common highways and forever free . . . without any tax, duty, impost, or toll therefor." This language, which is taken from the Northwest Ordinance of 1787 and is found in the admission acts of a number of the states, was construed by the United States Supreme Court in *Huse v. Glover*, 119 U.S. 543 (1886). In that case, the state of Illinois had constructed a lock and dam on the Illinois River and charged a toll for the passage of vessels through the lock. This charge was held not to violate the terms of the Ordinance. Citing *Cardwell v. American Bridge Company*, 113 U.S. 205 (1885), which had construed the same language in the California Admission Act, the court said that the object of this clause

was to preserve the rivers as highways equally open to all persons without preference to any, and unobstructed by duties or tolls, and thus prevent the use of the navigable streams by private parties to the exclusion of the public, and the exaction of toll for their navigation. . . . As thus construed the clause would prevent any exclusive use of the navigable waters of the State—a possible farming out of the privilege of navigating them to particular individuals, classes, or corporations, or by vessels of a particular character. 119 U.S. at 547–48.

The leasing program does not violate the clause as thus construed. It does not impose a charge for the use of the navigable waters as a highway, or tend to limit the privilege of navigation to any particular class of persons or vessels. It merely imposes a charge upon those who wish to occupy, to the exclusion of others, portions of the state's lands in pursuit of their own business activities. The fact that plaintiffs' business activities, or some of them, are dependent upon navigation does not immunize them from such a charge.

Application of the Leasing Program to Port Districts

Finally, plaintiff port districts contend that even if the leasing program is generally valid, it cannot be applied to them because the legislature has delegated to them the power to use or dispose of the state-owned submerged and submersible lands within their boundaries. The Court of Appeals held that the legislature's delegation to the port districts of authority relating to navigation did not constitute a surrender of the state's power to charge rental for the use of state lands. This issue was correctly resolved in the Board's favor.

In their petition for review, the plaintiff port districts stress the language of ORS 777.210(3), which authorizes the port to acquire, construct, maintain, or operate piers, wharves, docks, boat landings, and other facilities "with full power to lease and sell the same, together with the lands upon which they are situated, whether held by the port in its governmental capacity or not." Clearly, this authority to lease and sell the lands upon which navigational and other structures are situated is limited to those lands in which the ports have properly acquired the necessary interest. The statute simply grants to port districts the power to engage in activities of the kinds enumerated. It does not purport to be a grant of state lands for that purpose. The phrase "whether held by the port in its governmental capacity or not" was apparently intended to make it clear that the power to sell or lease port-owned facilities does not depend upon whether they are owned in a proprietary rather than a governmental capacity, as was assumed

in, for example, *Dix v. Port Oxford*, 131 Or. 157, 282 P. 109 (1929).

In ORS 777.120(1) each port is granted "full control of all bays, rivers and harbors within its limits, and between its limits and the sea," to the "full extent the State of Oregon might exercise control." There is here no express delegation of authority to occupy or dispose of the state's lands, and we do not believe such a delegation was intended. The statute as a whole discloses an intent to delegate to the ports only the state's power to regulate use of the navigable waters, not its proprietary interest in the lands under them.

In summary, then, we hold that the Court of Appeals correctly resolved the issues in this case, with two exceptions. First, its holding that the state owns the navigable waters themselves in a proprietary capacity was not necessary to the resolution of this case. We express no opinion as to whether that conclusion is correct. Second, we hold that the Board is not estopped by the decisions of this court to collect rentals for the occupation of state lands by structures (other than wharves within the purview of the wharfing statute) which were placed on those lands prior to the institution of the leasing program. There is, therefore, no need to remand the case, as the Court of Appeals ordered, for determination of which plaintiffs are entitled to a period of rent-free use of the lands.

In all other respects, the decision of the Court of Appeals is affirmed.

Questions

1. Assuming that the lease requirement is now valid, how would you develop a system to establish the fair market value of the submerged land rentals?

2. Were the property rights of the riparian landowners fairly addressed by the Oregon court? Would you have decided the case the same way?

Phillips Petroleum Company v. Mississippi, 484 U.S. 469 (1988)

JUSTICE WHITE delivered the opinion of the Court.

The issue here is whether the State of Mississippi, when it entered the Union in 1817, took title to lands lying under waters that were influenced by the tide running in the Gulf of Mexico, but were not navigable-in-fact.

I.

As the Mississippi Supreme Court eloquently put it: "Though great public interests and neither insignificant nor illegitimate private interests are present and in conflict, this in the end is a title suit." *Cinque Bambini Partnership v. State*, 491 So. 2d 508, 510 (1986). More specifically, in question here is ownership of forty-two acres of land underlying the north branch of Bayou LaCroix and eleven small drainage streams in southwestern Mississippi; the disputed tracts range from under one-half acre to almost ten acres in size. Although the waters over these lands lie several miles north of the Mississippi Gulf coast and are not navigable, they are nonetheless influenced by the tide, because they are adjacent and tributary to the Jourdan River, a navigable stream flowing into the Gulf. The Jourdan, in the area involved here, is affected by the ebb and flow of the tide. Record title to these tracts of land is held by petitioners, who trace their claims back to pre-statehood Spanish land grants.

The State of Mississippi, however, claiming that by virtue of the "equal footing doctrine" it acquired at the time of statehood and held in public trust all land lying under any waters influenced by the tide, whether navigable or not, issued oil and gas leases that included the property at issue. This quiet title suit, brought by petitioners, ensued.

The Mississippi Supreme Court, affirming the Chancery Court with respect to the lands at issue here, held that by virtue of becoming a state, Mississippi acquired "fee simple title to all lands naturally subject to tidal influence, inland to today's mean high water mark. . . ." Id., at 510. Petitioners' submission that the State acquired title only to lands under navigable waters was rejected.

We granted certiorari to review the Mississippi Supreme Court's decision, and now affirm the judgment below.

II.

As petitioners recognize, the "seminal case in American public trust jurisprudence is *Shively v. Bowlby*, 152 U.S. 1 (1894)." The issue in *Shively v. Bowlby* was whether the state of Oregon or a pre-statehood grantee from the United States of riparian lands near the mouth of the Columbia River at Astoria, Oregon, owned the soil below the high-water mark. Following an extensive survey of this Court's prior cases, the English common law, and various cases from the state courts, the Court concluded:

> At common law, the title and dominion in lands flowed by the tide water were in the King for the benefit of the nation. . . . Upon the American Revolution, these rights, charged with a like trust, were vested in the original States within their respective borders, subject to the rights surrendered by the Constitution of the United States.

> The new States admitted into the Union since the adoption of the Constitution have the same rights as the original States in the tide waters, and in the lands under them, within their respective jurisdictions. Id., at 57.

Shively rested on prior decisions of this Court, which had included similar, sweeping statements of States' dominion over lands beneath tidal waters. *Knight v. United States Land Association*, 142 U.S. 161, 183 (1891), for example, had stated,

> It is the settled rule of law in this court that absolute property in, and dominion and sovereignty over, the soils under the tide waters in the original States were reserved to the several States, and that the new States

since admitted have the same rights, sovereignty and jurisdiction in that behalf as the original States possess within their respective borders.

On many occasions, this Court has restated and reaffirmed these words from *Knight* and *Shively*.

Against this array of cases, it is not surprising that Mississippi claims ownership of all the tidelands in the State. Other states have done as much. The thirteen original states, joined by the Coastal States Organization (representing all coastal states), have filed a brief in support of Mississippi, insisting that ownership of thousands of acres of tidelands under non-navigable waters would not be disturbed if the judgment below were affirmed, as it would be if petitioners' navigability-in-fact test were adopted.

Petitioners rely on early state cases to indicate that the original States did not claim title to non-navigable tidal waters. But it has been long established that the individual States have the authority to define the limits of the lands held in public trust and to recognize private rights in such lands as they see fit. *Shively v. Bowlby*, 152 U.S., at 26. Some of the original States, for example, did recognize more private interests in tidelands than did others of the thirteen—more private interests than were recognized at common law, or in the dictates of our public trust cases. Because some of the cases which petitioners cite come from such States (i.e., from States which abandoned the common law with respect to tidelands), they are of only limited value in understanding the public trust doctrine and its scope in those States which have not relinquished their claims to all lands beneath tidal waters.

Finally, we note that several of our prior decisions have recognized that the States have interests in lands beneath tidal waters which have nothing to do with navigation. For example, this Court has previously observed that public trust lands may be reclaimed to create land for urban expansion. E.g., *Hardin v. Jordan*, 140 U.S. 371, 381–82 (1891); *Den v. Jersey Co.*, 15 How. 426, 432 (1854). Because of the State's ownership of tidelands, restrictions on the planting and har-

vesting of oysters there have been upheld. *McCready v. Virginia*, 94 U.S. 391, 395–97 (1877). It would be odd to acknowledge such diverse uses of public trust tidelands, and then suggest that the sole measure of the expanse of such lands is the navigability of the waters over them.

Consequently, we reaffirm our long-standing precedents which hold that the States, upon entry into the Union, received ownership of all lands under waters subject to the ebb and flow of the tide. Under the well-established principles of our cases, the decision of the Mississippi Supreme Court is clearly correct: the lands at issue here are "under tide waters," and therefore passed to the State of Mississippi upon its entrance into the Union.

III.

Petitioners do not deny that broad statements of public trust dominion over tidelands have been included in this Court's opinions since the early nineteenth century. Rather, they advance two reasons why these previous statements of the public trust doctrine should not be given their apparent application in this case.

A.

First, petitioners contend that these sweeping statements of State dominion over tidelands arise from an oddity of the common law, or more specifically, of English geography. Petitioners submit that in England practically all navigable rivers are influenced by the tide. See *The Propeller Genesee Chief v. Fitzhugh*, 12 How. 443, 454 (1852). Thus, "tidewater" and "navigability" were synonyms at common law. See *Illinois Central R. Co. v. Illinois*, 146 U.S. 387, 436 (1892). Consequently, in petitioners' view, the crown's ownership of lands beneath tidewaters actually rested on the navigability of those waters rather than the ebb and flow of the tide. Cf. Ibid. English authority and commentators are cited to show that the crown did not own the soil under any non-navigable waters. Petitioners also cite for support statements from this Court's opinions, such as *The Genesee Chief, supra,* and *Martin v. Lessee of Waddell,* 41 U.S. 367, (1842), which observed that it was "the navigable waters of England, and the soil under them, [which were] held by the Crown" at common law.

The cases relied on by petitioner, however, did not deal with tidal, non-navigable waters. And we will not now enter the debate on what the English law was with respect to the land under such waters, for it is perfectly clear how this court understood the common law of royal ownership, and what the Court considered the rights of the original and the later-entering States to be. As we discuss above, this Court has consistently interpreted the common law as providing that the lands beneath waters under tidal influence were given to the States upon their admission into the Union. It is true that none of these cases actually dealt with lands such as those involved in this case, but it has never been suggested in any of this Court's prior decisions that the many statements included therein—to the effect that the States owned all the soil beneath waters affected by the tide—were anything less than an accurate description of the governing law.

B.

Petitioners, in a related argument, contend that even if the common law does not support their position, subsequent cases from this Court developing the *American* public trust doctrine make it clear that navigability—and not tidal influences—has become the sine qua non of the public trust interest in tidelands in this country.

It is true that *The Genesee Chief, supra,* at 456–57, overruled prior cases of this Court which had limited admiralty jurisdiction to waters subject to tidal influence. The Court did sharply criticize the "ebb and flow" measure of admiralty inherited from England in *The Genesee Chief,* and instead insisted quite emphatically that the different topography of America—in particular, our "thousands of miles of public navigable water[s] . . . in which there is no

tide"—required that "jurisdiction [be] made to depend upon the navigable character of the water, and not upon the ebb and flow of the tide." Later, it came to be recognized as the "settled law of this country" that the lands under navigable freshwater lakes and rivers were within the public trust given the new States upon their entry into the Union, subject to the federal navigation easement and the power of Congress to control navigation on those streams under the Commerce Clause. *Barney v. Keokuk,* 94 U.S. 324, 338 (1877). See also *Illinois Central R. Co. v. Illinois, supra,* at 435–36.

The State's own freshwater river bottoms as far as the rivers are navigable, however, does not indicate that navigability is or was the prevailing test for state dominion over tidelands. Rather, this rule represents the American decision to depart from what it understood to be the English rule limiting crown ownership to the soil under tidal waters. In *Oregon ex rel. State Land Board v. Corvallis Sand & Gravel Co.,* 429 U.S. 363, 374 (1977), after recognizing the accepted doctrine that States coming into the Union had title to all lands under the tidewaters, the Court stated that *Barney v. Keokuk, supra,* had "extended the doctrine to waters which were nontidal but nevertheless navigable, consistent with [the Court's] earlier extension of admiralty jurisdiction."

This Court's decisions in *The Genesee Chief* and *Barney v. Keokuk* extended admiralty jurisdiction and public trust doctrine to navigable fresh waters and the lands beneath them. But we do not read those cases as simultaneously withdrawing from public trust coverage those lands which had been consistently recognized in this court's cases as being within that doctrine's scope: all lands beneath waters influenced by the ebb and flow of the tide. See *Mann v. Tacoma Land Co.,* 153 U.S. 273 (1894).

C.

Finally, we observe that not the least of the difficulties with petitioners' position is their concession that the States own the tidelands bordering the oceans, bays, and estuaries—even where these areas by no means could be considered navigable, as is always the case near the shore. It is obvious that these waters are part of the sea, and the lands beneath them are State property; ultimately, though, the only proof of this fact can be that the waters are influenced by the ebb and flow of the tide. This is undoubtedly why the ebb-and-flow test has been the measure of public ownership of tidelands for so long.

Admittedly, there is a difference in degree between the waters in this case and non-navigable waters on the seashore that are affected by the tide. But there is no difference in kind. For in the end, all tide waters are connected to the sea: the waters in this case, for example, by a navigable, tidal river. Perhaps the lands at issue here differ in some ways from tidelands directly adjacent to the sea; nonetheless, they still share those "geographical, chemical and environmental" qualities that make lands beneath tidal waters unique.

Indeed, we find the various alternatives for delineating the boundaries of public trust tidelands offered by petitioners and their supporting amici to be unpersuasive and unsatisfactory. As the State suggested at argument, and as recognized on several previous occasions, the ebb and flow rule has the benefit of "uniformity and certainty, and . . . eas[e] of application." We are unwilling, after its lengthy history at common law, in this Court, and in many state courts, to abandon the ebb and flow rule now, and seek to fashion a new test to govern the limits of public trust tidelands. Consequently, we hold that the lands at issue in this case were within those given to Mississippi when the State was admitted to the Union.

IV.

Petitioners in passing, and amici in somewhat greater detail, complain that the Mississippi Supreme Court's decision is "inequitable" and would upset "various . . . kinds of property ex-

pectations and interests [which] have matured since Mississippi joined the Union in 1817." They claim that they have developed reasonable expectations based on their record title for these lands, and that they (and their predecessors-in-interest) have paid taxes on these lands for more than a century.

We have recognized the importance of honoring reasonable expectations in property interests. Cf. *Kaiser Aetna v. United States, supra,* at 175. But such expectations can only be of consequence where they are "reasonable" ones. Here, Mississippi law appears to have consistently held that the public trust in lands under water includes "title to all the land under the tidewater." *Rouse v. Saucier's Heirs,* 166 Miss. 704, 713, 146 So. 291, 291–92 (1933). Although the Mississippi Supreme Court acknowledged that this case may be the first where it faced the question of the public trust interest in non-navigable tidelands, the clear and unequivocal statements in its earlier opinions should have been ample indication of the State's claim to tidelands. Moreover, cases which have discussed the State's public trust interest in these lands have described uses of them not related to navigability, such as bathing, swimming, recreation, fishing, and mineral development. These statements, too, should have made clear that the State's claims were not limited to lands under navigable waterways. Any contrary expectations cannot be considered reasonable.

We are skeptical of the suggestions by the dissent that a decision affirming the judgment below will have sweeping implications, either within Mississippi or outside that State. The State points out that only one other case is pending in its courts which raises the same issue. And as for the effect of our decision today in other States, we are doubtful that this ruling will do more than confirm the prevailing understanding—which in some States is the same as Mississippi's, and in others, is quite different. As this court wrote in *Shively v. Bowlby,* 152 U.S., at 26, "there is no universal and uniform law upon the subject; but ... each State has dealt with the lands under the tide waters within its borders according to its own views of justice and policy."

Consequently, our ruling today will not upset titles in all coastal states, as petitioners intimated at argument. As we have discussed, many coastal States as a matter of state law granted all or a portion of their tidelands to adjacent upland property owners long ago. Our decision today does nothing to change ownership rights in States which previously relinquished a public trust claim to tidelands such as those at issue here.

Indeed, we believe that it would be far more upsetting to settled expectations to reverse the Mississippi Supreme Court decision. As many land titles have been adjudicated based on the ebb-and-flow rule for tidelands, we cannot know how many titles would have to be adjusted if the scope of the public trust was now found to be limited to lands beneath navigable tidal waters only. If States do not own lands under non-navigable tidal waters, many State land grants based on our earlier decisions might now be invalid. Finally, even where States have given dominion over tidelands to private property owners, some States have retained for the general public the right to fish, hunt, or bathe on these lands. These long-established rights may be lost with respect to non-navigable tidal waters if we adopt the rule urged by petitioners.

The fact that petitioners have long been the record title holders, or long paid taxes on these lands, does not change the outcome here. How such facts would transfer ownership of these lands from the State to petitioners is a question of state law. Here, the Mississippi Supreme Court held that under Mississippi law, the State's ownership of these lands could not be lost via adverse possession, laches, or any other equitable doctrine. We see no reason to disturb the "general proposition [that] the law of real property is, under our Constitution, left to the

individual States to develop and administer." *Hughes v. Washington*, 389 U.S. 290, 295 (1968). Consequently, we do not believe that the equitable considerations petitioners advance divest the State of its ownership in the disputed tidelands.

V.

Because we believe that our cases firmly establish that the States, upon entering the Union, were given ownership over all lands beneath waters subject to the tide's influence, we affirm the Mississippi Supreme Court's determination that the lands at issue have became property of the State upon its admission to the Union in 1817. Furthermore, because we find no reason to set aside that court's state-law determination that subsequent developments did not divest the State of its ownership of these public trust lands, the judgment below is

Affirmed.

JUSTICE KENNEDY took no part in the consideration or decision of this case.

JUSTICE O'CONNOR, with whom JUSTICE STEVENS and JUSTICE SCALIA join, dissenting.

Breaking a chain of title that reaches back more than 150 years, the Court today announces a rule that will disrupt the settled expectations of landowners not only in Mississippi but in every coastal state. Neither our precedents nor equitable principles require this result, and I respectfully dissent from this undoing of settled history.

I.

As the Court acknowledges, this case presents an issue that we never have decided: whether a State holds in public trust all land underlying tidally influenced waters that are neither navigable themselves nor part of any navigable body of water. In holding that it does, the majority relies on general language in opinions that recognized state claims to land underlying tidewaters. But those cases concerned land lying beneath waters that were in fact navigable, e.g., *Shively v. Bowlby*, 152 U.S. 1 (1894) (Columbia River in Oregon), or beneath waters that were part of or immediately bordering a navigable body of water, e.g., *Mann v. Tacoma Land Co.*, 153 U.S. 273 (1894) (shallow tidelands in Commencement Bay in Washington). Until today, none of our decisions recognized a State's public trust title to land underlying a discrete and wholly non-navigable body of water that is properly viewed as separate from any navigable body of water.

In my view, the public trust properly extends only to land underlying navigable bodies of water and their borders, bays, and inlets. This Court has defined the public trust repeatedly in terms of navigability. It is true that these cases did not involve waters subject to the ebb and flow of the tide. But there is no reason to think that different tests of the scope of the public trust apply to salt and to fresh water. Navigability, not tidal influence, ought to be acknowledged as the universal hallmark of the public trust.

The public trust doctrine has its roots in English common law. Traditionally, all navigable waterways in England were by law common highways for the public. Both petitioners and respondents have made an effort to ascertain the extent of the king's rights under English common law.

Unfortunately, English cases of the late eighteenth and early nineteenth centuries did not directly address whether the king held title to lands underlying tidally influenced, non-navigable waters. Certainly the public's right of navigation was limited to waterways that were navigable in fact, and did not extend to every waterway subject to the ebb and flow of the tide.

American cases have developed the public trust doctrine in a way that is consistent with its common law heritage. Our precedents explain that the public trust extends to navigable waterways because its fundamental purpose is to preserve them for common use for transportation. "It is, indeed, the susceptibility to use as highways of commerce which gives sanction to the public right of control over navigation upon [navigable waterways], and consequently to the exclusion of private ownership, either of the waters or the soils under them." *Packer v. Bird*, 137 U.S. 661, 667 (1891). Similarly, the Court has emphasized that the public trust doctrine "is founded upon the necessity of preserving to the public the use of navigable waters from private interruption and encroachment." *Illinois Central R. Co. v. Illinois*, 146 U.S. 387, 436 (1892).

Although the States may commit public trust waterways to uses other than transportation, such as fishing or land reclamation, this exercise of sovereign discretion does not enlarge the scope of the public trust. Even the majority does not claim that the public trust extends to every waterway that can be used for fishing or for land reclamation. Nor does the majority explain why its tidal test is superior to a navigability test for the purpose of identifying waterways that are suited to these other uses.

Because the fundamental purpose of the public trust is to protect commerce, the scope of the public trust should parallel the scope of federal admiralty jurisdiction. This Court long ago abandoned the tidal test in favor of the navigability test for defining federal admiralty jurisdiction, describing the ebb-and-flow test as "purely artificial and arbitrary as well as unjust." *The Propeller Genesee Chief v. Fitzhugh*, 12 How. 443, 457 (1852). The Court recognized that whether waters are influenced by the tide is irrelevant to the purposes of admiralty jurisdiction, which are to facilitate commerce in times of peace and to administer the special rules of war. Subsequent admiralty cases confirm that "the ebb and flow of the tide do not constitute the usual test, as in England, or any test at all of the navigability of waters." *The Daniel Ball*, 77 U.S. 557, 563 (1871).

Having defined admiralty jurisdiction in terms of navigability, the Court applied the same reasoning to the problem of defining the public trust. The Court explained that "the public authorities ought to have entire control of the great passageways of commerce and navigation, to be exercised for the public advantage and convenience." *Barney v. Keokuk*, 94 U.S. 324, 338 (1877). And it sweepingly concluded that the tidal test "had no place in American jurisprudence since the decision in the case of *The Propeller Genesee Chief v. Fitzhugh*, 12 How. 443." *McGilvra v. Ross*, 215 U.S. 70, 78 (1909). These cases defined the public trust in the context of inland waterways. But the same reasoning applies to waterways influenced by the tide. Navigability, not tidal influence, characterizes the waterways that are suited to the purposes of the public trust.

Congress also has evidenced its belief that the States' public trusts are limited to lands underlying navigable waters. In 1953, Congress passed the Submerged Lands Act, 43 U.S.C. 1301–1315. Congress intended to confirm the States' existing rights to lands beneath navigable waters. The Act defines "lands beneath navigable waters" as including lands "covered by tidal waters." 43 U.S.C. 1301(a)(2). If tidal waters included discrete bodies of non-navigable water, this definition would be self-contradictory. Thus it appears that Congress understood "tidal waters" as referring to the boundaries of the navigable ocean. As Senator Cordon explained, "lands beneath navigable waters" identifies lands "as being under nontidal waters in the upper areas or being in tidal waters and—and I want this emphasized—outside inland waters." 99 Cong. Rec. 2632 (1953). Although the Submerged Lands Act is not at issue in this case, it is evidence of Congress's interpretation of the public trust doctrine, and that interpretation is entitled to consideration.

In sum, the purpose of the public trust, the analogy to federal admiralty jurisdiction, and the legislative history of the Submerged Lands Act all indicate that the States hold title only to lands underlying navigable waters. The term "navigable waters" is not self-defining, however. It must be construed with reference to cases in which this Court has described the boundaries of the public trust.

For public trust purposes, navigable bodies of water include the non-navigable areas at their boundaries. The question of whether a body of water is navigable is answered waterway by waterway, not inch by inch. The borders of the ocean, which certainly is navigable, extend to the mean high tide line as a matter of federal common law. Hence the States' public trusts include the ocean shore over which the tide ebbs and flows. This explains why there is language in our cases describing the public trust in terms of tidewaters: each of those cases concerned the shores of a navigable body of water. This does not imply, however, that all tidally influenced waters are part of the sea any more than it implies that the Missouri River is part of the Gulf of Mexico.

The Court holds today that the public trust includes not only tidewaters along the ocean shore, but also discrete bodies of water that are influenced by the tide but far removed from the ocean or any navigable tidal water, such as the separate little streams and bayous at issue here. The majority doubts whether a satisfactory test could be devised for distinguishing between the two types of tidally influenced waters. It therefore adopts a test that will include in the public trust every body of water that is interconnected to the ocean, even indirectly, no matter how remote it is from navigable water. This is wholly inconsistent with the federal law that identifies what inland fresh waters belong to the public trust. For example, if part of a freshwater river is navigable in fact, it does not follow that all continuous parts of the river belong to the public trust, no matter how distant they are from the navigable part. Conversely, federal law does not exclude from the public trust all non-navigable portions of a navigable river, such as shallow areas near the banks.

The question here is not with respect to a short interruption of navigability in a stream otherwise navigable, or of a negligible part, which boats may use, of a stream otherwise non-navigable. We are concerned with long reaches with particular characteristics of navigability or non-navigability." *United States v. Utah*, 283 U.S. 64, 77 (1831). See *Oklahoma v. Texas*, 258 U.S. 574 (1922, applying the navigability test to identify what parts of the Red and Arkansas rivers belong to the public trust).

To decide whether the tidewaters at issue in this case belong to the public trust, the Court should apply the same fact-specific navigability test that it applies to inland waters. It should distinguish between navigable bodies of water and connected, but discrete, bodies of tidally influenced water. To this end, Justice Field once applied the headland to headland test, a "universal rule governing the measurement of waters," and drew a boundary dividing the navigable waters of San Francisco Bay from the tidally influenced waters of Mission Creek. *Knight v. United States Land Assn.*, 142 U.S. 161, 207 (1891). Only waterways that are part of a navigable body of water belong to the public trust.

II.

The controversy in this case concerns more than cold legal doctrine. The particular facts of this case, to which the court's opinion gives short shrift, illustrate how unfortunate it is for the court to recognize a claim that appears belated and opportunistic.

Mississippi showed no interest in the disputed land from the time it became a State until the 1970s. Petitioners, or prior titleholders, recorded deeds on the land and paid property taxes throughout this period. In 1973, Mississippi passed the Coastal Wetlands Protection Law. Miss. Code Ann. 49-27-1 to 49-27-69 (Supp. 1987). This statute directed the Mississippi Marine Resources Council to prepare maps identifying state-owned wetlands. The maps, drawn from aerial photographs, were intended to show the probable scope of state-owned wetlands in order to aid state agencies in planning to protect them. 49-27-65. But the Mineral Lease Commission decided to use the maps as a basis for issuing oil and gas leases on what appeared to be state-owned lands. The Commission leased 600 acres to respondent Saga Petroleum U.S., Inc.

Petitioners, holders of record title, filed a complaint in Chancery Court to quiet title to the 600 contested acres and an additional 1,800 acres in the area. The Chancery Court decided that the public trust included lands underlying all tidally influenced waters. Even under this test, only 140.863 acres of the land belonged to the State of Mississippi. On appeal, the Supreme Court of Mississippi reduced Mississippi's claim by another 98 acres to account for land underlying two artificial lakes. The land now claimed by Mississippi consists of slightly more than 42 acres underlying the north branch of Bayou LaCroix and 11 small drainage streams.

These waterways are not used for commercial navigation. None of the drainage streams is more than a mile long; all are nameless. Mississippi is not pressing its claim for the sake of facilitating commerce, or even to protect the public's interest in fishing or other traditional uses of the public trust. Instead, it is leasing the land to a private party for exploitation of underlying minerals. Mississippi's novel undertaking has caused it to press for a radical expansion of the historical limits of the public trust.

The Court's decision today could dispossess thousands of blameless record owners and leaseholders of land that they and their predecessors in interest reasonably believed was lawfully theirs. The Court concludes that a decision favoring petitioners would be even more disruptive, because titles may have been adjudicated on the assumption that a tidal test defines the public trust. There is no way to ascertain, in a general matter, what assumptions about the public trust underlie existing property titles. What evidence there is suggests that the majority's rule is the one that will upset settled expectations. For example, the State of New

Jersey has decided to apply the Court's test. It now claims for its public trust all land underlying non-navigable tidal waters, and all land that has been under tidal waters at any time since the American Revolution.

Due to this attempted expansion of the [public trust] doctrine, hundreds of properties in New Jersey have been taken and used for state purposes without compensating the record owners or lien holders; prior homeowners of many years are being threatened with loss of title; prior grants and state deeds are being ignored; properties are being arbitrarily claimed and conveyed by the State to persons other than the record owners; and hundreds of cases remain pending and untried before the state courts awaiting processing with the National Resource Council. "Porro & Teleky, Marshland Title Dilemma: A Tidal Phenomenon," 3 Seton Hall L. Rev. 323, 325–26 (1972).

The Court's decision today endorses and encourages such action in other States.

Although there is no way to predict exactly how much land will be affected by the Court's decision, the magnitude of the problem is suggested by the fact that more than nine million acres have been classified as fresh or saline coastal wetlands. The Federal Government conveyed these lands to the States, which have conveyed many of them to individuals. To the extent that the conveyances to private parties purported to include public trust lands, the States may strike them down, if state law permits. The Court's broad definition of public trust lands will increase the amount of land that is vulnerable to such challenges.

The Court's suggestion that state law might honor the equitable considerations that support individual claims to public trust lands is not persuasive. Certainly the Mississippi Supreme Court's decision in this case attached little weight to petitioners' equitable claims. Although Mississippi collected taxes on the land and made no mention of its claim for over 150 years, the Mississippi Supreme Court held that Mississippi was not estopped from dispossessing petitioners. *Cinque Bambini Partnership v. State*, 491 So. 2d 508, 521 (1986). The stakes are high when the land lies over valuable oil, gas, or mineral deposits.

The Court's decision departs from our precedents, and I fear that it may permit grave injustice to be done to innocent property holders in coastal States. I dissent.

Questions

1. Do you find the holding in the *Phillips* case troubling in any respect?

2. Why were the other coastal states participating as amicus curiae?

3. Do you find the majority or the dissenting opinion more persuasive?

4. What is the "equal footing" doctrine?

5. Isn't it logical that admiralty jurisdiction was limited to navigable waters?

Borax Consolidated Ltd. v. City of Los Angeles, 296 U.S. 10 (1935)

CHIEF JUSTICE HUGHES delivered the opinion of the Court.

The City of Los Angeles brought this suit to quiet title to land claimed to be tideland of Mormon Island situated in the inner bay of San Pedro, now known as Los Angeles Harbor. The City asserted title under a legislative grant by the State. The Act of 1911 (Stats. 1911, c. 656, p. 1256) provided:

There is hereby granted to the city of Los Angeles, a municipal corporation of the State of California, and to its successors, all the right, title, and interest of the State of California, held by said state by virtue of its sovereignty, in and to all the tide lands and submerged lands, whether filled or unfilled, within the present boundaries of said city, and situated below the line of mean high tide of the Pacific Ocean, or of any harbor, estuary, bay or inlet within said boundaries.

Petitioners claimed under a preemption patent issued by the United States on December 30, 1881, to one William Banning. The District Court entered a decree, upon findings, dismissing the complaint upon the merits and adjudging that petioner, Borax Consolidated, Limited, was the owner in fee simple and entitled to the possession of the property. 5 F. Supp. 281. The Circuit Court of Appeals reversed the decree. 74 F. (2d) 901. Because of the importance of the questions presented, and of an asserted conflict with decisions of this Court, we granted certiorari, June 3, 1935.

Petitioners contest these rulings of the Court of Appeals. With respect to the ascertainment of the shoreline, they insist that the court erred in taking the "mean high tide line" and in rejecting "neap tides" as the criterion for ordinary high water mark.

1. The controversy is limited by settled principles governing the title to tidelands. The soils under tidewaters within the original States were reserved to them respectively, and the States since admitted to the Union have the same sovereignty and jurisdiction in relation to such lands within their borders as the original States possessed. *Martin v. Waddell*, 41 U.S. 367 (1842). This doctrine applies to tidelands in California. Upon the acquisition of the territory from Mexico, the United States acquired the title to tidelands equally with the title to upland, but held the former only in trust for the future States that might be erected out of that territory. *Knight v. United States Land Assn.*, 142 U.S. 161, 183.

2. As the District Court fell into a fundamental error in treating the survey and patent as conclusive, it was not incumbent upon the Court of Appeals to review the evidence and decide whether it showed, or failed to show, that the land in question was tideland. The court remanded the cause for a new trial in which the issues as to the boundary between upland and tideland, and as to the defenses urged by petitioners, are to be determined. In that disposition of the case we find no error.

3. There remains for our consideration, however, the ruling of the Court of Appeals in instructing the District Court to ascertain as the boundary "the mean high tide line" and in thus rejecting the line of "neap tides."

Petitioners claim under a federal patent which, according to the plat, purported to convey land bordering on the Pacific Ocean. There is no question that the United States was free to convey the upland, and the patent affords no ground for holding that it did not convey all the title that the United States had in the premises. The question as to the extent of this federal grant, that is, as to the limit of the land conveyed, or the boundary between the upland and the tideland, is necessarily a federal question. It is a question which concerns the validity and effect of an act done by the United States; it involves the ascertainment of the essential basis of a right asserted under federal law. Rights and interests in the tideland, which is subject to the sovereignty of the State, are matters of local law.

The tideland extends to the high water mark. This does not mean, as petitioners contend, a physical mark made upon the ground by the waters; it means the line of high water as determined by the course of the tides. By the civil law, the shore extends as far as the highest waves reach in winter. But by the common law, the shore "is confined to the flux and reflux of the sea at ordinary tides." It is the land "between ordinary high and low-water mark, the land over which the daily tides ebb and flow. When, therefore, the sea, or a bay, is named as a boundary, the line of ordinary high-water mark is always intended where the common law prevails." *United States v. Pacheco*, 2 Wall. 587, 590.

The range of the tide at any given place varies from day to day, and the question is, how is the line of "ordinary" high water to be determined? The range of the tide at times of new moon and full moon "is greater than the average," as "high water then rises higher and low water falls lower than usual." The tides at such times are called "spring tides." When the moon is in its first and third quarters, "the tide does not rise as high nor fall as low as on the average." At such times the tides are known as "neap tides." "Tidal Datum Plane," U.S. Coast and Geodetic Survey, Special Publication No. 135, p. 3. The view that "neap tides" should be taken as the ordinary tides had its origin in the statement of Lord Hale. In his classification, there are

three sorts of shores, or *littora marina*, according to the various tides: (1) the high spring tides, which are the fluxes of the sea at those tides that happen at the two equinoxials; (2) the spring tides, which happen twice every month at full and change of the moon; and (3) ordinary tides, or nepe tides, which happen between the full and change of the moon.

The last kind of shore, said Lord Hale, "is that which is properly littus maris." He thus excluded the "spring tides" of the month, assigning as the reason that "for the most part the lands covered with these fluxes are dry and maniorable," that is, not reached by the tides.

In California, the Acts of 1911 and 1917, upon which the City of Los Angeles bases its claim, grant the "tidelands and submerged lands" situated "below the line of mean high tide of the Pacific Ocean." Petitioners urge that "ordinary high water mark" has been defined by the state court as referring to the line of the neap tides. We find it unneccessary to review the cases cited or to attempt to determine whether they record a final judgment as to the construction of the state statute, which, of course, is a question for the state courts.

In determining the limit of the federal grant, we perceive no justification for taking neap high tides or the mean of those tides, as the boundary between upland and the tideland, and for thus excluding from the shore the land which is actually covered by the tides most of the time. In order to include the land that is thus covered, it is necessary to take the mean high tide line which, as the Court of Appeals said, is neither the spring tide nor the neap tide, but a mean of all the high tides.

In view of the definition of the mean high tide, as given by the United States Coast and Geodetic Survey, that "mean high water at any place is the average height of all the high waters at the place over a considerable period of time," and the further observation that "from theoretical considerations of an astronomical character" there should be a "periodic variation in the rise of water above sea level having a period of 18.6 years," the Court of Appeals directed that in order to ascertain the mean high tide line with requisite certainty in fixing the boundary of valuable tidelands, such as those here in question appear to be, "an average of 18.6 years should be determined as near as possible." We find no error in that instruction.

The decree of the Court of Appeals is affirmed.

Questions

1. What practical problems are presented by the application of the *Borax* rule? Can you think of a simpler method?

2. Would there be any problem if a state simply declared all beaches public?

State v. Ibbison, 448 A.2d 728, (R.I. 1982)

Defendants were convicted in the Fourth Division District Court of criminal trespass in violation of municipal code which prohibits a person from knowingly entering upon land of another without having been requested or invited to do so by owner or occupant of land, and they appealed. The Superior Court, Washington County, DeRobbio, J., granted defendants' motions to dismiss charges, and the State appealed those dismissals. The Supreme Court, Shea, J., held that: (1) for purposes of constitutional article governing fishery rights and shore privileges, mean high-tide line is landward boundary of shore; (2) dismissals would be affirmed on due process grounds; and (3) any municipality that intends to impose criminal penalties for trespass on waterfront property above mean-high-tide line must prove beyond reasonable doubt the defendant knew location of boundary line and intentionally trespassed across it.

Appeal denied and dismissed, granting of motion to dismiss charges affirmed.

Opinion

In this case, we consider a question involving the interpretation of a provision of our state constitution. Article I, section 17, of the Rhode Island Constitution, as amended by Art. XXXVII, secs. 1–2, provides that the people of the state "shall continue to enjoy and freely exercise all the rights of fishery, and the privileges of the shore, to which they have been heretofore entitled under the charter and usages of this state." The question raised is this: To what point does the shore extend on its landward boundary? The setting of this boundary will fix the point at which the land held in trust by the state for the enjoyment of all its people ends and private property belonging to littoral owners begins.

The defendants in this case, James Ibbison III, Don E. Morris, Allen E. Zumwalt, James W. Sminkey, Miles R. Stray, and William S. Gavitt were convicted in the Fourth Division District Court on February 2, 1979, of criminal trespass in violation of 19-17 of the Westerly Code. This section of the code prohibits a person from knowingly entering upon the land of another without having been requested or invited to do so by the owner or occupant of the land. The defendants were each fined $10 plus costs. They appealed their convictions to the Superior Court. On December 9, 1980, a justice of the Superior Court granted defendants' motion to dismiss the charges. The District and Superior Court justices reached different conclusions based on their fixing the boundary between the shore and littoral owners at different points. The state has appealed the dismissals.

Since this case is not before us after a trial in the Superior Court and we have no transcript of the District Court proceedings, there is no record of the facts other than the assertions of counsel. Fortunately, a lengthy recitation of facts is not necessary because the key fact needed for the resolution of this appeal has been stipulated to by the parties.

This dispute arose as defendants were engaged in a beach clean-up operation in Westerly. As defendants traveled along the beach, they were stopped by Wilfred Kay, a littoral owner, and Patrolman Byron Brown of the Westerly police department. Kay, believing his private property extended to the mean high-water line, had staked out that line previously. He informed defendants that they were not permitted to cross the landward side of it. The defendants, on the other hand, believed that their right to traverse the shore extended to the high-water mark. This line was defined by defendants in the Superior Court as a visible line on the shore indicated by the reach of an average high tide and further indicated by drifts and seaweed along the shore. It has been stipulated by the parties that defendants had crossed the mean high-tide line but were below the high-water mark at the time of their arrest. Also, at the time of the arrest, the mean high-tide line was under water.

We have referred to the term "high water mark" as used by defendants and accepted by the Superior Court. We shall now discuss the term "mean high tide line." This line is relied upon by the state as the proper boundary, and it is the line accepted by the District Court. The mean high tide is the arithmetic average of high-water heights observed over an 18.6-year Metonic cycle. It is the line that is formed by the intersection of the tidal plane of mean high tide with the shore.

The issue before us is in reality very narrow because the prior decided cases of this court have consistently recognized that the shore lies between high and low water.

The problem we face is that none of these cases have defined how the high-water line is to be calculated. Although no prior Rhode Island case explicitly resolves the question before us, there are two cases, however, that are somewhat helpful. In *Allen v. Allen*, 19 R.I. 114, 32 A. 166 (1895), this court stated that "[t]he State holds the legal fee of all lands below high water mark as a common law." Next, in *Jackvony v. Powel*, 67 R.I. 218, 21 A.2d 554 (1941), the court held unconstitutional under Art. I, sec. 17, a statute that would have permitted the city of Newport to erect a fence at Easton's Beach between the high- and low-water marks.

At various times in the *Jackvony* case, the court referred to the high-water line or mark, and at other times it referred to the mean high tide. Specifically, with regard to the privileges of the people on the shore, the court referred to the shores as "bordering on tidewaters and lying between the lines of mean high tide and mean low tide." We find that the *Jackvony* court used the two terms interchangeably.

The interesting point about the *Allen* case is the court's reliance on the common law in finding that the state holds title to all lands below the high-water mark, because at common law the boundary was the mean high-tide line. Here again, we believe that the *Allen* court uses these terms interchangeably.

It is difficult to discern any real difference between the two positions argued here. By definition, the mean high tide is, in reality, an average high tide. Similarly, defendants have defined the high-water mark in terms of an average. The defendants contend that their high-water mark is such, however, that it is readily observable because of drifts and the presence of seaweed. Our difficulty in accepting this position is that we have absolutely no evidence before us from which we could determine that this is generally true. As noted previously, we are handicapped by the absence of a record in this case. For this reason the only permissible action for us to take is to affix the boundary as was done at common law and which this court in *Allen* declared to be the settled policy of this state.

The common law background of this issue can be traced back several hundred years. Originally, land titles in England came from a grant from the crown beginning back during the reign of King John, which ended in 1216. These early grants were imprecise, however, especially because of the lack of definition of the seaward boundary of coastal grants. The grantees, however, no doubt viewed their property as extending to the sea.

In 1568–1569, Thomas Digges, a mathematician, engineer, astronomer, and lawyer, wrote a short treatise in which he concluded that the tidelands had not been included in the grants of the seacoasts by the crown. This work went largely unnoticed until 1670 when Sir Matthew Hale incorporated Digges's theory into his very influential treatise *De Jure Maris*. In this work Hale defined the shore as follows: "The shore is that ground that is between the ordinary high-water and low-water mark. This doth prima facie and of common right belong to the king, both in the shore of the sea and the shore of the arms of the sea."

After this time, the burden of proof was placed on landowners to show that their particular property extended to the low-water mark, and not the high-water mark. The burden placed this way made it very difficult for landowners to overcome.

This was the state of development of the law in England at the time of the colonization of the eastern shoreline of North America. After the Revolutionary War and the formation of our Republic, the individual states retained their own tidelands as they had previously. In a series of United States Supreme Court decisions beginning with *Martin v. Waddell*, 41 U.S. 367 (1842), and culminating with *Borax Consolidated Ltd. v. City of Los Angeles*, 296 U.S. 10 (1935), the Court confirmed individual state ownership of the tidelands.

There had been some uncertainty in the United States regarding whether the boundary was properly at the point of the mean high tide or the mean low tide, but this uncertainty was largely removed in 1935 when it was held in *Borax Consolidated, supra*, that the common law rule put the boundary between littoral owners and the state at the line of the mean high tide.

The Court noted that at common law the spring tides, the highest tides of the month, were excluded as the landward boundary of the shore since for the most part this land was dry and not reached by the tides. Presumably, the point reached by the spring tides is the same point as that argued by defendants as being the high-water mark evidenced by drifts and sea-weed.

Recognizing the monthly changes of the tides, the Court recited the following formula, used by the Court of Appeals, for finding the mean high-tide line:

From theoretical considerations of an astronomical character there should be a "periodic variation in the rise of water above sea level having a period of 18.6 years" the Court of Appeals directed that in order to ascertain the mean high tide line with requisite certainty in fixing the boundary of valuable tidelands, such as those here in question appear to be, "an average of 18.6 years should be determined as near as possible." We find no error in that instruction.

We concur in this analysis and apply the mean high-tide line as the landward boundary of the shore for the purposes of the privileges guaranteed to the people of this state by our constitution. This court has held that the common law governs the rights and obligations of the people of the state unless that law has been modified by our General Assembly. Here we apply the common law to govern the interpretation of a constitutional provision.

In fixing the landward boundary of the shore at the mean high-tide line, we are mindful that there is a disadvantage in that this point is not readily identifiable by the casual observer. We doubt, however, that any boundary could be set that would be readily apparent to an observer when we consider the varied topography of our shoreline. The mean-high-tide line represents the point that can be determined scientifically with the greatest certainty. Clearly, a line de-

termined over a period of years using modern scientific techniques is more precise than a mark made by the changing tides driven by the varying forces of nature. In *Luttes v. State*, 159 Tex. 500, 519, 324 S.W.2d 167, 179 (1958), the Texas court concluded that "common sense suggests a line based on a long-term average of daily highest water levels, rather than a line based on some theory of occasional or sporadic highest waters."

Additionally, we feel that our decision best balances the interests between littoral owners and all the people of the state. Setting the boundary at the point where the spring tides reach would unfairly take from littoral owners land that is dry for most of the month. Similarly, setting the boundary below the mean high-tide line at the line of the mean low tide would so restrict the size of the shore as to render it practically nonexistent.

Finally setting the boundary as we have done brings us in accord with many of the other states. We note that in a couple of these cases the term "high-water mark" is used in place of "mean high-tide line." However, this is inconsequential as each state defines the phrase in terms of the mean high tide.

This brings us to the actual disposition of this matter. In view of the lack of clarity in early decisions of this court regarding whether the landward boundary of the shoreline was to be computed as a mean or as an absolute high-water mark, we shall affirm the dismissals of the charges by the Superior Court justice but for different reasons.

We affirm the dismissals since basic due process provides that no man shall be held criminally responsible for conduct that he could not reasonably understand to be proscribed. Although this situation most often occurs when statutes are challenged for vagueness, we find that the facts of this case are such that these defendants are entitled to similar protection.

In the future, any municipality that intends to impose criminal penalties for trespass on waterfront property above the mean high-tide line must prove beyond reasonable doubt that the defendant knew the location of the boundary line and intentionally trespassed across it.

For the reasons stated, the appeal is denied and dismissed, the granting of the motion to dismiss is affirmed, and the papers of the court are remanded to the Superior Court.

Questions

1. What would you recommend to a waterfront property owner who wishes to exclude the public after *Ibbison*?

2. How would the *Ibbison* rule apply to waterfront property which has been filled and bulkheaded so that no intertidal zone remains?

Chapter 2

THE PUBLIC TRUST DOCTRINE

Illinois Central Railroad v. Illinois, 146 U.S. 387 (1892)

JUSTICE FIELD delivered the opinion of the court.

The object of the suit is to obtain a judicial determination of the title of certain lands on the east or lake front of the city of Chicago, situated between the Chicago River and Sixteenth Street, which have been reclaimed from the waters of the lake, and are occupied by the tracks, depots, warehouses, piers and other structures used by the railroad company in its business; and also of the title claimed by the company to the submerged lands, constituting the bed of the lake, lying east of its tracks, within the corporate limits of the city, for the distance of a mile, and between the south line of the south pier near the Chicago River extended eastwardly, and a line extended, in the same direction, from the south line of lot 21 near the company's roundhouse and machine shops. The determination of the title of the company will involve a consideration of its right to construct, for its own business, as well as for public convenience, wharves, piers, and docks in the harbor.

The State of Illinois was admitted into the Union in 1818 on an equal footing with the original States in all respects. Such was one of the conditions of the cession from Virginia of the territory northwest of the Ohio River, out of which the State was formed. But the equality prescribed would have existed if it had not been thus stipulated. There can be no distinction between the several States of the Union in the character of the jurisdiction, sovereignty, and dominion which they may possess and exercise over persons and subjects within their respective limits. The boundaries of the State were prescribed by Congress and accepted by the State in its original Constitution. They are given in the bill. It is sufficient for our purpose to observe that they include within their eastern line all that portion of Lake Michigan lying east of the main land of the State and the middle of the lake south of latitude forty-two degrees and thirty minutes.

It is the settled law of this country that the ownership of and dominion and sovereignty over lands covered by tidewaters, within the limits of the several States, belong to the respective States within which they are found, with the consequent right to use or dispose of any portion thereof, when that can be done without substantial impairment of the interest of the public in the waters, and subject always to the paramount right of Congress to control their navigation so far as may be necessary for the regulation of commerce with foreign nations and among the States. This doctrine has been often announced by this court, and is not questioned by counsel of any of the parties.

The same doctrine is in this country held to be applicable to lands covered by fresh water in the Great Lakes over which is conducted an extended commerce with different States and foreign nations. These lakes possess all the general characteristics of open seas, except in the freshness of their waters, and in the absence of the ebb and flow of the tide. In other respects they are inland seas, and there is no reason or principle for the assertion of dominion and sovereignty over and ownership by the State of lands covered by tidewaters that is not equally applicable to its ownership of and dominion and sovereignty over lands covered by the fresh waters of these lakes. At one time the existence of tidewaters was deemed essential in determining the admiralty jurisdiction of courts in England. That doctrine is now repudiated in this country as wholly inapplicable to our condition. In England the ebb and flow of the tide constitute the legal test of the navigability of waters. There no waters are navigable in fact, at least to any great extent, which are not subject to the tide. There, as said in the case of *Genesee Chief*, 12 How. 443, 455, "tide water and navigable water are unimportant exceptions, meant nothing more than public rivers, as contradistinguished from private ones"; and writers on the subject of admiralty jurisdiction "took the ebb and flow of the tide as the test because it was a convenient one, and more easily determined the character of the river. Hence the established doctrine in England, that the admiralty jurisdiction is confined to the ebb and flow of the tide. In other words, it is confined to public navigable waters."

But in this country the case is different. Some of our rivers are navigable for great distances above the flow of the tide—indeed, for hundreds of miles, by the largest vessels used in commerce. As said in the case cited:

There is certainly nothing in the ebb and flow of the tide that makes the waters peculiarly suitable for admiralty jurisdiction, nor anything in the absence of a tide that renders it unfit. If it is a public navigable water, on which commerce is carried on between different States or nations, the reason for the jurisdiction is precisely the same. And if a distinction is made on that account, it is merely arbitrary, without any foundation in reason; and, indeed, would seem to be inconsistent with it.

The Great Lakes are not in any appreciable respect affected by the tide, and yet on their waters, as said above, a large commerce is carried on, exceeding in many instances the entire commerce of States on the borders of the sea. When the reason of the limitation of admiralty jurisdiction in England was found inapplicable to the condition of navigable waters in this country, the limitation and all its incidents were discarded. So also, by the common law, the doctrine of the dominion over and ownership by the crown of lands within the realm under tide waters is not founded upon the existence of the tide over the lands, but upon the fact that the waters are navigable, tide waters and navigable waters, as already said, being used as synonymous terms in England. The public being interested in the use of such waters, the possession by private individuals of lands under them could not be permitted except by license of the crown, which could alone exercise such dominion over the waters as would insure freedom in their use so far as consistent with the public interest. The doctrine is founded upon the necessity of preserving to the public the use of navigable waters from private interruption and encroachment, a reason as applicable to navigable fresh waters as to waters moved by the tide. We hold, therefore, that the same doctrine as to the dominion and sovereignty over and ownership of lands under the navigable waters of the Great Lakes applies, which obtains at the common law as to the dominion and sovereignty over and ownership of lands under tide waters on the borders of the sea, and that the lands are held by the same trusts and limitations. Upon that theory we shall examine how far such dominion, sovereignty, and proprietary right have been encroached upon by the railroad company, and how far that company had, at the time, the assent of the State to such encroachment, and also the validity of the claim which the company asserts of a right to make further encroachments thereon by virtue of a grant from the State in April 1869.

We shall hereafter consider what rights the company acquired as a riparian owner from its acquisition of title to lands on the shore of the lake, but at present we are speaking only of what rights it acquired from the reclamation of the tract upon which the railroad and the works in connection with it are built. The construction of a pier or the extension of any land into navigable waters for a railroad or other purposes, by one not the owner of lands on the shore, does not give the builder of such pier or extension, whether an individual or corporation, any riparian rights. Those rights are incident to riparian ownership. They exist with such ownership and pass with the transfer of the land. And the land must not only be contiguous to the water, but in contact with it. Proximity without contact is insufficient. The riparian right attaches to land on the border of navigable water without any declaration to that effect from the former owner, and its designation in a conveyance by him would be surplusage. (See Gould on Waters, 148, and authorities there cited.)

The riparian proprietor is entitled, among other rights, as held in *Yates v. Milwaukee*, 10 Wall. 497, 504, to access to the navigable part of the water on the front of which lies his land, and for that purpose to make a landing, wharf, or pier for his own use or for the use of the public, subject to such general rules and regulations as the legislature may prescribe for the protection of the rights of the public. In the case cited the court held that this riparian right was property and valuable; and though it must be enjoyed in due subjection to the rights of the public, it could not be arbitrarily or capriciously impaired. It had been held in the previous case of *Dutton v. Strong*, 1 Black, 23, 33, that whenever the water of the shore was too shoal to be navigable, there was the same necessity for wharves, piers, and landing places as in the bays and arms of the sea; that where that necessity existed, it was difficult to see any reason for denying to the adjacent owner the right to supply it; but that the right must be understood as terminating at the point of navigability, where the necessity for such erections ordinarily ceased.

We proceed to consider the claim of the railroad company to the ownership of submerged lands in the harbor, and the right to construct such wharves, piers, docks, and other works therein as it may deem proper for its interest and business.

As to the grant of the submerged lands, the act declares that all the right and title of the State in and to the submerged lands, constituting the bed of Lake Michigan, and lying east of the tracks and breakwater of the company for the distance of one mile, and between the south line of the south pier extended eastwardly and a line extended eastwardly from the south line of lot 21, south of and near to the roundhouse and machine shops of the company "are granted in fee to the railroad company, its successors and assigns." The grant is accompanied with a proviso that the fee of the lands shall be held by the company in perpetuity, and that it shall not have the power to grant, sell, or convey the fee thereof. It also declares that nothing therein shall authorize obstructions to the harbor or impair the public right of navigation, or be construed to exempt the company from any act regulating the rates of wharfage and dockage to be charged in the harbor.

This clause is treated by the counsel of the company as an absolute conveyance to it of title to the submerged lands, giving it as full and complete power to use and dispose of the same, except in the technical transfer of the fee, in any manner it may choose, as if they were uplands, in no respect covered or affected by navigable waters, and not as a license to use the lands subject to revocation by the State. Treating it as such a conveyance, its validity must be determined by the consideration whether the legislature was competent to make a grant of the kind.

The act, if valid and operative to the extent claimed, placed under the control of the railroad company nearly the whole of the submerged lands of the harbor, subject only to the limitations that it should not authorize obstructions to the harbor or impair the public right of navigation, or exclude the legislature from regulating the rates of wharfage or dockage to be charged. With these limitations the act put it in the power of the company to delay indefinitely the improvement of the harbor, or to construct as many docks, piers, wharves, and other works as it might choose, and at such positions in the harbor as might suit its purposes, and permit any kind of business to be conducted thereon, and to lease them out on its own terms, for indefinite periods. The inhibition against the technical transfer of the fee of any portion of the submerged lands was of little consequence when it could make a lease for any period and renew it at its pleasure. And the inhibitions against authorizing obstructions to the harbor and impairing the public right of navigation placed no impediments upon the action of the railroad company which did not previously exist. A corporation created for one purpose, the construction and operation of a railroad between designated points, is, by the act, converted into a corporation to manage and practically control the harbor of Chicago, not simply for its own purpose as a railroad corporation, but for its own profit generally.

The circumstances attending the passage of the act through the legislature were on the hearing the subject of much criticism. As orig-

inally introduced, the purpose of the act was to enable the city of Chicago to enlarge its harbor and to grant to it the title and interest of the State to certain lands adjacent to the shore of Lake Michigan on the eastern front of the city, and place the harbor under its control, giving it all the necessary powers for its wise management. But during the passage of the act its purpose was changed. Instead of providing for the cessation of the submerged lands to the city, it provided for a cession of them to the railroad company. It was urged that the title of the act was not changed to correspond with its changed purpose, and an objection was taken to its validity on that account. But the majority of the court were of opinion that the evidence was insufficient to show that the requirement of the constitution of the State, in its passage, was not complied with.

The question, therefore, to be considered is whether the legislature was competent to thus deprive the State of its ownership of the submerged lands in the harbor of Chicago, and of the consequent control of its waters; or, in other words, whether the railroad corporation can hold the lands and control the waters by the grant, against any future exercise of power over them by the State.

That the State holds the title to the lands under the navigable waters of Lake Michigan, within its limits, in the same manner that the State holds title to soils under tidewater, by the common law, we have already shown, and that title necessarily carried with it control over the waters above them whenever the lands are subjected to use. But it is a title different in character from that which the State holds in lands intended for sale. It is different from the title which the United States holds in the public lands which are open to preemption and sale. It is a title held in trust for the people of the State that they may enjoy the navigation of the waters, carry on commerce over them, and have liberty of fishing therein freed from the destruction or interference of private parties. The interest of the people in the navigation of the waters and in commerce over them may be improved in many instances by the erection of wharves, docks, and piers therein, for which purpose the State may grant parcels of the submerged lands; and, so long as their disposition is made for such purpose, no valid objections can be made to the grants. It is grants of parcels of lands under navigable waters that may afford foundation for wharves, piers, docks, and other structures in aid of commerce, and grants of parcels which, being occupied, do not substantially impair the public interest in the lands and waters remaining that are chiefly considered and sustained in the adjudged cases as a valid exercise of legislative power consistently with the trust to the public upon which such lands are held by the State. But that is a very different doctrine from the one which would sanction the abdication of the general control of the State over lands under the navigable waters of an entire harbor or bay, or of a sea or lake. Such abdication is not consistent with the exercise of that trust which requires the government of the State to preserve such waters for the use of the public. The trust devolving upon the State for the public, and which can only be discharged by the management and control of property in which the public has an interest, cannot be relinquished by a transfer of the property. The control of the State for the purposes of the trust can never be lost, except as to such parcels as are used in promoting the interests of the public therein, or can be disposed of without any substantial impairment of the public interest in the lands and waters remaining. It is only by observing the distinction between a grant of such parcels for the improvement of the public interest, or which when occupied do not substantially impair the public interest in the lands and waters remaining, and a grant of the whole property in which the public is interested, that the language of the adjudged cases can be reconciled. General language sometimes found in opinions of the courts, expressive of absolute ownership and control by the State of lands under navigable waters, irrespective of any trust as to their use and disposition, must be read and construed with reference to the special facts of the particular cases. A grant of all the lands under the navigable waters of a State has never been adjudged to be within the legislative power; and any attempted grant of the kind would be held, if not absolutely void on its face, as subject to revocation. The State can no more abdicate its trust over property in which the whole people are interested, like navigable waters and soil under them, so as to leave them entirely under the use and control of private parties, except in the instance of parcels mentioned for the improvement of the navigation and use of the waters, or when parcels can be disposed of without impairment of the public interest in what remains, than it can abdicate its police powers in the administration of government and preservation of the peace. In the administration of government the use of such powers may for a limited period be delegated to a municipality or other body, but there always remains with the State the right to revoke those powers and exercise them in a more direct manner, and one more conformable to its wishes. So with trusts connected with public property, or property of a special character, like lands under navigable waters, they cannot be placed entirely beyond the direction and control of the State.

The harbor of Chicago is of immense value to the people of the State of Illinois in the facilities it affords to its vast and constantly increasing commerce; and the idea that its legislature can deprive the State of control over its bed and waters and place the same in the hands of a private corporation created for a different purpose, one limited to transportation of passengers and freight between distant points and the city, is a proposition that cannot be defended.

The area of the submerged lands proposed to be ceded by the act in question to the railroad company embraces something more than a thousand acres, being, as stated by counsel, more than three times the area of the outer harbor, and not only including all of that harbor but embracing adjoining submerged lands which will, in all probability, be hereafter included in the harbor. It is as large as that embraced by all the merchandise docks along the Thames at London; is much larger than that included in the famous docks and basins at Liverpool; is twice that of the port of Marseilles; and is nearly if not quite equal to the pier area along the waterfront of the city of New York. And the arrivals and clearings of vessels at the port exceed in number those of New York, and are equal to those of New York and Boston combined. Chicago has nearly 25 percent of the lake-carrying trade as compared with the arrivals and clearings of all the leading ports of our great inland seas. In the year ending June 30, 1886, the joint arrivals and clearances of vessels at that port amounted to 22,096, with a tonnage of over seven million; and in 1890 the tonnage of the vessels reached nearly nine million. As stated by counsel, since the passage of the Lake Front Act, in 1869, the population of the city has increased by nearly a million souls, and the increase of commerce has kept pace with it. It is hardly conceivable that the legislature can divest the State of the control and management of this harbor and vest it absolutely in a private corporation. Surely an act of the legislature transferring the title to its submerged lands and the power claimed by the railroad company to a foreign State or nation would be repudiated, without hesitation, as a gross perversion of the trust over the property under which it is held. So would a similar transfer to a corporation of another State. It would not be listened to that the control and management of the harbor of that great city—a subject of concern to the whole people of the State—should thus be placed elsewhere than in the State itself.

Any grant of the kind is necessarily revocable, and the exercise of the trust by which the property was held by the State can be resumed at any time. Undoubtedly there may be expenses incurred in improvements made under such a grant which the State ought to pay; but, be that as it may, the power to resume the trust whenever the State judges best is, we think, incon-

trovertible. The position advanced by the railroad company in support of its claim to the ownership of the submerged lands and the right to the erection of wharves, piers, and docks at its pleasure, or for its business in the harbor of Chicago, would place every harbor in the country at the mercy of a majority of the legislature of the State in which the harbor is situated.

We cannot, it is true, cite any authority where a grant of this kind has been held invalid, for we believe that no instance exists where the harbor of a great city and its commerce have been allowed to pass into the control of any private corporation. But the decisions are numerous which declare that such property is held by the State, by virtue of its sovereignty, in trust for the public. The ownership of the navigable waters of the harbor and of the lands under them is a subject of public concern to the whole people of the State. The trust with which they are held, therefore, is governmental and cannot be alienated, except in those instances mentioned of parcels used in the improvement of the interest thus held, or when parcels can be disposed of without detriment to the public interest in the lands and waters remaining.

The legislation which may be needed one day for the harbor may be different from the legislation that may be required at another day. Every legislature must, at the time of its existence, exercise the power of the State in the execution of the trust devolved upon it. We hold, therefore, that any attempted cession of the ownership and control of the State in and over the submerged lands in Lake Michigan, by the act of April 16, 1869, was inoperative to affect, modify, or in any respect to control the sovereignty and dominion of the State over the lands, or its ownership thereof, and that any such attempted operation of the act was annulled by the repealing act of April 15, 1873, which to that extent was valid and effective. There can be no irrepealable contract in a conveyance of property by a grantor in disregard of a public trust, under which he was bound to hold and manage it.

1. What motivated the state to make the grant in the first place?

2. Under what circumstances can title to submerged lands be transferred?

Boston Waterfront Dev. Corp. v. Commonwealth, 393 N.E.2d 356 (Mass. 1980)

QUIRICO, J.

This case arises from a dispute between the Boston Waterfront Development Corporation (BWDC) and the Commonwealth over the ownership of a small parcel of land at the end of a wharf extending into Boston Harbor. To resolve this dispute we must consider in historical perspective the allocation of rights among private parties, the Commonwealth, and the public to use, own, and enjoy one of the Commonwealth's most precious natural resources, its shore.

In 1964, the Commercial and Lewis Wharf Corporation, predecessor to BWDC, brought a petition to register title to a certain parcel of waterfront land under Lewis Wharf in the city of Boston, consisting of areas A, B, C, and F on an accompanying plan. After prolonged negotiations, BWDC, as substitute petitioner, and the Commonwealth stipulated that BWDC was the owner in fee simple of area A, that is, the land shoreward of the historic low water mark; and that BWDC would withdraw without prejudice its petition to register areas C and F. The only area remaining in dispute, area B, is the area between the low water mark and the currently existing seawall. This area is covered by the seaward end of a wharf constructed over filled land, partly occupied by the corner of an ancient granite building now renovated into modern shops, offices, restaurants, and condominiums. The parties agreed that the only issue to be decided by the Land Court was whether "the Petitioner obtained fee simple title to the soil beneath the fill" as a consequence of certain acts of the Legislature in the early nineteenth century shown collectively as the "Lewis Wharf statutes." The Land Court ruled that BWDC's predessor in title had obtained fee simple title, and entered a decree registering the land.

The Commonwealth appealed to the Appeals Court. Once again the issue framed was whether the petitioner had obtained fee simple title to the soil beneath the fill of area B as a result of the "Lewis Wharf statutes." The Appeals Court, in an opinion written by Goodman, J., agreed with the Land Court that BWDC's predecessors had been granted fee simple title to the disputed land, but added that it was held "subject to a condition subsequent that it be used in accordance with the purpose expressed in those statutes." We agree with the Appeals Court's decision.

Throughout history, the shores of the sea have been recognized as a special form of property of unusual value; and therefore subject to different legal rules from those which apply to inland property. At Roman law, all citizens held and had access to the seashore as a resource in common; in the words of Justinian, "they [the shores] cannot be said to belong to anyone as private property." With the collapse of the Roman Empire and its ordered system of law, public ownership of tidal areas gave way to a chaos of private fiefdoms. Under the English feudal law which emerged, ownership of the shore was claimed by the crown, which in turn had the power to grant out portions of its domain to the exclusive ownership and use of the private subjects who in fact possessed it.

The conflict between king and citizens that preceded the Magna Carta concerned, among other things, opposition to this absolute power of the crown to grant private rights in the shore, particularly as these rights interfered with the free navigation which was so essential to the rising commercial classes. After the Magna Carta, the competing interests were accommodated by a legal theory that divided the crown's rights to shore land below high water mark into two categories: a proprietary jus privatum, or ownership interest, and a governmental jus publicum, by which the king held the land in his sovereign capacity as a representative of all the people. This latter interest the crown could not convey into private hands, since it was "held as a public trust for all subjects and their free exercise of the common rights of navigation and fishery." The jus publicum was eventually understood to be under the control of Parliament, while the jus privatum belonged to the king. Since neither party held all the rights to the shore land, neither could convey it with free and clear title into private hands. These arrangements restored to the public some of the rights to the use of shore land which had been guaranteed by public ownership in Roman times.

These legal concepts are more than mere historical curiosities, because they were very much in the minds of the nineteenth-century legislators and judges who oversaw the development of Boston Harbor. When we attempt to interpret the significance of the legislative grants of rights in the Boston shoreline contained in the "Lewis Wharf statutes," we must remember that they were written by men who were familiar with the English common law history of the shore. The Supreme Judicial Court frequently referred in its opinions to the notion that the crown's ownership of shore land, from which all Massachusetts titles historically derived, was "in trust, for public uses." Legislative awareness of this historical background is evident, for example, in an 1850 report of the Senate Joint Committee on Mercantile Affairs and Insurance concerning the flats in Boston Harbor, in which the committee stated:

By the law of all civilized Europe, before the feudal system obtained in England, there was no such thing as property in tide waters. Tide waters were *res omnium*, that is, they were for the common use, like air and light. . . . In England, the fiction of a fee in the Crown, and the control of the trust in Parliament, we understand to have been a mode, suited to the times and the genius of the feudal law, for insuring to the

State the control over tide-waters. The Commonwealth succeeds to this right of control.

The first English settlers of what is now Massachusetts obtained their titles to land under grants from James I and Charles I which passed to the organized companies chartered to settle Plymouth and Massachusetts Bay colonies "absolute property in the land within the limits of the charter, the power of making laws for the government of the colony, and full dominion over all the ports, rivers, creeks, and havens, &c. in as full and ample a manner as they were before held by the crown of England." The jus privatum/jus publicum distinction in regard to shore land property was carried over to the New World, so that the company's ownership was understood to consist of a jus privatum which could be "parcelled out to corporations and individuals . . . as private property" and a jus publicum "in trust for public use of all those who should become inhabitants of said territory." *Commonwealth v. Roxbury*, 9 Gray 451, 483–84 (1857).

Land ownership in the colony was governed by the English common law, "which our ancestors brought with them, claiming it as their birthright." Owners of land bounded by the sea or salt water "could not by such boundary, hold any land below the ordinary low water mark; for all the land below belonged of common right to the king." Certain public rights to the use of such land were guaranteed by the 1641 colonial "Body of Libertyes" which provided that "every Inhabitant who is a householder shall have free fishing and fowling in any great ponds, bayes, Coves and Rivers . . . unless the freemen of the same Town or the General Court have otherwise appropriated them."

As to the land between high and low water marks, however, commonly referred to as the flats, the Massachusetts colonial law and practice deviated from the English law. Chief Justice Parsons explained this legal development very artfully in his opinion in *Storer v. Freeman*, *supra*, at 437:

When our ancestors emigrated to this country, their first settlements were on harbors or arms of the sea; and commerce was among the earliest objects of their attention. For the purposes of commerce, wharves erected below high water mark were necessary. But the colony was not able to build them at the public expense. To induce persons to erect them, the common law of England was altered by an ordinance, providing that the proprietor of land adjoining on the sea or salt water, shall hold to low water mark, where the tide does not ebb more than one hundred rods, but not more where the tide ebbs to a greater distance.

This alteration of common law ownership rules, perhaps originally just a matter of colonial custom, found official expression in the colonial ordinance of 1647, which declared that landowners adjoining "all *Creeks, Coves*, and other places, about and upon *Saltwater* . . . shall have propriety to the low water mark . . . [p]rovided that such proprietor shall not by this liberty, have power to stop or hinder the passage of boates or other vessels, in or through any Sea, Creeks, or Coves, to other mens' houses or lands." "The main object of the Massachusetts Colony ordinance has always been understood to induce the erection of wharves for the benefit of commerce." *Commonwealth v. Roxbury, supra*, at 503, 515.

Nineteenth-century opinions of the Supreme Judicial Court construed this colonial ordinance as granting "only a qualified property" in the flats to the upland owner, qualified by the public right of navigation. *Commonwealth v. Charlestown*, 1 Pick. 180, 184 (1822). Thus, for example, in the *Charlestown* case, *supra* at 184, the court held that "even the proprietor of the flats can lawfully erect nothing upon them, which will obstruct or hinder such passage [of boats]." Only the Legislature, according to the court, could authorize interference with the right of public passage, when necessary for a greater public good such as a bridge, dam, or mill:

[I]t is an unquestionable principle of the common law, that all navigable waters belong to the sovereign, or, in other words, to the public; and that no individual or corporation can appropriate them to their own use, or confine or obstruct them so as to impair the passage over them, without authority from the legislative power. *Commonwealth v. Charlestown, supra*, at 185–86.

It is against this background of historical and legal developments that the first proprietors of Lewis Wharf, predecessors in title to BWDC, built their wharf on Boston Harbor. A Lewis Wharf appears on Carleton's 1797 plan of Boston; by 1832, when the first of the "Lewis Wharf statutes" was passed, it was a long established feature of the harbor scene. Statute 1832, c. 102, declared that the "proprietors" of Lewis Wharf "are hereby authorized and empowered to extend and maintain the said wharf into the harbor channel," as far as to a described line which was seaward of low water mark, "*provided*, that so much of said wharf, as may be constructed in said channel [i.e., below low water], shall be built on piles. . . ." Two years later, these same proprietors and their associates were incorporated by an act of the Legislature into the "Lewis Wharf Company, with power to hold, in fee simple, or otherwise, all or any part of that real estate" lying within certain bounds around Lewis's and Hancock's Wharf, and were authorized within that area to

construct docks and wharves, lay vessels . . . , and receive dockage and wharfage therefor, erect buildings, lay out streets and passage ways, and improve and manage said property, as to them shall seem expedient: *provided*, that nothing herein contained shall be understood as authorizing said corporation in any way to interfere with the legal rights of any person or persons whomsoever. St. 1834, c. 115, 1.

A year later, this same Lewis Wharf Company was "authorized and empowered, to purchase and hold" the "land, wharf, and flats" of neighboring Snow's Wharf as well, "with all the powers and privileges, and subject to all the duties and requisitions" stated in the 1834 Act.

This series of statutes was but one of a multitude of similar acts passed in the 1810s, 1820s, and 1830s granting various parties wharf privileges in Boston Harbor. The wharfing statutes are themselves but one example of a larger class of statutes in which the Massachusetts Legislature granted property and privileges to private turnpike companies, canal companies, bridge- and dam-building companies, etc. as a means of stimulating private investment in economic development. The theory was that such "undertaking[s], although commenced with a view to the private advantage of the stockholders, promised to be of immense and certain utility to the State."

This convergence of private profit and public benefit stimulated such rapid commercial development in Boston Harbor that by 1835 the Legislature perceived a need for regulation of further harbor development. It passed a resolution appointing three commissioners to survey Boston Harbor and to define "such lines as they shall think expedient to establish, beyond which no wharves shall be extended into and over the tide waters of the Commonwealth...." Res. 1835, c. 40. These commissioners submitted their report in 1837, establishing a line beyond which wharves could not be extended into the harbor, and stating "*We leave all legal rights of private property as we found them*, only prescribing limits we think it expedient to establish beyond which they [wharves] cannot go further into the channel or tide-water, for the general good and preservation of the harbor." Report of the Commissioners for the Survey of Boston Harbor, 1837 Sen. Doc. No. 47, at 16 (emphasis added). This Commissioners' line was officially adopted by St. 1837, c. 229. In 1840 the Legislature gave the Lewis Wharf Company authority to extend its wharves into the harbor channel as far as this Commissioners' line, provided they were built upon piles. This line lies to the east of area B.

The question we must decide is whether the above statutes granted the Lewis Wharf Company a fee simple title to the land underneath the wharves which it was authorized to extend below low water mark. Preliminarily, we point

out that there is nothing in the actual language of these statutes making a grant of the title to land. The statutes give authority to "extend" wharves, power to "hold" real estate, to "improve" property, but nowhere do they explicitly convey land. Following the long-established principle of statutory construction that "in all grants, made by the government to individuals, of rights, privileges, and franchises, the words are to be taken most strongly against the grantee," these statutes on their face do not appear to sustain the petitioner's claim. However, a decision resting on the bare words of the statutes would ignore over one hundred years of judicial history interpreting similar grants. It is to examination of this precedent that we now turn.

The understanding of these cases concerning shore property is enhanced by following the historical development of Boston Harbor through the mid-nineteenth century. Legislative documents describe increasing concern with encroachment upon the harbor, as wharf property became very valuable, and great portions of the harbor were reclaimed as filled land. Investors who speculated in harbor property pressured the legislature to grant away the Commonwealth's flats to private owners. An 1850 report by the harbor commissioners considered whether or not to adopt such a policy and recommended against it, saying, "The demand for land is, in a great degree, an individual demand, the demand of companies engaged in speculations; while the demand for water is a demand of the public,—a demand of commerce, in which the State and nation have a deep and vital interest." The continuing pressure for development caused the Legislature in 1866 to create a permanent Board of Harbor Commissioners whose approval would be required for any proposed building or filling on the tidelands. In 1869, the Legislature declared that all "authority or license" thereafter granted to build, fill, or enclose tidelands was to be "revocable at any time, at the discretion of the legislature." One of the petitioner's arguments is that the passage of this 1869 legislation demonstrates that prior to 1869, such grants were not revocable licenses.

The question was first addressed in *Fitchburg R.R. v. Boston & Me. R.R.*, 3 Cush. 58 (1849), an action by Fitchburg for compensation for the Boston & Maine's taking of a strip of its wharf which lay below the low water line. Fitchburg had been authorized to extend its wharf below low water by a statute closely analogous to St. 1840, c. 18, of the "Lewis Wharf statutes" St. 1841, c. 35. The Boston & Maine contended that this authorization was but a revocable license, and that when the Legislature later authorized it to pass its rail in over the same land, this was an implied revocation of any of Fitchburg's rights. The court rejected this argument holding that "the statute of 1841 operated as a grant to the Charlestown Wharf Company [the predecessor of Fitchburg], and not as a mere revocable license." This interpretation was upheld in regard to other, very similar wharfage statutes in *Treasurer & Receiver Gen. v. Revere Sugar Refinery*, 247 Mass. 483, 489 (1924), the court stating that such a statute "operated as a legislative grant subject to the terms and conditions therein set forth, and not as a mere revocable license."

We see no reason to upset these interpretations; we agree that the "Lewis Wharf statutes" were grants rather than revocable licenses; but the salient question is: grants of what, and under what conditions? Examination of this question convinces us that what was granted was not a fee simple absolute title to the soil.

1. Having the right to build a wharf over tidal land does not necessarily mean having title to that land

Past decisions of this court have been inconsistent in their treatment of the relationship between wharfing privileges and ownership of the soil under the wharf. In *Boston v. Richardson*, 105 Mass. 351, 360–61 (1887), this court stated, "The title in the soil, and the right to wharf over and inclose flats, or the power to regulate such

wharfing, are not necessarily interdependent." The court pointed out that in many States, shoreland owners have a right to build wharves out to low water even without having title to the soil under them, and that such a right may have existed in colonial Massachusetts before the ordinance of 1647. The court does speculate that "[s]ince the general policy of granting the title in the flats to private proprietors, subject to the public right of navigation, has been manifested by the ordinance of 1647, a grant from the legislature of the right to erect a wharf over flats belonging to the Commonwealth *may* indeed carry with it a title in the flats" (emphasis added), but does not decide this point. The issue in the case was whether the city of Boston or certain neighboring private parties owned a disputed area of flats; the courts stated that the fact that the city had the authority to regulate wharfing in that area did not prove that it had title to the land.

In *Commonwealth Wharf Co. v. Winsor*, 146 Mass. 559, 563 (1888), the court's language also suggests a distinction between the authority to extend wharves and title to the soil. Commenting on the statutes (similar to the "Lewis Wharf statutes") which empowered the parties in that case to extend their docks below low water to the 1837 Commissioners' line, the court stated:

The establishment of the new harbor line did not carry out low-water mark, and the line of private ownership remained as it had been, at the old line of the harbor channel. The only private right either party had within the harbor channel was that given it by the statutes authorizing the extension of its wharf, namely, a right to extend into the harbor channel, within certain lines, a wharf built on piles.

An indirect, and somewhat cryptic hint that being authorized to extend one's wharf below low water was not equivalent to being granted title to the land underneath it occurs in *Gray v. Bartlett*, 20 Pick. 186, 194 (1838), where Chief Justice Shaw, who wrote many of the important decisions explicating rights to tideland property, comments, in dicta, that the part of the land under the plaintiff's wharf which is below low water is "a part of the public domain, and owned by neither of these parties."

In *Nichols v. Boston*, 98 Mass. 39, 42 (1867), on the other hand, the lessee of Lincoln's Wharf was held to have *title* to a dock lying below low water. The court commented that "the legislature may grant the title in the soil, or the right to build wharves thereon, below as well as above low water mark," leaving unclear how and when this distinction operated. In *Attorney Gen. v. Boston Wharf Co.*, 12 Gray 553, 562–63 (1859), a statute authorizing the Boston Wharf Company to extend its wharves out to the Commissioners' line, below low water, was said to give that company ownership of and "good title" to the flats within the boundaries described. In *Commonwealth v. Boston Terminal Co.*, 185 Mass. 281, 283–84 (1904), the court asserts, in dicta, that the Legislature can "pass its interest . . . in lands that are below extreme low water mark" free of any public trust, so that when these lands are "filled by the grantee [it] will extinguish the right of user by the public." The holding of *Boston Terminal*, however, is that the railroad must pay the Commonwealth for Commonwealth lands it acquired through the eminent domain power granted to it by the Legislature, since

[i]t cannot be held that the State, any more than an individual, parts with title in fee to real estate by implication alone; and if its land is to be granted in aid of private corporation, even if the public may thereby be more largely accommodated, this intention must clearly appear by the express words of the act under which the grant is claimed.

A trio of cases interpreting St. 1806, c. 18, which gave owners of land in New Bedford a right to extend their wharves below low water mark, leaves unclear the nature of the title granted by such a statute. In *Haskell v. New Bedford*, 108 Mass. 208, 209 (1871), the court refers to the plaintiff as "the owner in fee" of even that portion of the land and wharf below

low water; and in *Hamlin v. Pairpoint Mfg. Co.*, 141 Mass. 51, 57 (1886), the court construes the statute "as a legislative grant to the owners of lots of an *interest in the soil* between their lots and the channel of the river" (emphasis added). But the court also takes care to point out that "[w]hether it [the statute] gave them an absolute fee without any restrictions . . . it is not necessary to consider in this case. The act certainly gave them a possessory *title for the purpose of building wharves*, sufficient to enable them to maintain trespass if their rights are invaded" (emphasis added). In *Hastings v. Grimshaw*, 153 Mass. 497, 500 (1881), which cites to *Hamlin*, *supra*, saying it is again unnecessary to decide whether the statute of 1806 granted an absolute fee, the plaintiff's ownership interest is no longer described as a fee; rather he is called "the owner of the locus [below low water] described in the declaration, *so far as there could be private ownership of that property*" (emphasis added).

Read together, these cases establish no clear doctrine about the nature of the title, if any, granted to private owners by legislative acts giving authority to wharf below low water line. The only consistent theme appears to be that in any event this title is somehow in a special category, different from ordinary fee simple title to upland property. This difference is explored more fully below.

2. Title to land lying below the low water line is not equivalent to title to upland

In *Commonwealth v. Alger*, 7 Cush. 53 (1851), a wharf owner on Boston Harbor extended his wharf so that a triangular piece at the end of it lay *above* low water mark, but below the harbor commissioners' line below which no wharves were to reach. The Commonwealth indicted him for breaching the Commissioners' line; he answered that he owned the property down to low water mark and that the Commonwealth could not deprive him of the use of it without compensation. Chief Justice Shaw's opinion, after an exhaustive review of the relevant history and case law, concluded that by virtue of the ordinance of 1647 Alger held the land between high and low water "in fee, subject to a reserved easement [for navigation]." However, the court also held that it was competent for the Legislature, without compensation, to deprive Alger of the use of part of it, since "real estate . . . situated on the sea-shore, separating the upland from the sea, to which the public have a common and acknowledged right . . . should be held subject to somewhat more restrictive regulations in its use, than interior and upland estate." Similarly, in *Crocker v. Champlin*, 202 Mass. 437, 442 (1909), this court denied the plaintiff shore land owner's claim for compensation for the flooding of his flats by the Charles River Basin Commission, stating that if the Commonwealth flooded land above high water mark, compensation would have to be made, but that "the ordinance creating private property in flats reserved this right for the benefit of all the people."

In two cases in which private parties have sought to register title not, like BWDC, to land below low water mark, but to land between high and low water marks, this court has held that their title could only be registered with certain restrictions. In *Butler v. Attorney Gen.*, 195 Mass. 79, 84 (1907), a petitioner sought to register title to an unimproved beach on the shore at Gloucester. The Attorney General wished the Land Court to declare petitioner's title subject to certain reserved rights of the public. This court concluded that the public did not have a right to use petitioner's beach for bathing purposes, as the Attorney General had, among other things, requested, but held that

[w]e are of opinion that a decree should be entered that the premises are held by the petitioners in fee, subject, however, as to that portion between high and low water mark, to the easement of the public for the purposes of navigation and free fishing and fowling, and of passing freely over and through the water without any use of the land underneath, wherever the tide ebbs and flows.

This identical language was adopted in *Michaelson v. Silver Beach Improvement Assoc.*, 342 Mass. 251, 261 (1961), in registering petitioner's title to shore land on Wild Harbor.

If a restriction on the title is appropriate for land between high and low water mark, it is even more necessary for land below low water mark, which has traditionally been held to be inviolably committed to the public domain. Even assuming that the "Lewis Wharf statutes," like other statutes of its type, were not revocable licenses, and did grant an irrevocable right to the use of the described land for wharfage and related purposes, this does not lead to the conclusion that BWDC owns the soil at issue in unconditional fee simple title. The land was granted to BWDC's predecessors to fulfill a public need for commercial development of Boston Harbor, and the purpose of the grant, as explained below, is inextricably related to BWDC's ownership of the land.

3. The land below low water line can be granted by the State only to fulfill a public purpose, and the rights of the grantee to that land are ended when that purpose is extinguished

In 1869, the Illinois Legislature granted the Illinois Central Railroad in fee simple all land within a one mile–by–one mile square of the shoreline of Lake Michigan. In 1873, repenting its excessive generosity, the Legislature attempted to repeal this grant. The railroad challenged the validity of the attempted revocation and the case went to the United States Supreme Court. In ruling on this question, the Court pointed out that a State owns the soil under tide waters in trust for the people, but that "[t]he interest of the people in the navigation of the waters and in commerce over them may be improved in many instances by the erection of wharves, docks and piers therein, for which purpose the State may grant parcels of the submerged lands," and that "*so long as their disposition is made for such purpose*, no valid objections can be made to the grants" (emphasis added). *Illinois Central Railroad v. Illinois*, 146 U.S. 387, 452 (1892).

This requirement, that such lands be granted only for public purposes, was held by the Court to be central to the notion of governmental power:

The State can no more abdicate its trust over property in which the whole people are interested, so as to leave them entirely under the use and control of private parties, except in the instance of parcels mentioned for the improvement of the navigation and use of the waters, or when parcels can be disposed of without impairment of the public interest in what remains, than it can abdicate its police powers in the administration of government and the preservation of the peace.

Holding that any grant of the kind at issue was necessarily revocable, it upheld the Illinois statute revoking the railroad's ownership.

This court has also held that legislative acts must be for a public purpose. It has defined a public use as "one the enjoyment and advantage of which are open to the public on equal terms. The circumstances may be such that only a relatively small portion of the inhabitants may participate in the benefits, but the use or service must be of such nature that in essence it affects them as a community and not merely as individuals." *Opinion of the Justices*, 197 Mass. 567, 571 (1937).

The public purpose served by the "Lewis Wharf" and other similar statutes was defined by this court as: "to promote trade and commerce by enabling and encouraging the owners of flats to build wharves, warehouses, and other structures thereon for the use and convenience of those having occasion to resort to the ports and harbors. . . ." The Legislature expressed its intention to judge all requests for shore land grants by this standard of public use in an 1850 report of the Joint Committee on Mercantile Affairs and Insurance, saying that flats

should be granted, not for private benefit, not for public economical result, but strictly for the benefit of the harbors, where they are situated. Whenever a petition is presented for leave to occupy them, the single question should be, *as it always has been,—*will the grant benefit the harbor? or,—will the increased facilities, which will be given to commerce and commercial enterprise, *compensate* for any slight detriment of the harbor? . . . In other words, the flats in each and every harbor of the State should be devoted entirely to the benefit and improvement of that particular harbor. 1850 Sen. Doc. No. 119, at 4 (emphasis in original)

At that time, it was probably inconceivable to the men who sat in the Legislature or on the bench that the harbor would ever cease to be much used for commercial shipping, or that a wharf might be more profitable as a foundation for private condominiums and pleasure boats than as a facility serving public needs of commerce and trade. They did not speculate on what should become of the land granted to private proprietors to further development of maritime commerce if that very commerce should cease, because they did not envision it. But this court has held before that where a corporation was granted, even irrevocably, the use of certain previously public property for a public purpose, there was an implied condition in the grant that the company could not retain the granted locations without using them for the purpose for which they were granted. This court has also held that where the use of public or publicly granted land changes over time, the Legislature must approve the changed use.

Neither party to this litigation has addressed the question whether the present use of the disputed property is a public use consonant with the purposes for which the land was granted. This question remains open after our opinion today. We do hold, however, that BWDC's title to the land in area B is subject to that same public trust on which the Commonwealth originally held it, and that it may be used only for a purpose approved by the Legislature as a public use.

The essential import of this holding is that the land in question is not, like ordinary private land held in fee simple absolute, subject to development at the sole whim of the owner, but it is impressed with a public trust, which gives the public's representatives an interest and responsibility in its development. This concept is difficult to describe in language in complete harmony with the language of the law ordinarily applied to privately owned property. We are not dealing with the allocation of property rights between private individuals when we are concerned with a public resource such as Boston Harbor.

We believe that the formulation adopted by the Appeals Court appropriately expresses the intention underlying the grant made by the "Lewis Wharf statutes," and we endorse it. We therefore hold that BWDC has title to its property in fee simple, but subject to the condition subsequent that it be used for the public purpose for which it was granted.

The theory underpinning our holding was well expressed by professors Alfred E. McCordie and Wilson G. Crosby in their 1890 *Harvard Law Review* article, "The Right of Access and the Right to Wharf Out to Navigable Water," 4 Harv. L. Rev. 14, 24 (1890). After reviewing the history of tidelands development, they conclude:

The State, however, grants these lands for a particular purpose; namely, to further its commercial interests depending upon navigation. It is not unreasonable, therefore, to say that the grant is upon condition that the land be used for no other purposes than those of the commerce marine. If the property is used for any other purpose, the State should have the privilege of entering and determining the riparian proprietor's estate.

We hold, as did the Appeals Court, that BWDC's ownership of the land in question is subject to the condition that it be used for a public purpose related to the "promot[ion of] trade and commerce by enabling and encouraging the owners of flats to build wharves, warehouses, and other structures thereon for the use and convenience of those having occasion to resort to the ports and harbors. . . ." *Bradford v.*

McQuesten, 182 Mass. at 82. Whether BWDC's current use of the land is consistent with that public purpose, and if not, what the proper remedy might be, we leave for such further proceedings as the parties may deem appropriate or necessary.

So ordered.

BRAUCHER, J. dissenting.

The present decision leaves in limbo the ownership of the particular tract in litigation. The resulting uncertainty as to that tract may not be a matter of grave public concern, but we are told that there will be a similar mischievous effect on uncounted other parcels. In time the uncertainty may be alleviated by a broad interpretation of what uses are consistent with the "public purpose" embodied in the condition, or by the operation of G.L. c. 260, 31A. Meanwhile, however, the present decision creates a clog on the alienability of land contrary to a public policy that has prevailed for centuries.

I would affirm the decision of the Land Court.

Questions

1. What impact did this decision ultimately have on the development of the Boston waterfront?

2. Did the case "clog the availability of land" as the dissent predicted?

3. What "public use" is appropriate for old piers and warehouses built over public trust lands?

State of Vermont and City of Burlington v. Central Vermont Railway, 571 A.2d 1128 (Vt. 1989)

State and city brought action alleging public trust doctrine and challenging railroad's title to filled lands used for wharves on lakeshore. The Superior Court, Chittenden County, Stephen B. Martin, J., concluded that railroad had fee simple title and that land was to be used for public purpose. Appeal and cross-appeal were taken. The Supreme Court, Peck, J., held that: (1) railroad had title impressed with public trust and held fee simple subject to condition subsequent that land be used for railroad, wharf, or storage purposes; and (2) laches and equitable estoppel did not bar action by city and State.

PECK, JUSTICE

At issue in this case is title to a 1.1-mile strip of filled lands lying along the City of Burlington's waterfront. In response to recent efforts by the Central Vermont Railway (CVR) to sell this property to a real estate developer, the City and the State challenged CVR's title in the Chittenden Superior Court, invoking the public trust doctrine. The Court concluded that CVR has fee simple title to the parcel at issue but held that the land must always be used for a public purpose. CVR appeals, and the State and the City cross-appeal. We modify the trial court's order and, as modified, affirm.

In 1827, legislation was enacted that granted littoral owners on Lake Champlain the right to erect wharves by adding fill to submerged lands along the lakeshore. The 1827 Act provided that persons complying with the statute would have, with their heirs and assigns, the exclusive privilege of the use, benefit, and control of the wharves forever. The purpose of this legislation was to increase commerce and trade without an expenditure of public funds.

In 1849, the Vermont Central Railroad, a predecessor of CVR, used condemnation proceedings to obtain a strip of land along the lakeshore and began filling a substantial area lakeward from this strip. By 1851, this area had been used to bring a railroad line to the waterfront. Filling operations, first by Vermont Central and later by CVR, continued until 1972. CVR also purchased contiguous lands that had been filled by others. The railroad has paid property taxes on certain portions of the lands

and has sold other portions to the City and the federal government.

By the late 1970s, CVR's use of the area at issue had declined significantly. At the time of trial, the railroad had only one active customer on the waterfront.

CVR has pursued three major plans over the last decade for selling and/or developing its land along the lake, which now consists of the previously mentioned 1.1-mile strip centrally located on the City's waterfront. The first two of these plans failed to materialize, but, on December 10, 1986, the railroad entered into a purchase and sale agreement in which it agreed to sell or lease a large portion of the filled lands to a real estate developer.

The City and the State petitioned the Chittenden Superior Court for a declaratory judgment, challenging CVR's title on public trust grounds. After trial, the superior court concluded that CVR "holds the filled lands . . . in fee simple impressed with the public trust doctrine. This means that the railroad is free to convey such lands to any party, and those parties to any other parties, so long as such land is used for a public purpose." The court retained jurisdiction to resolve any dispute as to whether a proposed use of the property complies with the public purpose condition.

CVR brought the instant appeal, claiming that the trial court erred in concluding that its title is held subject to public trust limitations. CVR also argues that plaintiffs' claims are barred by estoppel and laches. The City and the State cross-appealed, urging: (1) that the trial court erred in holding that CVR has a fee simple interest in the filled lands; (2) that, even if CVR has such an interest, it is a fee simple determinable; (3) that, in any event, the legislature may revoke CVR's interest in the filled lands; (4) that only the state can act as public trustee; and (5) that allowing a private corporation to determine the uses of public trust property represents an unlawful delegation of legislative authority.

I.

Under the public trust doctrine, the lands submerged beneath navigable waters are "held by the people in their character as sovereign in trust for public uses for which they are adapted." Title to these lands is deemed to be "held in trust for the people of the State that they may enjoy the navigation of the waters, carry on commerce over them, and have liberty of fishing therein freed from the obstruction of interference of private parties." *Illinois Central Railroad v. Illinois*, 146 U.S. 387, 452 (1892). The character of this title is distinctive as compared to state-held title in other lands, and different legal rules therefore apply. *Boston Waterfront Development Corp. v. Commonwealth*, 378 Mass. 629, 631, 393 N.E.2d 356, 358 (1979).

The public trust doctrine is an ancient one, having its roots in the Justinian Institutes of Roman law. As one court has observed:

For centuries, land below the low water mark has been recognized as having a peculiar nature, subject to varying degrees of public demand for rights of navigation, passage, portage, commerce, fishing, recreation, conservation, and aesthetics. Historically, no developed western civilization has recognized absolute rights of private ownership in such land as a means of allocating this scarce and precious resource among the competing public demands. Though private ownership was permitted in the Dark Ages, neither Roman Law nor the English common law as it developed after the signing of the Magna Charta would permit it. *United States v. 1.58 Acres of Land*, 523 F.Supp. 120, 122–23 (D. Mass. 1981)

After the American Revolution, the people of each state acquired the "absolute right to all . . . navigable waters and the soils under them for their own common use." *Martin v. Waddell*, 41 U.S. 367, 410 (1842).

Despite its antediluvian nature, however, the public trust doctrine retains an undiminished vitality. The doctrine is not " 'fixed or static,' but one to 'be molded and extended to meet changing conditions and needs of the public it

was created to benefit.' " *Matthews v. Bay Head Improvement Assn.*, 95 N.J. 306, 326, 471 A.2d 355, 365 (1984; quoting *Borough of Neptune City v. Borough of Avon-by-the-Sea*, 61 N.J. 296, 309, 294 A.2d 47, 54 [1972]). The very purposes of the public trust have "evolved in tandem with the changing public perception of the values and uses of waterways." *National Audubon Society v. Superior Court of Alpine County*, 33 Cal.3d 419, 434, 658 P.2d 709, 719 (1983; en banc). Nor is the doctrine fixed in its form among jurisdictions, as "there is no universal and uniform law upon the subject." *Shively v. Bowlby*, 152 U.S. 1 (1894).

II.

In Vermont, the critical importance of public trust concerns is reflected in both case law and in the state constitution. Chapter II, sec. 67, of the Vermont Constitution provides that

the inhabitants of this State shall have liberty in seasonable times, to hunt and fowl on the lands they hold, and on other lands not inclosed, and in like manner to *fish in all boatable and other waters* (not private property) under proper regulations, to be made and provided by the General Assembly. (emphasis added)

Although Sec. 67 has no direct application here, it underscores the early emphasis placed upon the public interest in Vermont's navigable waters.

In 1918, this Court considered a miller's claimed right to raise and lower the level of Lake Morey by a few inches, an activity that the miller and his predecessors had been carrying out for 120 years. See *Hazen v. Perkins*, 92 Vt. at 416–17, 105 A. at 250. The miller accomplished these manipulations by altering a dam constructed by the state with legislative authority. After concluding that the waters of Lake Morey were boatable as a matter of law, the Court stated:

Being public waters according to the test afforded by the Constitution, the grants of land bounding upon the lake pass title only to the water's edge, or to low-water mark if there be a definite low-water line. The bed or soil of such boatable lakes in this State is held by the people in their character as sovereign in trust for public uses for which they are adapted. The [miller] did not, therefore, acquire any title to the waters of the lake, as such, nor to the lands covered by such waters, by grants from private sources. And the General Assembly cannot grant to private persons for private purposes, the right to control the height of the water of the lake . . . for such a grant would not be consistent with the exercise of that trust which requires the State to preserve such waters for the common and public use of all. The General Assembly being powerless to make such a grant, none can be intended as the basis of the decree.

Thus, while *Hazen* involved a claim of right to manipulate water levels rather than a claim of title, the case stands for the proposition that the legislature cannot grant rights in public trust property for private purposes. In several other states, this Court has invoked the public trust doctrine in rejecting claims of private rights with respect to public waters.

III.

It is against this legal and historical backdrop that we might judge CVR's assertion of title to the waterfront area at issue. The primary grounds for the railroad's claim lie in the provisions of two nineteenth-century legislative acts. The first, enacted in 1827, provides, in pertinent part:

That each and every person owning lands adjoining Lake Champlain, within this state, be . . . fully authorized and empowered to erect any wharf or wharves, store-house or store-houses, and to extend the same . . . into Lake Champlain, to any distance they may choose within this state. . . .

Provided also, That such wharf or wharves, store-house or store-houses shall not be extended so far into said lake as to impede the ordinary navigation in passing up and down said lake. . . .

That each and every person or persons, their heirs or assigns, shall have the exclusive privilege of the use, benefit and control of any wharf or wharves, store-house or store-houses, forever, which may hereafter be erected in said lake, agreeably to the provisions of this act.

The railroad also cites the provisions of legislation enacted in 1874, which provides:

Whenever any railroad company in this state shall have constructed their railroad beyond low water mark into Lake Champlain, or shall have built out into said lake any wharf, dock, pier or other structure in connection with such railroad, for its accommodation or use, which shall not impede ordinary navigation in passing up and down said lake, such building and structures are hereby declared to be lawful, and the legal title thereto is hereby confirmed to such railroad companies respectively, which built the same, or others lawfully claiming through them.

Contending that the 1874 Act is unequivocal as to ownership of the filled lands, CVR maintains that the trial court erred in holding that the railroad's title remains impressed with the public trust. We disagree.

We begin by observing that the public trust doctrine, particularly as it has developed in Vermont, raises significant doubts regarding legislative power to grant title to the lake bed free of the trust. As the Supreme Court of California has stated:

[T]he core of the public trust doctrine is the state's authority as sovereign to exercise a continuous supervision and control over the navigable waters of the state and the lands underlying those waters. . . . The corollary rule which evolved in tideland and lakeshore cases bar[s] conveyance of rights free of the trust except to serve trust purposes. . . . [P]arties acquiring rights in trust property generally hold those rights subject to the trust, and can assert no vested right to use those rights in a manner harmful to the trust. *National Audubon Society*, 33 Cal.3d at 425–26, 437, 658 P.2d at 712, 721

This rule obtains because the state's power to supervise trust property in perpetuity is coupled with the ineluctable duty to exercise this power. In the landmark case of *Illinois Central Railroad*, 146 U.S. 387, the United States Supreme Court declared:

The State can no more abdicate its trust over property in which the whole people are interested, like navigable waters and the soil under them, so as to leave them entirely under the use and control of private parties, . . . than it can abdicate its police powers in the administration of government and the preservation of the peace. In the administration of government the use of such powers may for a limited period be delegated to a municipality or other body, but there always remains with the State the right to revoke those powers and exercise them in a more direct manner, and one more comfortable to its wishes. So with trusts connected with public property, or property of a special character, like lands under navigable waters, they cannot be placed entirely beyond the direction and control of the State.

Citing dicta in *Illinois Central*, CVR argues that there are limited exceptions to the rule against alienation of public property. *Illinois Central* involved a legislative grant to a railroad company purportedly transferring title to the entire lake bed underlying the city of Chicago's harbor. The Court held that the grant was void on delegation grounds, observing,

The legislature could not give away nor sell the discretion of its successors in respect to matters, the government of which, from the very nature of things, must vary with varying circumstances. The legislation which may be needed one day for the harbor may be different from the legislation that may be required at another day. Every legislature must, at the time of its existence, exercise the power of the State in the execution of the trust devolved upon it. *Id.*, at 46.

In a preliminary discussion of the public trust doctrine, the Court noted the existence in "the adjudged cases" of two exceptions to the general rule against legislative alienation of trust property: grants of submerged parcels for purposes of aiding commerce or promoting the public interest and "grants of parcels which, being occupied, do not substantially impair the public interest in the lands and waters remaining." The first of these exceptions—which have never been espoused by this Court—does not provide guidance in situations where the grantee later seeks to abandon the public purpose for which the grant was made. CVR urges that the second exception establishes that grants of public trust property can sometimes be made

totally free of the trust; the State, on the other hand, argues that an unqualified grant of the lands at issue here would substantially impair the public interest in the lands and waters remaining.

We need not resolve this fundamental question of legislative power, however, because we hold that the legislature did not intend to grant the lands at issue free from the public trust. "[S]tatutes purporting to abandon the public trust are to be strictly construed; the intent to abandon must be clearly expressed or necessarily implied; and if any interpretation of the statute is reasonably possible which would retain the public interest in tidelands, the court must give the statute such an interpretation." *City of Berkeley v. Superior Court of Alameda County*, 26 Cal. 3d 515, 528, 606 P.2d 362, 369 *cert. denied*, 449 U.S. 840 (1980). As this Court observed in *Hazen*, "General words used in a statute will not apply to a state to the detriment of sovereign rights or interests unless such an intent clearly appears from the language used." *Hazen*, 92 Vt. at 420, 105 A. at 251.

First, we note that neither the 1827 Act nor the 1874 Act contains a clear expression of an intent to abandon the public trust interest in the lands covered by the wharves. The earlier statute gave littoral owners the right to create the wharves, and it granted "the exclusive privilege of the use, benefit and control" of those wharves to the persons who created them and "their heirs or assigns . . . forever." CVR contends that the words "heirs or assigns . . . forever" evince a legislative intent to grant a fee simple absolute in the lands now at issue. But these words do not refer to the submerged lands, or even to ownership of the wharves themselves; instead, they refer only to the privilege of using and controlling the wharves.

The 1874 Act comes no closer than the 1827 Act to an expression of legislative intent to abandon the public trust. To the extent that the language of the Act provides any guidance on this question, it implies that the legislature meant to ensure *preservation* of the trust: the

Act confirms only "legal title" in the railroads, and this term is common parlance in the law of trusts. The use of the term here suggests, if anything, legislative acknowledgment that beneficial title to the lands at issue was vested in the public.

Moreover, the historical context of the 1874 enactment is significant. In 1872, this Court considered a case in which a railroad company had filled submerged lands in Lake Champlain along shoreline that it did not own. See *Austin v. Rutland Railroad*, 45 Vt. 215 (1873). While the railroad's rights to the filled lands were not directly at issue, the Court implied that the true littoral owner might have a legal remedy against the railroad. Thus, it appears that the subsequent 1874 Act was intended to address this specific conflict between private parties rather than any question involving the public trust.

Nor do we find that an intention to abandon the public trust is necessarily implicit in either of the acts before us. The 1827 Act can be read as a simple grant of wharfing rights and privileges, while the 1874 Act actually employs the language of trust law. Neither of these enactments is inconsistent with a continuing adherence to public trust responsibilities on the part of the legislature.

The Supreme Judicial Court of Massachusetts was recently confronted with a strikingly similar factual situation. See *Boston Waterfront*, 378 Mass. at 630–37, 393 N.E.2d at 357–61. There, a series of early-nineteenth-century wharfing statutes had granted a wharf company the right to construct wharves into Boston Harbor and to hold them in fee simple. In recent years, a development corporation obtained the rights to these wharves and sought to register and confirm title to the lands beneath them. After an exhaustive review of the public trust doctrine, the court held that the development corporation had title to the property in fee simple, "but subject to the condition subsequent that it be used for the public purpose for which it was granted." In discussing the legis-

lative intent underlying the wharfing statutes, the court observed that:

> At that time, it was probably inconceivable to the men who sat in the Legislature . . . that the harbor would ever cease to be much used for commercial shipping, or that a wharf might be more profitable as a foundation for private condominiums and pleasure boats than as a facility serving public needs of commerce and trade. They did not speculate on what should become of the land granted to private proprietors to further development of maritime commerce if that very commerce should cease, because they did not envision it.

It is unlikely that the drafters of Vermont's 1827 Act were any more farsighted than Massachusetts's nineteenth-century legislators in this regard. With respect to the subsequent 1874 Act, which related to wharfs built for railroads, it seems equally improbable that the lawmakers of that era could have imagined that the newly laid rails would ever fall into disuse.

We are bound to interpret these enactments, if reasonably possible, to preserve the public's rights in the trust property. Therefore, we conclude that the legislature did not intend, through the provisions of either act, to grant a fee simple absolute in the lands at issue.

IV.

The exact nature of CVR's interest in the filled lands must still be determined. The State argues that the railroad's predecessors were granted only a franchise or an easement in the lands and that the grant was for an indefinite period of time. In support of this contention, the State cites *State v. Forehand*, 67 N.C.App. 148, 151, 312 S.E.2d 247, 249 (1984), in which the court held that a grant of submerged lands for wharf purposes "merely conveyed an appurtenant easement to erect wharves to the riparian owner."

Given the language of the two acts here, however, a similar interpretation cannot be sustained. First, the 1827 Act expressly states that the subject rights were granted "forever."

While this word does not render the grant unconditional, it surely makes its duration something more than indefinite. Second, although the 1874 Act's confirmation of "legal title" to the filled lands would not necessarily be inconsistent with the grant of a franchise or an easement, it appears to connote some greater right.

Nor does this Court's obligation to construe the acts to preserve the public trust mean that we are required to characterize them as grants of easements or franchises. As we have already observed, after considering the similar grants at issue in *Boston Waterfront*, the Supreme Judicial Court of Massachusetts concluded that they were intended by that state's legislature to convey fee simple title, but subject to the condition subsequent that the property be used for the public purpose for which it was granted. *Boston Waterfront*, 378 Mass. at 649, 393 N.E.2d at 367. We believe that such an interpretation here gives full effect to the words of the legislature while ensuring that its underlying intent to preserve the public trust is uncompromised.

Accordingly, we hold that CVR has a fee simple in the filled lands subject to the condition subsequent that the lands be used for railroad, wharf, or storage purposes. This means that the State has the right of reentry in the event that the condition is breached by the railroad.

CVR notes that, under 12 V.S.A. Sec. 4983, a condition must be clearly implied by the nature of the grant it qualifies in order to support forfeiture for nonperformance of that condition. As the foregoing discussion suggests, we conclude that a condition subsequent regarding use of the property is clearly implied by the nature and the subject matter of the two acts. Although conditions subsequent are not favored in the law, *Queen City Park Assn. v. Gale*, 110 Vt. 110, 116, 3 A.2d 529, 531 (1938), the public's sui generis interest in trust property "transcends the ordinary rules of property law." *Boston Waterfront*, 378 Mass. at 650, 393 N.E.2d at 367. Because we must interpret the acts reasonably to preserve the public's rights in the trust property, we do not hesitate to infer a condition subsequent here.

V.

Thus, the trial court was correct in concluding that the railroad's title is impressed with the public trust. The court prefaced this conclusion, however, by citing a number of cases from other jurisdictions that, in the aggregate, endorsed a wide variety of uses for land held under the public trust. The court stated that all of these uses—including restaurants, hotels, and shopping malls—were "examples of appropriate public uses that are encompassed by the contemporary public trust doctrine." Although the court retained jurisdiction to resolve disputes over proposed uses of the filled lands, it effectively gave CVR and its successors the right to choose among the listed uses for the property. On cross-appeal, the State and the City argue that this was erroneous, and we agree.

Lands held subject to the public trust may be used only for purposes approved by the legislature as public uses. See *Boston Waterfront*, 378 Mass. at 648–49, 393 N.E.2d at 366–67. Any substantial change in the filled lands must therefore be consistent with a legislative grant or mandate, subject to judicial review, and this legislative control cannot be delegated to others.

VI.

Because the railroad and its predecessors have occupied the lands at issue for 140 years and because the City has taxed portions of these lands, CVR maintains that the trial court erred by refusing to invoke the doctrine of laches as a bar to the claims made by the City and the State. CVR also argues that the railroad has relied to its detriment on the past acts and statements of the State and that the State should therefore be estopped from asserting any interest in the property. We disagree on both counts.

Laches arises where a claimant fails to assert a right for an unreasonable and unexplained period of time and where the delay has been prejudicial to the adverse party; under these circumstances, enforcement of the right is held to be inequitable. The doctrine of equitable estoppel has a similar foundation in principles of fair play: the purpose of the doctrine is to prevent a party " 'from asserting rights which may have existed against another party who in good faith has changed his or her position in reliance upon earlier representations.' " *Burlington Fire Fighter's Assn. v. City of Burlington*, 149 Vt. 293, 298–99, 543 A.2d 686, 690 (1988; quoting *Fisher v. Poole*, 142 Vt. 162, 168, 453 A.2d 408, 411 [1982]).

We hold that the claims asserted here cannot be barred through either laches or estoppel. As the Supreme Court of California has observed, the state acts as administrator of the public trust and has a continuing power that "extends to the revocation of previously granted rights or to the enforcement of the trust against lands long thought free of the trust." *National Audubon Society*, 33 Cal.3d at 440, 658 P.2d at 723. In *Thomas v. Sanders*, 65 Ohio App.2d 5, 413 N.E.2d 1224 (1979), the court considered a claim that a railroad's continued payment of property taxes evinced state recognition of its ownership of trust property. The court rejected the contention, opining that "the state or city cannot relinquish [the public trust property] by acquiescence and estoppel does not apply."

In any event, CVR could not prevail on either claim of error. Laches " 'is so much a matter of discretion by the lower court that action by that court should not be disturbed unless clearly shown to be wrong.' " *Stamato v. Quazzo*, 139 Vt. at 157, 423 A.2d at 1203 (1980) (quoting *Laird Properties New England Land Syndicate v. Mad River Corp.*, 131 Vt. 268, 282, 305 A.2d 562, 570 [1973]). Here, CVR did not pursue plans to sell the filled lands until 1978. Whatever delay occurred in the subsequent assertion of the claims by the City and State was not great enough to establish that the trial court was clearly wrong in rejecting the laches argument. Furthermore, the doctrine of equitable estoppel is rarely invoked against the government, being allowed only where the injustice that would otherwise result is of sufficient magnitude to justify any effect that the etoppel would have upon public interest or policy. *Burlington Fire Fighers' Assn. v. City of Burlington*, 149 Vt. at 299, 534 A.2d at 690 (1988). As a practical matter, this rule alone renders the doctrine of equitable estoppel inapplicable where the public trust is at stake. The trial court did not err in refusing to find either laches or estoppel.

VII.

In sum, the trial court correctly concluded that CVR does not hold title to the filled lands free of the public trust. The court erred, however, by enumerating permissible future uses of the property and by retaining jurisdiction to resolve disputes regarding those future uses. Accordingly, we modify the trial court's order and affirm.

Questions

1. What is meant by the term "condition subsequent" as a limitation on future land use?

2. Is the state legislature limited in any way when asked to specify what "public uses" are appropriate for the property?

3. Compare the concepts of laches and equitable estoppel and their role in this case.

Hall v. Nascimento, 594 A.2d 874, (R.I. 1991)

FAY, C. J.

This matter is before the Supreme Court on appeal by the defendants from a judgment entered in the Superior Court granting the plaintiffs, Warren H. and Catherine E. Hall, title to a particular tract of land in the town of Portsmouth located in an area known as Common Fence Point. The defendants, Alfred Nascimento, William Warren, Francis Shay, John Silva, and Jan Johnson, appeal in their capacities as trustees of the Common Fence Point Improvement Association (association). The association itself is also a named defendant in this action. The defendants assert that the trial justice misconceived evidence and consequently erred in holding that Mount Hope Bay formed the western boundary of the plaintiffs' property, that the plaintiffs' predecessors in title acquired littoral rights in the property, and that the plaintiffs had title to said land by deed or adverse possession. For the reasons set forth below, we reverse the trial justice's decision.

The property in question consists of two adjoining plots of land in the Hummock Point Beach area of Portsmouth known as lot Nos. 25 and 26 and an additional 270 lineal feet of land primarily created by fill from the dredging of Mount Hope Bay that extends from lot Nos. 25 and 26 to the shore of Mount Hope Bay. Prior to the dredge-and-fill operation a ten-foot-wide strip of beach area constituted the shoreline of Mount Hope Bay along the western boundary of lot Nos. 25 and 26. Lot No. 25 and lot No. 26 were deeded to plaintiffs' predecessors in 1921 and 1922, respectively, by the common grantor Henry A. Brown Corporation (Brown corporation). At the time of this initial conveyance the lots were part of the Hummock Point Beach Plan No. 1. Although no metes-and-bounds descriptions of the parcels appear in the deeds conveying the parcels and the deeds are silent regarding riparian or littoral rights, plan 1, which is referenced in the deeds, clearly defines the measurements and boundaries of the lots.

In 1926 Brown corporation, the common grantor, deeded to defendants' predecessors, the then-trustees of the association, "all right, title and interest of the said grantor in and to all land, marshes, sand bars, causeways, and riparian rights between high and low water marks on the shores of Mount Hope Bay and Sakonnet River, as shown on said Plans No. 1 and No. 2 Hummock Beach Point." The interest conveyed was to be held and maintained by the association in trust for "the sole use and benefit of all property owners, present or future, of all lots shown on said plans." In 1948 the Army Corps

of Engineers dredged a channel in Mount Hope Bay. The association was granted permission by the State of Rhode Island to place the fill from said dredging along the shore of the Common Fence Point area, thereby building up and greatly expanding the ten-foot-wide shoreline and beach area abutting lot Nos. 25 and 26. The fill increased the ten-foot strip by 260 feet, creating a 270-foot-wide area of shoreline between the waters of Mount Hope Bay and the original boundaries of lot Nos. 25 and 26 as shown on Plan 1. Following the dredge and fill along the shores of Common Fence Point the tax assessor for the town of Portsmouth represented the filled area as a public right-of-way. For taxing purposes, lot No. 25 and lot No. 26 were merged and labeled as lot No. 43. The original ten-foot strip is included in and designated as part of the right-of-way.

There is no dispute that plaintiffs are the owners of lot Nos. 25 and 26 as represented on Plan 1. The present challenge concerns the land abutting lot Nos. 25 and 26 to the west, which extends to Mount Hope Bay. It is therefore necessary for this court to examine not only the boundaries of the property as set forth in the deed conveying the title of lot Nos. 25 and 26 to plaintiffs' predecessors, but also the nature and history of the parcel of filled land claimed by both plaintiffs and defendants.

It has been established by this court that in cases such as this, in which the pertinent deeds do not contain detailed metes and bounds descriptions of the property being conveyed and a plat map is referenced describing the parcel, the maps and the deeds are to be considered together in determining the boundaries of the property. Plan 1, the plat map referenced in the original deeds conveying lot No. 25 and lot No. 26, contains two solid and separate lines divided by a ten-foot-wide area of land delineating the western boundary of the lots and the high-water mark of Mount Hope Bay, respectively. The solid lines indicate that the rights to the shoreline were not included in the original conveyance by Brown corporation. The fact that lot

No. 25 and lot No. 26 do not encompass the high-water mark is also reflected by the survey conducted at the behest of plaintiffs in 1987. The survey demonstrated that, as platted, the western boundary of plaintiffs' land does not extend to the high-water mark.

In *Bailey v. Burges*, 11 R.I. 330 (1876), we recognized that when a common grantor conveys shoreline property, he may retain the riparian rights to the property by keeping title to a strip of land above the high-water mark. The riparian rights will then attach to the property abutting the water and encompassing the high-water mark. We are aware of the fact that the matter before us involves littoral, not riparian, rights; but we are of the opinion that similar principles of law apply when either riparian or littoral rights are called into question. Therefore if the common grantor in the present case did not convey the area of land including the high-water mark, plaintiffs' predecessors did not acquire littoral rights. Furthermore plaintiffs acknowledged that the common grantor did not convey the ten-foot strip abutting lot Nos. 25 and 26 by referring to the area as "the old ten (10') foot area maintained as a beach for the use of all community association members."

It has been determined by this court that when a deed is silent regarding littoral rights, the boundary lines presented on the plat plan referenced in said deed determine the owner's rights to the shoreline property. Boundaries are deemed to be fixed by the plan whether they lie at the high-water mark or beyond. After examining the deeds pertinent to the property with which we are concerned, in conjunction with the appropriate plat map (Plan 1), we are of the opinion that definite western boundaries to both lot No. 25 and lot No. 26 are discernible. We conclude that the boundaries do not encompass the ten-foot strip of land that, prior to the dredging and filling of Mount Hope Bay, abutted the waters of the bay and consequently carried with it the littoral rights to that area. Therefore, we find that the trial justice erred in determining that plaintiffs' predecessors, and

subsequently plaintiffs, acquired title by deed to the land extending to the high-water mark.

To claim ownership rights in the filled area successfully, plaintiffs must prove that they, through their predecessors, were entitled to littoral rights to the tidelands that were filled. Such littoral rights could only be claimed if plaintiffs' predecessors had acquired title to the ten-foot strip. Because we have determined that plaintiffs' predecessors did not acquire rights to the ten-foot strip by deed, we conclude that plaintiffs do not hold title to the filled area abutting the ten-foot strip. This determination, however, does not conclude our consideration of the facts presented. We are now compelled to address the trial justice's alternative finding that plaintiffs hold title to the filled area by adverse possession.

Prior to the dredge-and-fill operation, the area, which is now claimed by both plaintiffs and defendants, was submerged land. Because we are dealing with tidelands and littoral rights in this instance, it is necessary to examine the ownership of this property in light of the public trust doctrine. The United States Supreme Court recognizes that in accordance with the public trust doctrine, the State holds title to property that lies below the high-water mark.

At common law, the title and dominion in lands flowed by the tide water were in the King for the benefit of the nation. . . . Upon the American Revolution, these rights, charged with alike trust, were vested in the original States within their respective borders, subject to the rights surrendered by the Constitution of the United States. *Phillips Petroleum Co. v. Mississippi*, 484 U.S. 469, 473–74, (1988; quoting *Shively v. Bowlby*, 152 U.S. 1, 57 [1894]).

It is well settled in Rhode Island that pursuant to the public trust doctrine the State maintains title in fee to all soil within its boundaries that lies below the high-water mark, and it holds such land in trust for the use of the public. *State v. Ibbison*, 448 A.2d 728, 730, 732–33 (R.I. 1982). The high-water mark on the original shoreline that existed prior to the 1948 dredge and fill was located within the bounds of the ten-foot strip of beach area, which, as we have already established, was retained by the association when lot No. 25 and lot No. 26 were conveyed to plaintiffs' predecessors. In *Carr v. Carpenter*, 22 R.I. 528, 529, 48 A. 805, 805 (1901), this court established that the owners of lands adjoining navigable waters have the right to " 'enjoy what remains of the rights and privileges in the soil beyond their strict boundary lines, after giving to the public the full enjoyment of their rights.' " The association, therefore, as owner of the land adjoining the waters, does not automatically lose all rights to the submerged soil and subsequently the filled area.

Such filled or submerged land owned in fee by the State and subject to the public trust doctrine may be conveyed by the State to a private individual by way of legislative grant, provided the effect of the transfer is not inconsistent with the precepts of the public trust doctrine.

The record before us is void of information evidencing such a legislative grant of the property to either plaintiffs or defendants. Because we have determined that defendants retained the strip of land that contained the high-water mark prior to the filling of the bay, and therefore acquired littoral rights to the then-submerged area, we find that defendants continue to maintain rights in that area as long as their use of the area is not inconsistent with the public trust. The defendants' rights, however, are subservient to the State's rights in the property because the State holds title in fee subject to the public trust doctrine.

Having established the ownership status of the State and the rights maintained by the association, we now address the trial justice's decision that the plaintiffs acquired title to the property by adverse possession. We are of the opinion that the trial justice erred in granting the plaintiffs title by adverse possession because a private party cannot adversely possess public property. Statutorily private individuals cannot adversely possess shoreline or waterfront property located within the State of Rhode Island because such property is maintained for public use. As established by the United States Supreme Court, however, this prohibition on adverse possession applies to all public lands owned by state governments and, therefore, is not limited to shoreline property. We therefore conclude that the plaintiffs do not hold title to the ten-foot beach area or the filled area by either deed or adverse possession.

For the reasons stated, the appeal of the defendants is sustained. The judgment appealed from is reversed, and the papers are remanded to the Superior Court.

Questions

1. Can a "legislative grant" be structured in such a way so as to avoid a subsequent public trust challenge?

2. Why does the doctrine of adverse possession fail to apply in this case?

3. Would the holding in this case have been any different if the filling had been done by the property owner seaward to a state harbor line?

Chapter 3

RIPARIAN RIGHTS AND THE NAVIGATIONAL SERVITUDE

Mentor Harbor Yachting Club v. Mentor Lagoons, Inc., 163 N.E.2d 373 (Ohio 1959)

MATHIAS, JUDGE

The facts as determined by the lower courts are substantially as follows:

In the late 1920s, the property now held by the parties to this action was owned by the Mentor Harbor Company, plaintiff's predecessor in title. The property, then in its natural state, consisted of marshlands in which there was located an inland body of water two or three hundred feet in diameter and fed by streams and drainage from the marsh. This body of water flowed into Lake Erie through a natural channel part of the time and at other times was separated from the lake by a sandbar formed in such channel as a result of the action of the waters of Lake Erie and the prevailing northwest winds.

While this area was in its natural state, it was used primarily by fishermen and hunters who obtained access thereto from Lake Erie through the natural passageway from the lake. However, at times of low water, it was sometimes neces-

sary for the fishermen and hunters to drag their boats over the seasonally existent sandbar.

The plan of the original owner, the Mentor Harbor Company, was to develop this area into a residential community with private dock and boating facilities similar to those found in Ft. Lauderdale, Florida. Pursuant to this plan, the company constructed a series of interconnected lagoons in the area which had comprised the marsh and widened and deepened the channel into Lake Erie, building concrete retaining walls along the side walls of the lagoons and channel. The area surrounding the lagoons was subdivided into lots, a few of which were sold, but the project was abandoned due to the economic conditions existing in the 1930s. Plaintiff, the Mentor Harbor Yachting Club, is the present owner of the land adjacent to the channel, while defendants, Mentor Lagoons, Inc., and Albert C. Nozik, and others are the owners of the property adjacent to the lagoons. The defendants claim a right to use the channel as a means of ingress and egress between the lagoons and Lake Erie.

This action was brought by plaintiff to enjoin defendants from trespassing on the channel. Injunctions were granted both by the trial court and by the Court of Appeals hearing the case de novo. The lower courts determined that defendants have no right to use this channel either by virtue of an easement or by virtue of the fact that it is navigable waters. Both the lower courts held as a matter of law that this channel constitutes non-navigable waters.

The question for determination is whether the Mentor Harbor watercourse flowing into Lake Erie constitutes a navigable body of water. If it is a naturally navigable watercourse it is public. In view of our determination of this question, a consideration of other issues presented in this cause is unnecessary.

The division of watercourses into navigable and non-navigable is merely a method of dividing them into public and private, which is the more natural classification. A modern concept of navigable waters was announced by this court in the recent case of *Coleman v. Schaeffer*, 1955, 163 Ohio St. 202, 126 N.E.2d 444. The syllabus of that case is as follows:

1. In determining the navigability of a stream, consideration may be given to its availability for boating or sailing for pleasure and recreation as well as for pecuniary profit.

2. Such navigability may be determined on the basis of not only the natural condition of the stream, but also of its availability for navigation after the making of reasonable improvements.

3. In determining the navigability of a stream, consideration may be given to its accessibility by public termini, but the presence or absence of such termini is not conclusive.

We shall, therefore, determine the navigability of the Mentor Harbor watercourse upon the basis of the following factors: (1) capacity for boating in its natural condition, (2) accessibility by public termini, (3) capacity for boating after the making of reasonable improvements, and (4) the capacity for boating for either recreation or commerce.

The natural condition of the watercourse in the *Coleman* case, *supra*, bore a marked resemblance to the condition of the waters of Mentor Harbor in

the early 1920s prior to the time any artificial improvements were made. In the *Coleman* case it was determined that Beaver Creek which flowed into Lake Erie near the city of Lorain, Ohio, was a navigable watercourse. The owner of the land adjacent to the opening of the creek at the point of its joinder with the lake employed a contractor in 1938 or 1939 to dredge out sand accumulated at the entrance to the creek. Such accumulation was caused by the natural action of the winds and waters of Lake Erie. An examination of the record in the *Coleman* case substantiates the similarity of the facts there to those herein. At the trial of that action, several witnesses testified regarding the natural condition of Beaver Creek. The appellee's brief discloses testimony which indicated that a sandbar was formed at the mouth of the creek in precisely the same manner as the one which appeared from time to time at the mouth of Mentor Harbor. In order to keep the creek open from year to year, the sand accumulation had to be dredged. Also, the appellee's brief cites the testimony of another witness to the effect that, prior to the dredging of Beaver Creek, the area had the appearance of a swamp or marsh.

A further resemblance in the natural condition of the two watercourses exists. Beaver Creek was navigable only for a distance of two miles from its mouth. At that point the creek became shallow and filled with vegetation and debris to the extent that even the smallest vessel could not navigate it. Similarly, in the instant case, the streams which fed the natural body of water at Mentor Harbor were navigable only for a short distance while that inland body of water itself was fully navigable.

In examining the natural condition of the Mentor Harbor watercourse, it was found by the Court of Appeals that a natural passage did in fact exist which connected the watercourse with Lake Erie. Prior to 1926, and before any improvements had been made, a number of vessels gained access to the inland waters by use of such passage. On these occasions the waters were variously used for hunting, fishing, and boating. At certain other times of the year, a sandbar was formed by the natural action of the wind and waves with the result that the inland waters were temporarily cut off from direct access to the lake. Periodically, the pressure of the inland waters would break a passage through the bar and the water would flow into the lake. We do not believe that such a natural temporary obstruction destroyed the otherwise navigable character of this watercourse. Navigability may exist despite the obstruction of falls, rapids, sand bars, carries, or shifting currents. *United States v. Appalachian Electric Power Co.*, 311 U.S. 377, 409 (1940). The same question is discussed in 56 American Jurisprudence, 649, Section 182, where this interesting language is found:

Navigability in the sense of the law is not destroyed because the watercourse is interrupted by occasional natural obstructions or portages.... There are but few freshwater rivers which did not originally present serious obstructions to uninterrupted navigation. The vital and essential point is whether the natural navigability of the river is such that it affords a channel for useful commerce. If this is so, *the river is navigable in fact, although its navigation may be encompassed with difficulties by reason of natural barriers, such as rapids and sand bars.* (emphasis added)

In *East Bay Sporting Club v. Miller*, 118 Ohio St. 360, 161 N.E. 12, this court recognized the principle that a body of water need not flow continuously in order to be properly characterized as a watercourse. The court in paragraph three of the syllabus stated:

A "watercourse" is a stream usually flowing in a particular direction in a definite channel having a bed, banks, or sides and discharging into some other stream or body of water. It need not flow continuously, and may sometimes be dry or the volume of such watercourse may sometimes be augmented by freshets or water backed into it from a lake or bay or other extraordinary causes; *but so long as it resumes its flow in a definite course in a recognized channel and between recognized banks such stream constitutes a watercourse.* (emphasis added)

The *East Bay* case is cited and quoted above only for approval and adoption of the definition of "watercourse." In other respects, that case is to be distinguished from the case at bar. The court in the *East Bay* case determined, inter alia, that two very shallow streams whose beds and banks were under single ownership and which flowed into Sandusky Bay were private and non-navigable. The court's conclusion was based on the fact that neither stream was capable of supporting commercial navigation. As we have pointed out, the test for determining the navigability of a watercourse has been considerably liberalized; and a stream's capacity for serving as a "highway for commerce" is no longer the exclusive question for consideration as it was in the *East Bay* case.

As announced by this court in the *Coleman* case, a factor which may be considered in determining the navigability of a watercourse is its accessibility by public termini. The presence or absence of such termini is not conclusive. However, it should be observed that the watercourse in question is bounded on the north by the public waters of Lake Erie. In its present condition, the Mentor Harbor watercourse is easily accessible from the lake, and in its natural condition it was accessible, except during the intervals of sand accumulation at the mouth of the channel.

In its present state, the watercourse in controversy consists of a deep channel joining Lake Erie with an elaborate system of extensive artificial lagoons. This watercourse is presently used, and has been used for many years, for sailing and mooring of yachts and various other craft of considerable size. There can be little doubt of the excellence of the place, in its present condition, for recreational boating. In the plaintiff's own words, "the obvious suitability of the artificial waterways for use by boats is not in dispute." To emphasize the present capacity of the watercourse for boating, it is interesting to note that the plaintiff admits the mooring of over sixty of its members' vessels at various places along the lagoons adjacent to the property owned by the defendants herein.

The abundant and continued public use of

this watercourse finds strong substantiation in the recent case of *State v. Pierce*, 164 Ohio St. 482, 132 N.E.2d 102. That controversy related to an alleged violation of a township zoning resolution governing the use of the Mentor Harbor Lagoon property, the same property with which we are now concerned. Judge Hart, in the opinion in that case in 164 Ohio St. at page 485, 132 N.W.2d 102, referred to the acknowledged public use of the property in question which use, it was stated, was for the purposes of hunting, fishing, and boating and had continued down through the years without objection from the owners of the land.

The plaintiff here claims that the deepening and widening of the channel in question was an improvement different in kind from the "reasonable improvement" involved in the *Coleman* case. This is true, the plaintiff contends, because of the large cost of the operation and because of the fact that the construction was undertaken in a "marsh-like" area. Thus, the plaintiff concludes that the dredging and maintenance of its channel do not constitute such a reasonable improvement. Our conclusion is to the contrary. As previously pointed out, the record in the *Coleman* case confirms the fact that the dredging of Beaver Creek and the dredging of Mentor Harbor were undertakings of a very similar nature. Both operations involved the dredging of sand accumulated because of identical causes. Both operations were conducted in areas which prior to such dredgings had the appearance of swamps or marshes, the latter feeding and draining into the navigable parts of the watercourses.

A natural watercourse does not lose its character as a public watercourse because a part of its channel has been artificially created. Nor is the channel of a naturally navigable watercourse made private because of reasonable improvements put upon it. Similarly, in the instance case, the lagoons, which are artificial extensions of the naturally navigable channel, became a part thereof and are public waters.

As revealed in the *Coleman* case, *supra*, this court has extended the criteria for determining navigability beyond the so-called "commercial usage" test as applied in paragraph two of the syllabus in the *East Bay Sporting Club* case, *supra*. To decide navigability solely upon the basis of such use fails to take cognizance of the tremendous increase in the public use of waterways. The capacity of a watercourse for recreational boating is also a factor which may now be considered. The Department of Natural Resources of this state estimates that over one million Ohio citizens make use of our waters. This department also estimates that a total annual expenditure of approximately $50 million is being made in Ohio directly pursuant to such public use. And this increased recreational use of our waters has been accompanied by a corresponding lessening of their use for commerce. We are in accord with the modern view that navigation for pleasure and recreation is as important in the eyes of the law as navigation for a commercial purpose.

We agree with defendant Nozik's assertion, when he urges us to comply with such a modern concept of navigable waters and to "declare these waters navigable; not only the waters of the plaintiff, which control the waters of the channel, but all the waters of the entire lagoons. These belong to the people. These are public."

We hold that the Mentor Harbor watercourse in its present state, including both the channel and the lagoons, is navigable and, hence, public waters.

The judgment of the Court of Appeals is reversed and final judgments are rendered for the defendants.

Questions

1. What was the practical impact of the finding that the waters were navigable?

2. Under the *Mentor Harbor* four-part navigability test, under what circumstances could you still find that a body of water is private?

Nugent v. Vallone, 161 A.2d 802 (R.I. 1960)

CONDON, CHIEF JUSTICE

This is a bill in equity to enjoin the Commerce Oil Refining Corporation from building a pier in the east passage of Narragansett Bay about nine hundred feet from the east shore of Conanicut Island opposite the end of Eldred Avenue in the town of Jamestown. The bill also prays that Joseph M. Vallone, state director of public works, and Henry Ise, chief of the state division of harbors and rivers, be enjoined from further approving or authorizing the building of such structure and expending any public funds in connection therewith. Certain citizens and taxpayers of Jamestown brought the bill originally in their own right, but later by leave of the superior court they substituted therefor an amended bill in the name of the attorney general on their relation and with his express consent. After a hearing thereon before a justice of that court, a decree was entered denying and dismissing the bill. The cause is there on the relators' appeal from such decree.

The amended bill seeks relief from threatened violation of public rights in the public waters of the state by the construction of the proposed pier. The relators do not allege any special injury peculiar to themselves or their property that would result therefrom. The main relief prayed for in the bill is that "said respondent, Commerce Oil Refining Corporation, be restrained temporarily and permanently from interfering with or encroaching upon public rights in and to the public waters and public lands adjacent to the area in question, namely, that area immediately east of Eldred Avenue in said Town of Jamestown," and also "from interfering with the riparian rights of the public in and to said Eldred Avenue and in and to the tidewaters and tidelands beyond the high-water mark in said Narragansett Bay."

In substance, the relators contend that the proposed pier will be an interference with navigation; that it will constitute an unlawful appropriation of the public domain under the waters of the east passage; that respondents Vallone and Ise were without lawful authority to assent to the construction of said pier; that the provisions of General Laws 1956, 46-6-2, under which they purported to act, are unconstitutional and void if construed so as to confer such authority; that the respondent corporation has no title to the shore at the easterly end of Eldred Avenue, but such title is in the state in trust for the public; that the proposed pier will encroach upon and interfere with the riparian rights of the public at that point; and finally that said pier will be a public nuisance. In this decision the trial justice considered such contentions expressly or impliedly and rejected them.

The evidence shows that respondent corporation is the owner of the entire east shore directly opposite the proposed pier including the easterly end of Eldred Avenue. There is no merit in relators' contention that the title thereto is in the state. That portion of Eldred Avenue was formally abandoned as a public highway by the Town of Jamestown. Since respondent corporation is the sole abutting owner of the land on either side of such abandoned highway, it is presumed to own the fee thereto. In this state there is a presumption that ownership of land abutting a highway carries with it the fee to the center line thereof. The mere fact that Eldred Avenue may have been originally an ancient colonial highway, as the relators contend, does not alter that rule.

As the sole riparian owner of the east shore, respondent corporation therefore had the right to wharf out into the east passage to avail itself of the full advantage of navigation. Many years ago this court observed in *Clark v. Peckham*, 10 R.I. 35, at page 36, "that while the shore itself, and the space between high- and low-water mark is public for passage, the riparian owner has a right of access to the great highway of nations, of which he cannot be deprived, is recognized by a great number of cases." Indeed it appears to have been long recognized in this state that this right to wharf out is a common law right which, in the absence of statute to the contrary, will not be denied, provided that the exercise thereof does not interfere with navigation or the rights of other riparian proprietors. And in *Yates v. City of Milwaukee*, 77 U.S. 497, 504, the Supreme Court speaking of the rights of riparian owners said, "Among those rights are access to the navigable part of the river from the front of his lot, the right to make a landing, wharf, or pier for his own use or for the use of the public, subject to such general rules and regulations as the legislature may see proper to impose for the protection of the rights of the public, whatever those may be."

In the case at bar respondent corporation did not assert its right until it had submitted its proposal to the duly constituted federal and state authorities for approval. The chief of the corps of engineers of the United States Army on behalf of the federal government certified that the proposed pier would not be a hazard to navigation. The respondents Vallone and Ise did likewise and gave their assent pursuant to the provisions of G.L. 1956, 46-6-2, which read as follows:

Approval of plans for construction of wharves and piers.

All persons who shall build into or over public tidewaters, by authority of said department or by authority of the general assembly, any wharf, pier, bridge, or other structure, or drive any piles into the land under public tidewater, or fill any flats, shall, before beginning such work, give written notice to the department of public works of the work they intend to do, and submit plans of any proposed wharf or other structure and of the flats to be filled, and of the mode in which the work is to be performed; and no such work shall be commenced until the plan and mode of performing the same shall be approved in writing by the director of public works; and said director may alter the said plans at his discretion and may prescribe the direction, limits, and mode of building the wharves or other structures; provided, that nothing herein contained shall be construed to impair the rights of any riparian proprietors to erect wharves authorized to be erected under any of the

laws establishing harbor lines within the state, or otherwise by the general assembly.

However, relators contend that respondents Vallone and Ise could not validly assent thereunder as such assent would be tantamount to giving away the soil under the waters of the east passage which the state holds in trust for the public. They argue further that if 46-6-2 is construed to grant such authority, it is violative of article I, sec. 17, article III, and article IV, secs. 1, 2, and 14, of the state constitution.

There is no merit in any of those contentions. It is true that the state holds title to the soil under the public waters of the state. However it holds such title not as a proprietor but only in trust for the public to preserve their rights of fishery, navigation, and commerce in such waters. The duly constituted public authorities have certified that the proposed pier will not interfere with any of those public rights. It was evidently for the purpose of assuring, in advance of any actual wharfing out, the full protection of such rights by lawful and reasonable regulation that the legislature enacted G.L. 1956, 46-6-2.

Therefore we must assume that respondents Vallone and Ise acted in the exercise of such regulatory authority. Their assent to the proposed pier was sufficient, as far as the state was concerned, to warrant respondent corporation's exercise of its common law right as a riparian owner to wharf out in order to obtain suitable access to the sea. And as far as the federal government's control over navigable waters was concerned, the permit from the corps of engineers removed any possible objection on that score.

Insofar as relators claim that the pier will be a public nuisance they take nothing by such contention. The approval of the pier by respondents Vallone and Ise on behalf of the state and by the chief of the corps of engineers on behalf of the federal government precludes relators from arguing that it will be either an interference with supposed riparian rights of the public or a hazard to navigation. Exercise of the right to do that which the law authorizes cannot be a public nuisance. In view of the absence of disapproval on the part of those public officials authorized to do so, the mere construction of the proposed pier was rightly held by the trial justice not to be unlawful and hence not a public nuisance. Whether the manner in which the pier is hereafter used will amount to such a nuisance is quite another question and non sub judice at this time.

The relators' appeal is denied and dismissed, the decree appealed from is affirmed, and the cause is remanded to the superior court for further proceedings.

Questions

1. What limits did the court recognize on the property owner's riparian rights?

2. Would the case have been decided differently if evidence had been introduced regarding shellfish beds which would have been covered by the pier construction?

Kaiser Aetna v. United States, 100 U.S. 383 (1979)

The Hawaii Kai Marina was developed by the dredging and filling of Kuapa Pond, which was a shallow lagoon separated from Maunalua Bay in the Pacific Ocean by a barrier beach. Although under Hawaii law Kuapa Pond was private property, the Court of Appeals for the Ninth Circuit held that when petitioners converted the pond into a marina and thereby connected it to the bay, it became subject to the "navigational servitude" of the Federal Government. Thus, the public acquired a right of access to what was once petitioners' private pond. We granted certiorari because of the importance of the issue and a conflict concerning the scope and nature of the servitude.

I. Kuapa Pond was apparently created in the late Pleistocene Period, near the end of the ice age, when the rising sea level caused the shoreline to retreat, and partial erosion of the headlands adjacent to the bay formed sediment that accreted to form a barrier beach at the mouth of the pond, creating a lagoon. It covered 523 acres on the island of Oahu, Hawaii, and extended approximately two miles inland from Maunalua Bay and the Pacific Ocean. The pond was contiguous to the bay, which is a navigable waterway of the United States, but was separated from it by the barrier beach.

Early Hawaiians used the lagoon as a fish pond and reinforced the natural sandbar with stone walls. Prior to the annexation of Hawaii, there were two openings from the pond to Maunalua Bay. The fish pond's managers placed removable sluice gates in the stone walls across these openings. Water from the bay and ocean entered the pond through the gates during high tide, and during low tide the current flow reversed toward the ocean. The Hawaiians used the tidal action to raise and catch fish such as mullet.

Kuapa Pond, and other Hawaiian fish ponds, have always been considered to be private property by landowners and by the Hawaiian government. Such ponds were once an integral part of the Hawaiian feudal system. And in 1848 they were allotted as parts of large land units, known as *ahupuaas*, by King Kamehameha III during the Great Mahele, or royal land division. Titles to the fish ponds were recognized to the same extent and in the same manner as rights in more orthodox fast land. Kuapa Pond was part of an *ahupuaa* that eventually vested in Bernice Pauahi Bishop and on her death formed a part of the trust corpus of petitioner Bishop Estate, the present owner.

In 1961, Bishop Estate leased a six thousand-acre area, which included Kuapa Pond, to petitioner Kaiser Aetna for subdivision development. The development is now known as Hawaii Kai. Kaiser Aetna dredged and filled parts of Kuapa Pond, erected retaining walls and built bridges within the development to create the Hawaii Kai Marina. Kaiser Aetna increased the average depth of the channel from two to six feet. It also created accommodations for pleasure boats and eliminated the sluice gates. When petitioners notified the Corps of Engineers of their plans in 1961, the Corps advised them they were not required to obtain permits for the development of and operations in Kuapa Pond. Kaiser Aetna subsequently informed the Corps that it planned to dredge an eight-foot-deep channel connecting Kuapa Pond to Maunalua Bay and the Pacific Ocean, and to increase the clearance of a bridge of the Kalanianaole Highway—which had been constructed during the early 1900s along the barrier beach separating Kuapa Pond from the bay and ocean—to a maximum of 13.5 feet over the mean sea level. These improvements were made in order to allow boats from the marina to enter into and return from the bay, as well as to provide better waters. The Corps acquiesced in the proposals, its chief of construction commenting only that the "deepening of the channel may cause erosion of the beach."

At the time of trial, a marina-style community of approximately 22,000 persons surrounded Kuapa Pond. It included approximately 1,500 marine waterfront lot lessees. The waterfront lot lessees, along with at least 86 non-marina lot lessees from Hawaii Kai and boat owners who are not residents of Hawaii Kai, pay fees for maintenance of the pond and for patrol boats that remove floating debris, enforce boating regulations, and maintain the privacy and security of the pond. Kaiser Aetna controls access to and use of the marina. It has generally not permitted commercial use, except for a small vessel, the Marina Queen, which could carry twenty-five passengers and was used for about five years to promote sales of marina lots and for a brief period by marina shopping center merchants to attract people to their shopping facilities.

In 1972, a dispute arose between petitioners and the Corps concerning whether: (1) petitioners were required to obtain authorization from the Corps, in accordance with Sec. 10 of the Rivers and Harbors Act, 33 U.S.C. Sec. 403,

for future construction, excavation, or filling in the marina, and (2) petitioners were precluded from denying the public access to the pond because, as a result of the improvements, it had become a navigable water of the United States. The dispute foreseeably ripened into a lawsuit by the United States Government against petitioners in the United States District Court for the District of Hawaii. In examining the scope of Congress's regulatory authority under the Commerce Clause, the District Court held that the pond was "navigable water of the United States" and thus subject to regulation by the Corps under Sec. 10 of the Rivers and Harbors Act. 408 F.Supp. 42, 53 (D. Haw. 1976). It further held, however, that the government lacked the authority to open the now dredged ponds to the public without payment of compensation to the owner. In reaching this holding the District Court reasoned that although the pond was navigable for the purpose of delimiting Congress's regulatory power, it was not navigable for the purpose of defining the scope of the federal "navigational servitude" imposed by the Commerce Clause. Thus, the District Court denied the Corps's request for an injunction to require petitioners to allow public access and to notify the public of the fact of the pond's accessibility.

The Court of Appeals agreed with the District Court's conclusion that the pond fell within the scope of Congress's regulatory authority, but reversed the District Court's holding that the navigational servitude did not require petitioners to grant the public access to the pond. 584 F.2d 378 (9th Cir. 1978).

The Court of Appeals reasoned that the "federal regulatory authority over navigable waters . . . and the right of public use cannot consistently be separated. It is the public right of navigational use that renders regulatory control necessary in the public interest." The question before us is whether the Court of Appeals erred in holding that petitioners' improvements to Kuapa Pond caused its original character to be so altered that it became subject to an overriding federal navigational servitude, thus converting into a public aquatic park that which petitioners had invested millions of dollars in improving on the assumption that it was a privately owned pond leased to them.

II. The Government contends that petitioners may not exclude members of the public from the Hawaii Kai Marina because "the public enjoys a federally protected right of navigation over the navigable waters of the United States." It claims the issue in dispute is whether Kuapa Pond is presently a "navigable water of the United States." When petitioners dredged and improved Kuapa Pond, the government continues, the pond—although it may once have qualified as fast land—became navigable water of the United States. The public thereby acquired a right to use Kuapa Pond as a continuous highway for navigation, and the Corps of Engineers may consequently obtain an injunction to prevent petitioners from attempting to reserve the waterway to themselves.

The position advanced by the Government, and adopted by the Court of Appeals below, presumes that the concept of "navigable waters of the United States" has a fixed meaning that remains unchanged in whatever context it is being applied.

· · ·

It is true that Kuapa Pond may fit within definitions of "navigability" articulated in past decisions of this Court. But it must be recognized that the concept of navigability in these decisions was used for purposes other than to delimit the boundaries of the navigational servitude: for example, to define the scope of Congress's regulatory authority under the Interstate Commerce Clause, to determine the extent of the authority of the Corps of Engineers under the Rivers and Harbors Act of 1899, and to establish the limits of the jurisdiction of federal courts, conferred by Art. III, Sec. 2, of the United States Constitution, over admiralty and maritime cases. Although the Government is clearly correct in maintaining that the now dredged Kuapa Pond falls within the definition

of "navigable waters" as this Court has used that term in delimiting the boundaries of Congress's regulatory authority under the Commerce Clause, . . . this Court has never held that the navigational servitude creates a blanket exception to the Takings Clause whenever Congress exercises its Commerce Clause authority to promote navigation. Thus, while Kuapa Pond may be subject to regulation by the Corps of Engineers, acting under the authority delegated it by Congress in the Rivers and Harbors Act, it does not follow that the pond is also subject to a public right of access.

A. Reference to the navigability of a waterway adds little if anything to the breadth of Congress's regulatory power over interstate commerce. It has long been settled that Congress has extensive authority over this Nation's waters under the Commerce Clause. Early in our history this Court held that the power to regulate commerce necessarily includes power over navigation. *Gibbons v. Ogden*, 22 U.S. 1 (1824). As stated in *Gilman v. Philadelphia*, 70 U.S. 713, 724–25:

Commerce includes navigation. The power to regulate Commerce comprehends the control for that purpose, and to the extent necessary, of all the navigable waters of the United States which are accessible from a state other than those in which they lie. For this purpose, they are the public property of the nation, and subject to all the requisite legislation by Congress.

The pervasive nature of Congress's regulatory authority over national waters was more fully described in *United States v. Appalachian Power Co., supra*, 311 U.S., at 426–27:

[I]t cannot properly be said that the constitutional power of the United States over its waters is limited to control for navigation. . . . In truth the authority of the United States is the regulation of commerce on its waters. Navigability . . . is but a part of this whole. Flood protection, watershed development, recovery of the cost of improvements through utilization of power are likewise parts of commerce control. . . . [The] authority is as broad as the needs of commerce. . . . The point is that navigable waters are subject to national planning and control in the broad regulation of commerce granted the Federal Government.

Appalachian Power Co. indicates that congressional authority over the waters of this Nation does not depend on a stream's "navigability."

· · ·

B. In light of its expansive authority under the Commerce Clause, there is no question but that Congress could assure the public a free right of access to the Hawaii Kai Marina if it so chose. Whether a statute or regulation that went so far amounted to a "taking," however, is an entirely separate question. As was recently pointed out in *Penn. Central Transportation Co. v. City of New York*, 438 U.S. 104 (1978), this Court has generally "been unable to develop any 'set formula' for determining when 'justice and fairness' require that economic injuries caused by public action be compensated by the Government, rather than remain disproportionately concentrated on a few persons." Rather, it has examined the "taking" question by engaging in essentially ad hoc, factual inquiries that have identified several factors— such as the economic impact of the regulation, its interference with reasonable investment backed expectations, and the character of the governmental action—that have particular significance. When the "taking" question has involved the exercise of the public right of navigation over interstate waters that constitute highways for commerce, however, this Court has held in many cases that compensation may not be required as a result of the federal navigational servitude. See, e.g., *United States v. Chandler-Dunbar*, 229 U.S. 53 (1913).

C. The navigational servitude is an expression of the notion that the determination whether a taking has occurred must take into consideration the important public interest in the flow of interstate waters in their natural condition are in fact capable of supporting public navigation. Thus, in *United States v. Chandler-Dunbar Co.*, *supra*, 229 U.S., at 69, this Court stated "that

the running water in a great navigable stream is [in]capable of private ownership. . . . " And, in holding that a riparian landowner was not entitled to compensation when the construction of a pier cut off his access to navigable water, this Court observed:

The primary use of the waters and the lands under them is for purposes of navigation, and the erection of the piers in them to improve navigation for the public is entirely consistent with such use, and infringes no right of the riparian owners. Whatever the nature of the interest of a riparian owner in the submerged lands in front of his upland bordering on a public navigable water, his title is not as full and complete as his title to fast land which has no direct connection with the navigation of such water. It is a qualified title, a bare technical title, not at his absolute disposal, as is his upland, but to be held at all times subordinate to such use of the submerged lands and of the waters flowing under them as may be consistent with or demanded by the public right of navigation.

For over a century, a long line of cases decided by this court involving government condemnation of "fast lands" delineated the elements of compensable damages that the government was required to pay because the lands were riparian to navigable streams. The Court was often deeply divided, and the results frequently turned on what could fairly be described as quite narrow distinctions. But this is not a case in which the government recognizes any obligation whether to condemn "fast lands" and pay just compensation under the Eminent Domain Clause of the Fifth Amendment to the Bill of Rights of the United States Constitution. It is instead a case in which the owner of what was once a private pond, separated from concededly navigable water by a barrier beach and used for aquatic agriculture, has invested substantial amounts of money in making improvements. The government contends that as a result of one of these improvements, the pond's connection to the navigable water in a manner approved by the Corps of Engineers, the owner has somehow lost one of the most essential sticks in the bundle of rights that are commonly characterized as property—the right to exclude others.

The navigational servitude, which exists by virtue of the Commerce Clause in navigable streams, gives rise to an authority in the Government to assure that such streams retain their capacity to serve as continuous highways for the purpose of navigation in interstate commerce. Thus, when the Government acquires fast lands to improve navigation, it is not required under the Eminent Domain Clause to compensate landowners for certain elements of damage attributable to riparian location, such as the land's value as a hydroelectric site or a port site. But none of these cases ever doubted that when the Government wished to acquire fast lands, it was required by the Eminent Domain Clause of the Fifth Amendment to condemn and pay fair value for that interest.

Here the Government's attempt to create a public right of access to the improved pond goes so far beyond ordinary regulation or improvement for navigation as to amount to a taking under the logic of *Pennsylvania Coal Co. v. Mahon, supra.* More than one factor contributes to this result. It is clear that prior to its improvement, Kuapa Pond was incapable of being used as a continuous highway for the purpose of navigation in interstate commerce. Its maximum depth at high tide was a mere two feet, it was separated from the adjacent bay and ocean by a natural barrier beach, and its principal commercial value was limited to fishing. It consequently is not the sort of "great navigable stream" that this Court has previously recognized as being "[in]capable of private ownership." And, as previously noted, Kuapa Pond has always been considered to be private property under Hawaiian law. Thus, the interest of petitioners in the now dredged marina is strikingly similar to that of owners of fast land adjacent to navigable water.

We have not the slightest doubt that the Government could have refused to allow such dredging on the ground that it would have impaired navigation in the bay, or could have conditioned its approval of the dredging on petitioners' agreement to comply with various measures that it deemed appropriate for the promotion of navigation. But what petitioners now have is a body of water that was private property under Hawaiian law, linked to navigable water by a channel dredged by them with the consent of the respondent. While the consent of individual officials representing the United States cannot "estop" the United States, it can lead to the fruition of a number of expectancies embodied in the concept of "property,"—expectancies that, if sufficiently important, the Government must condemn and pay for before it takes over the management of the landowner's property. In this case, we hold that the "right to exclude," so universally held to be a fundamental element of the property right, falls within this category of interests that the Government cannot take without compensation. This is not a case in which the Government is exercising its regulatory power in a manner that will cause an insubstantial devaluation of petitioners' private property; rather, the imposition of the navigational servitude in this context will result in an actual physical invasion of the privately owned marina.

If the Government wishes to make what was formerly Kuapa Pond into a public aquatic park after petitioners have proceeded as far as they have here, it may not, without invoking its eminent domain power and paying just compensation, require them to allow free access to the dredged pond while petitioners' agreement with their customers calls for an annual $72 regular fee.

Accordingly the judgment of the Court is Appeals is

Reversed.

Questions

1. Did the Army Corps "drop the ball" in this case when they granted the original permit?

2. Does the special nature of Hawaiian law with regard to ownership of ponds affect this case's precedential value?

U.S. v. Sasser, 967 F.2d 993 (4th Cir. 1992)

ERVIN, CHIEF JUDGE

In 1987, the United States Army Corps of Engineers ("the Corps") ordered Marshall C. Sasser to remove barriers blocking access to two streams on his property. Sasser refused to comply, and the government sued Sasser for injunctive relief in the district court below. The district court ruled in the government's favor and ordered Sasser to remove the barriers. 711 F.Supp. 720. The district court found that the Corps had jurisdiction over this matter based on the fact that the two streams were subject to the ebb and flow of the tide. Sasser argues that the Corps lacked subject matter jurisdiction, that the Corps did not follow its own regulations, and that the removal of the barriers would constitute a compensable taking of his property. We now affirm.

I.

In 1980, Sasser purchased property in coastal Georgetown County, South Carolina, that was formerly a rice plantation. Sasser had spent time on the property and surrounding land since 1950, when his father had purchased some of the land. In 1980, Sasser purchased his present property for $350,000. Sasser claims that he only obtained the property in order to create a private duck hunting club. He has since spent an additional $150,000 to build a clubhouse and make other improvements, and he has sold twelve memberships in his club.

This case concerns two streams. One empties into the Intracoastal Waterway, and the other empties into the Pee Dee River. The Intracoastal Waterway and the Pee Dee River are navigable waters of the United States. The two streams in question are natural bodies of water that originate on privately owned land and serve to drain the old rice fields. The parties have stipulated that both streams are subject to the ebb and flow of the tide. The two streams are also very shallow, subject only to use by canoes and john boats. Since at least the early 1940s, landowners have blocked access to the streams by placing wood and metal gates near the points where they meet the larger bodies of water (the Pee Dee River and the Intracoastal Waterway). In recent years, boaters have continually damaged the gates, and Sasser has repeatedly repaired them. In 1987, after receiving a number of letters and a petition requesting action, the Corps intervened in this feud, ordering Sasser and five other landowners who had blocked off similar streams to remove the barriers. The other five complied, but Sasser refused. The government claims that it sought the removal of the barriers in order to end the boater–landowner dispute and also to allow fishing, bird-watching, wildlife photography, and pleasure boating on the streams.

II.

Sasser first argues that the Corps lacked jurisdiction over the two streams. The Rivers and Harbors Appropriation Act of 1899, 33 U.S.C. Sec. 403, provides that "[t]he creation of any obstruction not affirmatively authorized by Congress to the navigable capacity of any of the waters of the United States is prohibited." The Act also authorizes the government to enforce the removal of any such obstruction in the district courts. 33 U.S.C. Sec. 406. By its terms, the Act "does not apply to . . . waters that are not subject to the ebb and flow of the tide and that are not used and are not susceptible to use in their natural condition or by reasonable improvement as a means to transport interstate or foreign commerce." 33 U.S.C. Sec. 401. The Army Corps of Engineers is the agency charged with enforcing the Act. Consistent with the Act, the Corps' jurisdiction extends to "navigable waters of the United States," which are defined as "those waters that are subject to the ebb and flow of the tide and/or are presently used, or

have been used in the past, or may be susceptible for use to transport interstate or foreign
commerce." 33 C.F.R. Sec. 329.4.

In arguing that the Corps lacked jurisdiction,
Sasser relies on *The Daniel Ball*, 77 U.S. 577
(1871), for the proposition that the "ebb and
flow" test may no longer be used to establish
jurisdiction over waters of the United States. In
The Daniel Ball, the Supreme Court defined
"navigable waters" as waters that:

form in their ordinary condition by themselves, or by
uniting with other waters, a continued highway over
which commerce is or may be carried on with other
States or foreign countries, in the customary modes
in which such commerce is conducted by water.

Id. 77 U.S. at 563. Sasser's theory is that the
Corps lacked jurisdiction over the two streams
in question, because they cannot really be used
for interstate commerce, at least not nowadays.
Therefore, he claims that the Corps had no
power to order him to remove the gates blocking access to the streams.

The Fourth Circuit recently adopted *The
Daniel Ball* test as its definition of admiralty jurisdiction:

We thus define navigable water for purposes of admiralty jurisdiction as a body of water which, in its
present configuration, constitutes a highway of commerce, alone or together with another body of water,
between the states or with foreign countries over
which commerce in its current mode is capable of
being conducted.

Alford v. Appalachian Power Co., 951 F.2d 30,
32 (4th Cir. 1991). Although *The Daniel Ball* is
thus still good law, it does not support Sasser's
theory because it does not apply to this case.
Later language in *Alford* exposes the flaw in
Sasser's argument:

Admiralty, though, is not concerned with the maintenance of rivers or other bodies of water, but rather
with the conduct of those who use them, and it does
not extend to the limits of federal power over waters
of the United States. Other federal interests may and
do justify federal jurisdiction over waters which are
defined as navigable for other purposes.

Id. at 33 (citing *Kaiser-Aetna v. United States*,
100 S.Ct. 383 [1979]). The *Alford* court pointed
out that admiralty jurisdiction does not cover
the maintenance of bodies of water, which is
what this case involves. The jurisdiction that
does cover maintaining bodies of water is based
on the interstate commerce power. In other
words, admiralty jurisdiction (*The Daniel Ball*)
and jurisdiction based on the interstate commerce power are defined differently, and Sasser's reliance on the definition of admiralty
jurisdiction is misplaced.

Sasser's argument that *The Daniel Ball*
sounded the death knell for the "ebb and flow"
test is without support, in cases such as this one
that involve coastal, rather than inland, waters.
The Supreme Court has noted that there are at
least four tests for determining whether bodies
of water are "navigable waters of the United
States." *Kaiser Aetna v. United States*, 100 S.Ct.
383 (1979). The tests are: (1) ebb and flow, (2)
connection with a continuous interstate waterway, (3) navigable capacity, and (4) navigable in
fact. While the Court has not faced the precise
argument that Sasser raises, several Circuit
Courts of Appeals have, and all have held that
whether waters are subject to the ebb and flow
of the tide is a valid test for determining the
Corps' jurisdiction over coastal waters. See, e.g.,
United States v. DeFelice, 641 F.2d 1169, 1173–
75 (5th Cir. 1981); *Leslie Salt Co. v. Froehlke*,
578 F.2d 742, 749–53 (9th Cir. 1978); *United
States v. Stoeco Homes, Inc.*, 498 F.2d 597, 608–
10 (3d Cir. 1974). Those courts reasoned that
the "ebb and flow" test and *The Daniel Ball*
definition of "navigable waters" logically coexist
because *The Daniel Ball* actually expanded admiralty jurisdiction, while abandoning the "ebb
and flow" test in coastal waters would serve to
contract federal jurisdiction. Moreover, those
courts have noted that defining "navigable waters of the United States" to include waters subject to the ebb and flow of the tide is well
within the limits of the interstate commerce
power. Finding the caselaw from other circuits
persuasive, we hold that the "ebb and flow" test

is a valid means of determining the Corps' jurisdiction over tidal waters.

Next, Sasser argues that the grandfather clause in the Corps' own regulations guarantees the continued existence of the two gates. Under 33 C.F.R. Sec. 330.3(b), no further permits are required for structures when (1) they were completed before December 18, 1968; (2) the Corps had not asserted jurisdiction at the time the activity occurred; and (3) the structures do not interfere with navigation. Both parties agree that this three-part test applies and that all three requirements must be met; they differ only as to the application of the test. There is no dispute over the second requirement, because the Corps did not assert jurisdiction when the gates were first constructed. As for the first requirement, the government argues that the barriers were not completed before 1968, because Sasser has had to repair and replace them continually since that time. Sasser maintains that gates have stood at the same sites since the early 1940s, so that they *were* completed before 1968. Because the record as to the existence of the gates since 1968 is unclear, we decline to rule on this requirement.

A better basis for deciding this issue is the third part of the grandfather test: whether the gates interfere with navigation. The gates clearly interfere with navigation at the present time, because they prevent boaters from going up the streams. However, Sasser argues that their interference with navigation should be evaluated as of the time they were built—the early 1940s. Sasser's theory is meritless. The regulation does not state that the interference with navigation should be measured as of the time the activity first occurred. In fact, the regulation's plain language ("there is no interference with navigation") indicates that the lack of interference must exist at the present time. Also, the regulation applies to a wide range of structures, not just those that interfere with navigation. It makes sense for the regulation to waive future permit requirements only for those existing structures that do not currently inter-

fere with navigation. After all, one purpose of the Rivers and Harbors Act, upon which the regulation is based, is to direct the Corps to prevent and remove obstacles to navigation. In addition, caselaw supports the government's position. See *Fisher v. Danos*, 595 F.Supp. 461, 466–67 (E.D.La. 1984), *aff'd*, 774 F.2d 1158 (5th Cir. 1985). We therefore hold that the gates are not grandfathered under the Corps' regulations, because the gates currently interfere with navigation.

Sasser next argues that the Corps failed to comply with its own regulations and that this failure prevents the government from bringing this action. Sasser bases this argument on 33 C.F.R. Sec. 329.14, which requires the Corps to investigate questions of jurisdiction and navigability by following certain procedures. Sasser cites a number of cases for the proposition that agencies are required to follow their own regulations. However, the regulation in question only requires the Corps to go through the procedures "when jurisdictional questions arise." 33 C.F.R. Sec. 329.14(a). As discussed above, the parties here stipulated that the streams in question are subject to the ebb and flow of the tide, removing any real question of jurisdiction. Sasser's reliance on *The Daniel Ball* did not by itself create a jurisdictional question within the meaning of the regulation. In addition, the government argues that it was justified in bypassing administrative procedures, citing *United States v. Zweifel*, 508 F.2d 1150 (10th Cir. 1975) (holding government may proceed in administrative tribunal or, under statute, in district court to clear title to public lands). The Rivers and Harbors Appropriation Act of 1899, 33 U.S.C. Secs. 406, 416, states that the Department of Justice and the Attorney General shall conduct the legal proceedings necessary for enforcing the Rivers and Harbors Act. The Act does not require any prior administrative action. Therefore, either because no actual jurisdictional question arose, or under the terms of the Rivers and Harbors Appropriation Act, the Corps' failure to investigate its jurisdiction in this case was immaterial.

Finally, Sasser argues that the government will have effected a compensable taking, if we affirm the district court and allow the Corps to remove the gates blocking access to the streams. He points to the $500,000 he has spent in expectation that he would continue to have a private duck hunting club, and he states that allowing pleasure boaters to use the streams will destroy the value of his property. The gates were necessary in the first place, Sasser states, to keep poachers and other trespassers off his land. Sasser relies primarily on *Kaiser Aetna v. United States*, 100 S.Ct. 383 (1979). In *Kaiser Aetna*, developers in Hawaii converted a land-locked lake into a marina with access to the ocean. They planned to charge boat owners $72 per year to use the marina. The government first gave its approval to the developers' plan but then later required the owners to allow free access to the marina. In finding that there was a compensable taking, the Court reasoned that, although the government could not be estopped by its earlier approval, the government's actions had led the marina owners to expect that they had the right to exclude others. This case differs from *Kaiser Aetna* in two important respects. First, the Corps in this case did nothing to give Sasser an expectation that he had the right to exclude others. The Rivers and Harbors Act and Corps regulations at issue were in effect before Sasser purchased his property in 1980, and the government at no time gave any approval to Sasser's project. Second, it was important in *Kaiser Aetna* that Hawaiian state law defined the property in question as private. Here, in contrast, the South Carolina Supreme Court has held that other old rice plantation canals in Georgetown County are navigable waters subject to public use. *South Carolina v. South Carolina Coastal Council*, 346 S.E.2d 716, 719 (S.C. 1986). Therefore, we hold that *Kaiser Aetna* does not require a finding that the Corps has effected a compensable taking.

In addition, later Supreme Court cases make

it clear that Sasser should seek any possible relief under the Tucker Act in the Court of Claims. See *Preseault v. I.C.C.*, 494 U.S. 1, 110 S.Ct. 914, 108 L.Ed.2d 1 (1990); *United States v. Riverside Bayview Homes*, 474 U.S. 121, 106 S.Ct. 455, 88 L.Ed.2d 419 (1985). In *Preseault*, the Court found a takings claim premature because the appellants had not made use of their Tucker Act remedy. 494 U.S. at 17, 110 S.Ct. at 924. In *Riverside Bayview Homes*, the Court reversed a lower court's decision that the Corps' regulatory jurisdiction over wetlands should be construed narrowly to avoid a takings question. The Court found that requiring or denying a permit to fill wetlands was not necessarily a taking, and that the Tucker Act remedy was available to provide compensation for takings that might result from the Corps' regulatory acts. Moreover, Sasser's damages are purely speculative at this point; it is impossible to predict whether and to what extent pleasure boaters will adversely affect the value of his duck hunting preserve. We therefore hold that Sasser must bring any future takings action in the Court of Claims.

For the reasons expressed above, the judgment of the district court is hereby AFFIRMED.

Questions

1. Did the court successfully distinguish the facts of this case with those in *Kaiser Aetna*?

2. Is it really "speculative," as the court suggests, that pleasure boaters and duck hunters represent a potentially significant multiple-use conflict?

3. Will Sasser succeed with his "takings" argument at the Court of Claims? How would the value be placed on what he argues has been lost?

Dardar v. Lafourche Realty Co., Inc., 985 F.2d 824 (5th Cir. 1993)

W. EUGENE DAVIS, CIRCUIT JUDGE

Plaintiffs, commercial fishermen, sued the

Lafourche Realty Co., Inc., seeking the right to use a system of navigable waters controlled by Lafourche Realty through an arrangement of fences, gates, and levees. The State of Louisiana intervened, asserting a right of public use of the waters and claiming title to the water bodies and over twelve thousand acres of land under the waters.

Lafourche Realty, the record owner of the property, counterclaimed, asserting title to all property located within its patents, including the water bottoms. Lafourche Realty contends that the digging of a canal in 1948 and various more recent improvements have artificially created the waterways which remain privately owned. The district court found for Lafourche Realty, rejecting the State's title claim and, in a separate trial, denying plaintiffs and the State any access to the water bodies. We affirm in part and vacate and remand in part.

I. Louisiana's Claim to Title

We first address the State's title claim. The disputed property lies in southeast Louisiana in Lafourche Parish, east of Bayou Lafourche, northwest of Caminada Bay, several miles from the Gulf coast. According to joint trial stipulations, Lafourche Realty is the record owner of the land. Originally federal property, the property was selected by and approved to the State of Louisiana under one or more of the Swamp Land Grant Acts of 1849 and 1850, by which the United States conveyed to Louisiana "swamplands subject to overflow." Louisiana authorized the State's alienation of lands "donated by Congress to the State of Louisiana, designated as sea marsh or prairie, subject to tidal overflow." The State conveyed the water bottoms by various transfers to Lafourche Realty's ancestors-in-title between 1861 and 1901. The State now argues that it nevertheless owns the water bottoms by virtue of its inherent sovereignty.

A. Public Trust Lands and Waters

The State bases its title claim, first, on public trust jurisprudence and the "equal footing" doc-

trine. On equal footing with the original thirteen states, Louisiana, upon attaining statehood, received ownership of all navigable waters within its borders and all tide waters and the lands under them from the United States in public trust. See *Phillips Petroleum Co. v. Mississippi*, 484 U.S. 469 (1988). Thus, the first element of Louisiana's claim based on the equal footing doctrine depends upon whether waters that were navigable or subject to the ebb and flow of the tide covered any of the property in the year of Louisiana's statehood, 1812. The court rejected this claim upon finding that no natural navigable water bodies existed on the property in 1812 and that the land was not then subject to the ebb and flow of the tide. Appellants challenge both the factual finding and the legal standard employed by the district court.

1. No Navigable Waters in 1812

The district court found that in 1812 none of the Lafourche Realty property was under waters that were navigable in fact. This Court does not set aside a district court's factual findings unless they are clearly erroneous. . . . Unless we are left with the definite and firm conviction that a mistake has been committed, we accept the trial court's findings.

The court's finding of non-navigability is supported by the testimony of Lafourche Realty's expert, Sherwood M. Gagliano, Ph.D., and official township surveys from later in the 1800s that do not depict any navigable water bodies on the property.

The State disparages the township surveys on the basis of its expert witness and nineteenth-century maps showing the existence of lakes and streams northwest of Caminada Bay. The State's expert, Mr. Charles Coates, discredited the absence of water bodies on the township surveys. He explained that those early surveyors did not meander the waters either because of the instability of the terrain or because the interior marsh was not considered saleable. The State also strongly urges reliance upon Captain G. W. Hughes's 1842 Map of Military Reconnaissance and Survey, allegedly depicting lakes and streams corresponding in location to some of the contested water bodies; this lake complex reappears in later maps until 1870, a couple of years before the official township survey.

The court found, however, that the "complex of three to four lakes that some nineteenth-century maps portray . . . are fictitious, at least to the extent the maps purport that any such water bodies lay within the Lafourche Realty Property." This finding was supported by Dr. Gagliano, who concluded that the four shallow lakes linked by a stream appearing on the Hughes map were sketched in "as an afterthought." The lack of detail on the Hughes map for the lakes shown on the subject property is striking. In contrast, other water bodies on the Hughes map (beyond the boundaries of the Lafourche Realty property) were depicted in minute detail with measured depths and with more meticulous renditions of the surrounding topography. Dr. Gagliano based his opinion in part on Captain Hughes's detailed field notes, which were devoid of a description of the four shallow lakes shown on the Hughes map. Dr. Gagliano also regarded the series of maps drafted after the Hughes map from 1842 until about 1872 as "copy-cat maps"; they picked up the lakes sketched on the Hughes map, but the configuration of lakes on such maps was "derived from very poor information." Dr. Gagliano opined that the Lafourche Realty property was historically floating trembling prairie, a category of land. Finally, some evidence suggested that the township surveyors indeed meandered the water bodies in preparing the official surveys, contrary to Mr. Coates's opinion.

2. Test of Navigability

The State next argues that the district court applied an incorrect legal standard to determine navigability. The State urges that the court ignored the test of *Ramsey River Road Property Owners Assn. Inc. v. Reeves*, 396 So.2d 873 (La. 1981), namely, whether a water body may be used in its ordinary condition as a highway for commerce over which trade and travel may be conducted in the customary modes of trade and travel on water *given the means of navigation at that time.* Considering nineteenth-century means of navigation in south Louisiana, the State argues, the court should have easily found navigability.

The district court, specifically noting that under *Ramsey River* "certain shallow water bodies may be wide enough and contain enough water flow . . . to sustain commercial activity such as floating lumber from a nearby sawmill," found, "the Lafourche Realty Property before 1902 did not contain any such water body." Even under a floating-lumber test of navigability, the court determined that no navigable water bodies existed on the property. The State's claim that the court exacted too strict a standard of navigability is without merit. Accordingly, there is no error in the finding and conclusion that Louisiana acquired none of the Lafourche Realty property as navigable water bottoms in 1812.

3. Ebb-and-Flow Tidelands at Statehood

Phillips Petroleum held that lands beneath waters influenced by the ebb and flow of the tide, whether navigable or not, were within the public trust and transferred to the new states upon their entry into the Union. The State contests the district court's finding that none of the land was subject to the ebb and flow of the tides in 1812. We need not address this factual finding. The State owned all the land at the time it transferred the parcels to Lafourche Realty's ancestors-in-title, either under the equal footing doctrines (described in *Phillips Petroleum*) or under the Swamp Land Grant Act, which conveyed "swamp lands subject to overflow" to the State. Whether the State continues to own any ebb-and-flow tidelands is a question of alienability, not acquisition.

B. Did the State Transfer Inalienable Public Trust Land?

The State transferred title by the issuance of various patents to Lafourche Realty's ancestors-in-title from 1861 to 1901. The State next contends that it could not have legally divested itself of the disputed property, because the property was inalienable public trust land—either tidelands or navigable water bottoms—during the years of the putative transfers of title. The district court resolved this issue by finding that none of the Lafourche Realty property contained navigable waters or was subject to tidal ebb and flow from the Gulf of Mexico from 1812 through 1901—*after* the last alienation by the State. The district court concluded that the State did not run afoul of any restriction on alienation of public things.

1. The Findings

As with the findings regarding the year 1812, the State challenges the district court's finding that the property contained no tide lands or waters that were navigable or subject to the ebb and flow of the tide until 1902. The trial court found:

At no time between 1812 and 1902 was any of the Lafourche Realty Property navigable in fact, capable of sustaining maritime or waterborne commerce, [or] more than at most two or three feet in water depth (and then only in isolated spots), or subject to salt or brackish water intrusion through tidal ebb and flow from the Gulf of Mexico. No evidence was presented of any sustained human habitation or activity including hunting, trapping, or fishing on the property during this period. While small portions of the property, namely, Bays Rambo and Jaque, may have been indirectly and slightly subject to freshwater tidal influences (as opposed to the direct, open coastal ebb and flow of tides) as early as 1901, none was in 1812. Although the entire area was subject to annual water overflow in and after 1812, this overflow was of fresh water from the Mississippi River; the actual waters of the Gulf did not, and still do not, "spread over" any of the Lafourche Realty Property. Further, this overflow would distribute in an even sheet fashion, and was not channeled along the relict channels that once connected to Bayou Lafourche.

Again, the State simply argues that its evidence was persuasive and attempts to discredit Lafourche Realty's evidence. The trial court heard the evidence, made credibility determinations, and found that none of the land was subject to coastal tidal influence or under navigable waters until after 1901. We will not second-guess the trial court's view of the evidence. The findings of non-navigability and lack of coastal tide waters through 1902 are supported by substantial evidence, including Dr. Gagliano's analysis of the paleography of the area.

2. No Impermissible Transfer of Navigable Water Bottoms

We need not reach the State's argument that navigability of certain waterways at the time of the transfers to private owners rendered the water bottoms inalienable. As noted above, the court found that the property contained no navigable waters until 1902, after the property was alienated to private ownership.

We turn next to the State's argument that the land and waters influenced by the tides were inalienable.

3. Louisiana's Retained Tidelands: Seashore Not Overflow

The State also complains that the district court erred in distinguishing between "indirect" freshwater tidal influences and "direct" coastal ebb and flow from the gulf. The State argues that land overflowed in either manner is inalienable public trust land.

Phillips Petroleum teaches that Louisiana law governs the alienability of tidelands. " '[T]here is no universal . . . law upon the subject; but . . . each State has dealt with the lands under the tide waters within its borders according to its own view of justice and policy.' " *Phillips Petroleum*, 484 U.S. at 483 (quoting *Shively v. Bowlby*, 152 U.S. 1, 26 [1894]). Thus, Louisiana may transfer ownership of tidelands to private parties if permitted by state law.

Louisiana has retained some of the tidelands it acquired in public trust as public property. The Civil Code declares that "[p]ublic things" are owned by the State or its political subdivisions and are subject to public use." La.Civ.Code Ann. arts. 450 and 452 (West 1980). The State owns "[p]ublic things . . . such as running waters, the waters and bottoms of natural navigable water bodies, the territorial sea, and the seashore." "Seashore" is defined as the space of land over which the waters of the sea spread in the highest tide during the winter season. Thus, tidelands comprising the seashore or sea bottoms are still owned by the State.

Tidelands which Louisiana acquired through the equal footing doctrine that are not seashore or sea bottoms, however, may be privately owned. Inland non-navigable water bodies and swamp land subject to indirect tidal overflow, but not direct coastal ebb and flow, may be privately owned under Louisiana law. Accordingly, we conclude that the district court properly distinguished "direct" coastal ebb and flow from "indirect" freshwater tidal influence. The question narrows to whether any of the subject land is properly characterized as the seashore or any of the water as the sea.

The district court found that the entire area comprising the Lafourche Realty property was subject to annual freshwater overflow from the Mississippi River. The court correctly ruled that this characteristic does not render the land inalienable seashore under Louisiana law. That tides may cause other water bodies to rise and spread over the area is insufficient to characterize the land as seashore.

The court found that Bays Rambo and Jaque may have been subject to freshwater tidal influences as early as 1901, but not direct coastal ebb and flow. Such freshwater tidal influence, without ebb and flow from the gulf, is not enough to identify the bays as the sea or arms of the sea.

Upon finding that none of the Lafourche Realty property constituted the "bottoms of natural navigable water bodies . . . [or] the seashore," the district court concluded that the State did not run afoul of any restriction on alienation of public things. This conclusion was correct. At the time of the issuance of patents,

the property consisted of only inland non-navigable water bodies and swamp land subject to overflow—neither of which is inalienable public property under the Code.

C. Subsequent Navigability or Tides

The State also assigns for review the question whether "waters which are today saline, subject to ebb and flow of the tide, and de facto used in commercial navigation" are State-owned. The State brief suggests only that navigable water bodies are "now" considered public things under the 1978 revisions of the Civil Code and that the State owns lands influenced by the tides to "today's high water mark" under *Phillips Petroleum Co. v. Mississippi.* Questions posed for appellate review but inadequately briefed are considered abandoned.

We note, nevertheless, that the district court properly focused its inquiry regarding ownership and riparian rights upon the status of the waterways in 1812. As for the effect of the tide today, sympathetic tidal influence in inland waterways does not make the waterways "sea" or their banks "seashore." Under the court's findings, the land is still not sea bottom or seashore, and so cannot become public property as such.

II. Claim for a Right of Use or Access

We next consider the State's and the private Plaintiff's right-of-use claims. The Appellants assert a navigational servitude over the water bodies under federal or state law.

A. Federal Navigational Servitude

Appellants argue first that the navigable streams in this case are subject to a federal navigational servitude which gives the public unrestricted access. The navigational servitude arises by virtue of the Commerce Clause in some navigable waters. *Kaiser Aetna v. United States*, 444 U.S. 164, 178 (1979), made it clear, however, that the navigational servitude does not extend to all navigable waters. When a navigational servitude exists, it gives rise to the right of the public to use those waterways as "continuous highways for the purpose of navigation in interstate commerce."

In *Kaiser Aetna*, the Court was concerned with the public's right of access to Kuapa Pond, a large lagoon contiguous to a navigable bay but separated from that bay by a barrier beach. Kuapa Pond was two feet deep and had been considered private property under Hawaiian law. Kaiser Aetna developed a marina around the pond. In developing the marina, Kaiser Aetna dredged Kuapa Pond to a depth of six feet, dredged an eight-foot-deep channel through the barrier beach into the nearby bay, and increased the clearance of an overhead bridge to allow boats to pass from the marina to the bay. Kaiser Aetna then allowed access to the pond only to those who paid a fee.

The Army Corps of Engineers, which had earlier consented to the improvement, declared the pond to be navigable water of the United States and demanded that Kaiser Aetna allow the public free access to the pond. The district court concluded that imposition of free public access to Kuapa Pond would be a taking of private property for which just compensation must be paid. *United States v. Kaiser Aetna*, 408 F.Supp. 42, 54 (D.Haw. 1976). The Court of Appeals reversed *United States v. Kaiser Aetna*, 584 F.2d 378 (9th Cir. 1978), holding that, as a navigable water of the United States, Kuapa Pond was subject to a public right of use. The Supreme Court reversed. 444 U.S. 164 (1979).

The majority reasoned that not all navigable waters are subject to a navigational servitude, and unless a navigational servitude is imposed on a waterway, the public has no right to use it. A navigational servitude recognizes "the important public interest in the flow of interstate waters that in their natural condition are in fact capable of supporting public navigation." The Court identified several factors that convinced it that no navigational servitude was imposed on Kuapa Pond: (1) Kuapa Pond in its natural state could not have been navigated and was not comparable to the major natural bodies of water to which the servitude had earlier been applied;

(2) the pond was private property under Hawaiian law; (3) the pond had been converted to a navigable body of water by the petitioners through the investment of private funds; and (4) the Corps had earlier consented to the conversion.

In a companion case, *Vaughn v. Vermilion Corp.*, 444 U.S. 206 (1979), the Court considered whether the public was entitled to access to a canal dredged on private property with private funds. The Supreme Court, relying on *Kaiser Aetna*, held that to the extent the artificial canal had not displaced natural waterways, the public had no right of access to it.

Applying *Kaiser Aetna* and *Vaughn* to the facts of today's case, we conclude that plaintiffs have no right of access to Tidewater Canal. That canal was dredged on private property with private funds. The district court specifically found that the construction of the canal did not interfere with or obstruct preexisting navigable waterways. Plaintiffs have not shown that this finding was clearly erroneous.

Unfortunately, the record in this case does not permit us to determine whether the other navigable bodies at issue in this case are subject to a navigational servitude. One of the factors enumerated by the court in *Kaiser Aetna* is clear: we are satisfied that under Louisiana law the water bodies, all of which were nonnavigable or nonexistent in 1812 or even as late as 1902, were private property. The other factors, however, are not so clear.

First, it is not plain to us whether the remaining navigable water bodies at issue are navigable in their "natural state." The district court found that some of the other water bodies became navigable from the increased water flow of Tidewater Canal. In 1948, the Tidewater Canal was dug from near Bayou Lafourche northeasterly. The trial court found that

when dug, its path intersected no identifiable continuous waterway, whether navigable or otherwise. Thereafter, the canal was further extended, drill slips and further canals were dug, and preexisting waterways were deepened and widened—all with the approval of the U.S. Army Corps of Engineers and all on private property. Together, these interconnecting waterways made it possible for large oil rigs and barges to be brought into the area from Bayou Lafourche to the west or from Caminada Bay (and ultimately the Gulf of Mexico) to the southeast.

The wide interconnections have increased the channelized water flow, which has promoted scouring of the waterways. Further, these interconnections have allowed salt water from the bays to the south and east to permeate all the waterways in the area. The salt water in turn has caused the freshwater vegetation, which had helped prevent erosion, to die and thus has led to further accelerated loss of land surface. Wave wash from passing vessels has contributed significantly to this erosion as well.

The court thus found that their banks and beds were gradually eroded and scoured from the effects of increased water flow, saltwater intrusion, and wave wash. The district court did not consider whether waterways that become navigable through such a process are considered interstate navigable waters in their "natural" condition. We are persuaded that waterways made navigable through erosion are "naturally" navigable even though the erosion is caused by increased water flow from a connecting dredged canal.

The district court found that the landowner dredged other canals and deepened and widened some preexisting water bodies. The court made no findings on the timing or extent of that dredging, except that Bayou Ferblanc was dredged in the 1950s to make a pirogue trail.

On remand, if the district court finds that the landowners' dredging activity on any of these waterways initially rendered that body navigable, then we would reach the same conclusion with respect to that water body as we do with Tidewater Canal. However, if such dredging activity did not initially render the water body navigable, the court should make additional findings and conclusions. As to each of the waterways at issue, the district court should make findings on the factors the Court considered important in *Kaiser Aetna* and determine whether a navigational servitude is imposed.

In sum, a navigational servitude is ordinarily imposed on a naturally navigable waterway. To negate the existence of a navigable servitude on a naturally navigable waterway, the landowner must demonstrate through the factors discussed in *Kaiser Aetna* that its interests outweigh those of the public.

B. No State Servitude

Appellants claim entitlement under Louisiana law to use the waterways on the Lafourche Realty property as "public things" either because they are navigable now or because they contain "running waters." Appellants argue that *Chaney v. State Mineral Board*, 444 So.2d 105 (La. 1983), identifies a public right of use of nontidal, non-navigable bodies of water. We think the district court correctly distinguished *Chaney*, a possessory action in which riparian landowners along a non-navigable stream were trying to establish the extent of their possession. Such arguments have failed to carry the day in Louisiana courts.

Finally, Appellants rely on the Civil Code articles pertaining to alluvion, dereliction, and abandoned riverbeds as providing a servitude. Article 499 grants to the riparian owner any accretion formed on a riverbank or dereliction formed by water receding from a bank; article 504 provides for ownership of an abandoned riverbed upon a change in the river's course. None of the circumstances contemplated by these articles occurred here, so these articles have no application.

III. Plaintiffs' Other Expert

Plaintiffs also assert error in the district court's failure to mention in its rulings the opinion of Professor James D. Gosselink. The trial court expressed in both opinions that it gave considerable weight to the testimony of Dr. Gagliano. We do not require a district court to mention each witness by name in reciting its findings.

IV. Bifurcation

The district court ordered that the title dispute and the claims to a navigational servitude be separately tried under Federal Rule 42(b). Appellants assert that bifurcation of the title issue from the navigational servitude issue prejudiced them. We find no prejudice in the bifurcation of the trial and no abuse of discretion in the order for separate trials.

V. Conclusion

The district court's careful, considered opinion on title rested on findings of fact amply supported by the record. The record ownership of Lafourche Realty Company was properly sustained. Appellants also failed to demonstrate any reversible error in the findings and conclusions that Lafourche Realty's title is unburdened by any state servitude. No federal navigational servitude exists on the Tidewater Canal. The judgment of the district court in all of these respects is affirmed. Consistent with our earlier discussion, we remand the case for further consideration (following an additional hearing, if the district court thinks it necessary) of whether a federal navigational servitude encumbers other waterways.

AFFIRMED IN PART; VACATED IN PART and REMANDED.

Questions

1. Are the *Sasser and Dardar* opinions consistent in their interpretation of the *Kaiser Aetna* rule?

2. Why did Lafourche Realty object to the use of the waterways by the commercial fishermen plaintiffs?

3. Was a test case involving Louisiana law almost inevitable after the state of Mississippi's success against *Phillips Petroleum*?

Chapter 4

PUBLIC ACCESS TO THE SHORELINE

Neptune City v. Borough of Avon-by-the-Sea, 294 A.2d 47 (N.J. 1972)

HALL, J.

The question presented by this case is whether an oceanfront municipality may charge nonresidents higher fees than residents for the use of its beach area. The challenge came from plaintiffs Borough of Neptune City, an adjacent inland municipality, and two of its residents. We granted plaintiffs' motion to certify their appeal to the Appellate Division before argument in that tribunal. The question posed is of ever-increasing importance in our metropolitan area. We believe that the answer to it should turn on the application of what has become known as the public trust doctrine.

Avon, in common with other New Jersey municipalities bordering on the Atlantic Ocean, is a seasonal resort-oriented community. The attraction to the influx of temporary residents and day visitors in the summer months is, of course, the ocean beach for bathing and associated recreational pleasures and benefits. According to the stipulation of facts, Avon's year-round population of 1,850, resident within its approximately seven-square-block area, is increased in the summertime to about 5,500 people (not counting day visitors), with the seasonal increase living in four hotels, forty rooming and boarding houses, and innumerable rented and owned private dwellings.

The municipality borders on the ocean for its full north-south length. Ocean Avenue, a county highway, is the easternmost street. Municipal east-west streets end at Ocean Avenue. Between it and the ordinary high-water line or mark of the ocean waters are located an elevated boardwalk and a considerable stretch of sand, dry except in time of storms and exceptionally high tides. This stretch, as well as the boardwalk, is owned and maintained by the municipality and has been for many years. Although the derivation of the borough's title is not contained in the record, there is no dispute that the sand area has been dedicated for public beach recreational purposes—in effect, a public park—and is used for access by bathers to the water, as well as for sunning, lounging, and other usual beach activities. The tide-flowed land lying between the mean high- and low-water marks, as well as the ocean-covered land seaward thereof to the state's boundary, is owned by the State in fee simple, *Bailey v. Driscoll*, 19 N.J. 363, 367–68, 117 A.2d 265 (1955). There has been no alienation in any respect of that land bordering Avon; even if this state-owned land had been conveyed to Avon, it would be required to maintain that land as a public park for public use, resort, and recreation.

Years ago Avon's beach, like the rest of the New Jersey shore, was free to all comers. As the trial court pointed out, "with the advent of automobile traffic and the ever-increasing number of vacationers, the beaches and bathing facilities became overcrowded and the beachfront municipalities began to take steps to limit the congestion by regulating the use of the beach facilities and by charging fees." It also seems obvious that local financial considerations entered into the picture. Maintenance of beachfronts is expensive and adds substantially to the municipal tax levy if paid for out of property taxes. Not only are there the costs of lifeguards, policing, cleaning, and the like, but also involved are capital expenses to prevent or repair erosion and storm damage through the construction of jetties, groins, bulkheads, and similar devices. (Construction of the latter is generally aided in considerable part, as it has been in Avon, by state and other governmental funds.) In addition, the seasonal population increase requires the expansion of municipal services and personnel in the fields of public safety, health and order. On the other hand, the values of real estate in the community, both commercial and residential, are undoubtedly greater than those of similar properties in inland municipalities by reason of the proximity of the ocean and the accessibility of the beach. And commercial enterprises located in the town are more valuable because of the patronage of large numbers of summer visitors. (Avon does not have, in contrast with many other shore communities, extensive boardwalk stores and amusements.)

Legislative authority to municipalities to charge beach user fees, for revenue purposes, was granted by two identical statutes—the first applicable only to boroughs, and the second applicable to all municipalities.

. . .

Until 1970 Avon's ordinance, adopted pursuant to the quoted statute, made no distinction in charges as between residents and nonresidents. The scheme then and since is that of registration and issuance of season, monthly, or daily identification badges for access to and use of the beach area east of the boardwalk. (The boardwalk is open and free to all.) The amounts of money involved are substantial. In 1969, 32,741 badges of all categories were issued, and the revenue from beachfront operations totalled $149,758.15, which went into the borough's general revenues.

The distinction between residents and nonresidents was made by an amendment to the ordinance in 1970, the enactment which is attacked in this case. It was accomplished by making the rate for a monthly badge the same as that charged for a full season's badge ($10) by restricting the sale of season badges to residents and taxpayers of Avon and the members of their immediate families, and also apparently by substantially increasing the rates for daily badges (from $1 and $1.25 to $1.50 and $2.25). A "resident" is defined as a person living within the territorial boundaries of the borough for not less than sixty consecutive days in the particular calendar year. The result is considerably higher charges for nonresidents under the definition than for permanent residents, taxpayers, and those staying sixty days or more. Residents of Neptune City, for example, using the beach daily, would pay twice as much for the season (two monthly badges) as residents of Avon.

Plaintiffs attacked the ordinance on several grounds, including the claim of a common law right of access to the ocean in all citizens of the state. This in essence amounts to reliance upon the public trust doctrine, although not denominated by plaintiffs as such. Avon, although inferentially recognizing some such right, defended its amendatory ordinance on the thesis, accepted by the trial court, that its property taxpayers should nevertheless not be called upon to bear the expense, above nondiscriminating beach user fees received, of the cost of operating and maintaining the beachfront, claimed to result from use by nonresidents, and that consequently the discrimination in fees was not irrational or invidious. All recognized that an oceanfront municipality may not absolutely exclude nonresidents from the use of its dedicated beach, including, of course, land seaward of the mean high-water mark; a trial court decision, *Brindley v. Lavallette*, 33 N.J. Super. 344, 348–49, 110 A.2d 157 (Law Div. 1954), had so held, although not by reliance upon the public trust doctrine. We approve that holding.

. . .

We prefer, however, not to treat the case on this basis, but rather, as we indicated at the outset, to approach it from the more fundamental viewpoint of the modern meaning and application of the public trust doctrine.

That broad doctrine derives from the ancient principle of English law that land covered by tidal waters belonged to the sovereign, but for the common use of all the people. Such lands passed to the respective states as a result of the American Revolution.

. . .

There is not the slightest doubt that New Jersey has always recognized the trust doctrine. The basic case is *Arnold v. Mundy*, 6 N.J.L. 1 (Sup. Ct. 1821), where Chief Justice Kirkpatrick spoke as follows:

Everything susceptible of property is considered as belonging to the nation that possesses the country, and as forming the entire mass of its wealth. But the nation does not possess all those things in the same manner. But very far the greater part of them are divided among the individuals of the nation, and become *private property*. Those things not divided among the individuals still belong to the nation, and are called *public property*. Of these, again, some are reserved for the necessities of the state, and are used for the public benefits, and those are called "*the do-*

main of the crown or of the republic"; others remain common to all the citizens, who take of them and use them, each according to his necessities, and according to the laws which regulate their use, and are called *common property*. Of this latter kind, according to the writers upon the law of nature and of nations, and upon the civil law, are the air, the running water, the sea, the fish, and the wild beasts. But inasmuch as the things which constitute this *common property* are things in which a sort of transient usufructary possession, only, can be had; and inasmuch as the title to them and to the soil by which they are supported, and to which they are appurtenant, cannot well, according to the common law notion of title, be vested in all the people; therefore, the wisdom of that law has placed it in the hands of the sovereign power, to be held, protected, and regulated for the common use and benefit. But still, though this title, strictly speaking, is in the sovereign, yet the use is common to all the people.

. . .

And I am further of opinion, that, upon the Revolution, all these royal rights became vested in *the people of New Jersey* as the sovereign of the country, and are now in their hands; and that they, having, themselves, both the legal title and the usufruct, may make such disposition of them, and such regulation concerning them, as they may think fit; that this power of disposition and regulation must be exercised by them in their sovereign capacity; that the legislature is their rightful representative in this respect, and, therefore, that the legislature, in the exercise of this power, may lawfully erect ports, harbors, basins, docks, and wharves on the coasts of the sea and in the arms thereof, and in the navigable rivers; that they may bank off those waters and reclaim the land upon the shores; that they may build dams, locks, and bridges for the improvement of the navigation and the ease of passage; that they may clear and improve fishing places, to increase the product of the fishery; that they may create, enlarge, and improve oyster beds, by planting oysters therein in order to procure a more ample supply; that they may do these things, themselves, at the public expense, or they may authorize others to do it by their own labor, and at their own expense, giving them reasonable tolls, rents, profits, or exclusive and temporary enjoyments; but still this power, which may be thus exercised by the sovereignty of the state, is nothing more than what is called the jus regium, the right of regulating, improving, and securing for the common benefit of every individual citizen. The sovereign power itself, therefore, cannot, consistently with the principles of the law of nature and the constitution of a well-ordered society, make a direct and absolute grant of the waters of the state, divesting all the citizens of their common right. It would be a grievance which never could be long borne by a free people.

Similar expressions are found throughout our decisions down through the years.

. . .

It is safe to say, however, that the scope and limitations of the doctrine in this state have never been defined with any great degree of precision. That it represents a deeply inherent right of the citizenry cannot be disputed. Two aspects should be particularly mentioned, one only tangentially involved in this case and the latter directly pertinent. The former relates to the lawful extent of the power of the legislature to alienate trust lands to private parties; the latter to the inclusion within the doctrine of public accessibility to and use of such lands for recreation and health, including bathing, boating, and associated activities. Both are of prime importance in this day and age. Remaining tidal water resources still in the ownership of the State are becoming very scarce, demands upon them by reason of increased population, industrial development, and their popularity for recreational uses and open space are much heavier, and their importance to the public welfare has become much more apparent. All of these factors mandate more precise attention to the doctrine.

Here we are not directly concerned with the extent of legislative power to alienate tidal lands because the lands seaward of the mean high-water line remain in state ownership, the municipality owns the bordering land, which is dedicated to park and beach purposes, and no problem of physical access by the public to the

ocean exists. The matter of legislative alienation in this state should, nonetheless, be briefly adverted to since it has a tangential bearing. As the earlier quotations indicate, it has always been assumed that the State may convey or grant rights in some tidal lands to private persons where the use to be made thereof is consistent with and in furtherance of the purposes of the doctrine. . . . We mention this alienation aspect to indicate that, at least where the upland sand area is owned by a municipality—a political subdivision and creature of the state—and dedicated to public beach purposes, a modern court must take the view that the public trust doctrine dictates that the beach and the ocean waters must be open to all on equal terms and without preference and that any contrary state or municipal action is impermissible.

We have no difficulty in finding that, in this latter half of the twentieth century, the public rights in tidal lands are not limited to the ancient prerogatives of navigation and fishing, but extend as well to recreational uses, including bathing, swimming, and other shore activities. The public trust doctrine, like all common law principles, should not be considered fixed or static, but should be molded and extended to meet changing conditions and needs of the public it was created to benefit. The legislature appears to have had such an extension in mind in enacting N.J.S.A. 12:3–33, 34, previously mentioned. Those sections, generally speaking, authorize grants to governmental bodies of tide-flowed lands which front upon a public park extending to such lands, but only upon condition that any land so granted shall be maintained as a public park for public use, resort, and recreation.

Other states have readily extended the doctrine, beyond the original purposes of navigation and fishing, to cover other public uses, and especially recreational uses. In Massachusetts, it was held many years ago that "it would be too strict a doctrine to hold that the trust for the public, under which the state holds and controls navigable tide waters and the land under them, beyond the line of private ownership, is for navigation alone. It is wider in its scope, and it includes all necessary and proper uses, in the interest of the public." *Home for Aged Women v. Commonwealth*, 202 Mass. 422, 89 N.E. 124, 129 (1909). Wisconsin, where the doctrine covers all navigable waters, has long held that it extends to all public uses of water including pleasure boating, sailing, fishing, swimming, hunting, skating, and enjoyment of scenic beauty. Courts in several other states have recently recognized the vital public interest in the use of the seashore for recreational purposes and have, under various theories consistent with their own law, asserted the public rights in such land to be superior to private or municipal interests. Modern text writers and commentators assert that the trend of the law is, or should be, in the same direction.

We are convinced it has to follow that, while municipalities may validly charge reasonable fees for the use of their beaches, they may not discriminate in any respect between their residents and nonresidents. The Avon amendatory ordinance of 1970 clearly does so by restricting the sale of season badges to residents, as defined in the ordinance, resulting in a lower fee to them. In addition, the fee for daily badges, which would be utilized mostly by nonresidents, may have been as well discriminatorily designated with respect to the amount of the charge. Since we cannot tell what fee schedule the municipality would have adopted when it passed this ordinance in 1970 if it had to do so on the basis of equal treatment for all, we see no other course but to set aside the entire amendatory enactment.

. . .

The judgment of the Law Division is reversed and the cause is remanded to that tribunal for the entry of a judgment consistent with this opinion.

Questions

1. In this instance, and many others, the community in question shows a net profit for the beach operation. But what about the example where local property-tax dollars are used to subsidize a less popular beach? Could a fee differential be defended there?

2. Is the New Jersey view of the public trust doctrine the general rule for most coastal states? Read the next case before you answer.

Matthews v. Bay Head Association, 471 A.2d 355 (N.J. 1984)

The major issue in this case is whether, ancillary to the public's right to enjoy the tidal lands, the public has a right to gain access through and to use the dry sand area not owned by a municipality but by a quasi-public body.

. . .

Facts

The Borough of Bay Head (Bay Head) borders the Atlantic Ocean. Adjacent to it on the north is the Borough of Point Pleasant Beach, on the south the Borough of Mantoloking, and on the west Barnegat Bay. Bay head consists of a fairly narrow strip of land, 6,667 feet long (about 1¼ miles). A beach runs along its entire length adjacent to the Atlantic Ocean. There are seventy-six separate parcels of land that border the beach. All except six are owned by private individuals. Title to those six is vested in the Association.

The Association was founded in 1910 and incorporated as a nonprofit corporation in 1932. Its certificate of incorporation states that its purposes are

the improving and beautifying of the Borough of Bay Head, New Jersey, cleaning, policing and otherwise making attractive and safe the bathing beaches in said Borough, and the doing of any act which may be found necessary or desirable for the greater convenience, comfort, and enjoyment of the residents.

Its constitution delineates the Association's object to promote the best interests of the Borough and "in so doing, to own property, operate bathing beaches, hire lifeguards, beach cleaners, and policemen."

Nine streets in the Borough, which are perpendicular to the beach, end at the dry sand. The Association owns the land commencing at the end of seven of these streets for the width of each street and extending through the upper dry sand to the mean high-water line, the beginning of the wet-sand area or foreshore. In addition, the Association owns the fee in six shorefront properties, three of which are contiguous and have a frontage aggregating 310 feet. Many owners of beachfront property executed and delivered to the Association leases of the upper dry-sand area. These leases are revocable by either party to the lease on thirty days' notice. Some owners have not executed such leases and have not permitted the Association to use their beaches. Some also have acquired riparian grants from the State extending approximately one thousand feet east of the high-water line.

The Association controls and supervises its beach property between the third week in June and Labor Day. It engages about forty employees who serve as lifeguards, beach police, and beach cleaners. Lifeguards, stationed at five operating beaches, indicate by use of flags whether the ocean condition is dangerous (red), requires caution (yellow), or is satisfactory (green). In addition to observing and, if need be, assisting those in the water, when called upon lifeguards render first aid. Beach cleaners are engaged to rake and keep the beach clean of debris. Beach police are stationed at the entrances to the beaches where the public streets lead into the beach to ensure that only Association members or their guests enter. Some beach police patrol the beaches to enforce its membership rules.

Membership is generally limited to residents of Bay Head. Class A members are property owners. Class B are nonowners. Large families (six or more) pay $90 per year and small families pay $60 per year. Upon application residents are routinely accepted. Membership is evidenced by badges that signify permission to use the beaches. Members, which include local hotels, motels, and inns, can also acquire badges for guests. The charge for each guest badge is $12. Members of the Bay Head Fire Company, Bay Head Borough employees, and teachers in the municipality's school system have been issued beach badges irrespective of residency.

Except for fishermen, who are permitted to walk through the upper dry sand area to the foreshore, only the membership may use the beach between 10:00 A.M. and 5:30 P.M. during the summer season. The public is permitted to use the Association's beach from 5:30 P.M. to 10:00 A.M. during the summer and, with no hourly restrictions, between Labor Day and mid-June.

No attempt has ever been made to stop anyone from occupying the terrain east of the high-water mark. During certain parts of the day, when the tide is low, the foreshore could consist of about fifty feet of sand not being flowed by the water. The public could gain access to the foreshore by coming from the Borough of Point Pleasant Beach on the north or from the Borough of Mantoloking on the south.

Association membership totals between 4,800 and 5,000. The Association president testified during depositions that its restrictive policy, in existence since 1932, was due to limited parking facilities and to the overcrowding of the beaches. The Association's avowed purpose was to provide the beach for the residents of Bay Head.

There is also a public boardwalk, about one-third of a mile long, parallel to the ocean on the westerly side of the dry-sand area. The boardwalk is owned and maintained by the municipality.

· · ·

The Public Trust

In *Borough of Neptune City v. Borough of Avon-by-the-Sea*, 61 N.J. 296, 303, 294 A.2d 47 (1972), Justice Hall alluded to the ancient principle "that land covered by tidal waters belonged to the sovereign, but for the common use of all the people." The genesis of this principle is found in Roman jurisprudence, which held that "[b]y the law of nature the air, running water, the sea, and consequently the shores of the sea," were "common to mankind." Justinian, *Institutes* 2.1.1 (T. Sandars trans. 1st Am. ed. 1876). No one was forbidden access to the sea, and everyone could use the seashore "to dry his nets there, and haul them from the sea." The seashore was not private property, but "subject to the same law as the sea itself, and the sand or ground beneath it." Id. This underlying concept was applied in New Jersey in *Arnold v. Mundy*, 6 N.J.L. 1 (Sup. Ct. 1821).

. . .

In *Avon*, Justice Hall reaffirmed the public's right to use the waterfront as announced in *Arnold v. Mundy*. He observed that the public has a right to use the land below the mean average high-water mark.

. . .

In *Van Ness v. Borough of Deal*, 78 N.J. 174, 393 A.2d 571 (1978), we stated that the public's right to use municipally owned beaches was not dependent upon the municipality's dedication of its beaches to use by the general public. The Borough of Deal had dedicated a portion of such beach for use by its residents only. We found such limited dedication "immaterial" given the public trust doctrine's requirement that the public be afforded the right to enjoy all dry-sand beaches owned by a municipality. 78 N.J. at 179–80, 393 A.2d 571.

Public Rights in Privately Owned Dry Sand Beaches

In *Avon* and *Deal* our finding of public rights in dry sand areas was specifically and appropriately limited to those beaches owned by a municipality. We now address the extent of the public's interest in privately owned dry-sand beaches. This interest may take one of two forms. First, the public may have a right to cross privately owned dry-sand beaches in order to gain access to the foreshore. Second, this interest may be of the sort enjoyed by the public in municipal beaches under *Avon* and *Deal*, namely, the right to sunbathe and generally enjoy recreational activities.

Beaches are a unique resource and are irreplaceable. The public demand for beaches has increased with the growth of population and improvement of transportation facilities. Furthermore the projected demand for saltwater swimming will not be met "unless the existing swimming capacities of the four coastal counties are expanded." Department of Environmental Protection, Statewide Comprehensive Outdoor Recreation Plan 200 (1977). The DEP estimates that, compared to 1976, the State's saltwater swimming areas "must accommodate 764,812 more persons by 1985 and 1,021,112 persons by 1995."

Exercise of the public's right to swim and bathe below the mean high-water mark may depend upon a right to pass across the upland beach. Without some means of access the public right to use the foreshore would be meaningless. To say that the public trust doctrine entitles the public to swim in the ocean and to use the foreshore in connection therewith without assuring the public of a feasible access route would seriously impinge on, if not effectively eliminate, the rights of the public trust doctrine. This does not mean the public has an unrestricted right to cross at will over any and all property bordering on the common property. The public interest is satisfied so long as there is reasonable access to the sea.

The bather's right in the upland sands is not limited to passage. Reasonable enjoyment of the foreshore and the sea cannot be realized unless some enjoyment of the dry-sand area is also allowed. The complete pleasure of swimming must be accompanied by intermittent periods of rest and relaxation beyond the water's edge. The unavailability of the physical sites for such rest and relaxation would seriously curtail and in many situations eliminate the right to the recreational use of the ocean.

Precisely what privately owned upland sand area will be available and required to satisfy the public's right under the public trust doctrine will depend on the circumstances. Location of the dry sand area in relation to the foreshore, extent and availability of publicly owned upland sand area, nature and extent of the public demand, and usage of the upland sand land by the owner are all factors to be weighed and considered in fixing the contours of the usage of the upper sand.

Today, recognizing the increasing demand for our State's beaches and the dynamic nature of the public trust doctrine, we find that the public must be given both access to and use of privately owned dry sand areas as reasonably necessary. While the public's right in private beaches are not coextensive with the rights enjoyed in municipal beaches, private landowners may not in all instances prevent the public trust doctrine. The public must be afforded reasonable access to the foreshore as well as a suitable area for recreation on the dry sand.

Questions

1. What is a "quasi-public" body, and is the court's holding limited to organizations of that type?

2. What limits are placed on the public's right to use upland areas as part of their "reasonable enjoyment of the foreshore and the sea"?

State ex rel. Thornton v. Hay, 462 P.2d 671 (Oreg. 1969).

GOODWIN, JUSTICE

William and Georgianna Hay, the owners of a tourist facility at Cannon Beach, appeal from a decree which enjoins them from constructing fences or other improvements in the dry-sand area between the sixteen-foot elevation contour line and the ordinary high-tide line of the Pacific Ocean.

The issue is whether the state has the power to prevent the defendant landowners from enclosing the dry-sand area contained within the legal description of their oceanfront property.

The defendant landowners concede that the State Highway Commission has standing to represent the rights of the public in this litigation, and that all tideland lying seaward of the ordinary, or mean high-tide, line is a state recreation area.

Below, or seaward of, the mean high-tide line, is the state-owned foreshore, or wet-sand area, in which the landowners in this case concede the public's paramount right, and concerning which there is no justiciable controversy.

The only issue in this case, as noted, is the power of the state to limit the record owner's use and enjoyment of the dry-sand area, by whatever boundaries the area may be described.

The dry-sand area in Oregon has been enjoyed by the general public as a recreational adjunct of the wet-sand or foreshore area since the beginning of the state's political history. The first European settlers on these shores found the aboriginal inhabitants using the foreshore for clam digging and the dry-sand area for their cooking fires. The newcomers continued these customs after statehood. Thus, from the time of the earliest settlement to the present day, the general public has assumed that the dry-sand area was a part of the public beach, and the public has used the dry-sand area for picnics, gathering wood, building warming fires, and generally as a headquarters from which to supervise children or to range out over the foreshore as the tides advance and recede. In the Cannon Beach vicinity, state and local officers have policed the dry sand, and municipal sanitary crews have attempted to keep the area reasonably free from man-made litter.

Perhaps one explanation for the evolution of

the custom of the public to use the dry-sand area for recreational purposes is that the area could not be used conveniently by its owners for any other purpose. The dry-sand area is unstable in its seaward boundaries, unsafe during winter storms, and for the most part unfit for the construction of permanent structures. While the vegetation line remains relatively fixed, the western edge of the dry-sand area is subject to dramatic moves eastward or westward in response to erosion and accretion. For example, evidence in the trial below indicated that between April 1966 and August 1967 the seaward edge of the dry-sand area involved in this litigation moved westward 180 feet. At other points along the shore, the evidence showed, the seaward edge of the dry-sand area could move an equal distance to the east in a similar period of time.

Until very recently, no question concerning the right of the public to enjoy the dry-sand area appears to have been brought before the courts of this state. The public's assumption that the dry sand as well as the foreshore was "public property" had been reinforced by early judicial decisions.

. . .

In 1935, the United States Supreme Court held that a federal patent conveyed title to land farther seaward, to the mean high-tide line. *Borax Consolidated, Ltd. v. Los Angeles*, 296 U.S. 10 (1935). While this decision may have expanded seaward the record ownership of upland landowners, it was apparently little noticed by Oregonians. In any event, the *Borax* decision had no discernible effect on the actual practices of Oregon beachgoers and upland property owners.

Recently, however, the scarcity of oceanfront building sites has attracted substantial private investments in resort facilities. Resort owners like these defendants now desire to reserve for their paying guests the recreational advantages that accrue to the dry-sand portions of their deeded property. Consequently, in 1967, public debate and political activity resulted in legisla-

tive attempts to resolve conflicts between public and private interests in the dry-sand area. ORS 390.610:

1. The Legislative Assembly hereby declares it is the public policy of the State of Oregon to forever preserve and maintain the sovereignty of the state heretofore existing over the seashore and ocean beaches of the state from the Columbia River on the north to the Oregon-California line on the south so that the public may have the free and uninterrupted use thereof.

2. The Legislative Assembly recognizes that over the years the public has made frequent and uninterrupted use of lands abutting, adjacent and contiguous to the public highways and state recreation areas and recognizes, further, that where such use has been sufficient to create easements in the public through dedication, prescription, grant, or otherwise, that it is in the public interest to protect and preserve such public easements as a permanent part of Oregon's recreational resources.

3. Accordingly, the Legislative Assembly hereby declares that all public rights and easements in those lands described in subsection (2) of this section are confirmed and declared vested exclusively in the State of Oregon and shall be held and administered in the same manner as those lands described in ORS 390.720.

. . .

The state concedes that such legislation cannot divest a person of his rights in land, and that the defendants' record title, which includes the dry-sand area, extends seaward to the ordinary or mean high-tide line.

The landowners likewise concede that since 1899 the public's rights in the foreshore have been confirmed by law as well as by custom and usage. Oregon Laws 1899, p. 3, provided "that the shore of the Pacific ocean, between ordinary high and extreme low tides, and from the Columbia River on the north to the south boundary line of Clatsop County on the south, is hereby declared a public highway, and shall forever remain open as such to the public."

The disputed area is sui generis. While the foreshore is "owned" by the state, and the upland is "owned" by the patentee or record-title holder, neither can be said to "own" the full bundle of rights normally connoted by the term "estate in fee simple."

In addition to the sui generis nature of the land itself, a multitude of complex and sometimes overlapping precedents in the law confronted the trial court. Several early Oregon decisions generally support the trial court's decision, i.e., that the public can acquire easements in private land by long-continued use that is inconsistent with the owner's exclusive possession and enjoyment of his land. A citation of the cases could end the discussion at this point. But because the early cases do not agree on the legal theories by which the results are reached, and because this is an important case affecting valuable rights in land, it is appropriate to review some of the law applicable to this case.

One group of precedents relied upon in part by the state and by the trial court can be called the "implied-dedication" cases. The doctrine of implied dedication is well known to the law in this state and elsewhere. Dedication, however, whether express or implied, rests upon an intent to dedicate. In the case at bar, it is unlikely that the landowners thought they had anything to dedicate, until 1967, when the notoriety of legislative debates about the public's rights in the dry-sand area sent a number of oceanfront landowners to the offices of their legal advisers.

A second group of cases relied upon by the state, but rejected by the trial court, deals with the possibility of a landowner's losing the exclusive possession and enjoyment of his land through the development of prescriptive easements in the public.

In Oregon, as in most common-law jurisdictions, an easement can be created in favor of one person in the land of another by uninterrupted use and enjoyment of the land in a particular manner for the statutory period, so long as the use is open, adverse, under claim of right, but without authority of law or consent of the owner. In Oregon, the prescriptive period is ten years. The public use of the disputed land in the case at bar is admitted to be continuous for more than sixty years. There is no suggestion in the record that anyone's permission was sought or given; rather, the public used the land under a claim of right. Therefore, if the public can acquire an easement by prescription, the requirements for such an acquisition have been met in connection with the specific tract of land involved in this case.

The owners argue, however, that the general public, not being subject to actions in trespass and ejectment, cannot acquire rights by prescription, because the statute of limitations is irrelevant when an action does not lie.

While it may not be feasible for a landowner to sue the general public, it is nonetheless possible by means of signs and fences to prevent or minimize public invasions of private land for recreational purposes. In Oregon, moreover, the courts and the Legislative Assembly have both recognized that the public can acquire prescriptive easements in private land, at least for roads and highways.

Another statute codifies a policy favoring the acquisition by prescription for public recreational easements in beach lands. While such a statute cannot create public rights at the expense of a private landowner the statute can, and does, express legislative approval of the common-law doctrine of prescription where the facts justify its application. Consequently, we conclude that the law in Oregon, regardless of the generalizations that may apply elsewhere, does not preclude the creation of prescriptive easements in beach land for public recreational use.

Because many elements of prescription are present in this case, the state has relied upon the doctrine in support of the decree below. We believe, however, that there is a better legal basis for affirming the decree. The most cogent basis for the decision in this case is the English doctrine of custom. Strictly construed, prescription applies only to the specific tract of land before the court, and doubtful prescription cases could fill the courts for years with tract-by-tract litigation. An established custom, on the other hand, can be proven with reference to a larger region. Oceanfront lands from the northern to the southern border of the state ought to be treated uniformly.

The other reason which commends the doctrine of custom over that of prescription in this case is the unique nature of the lands in question. This case deals solely with the dry-sand area along the Pacific shore, and this land has been used by the public as public recreational land according to an unbroken custom running back in time as long as the land has been inhabited.

A custom is defined in 1 Bouv. Law Dict., Rawle's Third Revision, p. 742, as "such a usage as by common consent and uniform practice has become the law of the place, or of the subject matter to which it relates."

In 1 Blackstone, *Commentaries* Sec. 75–78, Sir William Blackstone set out the requisites of a particular custom.

Paraphrasing Blackstone, the first requirement of a custom, to be recognized as law, is that it must be ancient. It must have been used so long "that the memory of man runneth not to the contrary." Professor Cooley footnotes his edition of Blackstone with the comment that "long and general" usage is sufficient. In any event, the record in this case at bar satisfies the requirement of antiquity. So long as there has been an institutionalized system of land tenure in Oregon, the public has freely exercised the right to use the dry-sand area up and down the Oregon coast for the recreational purposes noted earlier in this opinion.

The second requirement is that the right be exercised without interruption. A customary right need not be exercised continuously, but it must be exercised without an interruption caused by anyone possessing a paramount right. In the case at bar, there was evidence that the public's use and enjoyment of the dry-sand area had never been interrupted by private landowners.

Blackstone's third requirement, that the cus-

tomary use be peaceable and free from dispute, is satisfied by the evidence which related to the second requirement.

The fourth requirement, that of reasonableness, is satisfied by the evidence that the public has always made use of the land in a manner appropriate to the land and to the usages of the community. There is evidence in the record that when inappropriate uses have been detected, municipal police officers have intervened to preserve order.

The fifth requirement, certainty, is satisfied by the visible boundaries of the dry-sand area and by the character of the land, which limits the use thereof to recreational uses connected with the foreshore.

The sixth requirement is that a custom must be obligatory; that is, in the case at bar, not left to the option of each landowner, whether or not he will recognize the public's right to go upon the dry-sand area for recreational purposes. The record shows that the dry-sand area in question has been used, as of right, uniformly with similarly situated lands elsewhere, and that the public's use has never been questioned by an upland owner so long as the public remained on the dry sand and refrained from trespassing upon the lands above the vegetation line.

Finally, a custom must not be repugnant, or inconsistent, with other customs or with other law. The custom under consideration violates no law, and is not repugnant.

Two arguments have been arrayed against the doctrine of custom as a basis for decision in Oregon. The first argument is that custom is unprecedented in this state, and has only scant adherence elsewhere in the United States. The second argument is that because of the relative brevity of our political history it is inappropriate to rely upon an English doctrine that requires greater antiquity than a newly settled land can muster. Neither of these arguments is persuasive.

The custom of the people of Oregon to use the dry-sand area of the beaches for public recreational purposes meets every one of Blackstone's requisites. While it is not necessary to rely upon precedent from other states, we are not the first state to recognize custom as a source of law.

On the score of the brevity of our political history, it is true that the Anglo-American legal system on this continent is relatively new. Its newness has made it possible for government to provide for many of our institutions by written law rather than by customary law. This truism does not, however, militate against the validity of a custom when the custom does in fact exist. If antiquity were the sole test of validity of a custom, Oregonians could satisfy that requirement by recalling that the European settlers were not the first people to use the dry-sand area as public land.

Finally, in support of custom, the record shows that the custom of the inhabitants of Oregon and of visitors in the state to use the dry sand as a public recreation area is so notorious that notice of the custom on the part of persons buying land along the shore must be presumed. In the case at bar, the landowners conceded their actual knowledge of the public's long-standing use of the dry-sand area, and argued that the elements of consent present in the relationship between the landowners and the public precluded the application of the law of prescription. As noted, we are not resting this decision on prescription, and we leave open the effect upon prescription of the type of consent that they have been present in this case. Such elements of consent are, however, wholly consistent with the recognition of public rights derived from custom.

Because so much of our law is the product of legislation, we sometimes lose sight of the importance of custom as a source of law in our society. It seems particularly appropriate in the case at bar to look to an ancient and accepted custom in this state as the source of a rule of law. The rule in this case, based upon custom, is salutary in confirming a public right, and at the same time it takes from no man anything

which he has had a legitimate reason to regard as exclusively his.

For the foregoing reasons, the decree of the trial court is affirmed.

Questions

1. The court introduces, and then dismisses, the use of concepts of implied dedication and easement by prescription in this case. How can the concepts be distinguished, and what are their strengths and weaknesses?

2. The court acknowledged that its use of the doctrine of custom was controversial. Do you agree with its application, or do you sense that the court was "reaching" for an argument to support a desired conclusion?

Gion v. City of Santa Cruz, 465 P.2d 50 (Cal. 1970)

PER CURIAM

We consider these two cases together because both raise the question of determining when an implied dedication of land has been made.

Gion v. City of Santa Cruz concerns three parcels of land on the southern, or seaward, side of West Cliff Drive, between Woodrow and Columbia streets in Santa Cruz. The three lots contain a shoreline of approximately 70 feet to approximately 160 feet. Two of the three lots are contiguous; the third is separated from the first two by approximately fifty feet. Each lot has some area adjoining and level with the road (thirty to forty feet above the sea level) on which vehicles have parked for the last sixty years. This parking area extends as far as sixty feet from the road on one parcel, but on all three parcels there is a sharp cliff-like drop beyond the level area onto a shelf area and then another drop into the sea. The land is subject to continuous, severe erosion. Two roads previously built by the city have been slowly eroded by the sea. To prevent future erosion the city has filled in small amounts of the land

and placed supporting riprap in weak areas. The city also put an emergency alarm system on the land and in the early 1960s paved the parking area. No other permanent structures have ever been built on this land.

Since 1880, the City of Santa Cruz has had fee title to a road at some location near the present road. Also since 1880, there has been an area south, or seaward, of the road area that has been in private hands. As the area south of the road eroded, the city moved its road a short distance to the north. In 1932, after moving the road to its present location, the city gave a quit-claim deed for the land previously covered by the road, but no longer used as a road, to G. H. Normand, the owner and developer of the surrounding property. The area presently under dispute, therefore, includes an old roadbed. Most of the area, however, has never been used for anything but the pleasure of the public.

Since at least 1900, various members of the public have parked vehicles on the level area, and proceeded toward the sea to fish, swim, picnic, and view the ocean. Such activities have proceeded without any significant objection by the fee owners of the property. M. P. Bettencourt, who acquired most of the property in dispute in 1941 and sold it to Gion in 1958 and 1961, testified that during his twenty years of ownership he had occasionally posted signs that the property was privately owned. He conceded, however, that the signs quickly blew away or were torn down, that he never told anyone to leave the property, and that he always granted permission on the few occasions when visitors requested permission to go on it. In 1957, he asked a neighbor to refrain from dumping refuse on the land. The persons who owned the land prior to Bettencourt paid even less attention to it than did Bettencourt. Every witness who testified about the use of the land before 1941 stated that the public went upon the land freely without any thoughts as to whether it was public or privately owned. In fact, counsel for Gion offered to stipulate at trial that since 1900 the public has fished on the property and that no one ever asked or told anyone to leave it.

The City of Santa Cruz has taken a growing interest in this property over the years and has acted to facilitate the public's use of the land. In the early 1900s, for instance, the Santa Cruz school system sent all the grammar and high school students to this area to plant ice plant, to beautify the area and keep it from eroding. In the 1920s, the city posted signs to warn fishermen of the dangers from eroding cliffs. In the 1940s, the city filled in holes and built an embankment on the top level area to prevent cars from driving into the sea. At that time, the city also installed an emergency alarm system that connected a switch near the cliff to an alarm in the firehouse and police station. The city replaced a washed-out guardrail and oiled the parking area in the 1950s, and in 1960–61, the city spent $500,000 to prevent erosion in the general area. On the specific property now in dispute, the city filled in collapsing tunnels and placed boulders in weak areas to counter the eroding action of the waves. In 1963, the city paved all of the level area on the property, and in recent years the sanitation department has maintained trash receptacles thereon and cleaned it after weekends of heavy use.

. . .

In *Dietz v. King*, plaintiffs, as representatives of the public, asked the court to enjoin defendants from interfering with the public's use of Navarro Beach in Mendocino County and an unimproved dirt road, called the Navarro Beach Road, leading to that beach. The beach is a small sandy peninsula jutting into the Pacific Ocean. It is surrounded by cliffs at the south and east, and is bounded by the Navarro River and the Navarro Beach Road (the only convenient access to the beach by land) on the north. The Navarro Beach Road branches from a county road that parallels State Highway 1. The road runs in a southwesterly direction along the Navarro River for 1,500 feet and then turns for the final 1,500 feet due south to the beach. The road first crosses for a short distance land owned by the Carlyles, who maintain a residence adjacent to the road. It then crosses land owned by Mae Crider and Jack W. Sparkman, proprietors of an ancient structure called the Navarro-by-the-Sea Hotel, and, for the final 2,200 feet, land now owned by defendants.

The public has used the beach and the road for at least one hundred years. Five cottages were built on the high ground of the ocean beach about one hundred years ago. A small cemetery plot containing the remains of shipwrecked sailors and natives of the area existed there. Elderly witnesses testified that persons traveled over the road during the closing years of the last century. They came in substantial numbers to camp, picnic, collect and cut driftwood for fuel, and fish for abalone, crabs, and finned fish. Others came to the beach to decorate the graves, which had wooden crosses upon them. Indians, in groups of fifty to seventy-five, came from as far away as Ukiah during the summer months. They camped on the beach for weeks at a time, drying kelp and catching and drying abalone and other fish. In decreasing numbers they continued to use the road and the beach until about 1950.

In more recent years the public use of Navarro Beach has expanded. The trial court found on substantial evidence that "for many years members of the public have used and enjoyed the said beach for various kinds of recreational activities, including picnicking, hiking, swimming, fishing, skin diving, camping, driftwood collecting, firewood collecting, and related activities." At times as many as one hundred persons have been on the beach. They have come in automobiles, trucks, campers, and trailers. The beach has been used for commercial fishing, and during good weather a school for retarded children has brought its students to the beach once every week or two.

None of the previous owners of the King property ever objected to public use of Navarro Beach Road. The land was originally owned by a succession of lumber and railroad companies, which did not interfere with the public's free use of the road and beach. The Southern Pacific Land Company sold the land in 1942 to Mr. and Mrs. Oscar J. Haub who in turn sold it to the Kings in 1959. Mrs. Haub testified by deposition that she and her husband encouraged the public to use the beach. "We intended," she said, "that the public would go through and enjoy that beach without any charge and just for the fun of being out there." She also said that it "was a free beach for anyone to go down there . . . you could go in and out as you pleased," and "[w]e intended that the beach be free for anybody to go down there and have a good time." Only during World War II, when the U.S. Coast Guard took over the beach as a base from which to patrol the coast, was the public barred from the beach.

In 1960, a year after the Kings acquired the land, they placed a large timber across the road at the entrance to their land. Within two hours it was removed by persons wishing to use the beach. Mr. King occasionally put up "No Trespassing" signs, but they were always removed by the time he returned to the land, and the public continued to use the beach until August 1966. During that month, Mr. King had another large log placed across the road at the entrance to his property. That barrier was, however, also quickly removed. He then sent in a Caterpillar crew to permanently block the road. That operation was stopped by the issuance of a temporary restraining order.

The various owners of the Navarro-by-the-Sea property have at times placed an unlocked chain across the Navarro Beach Road on that property. One witness said she saw a chain between 1911 and 1920. Another witness said the chain was put up to discourage cows from straying and eating poisonous weeds. The chain was occasionally hooked to an upright spike, but was never locked in place and could be easily removed. Its purpose apparently was to restrict cows, not people, from the beach. In fact, the chain was almost always unhooked and lying on the ground.

From about 1949 on, a proprietor of the Navarro-by-the-Sea Hotel maintained a sign at the posts saying, "Private Road—Admission 50 Cents—please pay at hotel." With moderate success, the proprietor collected tolls for a relatively short period of time. Some years later, another proprietor resumed the practice. Most persons ignored the sign, however, and went to the beach without paying. The hotel operators never applied any sanctions to those who declined to pay. In a recorded instrument the present owners of the Navarro-by-the-Sea property acknowledged that "for over one hundred years there has existed a public easement and right of way" in the road as it crosses their property. The Carlyles and the previous owners of the first stretch of the Navarro Beach Road never objected to its use over their property and do not now object.

. . .

In our most recent discussion of common-law dedication, *Union Transp. Co. v. Sacramento County*, 42 Cal.2d 235, 240–41, 267 P.2d 10, (1954) we noted that a common-law dedication of property to the public can be proved either by showing acquiescence of the owner in use of the land under circumstances that negate the idea that the use is under license or by establishing open and continuous use by the public for the prescriptive period. When dedication by acquiescence for a period of less than five years is claimed, the owner's actual consent to the dedication must be proved. The owner's intent is the crucial factor. When, on the other hand, a litigant seeks to provide dedication by adverse use, the inquiry shifts from the intent and activities of the owner to those of the public. The question then is whether the public has used the land "for a period of more than five years with full knowledge of the owner, without asking or receiving permission to do so and without objection being made by anyone." As other cases have stated, the question is whether the public has engaged in "long-continued adverse use" of the land sufficient to raise the "conclusive and undisputable presumption of knowl-

edge and acquiescence, while at the same time it negatives the idea of a mere license."

In both cases at issue here, the litigants representing the public contend that the second test has been met. Although there is evidence in both cases from which it might be inferred that owners preceding the present fee owners acquiesced in the public use of the land, that argument has not been pressed before this court. We therefore turn to the issue of dedication by adverse use.

Three problems of interpretation have concerned the lower courts with respect to proof of dedication by adverse use: (1) When is a public use deemed to be adverse? (2) Must a litigant representing the public prove that the owner did not grant a license to the public? (3) Is there any difference between dedication of shoreline property and other property?

In determining the adverse use necessary to raise a conclusive presumption of dedication, analogies from the law of adverse possession and easement by prescriptive rights can be misleading. An adverse possessor or a person gaining a personal easement by prescription is acting to gain a property right in himself, and the test in those situations is whether the person acted as if he actually claimed a personal legal right in the property. Such a personal claim of right need not be shown to establish a dedication because it is a public right that is being claimed. What must be shown is that persons used the property believing the public had a right to such use. This public use may not be "adverse" to the interests of the owner in the sense that the word is used in adverse possession cases. If a trial court finds that the public has used land without objection or interference for more than five years, it need not make a separate finding of "adversity" to support a decision of implied dedication.

Litigants, therefore, seeking to show that land has been dedicated to the public need only produce evidence that persons have used the land as they would have used public land. If the land involved is a beach or shoreline area, they should show that the land was used as if it were a public recreation area. If a road is involved, the litigants must show that it was used as if it were a public road. Evidence that the users looked to a governmental agency for maintenance of the land is significant in establishing an implied dedication to the public.

Litigants seeking to establish dedication to the public must also show that various groups of persons have used the land. If only a limited and definable number of persons have used the land, those persons may be able to claim a personal easement but not dedication to the public. An owner may well tolerate use by some persons but object vigorously to use by others. If the fee owner proves that use of the land fluctuated seasonally, on the other hand, such a showing does not negate evidence of adverse user. "[T]he thing of significance is that whoever wanted to use [the land] did so . . . when they wished to do so without asking permission and without protest from the land owners." *Seaway Company v. Attorney General* (Tex. Civ. App., *supra*), 375 S.W.2d 923, 936.

The second problem that has concerned lower courts is whether there is a presumption that use by the public is under a license by the fee owner, a presumption that must be overcome by the public with evidence to the contrary.

Counsel for the fee owners have argued that the following language from *F.A. Hihn Co. v. City of Santa Cruz* (1915) 170 Cal. 436, 448, 150 P. 62, 68 is controlling:

"where land is unenclosed and uncultivated, the fact that the public has been in the habit of going upon the land will ordinarily be attributed to a license on the part of the owner, rather than to his intent to dedicate. This is more particularly true where the use by the public is not over a definite and specified line, but extends over the entire surface of the tract. It will not be presumed, from mere failure to object, that the owner of such land so used intends to create in the public a right which would practically destroy his own right to use any part of the property.

We rejected that view, however, in *O'Banion v.*

Borba, supra, 32 Cal.2d 145, 195 P.2d 10. With regard to the question of presumptions in establishing easements by prescription we said: "There has been considerable confusion in the case involving the acquisition of easements by prescription, concerning the presence or absence of a presumption that the use is under a claim of right adverse to the owner of the servient tenement, and of which he has constructive notice, upon the showing of an open, continuous, notorious, and peaceable use for the prescriptive period. Some cases hold that from that showing a presumption arises that the use is under a claim of right adverse to the owner. It has been intimated that the presumption does not arise when the easement is over unenclosed and unimproved land. Other cases hold that there must be specific direct evidence of an adverse claim of right, and in its absence, a presumption of permissive use is indulged. The preferable view is to treat the case the same as any other, that is, the issue is ordinarily one of fact, giving consideration to all the circumstances and the inferences that may be drawn therefrom. The use may be such that the trier of fact is justified in inferring an adverse claim and user and imputing constructive knowledge thereof to the owner. There seems to be no apparent reason for discussing that matter from the standpoint of presumptions."

No reason appears for distinguishing proof of implied dedication by invoking a presumption of permissive use. The question whether public use of privately owned lands is under a license of the owner is ordinarily one of fact. We will not presume that owners of property today knowingly permit the general public to use their lands and grant a license to the public to do so. For a fee owner to negate a finding of intent to dedicate based on uninterrupted public use for more than five years, therefore, he must either affirmatively prove that he has granted the public a license to use his property or demonstrate that he has made a bona fide attempt to prevent public use. Whether an owner's efforts to halt public use are adequate in a particular case will turn on the means the owner uses in relation to the character of the property and the extent of public use. Although "No Trespassing" signs may be sufficient when only an occasional hiker traverses an isolated property, the same action cannot reasonably be expected to halt a continuous influx of beach users to an attractive seashore property. If the fee owner proves that he has made more than minimal and ineffectual efforts to exclude the public, then the trier of fact must decide whether the owner's activities have been adequate. If the owner has not attempted to halt public use in any significant way, however, it will be held as a matter of law that he intended to dedicate the property or an easement therein to the public, and evidence that the public used the property for the prescriptive period is sufficient to establish dedication.

A final question that has concerned lower courts is whether the rules governing shoreline property differ from those governing other types of property, particularly roads. Most of the case law involving dedication in this state has concerned roads and land bordering roads.

. . .

This emphasis on roadways arises from the ease with which one can define a road, the frequent need for roadways through private property, and perhaps also the relative frequency with which express dedications of roadways are made. The rules governing implied dedication apply with equal force, however, to land used by the public for purposes other than as a roadway.

Even if we were reluctant to apply the rules of common-law dedication to open recreational areas, we must observe the strong policy expressed in the constitution and statutes of this state of encouraging public use of shoreline recreational areas.

Among the statutory provisions favoring public ownership of shoreline areas is Civil Code, section 830. That section states that absent specific language to the contrary, private ownership of uplands ends at the high-water mark. The decisions of this court have interpreted this provision to create a presumption in favor of public ownership of land between high and low tide.

There is also a clearly enunciated public policy in the California Constitution in favor of allowing the public access to shoreline areas:

"No individual, partnership, or corporation, claiming or possessing the frontage of tidal lands of a harbor, bay, inlet, estuary, or other navigable water in this State, shall be permitted to exclude the right of way to such water whenever it is required for any public purpose, nor to destroy or obstruct the free navigation of such water." Art. XV, section 2.

Recreational purposes are among the "public purposes" mentioned by this constitutional provision.

This court has in the past been less receptive to arguments of implied dedication when open beach lands were involved than it has when well defined roadways are at issue.

With the increased urbanization of this state, however, beach areas are now as well defined as roadways. This intensification of land use combined with the clear public policy in favor of encouraging and expanding public access to and use of shoreline areas leads us to the conclusion that the courts of this state must be as receptive to a finding of implied dedication of shoreline areas as they are to a finding of implied dedication of roadways. (For a similar result see *State ex rel. Thornton v. Hay*, 462 P.2d 671 [Oreg. 1969].)

We conclude that there was an implied dedication of property rights in both cases. In both cases the public used the land "for a period of more than five years with full knowledge of the owner, without asking or receiving permission to do so and without objection being made by anyone."

In both cases the public used the land in public ways, as if the land was owned by a government, as if the land were a public park.

In *Gion v. City of Santa Cruz*, the public use of the land is accentuated by the active participation of the city in maintaining the land and helping the public to enjoy it. The variety and long duration of these activities indicate conclusively that the public looked to the city for maintenance and care of the land and that the city came to view the land as public land.

No governmental agency took an active part in maintaining the beach and road involved in *Dietz v. King*, but the public nonetheless treated the land as land they were free to use as they pleased. The evidence indicates that for over a hundred years persons used the beach without regard to who owned it. A few persons may have believed that the proprietors of the Navarro-by-the-Sea Hotel owned or supervised the beach, but no one paid any attention to any claim of the true owners. The activities of the Navarro-by-the-Sea proprietors in occasionally collecting tolls has no effect on the public's rights in the property because the question is whether the public's use was free from interference or objection by the fee owner or persons acting under his direction and authority.

The rare occasions when the fee owners came onto the property in question and casually granted permission to those already there have, likewise, no effect on the adverse use of the public. By giving permission to a few, an owner cannot deprive the many, whose rights are claimed totally independent of any permission asked or received of their interest in the land. If a constantly changing group of persons use land in a public way without knowing or caring whether the owner permits their presence, it makes no difference that the owner has informed a few persons that their use of the land is permissive only.

The present fee owners of the lands in question have of course made it clear that they do not approve of the public use of the property. Previous owners, however, by ignoring the widespread public use of the land for more than five years have impliedly dedicated the property to the public. Nothing can be done by the present owners to take back that which was previously given away. In each case the trial court found the elements necessary to implied dedication were present—use by the public for the prescriptive period without asking or receiving permission from the fee owner. There is no ev-

idence that the respective fee owners attempted to prevent or halt this use. It follows as a matter of law that a dedication to the public took place. The judgment in *Gion* is affirmed.

Questions

1. Does the court's decision place too great a burden on property owners of large tracts of land?

2. How does a "license" defeat prescription?

Daytona Beach v. Tona-Rama, Inc., 271 So.2d 765 (App.Fla. 1973)

In the case sub judice, the land in issue is occupied in part by the Main Street pier, a landmark of the Daytona Beach oceanfront for many years, and the land and pier are owned by the defendant. The pier is used as a recreation center and tourist attraction. It is utilized for fishing and dances, and offers a skylift and helicopter flights by the present owner.

That portion of the land owned by defendant which is not occupied by the pier has been left free of obstruction and has been utilized by sunbathing tourists for untold decades. These visitors to Daytona Beach, including those who have relaxed on the white sands of the subject lands, are the lifeblood of the pier. As such, they have not been opposed, but have been welcomed to utilize the otherwise unused sands of petitioner's oceanfront parcel of land.

The sky tower, which was substantially completed when the trial judge's order halted it, consists of a metal tower rising 176 feet above the ocean and a 25-passenger, air-conditioned gondola which was to be boarded from the pier to rise, rotating slowly, to the top of the tower, remain rotating at the top for a few minutes, and then descend. The tower utilizes a circle of sand only 17 feet in diameter. A building permit was issued in October 1969, and the project was completed, representing an investment of over $125,000, by the time the hearings were held.

The trial judge held that the land upon which

the owner has constructed was "a public thoroughfare, public bathing beach, recreation area and playground."

Upon this finding, the trial judge declared that the lands had been rendered public by prescriptive right. The District Court of Appeal, First District, affirmed, thus approving the destruction of the $125,000 investment and dooming any meaningful use of the property by the owner. In effect, the owner of the land is paying taxes for the sole benefit of the public.

As noted above, such prescriptive right has been recognized by this Court, and under proper circumstances is just. However, such a situation is not presented in the case sub judice.

The District Court of Appeal, First District, opined:

It is our view that the sporadic exercise of authority and dominion by the owners over the parcel in question was not sufficient to preserve their rights as against the prescriptive rights which accrued to the benefit of the public by its use of the beach area. *City of Daytona Beach v. Tona-Rama, Inc.*, 271 So.2d 765, p. 767.

The public has continuously, and over a period of several decades, made uninterrupted use of the lands in issue. However, neither the trial court, nor the District Court, reached the other requirement for prescription to be properly effective—adverse possession inconsistent with the owner's use and enjoyment of the land.

The use of property by the public was not against, but was in furtherance of, the interest of the defendant owner. Such use was not injurious to the owner and there was no invasion of the owner's right to the property. Unless the owner loses something, the public could obtain no easement by prescription.

Even if it should be found that such an easement had been acquired by prescription, the defendant-owner could make any use of the land consistent with, or not calculated to interfere with, the exercise of the easement by the public. The erection of the sky tower was

consistent with the recreational use of the land by the public and could not interfere with the exercise of any easement the public may have acquired by prescription, if such were the case.

The beaches of Florida are of such a character as to use and potential development as to require separate consideration from other lands with respect to the elements and consequences of title. The sandy portion of the beaches are of no use for farming, grazing, timber production, or residency—the traditional uses of land—but has served as a thoroughfare and haven for fishermen and bathers, as well as a place of recreation for the public. The interest and rights of the public to the full use of the beaches should be protected. Two states, Oregon and Hawaii, have used the "customary rights doctrine" to afford the rights in beach property.

As stated in *Tiffany Real Property*, (3d ed.), vol. 3, section 935:

In England, persons of a certain locality or of a certain class may have, by immemorial custom, a right to make use of land belonging to an individual. Thus, there may be a custom for the inhabitants of a certain town to dance or play games on a particular piece of land belonging to an individual, or to go thereon in order to get water. So there may be a custom for fishermen to dry nets on certain land, or for persons in a certain trade (victualers) to erect booths upon certain privatage land during a fair. The custom, to be valid, "must have continued from time immemorial, without interruption, and as of right; it must be certain as to the place, and as to the persons; and it must be certain and reasonable as to the subject matter or rights created."

. . .

Occasionally in this country it has been decided that rights to use private land cannot thus be created by custom, for the reason that they would tend so to burden land as to interfere with its improvement and alienation, and also because there can be no usage in this country of an immemorial character. In one state, on the other hand, the existence of such customary rights is affirmed, and in others this is assumed in decisions adverse to the existence of the right in the particular case.

If the recreational use of the sandy area adjacent to mean high tide has been ancient, reasonable, without interruption, and free from dispute, such use, as a matter of custom, should not be interfered with by the owner. However, the owner may make any use of his property which is consistent with such public use and not calculated to interfere with the exercise of right of the public to enjoy the dry-sand area as a recreational adjunct of the wet-sand, or foreshore, area.

This right of customary use of the dry-sand area of the beaches by the public does not create any interest in the land itself. Although this right of use cannot be revoked by the landowner, it is subject to appropriate governmental regulation and may be abandoned by the public.

Testimony was presented that the public's presence on the land and its use of the land was not adverse to the interest of defendant, but rather that the defendant's Main Street pier relied on the presence of such seekers of the sea for its business. Thus, the issue of adversity was clearly raised and the evidence failed to show any adverse use by the public. In fact, the construction of the sea tower was consistent with the general recreational use by the public. The general public may continue to use the dry-sand area for their usual recreational activities, not because the public has any interest in the land itself, but because of a right gained through custom to use this particular area of the beach as they have without dispute and without interruption for many years.

The decision of the District Court of Appeal is quashed and this cause is remanded to the District Court with instructions to further remand the same to the trial court for the purpose of entering final judgment for defendant.

It is so ordered.

BOYD, JUSTICE, dissenting.

I respectfully dissent.

Historians estimate that the North American continent has been inhabited by man for at least ten thousand years, and that, at the time Columbus discovered America, twenty-five thousand Indians lived in Florida.

One does not have to be a Chamber of Commerce publicity director to assume that these earliest of Floridians enjoyed the beautiful sandy beaches at Daytona. They were followed by countless Europeans, and, for many decades, the City of Daytona Beach has exercised dominion over the beaches, as if the beaches were owned and controlled by the City government. Thus, the case before us obviously presents a unique situation in which the land has been treated by the public and local government for many decades as publicly owned land. The public has used it for swimming, hiking, auto driving, and related purposes for a period much longer than twenty years, without interruption. The City has furnished police, sanitation, lifeguards, and other municipal services, normally provided to City-owned beach property, during said time. With the exceptions of being registered in the public records as privately owned, and the payment of taxes, the property has had all the attributes of a publicly owned beach continuously for more than twenty years. Surely, when the present owner purchased the land in question, it was common knowledge that the public had, for centuries, used both the wet and dry sand near the ocean for recreational purposes.

If this building be permitted to stand, then the owner might well next decide to erect a gargantuan hotel on the property, and the adjoining property owners, demanding equal protection of the law, might then begin to construct a series of hotels along the waterfront—similar to the series that now exists along the east side of Collins Avenue in Miami Beach. This would form a concrete wall, effectively cutting off any view of the Atlantic Ocean from the public. A repetition of the concrete wall created by such buildings would be extremely detrimental to the people of this State and to our vital tourism industry.

In my opinion, the trial court and the District Court of Appeal, First District, were correct in ordering the structure removed, for the reason that it encroaches upon the prescriptive rights of the public.

The record shows that the building was constructed, with a building permit granted by the City of Daytona Beach, apparently in good faith by the owner of record, who has been paying taxes on the property, and whose equitable rights should not be completely ignored. The trial court should require an accounting of all costs expended and all income received from this recreational structure, and if the money received thus far from the investment has not reimbursed all of those who have invested in the facility in good faith, they should be allowed to recoup their investments before removal of the structure. The equitable principles involved in the elimination of a nonconforming use would apply here.

The majority opinion ably defines the law generally applicable to beach properties. The intermittent, occasional use of dry-sand beach property by individuals or groups for recreational purposes does not establish prescriptive easements. If such were the law of this state, countless thousands of beach lots would have questionable titles. I dissent to the majority opinion only because the property here in question is totally unique in character by its treatment and use as a public beach for many decades. Only property having the same unique characteristics should be affected by any decision against this owner.

I offer no comment or opinion as to how far back from the wet sand the owner should be denied building privileges, but I don't think the government can collect taxes while denying the owner some reasonable use of the property not in conflict with the prescriptive rights of the public.

Therefore, I respectfully dissent to the majority opinion, and would affirm the decision of the District Court of Appeal, First District.

Questions

1. Does the erection of the tower, as the dissent argues, foretell the construction of a "gar-gantuan hotel" on the property? Would it be that simple?

2. Did the court adequately develop the argument that the doctrine of custom should apply here? How does this compare to the Oregon example in *Thornton v. Hay*?

Bell v. Town of Wells, 557 A.2d 168, (Me. 1989)

MCKUSICK, CHIEF JUSTICE

In their quiet title action initiated in 1984 against the Town of Wells, the State Bureau of Public Lands, and various individuals, Edward B. Bell and other owners of land bounded by the sea at Moody Beach in Wells sought a judicial declaration and injunction limiting the use the public may make of the beach. After a four-week bench trial, the Superior Court on October 1, 1987, entered judgments in plaintiffs' favor declaring the state of the legal title to Moody Beach. In doing so, the court reviewed and applied the rules of property law governing the ownership of intertidal land in Maine, declared the Public Trust in Intertidal Land Act unconstitutional, and made a factual determination that the public had acquired no easement over Moody Beach by local custom or otherwise. On the present appeal, we affirm.

We agree with the Superior Court's declaration of the state of the legal title to Moody Beach. Long and firmly established rules of property law dictate that the plaintiff oceanfront owners at Moody Beach hold title in fee to the intertidal land subject to an easement, to be broadly construed, permitting public use only for fishing, fowling, and navigation (whether for recreation or business), and any other uses reasonably incidental or related thereto. Although contemporary public needs for recreation are clearly much broader, the courts and the legislature cannot simply alter these long-established property rights to accommodate new recreational needs; constitutional prohibitions on the taking of private property without compensation must be considered. On this basis we agree with the Superior Court's conclusion that the Public Trust in Intertidal Land Act, which declares an unlimited right in the public to use the intertidal land for "recreation," is unconstitutional. Finally, on the record in this case no public easement by local custom has been proven to exist at Moody Beach, even assuming—as need not be decided in this case—that in Maine a public easement may be acquired over privately owned land by local custom.

The Facts

Moody Beach is a sandy beach located within the Town of Wells. It is about a mile long and lies between Moody Point on the north, the Ogunquit town line on the south, the Atlantic Ocean on the east, and a seawall on the west. Moody Beach has a wide intertidal zone with a strip of dry sand above the mean high-water mark. More than one hundred privately owned lots front on the ocean at Moody Beach. In addition, the Town of Wells in the past has acquired by eminent domain three lots which it uses for public access to the ocean. Each plaintiff now before the court owns a house or cottage situated on one of twenty-eight private oceanfront lots. Each lot is about fifty feet wide and is bordered on the west by Ocean Avenue. At trial, the parties stipulated that the plaintiff oceanfront owners hold title to the parcels described in their deeds in fee simple absolute and that their parcels were bounded on the Atlantic Ocean. A public beach, now known as Ogunquit Beach, lies immediately to the south of Moody Beach; the Village of Ogunquit acquired that beach by eminent domain in 1925.

The evidence at trial regarding the history of public recreational use of Moody Beach was inconclusive. Dr. Edwin Churchill, chief curator of the Maine State Museum, testified that visitors to seventeenth-century Maine used the beaches and a number of hotels were operating in the Wells area by the latter half of the nineteenth century. An 1865 history of Wells specifically refers to a "large hotel on the beach which is much patronized in summer by persons who are in search of sea air and bathing." Dr. Churchill testified that the beach in question was Wells Beach but that Wells Beach then encompassed the areas now known as Ogunquit, Moody, and Wells beaches. Recreational activities took place on the beaches of Cape Elizabeth and Kennebunk, and Dr. Churchill inferred that similar activities occurred on the beaches of Wells in the nineteenth century. Dr. Churchill, however, found no specific reference to recreational activity in the particular area now known as Moody Beach.

The testimony regarding more recent public recreational use of Moody Beach was conflicting. Defendants' witnesses testified that they always had considered Moody Beach public and that the public had used the beach for as long as they could remember. On the whole evidence, however, the Superior Court found:

The only open and continuous public use . . . proved to exist in this case for the twenty years preceding the filing of this lawsuit . . . was the public's (and the plaintiffs' for that matter) consistent habit of strolling up and down the length of Moody Beach. All of the plaintiffs testified that they were perfectly willing to permit this, never complained about it and would continue to permit this activity in the future.

I. The Public Easement in the Privately Owned Intertidal Land Does Not Extend beyond that Reserved in the Colonial Ordinance Broadly Construed

A. The Upland Owner's Fee Title to Intertidal Land

On the first appeal in this case, we examined in detail the historical sources of the legal regime governing the ownership of intertidal land in Maine. *Bell v. Town of Wells*, 510 A.2d 509 (Me. 1986) (*Bell I*). The elaborate legal and historical researches reflected in the extensive briefs filed with us on this second appeal fail to demonstrate any error in the conclusions we reached less than three years ago.

Long before 1820 it was established in the

common law of Massachusetts, applicable to its entire territory including the District of Maine, that the owner of shoreland above the mean high-water mark presumptively held title in fee to intertidal land subject only to the public's right to fish, fowl, and navigate. That rule of law governing titles to intertidal land had its origin in the Colonial Ordinance of 1641–47 of the Massachusetts Bay Colony and long before the separation of Maine was received into the common law of Massachusetts by long usage and practice throughout the jurisdiction of the Commonwealth. Then, by force of Article X, Section 3, of the Maine Constitution, that property rule was confirmed as the law of the new State of Maine. Only eleven years later, this court speaking through Chief Justice Mellen categorically rejected an argument that the rule of real property law taken into the common law from the Colonial Ordinance did not prevail in Maine: "Ever since [the 1810 decision in *Storer v. Freeman*], as well as long before, *the law on this point has been considered as perfectly at rest*; and we do not feel ourselves at liberty to discuss it as an open question." *Lapish v. Bangor Bank*, 8 Me. 85, 93 (1931) (emphasis added). The very next year the Massachusetts Supreme Judicial Court, speaking through Chief Justice Shaw, stated of the rule vesting fee ownership of intertidal land in the upland owner: "[T]he rule in question . . . being a settled rule of property, it would be extremely injurious to the stability of titles, and to the peace and interests of the community, to have it seriously drawn in question."

The pioneer Supreme Court opinion on coastal property rights, *Shively v. Bowlby*, 152 U.S. 1, 14 S.Ct. 548, 38 L.Ed. 331 (1894), written by Justice Gray, formerly Chief Justice of the Massachusetts Supreme Judicial Court, emphasizes the uniqueness of the Maine and Massachusetts legal rule governing title to intertidal land or flats:

In Massachusetts, by virtue of an ancient colonial enactment, commonly called the Ordinance of 1641, but really passed in 1647, and remaining in force to this day, the title of the owner of land bounded by tidewater extends from high-water mark over the shore or flats to low-water mark, if not beyond one hundred rods. The private right thus created in the flat is not a mere easement, but a title in fee, which will support a real action, or an action of trespass quare clausum fregit, and which may be conveyed by its owner with or without the upland; and which he may build upon or enclose, provided he does not impede the public right of way over it for boats or vessels. But his title is subject to the public rights of navigation and fishery; and therefore, so long as the flats have not been built upon or enclosed, those public rights are not restricted or abridged. . . . It is because of the ordinance vesting the title in fee of the flats in the owner of the upland, that a conveyance of his land bounding on the tidewater, by whatever name, whether "sea," "bay," "harbor," or "river," has been held to include the land below high-water mark as far as the grantor owns.

The brief of the amici curiae contends that the State of Maine on coming into the Union on separation from Massachusetts "obtained title to its intertidal lands under the 'equal footing' doctrine," a doctrine that has been most recently discussed by the United States Supreme Court in *Phillips Petroleum Co. v. Mississippi*, 484 U.S. 469 (1988). Any such revisionist view of history comes too late by at least 157 years. Prior to separation the Commonwealth of Massachusetts had already granted to the upland owners fee title in the intertidal land within its entire territory including the District of Maine. Contrary to the amicus argument, there was nothing in the pre-1820 Massachusetts common law governing title to the intertidal zone that was repugnant to the constitution of the new State. As already noted, in absence of such repugnance, Article X, Section 3, of the Maine Constitution declared that all laws in force in the District of Maine in 1820 would remain in force in the new State.

Maine has no reported case where a claim of a public easement for general recreation such as bathing, sunbathing, and walking on privately owned intertidal land has even been asserted. We cannot accept the argument of the Town of Wells that the absence of precise prior authority in Maine leaves it open for us to disregard the language of the Colonial Ordinance and to fashion a "no more burdensome" public easement that will meet the undoubted needs of modern society for more public recreational facilities. The absence of direct Maine authority is, at best for the Town, a neutral factor in our decision. Furthermore, we do have case authority squarely on point to guide us in deciding the question presented to us in Maine for the first time. Two Massachusetts Supreme Judicial Court cases, decided in 1907 and 1961, as well as the 1974 unanimous advisory opinion of its justices that is quoted above, have considered the exact question raised by this appeal and have ruled adversely to the claim now made by the Town of Wells.

Butler v. Attorney General, 195 Mass. 79, 80 N.E. 688 (1907), held that the public easement in intertidal land does not extend to public bathing. The Massachusetts court noted that the Colonial Ordinance mentioned no public rights except for fishing, fowling, and navigation. It reasoned as follows:

In the seashore the entire property, under the colonial ordinance, is in the individual, subject to the public rights. Among these is, of course, the right of navigation, with such incidental rights as pertain thereto. We think that there is a right to swim or float in or upon public waters as well as to sail upon them. But we do not think that this includes a right to use for bathing purposes, as these words are commonly understood, that part of the beach or shore above low-water mark, where the distance to high-water mark does not exceed one hundred rods, whether covered with water or not. It is plain, we think, that under the law of Massachusetts there is no reservation or recognition of bathing on the beach as a separate right of property in individuals or the public under the colonial ordinance.

Michaelson v. Silver Beach Improvement Assn., 342 Mass. 251, 259, 173 N.E.2d 273, 278 (1961), held that an artificial beach in front of the plaintiffs' seashore property created by public dredging became the private property of the plaintiffs by the doctrine of accretion, and held further that the defendant Association of other property owners in the vicinity should be enjoined from using the plaintiffs' newly created beach "for usual bathing purposes, down to the low-water mark." Finally, in 1974 the justices of the Massachusetts court rendered a well-reasoned opinion that walking along privately owned intertidal land, except to the extent it is incidental to fishing, fowling, or navigation, does not fall within the public easement reserved out of the grant of private ownership by the Colonial Ordinance. *Opinion of the Justices*, 365 Mass. 681, 313 N.E.2d 561. The Massachusetts justices unanimously informed the Massachusetts House of Representatives that a proposed statute creating a "public on-foot free right-of-passage" along the state's seashore between the mean high-water line and the extreme low-water line would constitute an unconstitutional taking of private property.

The Maine common-law rules defining the property interests in intertidal land come from the same Colonial Ordinance source as the Massachusetts common-law rules on that subject, and the Maine case development on the subject has in no significant respect departed from that in Massachusetts. The public need for access along the seashore was certainly as strong in Massachusetts in 1974 as in Maine today. In these circumstances, the three unanimous Massachusetts opinions, addressing the precise issue here raised in Maine for the first time, are persuasive precedent in the case at bar.

A public easement for bathing, sunbathing, and recreational walking cannot be justified on the factual assumption that it is "no more burdensome" on the private landowner than the Colonial Ordinance easement for fishing, fowling, and navigation. To justify adding a further easement on the ground it is "no more burdensome" is on its face self-contradictory. No one suggests or could suggest that any such public easement for bathing, sunbathing, and recreational walking is to be substituted for the ancient easement. Fishing, fowling, and navigation remain important uses of the Maine coast. If the private landowner now has ten fishermen, fowlers, and boaters using his land, adding ten bathers, sunbathers, and walkers obviously makes the aggregate public easement more burdensome. Furthermore, one would expect that a direct comparison of the magnitude of the relative burdens would show that at Moody Beach a substitution of bathers, sunbathers, and walkers for the fishermen, fowlers, and boaters using the beach would in fact result in a much greater burden upon the fee owner.

A court would have other difficulties as well with declaring a public easement for bathing, sunbathing, and recreational walking on the privately owned intertidal land. On the one hand, those uses fall considerably short of the comprehensive recreational use the Town of Wells urges as the scope of the modern public need, and also considerably short of the routine uses to which public beaches are put. We can find no principle basis for allowing bathing, sunbathing, and walking on privately owned intertidal land, and not allowing picnics and Frisbee-throwing and the many other activities people regularly engage in on the beach. But there is no basis in law or history for declaring a public easement for general recreation. That would turn the intertidal zone of Moody Beach into a public recreational area indistinguishable from the adjacent Ogunquit Beach, which the Village of Ogunquit acquired in its entirely by eminent domain.

The foregoing considerations demonstrate why a court cannot extend a public easement in the privately owned intertidal land beyond that reserved in the Colonial Ordinance and defined by over 340 years of history. To declare a general recreational easement, the court would be engaging in legislating, and it would do so without the benefit of having had the political processes define the nature and extent of the public need. It would also do so completely free of the practical constraints imposed on the legislative branch of government by the necessity of its raising the money to pay for any easement taken from private landowners. The objectives of the Town of Wells are better achieved by a public taking of a public easement tailored to its specific public need.

Thus, as we have seen, the legal regime governing the ownership of intertidal land was firmly established in the District of Maine prior to Statehood. It has been so declared in 1810 by the Massachusetts Supreme Judicial Court in a case involving intertidal land in Cape Elizabeth. *Storer v. Freeman*, 6 Mass. 435. As previously noted, in 1820 the Maine Constitution both confirmed the grant of the intertidal land in fee to the upland owners and took over as the law of Maine the reserved public easement limited to fishing, fowling, and navigation. Over a century ago, this court emphatically rejected the argument "that the court may change [that legal regime] if satisfied that it does not operate beneficially under present circumstances." *Barrows v. McDermott*, 73 Me. at 449. The judicial branch is bound, just as much as the legislative branch, by the constitutional prohibition against the taking of private property for public use without compensation.

II. The Public Trust in Intertidal Land Act Constitutes an Unconstitutional Taking

The legislature, by enacting in 1986 the Public Trust in Intertidal Land Act, declared that "the intertidal lands of the State are impressed with a public trust," and that those rights of the public include a "right to use intertidal land for recreation." The legislature thus imposed upon all intertidal land (defined by the Act in accordance with the Colonial Ordinance) an easement for use by the general public for "recreation" without limitation. The Superior Court held the Public Trust in Intertidal Land Act unconstitutional as a violation of the separation of powers provision of the Maine Constitution, Art. III. We do not reach the separation of powers question because the Act takes for public use much greater rights in the intertidal zone than are reserved by the common law and therefore the Act on its face constitutes an unconstitutional taking of private property. We agree therefore with the Superior Court that the Act is unconstitutional, but we ground our holding on the violation of the Takings Clauses of both the Maine and the United States Constitutions.

The Public Trust in Intertidal Land Act in creating a public easement for "recreation" leaves that term both undefined and unlimited—with the sole exceptions that the public recreation may not interfere with any structure or improvement lawfully maintained on intertidal land, nor may motorized vehicles other than watercraft be used there unless authorized by the State or municipality. The very nature of those exceptions emphasizes the all-inclusive recreational easement created by the Act over intertidal land owned in fee by the upland property holders. By its use of the unqualified term "recreation," the Act permits both individual and organized recreation of any form and nature. Members of the public in unrestricted numbers are thus given the right to come on this private property, not only for bathing, sunbathing, and walking as general recreation, but also for any other recreational activity whatever including, for example, ball games and athletic competitions, camping for extended hours, operation of vehicles (including even ATVs and other motorized vehicles, with State or municipal authorization), nighttime beach parties, and horseback riding. This comprehensive easement for public recreation sharply differs in nature and magnitude from the easement for fishing, fowling, and navigation and related uses that the common law alone reserved in favor of the public out of the fee ownership of intertidal land it at the same time vested in the upland owners. The Act thus constitutes a taking of private property for a public use. Since the Act provides no compensation for the landowners whose property is burdened by the general recreational easement taken for public use, it vio-

lates the prohibition contained in both our State and Federal Constitutions against the taking of private property for public use without just compensation.

Our analysis and conclusion are the same under both Constitutions. Long ago this court said:

[The Takings Clause] was designed to operate and it does operate to prevent the acquisition of any title to land *or to an easement in it* or to a permanent appropriation of it, from an owner for public use, without the actual payment or tender of a just compensation for it. *Cushman v. Smith*, 34 Me. 247, 265 (1852) (emphasis added)

In their 1974 *Opinion of the Justices* already discussed above, the justices of the Massachusetts court have already answered the very question now before us. They declared that a proposed statute merely to create a public footpath along the intertidal zone, a much more limited and less intrusive public easement than that taken by the Maine Act, would constitute an unconstitutional taking of property from the owners of the fee. The Massachusetts justices' reasoning has precise relevance to the case at bar:

The elusive border between the police power of the State and the prohibition against taking of property without compensation has been the subject of extensive litigation and commentary. But these difficulties need not concern us here. The permanent physical intrusion into the property of private persons, which the bill would establish, is a taking of property within even the most narrow construction of that phrase possible under the Constitutions of the Commonwealth and of the United States.

It is true that the bill does not completely deprive private owners of all use of their seashore property in the sense that a formal taking does. But the case is readily distinguishable from such regulation as merely prohibits some particular use or uses which are harmful to the public. Their interference with private property here involves a wholesale denial of an owner's right to exclude the public. If a possessory interest in real property has any meaning at all it must include the general right to exclude others.

The public recreational easement taken by the Maine Act over oceanfront owners' land must be distinguished from the governmental action regulating private land use that we have in recent years examined under the Takings Clause. In those cases of "regulatory taking" we make "a factual inquiry into the substantiality of the diminution in value of the property involved." That analysis becomes appropriate, however, when the issue before us is the constitutionality of a statute that authorizes a physical invasion of private property. As one scholar has written:

The modern significance of physical occupation is that courts, while they sometimes do hold nontrespassory injuries compensable, never deny compensation for a physical takeover. Michelman, "Property, Utility, and Fairness: comments on the Ethical Foundations of 'Just Compensation' Law," 80 Harv. L. Rev. 1165, 1184 (1967)

In *Nollan v. California Coastal Comm'n*, 483 U.S. 825, 107 S.Ct. 3141, 97 L.Ed.2d 677 (1987), where California had conditioned a seaside building permit upon the private owners' "mak[ing] an easement across their beachfront available to the public on a permanent basis," the Court found an unconstitutional taking, however slight the adverse economic impact on the owners, saying:

We think a "permanent physical occupation" has occurred, for purposes of that rule, where individuals are given a permanent and continuous right to pass to and fro, so that the real property may continuously be traversed, even though no particular individual is permitted to station himself permanently upon the premises.

The fact that the common law already has reserved to the public an easement in intertidal land for fishing, fowling, and navigation, and for related uses (even though the specific objects of that easement may be pursued for recreation as well a sustenance and profit) does not mean that the State can, without paying compensation to the private landowners, take in addition a public easement for general recreation. The common law has reserved to the public only a limited easement; the Public Trust in Intertidal Land Act takes a comprehensive easement for "recreation" without limitation. The absence of any compensation to the fee owners renders the Act unconstitutional.

Conclusion

As development pressures on Maine's real estate continue, the public will increasingly seek shorefront recreational opportunities of the twentieth- and twenty-first century variety, not limited to fishing, fowling, and navigation. No one can be unsympathetic to the goal of providing such opportunities to everyone, not just to those fortunate enough to own shore frontage. The solution under our constitutional system, however, is for the State or municipalities to purchase the needed property rights or obtain them by eminent domain through the payment of just compensation, not to take them without compensation through legislative or judicial decree redefining the scope of private property rights. Here, whatever various visitors to Moody Beach may have thought, the state of the title to the intertidal land was never in any doubt under the Maine Constitution and relevant case law, and owners, occupiers, buyers, and sellers of shorefront land were entitled to rely upon their property rights as so defined. In the absence of State regulation to the extent permitted by the police power, that is the meaning of our constitutional prohibitions against the taking of private property without just compensation.

The entry is: Judgments affirmed.

WATHEN, JUSTICE with whom ROBERTS and CLIFFORD, JUSTICES, join, dissenting.

I do not agree that public recreational rights in the Maine coast are confined strictly to "fishing," "fowling," and "navigation," however "sympathetically generous" the interpretation of those terms might be. The Court concludes that the shoreowners have the unrestricted right to exclude any member of the public from the intertidal lands unless that person is engaged in fishing, fowling, or navigation. That conclusion is premised upon the erroneous assumption that the Colonial Ordinance is the exclusive and preeminent source of all public rights. In fact, public rights in the intertidal lands existed at common law, long before the Ordinance. Those common-law rights were not displaced by the Ordinance and are broad enough to permit the activities described in the Public Trust in Intertidal Land Act. Because I interpret the common-law right of use more flexibly and expansively than the Court does, I would vacate the judgment and uphold the constitutionality of the Act on the basis that it merely confirms recreational rights existing as a matter of common law.

Any attempt to fairly and justly resolve this important controversy is made more difficult by the need for an accurate and faithful reconstruction of the relevant aspects of more than three hundred years of human activity and common-law development. Rarely is there such a gap in the development of the law that a court confronts a significant issue of first impression concerning an ordinance enacted as long ago as 1641. My review of the relevant history, both social and legal, persuades me that the opinion of the Court does not accurately define the public's right to use the Maine shore.

With the advantage of hindsight, it is now established beyond doubt that the determination of public and private rights in the intertidal land is fundamentally a matter of state law. This conclusion derives from the prevailing interpretation of the English common law regarding ownership of the intertidal lands. Under that interpretation, the king held title to all the lands below the high-water mark which were affected by the ebb and flow of the tides. The king's ownership of those lands was qualified. The lands were thought "incapable of ordinary and private occupation, cultivation, and improvement" and more appropriately devoted to public uses such as navigation, commerce, and fishing. *Shively v. Bowlby*, 152 U.S. at 11. The king's ownership of the intertidal lands was therefore of two types. He held the title, or jus privatum, absolutely. As sovereign he also held

the public rights or jus publicum in trust for the benefit of the public. Id. Although the king possessed the power to convey the lands below the high-water mark, any conveyance to a private individual was subject to the jus publicum. Following the American Revolution, "the people of each state became themselves sovereign; and in that character hold the absolute right to all their navigable waters and the soils under them for their own common use, subject only to the rights since surrendered by the Constitution to the general government." *Martin v. Lessee of Waddell*, 41 U.S. 367, 410 (1842). In a recent case, the Supreme Court of the United States restated the principle and held that the original thirteen states and all new states, upon entering the Union, acquired title to all lands under waters subject to the ebb and flow of the tides. *Phillips Petroleum Co. v. Mississippi*, 484 U.S. 469 (1988). As sovereign, those states, like the king, hold the intertidal lands in trust for the public.

It is now certain that unless the common law has been modified, ownership of the intertidal lands lies in the state. It is also established "that the individual states have the authority to define the limits of the lands held in public trust and to recognize private rights in such lands as they see fit." The Massachusetts Bay Colony altered the common law regarding sovereign ownership by the enactment of a Colonial Ordinance and the subsequent adoption of that Ordinance as part of the common law. Maine entered the Union as part of the State of Massachusetts and, after achieving independent statehood purported to adopt the Massachusetts usage as part of the common law of Maine. The issue thus becomes: what change in the common-law rights of the public has been wrought by the scheme of private ownership that arose from the Colonial Ordinance and the customary law resulting from that Ordinance?

Enactment of Colonial Ordinance

In 1620 James I, king of England, granted to the Council of Plymouth "for the planting, ruling, ordering, and governing of Newe England in America . . . all the Firme Landes, Soyles, Groundes, Havens, Portes, Rivers, Waters, Fishing. . . ." The Charter of the Massachusetts Bay (March 4, 1629), reprinted in R. Perry, *Sources of Our Liberties* 82 (1960; reciting prior grant by James I). This grant was confirmed and reiterated eight years later by Charles I in the Charter of Massachusetts Bay and embraced the whole of New England. The Charter empowered the officers of the Massachusetts Bay Company "to make Lawes and Ordinnces [*sic*] for the Good and Welfare of the saide Company. . . ." On the basis of the authority so conferred, the General Court appointed a committee to prepare a draft of laws to place a limitation on the discretionary power of the magistrates. As a concession to the magistrates who vigorously resisted the enactment of laws, it was agreed that the initial set of laws would remain in force for three years only. The Body of Liberties of 1641 was enacted on that temporary basis. Section 16 of the Body of Liberties, the predecessor of the Colonial Ordinance, gave to all inhabitants the right of free fishing and fowling. Section 16 provided:

Every inhabitant that is an howse holder shall have free fishing and fowling in any great ponds and Bayes, Coves and Rivers, so farre as the sea ebbes and flowes within the presincts of the towne where they dwell, unlesse the free men of the same Towne or the Generall Court have otherwise appropriated them, provided that this shall not be extended to give leave to any man to come upon others proprietie without there leave. Massachusetts Body of Liberties, Section 16 (December 10, 1641), reprinted in R. Perry at 148, 150

Six years later, the Body of Liberties was amended and made more comprehensive. Section 2 of the "Liberties Common" replaced Section 16 and provided as follows:

Everie Inhabitant who is an hous-holder shall have free fishing and fowling, in any great Ponds, Bayes, Coves and Rivers so far as the Sea ebbs and flows, within the precincts of the town where they dwell, unles the Free-men of the same town, or the General Court have otherwise appropriated them. Provided that no town shall appropriate to any particular person or persons, any great Pond containing more than ten acres of land: and that no man shall come upon anothers proprietie without their leave otherwise then as hereafter expressed; the which clearly to determine, it is declared that in all creeks, coves, and other places, about and upon salt water where the Sea ebbs and flows, the Proprietor of the land adjoyning shall have propriete to the low water mark where the Sea doth not ebb above a hundred rods, and not more wheresoever it ebbs farther. Provided that such Proprietor shall not by this libertie have power to stop or hinder the passage of boats or other vessels in, or through any sea creeks, or coves to other mens houses or lands. And for great Ponds lying in common though within the bounds of some town, it shall be free for any man to fish and fowl there, and may passe and repasse on foot through any mans propriete for that end, so they trespasse not upon any mans corn or meadow. Liberties Common, Section 2, *The Book of the General Lawes and Libertyes Concerning the Inhabitants of Massachusetts* (Boston, 1647; facimile reprint in 1 D. Cushing, *The Laws and Liberties of Massachusetts 1641–1691*, at 41, 1976)

Section 2 of the Liberties Common has come to be known as the Colonial Ordinance. It grants "propriete" to the adjoining upland owner to the low-water mark of tidal waters, not to exceed one hundred rods. The ordinance in terms preserves to inhabitants the right of free fishing and fowling. It provides further that the fee title of the upland owner in the intertidal lands does not give him the right to "hinder the passage of boats or other vessels." The courts have construed this clause as a reservation to the public of the right of navigation.

Public Ownership and Evolving Concepts of Public Rights

The "grant of land" occasioned by the Ordinance was designed to promote commerce by encouraging the construction of wharves at private expense. "To induce persons to erect them, the common law of England was altered by an ordinance, providing that the proprietor of land adjoining on the sea or salt water, shall hold to lower water mark." *Storer v. Freeman*, 6 Mass. 435, 438 (1810). Notwithstanding that limited purpose, this court has followed the lead of Massachusetts in describing the rights of the riparian owner expansively in terms of fee simple ownership. Chief Justice Shaw emphasized the substantial nature of the owner's interest in *Commonwealth v. Alger*, 61 Mass. (7 Cush.) 53 (1851), one of the leading cases construing the ordinance. According to that court, the ordinance "imports not an easement, an incorporeal right, license, or privilege, but a jus in re, a real or proprietary title to, and interest inn, the soil itself, in contradistinction to a usufruct, or an uncertain and precarious interest." Moreover, the fee holder could use traditional forms of action against persons who attempted to interfere with his rights of ownership. "[H]e may maintain trespass for unlawful entry thereon, or trespass on the case for obstructing his rights of fishery, or a writ of entry against a disseizor." *Marshall v. Walker*, 93 Me. 532, 537, 45 A. 497, 498 (1900). Subject to the rights of fishing, fowling, and navigation expressly reserved to the public in the ordinance, the riparian owner's "title to the shore [is] as ample as to the upland." *State v. Wilson*, 42 Me. 9, 29 (1856).

The substantial nature of the interest accorded to the littoral owner is illustrated by this Court's decision in *Sawyer v. Beal*, 97 Me. 356, 54 A. 848 (1903). In that case, the plaintiff, littoral owner brought suit to recover a statutorily prescribed penalty under R.S. ch. 3, section 63 (1885). That statute prohibited the erection of fish weirs or wharves in tide water "in front of the shore or flats" of the riparian owner. The precise issue was the construction of the phrase "in front of the shore or flats." The Court analyzed the issue with reference to the purpose of the statute which was to protect the rights of the littoral owner and concluded that the statute prohibited fish weirs which were "so near the shore of another as to injure of injuriously affect the latter in the enjoyment of his rights as such

owner." The Court stressed the fact that the statute created no new rights in the owner. Rather its purpose was to "extend to him additional protection" in the enjoyment of his existing rights, and to provide him with a means of redressing non-trespassory interferences with the "use and enjoyment of his land." In this case we described the right of the littoral owner as follows: "Within the limits of his ownership he has all the exclusive rights of an owner."

In *Marshall v. Walker*, 93 Me. 532, 45 A. 497 (1900), we suggested that the owner of the flats might appropriate the flats to himself by building on them or filling them and thereby cut off public rights provided only that navigation is not unreasonably impaired by this action.

[The] ordinance has become a part of our common law, and by it, the proprietor of the main holds the shore to low water not exceeding one hundred rods. *He holds it in fee, like other lands*, subject, however, to the jus publicum, the right of the public to use it for the purposes of navigation and fishery, not, however, to interfere with his right of exclusive appropriation that shall not unreasonably impede navigation by filling and turning it into upland, or by building wharves or other structures upon it, so that necessarily the public would be excluded thereby.

In addition, we have held that the lands of the riparian owner may be increased by natural accretion, *King v. Young*, 76 Me. 76 (1884), and that he may convey the flats yet retain the upland or vice versa, or convey both separately.

Looking at the other side of the ledger, we have consistently characterized the public's interest as an easement. It is true, however, that it is an easement that has undergone significant change since its inclusion in the Ordinance. By its terms the Ordinance extended the liberties of fishing and fowling only to inhabitants who were householders. Perhaps as a result of the preexisting common law or a recognition of contrary usage the early opinions of this court described the liberties as a public right. Although the liberties secured by the Ordinance grew out of the necessity to provide sustenance, they were soon expanded to include recreational fishing and fowling. In 1882, this court acknowledged the possibility that the liberties were "now chiefly exercised by pleasure seekers and idle tramps who might be more profitably employed." Moreover, the public's easement for fishing has expanded to include activities such as digging for worms, *State v. Lemar*, 147 Me. 405, 87 A.2d 886 (1952), digging for shellfish, *Moulton v. Libbey*, 37 Me. 472 (1854), and digging for clams, *State v. Levitt*, 105 Me. 76, 72 A. 875 (1909). The public rights of navigation now include the right to use the waters as a public highway even when frozen, *French v. Camp*, 18 Me. 433 (1841), and include travel for recreational purposes.

This Court summed up the public rights in the intertidal flats at the beginning of this century in *Marshall v. Walker*, 93 Me. 532, 45 A. 497 (1900). The public "may sail over them, may moor their craft upon them, may allow their vessels to rest upon the soil when bare, may land and walk upon them, may ride or skate over them when covered with water bearing ice, may fish in the water over them, [and] may dig shellfish in them."

The last time this Court examined any of the public rights in intertidal lands we adopted an expansive view of the right of navigation. In *Andrews v. King*, 124 Me. 361, 129 A. 298 (1925), the shore owner claimed that the defendant, operator of a small power boat for hire, had no right to land passengers on his flats between high- and low-water mark. The plaintiff argued that under the express terms of the Ordinance, the right of navigation was limited to the stated purpose of passage to "other men's houses" or navigation for the purposes of fishing and fowling. We rejected this rigid construction of the Ordinance and held that the reservation in the Ordinance encompassed a general right of navigation. More significantly, we noted that the right of navigation included the mooring of vessels, and the discharging and taking in of cargoes, provided the flats are unoccupied. In addition, members of the public were permitted to make

such uses of the privately owned flats "[i]n the pursuit of [their] private affairs, of business *as well as pleasure*" (emphasis added).

This Court has imposed limitations on the right of the public to use the intertidal flats for certain purposes. Significantly, however, we have not held, nor even suggested, that the scheme of ownership established by the Ordinance precludes the public from using the intertidal zone for common recreational beach activities. In *Moore v. Griffin*, 22 Me. 350 (1843), this Court held that "[n]either the ordinance nor the common law would authorize the taking of 'muscle-bed [sic] manure' from the land of another person." The plaintiff in *Moore* brought an action in trespass quare clausum against defendant for entry upon his river flats between high- and low-water mark and removal of six gondola loads of mussel-bed manure. The Court rejected the defendant's contention that the Ordinance reserves not only the rights of fishing and fowling but also permits taking sand, sea manure, and ballast, as a right of soil in the flats. Rather, the Court held: "No such practice can be recognized as depriving the legal owner of his rights according to his title, unless supported by proof, that would establish a common right. The language of the reservation in the ordinance cannot be extended beyond the obvious meaning of the words fishing and fowling." The decision in *Moore* was approved more than forty years later by this Court in *King v. Young*, 76 Me. 76 (1884).

Similarly, we have prohibited the taking of seaweed from the flats of another. "[T]he title to the seaweed is in the owner of the flats." *Hill v. Lord*, 48 Me. 83, 86 (1861). Although we have not decided the question, at least one commentator has suggested that the scheme of ownership established by the ordinance also prohibits the public from taking sand and empty shells from the flats. See Comment, "The Public Trust Doctrine in Maine's Submerged Lands: Public Rights, State Obligation and the Role of the Courts," 37 Me. L. Rev. 105, 114 (1985).

In addition to prohibiting the taking of certain substances from the flats, we have also prohibited the deposit of substances on the flats. For example, in *McFadden v. Haynes and DeWitt Ice Co.*, 86 Me. 319, 29 A. 1068 (1894), this Court held that the defendant ice company, a member of the public, had no right to deposit snow upon the plaintiff's flats between high- and low-water mark. The defendant argued that since a fisherman had the right to engage in certain activities on the flats such as anchoring his boat there or placing an iceboat or hut on the frozen surface, "an ice cutter, by analogy, should be allowed temporarily to encumber another's flats with snow scraped from his ice." We disagreed, however, and took a more restrictive view of the public's right to encumber the flat.

Property rights cannot be established by analogy alone. The fisherman has a right to go upon another's flats to take his fish, because the ordinance of 1647 . . . expressly reserved the right of fishery. The fisherman has a right to go upon another's flats because it is one of his reserved rights. But no such right was reserved to the ice cutter. . . . And we fail to perceive how an ice company, operating upon one of our navigable rivers, can possess the right to deposit the snow scraped from its ice upon the flats of an adjoining owner, without the latter's consent. It is not among the reserved rights mentioned in the ordinance of 1647, nor . . . has the right to thus encumber another's land been recognized or affirmed by judicial decision.

In modern times this Court, sitting as the Law Court, has not been called upon to further define and delineate the public right. We have, however, expressed the view that public rights in intertidal lands are dynamic. In *Opinion of the Justices*, 437 A.2d 597 (Me. 1981) the question posed to the Justices concerned the constitutionality of a bill releasing the state's interest in filled submerged and intertidal lands. In commenting on the reasonableness of the legislation, the individual Justices recognized that the rights of the public in submerged and intertidal lands must evolve with the passage of time.

Navigation, fishing, and fowling were the historical purposes for which the public trust principle was developed in the common law. Those public uses of intertidal and submerged lands remain important, but others have grown up as well. The press of an increasing population has lead to heavy demands upon Maine's great ponds and seacoast for recreation uses.

The Law Court later noted that the Justices had stated that "the needs of a growing society may lead to a wider variety of public uses" of submerged lands. *Harding v. Commissioner*, 510 A.2d 533, 537 (Me. 1986).

In 1925, when this Court decided *Andrews*, we expanded the right of navigation and in doing so we noted that plaintiff's flats had been used as a landing place for fifty years. *Andrews v. King*, 124 Me. at 364, 129 A. 298. We rejected a rigid application of the terms of the Ordinance and resorted to contemporary notions of usage and public acceptance in order to strike a rational and fair balance between private ownership and public rights. Similarly, in the present controversy we should consider current notions of usage and public acceptance. Although the practice of fishing, fowling, and navigation, as classically defined, may have become less important, other recreational uses have developed and received public acceptance within the past sixty years. I am persuaded that this Court and the Superior Court erred in arresting further development in the law by effectively confining public rights to those that had been recognized prior to 1925. Although we must avoid placing any additional burden upon the shoreowner, there is no reason to confine, nor have we in the past confined, the rights of the public strictly to the usage prevailing in the seventeenth century. Neither reason nor logic supports the necessary and unfortunate conclusion flowing from this Court's analysis; namely, that the common-law rights of the public would be extinguished if fishing, fowling, and navigation were no longer practiced. When the necessities of the seventeenth century disappear and the emphasis moves from those historic activities to other uses no more burdensome, the common-law rights of the public should remain vital. The citizens of Maine are still in need of sustenance, albeit, in a different form.

The genius of the common law has been its ability to adapt legal doctrine to changing needs and circumstances. As we noted long ago: "The common law would ill deserve its familiar panegyric as the 'perfection of human reason' if it did not expand with the progress of society and develop with new ideas or right and justice." In re *Robinson*, 88 Me. 17, 23, 33 A. 652, 654 (1895). The increased importance of recreational use of the shore is evident. The power of the Maine coast to restore body and mind is well known. The Maine Legislature has specifically recognized that "recreational uses are among the most important to the Maine people today who use intertidal land for relaxation from the pressures of modern life and for enjoyment of nature's beauty." Such a public resource is not, and never has been, the subject of exclusive ownership. I firmly believe that it is primarily the intensity of the modern use rather than the nature of the use that provides the impetus for this litigation. Given similar degrees of intensity of use, one would imagine that a shore owner might prefer the presence of sunbathers, swimmers, and strollers over fowlers and fishermen. Further, as has been suggested elsewhere, the narrow view adopted by the Court today results in absurd and easily thwarted distinctions between permissible and impermissible activities:

[A] narrow view would recognize the right to picnic in a rowboat while resting on the foreshore but brand as a trespass the same activities performed while sitting on a blanket spread on the foreshore. The narrow view taken by the Massachusetts court does not exclude the public from walking on the foreshore as it purports; it merely requires that a person desiring to stroll along the foreshores of that state take with him a fishing line or net. In keeping with the apparent purpose of the Colony Ordinance and its past decisions, the Maine Supreme Judicial Court can refuse to draw such a delicate distinction between the rights

expressly reserved in the ordinance and similar recreational activities. With such a refusal the court will avoid the anomalous result of "declaring the same man a trespasser for bathing, who was no trespasser when up to his knees or neck in water, in search of a lobster, a crab, or a shrimp." Comment, *Coastal Recreation* at 83

In the context of this case, I would not attempt to provide a comprehensive definition of the recreational activities that could fall within the common-law rights of the public. The plaintiffs requested a declaration that their ownership was subject only to the rights of fishing, fowling, and navigation. The Superior Court granted their request, confining the public rights to those previously recognized by this Court and denying any further judicial development of those rights. I conclude that the court was in error. The rights of the public are, at a minimum, broad enough to include such recreational activities as bathing, sunbathing, and walking. As ordinarily practiced, such activities involve no additional burden on the shore owners and nothing is taken from or deposited on the intertidal lands. The present litigation does not require that we delineate the outer limits of the public rights. On the record before us it is only necessary to rule that the plaintiffs are not entitled to a declaration restricting the public rights to fishing, fowling, and navigation. Any further refinement should await common-law development or legislative action.

Conclusion

Twice in its opinion this Court mentions the finding of the Superior Court concerning the public's habit of "strolling" up and down the length of Moody Beach and the acquiescence of the private owners. Despite the shore owners' testimony that they would continue to permit this activity in the future, they are not bound to do so, and the Superior Court order, affirmed by this Court, does not acknowledge any right on the part of the public to stroll on the beach. This Court's opinion does nothing to dispel the obvious conclusion that from this moment on, at Moody Beach and every other private shore in Maine, the public's right even to stroll upon the intertidal lands hangs by the slender thread of the shore owners' consent. I will not hazard a guess whether that consent will be forthcoming. In my judgment, the public rights should not be so quickly and completely extinguished. I admit that the Court has assiduously followed the path taken by the courts of Massachusetts but, for me, that is not the goal. By interpreting Maine history, without attempting to revise it, I find a legally sufficient basis for recognizing limited public recreational rights in the Maine seashore. I am strengthened in my conviction by the fact that those same rights have been recognized by the Maine Legislature. I would vacate the judgment.

Therefore, I respectfully dissent to the majority opinion, and would affirm the decision of the District Court of Appeal, First District.

Questions

1. In a headline story on August 14, 1989, the *National Law Journal* reported that all four justices composing the majority in this case had failed to disclose that they owned homes along the coast. The dissenters did not. Was this a mere coincidence, or should Maine adopt tougher canons of ethics for the judiciary?

2. Which activity does the majority opinion favor: walking along the beach, holding a child's hand, or a shotgun? Watching birds with binoculars, or blasting them out of the sky with bird shot?

3. Compare the public's right to the shore in Oregon, New Jersey, California, and Maine. How can you explain the tremendous variations in permissible uses and the broad number of theories used to support them?

Chapter 5

REGULATING DEVELOPMENT IN THE COASTAL ZONE: THE COASTAL ZONE MANAGEMENT ACT OF 1972

As regulatory programs go, the federal coastal zone management program is of fairly recent vintage. However, its roots can be traced back nearly two thousand years, to the Sermon on the Mount:

So whoever hears these words of mine and acts on them is like a man who had the sense to build his house on rock. The rain came down, the floods rose, the winds blew and beat upon that house but it did not fall, because its foundations were on rock. And whoever hears these words of mine and does not act on them is like a man who was foolish enough to build his house on sand. The rain came down, the floods rose, the winds blew and battered against that house; and it fell with a great crash.

Matthew 7:24–27

Despite that biblical admonition, our beaches and shores have become highly developed and routinely suffer significant damage from the forces of nature. One major effort to control that development was the Coastal Zone Management Act (16 U.S.C. Secs. 1451, *et seq.*) of 1972.

Selected Provisions of the Coastal Zone Management Act of 1972, as Amended through 1990

Sec. 1451. Congressional Findings

The Congress finds that:

(a) There is a national interest in the effective management, beneficial use, protection, and development of the coastal zone.

(b) The coastal zone is rich in a variety of natural, commercial, recreational, ecological, industrial, and esthetic resources of immediate and potential value to the present and future well-being of the Nation.

(c) The increasing and competing demands upon the lands and waters of our coastal zone occasioned by population growth and economic development, including requirements for industry, commerce, residential development, recreation, extraction of mineral resources and fossil fuels, transportation and navigation, waste disposal, and harvesting of fish, shellfish, and other living marine resources, have resulted in the loss of living marine resources, wildlife, nutrient-rich areas, permanent and adverse changes to ecological systems, decreasing open space for public use, and shoreline erosion.

(d) The habitat areas of the coastal zone, and the fish, shellfish, other living marine resources, and wildlife therein, are ecologically fragile and consequently extremely vulnerable to destruction by man's alterations.

(e) Important ecological, cultural, historic, and esthetic values in the coastal zone which are essential to the well-being of all citizens are being irretrievably damaged or lost.

(f) New and expanding demands for food, energy, minerals, defense needs, recreation, waste disposal, transportation, and industrial activities in the Great Lakes, territorial sea, exclusive economic zone, and Outer Continental Shelf are placing stress on these areas and are creating the need for resolution of serious conflicts among important and competing uses and values in coastal and ocean waters.

(g) Special natural and scenic characteristics are being damaged by ill-planned development that threatens these values.

(h) In light of competing demands and the urgent need to protect and to give high priority to natural systems in the coastal zone, present state and local institutional arrangements for planning and regulating land and water uses in such areas are inadequate.

(i) The key to more effective protection and use of the land and water resources of the coastal zone is to encourage the states to exercise their full authority over the lands and waters in the coastal zone by assisting the states, in cooperation with Federal and local governments and other vitally affected interests, in developing land and water use programs for the coastal zone, including unified policies, criteria, standards, methods, and processes for dealing with land and water use decisions of more than local significance.

(j) The national objective of attaining a greater degree of energy self-sufficiency would be ad-

vanced by providing Federal financial assistance to meet state and local needs resulting from new or expanded energy activity in or affecting the coastal zone.

(k) Land uses in the coastal zone, and the uses of adjacent lands which drain into the coastal zone, may significantly affect the quality of coastal waters and habitats, and efforts to control coastal water pollution from land use activities must be improved.

(l) Because global warming may result in a substantial sea level rise with serious adverse effects in the coastal zone, coastal states must anticipate and plan for such an occurrence.

(m) Because of their proximity to and reliance upon the ocean and its resources, the coastal states have substantial and significant interests in the protection, management, and development of the resources of the exclusive economic zone that can only be served by the active participation of coastal states in all Federal programs affecting such resources and, wherever appropriate, by the development of state ocean resource plans as part of their federally approved coastal zone management programs.
(As amended November 5, 1990, P.L. 101–508, Title VI, Subtitle C, Sec. 6203[a], 104 State. 1388–300.)

Sec. 1453. Definitions

For the purposes of this title:

(1) The term "coastal zone" means the coastal waters (including the lands therein and thereunder) and the adjacent shorelands (including the waters therein and thereunder), strongly influenced by each other and in proximity to the shorelines of the several coastal states, and includes islands, transitional and intertidal areas, salt marshes, wetlands, and beaches. The zone extends, in Great Lakes waters, to the international boundary between the United States and Canada and, in other areas, seaward to [the outer limit of] the outer limit of State title and ownership under the Submerged Lands Act (43 U.S.C. 1301 et seq.), the Act of

March 2, 1917 (48 U.S.C. 749), the Covenant to Establish a Commonwealth of the Northern Mariana Islands in Political Union with the United States of America, as approved by the Act of March 24, 1976 (48 U.S.C. 1681 note), or section 1 of the Act of November 20, 1963 (48 U.S.C. 1705), as applicable. The zone extends inland from the shorelines only to the extent necessary to control shorelands, the uses of which have a direct and significant impact on the coastal waters, and to control those geographical areas which are likely to be affected by or vulnerable to sea level rise. Excluded from the coastal zone are lands the use of which is by law subject solely to the discretion of or which is held in trust by the Federal Government, its officers or agents.

Sec. 1454. Management Program Development Grants

(a) *Authorization.* The Secretary may make grants to any coastal state:

(1) under subsection (c) for the purpose of assisting such state in the development of a management program for the land and water resources of its coastal zone; and

(2) A definition of what shall constitute permissible land uses and water uses within the coastal zone which have a direct and significant impact on the coastal waters.

(3) An inventory and designation of areas of particular concern within the coastal zone.

(4) An identification of the means by which the state proposes to exert control over the land uses and water uses referred to in paragraph (2), including a listing of relevant constitutional provisions, laws, regulations, and judicial decisions.

(5) Broad guidelines on priorities of uses in particular areas, including specifically those uses of lowest priority.

(6) A description of the organizational structure proposed to implement such management program, including the responsibilities and interrelationships of local, area-wide, state, re-

gional, and interstate agencies in the management process.

(7) A definition of the term "beach" and a planning process for the protection of, and access to, public beaches and other public coastal areas of environmental, recreational, historical, esthetic, ecological, or cultural value.

(8) A planning process for energy facilities likely to be located in, or which may significantly affect, the coastal zone, including, but not limited to, a process for anticipating and managing the impacts from such facilities.

(9) A planning process for (A) assessing the effects of shoreline erosion (however caused), and (B) studying and evaluating ways to control, or lessen the impact of, such erosion, and to restore areas adversely affected by such erosion.

Sec. 1455. Administrative Grants

(a) The Secretary may make grants to any coastal state for the purpose of administering that state's management program, if the state matches any such grant according to the following ratios of Federal-to-State contributions for the applicable fiscal year:

(1) For those States for which programs were approved prior to enactment of the Coastal Zone Act Reauthorization Amendments of 1990 [enacted Nov. 5, 1990], 1 to 1 for any fiscal year.

(2) For programs approved after enactment of the Coastal Zone Act Reauthorization Amendments of 1990 [enacted Nov. 5, 1990], 4 to 1 for the first fiscal year, 2.3 to 1 for the second fiscal year, 1.5 to 1 for the third fiscal year, and 1 to 1 for each fiscal year thereafter.

(b) The Secretary may make a grant to a coastal state under subsection (a) only if the Secretary finds that the management program of the coastal state meets all applicable requirements of this title and has been approved in accordance with subsection (d).

(c) Grants under this section shall be allocated to coastal states with approved programs based on rules and regulations promulgated by the Secretary which shall take into account the extent and nature of the shoreline and area covered by the program, population of the area, and other relevant factors.

Section 1456. Coordination and Cooperation

(a) *Federal Agencies.* In carrying out his functions and responsibilities under this title, the Secretary shall consult with, cooperate with, and, to the maximum extent practicable, coordinate his activities with other interested Federal agencies.

(b) *Adequate Consideration of Views of Federal Agencies.* The Secretary shall not approve the management program submitted by a state pursuant to section 306 [16 USCS Sec. 1455] unless the views of Federal agencies principally affected by such program have been adequately considered.

(c) *Consistency of Federal Activities with State Management Programs; Certification.*

(1) (A) Each Federal agency activity within or outside the coastal zone that affects any land or water use or natural resource of the coastal zone shall be carried out in a manner which is consistent to the maximum extent practicable with the enforceable policies of approved State management programs. A Federal agency activity shall be subject to this paragraph unless it is subject to paragraph (2) or (3).

(2) Any Federal agency which shall undertake any development project in the coastal zone of a state shall insure that the project is, to the maximum extent practicable, consistent with the enforceable policies of approved state management programs.

(3) (A) After final approval by the Secretary of a state's management program, any applicant for a required Federal license or permit to conduct an activity, in or outside of the coastal zone, affecting any land or water use or natural resource of the coastal zone of that state shall provide in the application to the licensing or permitting agency a certification that the proposed activity complies with the enforceable policies of the state's approved program and that such activity will be conducted in a manner consistent with the program.

(B) After the management program of any coastal state has been approved by the Secretary under section 306 [16 USCS Sec. 1455], any person who submits to the Secretary of the Interior any plan for the exploration or development of, or production from, any area which has been leased under the Outer Continental Shelf Lands Act (43 U.S.C. 1331 et seq.) and regulations under such Act shall, with respect to any exploration, development, or production described in such plan and affecting any land or water use or natural resource of the coastal zone of such state, attach to such plan a certification that each activity which is described in detail in such plan complies [with the enforceable policies of] such state's approved management program and will be carried out in a manner consistent with such program.

American Petroleum Institute v. Knecht, 456 F.Supp. 889 (C.D.Cal. 1978), affirmed, 609 F.2d 1306 (9th Cir. 1979)

MEMORANDUM OF DECISION AND ORDER

KELLEHER, DISTRICT JUDGE

Plaintiffs American Petroleum Institute, Western Oil and Gas Association, and certain oil company members of the aforesaid Institute and Association brought this action against three federal officials ("the federal defendants") in their official capacities as Secretary of Commerce, Administrator of the National Oceanic and Atmospheric Administration ("NOAA"), and Acting Associate Administrator of the Office of Coastal Zone Management ("OCZM"), seeking declaratory and injunctive relief against defendants' imminent grant of "final approval" of the California Coastal Zone Management Program ("CZMP") pursuant to Sec. 306 of the Coastal Zone Management Act of 1972 and seeking further relief in the nature of mandamus directing the federal defendants to grant "preliminary approval" to the CZMP pursuant to Sec. 301 (d) of the Act.

In brief, plaintiffs contend that the California Program cannot lawfully be approved by the federal defendants under Sec. 306 of the CZMA, principally for two reasons. First, the CZMP is not a "management program" within the meaning of Sec. 304(11) of the Act in that (a) it fails to satisfy the requirements of Secs. 305(b) and 306(c), (d), and (e), and regulations promulgated thereunder, as regards content specificity;...

. . .

For reasons set forth below, the Court affirms the federal defendants' Sec. 306 approval of the CZMP and grants judgment for defendants and against plaintiffs.

The Court has before it for determination both preliminary and for ultimate disposition questions of the highest importance, greatest complexity, and highest urgency. They arise as the result of high legislative purpose, low bureaucratic bungling, and present inherent difficulty in judicial determination. In other words, for the high purpose of improving and maintaining felicitous conditions in the coastal areas of the United States, the Congress has undertaken a legislative solution, the application of which is so complex as to make it almost wholly unmanageable. In the course of the legislative process, there obviously came into conflict many competing interests which, in typical fashion, the Congress sought to accommodate, only to create thereby a morass of problems between the private sector, the public sector, the federal bureaucracy, the state legislature, the state bureaucracy, and all of the administrative agencies appurtenant thereto. Because the action taken gives rise to claims public and private which must be adjudicated, this matter is now involved in the judicial process.

LEGISLATIVE HISTORY OF THE CZMA

A seemingly unbridgeable gulf between the parties concerning the proper construction of the CZMA establishes the cutting edge of this action. First, noted at the outset of this memorandum of decision, plaintiffs complain that the California Program fails to qualify for final approval under Sec. 306 because it lacks the requisite specificity Congress intended management programs to embody, especially with respect to the substantive requirements of Secs. 305(b) and 306(c), (d), and (e), so as to enable private users in the coastal zone subject to an approved program to be able to predict with reasonable certainty whether or not their proposed activities will be found to be "consistent" with the program under Sec. 307(c). Second, plaintiffs contend that a proper understanding of Sec. 306(c)(8), particularly in light of the 1976 Amendments, compels the conclusion that in requiring "adequate consideration" Congress intended that an approvable program affirmatively accommodate the national interest in planning for and siting energy facilities and that the CZMP fails to do so. The Court here addresses each of these contentions.

A. The Definition of "Management Program"

Any attempt to resolve this underlying dispute, out of which most of the issues in this lawsuit arise, must begin with Congress's definition of a "management program" in Sec. 304(11) of the Act:

The term "management program" includes, but is not limited to, a comprehensive statement in words, maps, illustrations, and other media of communication, prepared and adopted by the state in accordance with the provisions of this title, setting forth *objectives, policies and standards to guide* public and private uses of land and waters in the coastal zone. (emphasis added)

This definition is exactly as originally contained in the Senate version of the CZMA (S.3507). In its report on S.3507, the Committee on Commerce stated:

"Management program" is the term to refer to the *process* by which a coastal State . . . proposes . . . to manage land and water uses in the coastal zone so as to reduce or minimize a direct, significant, and adverse effect upon those waters, including the development of criteria and of the governmental structure capable of implementing such a program. In adopting the term "management program" the committee seeks to convey the importance of a *dynamic* quality to the planning undertaken in this Act that permits adjustments as more knowledge is gained, as new technology develops, and as social aspirations are more clearly defined. The Committee does not intend to provide for management programs that are static but rather to create a *mechanism for continuing review* of coastal zone programs on a regular basis and to provide a framework for the allocation of resources that are available to carry out these programs. S.Rep.No. 753, 92nd Cong., 2nd Sess. (1972), U.S. Code Cong. & Admin. News 1972, pp. 4776, 4784, reprinted in Senate Committee on Commerce, Legislative History of the CZMA 201–202 (Comm. Print 1976) ("Legislative History"). (emphasis added)

The House version (H.R. 14146) did not contain a definition of "management program" and the Conference Report (H. Rep. No. 921544, 92nd Cong., 2nd Sess. [1972] [Legislative History at 4431]) failed to add anything further to the above explanation.

The Court agrees with defendants that Congress never intended that to be approvable under Sec. 306, a management program must provide a "zoning map" which would inflexibly commit the state in advance of receiving specific proposals to permitting particular activities in a specific area. Nor did Congress intend by using the language of "objectives, policies, and standards" to require that such programs establish such detailed criteria that private users be able to rely on them as predictive devices for determining the fate of projects without interaction between the relevant state agencies and the user. To satisfy the definition in the Act, a program need only contain standards of suffi-

cient specificity "to guide public and private uses."

The CZMA was enacted primarily with a view to encouraging the coastal states to plan for the management, development, preservation, and restoration of their coastal zones by establishing rational processes by which to regulate uses therein. Although sensitive to balancing competing interests, it was first and foremost a statute directed to and solicitous of environmental concerns. See Secs. 302 and 303. "The key to more effective use of the coastal zone in the future is introduction of management systems permitting conscious and informed choices among the various alternatives. The aim of this legislation is to assist in this very critical goal." S. Rep. No. 753, U.S. Code Cong. & Admin. News 1972, p. 4781 (Legislative History at 198).

The Amendments of 1976 made clear the national interest in the planning for, and siting of, energy facilities (to be discussed *infra*). Apparently neither the Act nor the Amendments thereto altered the primary focus of the legislation: the need for a rational planning process to enable the state, not private users of the coastal zone, to be able to make "hard choices." "If those choices are to be rational and devised in such a way as to preserve future options, the program must be established to provide guidelines which will enable the selection of those choices." H. Rep. No. 1049 (Legislative History at 315). The 1976 Amendments do not require increased specificity with regard to the standards and objectives contained in a management program.

In conclusion, to the extent plaintiffs' more specific challenges to the Acting Administrator's Sec. 306 approval are premised on an interpretation of congressional intent to require that such programs include detailed criteria establishing a sufficiently high degree of predictability to enable a private user of the coastal zone to say with certainty that a given project must be deemed "consistent" therewith, the Court rejects plaintiffs' contention.

. . .

B. Adequate Consideration of the National Interest

Plaintiffs' fundamental grievance with the California Program stems from its assertion that the Program fails to satisfy the mandate of Sec. 306(c)(8) that before the Secretary grant approval to a management program under Sec. 306 she find that it provides for adequate consideration of the national interest involved in planning for, and in the siting of, facilities (including energy facilities in, or which significantly affect, such state's coastal zone) which are necessary to meet requirements which are other than local in nature.

Plaintiffs urge that the CZMA, particularly in light of the 1976 Amendments, requires an "affirmative commitment" on the part of the state before Sec. 306 approval is proper. The California Program allegedly fails adequately to make that commitment in that its general lack of specificity, coupled with what plaintiffs characterize as California's overall antipathy to energy development (as embodied in the policies and practices of its Coastal Commission), combine to give the Coastal Commission a "blank check" effectively to veto any or all exploration and development activities subject to Sec. 307(c)(3) simply by finding such activity not to be "consistent" with the CZMP.

Defendants, beyond taking issue with plaintiffs' characterization of California's energy posture, assert first, that plaintiffs' premise that the Act requires an affirmative commitment is incorrect as a matter of law and second, that the Program contains adequate consideration of national energy interests. Defendants contend that the CZMP contains "performance standards and criteria" more than adequate to satisfy the requirements of the CZMA and serve as a guide to plaintiffs in planning their activities in the coastal zone. Implicit in the various provisions of the Coastal Act (and in particular those in Secs. 30001.2 and 30260-64) and in Chapter 11 of the Program Description is a wholly adequate consideration of the national energy interest.

Plaintiffs apparently focus on language in H. Rep. No. 92-1049 (which accompanied H.R. 14146) to the effect that, "if the program as developed is to be approved and thereby enable the State to receive funds assistance under this title, the State *must take into account and must accommodate* its program to the specific requirements of various Federal laws which are applicable to its coastal zone." Legislative History at 321. The report continues:

To the extent that a State program does not recognize these overall national interests, as well as the specific national interest in the generation and distribution of electric energy . . . or is construed as conflicting with any applicable statute, the Secretary may not approve the State program until it is amended to recognize those Federal rights, powers, and interests. Id. at 322

It is to be noted that the reference in the House Report to the state's need to "accommodate" its program is to "the specific requirements of various (applicable) Federal laws." It is not a requirement that the state program expressly "accommodate" energy interests. In the program approval regulations published on January 9, 1975 (40 Fed. Reg. 1683), NOAA stated that, "A management program which integrates . . . the siting of facilities meeting requirements which are of greater than local concern into the determination of uses and areas of Statewide concern will meet the requirements of Section 306(c)(8)." (15 C.F.R. Sec. 923.15[a]) In subsection (b) NOAA amplified on the above requirement.

[T]he requirement should not be construed as compelling the States to propose a program which accommodates certain types of facilities, but to assure that such national concerns are included at an early state in the State's planning activities and that such facilities not be arbitrarily excluded or unreasonably restricted in the management program without good and sufficient reasons. . . . No separate national interest "test" need be applied and submitted other than evidence that the listed national interest facilities have been considered in a manner similar to all other uses, and that appropriate consultation with the Federal agencies listed has been conducted.

The Coastal Zone Management Act Amendments of 1976, Pub. L. 94-370 ("1976 Amendments"), while largely prompted by the 1973 Arab oil embargo and while expressly recognizing the national interest in the planning for and siting of energy facilities, nevertheless did not alter the requirement of "adequate consideration" in Sec. 306(c)(8) or make any changes in the degree of specificity required under the Act. Rather, recognizing that coastal states like California were currently burdened by the onshore impacts of Federal offshore (OCS) activities and likely to be burdened further by the plans for increased leases on the OCS, Congress sought to encourage or induct the affected states to step up their plans vis-à-vis such facilities.

The primary means chosen to accomplish this result was the Coastal Energy Impact Program ("CEIP") contained in new Sec. 308. . . . The Congress was particularly careful to circumscribe the role of the federal government in particular siting decisions. Thus, Sec. 308(i) provides: "The Secretary shall not intercede in any land use or water use decision of any coastal state with respect to the siting of any energy facility or public facility by making siting in a particular location a prerequisite to, or a condition of, financial assistance under this section."

This provision is consistent with the approach of the CZMA as a whole to leave the development of, and decisions under, a management program to the state, subject to the Act's more specific concern that the development and decision-making process occur in a context of cooperative interaction, coordination, and sharing of information among affected agencies, both local, state, regional, and federal. This last, especially as regards energy facility planning, is the policy behind the Energy Facility Planning Process ("EFPP") of Sec. 305(b)(8) and the Interstate Grants provision of new Sec. 309 (which encourages the coastal states to give high priority to coordinating coastal zone planning utilizing "interstate agreements or compacts"). It should be noted that the only amendment to the national interest requirement of Sec. 306(c)(8) effectuated by the 1976 Amendments is the additional requirement that in fulfilling its obligation to provide "adequate consideration of the national interest" in the case of energy facilities, the state also give such consideration "to any applicable interstate energy plan or program" established under Sec. 309.

The Court rejects plaintiffs' argument that affirmative accommodation of energy facilities was made a quid pro quo for approval under Sec. 306 by the 1976 Amendments. In addition to the above, the court notes that Congress itself did not assume that such siting was automatically to be deemed necessary in all instances. For instance, in its report on H.R. 3981, the committee on Merchant Marine and Fisheries stated that the addition of the EFPP in Sec. 305(b)(8)

reflects the Committee's finding that increasing involvement of coastal areas in providing energy for the nation is likely, as can be seen in the need to expand the Outer Continental Shelf petroleum development. State coastal zone programs should, therefore, specifically address how major energy facilities are to be located in the coastal zone if such siting is necessary. Second, the program shall include methods of handling the anticipated impacts of such facilities. The Committee in no way wishes to accelerate the location of energy facilities in the coasts; on the contrary, it feels a disproportionate share are there now. . . . There is no intent here whatever to involve the Secretary of Commerce in specific siting decisions.

The concern that the CEIP not encourage the siting in the coastal zone of energy facilities which could be located elsewhere is embodied in Sec. 308.

The Senate Committee on Commerce, in reporting S.586 to the full Senate, stated:

The Secretary of Commerce (through NOAA) should provide guidance and assistance to States under this section 305(b)(8), and under section 306, to enable them to know what constitutes "adequate consideration of the national interest" in the siting of facilities necessary to meet requirements other than local in nature. The committee wishes to emphasize, consistent with the overall intent of the Act, that this new paragraph (8) requires a State to develop, and maintain a planning process, but does not imply intercession in specific siting decisions. *The Secretary of Commerce (through NOAA), in determining whether a coastal State has met the requirements, is restricted to evaluating the adequacy of that process.* (emphasis added)

Consistent with this mandate, NOAA has promulgated revised program approval regulations (43 Fed. Reg. 8378, March 1, 1978). These interim final rules follow the submission of comments on the proposed rules published on August 29, 1977 (42 Fed. Reg. 43552). The Court looks to the revised regulations because they reflect NOAA's interpretation of any changes wrought by the 1976 Amendments, the former regulations against which the California Program was tested having been promulgated after the Arab oil embargo but before the 1976 Amendments.

In its response to several reviewers' suggestion that Sec. 306(c)(8) be interpreted to require that facilities be accommodated in a State's coastal zone, the agency reiterated the position it has maintained since the inception of the CZMA that

the purpose of "adequate consideration" is to achieve the act's "spirit of equitable balance between State and national interests." As such, consideration of facilities in which there may be a national interest must be undertaken within the context of the act's broader finding of a "national interest in the . . . beneficial use, protection, and development of the coastal zone" (Section 302[a]). Subsection 302(g) of the Act gives "high priority" to the protection of natural systems. Accordingly, while the primary focus of subsection 306(c)(8) is on the planning for and siting of facilities, adequate consideration of the national interest in these facilities must be based on a balancing of these

interests relative to the wise use, protection, and other development of the coastal zone. As the Department of Energy noted in its comments on the proposed regulations: "The Act presumes a balancing of the national interest in energy self-sufficiency with State and local concerns involving adverse economic, social, or environmental impacts." 43 Fed. Reg. 8379

Section 306(c)(8) is treated at length in 15 C.F.R. Sec. 923.52. After generally noting that one "need not conclude . . . that any and all such facilities proposed for the coastal zone need be sited therein," the regulation proceeds to set forth requirements which must be met by the management program in order to satisfy Sec. 306(c)(8).

The court notes further in this regard that the standards established by the Coastal Act for making energy facilities siting decisions, in the words of the Coastal Commission staff, "establish the general findings that must be made to authorize coastal dependent industrial facilities, liquefied natural gas terminals, oil and gas developments, refineries, petrochemical facilities and electric power plants." FEIS, Part II (Chapter 9) at 66. The key to the California approach, and one which the Acting Administrator and this Court find acceptable under the CZMA, is that the standards require that "findings" be made upon which specific siting decisions ensue. For instance, in dealing with the siting of oil tanker facilities, Sec. 30261(a) requires that

[t]anker facilities shall be designed to (1) minimize the total volume of oil spilled, (2) minimize the risk of collision from movement of other vessels, (3) have ready access to the most effective feasible containment and recovery equipment for oil spills, and (4) have onshore deballasting facilities to receive any fouled ballast water from tankers where operationally or legally required.

As can readily be seen from these provisions, whether a particular tanker facility siting proposal will be deemed "consistent" with these requirements of the California Program will turn on specific findings of a factual nature. The

California Program sensibly does not attempt to map out in advance precisely what type or size tanker facilities will be found to meet these requirements in particular areas of its almost one thousand-mile coastline. Rather, by its very nature, the coastal Act encourages plaintiffs with a particular facility in mind to address themselves to the standards set forth in the Coastal Act and to plan such a facility in cooperation and communication with the Coastal commission from the inception. This approach seems consonant with the overall approach of the CAMA itself.... To the extent plaintiffs seek not guidance with respect to the way in which coastal resources will be managed but instead a "zoning map" which would implicitly avoid the need to consult with the state regarding planned activities in or affecting its coastal zone, the Court rejects their position. While wholly sympathetic to the legitimate concerns of corporate officers and planners who must conform their activities to the standards of the CZMP, the Court nevertheless concludes that the Acting Administrator's finding that the Program satisfies 306(c)(8) is supportable and hence not arbitrary or capricious. It proceeds from a correct interpretation of the CZMA.

Finally, the court notes that both the California Program and the CZMA contain safeguards to protect plaintiffs from arbitrary exercise by the Coastal Commission of its Sec. 307 consistency powers. First, plaintiffs under the Coastal Act may seek judicial review of a decision of the Coastal Commission finding a specific proposed activity of plaintiffs to be inconsistent with the CZMP. Such review certainly may encompass a challenge to the Commission's interpretation of the California Program as well as a challenge to specific findings upon which the determination presumably would be based. Second, with respect to an adverse consistency determination regarding any proposed activity for which a federal license or permit is required or which involves an OCS plan, the party against whose activity such a determination has been made may seek review by the Secretary of

Commerce (who could also undertake review on her own initiative) on the grounds that "the activity is consistent with the objectives of this title or is otherwise necessary in the interest of national security." Sec. 307(c)(3)(A) and (B). Third, under Sec. 312(a) the Secretary is obliged to conduct "a continuing review of (1) the management programs of the coastal states and the performance of such states with respect to coastal zone management; and (2) the coastal energy impact program provided for under section 308." Subsection (b) provides: "The Secretary shall have the authority to terminate any financial assistance extended under section 306 ... if (1) (s)he determines that the state is failing to adhere to and is not justified in deviating from the program approved by the Secretary."

In short, both as regards specific determinations of inconsistency and as regards general trends in and manner of issuance of such determinations, plaintiffs are amply protected by and have various forms of recourse under the California Program itself and Secs. 307 and 312 of the CZMA.

[T]he length, complexity and convolutions of this memorandum and of the findings and conclusions set forth herein speak louder and much more eloquently than the words themselves. The message is as clear as it is repugnant: under our so-called federal system, Congress is constitutionally empowered to launch programs the scope, impact, consequences, and workability of which are largely unknown, at least to Congress, at the time of enactment; the federal bureaucracy is legally permitted to execute the congressional mandate with a high degree of befuddlement as long as it acts no more befuddled than Congress must reasonably have anticipated; if ultimate execution of the congressional mandate requires interaction between federal and state bureaucracy, the resultant maze is one of the prices required under the system.

The foregoing shall constitute the court's findings of fact and conclusions of law.

The administrative action is affirmed; the petition is denied, each side to bear its costs.

Questions

1. Although the court ruled in favor of the government, the judge expressed frustration with both the legislative and executive branches. What were his principal criticisms? Could the system have been designed more effectively?

2. The American Petroleum Institute feared that this new federal program would unduly restrict its members' operations. Has history shown that their fears were justified?

Secretary of the Interior v. California, 464 U.S. 312 (1984)

JUSTICE O'CONNOR delivered the opinion of the court.

This case arises out of the Department of the Interior's sale of oil and gas leases on the outer continental shelf off the coast of California. We must determine whether the sale is an activity "directly affecting" the coastal zone under section 307(c)(1) of the Coastal Zone Management Act (CZMA). That section provides in its entirety:

Each Federal agency conducting or supporting activities directly affecting the coastal zone shall conduct or support those activities in a manner which is, to the maximum extent practicable, consistent with approved state management programs. 16 U.S.C. section 1456(c)(1).

We conclude that the Secretary of the Interior's sale of outer continental shelf oil and gas leases is not an activity "directly affecting" the coastal zone within the meaning of the statute.

I.

CZMA defines the "coastal zone" to include state but not federal land near the shorelines of the several coastal states, as well as coastal waters extending "seaward to the outer limit of the United States territorial sea." 16 U.S.C. section 1453(1). The territorial sea for the states bordering on the Pacific or Atlantic oceans extends three geographical miles seaward from the coastline. Submerged lands subject to the jurisdiction of the United States that lie beyond the territorial sea constitute the "outer continental shelf" (OCS). By virtue of the Submerged Lands Act, passed in 1953, the coastal zone belongs to the states, while the OCS belongs to the federal government. 43 U.S.C. sections 1302, 1311.

CZMA was enacted in 1972 to encourage the prudent management and conservation of natural resources in the coastal zone. Congress found that the "increasing and competing demands upon the lands and waters of our coastal zone" had "resulted in the loss of living marine resources, wildlife, nutrient-rich areas, permanent and adverse changes to ecological systems, decreasing open spaces for public use, and shoreline erosion." 16 U.S.C. section 1451(c). Accordingly, Congress declared a national policy to protect the coastal zone, to encourage the states to develop coastal zone management programs, to promote cooperation between federal and state agencies engaged in programs affecting the coastal zone, and to encourage broad participation in the development of coastal zone management programs. 16 U.S.C. section 1452.

Through a system of grants and other incentives, CZMA encourages each coastal state to develop a coastal management plan. Further grants and other benefits are made available to a coastal state after its management plan receives federal approval from the Secretary of Commerce. To obtain such approval a state plan must adequately consider the "national interest" and "the view of the Federal agencies principally affected by such program." 16 U.S.C. sections 1455(c)(8), 1456(b).

Once a state plan has been approved, CZMA section 307(c)(1) requires federal activities "conducting or supporting activities directly affecting the coastal zone" to be "consistent" with the state plan "to the maximum extent practicable." 16 U.S.C. section 1456(c)(1). The Commerce Department has promulgated regulations implementing that provision. Those regulations require federal agencies to prepare a "consistency determination" document in support of any activity that will "directly affect" the coastal zone of a state with an approved management plan. The document must identify the "direct effects" of the activity and inform state agencies how the activity has been tailored to achieve consistency with the state program. 15 CFR section 930.34, .39 (1983).

II.

OCS lease sales are conducted by the Department of the Interior (Interior). Oil and gas companies submit bids and the high bidders receive priority in the eventual exploration and development of oil and gas resources situated in the submerged lands on the OCS. A lessee does not, however, acquire an immediate or absolute right to explore for, develop, or produce oil or gas on the OCS; those activities require separate, subsequent federal authorization.

In 1977, the Department of Commerce approved the California Coastal Management Plan. The same year, Interior began preparing Lease Sale No. 53—a sale of OCS leases off the California coast near Santa Barbara. Interior first asked several state and federal agencies to report on potential oil and gas resources in this area. The Agency then requested bidders, federal and state agencies, environmental organizations, and the public to identify which of 2,036 tracts in the area should be offered for lease. In October 1978, Interior announced the tentative selection of 243 tracts, including 115 tracts situated in the Santa Maria Basin located off western Santa Barbara. Various meetings were then held with state agencies. Consultations with other federal agencies were also initiated. Interior issued a Draft Environmental Impact Statement in April 1980.

On July 8, 1980, the California Coastal Commission informed Interior that it had determined Lease Sale No. 53 to be an activity "directly affecting" the California coastal zone. The state commission therefore demanded a consistency determination—a showing by In-

terior that the lease sale would be "consistent" to the "maximum extent practicable" with the state coastal zone management program. Interior responded that the Lease Sale would not "directly affect" the California coastal zone. Nevertheless, Interior decided to remove 128 tracts, located in four northern basins, from the proposed lease sale, leaving only the 115 tracts in the Santa Maria Basin. In September 1980, Interior issued a final Environmental Impact Statement. On October 27, 1980, it published a proposed notice of sale, limiting bidding to the remaining 115 blocks in the Santa Maria Basin. 45 Fed. Reg. 71140 (1980).

On December 16, 1980, the state commission reiterated its view that the sale of the remaining tracts in the Santa Maria Basin "directly affected" the California coastal zone. The commission expressed its concern that oil spills on the OCS could threaten the southern sea otter, whose range was within twelve miles of the thirty-one challenged tracts. The commission explained that it "has been consistent in objecting to proposed offshore oil development within specific buffer zones around special sensitive marine mammal and seabird breeding areas." App. 77. The commission concluded that thirty-one more tracts should be removed from the sale because "leasing within twelve miles of the sea otter range in Santa Maria Basin would not be consistent" with the California Coastal Management Program. California Governor Brown later took a similar position, urging that thirty-four more tracts be removed.

Interior rejected the State's demands. In the Secretary's view, no consistency review was required because the lease sale did not engage CZMA section 307(c)(1), and the Governor's request was not binding because it failed to strike a reasonable balance between the national and local interests. On April 10, 1981, Interior announced that the lease sale of the 115 tracts would go forward, and on April 27 issued a final notice of sale.

Respondents filed two substantially similar suits in federal district court to enjoin the sale of twenty-nine tracts situated within twelve miles of the sea otter range. Both complaints alleged, inter alia, Interior's violation of section 307(c)(1) of CZMA. They argued that leasing sets in motion a chain of events that culminates in oil and gas development, and that leasing therefore "directly affects" the coastal zone within the meaning of section 307(c)(1).

The district court entered a summary judgment for respondents on the CZMA claim. The Court of Appeals for the Ninth Circuit affirmed that portion of the district court judgment that required a consistency determination before the sale. We granted certiorari, and we now reverse.

III.

Whether the sale of leases on the OCS is an activity "directly affecting" the coastal zone is not self-evident. As already noted, OCS leases involve submerged lands outside the coastal zone, and as we shall discuss, an OCS lease authorizes the holder to engage only in preliminary exploration; further administrative approval is required before full exploration or development may begin. Both sides concede that the preliminary exploration itself has no significant effect on the coastal zone. Both also agree that a lease sale is one in a series of decisions that may culminate in activities directly affecting that zone.

A.

We are urged to focus first on the plain language of section 307(c)(1). Interior contends that "directly affecting" means "having a direct, identifiable impact on the coastal zone." Respondents insist that the phrase means "initiating a series of events of coastal management consequences." But CZMA nowhere defines or explains which federal activities should be viewed as "directly affecting" the coastal zone, and the alternative verbal formulations proposed by the parties, both of which are superficially plausible, find no support in the Act itself.

We turn therefore to the legislative history. A fairly detailed review is necessary, but that review persuades us that Congress did not intend OCS lease sales to fall within the ambit of CZMA Sec. 307(c)(1).

In the CZMA bills first passed by the House and Senate, Sec. 307(c)(1)'s consistency requirements extended only to federal activities "in" the coastal zone. The "directly affecting" standard appeared nowhere in Sec. 307(c)(1)'s immediate antecedents. It was the House-Senate Conference committee that replaced "in the coastal zone" with "directly affecting the coastal zone." Both chambers then passed the conference bill without discussing or even mentioning the change.

At first sight, the conference's adoption of "directly affecting" appears to be a surprising, unexplained, and subsequently unnoticed expansion in the scope of Sec. 307(c)(1), going beyond what was required by either of the versions of Sec. 307(c)(1) sent to conference. But a much more plausible explanation for the change is available.

The explanation lies in the two different definitions of the "coastal zone." The bill the Senate sent to the Conference defined the coastal zone to exclude "lands the use of which is by law subject solely to the discretion of or which is held in trust by the Federal Government, its officers, or agents." This exclusion would reach federal parks, military installations, Indian reservations, and other federal lands that would lie within the coastal zone but for the fact of federal ownership. Under the Senate bill, activities on these lands would thus have been entirely exempt from compliance with state management plans. By contrast, the House bill's definition of "coastal zone" included lands under federal jurisdiction; thus federal activities on those lands were to be fully subject to section 307(c)(1)'s consistency requirement. Under both bills, however, submerged lands on the OCS were entirely excluded from the coastal zone, and federal agency activities in those areas thus exempt from section 307(c)(1)'s consistency requirement.

Against this background, the Conference Committee's change in section 307(c)(1) has all the markings of a simple compromise. The Conference accepted the Senate's narrower definition of the "coastal zone," but then expanded section 307(c)(1) to cover activities on federal lands not "in" but nevertheless "directly affecting" the zone. By all appearances, the intent was to reach at least some activities conducted in those federal enclaves excluded from the Senate's definition of the "coastal zone."

Though cryptic, the Conference Report's reference to the change in section 307(c)(1) fully supports this explanation. "The Conferees . . . adopted the Senate language . . . which made it clear that Federal lands are not included within a state's coastal zone. *As to the use of such lands which would affect a state's coastal zone, the provisions of section 307(c) would apply*" (emphasis added). In the entire Conference report, this is the only mention of the definition of the coastal zone chosen by the Conference, and the only hint of an explanation for the change in section 307(c)(1). The "directly affecting" language was not deemed worthy of note by any member of Congress in the subsequent floor debates. The implication seems clear: "directly affecting" was used to strike a balance between two definitions of the "coastal zone." The legislative history thus strongly suggests that OCS leasing, covered by neither the House nor the Senate version of section 307(c)(1), was also intended to be outside the coverage of the Conference's compromise.

Nonetheless, the internal language of section 307(c)(1), read without reference to its history, is sufficiently imprecise to leave open the possibility that some types of federal activities conducted on the OCS could fall within section 307(c)(1)'s ambit. We need not, however, decide whether any OCS activities other than oil and gas leasing might be covered by section 307(c)(1), because further investigation reveals that in any event Congress expressly intended

to remove the control of OCS resources from CZMA's scope.

B.

If section 307(c)(1) and its history standing alone are less than crystalline, the history of other sections of the original CZMA bills impel a narrow reading of that clause. Every time it faced the issue in the CZMA debates, Congress deliberately and systematically insisted that no part of CZMA was to reach beyond the three-mile territorial limit.

There are, first, repeated statements in the House and Senate floor debates that CZMA is concerned only with activities on land or in the territorial sea, not on the outer continental shelf, and that the allocation of state and federal jurisdiction over the coastal zone and the OCS was not to be changed in any way. But Congress took more substantial and significant action as well. Congress debated and firmly rejected at least four proposals to extend parts of CZMA to reach OCS activities.

Section 313 of the House CZMA bill, as reported by committee and passed by the House, embodies the most specific of these proposals. That section would have achieved explicitly what respondents now contend section 307(c)(1) achieves implicitly. It provided:

The Secretary shall develop . . . a program for the management of the area outside the coastal zone and within twelve miles of the [coast]. . . .

To the extent that any part of the management program . . . shall apply to any high seas area, the subjacent seabed and subsoil of which lies within the seaward boundary of a coastal state, . . . the program shall be coordinated with the state involved. . . .

The Secretary shall, to the maximum extent practicable, apply the program . . . to waters which are adjacent to specific areas in the coastal zone which have been designated by the states for the purpose of preserving or restoring such areas for their conservation, recreational, ecological, or esthetic values.

Congressman Anderson of California, the drafter of this section and coauthor of the House CZMA bill, explained the section's purpose on the floor of the House. In light of the instant litigation, his comments were remarkably prescient. By 1972, Congressman Anderson pointed out, California had established seven marine sanctuaries, including one located near Santa Barbara, California, in the area allegedly threatened by the leases here in dispute.

These State-established sanctuaries, which extend from the coastline seaward to three miles, account for nearly a fourth of the entire California coast.

However, the Federal Government has jurisdiction outside the State area, from three miles to twelve miles at sea. All too often, the Federal Government has allowed development and drilling to the detriment of the State program.

A case in point is Santa Barbara where California established a marine sanctuary banning the drilling of oil in the area under State authority.

Yet, outside the sanctuary—in the federally controlled area—the Federal Government authorized drilling which resulted in the January 1969 blowout. This dramatically illustrated the point that oil spills do not respect legal jurisdictional lines.

House section 313, Congressman Anderson went on to explain, would play the crucial role of encouraging federal OCS oil and gas leasing to be conducted in a manner consistent with state management programs.

Since House section 313 would have provided respondents with precisely the protection they now seek here, it is significant that the Conference Committee, and ultimately Congress as a whole, flatly rejected the provision. And the reason for the rejection, as explained in the Conference Report, was to forestall conflicts of the type before us now. "The Conferees . . . excluded [House section 313] authorizing a Federal management program for the contiguous zone of the United States, because the provisions relating thereto did not prescribe sufficient standards or criteria *and would create potential conflicts with legislation already in existence concerning Continental Shelf resources*" (emphasis added).

The House bill included another similar provision that would have been almost equally fa-

vorable to respondents here—had it not been rejected by the Conference and subsequently by Congress as a whole. Section 312(b), (c), of the House bill invited the Secretary of Commerce to extend coastal zone marine sanctuaries established by the states into the OCS region. But the Conference Committee rejected House section 312 as well. The Conference Report explained: "The Conferees agreed to delete the provisions of the House version relating to extension of estuarine sanctuaries, in view of the fact that the need for such provisions appears to be rather remote and could cause problems since they would extend beyond the territorial limits of the United States."

When the Conference bill returned to the House, with House sections 312 and 313 deleted, Congressman Anderson expressed his dismay.

I am deeply disappointed that the Senate conferees would not accept the position of the House of Representatives regarding the extension of State-established marine sanctuaries to areas under Federal jurisdiction.

. . . [W]e were successful, in committee, in adding a provision which I authored designed to protect State-established sanctuaries, such as exist off Santa Barbara, Calif., from federally authorized development.

This provision would have required the Secretary to apply the coastal zone program to waters immediately adjacent to the coastal waters of a State, which that State has designated for specific preservation purposes.

It was accepted overwhelmingly by the House of Representatives despite the efforts of the oil and petroleum industry to defeat it.

But what they failed to accomplish in the House, they accomplished in the conference committee. . . .

In light of these comments by Congressman Anderson, and the express statement in the Conference report that House section 313 was removed to avoid "conflicts with legislation already in existence concerning Continental Shelf resources," it is fanciful to suggest that the conferees intended the "directly affecting" language of section 307(c)(1) to substitute for the House section 313's specific and considerably more detailed language. Certainly the author of House section 313 recognized that the amended section 307(c)(1) could not serve that purpose.

Two similar attempts to extend CZMA's reach beyond the coastal zone were made in the Senate. These, as well, were firmly rejected on the Senate floor or in Conference.

C.

To recapitulate, the "directly affecting" language in section 307(c)(1) was, by all appearances, only a modest compromise, designed to offset in part the narrower definition of the coastal zone favored by the Senate and adopted by the Conference Committee. Section 307(c)(1)'s "directly affecting" language was aimed at activities conducted or supported by federal agencies on federal lands physically situated in the coastal zone but excluded from the zone as formally defined by the Act. Consistent with this view, the same Conference Committee that wrote the "directly affecting" language rejected two provisions in the House bill that would have required precisely what respondents seek here—coordination of federally sponsored OCS activities with state coastal management and conservation programs. In light of the Conference Committee's further, systematic rejection of every other attempt to extend the reach of CZMA to the OCS, we are impelled to conclude that the 1972 Congress did not intend section 307(c)(1) to reach OCS lease sales.

IV.

A broader reading of section 307(c)(1) is not compelled by the thrust of other CZMA provisions. First, it is clear beyond peradventure that Congress believed that CZMA's purposes could be adequately effectuated without reaching federal activities conducted outside the coastal zone. Both the Senate and House bills were originally drafted, debated, and passed, with

section 307(c)(1) expressly limited to federal activities in the coastal zone. Broad arguments about CZMA's structure, the Act's incentives for the development of state management programs, and the Act's general aspirations for state-federal cooperation thus cannot support the expansive reading of section 307(c)(1) urged by respondents.

Moreover, a careful examination of the structure of CZMA section 307 suggests that lease sales are a type of federal agency activity not intended to be covered by section 307(c)(1) at all.

Section 307(c) contains three coordinated parts. Paragraph (1) refers to activities "conduct[ed] or support[ed]" by a federal agency. Paragraph (2) covers "development projects undertake[n]" by a federal agency. Paragraph (3) deals with activities by private parties authorized by a federal agency's issuance of licenses and permits. The first two paragraphs thus reach activities in which the federal agency is itself the principal actor, the third reaches the federally approved activities of third parties. Plainly, Interior's OCS lease sales fall in the third category. Section 307(c)(1) should therefore be irrelevant to OCS lease sales, if only because drilling for oil or gas on the OCS is neither "conduct[ed]" nor "support[ed]" by a federal agency. Section 307(c)(3), not section 307(c)(1), is the more pertinent provision. Respondents' suggestion that the consistency review requirement of section 307(c)(3) is focused only on the private applicants for permits or licenses, not federal agencies, is squarely contradicted by abundant legislative history and the language of section 307(c)(3) itself.

CZMA section 307(c)(3) definitely does not require consistency review of OCS lease sales. As enacted in 1972, that section addressed the requirements to be imposed on federal licensees whose activities might affect the coastal zone. A federal agency may not issue a "license or permit" for any activity "affecting land or water uses in the coastal zone" without ascertaining that the activity is consistent with the state program or otherwise in the national interest. Each affected state with an approved management program must concur in the issuance of the license or permit; a state's refusal to do so may be overridden only if the Secretary of Commerce finds that the proposed activity is consistent with CZMA's objectives or otherwise in the interest of national security. Significantly, section 307(c)(3) contained no mention of consistency requirements in connection with the sale of a lease.

In 1976, Congress expressly addressed—and preserved—that omission. Specific House and Senate committee proposals to add the word "lease" to section 307(c)(3) were rejected by the House and ultimately by Congress as a whole. It is surely not for us to add to that statute what Congress twice decided to omit.

Instead of inserting the word "lease" in section 307(c)(3), the House-Senate Conference Committee renumbered the existing section 307(c)(3) as section 307(c)(3)(A), and added a second paragraph, section 307(c)(3)(B). Respondents apparently concede that of these two subparagraphs, only the latter is now relevant to oil and gas activities on the OCS. The new paragraph section 307(c)(3)(B), however, provides only that applicants for federal licenses or permits to explore, produce, or develop oil or gas on the OCS must first certify consistency with affected state plans. Again, there is no suggestion that a lease sale by Interior requires any review of consistency with state management plans.

A.

If the distinction between a sale of a "lease" and the issuance of a permit to "explore," "produce," or "develop" oil or gas seems excessively fine, it is a distinction that Congress has codified with great care. CZMA section 307(c)(3)(B) expressly refers to the Outer Continental Shelf Lands Act of 1953, 43 U.S.C. section 1331 et seq., (OCSLA), so it is appropriate to turn to that Act for a clarification of the differences between a lease sale and the approval of a plan for "exploration," "development," or "production."

OCSLA was enacted in 1953 to authorize federal leasing of the OCS for oil and gas development. The Act was amended in 1978 to provide for the "expeditious and orderly development, subject to environmental safeguards," of resources on the OCS. As amended, OCSLA confirms that at least since 1978 the sale of a lease has been a distinct stage of the OCS administrative process, carefully separated from the issuance of a federal license or permit to explore, develop, or produce gas or oil on the OCS.

Before 1978, OCSLA did not define the terms "exploration," "development," or "production." But it did define a "mineral lease" to be "any form of authorization for the exploration for, or development or removal of deposits of, oil, gas, or other minerals. . . ." The pre-1978 OCSLA did not specify what, if any, rights to explore, develop, or produce were transferred to the purchaser of a lease; the Act simply stated that a lease should "contain such rental provisions and such other terms and provisions as the Secretary may prescribe at the time of offering the area for lease." Thus before 1978 the sale by Interior of an OCS lease might well have engaged CZMA section 307(c)(3)(B) by including express or implied federal approval of a "plan for the exploration or development of, or production from" the leased tract.

The leases in dispute here, however, were sold in 1981. By then it was clear that a lease sale by Interior did not involve the submission or approval of "any plan for the exploration or development of, or production from" the leased tract. Under the amended OCSLA, the purchase of a lease entitled the purchaser only to priority over other interested parties in submitting for federal approval a plan for exploration, production, or development. Actual submission and approval or disapproval of such plans occurs separately and later.

Since 1978 there have been four distinct statutory stages to developing an offshore oil well:

(1) formulation of a five-year leasing plan by the Department of the Interior; (2) lease sales; (3) exploration by the lessees; (4) development and production. Each stage involves separate regulatory review that may, but need not, conclude in the transfer to lease purchasers of rights to conduct additional activities on the OCS. And each stage includes specific requirements for consultation with Congress, between federal agencies, or with the States. Formal review of consistency with state coastal management plans is expressly reserved for the last two stages.

(1) *Preparation of a leasing program.* The first stage of OCS planning is the creation of a leasing program. Interior is required to prepare a five-year schedule of proposed OCS lease sales. During the preparation of that program Interior must solicit comments from interested federal agencies and the governors of affected states, and must respond in writing to all comments or requests received from the state governors. The governor of any affected state is given a formal opportunity to submit recommendations regarding the "size, timing, or location" of a proposed lease sale. Interior is required to accept these recommendations if it determines they strike a reasonable balance between the national interest and the well-being of the citizens of the affected state. Local governments are also permitted to submit recommendations, and the Secretary "may" accept these. The proposed leasing program is then submitted to the President and Congress, together with comments received by the Secretary from the governor of the affected state.

Plainly, prospective lease purchasers acquire no rights to explore, produce, or develop at this first stage of OCSLA planning, and consistency review provisions of CZMA section 307(c)(3)(B) are therefore not engaged. There is also no suggestion that CZMA section 307(c)(1) consistency requirements operate here, though we note that preparation and submission to Congress of the leasing program could readily be characterized as "initiating a series of events of coastal management consequence."

(2) *Lease sales.* The second stage of OCS planning—the stage in dispute here—involves the solicitation of bids and the issuance of offshore leases. Requirements of the National Environmental Protection Act and the Endangered Species Act must be met first. The Secretary may then proceed with the actual lease sale. Lease purchasers acquire the right to conduct only limited "preliminary" activities on the OCS—geophysical and other surveys that do not involve seabed penetrations greater than three hundred feet and that do not result in any significant environmental impacts.

Again, there is no suggestion that these activities in themselves "directly affect" the coastal zone. But by purchasing a lease, lessees acquire no right to do anything more. Under the plain language of OCSLA, the purchase of a lease entails no right to proceed with full exploration, development, or production that might trigger CZMA section 307(c)(3)(B); the lessee acquires only a priority in submitting plans to conduct those activities. If these plans, when ultimately submitted, are disapproved, no further exploration or development is permitted.

(3) *Exploration.* The third stage of OCS planning involves review of more extensive exploration plans submitted to Interior by lessees. Exploration may not proceed until an exploration plan has been approved. A lessee's plan must include a certification that the proposed activities comply with any applicable state management program developed under CZMA.

There is, of course, no question that CZMA consistency review requirements operate here. CZMA section 307(c)(3)(B) expressly applies, and as noted, OCSLA itself refers to the applicable CZMA provision.

(4) *Development and production.* The fourth and final stage is development and production. The lessee must submit another plan to Interior. The Secretary must forward the plan to the governor of any affected state and, on request, to the local governments of affected states, for

comment and review. Again, the governor's recommendations must be accepted, and the local governments' may be accepted, if they strike a reasonable balance between local and national interests. Reasons for accepting or rejecting a governor's recommendations must be communicated in writing to the governor. In addition, the development and production plan must be consistent with the applicable state coastal management program. The State can veto the plan as "inconsistent," and the veto can be overridden only by the Secretary of Commerce. A plan may also be disapproved if it would "probably cause serious harm or damage . . . to the marine, coastal, or human environments." If a plan is disapproved for the latter reason, the lease may again be cancelled and the lessee is entitled to compensation.

Once again, the applicability of CZMA to this fourth stage of OCS planning is not in doubt. CZMA section 307(c)(3)(B) applies by its own terms, and is also expressly invoked by OCSLA.

Congress has thus taken pains to separate the various federal decisions involved in formulating a leasing program, conducting lease sales, authorizing exploration, and allowing development and production. Since 1978, the purchase of an OCS lease, standing alone, entails no right to explore, develop, or produce oil and gas resources on the OCS. The first two stages are not subject to consistency review; instead, input from State governors and local governments is solicited by the Secretary of the Interior. The last two stages invite further input for governors or local governments, but also require formal consistency review. States with approved CZMA plans retain considerable authority to veto inconsistent exploration or development and production plans put forward in those latter stages. The stated reason for this four-part division was to forestall premature litigation regarding adverse environmental effects that all agree will flow, if at all, only from the latter stages of OCS exploration and production.

Having examined the coordinated provisions

of CZMA section 307(c)(3) and OCSLA we return to CZMA section 307(c)(1).

As we have noted, the logical paragraph to examine in connection with a lease sale is not 307(c)(1), but 307(c)(3). Nevertheless, even if OCS lease sales are viewed as involving an OCS activity "conduct[ed]" or "support[ed]" by a federal agency, lease sales can no longer aptly be characterized as "directly affecting" the coastal zone. Since 1978 the sale of a lease grants the lessee the right to conduct only very limited, "preliminary activities" on the OCS. It does not authorize full-scale exploration, development, or production. Those activities may not begin until separate federal approval has been obtained, and approval may be denied on several grounds. If approval is denied, the lease may then be cancelled, with or without the payment of compensation to the lessee. In these circumstances, the possible effects on the coastal zone that may eventually result from the sale of a lease cannot be termed "direct."

It is argued, nonetheless, that a lease sale is a crucial step. Large sums of money change hands, and the sale may therefore generate momentum that makes eventual exploration, development, and production inevitable. On the other side, it is argued that consistency review at the lease sale stage is at best inefficient, and at worst impossible: leases are sold before it is certain if, where, or how exploration will actually occur.

The choice between these two policy arguments is not ours to make; it has already been made by Congress. In the 1978 OCSLA amendments Congress decided that the better course is to postpone consistency review until the two later stages of OCS planning, and to rely on less formal input from State governors and local governments in the two earlier ones. It is not for us to negate the lengthy, detailed, and coordinated provisions of CZMA section 307(c)(3)(B), and OCSLA sections 1344–46 and 1351, by a superficially plausible but ultimately unsupportable construction of two words in CZMA section 307(c)(1).

V.

Collaboration among state and federal agencies is certainly preferable to confrontation in or out of the courts. In view of the substantial consistency requirements imposed at the exploration, development, and production stages of OCS planning, the Department of the Interior, as well as private bidders on OCS leases, might be well advised to ensure in advance that anticipated OCS operations can be conducted harmoniously with state coastal management programs. But our review of the history of CZMA section 307(c)(1), and the coordinated structures of the amended CZMA and OCSLA, persuades us that Congress did not intend section 307(c)(1) to mandate consistency review at the lease sale stage.

Accordingly, the decision of the Court of Appeals for the Ninth Circuit is reversed insofar as it requires petitioners to conduct consistency review pursuant to CZMA section 307(c)(1) before proceeding with Lease Sale No. 53.

It is so ordered.

JUSTICE STEVENS, with whom JUSTICE BRENNAN, JUSTICE MARSHALL, and JUSTICE BLACKMUN join, dissenting.

In this case, the State of California is attempting to enforce a federal statutory right. Its coastal zone management program was approved by the Federal Government pursuant to a statute enacted in 1972. In section 307(c)(1) of that statute, the Coastal Zone Management Act (CZMA), the Federal Government made a promise to California: "Each Federal agency conducting or supporting activities directly affecting the coastal zone shall conduct or support those activities in a manner which is, to the maximum extent practicable, consistent with approved state management programs."

The question in this case is whether the Secretary of the Interior was conducting an activity directly affecting the California Coastal Zone when he sold oil and gas leases in the Pacific Ocean and area immediately adjacent to that zone. One would think that this question could be easily answered simply by reference to a question of fact—does this sale of leases directly affect the coastal zone? The District Court made a finding that it did, which the Court of Appeals affirmed, and which is not disturbed by the Court. Based on a straightforward reading of the statute, one would think that that would be the end of the case.

The Court reaches a contrary conclusion, however, based on either or both of these two theories: (1) section 307(c)(1) only applies to federal activities that take place within the coastal zone itself or in a federal enclave within the zone—it is wholly inapplicable to federal activities on the outer continental shelf no matter how seriously they may affect the coastal zone; (2) even if the sale of oil leases by the Secretary of the Interior would have been covered by section 307(c)(1) when the CZMA was enacted in 1972, amendments to an entirely different statute adopted in 1978 mean that the leases cannot directly affect the coastal zone notwithstanding the fact that those amendments merely imposed additional obligations on private lessees and did not purport to cut back on any obligation previously imposed on federal agencies.

The Court's first theory is refuted by the plain language of the 1972 Act, its legislative history, the basic purpose of the Act, and the findings of the District Court. The Court's second theory, which looks at post-1972 legislative developments, is simply overwhelmed by a series of unambiguous legislative pronouncements that consistently belie the Court's interpretation of the intent of Congress.

I.

Because there is so much material refuting the Court's reading of the 1972 Act, an index of what is to follow may be useful. I shall first note that the plain language of section 307(c)(1) draws no distinction between activities that take place outside the coastal zone and those that occur within the zone; it is the effect of the activities rather than their location that is relevant. I shall then review the legislative history which demonstrates that the words "directly affecting" were included in the section to make sure that the statute covered activities occurring outside the coastal zone if they are the functional equivalent of activities occurring within the zone. I shall then identify some of the statutory provisions indicating that Congress intended to require long-range, advance planning. I shall conclude part I with a description of the findings that bring this case squarely within the congressional purpose.

Plain Language

In statutory construction cases, the Court generally begins its analysis by noting that "[t]he starting point in every case involving construction of a statute is the language itself." Not much is said, however, about the plain language of section 307(c)(1) in the opinion of the Court, and no wonder. The words "activities directly affecting the coastal zone" make it clear that section 307(c)(1) applies to activities that take place outside the zone itself as well as to activities conducted within the zone. There are federal enclaves inside the boundaries of the coastal zone that, as a matter of statutory definition, are excluded from the zone itself. Moreover, the ocean areas on the outer continental shelf (OCS) that are adjacent to, and seaward of, the coastal zone are subject to the exclusive jurisdiction of the Federal Government. Quite plainly, the federal activities that may directly affect the coastal zone can be conducted in the zone itself, in a federal enclave, or in an adjacent federal area. The plain meaning of the words thus indicates that the words "directly affecting" were intended to enlarge the coverage of section 307(c)(1) to encompass activities conducted outside as well as inside the zone. In light of this language it is hard to see how the court can hold, as it does, that federal activities in the OCS can never fall within the statute because they are outside the outer boundaries of the coastal zone.

Legislative History

The plain meaning of the Act is confirmed by its legislative history. Both the House and Senate versions of the CZMA originally applied only to federal agencies conducting "activities in the coastal zone." At the same time, Congress clearly recognized that the most fundamental purpose of the CZMA was "to preserve, protect, develop, and where possible, to restore or enhance, the resources of the Nation's coastal zone for this and succeeding generations." In writing the versions of the CZMA that went to conference, both Houses stated that their purpose was to prevent adverse effects on the coastal zone. Yet it plainly would have been impossible to achieve this purpose without considering activities outside of the zone which nevertheless could have a devastating impact on it—activities such as those that led to the 1969 Santa Barbara, California, oil spill, which occurred in the OCS but which had a devastating impact on the adjacent California coast. When the conferees adopted the definition of "coastal zone" that excluded federal enclaves, they recognized the need to expand the description of federal activities that should be conducted in a manner that is consistent with an approved state program. The substitution of the words "directly affecting" for the word "in" accomplished this purpose. Thus, if an activity outside the zone has the same kind of effect on the zone as if it had been conducted in the zone, it is covered by section 307(c)(1).

The House version of the CZMA clearly recognized that activities outside the coastal zone could have a critical impact upon the coastal zone, and therefore had to be covered by management plans. It defined the coastal zone to extend inland to areas which could have an impact on it, in order to enable the CZMA to achieve "its underlying purpose, that is the management of and the protection of the coastal waters. It would not be possible to accomplish that purpose without to some degree extending the coverage to the shore lands which have an impact on those waters." The House bill did not extend the zone seaward because it instead required the Secretary of Commerce to develop a management program for activities on the OCS that was consistent with the management program of the adjacent State. Section 313 was thus specifically premised on the recognition that federal activities in the OCS, particularly the sale of oil and gas leases, could have a direct impact on the coastal zone. The House further recognized the need to regulate federal OCS activities to protect the coastal zone in section 312 of its bill, which provided for the expansion of coastal zone marine sanctuaries established by state management plans into the OCS, in order to fully protect the coastal zone. The House showed its concern about the impact of federal activities in the OCS on the coastal zone by rejecting an amendment to section 312 which would have made it permissive rather than mandatory for the Federal Government to establish sanctuaries in areas adjacent to state sanctuaries, and another amendment that would have deleted section 312 altogether. Thus it is plainly evident that the House did wish to protect the integrity of state coastal zone management with respect to federal activities in the OCS.

The Senate shared the House's concern that State management plans must apply to federal activities in areas adjacent to the coastal zone. The Senate Report on its version of the CZMA stated that its version was derived from a bill it had reported favorably during the previous year, S. 582. In particular, the 1971 Senate version of the CZMA used exactly the same language in framing the consistency obligation as did the 1972 version. The report on the 1971 bill construed this language to extend the consistency obligation to federal activities in waters outside of the coastal zone which functionally interact with the zone:

[A]ny lands or waters under Federal jurisdiction and control, where the administering Federal agency determines them to have a functional interrelationship from an economic, social, or geographic standpoint with lands and waters within the territorial sea, should be administered consistent with approved State management programs except in cases of overriding national interest as determined by the President.

Since the 1972 Senate CZMA used identical language to describe the consistency requirement, and nothing in the 1972 Senate report indicates that this language should be construed differently than the 1971 language, it follows that the 1972 Senate version placed a consistency obligation upon federal activities in the OCS which affects the coastal zone.

Thus, the Court is simply wrong to say that both versions of the CZMA sent to conference displayed no interest in regulating federal activities occurring outside of the exterior boundaries of the coastal zone. The conferees' adoption of the "directly affecting" language merely clarified the scope of the consistency obligation. The House surrendered the requirements that the Federal Government develop its own management plan for OCS activities and that federal lands within the coastal zone be included in the zone, but in return ensured that any federal activities "directly affecting" the coastal zone would be subject to the consistency requirement of section 307(c)(1). The only explanations of this compromise to be found in the legislative history can be briefly set out. The conferees wrote:

[A]s to federal agencies involved in any activities directly affecting the state coastal zone and any Federal participation in development projects in the coastal zone, *the Federal agencies must make certain that their activities are to the maximum extent practicable consistent with approved state management programs.* (emphasis added)

Senator Hollings, the floor manager of the CZMA, said when he presented the conference report to the Senate: "The bill provides States with national policy goals to control those land uses which have a direct and significant impact on coastal waters." That is the entire history of the conference compromise. There is not the slightest indication that Congress intended to adopt the strange rule which the Court announces today—that OCS leasing cannot be subject to consistency requirements. To the contrary, these statements indicate that any federal activity is covered as long as it directly affects the coastal zone. The conferees' reference to federal rights in "submerged lands" further indicates that it recognized that the statute could be applied to the OCS. The inescapable conclusion is that sections 312 and 313 were deleted precisely because section 307(c)(1) had been strengthened so as to protect the coastal zone from federal OCS activities, which obviated the need for these sections. There is no indication whatsoever that the deletion occurred because Congress rejected any application of state management plans to federal activities in the OCS.

In sum, the substitution of the words "directly affecting the coastal zone" for the words "in the coastal zone" plainly effectuated the congressional intent to cover activities outside the zone that are the functional equivalent of activities within the zone, thereby addressing the concern of both Houses that the consistency requirement extend to federal OCS activities. There is simply no evidence that section 307(c)(1) was not intended to reach federal OCS activities which directly affect the coastal zone.

Purposes of the CZMA

An examination of the underlying purposes of the CZMA confirms that the most obvious reading of section 307(c)(1), which would apply its consistency obligation to federal OCS leasing that directly affects the coastal zone, is fully justified.

The congressional findings in section 302 of the CZMA first identify the "national interest in the effective management, beneficial use, protection, and development of the coastal zone," and then recite the various conflicting demands on the valuable resources in such zones, including those occasioned by the "extraction of min-

eral resources and fossil fuels." Congress found that special natural and scenic characteristics are "being damaged by ill-planned development" and that "present state and local institutional arrangements for planning and regulating land and water use in such areas are inadequate." Finally, Congress found that the effective protection of resources in the coastal zone required the development of "land and water use programs for the coastal zone, including unified policies, criteria, standards, methods, and processes for dealing with land and water use decisions of more than local significance." The declaration of national policy in section 303 of the 1972 CZMA unambiguously exhorted "all Federal agencies engaged in programs affecting the coastal zone to cooperate and participate with state and local governments and regional agencies in effectuating the purposes of this title." The policy declaration concluded:

With respect to implementation of such management programs, it is the national policy to encourage cooperation among the various state and regional agencies including establishment of interstate and regional agreements, cooperative procedures, and joint action particularly regarding environmental problems.

These provisions surely indicate a congressional preference for long-range planning and for close cooperation between federal and state agencies in conducting or supporting activities that directly affect the coastal zone. Statutes should be construed in a manner consistent with their underlying policies and purposes. By applying the consistency obligation to the first critical step in OCS development, the decision to lease, the statute is construed in a manner consistent with its underlying purpose.

The majority's construction of section 307(c)(1) is squarely at odds with this purpose. Orderly, long-range, cooperative planning dictates that the consistency requirement must apply to OCS leasing decisions. The sale of OCS leases involves the expenditure of millions of dollars. If exploration and development of the leased tracts cannot be squared with the requirements of the CZMA, it would be in everyone's interest to determine that as early as possible. On the other hand, if exploration and development of the tracts would be consistent with the state management plan, a pre-leasing consistency determination would provide assurances to prospective purchasers and hence enhance the value of the tracts to the Federal Government and, concomitantly, the public. Advance planning can only minimize the risk of either loss or inconsistency that may ultimately confront all interested parties. It is directly contrary to the legislative scheme not to make a consistency determination at the earliest point. It is especially incongruous since the Court agrees that all federal activity "in" the coastal zone is subject to consistency review. If activity in the OCS directly affects the zone—if it is in fact the functional equivalent of activity "in" the zone—it is inconceivable that Congress would have wanted it to be treated any differently.

The only federal activity that ever occurs with respect to OCS oil and gas development is the decision to lease; all other activities in the process are conducted by lessees and not the Federal Government. If the leasing decision is not subject to consistency requirements, then the intent of Congress to apply consistency review to federal OCS activities would be defeated and this part of the statute rendered nugatory. Such a construction must be rejected.

The Direct Effects

The lease sales at issue in this case are in fact the functional equivalent of an activity conducted in the zone. There is no dispute about the fact that the Secretary's selection of lease tracts and lease terms constituted decisions of major importance to the coastal zone. . . . It cannot be denied that in reality OCS oil and gas leasing "directly" looks toward development of the OCS, and the consequences for the coastal

zone that the District Court found development would entail. Development is the expected consequence of leasing; if it were not, purchasers would never commit millions of dollars to the acquisition of leases. Congress views leasing in exactly this way; it has defined the lease acquired by purchasers as a "form of authorization . . . which authorized exploration for, and development and production of, minerals. . . ." 43 U.S.C. section 1331(c) (1976 ed., Supp. V). As the Court of Appeals observed, leasing sets into motion a chain of events designed and intended to lead to exploration and development. When the intended and most probable consequence of a federal activity is oil and gas production that will dramatically affect the adjacent coastal zone, that activity is one "directly affecting" the coastal zone within the meaning of section 307(c)(1).

. . .

In sum, the intent of Congress expressed in the plain language of the Statutes and in its long legislative history unambiguously requires consistency review if an OCS lease sale directly affects the coastal zone. The affirmative findings of fact made by the lower courts on that score are amply supported and are not disturbed by the Court today.

I therefore respectfully dissent.

Questions

1. It is rare that two simple words like "directly affecting" end up the focus of a hotly contested 5-4 U.S. Supreme Court decision. Which side of the argument do you find persuasive?

2. As you may have noted in your earlier reading of the statute, Congress changed the phrase "directly affecting" to "that affects" in the 1990 reauthorization of the law. Does that finally settle the question?

Chapter 6

WHEN DOES REGULATION GO TOO FAR? THE TAKINGS ISSUE

... nor shall private property be taken for public use, without just compensation.

Fifth Amendment to the United States Constitution

Nollan v. California Coastal Commission, 483 U.S. 825 (1987)

JUSTICE SCALIA delivered the opinion of the Court.

James and Marilyn Nollan appeal from the decision of the California Court of Appeal ruling that the California Coastal Commission could condition its grant of permission to rebuild their house on their transfer to the public of an easement across their beachfront property. The California court rejected their claim that imposition of that condition violates the Takings Clause of the Fifth Amendment, as incorporated against the States by the Fourteenth Amendment. We noted probable jurisdiction.

I.

The Nollans own a beachfront lot in Ventura County, California. A quarter-mile north of their property is Faria County Park, an oceanside public park with a public beach and recreation area. Another public beach area, known locally as "the Cove," lies 1,800 feet south of their lot. A concrete seawall approximately eight feet high separates the beach portion of the Nollans' property from the rest of the lot. The historic mean high-tide line determines the lot's oceanside boundary.

The Nollans originally leased their property with an option to buy. The building on the lot was a small bungalow, totaling 504 square feet, which for a time they rented to summer vacationers. After years of rental use, however, the building had fallen into disrepair, and could no longer be rented out.

The Nollans' option to purchase was conditioned on their promise to demolish the bungalow and replace it. In order to do so, under California Public Resources Code sections 30106, 30212, and 30600 (West 1986), they were required to obtain a coastal development permit from the California Coastal Commission. On February 25, 1982, they submitted a permit application to the Commission in which they proposed to demolish the existing structure and replace it with a three-bedroom house in keeping with the rest of the neighborhood.

The Nollans were informed that their application had been placed on the administrative calendar, and that the Commission staff had recommended that the permit be granted subject to the condition that they allow the public an easement to pass across a portion of their property bounded by the mean high-tide line on one side, and their seawall on the other side. This would make it easier for the public to get to Faria County Park and the Cove. The Nollans protested imposition of the condition, but the Commission overruled their objections and granted the permit subject to their recordation of a deed restriction granting the easement.

On June 3, 1982, the Nollans filed a petition for writ of administrative mandamus asking the Ventura County Superior Court to invalidate the access condition. They argued that the condition could not be imposed absent evidence that their proposed development would have a direct adverse impact on public access to the beach. The court agreed, and remanded the case to the Commission for a full evidentiary hearing on that issue.

On remand, the commission held a public hearing, after which it made further factual findings and reaffirmed its imposition of the condition. It found that the new house would increase blockage of the view of the ocean, thus contributing to the development of "a 'wall' of residential structures" that would prevent the public "psychologically . . . from realizing a stretch of coastline exists nearby that they have every right to visit." These effects of construction of the house, along with other area development, would cumulatively "burden the public's ability to traverse to and along the shorefront." Therefore, the Commission could properly require the Nollans to offset that burden by providing additional lateral access to the public beaches in the form of an easement across their property. The Commission also noted that it had similarly conditioned forty-three out of sixty coastal development permits

along the same tract of land, and that of the seventeen not so conditioned, fourteen had been approved when the Commission did not have administrative regulations in place allowing imposition of the condition, and the remaining three had not involved shorefront property.

The Nollans filed a supplemental petition for a writ of administrative mandamus with the Superior Court, in which they argued that imposition of the access condition violated the Takings Clause of the Fifth Amendment, as incorporated against the States by the Fourteenth Amendment. The Superior Court ruled in their favor on statutory grounds, finding, in part to avoid "issues of constitutionality," that the California Coastal Act of 1976 authorized the Commission to impose public access conditions on coastal development permits for the replacement of an existing single-family home with a new one only where the proposed development would have an adverse impact on public access to the sea. In the Court's view, the administrative record did not provide an adequate factual basis for concluding that replacement of the bungalow with the house would create a direct or cumulative burden on public access to the sea. Accordingly, the Superior Court granted the writ of mandamus and directed that the permit condition be struck.

The Commission appealed to the California Court of Appeal. While that appeal was pending, the Nollans satisfied the condition on their option to purchase by tearing down the bungalow and building the new house, and bought the property. They did not notify the Commission that they were taking that action.

The Court of Appeal reversed the Superior Court. It disagreed with the Superior Court's interpretation of the Coastal Act, finding that it required that a coastal permit for the construction of a new house whose floor area, height, or bulk was more than 10 percent larger than that of the house it was replacing be conditioned on a grant of access. It also ruled that that requirement did not violate the Constitution under the reasoning of an earlier case of the Court of Appeal, *Grupe v. California Coastal Comm'n*, 166 Cal. App. 3d 148, 212 Cal. Rptr. 578 (1985). In that case, the court had found that so long as a project contributed to the need for public access, even if the project standing alone had not created the need for access, and even if there was only an indirect relationship between the access exacted and the need to which the project contributed, imposition of an access condition on a development permit was sufficiently related to burdens created by the project to be constitutional. The Court of Appeal ruled that the record established that that was the situation with respect to the Nollans' house. It ruled that the Nollans' taking claim also failed because, although the condition diminished the value of the Nollans' lot, it did not deprive them of all reasonable use of their property. Since, in the Court of Appeals's view, there was no statutory or constitutional obstacle to imposition of the access condition, the Superior Court erred in granting the writ of mandamus. The Nollans appealed to this Court, raising only the constitutional question.

II.

Had California simply required the Nollans to make an easement across their beachfront available to the public on a permanent basis in order to increase public access to the beach, rather than conditioning their permit to rebuild their house on their agreeing to do so, we have no doubt there would have been a taking. To say that the appropriation of a public easement across the landowner's premise does not constitute the taking of a property interest but rather, (as Justice Brennan contends), "a mere restriction on its use," is to use words in a manner that deprives them of all their ordinary meaning. Indeed, one of the principal uses of the eminent domain power is to assure that the government be able to require conveyance of just such interests, so long as it pays for them. We have repeatedly held that, as to property reserved by its owner for private use, "the right to exclude [others is] 'one of the most essential

sticks in the bundle of rights that are commonly characterized as property.'" We think a "permanent physical occupation" has occurred, for purposes of that rule, where individuals are given a permanent and continuous right to pass to and fro, so that the real property may continuously be traversed, even though no particular individual is permitted to station himself permanently upon the premises. . . .

Given, then, that requiring uncompensated conveyance of the easement outright would violate the Fourteenth Amendment, the question becomes whether requiring it to be conveyed as a condition for issuing a land use permit alters the outcome. We have long recognized that land use regulation does not effect a taking if it "substantially advance[s] legitimate state interests" and does not "den[y] an owner economically viable use of his land." *Agins v. Tiburon*, 447 U.S. 255, 260 (1980). See also *Penn Central Transportation Co. v. New York City*, 438 U.S. 104, 127 (1978) ("a use restriction may constitute a 'taking' if not reasonably necessary to the effectuation of a substantial government purpose"). Our cases have not elaborated on the standards for determining what constitutes a "legitimate state interest" or what type of connection between the regulation and the state interest satisfies the requirement that the former "substantially advance" the latter. They have made clear, however, that a broad range of governmental purposes and regulations satisfies these requirements. The Commission argues that among these permissible purposes are protecting the public's ability to see the beach, assisting the public in overcoming the "psychological barrier" to using the beach created by a developed shorefront, and preventing congestion on the public beaches. We assume, without deciding, that this is so—in which case the Commission unquestionably would be able to deny the Nollans their permit outright if their new house (alone, or by reason of the cumulative impact produced in conjunction with other construction) would substantially impede these purposes, unless the denial would interfere so drastically with the Nollans' use of their property as to constitute a taking.

The Commission argues that a permit condition that serves the same legitimate police-power purpose as a refusal to issue the permit should not be found to be a taking if the refusal to issue the permit would not constitute a taking. We agree. Thus, if the Commission attached to the permit some condition that would have protected the public's ability to see the beach notwithstanding construction of the new house—for example, a height limitation, a width restriction, or a ban on fences—so long as the Commission could have exercised its police power (as we have assumed it could) to forbid construction of the house altogether, imposition of the condition would also be constitutional. Moreover (and here we come closer to the facts of the present case), the condition would be constitutional even if it consisted of the requirement that the Nollans provide a viewing spot on their property for passersby with whose sighting of the ocean their new house would interfere. Although such a requirement, constituting a permanent grant of continuous access to the property, would have to be considered a taking if it were not attached to a development permit, the commission's assumed power to forbid construction of the house in order to protect the public's view of the beach must surely include the power to condition construction upon some concession by the owner, even a concession of property rights, that serves the same end. If a prohibition designed to accomplish that purpose would be a legitimate exercise of the police power rather than a taking, it would be strange to conclude that providing the owner an alternative to that prohibition which accomplishes the same purpose is not.

The evident constitutional propriety disappears, however, if the condition substituted for the prohibition utterly fails to further the end advanced as the justification for the prohibition. When that essential nexus is eliminated, the situation becomes the same as if California law forbade shouting "fire" in a crowded theater, but granted dispensations to those willing to contribute $100 to the state treasury. While a ban on shouting "fire" can be a core exercise of the State's police power to protect the public safety, and can thus meet even our stringent standards for regulation of speech, adding the unrelated condition alters the purpose to one which, while it may be legitimate, is inadequate to sustain the ban. Therefore, even though, in a sense, requiring a $100 tax contribution in order to shout fire is a lesser restriction on speech than an outright ban, it would not pass constitutional muster. Similarly here, the lack of nexus between the condition and the original purpose of the building restriction converts that purpose to something other than what it was. The purpose then becomes, quite simply, the obtaining of an easement to serve some valid governmental purpose, but without payment of compensation. Whatever may be the outer limits of "legitimate state interests" in the takings and land use context, this is not one of them. In short, unless the permit condition serves the same governmental purpose as the development ban, the building restriction is not a valid regulation of land use but "an out-and-out plan of extortion."

III.

The Commission claims that it concedes as much, and that we may sustain the condition at issue here by finding that it is reasonably related to the public need or burden that the Nollans' new house creates or to which it contributes. We can accept, for purposes of discussion, the Commission's proposed test as to how close a "fit" between the condition and the burden is required, because we find that this case does not meet even the most untailored standards. The Commission's principal contention to the contrary essentially turns on a play on the word "access." The Nollans' new house, the Commission found, will interfere with "visual access" to the beach. That in turn (along with other shorefront development) will interfere with the desire of people who drive past the

Nollans' house to use the beach, thus creating a "psychological barrier" to "access." The Nollans' new house will also, by a process not altogether clear from the Commission's opinion but presumably potent enough to more than offset the effects of the psychological barrier, increase the use of the public beaches, thus creating the need for more "access." These burdens on "access" would be alleviated by a requirement that the Nollans provide "lateral access" to the beach.

Rewriting the argument to eliminate the play on words makes clear that there is nothing to it. It is quite impossible to understand how a requirement that people already on the public beaches be able to walk across the Nollans' property reduces any obstacles to viewing the beach created by the new house. It is also impossible to understand how it lowers any "psychological barrier" to using the public beaches, or how it helps to remedy any additional congestion on them caused by construction of the Nollans' new house. We therefore find that the Commission's imposition of the permit condition cannot be treated as an exercise of its land use power for any of these purposes. Our conclusion on this point is consistent with the approach taken by every other court that has considered the question, with the exception of the California state courts.

Justice Brennan argues that imposition of the access requirement is not irrational. In his version of the Commission's argument, the reason for the requirement is that in its absence, a person looking toward the beach from the road will see a street of residential structures including the Nollans' new home and conclude that there is no public beach nearby. If, however, that person sees people passing and repassing along the dry sand behind the Nollans' home, he will realize that there is a public beach somewhere in the vicinity. The Commission's action, however, was based on the opposite factual finding that the wall of houses completely blocked the view of the beach and that a person looking from the road would not be able to see it at all.

Even if the Commission had made the finding that Justice Brennan proposed, however, it is not certain that it would suffice. We do not share Justice Brennan's confidence that the Commission "should have little difficulty in the future in utilizing its expertise to demonstrate a specific connection between provisions for access and burdens on access," that will avoid the effect of today's decision. We view the Fifth Amendment's property clause to be more than a pleading requirement, and compliance with it to be more than an exercise in cleverness and imagination. As indicated earlier, our cases describe the condition for abridgement of property rights through the police power as a "*substantial* advanc[ing]" of a legitimate State interest. We are inclined to be particularly careful about the adjective where the actual conveyance of property is made a condition to the lifting of a land use restriction, since in that context there is heightened risk that the purpose is avoidance of the compensation requirement, rather than the stated police-power objective.

We are left, then, with the Commission's justification for the access requirement unrelated to land use regulation:

Finally, the commission notes that there are several existing provisions of pass and repass lateral access benefits already given by past Faria Beach Tract applicants as a result of prior coastal permit decisions. The access required as a condition of this permit is part of a comprehensive program to provide continuous public access along Faria Beach as the lots undergo development or redevelopment. App. 68.

That is simply an expression of the Commission's belief that the public interest will be served by a continuous strip of publicly accessible beach along the coast. The Commission may well be right that it is a good idea, but that does not establish that the Nollans (and other coastal residents) alone can be compelled to contribute to its realization. Rather, California is free to advance its "comprehensive program," if it wishes, by using its power of eminent domain for this "public purpose," but if it wants an easement across the Nollans' property, it must pay for it.

Reversed

JUSTICE BRENNAN, with whom JUSTICE MARSHALL joins, dissenting.

Appellants in this case sought to construct a new dwelling on their beach lot that would both diminish visual access to the beach and move private development closer to the public tidelands. The Commission reasonably concluded that such "buildout," both individually and cumulatively, threatens public access to the shore. It sought to offset this encroachment by obtaining assurance that the public may walk along the shoreline in order to gain access to the ocean. The Court finds this an illegitimate exercise of the police power, because it maintains that there is no reasonable relationship between the effect of the development and the condition imposed.

The first problem with this conclusion is that the Court imposes a standard of precision for the exercise of a State's police power that has been discredited for the better part of this century. Furthermore, even under the Court's cramped standard, the permit condition imposed in this case directly responds to the specific type of burden on access created by appellants' development. Finally, a review of those factors deemed most significant in takings analysis makes clear that the Commission's action implicates none of the concerns underlying the Takings Clause. The Court has thus struck down the commission's reasonable effort to respond to intensified development along the California coast, on behalf of landowners who can make no claim that their reasonable expectations have been disrupted. The Court has, in short, given appellants a windfall at the expense of the public.

I.

The Court's conclusion that the permit condition imposed on appellants is unreasonable cannot withstand analysis. First, the Court de-

mands a degree of exactitude that is inconsistent with our standard for reviewing the rationality of a state's exercise of its police power for the welfare of its citizens. Second, even if the nature of the public access condition imposed must be identical to the precise burden on access created by appellants, this requirement is plainly satisfied.

A.

There can be no dispute that the police power of the States encompasses the authority to impose conditions on private development. It is also by now commonplace that this Court's review of the rationality of a State's exercise of its police power demands only that the State *"could rationally have decided"* that the measure adopted might achieve the State's objective. In this case, California has employed its police power in order to condition development upon preservation of public access to the ocean and tidelands. The Coastal Commission, if it had so chosen, could have denied the Nollans' request for a development permit, since the property would have remained economically viable without the requested new development. Instead, the State sought to accommodate the Nollans' desire for new development, on the condition that the development not diminish the overall amount of public access to the coastline. Appellants' proposed development would reduce public access by restricting visual access to the beach, by contributing to an increased need for community facilities, and by moving private development closer to public beach property. The Commission sought to offset this diminution in access, and thereby preserve the overall balance of access, by requesting a deed restriction that would ensure "lateral" access: the right of the public to pass and repass along the dry sand parallel to the shoreline in order to reach the tidelands and the ocean. In the expert opinion of the Coastal Commission, development conditioned on such a restriction would fairly attend to both public and private interests.

The Court finds fault with this measure because it regards the condition as insufficiently tailored to address the precise type of reduction in access produced by the new development. The Nollans' development blocks visual access, the Court tells us, while the Commission seeks to preserve lateral access along the coastline. Thus, it concludes, the State acted irrationally. Such a narrow conception of rationality, however, has long since been discredited as a judicial abrogation of legislative authority. . . .

The Commission is charged by both the state constitution and legislature to preserve overall public access to the California coastline. The Commission has sought to discharge its responsibilities in a flexible manner. It has sought to balance private and public interests and to accept tradeoffs: to permit development that reduces access in some ways as long as other means of access are enhanced. In this case, it has determined that the Nollans' burden on access would be offset by a deed restriction that formalizes the public's right to pass along the shore. In its informed judgment, such a tradeoff would preserve the net amount of public access to the coastline. The Court's insistence on a precise fit between the forms of burden and condition on each individual parcel along the California coast would penalize the Commission for its flexibility, hampering the ability to fulfill its public trust mandate.

The Court's demand for this precise fit is based on the assumption that private landowners in this case possess a reasonable expectation regarding the use of their land that the public has attempted to disrupt. In fact, the situation is precisely the reverse: it is private landowners who are the interlopers. The public's expectation of access considerably antedates any private development on the coast. Article X, Section 4 of the California Constitution, adopted in 1879, declares:

No individual, partnership, or corporation, claiming or possessing the frontage or tidal lands of a harbor, bay, inlet, estuary, or other navigable water in this State shall be permitted to exclude the right of way

to any such water whenever it is required for any public purpose, nor to destroy or obstruct the free navigation of such water; and the Legislature shall enact such laws as will give the most liberal construction to this provision, so that access to the navigable waters of this State shall always be attainable for the people thereof.

It is therefore private landowners who threaten the disruption of settled public expectations. Where a private landowner has had a reasonable expectation that his or her property will be used for exclusively private purposes, the disruption of this expectation dictates that the government pay if it wishes the property to be used for a public purpose. In this case, however, the State has sought to protect *public* expectations of access from disruption by private land use. The State's exercise of its police power for this purpose deserves no less deference than any other measure designed to further the welfare of state citizens.

Congress expressly stated in passing the CZMA that "[i]n light of competing demands and the urgent need to protect and to give high priority to natural systems in the coastal zone, present state and local institutional arrangements for planning and regulating land and water uses in such areas are inadequate." 16 U.S.C. section 1451(h). It is thus puzzling that the Court characterizes as a "non-land-use justification," the exercise of the police power to " 'provide continuous public access along Faria Beach as the lots undergo development or redevelopment.' " The Commission's determination that certain types of development jeopardize public access to the ocean, and that such development should be conditioned on preservation of access, is the essence of responsible land use planning. The Court's use of an unreasonably demanding standard for determining the rationality of state regulation in this area thus could hamper innovative efforts to preserve an increasingly fragile national resource.

B.

Even if we accept the Court's unusual demand for a precise match between the condition imposed and the specific type of burden on access created by the appellants, the State's action easily satisfies this requirement. First, the lateral access condition serves to dissipate the impression that the beach that lies behind the wall of homes along the shore is for private use only. It requires no exceptional imaginative powers to find plausible the Commission's point that the average person passing along the road in front of a phalanx of imposing permanent residences, including the appellants' new home, is likely to conclude that this particular portion of the shore is not open to the public. If, however, that person can see that numerous people are passing and repassing along the dry sand, this conveys the message that the beach is in fact open for use by the public. Furthermore, those persons who go down to the public beach a quarter-mile away will be able to look down the coastline and see that persons have continuous access to the tidelands, and will observe signs that proclaim the public's right of access over the dry sand. The burden produced by the diminution in visual access—the impression that the beach is not open to the public—is thus directly alleviated by the provision for public access over the dry sand. The Court therefore has an unrealistically limited conception of what measures could reasonably be chosen to mitigate the burden produced by a diminution of visual access.

The second flaw in the Court's analysis of the fit between burden and exaction is more fundamental. The Court assumes that the only burden with which the Coastal Commission was concerned was blockage of visual access to the beach. This is incorrect. The Commission specifically stated in its report in support of the permit condition that "[t]he Commission finds that the applicants' proposed development would present an increase in view blockage, *an increase in private use of the shorefront*, and that this impact would burden the public's ability to traverse to and along the shorefront" (emphasis added). It declared that the possibility that "the public may get the impression that the beach-

front is no longer available for public use" would be "due to *the encroaching nature of private use immediately adjacent to the public use*, as well as the visual 'block' of increased residential build-out impacting the visual quality of the beachfront" (emphasis added).

The record prepared by the Commission is replete with references to the threat to public access along the coastline resulting from the seaward encroachment of private development along a beach whose mean high-tide line is constantly shifting. As the Commission observed in its report, "The Faria Beach shoreline fluctuates during the year depending on the seasons and accompanying storms, and the public is not always able to traverse the shoreline below the mean high-tide line." As a result, the boundary between publicly owned tidelands and privately owned beach is not a stable one, and "[t]he existing seawall is located very near to the mean high-water line." When the beach is at its largest, the seawall is about ten feet from the mean high-tide mark; "[d]uring the period of the year when the beach suffers erosion, and the mean high-water line appears to be located either on or beyond the existing seawall." Expansion of private development on appellants' lot toward the seawall would thus "increase private use immediately adjacent to public tidelands, which has the potential of causing adverse impacts on the public's ability to traverse the shoreline."

The deed restriction on which permit approval was conditioned would directly address this threat to the public's access to the tidelands. It would provide a formal declaration of the public's right of access, thereby ensuring that the shifting character of the tidelands, and the presence of private development immediately adjacent to it, would not jeopardize enjoyment of that right. The imposition of the permit condition was therefore directly related to the fact that appellants' development would be "located along a unique stretch of coast where lateral access is inadequate due to the construction of private residential structures and shoreline protective devices along a fluctuating shoreline." The deed restriction was crafted to deal with the particular character of the beach along which appellants sought to build, and with the specific problems created by expansion of development toward the public tidelands. In imposing the restriction, the State sought to ensure that such development would not disrupt the historical expectation of the public regarding access to the sea.

The court is therefore simply wrong that there is no reasonable relationship between the permit condition and the specific type of burden on public access created by the appellants' proposed development. Even were the Court desirous of assuming the added responsibility of closely monitoring the regulation of development along the California coast, this record reveals rational public action by any conceivable standard.

II.

The fact that the Commission's action is a legitimate exercise of the police power does not, of course, insulate it from a takings challenge, for when "regulation goes too far it will be recognized as a taking." *Pennsylvania Coal Co. v. Mahon*, 260 U.S. 393, 415 (1922). Conventional takings analysis underscores the implausibility of the Court's holding, for it demonstrates that this exercise of California's police power implicates none of the concerns that underlie our takings jurisprudence.

In reviewing a Takings Clause claim, we have regarded as particularly significant the nature of the governmental action and the economic impact of regulation, especially the extent to which regulation interferes with investment-backed expectations. The character of the government action in this case is the imposition of a condition on permit approval, which allows the public to continue to have access to the coast. The physical intrusion permitted by the deed restriction is minimal. The public is permitted the right to pass and repass along the coast in an area from the seawall to the mean high-tide mark. This area is at its *widest* ten

feet, which means that *even without the permit condition*, the public's right of access permits it to pass on average within a few feet of the seawall. Passage closer to the eight-foot high rocky seawall will make the appellants even less visible to the public than passage along the high-tide area farther out on the beach. The intrusiveness of such passage is even less than the intrusion regulating from the required dedication of a sidewalk in front of private residences, exactions which are commonplace conditions on approval of development. Furthermore, the high-tide line shifts throughout the year, moving up to and beyond the seawall, so that public passage for a portion of the year would either be impossible or would not occur on appellants' property. Finally, although the Commission had the authority to provide for either passive or active recreational use of the property, it chose the least intrusive alternative: a mere right to pass and repass. As this Court made clear in *Prune Yard Shopping Center v. Robins*, 447 U.S. 74, 83 (1980), physical access to private property in itself creates no takings problem if it does not "unreasonably impair the value or use of [the] property." Appellants can make no tenable claim that either their enjoyment of their property or its value is diminished by the public's ability merely to pass and repass a few feet closer to the seawall beyond which appellants' house is located.

Prune Yard is also relevant in that we acknowledge in that case that public access rested upon a "state constitutional . . . provision that had been construed to create rights to the use of private property by strangers." Id., at 81. In this case, of course, the State is also acting to protect a state constitutional right. The constitutional provision guaranteeing public access to the ocean states that "the Legislature shall enact such laws as will give *the most liberal construction to this provision* so that access to the navigable waters of this State shall be always attainable for the people thereof" (emphasis added). This provision is the explicit basis for the statutory directive to provide for public access along the coast in new development projects, and has been construed by the state judiciary to permit passage over private land where necessary to gain access to the tidelands. *Grupe v. California Coastal Comm'n*, 166 Cal. App. 3d 148, 171–72, 212 Cal. Rptr. 578, 592–93 (1985). The physical access to the perimeter of appellants' property at issue in this case thus results directly from the State's enforcement of the state constitution.

Finally, the character of the regulation in this case is not unilateral government action, but a condition of approval on a development request submitted by appellants. The State has not sought to interfere with any preexisting property interest, but has responded to appellants' proposal to intensify development on the coast. Appellants themselves chose to submit a new development application, and could claim no property interest in its approval. They were aware that approval of such development would be conditioned on preservation of adequate public access to the ocean. The State has initiated no action against appellants' property; had the Nollans not proposed more intensive development in the coastal zone, they would never have been subject to the provision that they challenge.

Examination of the economic impact of the Commission's action reinforces the conclusion that no taking has occurred. Allowing appellants to intensify development along the coast in exchange for ensuring public access to the ocean is a classic instance of government action that produces a "reciprocity of advantage." Appellants have been allowed to replace a one-story 521-square-foot beach home with a two story 1,674-square-foot residence and an attached two-car garage, resulting in development covering 2,464 square feet of the lot. Such development obviously significantly increases the value of appellants' property; appellants make no contention that this increase is offset by any diminution in value resulting from the deed restriction, much less that the restriction made the property less valuable than it would have

been without the new construction. Furthermore, appellants gain an additional benefit from the Commission's permit condition program. They are able to walk along the beach beyond the confines of their own property only because the Commission has required deed restrictions as a condition of approving other new beach developments. Thus, appellants benefit both as private landowners and as members of the public from the fact that new development permit requests are conditioned on preservation of public access.

Ultimately, appellants' claim of economic injury is flawed because it rests on the assumption of entitlement to the full value of their new development. Appellants submitted a proposal for more intensive development of the coast, which the Commission was under no obligation to approve, and now argue that a regulation designed to ameliorate the impact of that development deprives them of the full value of their improvements. Even if this novel claim were somehow cognizable, it is not significant. "[T]he interest in anticipated gains has traditionally been viewed as less compelling than other property-related interests." *Andrus v. Allard*, 444 U.S. 51, 66 (1979).

With respect to appellants' investment-backed expectations, appellants can make no reasonable claim to any expectation of being able to exclude members of the public from crossing the edge of their property to gain access to the ocean. It is axiomatic, of course, that state law is the source of those strands that constitute a property owner's bundle of property rights. "[A]s a general proposition[,] the law of real property is, under our Constitution, left to the individual States to develop and administer." In this case, the state constitution explicitly states that no one possessing the "frontage" of any "navigable water in this State, shall be permitted to exclude the right of way to such water whenever it is required for any public purpose." Cal. Const. Art. X, section 4. The state Code expressly provides that, save for exceptions not relevant here, "[p]ublic access from the nearest public roadway to the shoreline and along the coast shall be provided in new development projects." Cal. Pub. Res. Code Ann. section 30212 (1986). The Coastal Commission Interpretative Guidelines make clear that fulfillment of the Commission's constitutional and statutory duty require that approval of new coastline development be conditioned upon provisions ensuring lateral public access to the ocean. At the time of appellants' permit request, the Commission had conditioned all forty-three of the proposals for coastal new development in the Faria Family Beach Tract on the provision of deed restrictions ensuring lateral access along the shore. Finally, the Faria family had leased the beach property since the early part of this century, and "the Faria family and their lessees [including the Nollans] had not interfered with public use of the beachfront within the Tract, so long as public use was limited to pass and repass lateral access along the shore." California therefore has clearly established that the power of exclusion for which appellants seek compensation simply is not a strand in the bundle of appellants' property rights, and appellants have never acted as if it were. Given this state of affairs, appellants cannot claim that the deed restriction has deprived them of a reasonable expectation to exclude from their property persons desiring to gain access to the sea.

Even were we somehow to concede a preexisting expectation of a right to exclude, appellants were clearly on notice when requesting a new development permit that a condition of approval would be a provision ensuring public lateral access to the shore. Thus, they surely could have had no expectation that they could obtain approval of their new development and exercise any right of exclusion afterward. . . .

Standard Taking Clause analysis thus indicates that the Court employs its unduly restrictive standard of police power rationality to find a taking where neither the character of governmental action nor the nature of the private interest affected raise any takings concern. The result is that the Court invalidates regulation

that represents a reasonable adjustment of the burdens and benefits of development along the California coast.

III.

The foregoing analysis makes clear that the State has taken no property from appellants. Imposition of the permit condition in this case represents the State's reasonable exercise of its police power. The Coastal Commission has drawn on its expertise to preserve the balance between private development and public access, by requiring that any project that intensifies development on the increasingly crowded California coast must be offset by gains in public access. Under the normal standard for review of the police power, this provision is eminently reasonable. Even accepting the Court's novel insistence on a precise quid pro quo of burdens and benefits, there is a reasonable relationship between the public benefit and the burden created by appellants' development. The movement of development closer to the ocean creates the prospect of encroachment on public tidelands, because of fluctuation in the mean high-tide line. The deed restriction ensures that disputes about the boundary between private and public property will not deter the public from exercising its right to have access to the sea.

Furthermore, consideration of the Commission's action under traditional takings analysis underscores the absence of any viable takings claim. The deed restriction permits the public only to pass and repass along a narrow strip of beach, a few feet closer to a seawall at the periphery of appellants' property. Appellants almost surely have enjoyed an increase in the value of their property even with the restriction, because they have been allowed to build a significantly larger new home with garage on their lot. Finally, appellants can claim the disruption of no expectation interest, both because they have no right to exclude the public under state law, and because, even if they did, they had full advance notice that new development along the coast is conditioned on provisions for continued public access to the ocean.

Fortunately, the Court's decision regarding this application of the Commission's permit program will probably have little ultimate impact either on this parcel in particular or the Commission program in general. A preliminary study by a Senior Lands Agent in the State Attorney General's Office indicates that the portion of the beach at issue in this case likely belongs to the public. Since a full study had not been completed at the time of appellants' permit application, the deed restriction was requested "without regard to the possibility that the applicant is proposing development on public land." Furthermore, analysis by the same Land Agent also indicated that the public had obtained a prescriptive right to the use of Faria Beach from the seawall to the ocean. The Superior Court explicitly stated in its ruling against the Commission on the permit condition issue that "no part of this opinion is intended to foreclose the public's opportunity to adjudicate the possibility that public rights in [appellants] beach have been acquired through prescriptive use." Id., at 420.

With respect to the permit condition program in general, the Commission should have little difficulty in the future in utilizing its expertise to demonstrate a specific connection between provisions for access and burdens on access produced by new development. Neither the Commission in its report nor the State in its briefs and at argument highlighted the particular threat to lateral access created by appellants' development project. In defending its action, the State emphasized the general point that overall access to the beach had been preserved, since the diminution of access created by the project had been offset by the gain in lateral access. This approach is understandable, given that the State relied on the reasonable assumption that its action was justified under the normal standard of review for determining legitimate exercises of a State's police power. In the future, alerted to the Court's apparently

more demanding requirement, it need only make clear that a provision for public access directly responds to a particular type of burden on access created by a new development. Even if I did not believe that the record in this case satisfies this requirement, I would have to acknowledge that the record's documentation of the impact of coastal development indicates that the Commission should have little problem presenting its findings in a way that avoids a takings problem.

Nonetheless it is important to point out that the Court's insistence on a precise accounting system in this case is insensitive to the fact that increasing intensity of development in many areas calls for farsighted, comprehensive planning that takes into account both the interdependence of land uses and the cumulative impact of development. As one scholar has noted:

Property does not exist in isolation. Particular parcels are tied to one another in complex ways, and property is more accurately described as being inextricably part of a network of relationships that is neither limited to, nor usefully defined by, the property boundaries with which the legal system is accustomed to dealing. Frequently, use of any given parcel of property is at the same time effectively a use of, or a demand upon, property beyond the border of the user. Sax, Takings, Private Property, and Public Rights, 81 Yale L.J. 149, 152 (1971) (footnote omitted)

As Congress has declared, "The key to more effective protection and use of the land and water resources of the coast [is for the states to] develo[p] land and water use programs for the coastal zone, including unified policies, criteria, standards, methods, and processes for dealing with land and water use decisions of more than local significance." 16 U.S.C. section 1451(i). This is clearly a call for a focus on the overall impact of development on coastal areas. State agencies therefore require considerable flexibility in responding to private desires for development in a way that guarantees the preservation of public access to the coast. They should be encouraged to regulate development in the context of the over all balance of competing uses of the shoreline. The Court today does precisely the opposite, overruling an eminently reasonable exercise of an expert state agency's judgment, substituting its own narrow view of how this balance should be struck. Its reasoning is hardly suited to the complex reality of natural resource protection in the twentieth century. I can only hope that today's decision is an aberration, and that a broader vision ultimately prevails.

I dissent.

Questions

1. After agreeing to the public passage easement as the sole condition of the permit which allowed them to quadruple the size of their home, was it fair to the Coastal Commission to later challenge that condition *after* the house was built and visual access blocked?

2. What other means could be used to secure the public's right to use the beach in question?

3. Would you concur with Justice Scalia's view that this was an act of "out and out extortion"?

Annicelli v. Town of South Kingstown, 463 A.2d 133, (R.I. 1983)

KELLEHER, JUSTICE

This is a case of first impression in Rhode Island which pits a landowner's constitutional rights against the ecological primacy of a barrier beach. The defendant, town of South Kingstown (the town), appeals from the decision of a justice of the Superior Court granting the plaintiff, Ida Annicelli (Annicelli), declaratory relief from certain amendments to the town's zoning ordinance. As a result of those amendments, various segments of the town's shoreline were designated "High Flood Danger" districts (HFD zone). One such area encompassed Green Hill Beach where Annicelli's property is located.

Classification of the beach as an HFD zone effectively precluded Annicelli from constructing a single-family dwelling on the land. The trial justice found that the HFD zone, as applied to Annicelli's property, constituted an indirect confiscatory taking without compensation in violation of articles V and XIV of the amendments to the United States Constitution and article I, section 16, of the Rhode Island Constitution.

In his decision, the trial justice concluded that the town was obliged to exercise its powers of eminent domain to compensate Annicelli. He determined that the effect of the HFD zone was to return the beach property to its natural state for the public benefit and that, under these circumstances, it was inappropriate for the town to exercise its police powers. However, the judgment entered by the trial justice was inconsistent with his decision. Rather than order compensation pursuant to condemnation proceedings, the judgment enjoined the town from enforcing the applicable provisions of the ordinance against Annicelli's property and further directed the building inspector to issue the requested permit.

After a thorough review of the record, we are of the opinion that Annicelli has in fact established an action of inverse condemnation against the town and thus must be compensated for a constructive "taking" of her property. Before expounding upon the rationale underlying this conclusion, we shall recapitulate the factual situation.

On May 8, 1975, Annicelli, an out-of-state resident, signed a purchase-and-sale agreement with the owner of real estate on Green Hill Beach for the purpose of constructing a single-family dwelling there. The stated purchase price was $16,750. Among other stipulations, the agreement provided that Annicelli would relieve the seller of any responsibility toward successfully obtaining "all necessary building, sanitation, and coastal resources permits." Three weeks after the agreement was signed, the town council adopted the amendments to the zoning ordinance creating the HFD zone which gave rise to the instant controversy.

Approximately five months after the amendments were adopted, Annicelli took title and possession of the land. Immediately thereafter, Annicelli applied to the town building inspector for a permit to build a single-family dwelling on her property. She also applied for a permit from the Rhode Island Department of Health to construct an individual sewage-disposal system for her proposed dwelling. Although the permit from the health department was approved, the application for the building permit was denied on the ground that a single-family dwelling was not permitted in an HFD zone.

Rather than appeal the decision of the building inspector to the zoning board of review, Annicelli filed an action for declaratory judgment in the Superior Court on January 15, 1976. The trial justice denied a defense motion to dismiss the action for failure to exhaust administrative remedies. In denying the motion, the trial justice reasoned that the zoning board would have been powerless to grant Annicelli a special exception because none of the permitted uses within the HFD zone included residential dwellings. Indeed, section 14.53 of the ordinance, entitled "Uses and Structures Prohibited within the HFD Zoning District," provides in part as follows: "No residential dwelling designed or used for overnight human occupancy shall be constructed within the HFD Zoning District as defined herein. This prohibition shall apply even if the land within said HFD Zoning District is above the base flood elevation."

The trial justice further ruled that any attempt by Annicelli to obtain a variance as opposed to a special exception would have been a similarly futile exercise. The statute applicable at the time the action was brought authorized the board to grant a variance only for the reinstatement of a nonconforming use that was unavailable to Annicelli. It did not authorize so-called use variances. Entitled "An Act Relating to Zoning Ordinances for South Kingstown,"

ch. 101 of the 1973 Public Laws provided in section 18 that the zoning board of review shall have the power to: "(b) Grant a variance from the restrictions of the zoning ordinance other than use restrictions or requirements ... (c) Grant a variance from the use regulations or requirements of the zoning ordinance only where application is made for reinstatement of a nonconforming use...." The trial justice noted that P.L. 1973, ch. 101, section 18, was amended by P.L. 1976, ch. 11, section 1, subsequent to the filing date of Annicelli's complaint. The effect of the amendment was to eliminate the distinction between use variances and other types of variances, thereby empowering the board to grant the former under appropriate circumstances. Consequently, while her action was pending in Superior Court, Annicelli once again applied to the building inspector for a permit under the newly amended statute. To her chagrin she was once again summarily denied on the ground that the ordinance forbade such use of the property. Annicelli thereafter filed an amendment to her complaint, and trial commenced on June 13, 1977.

Not unexpectedly, Annicelli's witnesses indicated that the property was best suited for use as a single-family dwelling. This conclusion was based upon the belief that the permitted or excepted uses were completely impractical as applied to Annicelli's property because of the size and location of the lot and the nature of its topography. Permitted uses under section 14.41 and expected uses under section 14.42 of the ordinance include, among others, a horticultural nursery or greenhouse, a park or playground, a wildlife area or nature preserve, or a golf course or marina; also allowed were the raising of crops and animals, the storing of commercial vehicles, and the repairing of boats. Annicelli's appraiser estimated that the property was worth $1,000 in its present state because none of the enumerated uses was practical, and $1,000 was, as he put it, the "most anyone would pay ... for a spot to sit on the beach to go swimming." The town's appraiser opined that the property was probably worth $8,500. However, he conceded that several of the uses were impractical while denying that Annicelli was deprived of all reasonable or beneficial use of her property.

The testimony elicited at trial included an enlightened explanation of the role barrier beaches play in the ecological system. To comprehend fully and analyze fairly the matter before us, we shall review this testimony. In 1975 the town adopted an Environmental Master Plan (the plan) particularizing the town's recreational and environmental needs. The plan is part of the Comprehensive Community Plan that serves as the long-range planning device for the development of land-management policies in the town. It recommended that the town's barrier beaches, particularly Green Hill Beach, be classified as open space and conservation areas. To further these goals, the plan called for the creation of HFD zones to prevent construction of residences, to restrict uses that contribute to erosion, and to preclude development along the immediate oceanfront. However, the plan did not counsel the town to condemn barrier beachfront property or raze homes presently situated on Green Hill Beach. It simply advised the town to prohibit further development of any undeveloped lots on Green Hill Beach because the dunes there were dangerously low in profile. Further development of Green Hill Beach, according to the plan's predictions, would compound the erosion already taking place, thereby creating a hazard to the public health and safety.

At trial, expert witnesses testified that a barrier beach is a narrow strip of unconsolidated material consisting of sand or cobble extending roughly parallel to and below the shoreline. The beach is formed by the marine processes of currents and wave action and is usually separated from the mainland by a salt or freshwater pond. The record clearly reveals to the untutored mind the crucial role that barrier beaches play in harboring shorelines from storm erosion. In addition to performing this function, barrier beaches protect the coastal ponds behind them

which are highly productive resources that serve as spawning grounds for various species of fish and other aquatic life.

According to the uncontradicted testimony, barrier beaches are extremely fragile ecological systems that cannot tolerate construction or foot and vehicular traffic because such activities destroy the dune grass that actually stabilizes the dune itself. When destabilization occurs, the barrier beach's ability to play the protective role designed for it by nature is compromised. The area in which Green Hill Beach is located has been designated a "developed" as opposed to an "undeveloped" barrier beach because of the presence of approximately thirty existing homes on the dune.

With this factual background in mind, we turn to the merits of the arguments before us. The threshold issue to be resolved is whether Annicelli is properly before this court in view of the fact that she failed to take an appeal first from the building inspector's decision to the zoning board of review. General Laws 1956 (1980 Reenactment) section 45-24-16 provides for appeals to the board of review from decisions of the building inspector. The town's authority to hear appeals is specifically provided in its zoning-enabling legislation that is contained in ch. 101 of the Public Laws of January 1973. As mentioned above, section 18 thereof, which was amended in March 24, 1976, by ch. 11 of the Public Laws of January 1976, also authorizes the board to grant variances upon appeal.

The town contends that the trial justice should have dismissed and denied Annicelli's petition for declaratory judgment on the ground that Annicelli failed to exhaust her administrative remedies as provided by statute. We disagree. The case that the town believes dispositive of this issue, *Nardi v. City of Providence*, 89 R.I. 437, 153 A. 2d 136 (1959), is inapposite. In that case, the complainant seeking relief challenged the constitutionality of the ordinance only insofar as it applied to his property. Furthermore, the complainant in *Nardi* failed to apply for a permit under a claim of right to use his property in any way inconsistent with the provisions of the ordinance in question. In contrast, in the instant matter, Annicelli has challenged the ordinance as invalid on its face as well as in its application to her property. Additionally, as the trial justice noted, Annicelli, unlike the complaint in *Nardi*, asserted rights with respect to her property when she applied for the building permit that was subsequently denied.

In *Golden Gate Corp. v. Town of Narragansett*, 116 R.I. 552, 359 A.2d 321 (1976), we pointed out that the exhaustion-of-remedies principle adhered to in *Nardi* was applicable to cases in which a litigant contends only that an ordinance is unconstitutional in its application to his specific property. In such a situation, the court will avoid a needless judicial determination, where an application to the zoning board seeking a variance or an exception could meet with success. However, we went on to point out that no reasonable basis exists for forestalling a judicial inquiry when the ordinance is challenged as patently invalid. In that situation, the issue must of necessity be resolved in court rather than at the administrative level.

These sentiments were also echoed earlier in *Frank Ansuini, Inc. v. City of Cranston*, 107 R.I. 63, 264 A.2d 910 (1970), where we distinguished *Nardi* partly on the ground that the complainant failed to show any futility in appealing to the board of review. In *Ansuini*, as in the instant matter, it would have been futile for the complainant to have appealed to the board of review because the board lacked authority to grant the relief sought. "In such circumstances, the courts will not deny judicial relief on the ground that one invoking its protection has first failed to do that which would be futile." Id., at 73, 264 A.2d at 915–16.

The principles enunciated in *Ansuini* and reiterated in *Golden Gate* are not rendered impertinent because the trial justice in the instant action ruled, not that the HFD zone was invalid on its face, but that it was unconstitutional only

in its application to Annicelli's property. Consequently, the town is mistaken in asserting that the trial justice's decision was inconsistent with previous case law. The complaint sets forth the claim, and in the instant case Annicelli challenged the ordinance as patently unconstitutional on its face. Because by the clear and unambiguous language of the ordinance construction of single-family dwellings is flatly ruled out under all circumstances, we acquiesce with the trial justice's conclusion that any attempt to have the board of review grant a special exception or variance would have been futile.

Concerning the issue of Annicelli's standing to bring this case, we need only make brief reference to the well-established doctrine of equitable conversion. Annicelli became the equitable or beneficial owner of the property when she signed the purchase-and-sale agreement. As stated in the factual resume above, that agreement specifically placed the burden of obtaining all necessary permits on the purchaser and made no provision for rescission of the contract in the event of a zoning change.

The general rule to be applied when a zoning change occurs during the interim between the signing of the purchase-and-sale agreement and actual conveyance of the property has been articulated by Professor Corbin as follows:

> After a contract for the sale of land has been made, but before actual conveyance, it sometimes happens that a zoning ordinance is adopted limiting the uses to which the property may be put. . . . This change in the law may frustrate in part or in whole the purpose for which the purchaser agreed to buy the land. In the absence of some expression in the contract to the contrary, the risk of such a restriction by ordinance seems likely to be allocated to the purchaser. 6 Corbin, *Contracts* section 1361 at 492 (1962)

Heeding this advice, we have previously stated that one who has a binding contract to purchase property has standing to seek relief from a zoning ordinance. With this enunciation of the principle as our guide, we are led by the facts of this case to no other conclusion than Annicelli was aggrieved by the zoning change and thus had standing to bring suit.

Having disposed of these initial questions, we turn to the gravamen of the controversy before us and determine whether the town has in fact unconstitutionally taken Annicelli's property for public use without compensation by its designation of Green Hill Beach as an HFD zone. The trial justice answered this question in the affirmative, ruling that the ordinance as applied to Annicelli's property "constitute[d] an indirect, confiscatory taking of her property without just compensation, in violation of the United States and Rhode Island Constitutions."

The Fifth Amendment to the United States Constitution provides that "[n]o person shall be . . . deprived of . . . property, without due process of law; nor shall private property be taken for public use, without just compensation." This provision applies to the states and their subdivisions by the due-process clause of the Fourteenth Amendment. The Rhode Island Constitution in art. I, sec. 16, states that "[p]rivate property shall not be taken for public uses, without just compensation." We have ruled that use regulations that are reasonably necessary to protect the public health and safety are permissible exercises of the police power which do not require compensation, provided that they do not become arbitrary, destructive, or confiscatory. Furthermore, we have recognized that a zoning ordinance that deprives an owner of all beneficial use of his property is confiscatory and requires compensation.

When all beneficial use of property is deprived by governmental restrictions, there is no question that an unconstitutional taking can occur even in the absence of a physical entry. In such circumstances, an action in inverse condemnation lies because it permits recovery against a governmental entity that takes the property in fact without formally exercising the power of eminent domain. In other words, when a restriction is so great that the landowner ought not to bear the burden for the public

good, the restriction is looked upon as a constructive taking. This is so even though the actual use has not been transferred to the government in the traditional sense of a taking. "Whether a taking has occurred depends upon whether 'the restriction practically or substantially renders the land useless for all reasonable purposes.'" *Just v. Marinette County*, 56 Wis. 2d 7, 15, 201 N.W.2d 761, 767 (1972).

Given these guidelines, our task in the instant case is to determine whether the amendments adopted by the town council meet the test of constitutional exercise of the police power. We must balance the conflicting aims of the public interest in preserving barrier beaches in their natural state with Annicelli's asserted right to use her property as she pleases. Public rights may be protected by the exercise of the police power unless, as outlined above, the damage to the property owner becomes overbearing and amounts to a confiscation. Thus, the distinction between the exercise of the police power and the power of eminent domain is the use to which the property is put and the degree of damage to the property owner.

Throughout our analysis we must keep in mind the caveat that pecuniary loss or diminution in value is not controlling on the issue of confiscation because a property owner does not have a vested property right in maximizing the value of his property. In *Golden Gate Corp. v. Town of Narragansett*, 116 R.I. 552, 566, 359 A.2d 321, 328 (1976), we said that a zoning ordinance is not confiscatory merely because the property cannot be put to its most profitable use. Recently, the Supreme Court in *Agins v. City of Tiburon*, 447 U.S. 255 (1980), denied a challenge to the constitutionality of an ordinance in a situation in which the plaintiff's five acres of land were limited to only five dwellings. The Court found that the ordinance did not prevent the best use of the land but merely limited it.

In the instant controversy, the town contends that the denial of Annicelli's building permit constituted a valid exercise of the police power.

The town's argument is based on its conclusion that the proposed use was unsafe, that the construction of a residence would create a nuisance, and that Annicelli failed to show that she had been denied all reasonable and beneficial use of the property. The trial justice rejected each of these contentions. We are reminded at this juncture that it is a well-settled principle that we shall not overturn the rulings of the trial justice unless he overlooked or misconceived material evidence or was clearly wrong.

After reviewing the record, we cannot find fault with the trial justice's conclusions. Much of the transcript in this case is devoted to an exhaustive accounting of why each of the permissible or expected uses was impractical as applied to Annicelli's property. As noted by the trial justice, these uses can only reasonably be envisioned on a much larger tract. Indeed, in numerous instances, the town's witness conceded that the uses were unavailable to Annicelli. There is no question that this case is not one of mere diminution in value or use of property. The record demonstrates to us that all reasonable or beneficial use of Annicelli's property has been rendered an impossibility; consequently, under the standards promulgated by the Supreme Court, Annicelli must be compensated.

Our determination that the town should have exercised its power of eminent domain rather than its police power is further premised on the fact that the overall purpose of the ordinance in question is to benefit the public welfare by protecting vital natural resources, here barrier beaches, and preserving them for posterity. We glean this purpose from the testimony at trial and the preamble of the ordinance, which states that the ordinance is designed to:

A. Secure safety from . . . flood . . . and other dangers from natural . . . disaster;

. . .

H. Promote the conservation of open space, valuable natural resources, and ecological features and prevent urban sprawl and wasteful land development practices. . . .

Preserving barrier beaches is a worthy environmental goal that the town may lawfully pursue. However, as we have stated in our analysis above, the police power may properly regulate the use of property only where uncontrolled use would be harmful to the public. The instant controversy does not present a case in which a harmful use is prevented by the ordinance, such as the discharge of waste and pollutants into a "precariously balanced environment." The use to be prevented here, construction of a single-family dwelling in an area in which thirty such structures already exist, constitutes a taking for the public good rather than a taking to prevent a public harm.

Our ruling today that ecological or environmental legislation may constitute a taking when all beneficial use of the property is denied to the landowner to benefit the public welfare is in harmony with rulings involving similar fact situations in other jurisdictions. . . . In each case, the respective courts found that the ordinances so restricted the use of the property for the public welfare that the owners were denied all reasonable use and a taking was recognized.

In conclusion, although the public interest in preserving barrier beaches is commendable, particularly in consideration of the vital role they play in preserving and protecting our shoreline, that interest must not overshadow a cognizance of the danger that the exercise of the police power can result in a taking of one's property. Here, where the plaintiff's property has been taken for the benefit of the community welfare, the occasion is appropriate for an award of just compensation.

Accordingly, the plaintiff's appeal is sustained in part. So much of the judgment that finds that there has been a taking is affirmed. That portion of the judgment that enjoins the town from enforcing its ordinance and orders the issuance of a building permit is hereby vacated. The case is remanded to the Superior Court for entry of a new judgment and further proceedings in accordance with this opinion, including a hearing at which a determination will be made as to the fair market value of Annicelli's property.

Questions

1. Describe the distinctions between the use of the police power and the power of eminent domain.

2. Was Annicelli denied "all reasonable uses" of her property or just permission to build a house?

3. How can you distinguish "taking for the public good" from "taking to prevent a public harm"?

Lucas v. South Carolina Coastal Council, 112 S.Ct. 2886 (1992)

JUSTICE SCALIA delivered the opinion of the Court.

In 1986, petitioner David H. Lucas paid $975,000 for two residential lots on the Isle of Palms in Charleston County, South Carolina, on which he intended to build single-family homes. In 1988, however, the South Carolina Legislature enacted the Beachfront Management Act, S.C. Code Sec. 48-39-250 et seq. (Supp. 1990) (Act), which has the direct effect of barring petitioner from erecting any permanent habitable structures on his two parcels. A state trial court found that this prohibition rendered Lucas's parcels "valueless." This case requires us to decide whether the Act's dramatic effect on the economic value of Lucas's lots accomplished a taking of private property under the Fifth and Fourteenth Amendments requiring the payment of "just compensation." U.S. Const., Amdt. 5.

I.

A.

South Carolina's expressed interest in intensively managing development activities in the so-called "coastal zone" dates from 1977 when,

in the aftermath of Congress's passage of the federal Coastal Zone Management Act of 1972, the legislature enacted a Coastal Zone Management Act of its own. In its original form, the South Carolina Act required owners of coastal zone land that qualified as a "critical area" (defined in the legislation to include beaches and immediately adjacent sand dunes, Sec. 48-39-10[J]) to obtain a permit from the newly created South Carolina Coastal Council prior to committing the land to a "use other than the use the critical area was devoted to on [September 28, 1977]."

In the late 1970s, Lucas and others began extensive residential development of the Isle of Palms, a barrier island situated eastward of the City of Charleston. Toward the close of the development cycle for one residential subdivision known as "Beachwood East," Lucas in 1986 purchased the two lots at issue in this litigation for his own account. No portion of the lots, which were located approximately three hundred feet from the beach, qualified as a "critical area" under the 1977 Act; accordingly, at the time Lucas acquired these parcels, he was not legally obliged to obtain a permit from the Council in advance of any development activity. His intention with respect to the lots was to do what the owners of the immediately adjacent parcels had already done: erect single-family residences. He commissioned architectural drawings for this purpose.

The Beachfront Management Act brought Lucas's plans to an abrupt end. Under the 1988 legislation, the Council was directed to establish a "baseline" connecting the landward-most "point[s] of erosion . . . during the past forty years" in the region of the Isle of Palms that includes Lucas's lots. In action not challenged here, the Council fixed this baseline landward of Lucas's parcels. That was significant, for under the Act construction of occupiable improvements was flatly prohibited seaward of a line drawn twenty feet landward of, and parallel to, the baseline. The Act provided no exceptions.

B.

Lucas promptly filed suit in the South Carolina Court of Common Pleas, contending that the Beachfront Management Act's construction bar effected a taking of his property without just compensation. Lucas did not take issue with the validity of the Act as a lawful exercise of South Carolina's police power, but contended that the Act's complete extinguishment of his property's value entitled him to compensation regardless of whether the legislature had acted in furtherance of legitimate police-power objectives. Following a bench trial, the court agreed. Among its factual determinations was the finding that "at the time Lucas purchased the two lots, both were zoned for single-family residential construction and . . . there were no restrictions imposed upon such use of the property by either the State of South Carolina, the County of Charleston, or the Town of the Isle of Palms." The trial court further found that the Beachfront Management Act decreed a permanent ban on construction insofar as Lucas's lots were concerned, and that this prohibition "deprive[d] Lucas of any reasonable economic use of the lots, . . . eliminated the unrestricted right of use, and render[ed] them valueless." The court thus concluded that Lucas's properties had been "taken" by operation of the Act, and it ordered respondent to pay "just compensation" in the amount of $1,232,387.50.

The Supreme Court of South Carolina reversed. It found dispositive what it described as Lucas's concession "that the Beachfront Management Act [was] properly and validly designed to preserve . . . South Carolina's beaches." 304 S.C. 376, 379, 404 S.E.2d 895, 896 (1991). Failing an attack on the validity of the statute as such, the Court believed itself bound to accept the "uncontested . . . findings" of the South Carolina legislature that new construction in the coastal zone—such as petitioner intended—threatened this public resource. The Court ruled that when a regulation respecting the use of property is designed "to prevent serious public harm," no compensation is owing under the Takings Clause regardless of the regulation's effect on the property's value.

To the dissenters, the chief purposes of the legislation, among them the promotion of tourism and the creation of a "habitat for indigenous flora and fauna," could not fairly be compared to nuisance abatement. As a consequence, they would have affirmed the trial court's conclusion that the Act's obliteration of the value of petitioner's lots accomplished a taking.

We granted certiorari.

II.

As a threshold matter, we must briefly address the Council's suggestion that this case is inappropriate for plenary review. After briefing and argument before the South Carolina Supreme Court, but prior to issuance of that court's opinion, the Beachfront Management Act was amended to authorize the Council, in certain circumstances, to issue "special permits" for the construction or reconstruction of habitable structures seaward of the baseline. According to the Council, this amendment renders Lucas's claim of a permanent deprivation unripe, as Lucas may yet be able to secure permission to build on his property. "[The Court's] cases," we are reminded, "uniformly reflect an insistence on knowing the nature and extent of permitted development before adjudicating the constitutionality of the regulations that purport to limit it." *MacDonald, Sommer & Frates v. County of Yolo*, 477 U.S. 340, 351 (1986). Because petitioner "has not yet obtained a final decision regarding how [he] will be allowed to develop [his] property," the Council argues that he is not yet entitled to definitive adjudication of his takings claim in this Court.

We think these considerations would preclude review had the South Carolina Supreme Court rested its judgment on ripeness grounds, as it was (essentially) invited to do by the Council; see Brief for Respondent 9, n. 3. The South Carolina Supreme Court shrugged off the possibility of further administrative and trial proceedings, however, preferring to dispose of Lucas's takings claim on the merits. This unusual disposition does not preclude Lucas from applying for a permit under the 1990 amendment for *future* construction, and challenging, on takings grounds, any denial. But it does preclude, both practically and legally, any takings claim with respect to Lucas's *past* deprivation, i.e., for his having been denied construction rights during the period before the 1990 amendments. See generally *First English Evangelical Lutheran Church of Glendale v. County of Los Angeles*, 482 U.S. 304 (1987) (holding that temporary deprivations of use are compensable under the Takings Clause). Without even so much as commenting upon the consequences of the South Carolina Supreme Court's judgment in this respect, the Council insists that permitting Lucas to press his claim of a past deprivation on this appeal would be improper, since "the issues of whether and to what extent [Lucas] has incurred a temporary taking . . . have simply never been addressed." Yet Lucas had no reason to proceed on a "temporary taking" theory at trial, or even to seek remand for that purpose prior to submission of the case to the South Carolina Supreme Court, since as the Act then read, the taking was unconditional and permanent. Moreover, given the breadth of the South Carolina Supreme Court's holding and judgment, Lucas would plainly be unable (absent our intervention now) to obtain further state-court adjudication with respect to the 1988–1990 period.

In these circumstances, we think it would not accord with sound process to insist that Lucas pursue the late-created "special permit" procedure before his takings claim can be considered ripe. Lucas has properly alleged Article III injury-in-fact in this case, with respect to both the pre-1990 and post-1990 constraints placed on the use of his parcels by the Beachfront Management Act. That there is a discretionary "special permit" procedure by which he may regain—for the future, at least—beneficial use of his land goes only to the prudential "ripe-

ness" of Lucas's challenge, and for the reasons discussed we do not think it prudent to apply that prudential requirement here. We leave for decision on remand, of course, the questions left unaddressed by the South Carolina Supreme Court as a consequence of its categorical disposition.

III.

A.

Prior to Justice Holmes's exposition in *Pennsylvania Coal Co. v. Mahon*, 260 U.S. 393 (1922), it was generally thought that the Takings Clause reached only a "direct appropriation" of property, or the functional equivalent of a "practical ouster of [the owner's] possession." Justice Holmes recognized in *Mahon*, however, that if the protection against physical appropriations of private property was to be meaningfully enforced, the government's power to redefine the range of interests included in the ownership of property was necessarily constrained by constitutional limits. If, instead, the uses of private property were subject to unbridled, uncompensated qualification under the police power, "the natural tendency of human nature [would be] to extend the qualification more and more until at last private property disappear[ed]."

These considerations gave birth in that case to the oft-cited maxim that, "while property may be regulated to a certain extent, if regulation goes too far it will be recognized as a taking." Nevertheless, our decision in *Mahon* offered little insight into when, and under what circumstances, a given regulation would be seen as going "too far" for purposes of the Fifth Amendment. In seventy-odd years of succeeding "regulatory takings," jurisprudence, we have generally eschewed any " 'set formula' " for determining how far is too far, preferring to "engag[e] in . . . essentially ad hoc factual inquiries." We have, however, described at least two discrete categories of regulatory action as compensable without case-specific inquiry into the public interest advanced in support of the restraint. The first encompasses regulations that compel the property owner to suffer a physical "invasion" of his property. In general (at least with regard to permanent invitations), no matter how minute the intrusion, and no matter how weighty the public purpose behind it, we have required compensation.

The second situation in which we have found categorical treatment appropriate is where regulation denies all economically beneficial or productive use of land. As we have said on numerous occasions, the Fifth Amendment is violated when land-use regulation "does not substantially advance legitimate state interests or *denies an owner economically viable use of his land.*"

We have never set forth the justification for this rule. Perhaps it is simply, as Justice Brennan suggested, that total deprivation of beneficial use is, from the landowner's point of view, the equivalent of a physical appropriation. . . . Regulations that leave the owner of land without economically beneficial or productive options for its use—typically, as here, by requiring land to be left substantially in its natural state— carry with them a heightened risk that private property is being pressed into some form of public service under the guise of mitigating serious public harm. See, e.g., *Annicelli v. Town of South Kingstown*, 463 A.2d 133, 140–41 (R.I. 1983) (prohibition on construction adjacent to beach justified on twin grounds of safety and "conservation of open space").

We think, in short, that there are good reasons for our frequently expressed belief that when the owner of real property has been called upon to sacrifice all economically beneficial uses in the name of the common good, that is, to leave his property economically idle, he has suffered a taking.

B.

The trial court found Lucas's two beachfront lots to have been rendered valueless by respondent's enforcement of the coastal-zone con-

struction ban. Under Lucas's theory of the case, which rested upon our "no economically viable use" statements, that finding entitled him to compensation. Lucas believed it unnecessary to take issue with either the purposes behind the Beachfront Management Act, or the means chosen by the South Carolina Legislature to effectuate those purposes. The South Carolina Supreme Court, however, thought otherwise. In its view, the Beachfront Management Act was no ordinary enactment, but involved an exercise of South Carolina's "police powers" to mitigate the harm to the public interest that petitioner's use of his land might occasion. By neglecting to dispute the findings enumerated in the Act or otherwise to challenge the legislature's purposes, petitioner "concede[d] that the beach/dune area of South Carolina's shores is an extremely valuable public resource; that the erection of new construction, inter alia, contributes to the erosion and destruction of this public resource; and that discouraging new construction in close proximity to the beach/dune area is necessary to prevent a great public harm." In the court's view, these concessions brought petitioner's challenge within a long line of this Court's cases sustaining against Due Process and Takings Clause challenges the State's use of its "police powers" to enjoin a property owner from activities akin to public nuisances.

It is correct that many of our prior opinions have suggested that "harmful or noxious uses" of property may be proscribed by government regulation without the requirement of compensation. For a number of reasons, however, we think the South Carolina Supreme Court was too quick to conclude that the principle decides the present case. The "harmful or noxious uses" principle was the Court's early attempt to describe in theoretical terms why government may, consistent with the Takings Clause, affect property values by regulation without incurring an obligation to compensate—a reality we nowadays acknowledge explicitly with respect to the full scope of the State's police power.

"Harmful or noxious use" analysis was, in other words, simply the progenitor of our more contemporary statements that "land-use regulation does not effect a taking if it 'substantially advance[s] legitimate state interests.'. . ."

The transition from our early focus on control of "noxious" uses to our contemporary understanding of the broad realm within which government may regulate without compensation was an easy one, since the distinction between "harm-preventing" and "benefit-conferring" regulation is often in the eye of the beholder. It is quite possible, for example, to describe in *either* fashion the ecological, economic, and aesthetic concerns that inspired the South Carolina legislature in the present case. One could say that imposing a servitude on Lucas's land is necessary in order to prevent his use of it from "harming" South Carolina's ecological resources; or, instead, in order to achieve the "benefits" of an ecological preserve. Whether one or the other of the competing characterizations will come to one's lips in a particular case depends primarily upon one's evaluation of the worth of competing uses of real estate. A given restraint will be seen as mitigating "harm" to the adjacent parcels or securing a "benefit" for them, depending upon the observer's evaluation of the relative importance of the use that the restraint favors. See *Sax, Takings and the Police Power*, 74 Yale L.J. 36, 49 (1964) ("[T]he problem [in this area] is not one of noxiousness or harm-creating activity at all; rather, it is a problem of inconsistency between perfectly innocent and independently desirable uses.") Whether Lucas's construction of single-family residences on his parcels should be described as bringing "harm" to South Carolina's adjacent ecological resources thus depends principally upon whether the describer believes that the State's use interest in nurturing those resources is so important that any competing adjacent use must yield.

Where the State seeks to sustain regulation that deprives land of all economically beneficial use, we think it may resist compensation only if the logically antecedent inquiry into the nature of the owner's estate shows that the proscribed use interests were not part of his title to begin with. This accords, we think, with our "takings" jurisprudence, which has traditionally been guided by the understandings of our citizens regarding the content of, and the State's power over, the "bundle of rights" that they acquire when they obtain title to property.

Where "permanent physical occupation" of land is concerned, we have refused to allow the government to decree it anew (without compensation), no matter how weighty the asserted "public interests" involved, *Loretto v. Teleprompter Manhattan CATV Corp.*, 458 U.S., at 426—though we assuredly would permit the government to assert a permanent easement that was a preexisting limitation upon the landowner's title. We believe similar treatment must be accorded confiscatory regulations, i.e., regulations that prohibit all economically beneficial use of land: Any limitation so severe cannot be newly legislated or decreed (without compensation), but must inhere in the title itself, in the restrictions that background principles of the State's law of property and nuisance already place upon land ownership. A law or decree with such an effect must, in other words, do no more than duplicate the result that could have been achieved in the courts—by adjacent landowners (or other uniquely affected persons) under the State's law of private nuisance, or by the State under its complementary power to abate nuisances that affect the public generally, or otherwise.

On this analysis, the owner of a lake bed, for example, would not be entitled to compensation when he is denied the requisite permit to engage in a landfilling operation that would have the effect of flooding others' land. Nor the corporate owner of a nuclear generating plant, when it is directed to remove all improvements from its land upon discovery that the plant sits astride an earthquake fault. Such regulatory action may well have the effect of eliminating the land's only economically productive use, but it does not proscribe a productive use that was previously permissible under relevant property and nuisance principles. The use of these properties for what are now expressly prohibited purposes was always unlawful, and (subject to other constitutional imitations) it was open to the State at any point to make the implication of those background principles of nuisance and property law explicit. . . . When, however, a regulation that declares "off-limits" all economically productive or beneficial uses of land goes beyond what the relevant background principles would dictate, compensation must be paid to sustain it.

The "total taking" inquiry we require today will ordinarily entail (as the application of state nuisance law ordinarily entails) analysis of, among other things, the degree of harm to public lands and resources, or adjacent private property, posed by the claimant's proposed activities.

It seems unlikely that common-law principles would have prevented the erection of any habitable or productive improvements on petitioner's land; they rarely support prohibition of the "essential use" of land. . . . South Carolina must identify background principles of nuisance and property law that prohibit the uses he now intends in the circumstances in which the property is presently found. Only on this showing can the State fairly claim that, in proscribing all such beneficial uses, the Beachfront Management Act is taking nothing.

· · ·

The judgment is reversed and the case remanded for proceedings not inconsistent with this opinion.

So ordered.

JUSTICE KENNEDY, concurring in the Judgment.

The case comes to the Court in an unusual posture, as all my colleagues observe. After the suit was initiated but before it reached us,

South Carolina amended its Beachfront Management Act to authorize the issuance of special permits at variance with the Act's general limitations. See S.C. Code Sec. 48-39-290(D)(1) (Supp. 1991). Petitioner has not applied for a special permit but may still do so. The availability of this alternative, if it can be invoked, may dispose the petitioner's claim of a permanent taking. As I read the Court's opinion, it does not decide the permanent taking claim, but neither does it foreclose the Supreme Court of South Carolina from considering the claim or requiring petitioner to pursue an administrative alternative not previously available.

Although we establish a framework for remand, moreover, we do not decide the ultimate question of whether a temporary taking has occurred in this case. The facts necessary to the determination have not been developed in the record. Among the matters to be considered on remand must be whether petitioner had the intent and capacity to develop the property and failed to do so in the interim period because the State prevented him. Any failure by petitioner to comply with relevant administrative requirements will be part of that analysis.

The South Carolina Court of Common Pleas found that petitioner's real property has been rendered valueless by the State's regulation. The finding appears to presume that the property has no significant market value or resale potential. This is a curious finding, and I share the reservations of some of my colleagues about a finding that a beachfront lot loses all value because of a development restriction.

The finding of no value must be considered under the Takings Clause by reference to the owner's reasonable, investment-backed expectations. The Takings Clause, while conferring substantial protection on property owners, does not eliminate the police power of the State to enact limitations on the use of their property. *Mugler v. Kansas*, 123 U.S. 623, 669 (1887). The rights conferred by the Takings Clause and the police power of the State may coexist without conflict. Property is bought and sold, investments are made, subject to the State's power to regulate. Where a taking is alleged from regulations which deprive the property of all value, the test must be whether the deprivation is contrary to reasonable, investment-backed expectations.

In my view, reasonable expectations must be understood in light of the whole of our legal tradition. The common law of nuisance is too narrow a confine for the exercise of regulatory power in a complex and interdependent society. The State should not be prevented from enacting new regulatory initiatives in response to changing conditions, and courts must consider all reasonable expectations whatever their source. The Takings Clause does not require a static body of state property law; it protects private expectations to ensure private investment. I agree with the Court that nuisance prevention accords with the most common expectations of property owners who face regulation, but I do not believe this can be the sole source of state authority to impose severe restrictions. Coastal property may present such unique concerns for a fragile land system that the State can go further in regulating its development and use than the common law of nuisance might otherwise permit.

The Supreme Court of South Carolina erred, in my view, by reciting the general purposes for which the state regulations were enacted without a determination that they were in accord with the owner's reasonable expectations and therefore sufficient to support a severe restriction on specific parcels of property. The promotion of tourism, for instance, ought not to suffice to deprive specific property of all value without a corresponding duty to compensate. Furthermore, the means as well as the ends of regulation must accord with the owner's reasonable expectations. Here, the State did not act until after the property had been zoned for individual lot development and most other parcels had been improved, throwing the whole burden of the regulation on the remaining lots. This too must be measured in the balance.

With these observations, I concur in the judgment of the Court.

JUSTICE BLACKMUN, dissenting.

Today the Court launches a missile to kill a mouse.

The State of South Carolina prohibited petitioner Lucas from building a permanent structure on his property from 1988 to 1990. Relying on an unreviewed (and implausible) state trial court finding that this restriction left Lucas's property valueless, this Court granted review to determine whether compensation must be paid in cases where the State prohibits all economic use of real estate. According to the Court, such an occasion never has arisen in any of our prior cases, and the Court imagines that it will arise "relatively rarely" or only in "extraordinary circumstances." Almost certainly it did not happen in this case.

Nonetheless, the Court presses on to decide the issue, and as it does, it ignores its jurisdictional limits, remakes its traditional rules of review, and creates simultaneously a new categorical rule and an exception (neither of which is rooted in our prior case law, common law, or common sense). I protest not only the Court's decision, but each step taken to reach it. More fundamentally, I question the Court's wisdom in issuing sweeping new rules to decide such a narrow case. Surely, as Justice Kennedy demonstrates, the Court could have reached the result it wanted without inflicting this damage upon our Takings Clause jurisprudence.

My fear is that the Court's new policies will spread beyond the narrow confines of the present case. For that reason, I, like the Court, will give far greater attention to this case than its narrow scope suggests—not because I can intercept the Court's missile, or save the targeted mouse, but because I hope perhaps to limit the collateral damage.

I.

A.

In 1972 Congress passed the Coastal Zone Management Act, 16 U.S.C. Sec. 1451 et seq.

The Act was designed to provide States with money and incentives to carry out Congress's goal of protecting the public from shoreline erosion and coastal hazards. In the 1980 Amendments to the Act, Congress directed States to enhance their coastal programs by "[p]reventing or significantly reducing threats to life and the destruction of property by eliminating development and redevelopment in high-hazard areas."

South Carolina began implementing the congressional directive by enacting the South Carolina Coastal Zone Management Act of 1977. Under the 1977 Act, any construction activity in what was designated the "critical area" required a permit from the Council, and the construction of any habitable structure was prohibited. The 1977 critical area was relatively narrow.

This effort did not stop the loss of shoreline. In October 1986, the Council appointed a "Blue Ribbon Committee on Beachfront Management" to investigate beach erosion and propose possible solutions. In March 1987, the Committee found that South Carolina's beaches were "critically eroding," and proposed land-use restrictions. In response, South Carolina enacted the Beachfront Management Act on July 1, 1988. The 1988 Act did not change the uses permitted within the designated critical areas. Rather, it enlarged those areas to encompass the distance from the mean high-water mark to a setback line established on the basis of "the best scientific and historical data" available.

B.

Petitioner Lucas is a contractor, manager, and part owner of the Wild Dune development on the Isle of Palms. He has lived there since 1978. In December 1986, he purchased two of the last four pieces of vacant property in the development. The area is notoriously unstable. In roughly half of the last forty years, all or part of petitioner's property was part of the beach or flooded twice daily by the ebb and flow of the tide. Between 1957 and 1963, petitioner's property was under water. Between 1963 and 1973 the shoreline was 100 to 150 feet onto petitioner's property. In 1973 the first line of stable vegetation was about halfway through the property. Between 1981 and 1983, the Isle of Palms issued twelve emergency orders for sandbagging to protect property in the Wild Dune development. Determining that local habitable structures were in imminent danger of collapse, the Council issued permits for two rock revetments to protect condominium developments near petitioner's property from erosion; one of the revetments extends more than halfway onto one of his lots.

C.

The South Carolina Supreme Court found that the Beachfront Management Act did not take petitioner's property without compensation. The decision rested on two premises that until today were unassailable—that the State has the power to prevent any use of property it finds to be harmful to its citizens, and that a state statute is entitled to a presumption of constitutionality.

The Beachfront Management Act includes a finding by the South Carolina General Assembly that the beach/dune system serves the purpose of "protect[ing] life and property by serving as a storm barrier which dissipates wave energy and contributes to shoreline stability in an economical and effective manner." The General Assembly also found that "development unwisely has been sited too close to the [beach/dune] system. This type of development has jeopardized the stability of the beach/dune system, accelerated erosion, and endangered adjacent property."

If the state legislature is correct that the prohibition on building in front of the setback line prevents serious harm, then, under this Court's prior cases, the Act is constitutional.

Petitioner never challenged the legislature's findings that a building ban was necessary to protect property and life. Nor did he contend that the threatened harm was not sufficiently serious to make building a house in a particular location a "harmful" use, that the legislature had not made sufficient findings, or that the legislature was motivated by anything other than a desire to minimize damage to coastal areas.

Nothing in the record undermines the General Assembly's assessment that prohibitions on building in front of the setback line are necessary to protect people and property from storms, high tides, and beach erosion. Because that legislative determination cannot be disregarded in the absence of such evidence, and because its determination of harm to life and property from building is sufficient to prohibit that use under this Court's cases, the South Carolina Supreme Court correctly found no taking.

II.

My disagreement with the Court begins with its decision to review this case. This Court has held consistently that a land-use challenge is not ripe for review until there is a final decision about what uses of the property will be permitted. The ripeness requirement is not simply a gesture of goodwill to land-use planners. In the absence of "a final and authoritative determination of the type and intensity of development legally permitted on the subject property," utilization of state procedures for just compensation, there is no final judgment, and in the absence of a final judgment there is no jurisdiction.

This rule is "compelled by the very nature of the inquiry required by the Just Compensation Clause," because the factors applied in deciding a takings claim "simply cannot be evaluated until the administrative agency has arrived at a final, definitive position regarding how it will apply the regulations at issue to the particular land in question."

The Court admits that the 1990 amendments to the Beachfront Management Act allowing special permits preclude Lucas from asserting that his property has been permanently taken. The Court agrees that such a claim would not be ripe because there has been no final decision by respondent on what uses will be permitted. The

Court, however, will not be denied: it determines that petitioner's "temporary takings" claim for the period from July 1, 1988, to June 25, 1990, is ripe. But this claim also is not justiciable.

From the very beginning of this litigation, respondent has argued that the courts

lac[k] jurisdiction in this matter because the plaintiff has sought no authorization from Council for use of his property, has not challenged the location of the baseline or setback line as alleged in the Complaint, and because no final agency decision has been rendered concerning use of his property or location of said baseline or setback line.

Although the Council's plea has been ignored by every court, it is undoubtedly correct.

Under the Beachfront Management Act, petitioner was entitled to challenge the setback line or the baseline or erosion rate applied to his property in formal administrative, followed by judicial, proceedings. Because Lucas failed to pursue this administrative remedy, the Council never finally decided whether Lucas's particular piece of property was correctly categorized as a critical area in which building would not be permitted. This is all the more crucial because Lucas argued strenuously in the trial court that his land was perfectly safe to build on, and that his company had studies to prove it. If he was correct, the Council's final decision would have been to alter the setback line, eliminating the construction ban on Lucas's property.

That petitioner's property fell within the critical area as initially interpreted by the Council does not excuse petitioner's failure to challenge the Act's application to his property in the administrative process. The claim is not ripe until petitioner seeks a variance from that status.

Even if I agreed with the Court that there were no jurisdictional barriers to deciding this case, I still would not try to decide it. The Court creates its new taking jurisprudence based on the trial court's finding that the property had lost all economic value. This finding is almost certainly erroneous. Petitioner still can enjoy other attributes of ownership, such as the right to exclude others, "one of the most essential sticks in the bundle of rights that are commonly characterized as property." *Kaiser Aetna v. United States*, 444 U.S. 164, 176 (1979). Petitioner can picnic, swim, camp in a tent, or live on the property in a movable trailer. State courts frequently have recognized that land has economic value where the only residual economic uses are recreation or camping. Petitioner also retains the right to alienate the land, which would have value for neighbors and for those prepared to enjoy proximity to the ocean without a house.

Yet the trial court, apparently believing that "less value" and "valueless" could be used interchangeably, found the property "valueless." The court accepted no evidence from the State on the property's value without a home, and petitioner's appraiser testified that he never had considered what the value would be absent a residence. The appraiser's value was based on the fact that the "highest and best use of these lots . . . [is] luxury single-family detached dwellings." The trial court appeared to believe that the property could be considered "valueless" if it was not available for its most profitable use. Absent that erroneous assumption, I find no evidence in the record supporting the trial court's conclusion that the damage to the lots by virtue of the restrictions was "total."

Clearly, the Court was eager to decide this case. But eagerness, in the absence of proper jurisdiction, must—and in this case should have been—met with restraint.

III.

The Court's willingness to dispense with precedent in its haste to reach a result is not limited to its initial jurisdictional decision. The Court also alters the long-settled rules of review.

The South Carolina Supreme Court's deci-·sion to defer to legislative judgments in the absence of a challenge from petitioner comports with one of this Court's oldest maxims: "The existence of facts supporting the legislative judgment is to be presumed." *United States v. Carolene Products Co.*, 304 U.S. 144, 152 (1938). Indeed, we have said the legislature's judgment is "well-nigh conclusive."

Accordingly, this Court always has required plaintiffs challenging the constitutionality of an ordinance to provide "some factual foundation of record" that contravenes the legislative findings. In the absence of such proof, "the presumption of constitutionality must prevail." We only recently have reaffirmed that claimants have the burden of showing a state law constitutes a taking.

Rather than invoking these traditional rules, the Court decides the State has the burden to convince the courts that its legislative judgments are correct. Despite Lucas's complete failure to contest the legislature's findings of serious harm to life and property if a permanent structure is built, the Court decides that the legislative findings are not sufficient to justify the use prohibition. Instead, the Court "emphasize[s]" the State must do more than merely proffer its legislative judgments to avoid invalidating its law. In this case, apparently, the State now has the burden of showing the regulation is not a taking. The Court offers no justification for its sudden hostility toward state legislators, and I doubt that it could.

IV.

The Court does not reject the South Carolina Supreme Court's decision simply on the basis of its disbelief and distrust of the legislature's findings. It also takes the opportunity to create a new scheme for regulations that eliminate all economic value. From now on, there is a categorical rule finding these regulations to be a taking unless the use they prohibit is a background common-law nuisance or property principle.

A.

This Court repeatedly has recognized the ability of government, in certain circumstances, to regulate property without compensation no matter how adverse the financial effect on the owner may be. More than a century ago, the Court explicitly upheld the right of States to prohibit uses of property injurious to public health, safety, or welfare without paying compensation: "A prohibition simply upon the use of property for purposes that are declared, by valid legislation, to be injurious to the health, morals, or safety of the community, cannot, in any just sense, be deemed a taking or an appropriation of property." *Mugler v. Kansas*, 123 U.S. 623, 668–69 (1887). On this basis, the Court upheld an ordinance effectively prohibiting operation of a previously lawful brewery, although the "establishments will become of no value as property."

The Court recognizes that "our prior opinions have suggested that 'harmful or noxious uses' of property may be proscribed by government regulation without the requirement of compensation," but seeks to reconcile them with its categorical rule by claiming that the Court never has upheld a regulation when the owner alleged the loss of all economic value. Even if the Court's factual premise was correct, its understanding of the Court's cases is distorted. In none of the cases did the Court suggest that the right of a State to prohibit certain activities without paying compensation turned on the availability of some residual valuable use. Instead, the cases depended on whether the government interest was sufficient to prohibit the activity, given the significant private cost.

Until today, the Court explicitly had rejected the contention that the government's power to act without paying compensation turns on whether the prohibited activity is a common-law nuisance. The brewery closed in *Mugler* itself was not a common-law nuisance, and the Court specifically stated that it was the role of the legislature to determine what measures would be appropriate for the protection of the public health and safety.

The Court rejects the notion that the State always can prohibit uses it deems a harm to the public without granting compensation because

"the distinction between 'harm preventing' and 'benefit-conferring' regulation is often in the eye of the beholder." Since the characterization will depend "primarily upon one's evaluation of the worth of competing uses of real estate," the Court decides a legislative judgment of this kind no longer can provide the desired "objective, value-free basis" for upholding a regulation. The Court, however, fails to explain how its proposed common-law alternative escapes the same trap.

Even more perplexing, however, is the Court's reliance on common-law principles of nuisance in its quest for a value-free taking jurisprudence. In determining what is a nuisance at common law, state courts make exactly the decision that the Court finds so troubling when made by the South Carolina General Assembly today: they determine whether the use is harmful. Common-law public and private nuisance law is simply a determination whether a particular use causes harm. There is nothing magical in the reasoning of judges long dead. They determined a harm in the same way as state judges and legislatures do today. If judges in the eighteenth and nineteenth centuries can distinguish a harm from a benefit, why not judges in the twentieth century, and if judges can, why not legislators? There simply is no reason to believe that new interpretations of the hoary common-law nuisance doctrine will be particularly "objective" or "value-free."

B.

Finally, the Court justifies its new rule that the legislature may not deprive a property owner of the only economically valuable use of his land, even if the legislature finds it to be a harmful use, because such action is not part of the "long-recognized" "understandings of our citizens." These "understandings" permit such regulation only if the use is a nuisance under the common law. Any other course is "inconsistent with the historical compact recorded in the Takings Clause." It is not clear from the Court's opinion where our "historical compact" or "citizens' understanding" comes from, but it does not appear to be history.

The principle that the State should compensate individuals for property taken for public use was not widely established in America at the time of the Revolution.

Even into the nineteenth century, state governments often felt free to take property for roads and other public projects without paying compensation to the owners. There was an obvious movement toward establishing the just compensation principle during the nineteenth century, but "there continued to be a strong current in American legal thought that regarded compensation simply as a 'bounty given . . . by the State' out of 'kindness' and not out of justice."

Although, prior to the adoption of the Bill of Rights, America was replete with land use regulations describing which activities were considered noxious and forbidden, the Fifth Amendment's Takings Clause originally did not extend to regulations of property, whatever the effect.

Even when the courts began to consider that regulation in some situations could constitute a taking, they continued to uphold bans on particular uses without paying compensation, notwithstanding the economic impact, under the rationale that no one can obtain a vested right to injure or endanger the public.

In addition, state courts historically have been less likely to find that a government action constitutes a taking when the affected land is undeveloped.

Nor does history indicate any common-law limit on the State's power to regulate harmful uses even to the point of destroying all economic value. Nothing in the discussions in Congress concerning the Takings Clause indicates that the Clause was limited by the common-law nuisance doctrine. Common-law courts themselves rejected such an understanding. They regularly recognized that it is "for the legislature to interpose, and by positive enactment to

prohibit a use of property which would be injurious to the public."

In short, I find no clear and accepted "historical compact" or "understanding of our citizens" justifying the Court's new taking doctrine. Instead, the Court seems to treat history as a grab bag of principles, to be adopted where they support the Court's theory, and ignored where they do not. If the Court decided that the early common law provides the background principles for interpreting the Takings Clause, then regulation, as opposed to physical confiscation, would not be compensable. If the Court decided that the law of a later period provides the background principles, then regulation might be compensable, but the Court would have to confront the fact that legislatures regularly determined which uses were prohibited, independent of the common law, and independent of whether the uses were lawful when the owner purchased. What makes the Court's analysis unworkable is its attempt to package the law of two incompatible eras and peddle it as historical fact.

V.

The Court makes sweeping and, in my view, misguided and unsupported changes in our taking doctrine. While it limits these changes to the most narrow subset of government regulation— that eliminate all economic value from land— these changes go far beyond what is necessary to secure petitioner Lucas's private benefit. One hopes they do not go beyond the narrow confines the Court assigns them to today.

I dissent.

JUSTICE STEVENS, dissenting.

The Court's holding today effectively freezes the State's common law, denying the legislature much of its traditional power to revise the law governing the rights and uses of property. Until today, I had thought that we had long abandoned this approach to constitutional law. More than a century ago we recognized that "the great office of statutes is to remedy defects in the common law as they are developed, and to adapt it to the changes of time and circumstances." *Munn v. Illinois*, 94 U.S. 113, 134 (1877). As Justice Marshall observed about a position similar to that adopted by the Court today:

If accepted, that claim would represent a return to the era of *Lochner v. New York*, 198 U.S. 45 (1905), when common-law rights were also found immune from revision by State or Federal Government. Such an approach would freeze the common law as it has been constructed by the courts, perhaps at its nineteenth-century state of development. It would allow no room for change in response to changes in circumstance. The Due Process Clause does not require such a result. *PruneYard Shopping Center v. Robins*, 447 U.S. 74, 93 (1980) (concurring opinion)

Arresting the development of the common law is not only a departure from our prior decisions, it is also profoundly unwise. The human condition is one of constant learning and evolution—both moral and practical. Legislatures implement that new learning; in doing so, they must often revise the definition of property and the rights of property owners. Thus, when the Nation came to understand that slavery was morally wrong and mandated the emancipation of all slaves, it, in effect, redefined "property." On a lesser scale, our ongoing self-education produces similar changes in the rights of property owners: New appreciation of the significance of endangered species, see, e.g., *Andrus v. Allard*, 444 U.S. 51 (1979); the importance of wetlands, see, e.g., 16 U.S.C. Sec. 3801 et seq.; and the vulnerability of coastal lands, see, e.g., 16 U.S.C. Sec. 1451 et seq., shapes our evolving understandings of property rights.

Of course, some legislative redefinitions of property will effect a taking and must be compensated—but it certainly cannot be the case that every movement away from common law does so. There is no reason, and less sense, in such an absolute rule. We live in a world in which changes in the economy and the environment occur with increasing frequency and importance. If it was wise a century ago to allow

Government " 'the largest legislative discretion' " to deal with " 'the special exigencies of the moment,' *Mugler*, 123 U.S., at 669, it is imperative to do so today. The rule that should govern a decision in a case of this kind should focus on the future, not the past.

The Court's categorical approach rule will, I fear, greatly hamper the efforts of local officials and planners who must deal with increasingly complex problems in land-use and environmental regulation. As this case—in which the claims of an individual property owner exceed $1 million—well demonstrates, these officials face both substantial uncertainty because of the ad hoc nature of takings law and unacceptable penalties if they guess incorrectly about the law.

The rigid rules fixed by the Court today clash with this enterprise: "fairness and justice" are often disserved by categorical rules.

In view of all these factors, even assuming that petitioner's property was rendered valueless, the risk inherent in investments of the sort made by petitioner, the generality of the Act, and the compelling purpose motivating the South Carolina Legislature persuade me that the Act did not effect a taking of petitioner's property.

Accordingly, I respectfully dissent.

Statement of JUSTICE SOUTER.

I would dismiss the writ of certiorari in this case as having been granted improvidently. After briefing and argument it is abundantly clear that an unreviewable assumption on which this case comes to us is both questionable as a conclusion of Fifth Amendment law and sufficient to frustrate the Court's ability to render certain the legal premises on which its holding rests.

While the issue of what constitutes total deprivation deserves the Court's attention, as does the relationship between nuisance abatement and such total deprivation, the Court should confront these matters directly. Because it can neither do so in this case, nor skip over those preliminary issues and deal independently with defenses to the Court's categorical compensation rule, the Court should dismiss the instant writ and await an opportunity to face the total deprivation question squarely. Under these circumstances, I believe it proper for me to vote to dismiss the writ, despite the Court's contrary preference.

The Supreme Court of South Carolina, David H. Lucas, Respondent v. South Carolina Coastal Council, Appellant. Order on Remand (Nov. 20, 1992)

In 1986 David H. Lucas (Lucas) purchased two oceanfront lots on the Isle of Palms, South Carolina. At the time of purchase, both lots were zoned and suitable for single-family residential construction. Prior to Lucas's commencing construction on these lots, the legislature of this State enacted the 1988 Beachfront Management Act. Under the 1988 Act, the South Carolina Coastal Council (Coastal Council) was charged with establishing new baselines and setback lines for the coast. Lucas's lots are entirely seaward of the baseline and setback line drawn for the area in which Lucas's property is located. Thus, as a consequence of the 1988 Act, Lucas was restrained from constructing any more than a walkway or small deck on his property.

Lucas filed a summons and complaint in which he alleged that the 1988 Act constituted a permanent taking of his private property without just compensation. The trial judge held that the 1988 Act did constitute a permanent, total taking of private property without just compensation in contravention of the Fifth Amendment of the Constitution of the United States and Article I, Section 13, of the South Carolina Constitution. Coastal Council appealed.

During the pendency of the appeal, but after briefing and oral argument before this Court, the 1988 Act was amended to authorize Coastal Council to issue "Special Permits" for the construction of habitable structure seaward of the established baseline. This court declined to dismiss the action to determine whether coastal council would issue a special permit to allow Lucas to build a habitable structure under the

1990 Act. Instead, we elected to dispose of the case on its merits. A majority of the court determined that the 1988 Act sought to prevent serious public harm and thus was a permissible restriction of the use of Lucas's property. Accordingly, the majority held that Lucas had not suffered a "regulatory taking" entitling him to compensation. Lucas appealed this ruling to the United States Supreme Court, and that Court granted certiorari.

The United States Supreme Court reversed our opinion on June 29, 1992, in *Lucas v. South Carolina Coastal Council*. The United States Supreme Court ruled that Coastal Council had advanced no State interest sufficient to justify the total regulatory taking of Lucas's land and that, in fact, "[w]here the State seeks to sustain regulation that deprives land of all economically beneficial use . . . it may resist compensation only if logically antecedent inquiry into the nature of the owner's estate shows that the proscribed use interests were not part of its title to begin with." The court remanded this issue to allow Coastal Council the opportunity to "identify background principles of nuisance and property law" by which Lucas could be restrained from constructing a habitable structure on his land.

The inquiry does not end here. The Court also noted that, pursuant to the 1990 Act, Lucas may apply for a special permit to build seaward of the baseline. Clearly, Lucas has been only temporarily deprived of the use of his land if he can obtain a special permit to construct habitable structures on his lots. The court discerned, however, that our decision to dispose of the case on its merits "practically and legally" had precluded Lucas from asserting a claim with respect to his having been temporarily deprived of the right to build prior to the 1990 Act. Indeed absent the Court's intervention and reversal, Lucas would have been unable to obtain further state-court adjudication with respect to a temporary taking. Accordingly, the remand of this case from the United States Supreme Court has created for Lucas a cause of action for the temporary deprivation of the use of his property, unless Coastal Council can demonstrate that Lucas's intended use of his land was not part of the bundle of rights inhering in his title.

We have reviewed the record and heard arguments from the parties regarding whether Coastal Council possesses the ability under the common law to prohibit Lucas from constructing a habitable structure on his land. Coastal Council has not persuaded us that any common-law basis exists by which it could restrain Lucas's desired use of his land, nor has our research uncovered any such common-law principle. We hold that the sole issue on remand from this court to the circuit level is a determination of the actual damages . . . as the result of his being temporarily deprived of the use of his property.

In this regard, we grant leave to the parties to amend their pleadings and present evidence of the actual damages Lucas has sustained as a result of the temporary nonacquisitory taking of his property without just compensation. We direct the trial judge to make specific findings of damages appropriate to compensate Lucas for his temporary deprivation of the use of his property. To this end, we do not dictate any specific method of calculating the damages for the temporary nonacquisatory taking. We do find, however, that because Lucas was unable to assert a temporary taking claim until the United States Supreme Court overturned our prior disposition of the case, and because Lucas has been unable to act pending our order on remand, that Lucas has suffered a temporary taking deserving compensation commencing with the enactment of the 1988 Act and continuing through the date of this Order.

We are aware that, once Lucas applies for a special permit pursuant to the 1990 Act, Coastal Council could deny the special permit or place such restrictions on the permit that Lucas might contend that a subsequent unconstitutional taking has occurred. We emphasize that this Order is made without prejudice to the right of the parties to litigate any subsequent deprivations which may arise as the result of Coastal Council's actions in regard to the granting or nongranting of a special permit for future construction.

It is so ordered.

Questions

1. Justice Scalia's majority opinion gives us a new standard for takings cases: "When the owner of real property has been called upon to sacrifice all economically beneficial uses in the name of the common good." What, in Mr. Lucas's case, does that mean?

2. How could Lucas ever get this case to the Supreme Court without even applying for a building permit?

3. On remand, the South Carolina Supreme Court found a "temporary taking" from 1988 to 1992—how will *that* be calculated?

Chapter 7

STATE REGULATION OF FISHERIES AND INDIAN FISHING RIGHTS

Manchester v. Massachusetts, 139 U.S. 240 (1890)

By an act of the legislature of the Commonwealth of Massachusetts, approved May 6, 1886 (Laws of 1886, c. 192), entitled "An act for the protection of the fisheries in Buzzard's Bay," it was enacted as follows:

SECTION 1. No person shall draw, set, stretch or use any drag net, set net, or gill net, purse or sweep seine of any kind for taking fish anywhere in the waters of Buzzard's Bay within the jurisdiction of this Commonwealth, nor in any harbor, cove, or bight of said bay except as hereinafter provided.

. . . Under that statute, a complaint in writing under oath was made on behalf of the Commonwealth, before a trial justice in and for the county of Barnstable, in Massachusetts, that Arthur Manchester, at Falmouth, in the county of Barnstable, on the 19th day of July, in the year 1889, did then and there draw, set, stretch, and use a purse seine for the taking of fish in the waters of Buzzard's Bay, within the jurisdiction of the Commonwealth. Under a warrant issued on this complaint, Manchester was, on the 1st of August, 1889, brought before the trial justice, and pleaded not guilty. The justice found him guilty, on a hearing of the case, and imposed upon him a fine of $100, to the use of the Com-

monwealth, and costs, and ordered that, if the fine and costs should not be paid, he should be committed to jail, there to be kept until he should pay them, or be otherwise discharged by due course of law.

. . . The defendant did not dispute any of the testimony offered by the Commonwealth, but introduced evidence tending to show that he was engaged in fishing for menhaden only, and that he caught no other fish excepting menhaden; that menhaden is not a food fish and is only valuable for the purpose of bait and of manufacture into fish oil; and that the taking of said menhaden by seining does not tend in any way to decrease the quantity and variety of food fishes. The defendant offered evidence further tending to show that he was in the employ of the firm of Charles Cook and others, who were engaged in the State of Rhode Island in the business of seining menhaden to be sold for bait and to be manufactured into fish oil and fish manure. The defendant further offered testimony tending to show that it was impossible to discern objects across from one headland to the other at the mouth of Buzzard's Bay. The defendant's evidence showed that the said steamer was of Newport, Rhode Island, duly enrolled and licensed at that port, under the laws of the United States, for carrying on the menhaden fishery, and it was conceded by the Commonwealth that the defendant was employed upon the vessel described by said enrollment and license, and, at the time of the commission of the acts complained of, he and his associates were so in the employ of the vessel described in said license.

The principal contentions in this court on the part of the defendant are that, although Massachusetts, if an independent nation, could have enacted a statute like the one in question, which her own courts would have enforced and which other nations would have recognized, yet when she became one of the United States, she surrendered to the general government her right of control over the fisheries of the ocean, and transferred to it her rights over the waters adjacent to the coast and a part of the ocean; that, as by the Constitution, article 3, section 2, the judicial power of the United States is made to extend to all cases of admiralty and maritime jurisdiction, it is consistent only with that view that the rights in respect of fisheries should be regarded as national rights, and be enforced only in national courts; that the proprietary right of Massachusetts is confined to the body of the county; that the offence committed by the defendant was committed outside of that territory, in a locality where legislative control did not rest upon title in the soil and waters, but upon rights of sovereignty inseparably connected with national character, and which were intrusted exclusively to the enforcement in admiralty courts; that the Commonwealth has no jurisdiction upon the ocean within three miles of the shore; that it could not, by the statute in question, oust the United States of jurisdiction; that fishing upon the high seas is in its nature an integral part of national commerce, and its control and regulation are necessarily vested in Congress and not in the individual states; that Congress has manifested its purpose to take the regulation of coast fisheries, in the particulars covered by the Massachusetts statute in question, by the joint resolution of Congress of February 9, 1871 (16 State. 593), establishing the

Fish Commission, and by Title 51 of the Revised Statutes, entitled "Regulation of Fisheries," and by the act of February 28, 1887, c. 288 (24 Stat. 434), relating to the mackerel fisheries, and by acts relating to bounties, privileges, and agreements, and by granting the license under which the defendant's steamer was fishing; and that, in view of the act of Congress authorizing such license, no statute of a State could defeat the right of the defendant to fish in the high seas under it.

By the Public Statutes of Massachusetts, part 1, title 1, c. 1, sections 1 and 2, it is enacted as follows:

Section 1. The territorial limits of this Commonwealth extend one marine league from its seashore at low-water mark. When an inlet or arm of the sea does not exceed two marine leagues in width between its headlands, a straight line from one headland to the other is equivalent to the shore line. Section 2. The sovereignty and jurisdiction of the Commonwealth extend to all places within the boundaries thereof; subject to the rights of concurrent jurisdiction granted over places ceded to the United States.

The same Public Statutes, part 1, title 1, c. 22, section 1, contain the following provision: "The boundaries of counties bordering on the sea shall extend to the line of the Commonwealth, as defined in section one of chapter one." Section 11 of the same chapter is as follows: "The jurisdiction of counties separated by waters within the jurisdiction of the Commonwealth shall be concurrent upon and over such waters." By section 2 of chapter 196 of the acts of Massachusetts of 1881, it is provided as follows:

Section 2. The harbor and land commissioners shall locate and define the courses of the boundary lines between adjacent cities and towns bordering upon the sea and upon arms of the sea from high-water mark outward to the line of the Commonwealth, as defined in said section one, [section one of chapter one of the General Statutes], so that the same shall conform as nearly as may be to the course of the boundary lines between said adjacent cities and towns on the land; and they shall file a report of their doings with suitable plans and exhibits, showing the boundary lines of any town by them located and defined, in the registry of deeds in which deeds of real estate situated in such town are required to be recorded, and also in the office of the secretary of the Commonwealth.

The report of the Superior Court states that the point where the defendant was using the seine was within that part of Buzzard's Bay which the harbor and land commissioners, acting under the provisions of the act of 1881, had, so far as they were capable of doing so, assigned to and made part of the town of Falmouth; that the distance between the headlands at the mouth of Buzzard's Bay "was more than one and less than two marine leagues"; that "the distance across said bay, at the point where the acts of the defendant were done, is more than two marine leagues, and the opposite points are in different counties"; and that "the place where the defendant was so engaged with said seine was about, and not exceeding, one mile and a quarter from a point on the shore midway from the north line of" the town of Falmouth "to the south line" of that town.

Buzzard's Bay lies wholly within the territory of Massachusetts, having Barnstable County on the one side of it, and the counties of Bristol and Plymouth on the other. The defendant offered evidence that he was fishing for menhaden only, with a purse seine; that "the bottom of the sea was not encroached upon or disturbed"; "that it was impossible to discern objects across from one headland to the other at the mouth of Buzzard's Bay"; and that the steamer was duly enrolled and licensed at the port of Newport, Rhode Island, under the laws of the United States, for carrying on the menhaden fishery.

By section 1 of chapter 196 of the laws of Massachusetts of 1881, it was enacted as follows: "Section 1. The boundaries of cities and towns bordering upon the sea shall extend to the line of the Commonwealth as the same is defined in section 1 of chapter 1 of the General Statutes." Section 1 of chapter 1 of the General Statutes contains the provisions before recited as now contained in the Public Statutes, chapter 1, section 1, and chapter 22, sections 1 and 11. Buzzard's Bay was undoubtedly within the territory described in the charter of the Colony of New Plymouth and the Province charter. By the definitive treaty of peace of September 3, 1783, between the United States and Great Britain (8 Stat. 81), His Britannic Majesty acknowledged the United States, of which Massachusetts Bay was one, to be free, sovereign, and independent States, and declared that he treated with them as such, and, for himself, his heirs, and successors, relinquished all claims to the government, propriety, and territorial rights of the same and every part thereof. Therefore, if Massachusetts had continued to be an independent nation, her boundaries on the sea, as defined by her statutes, would unquestionably be acknowledged by all foreign nations, and her right to control the fisheries within those boundaries would be conceded. The limits of the right of a nation to control the fisheries on its seacoasts, and in the bays and arms of the sea within its territory, have never been placed at less than a marine league from the coast on the open sea; and bays wholly within the territory of a nation, the headland of which are not more than two marine leagues, or six geographical miles, apart, have always been regarded as a part of the territory of the nation in which they lie.

On this branch of the subject the case of *The Queen v. Keyn*, 2 Ex.D. 63, is cited for the plaintiff in error, but there the question was not as to the extent of the dominion of Great Britain over the open sea adjacent to the coast, but only as to the extent of the existing jurisdiction of the Court of Admiralty in England over offenses committed on the open sea; and the decision had nothing to do with the right of control over fisheries in the open sea or in bays or arms of the sea. In all the cases cited in the opinions delivered in *The Queen v. Keyn*, wherever the question of the right of fishery is referred to, it is conceded that the control of fisheries, to the extent of at least a marine league from the shore, belongs to the nation on whose coast the fisheries are prosecuted.

We think it must be regarded as established that, as between nations, the minimum limit of the territorial jurisdiction of a nation over tidewaters is a marine league from its coast; that bays wholly within its territory not exceeding two marine leagues in width at the mouth are within this limit; and that included in this territorial jurisdiction is the right of control over fisheries, whether the fish be migratory, free-swimming fish, or free-moving fish, or fish attached to or embedded in the soil. The open sea within this limit is, of course, subject to the common right of navigation; and all governments, for the purpose of self-protection in time of war or for the prevention of frauds on its revenue, exercise an authority beyond this limit.

It is further insisted by the plaintiff in error that the control of the fisheries of Buzzard's Bay is, by the Constitution of the United States, exclusively with the United States, and that the statute of Massachusetts is repugnant to that Constitution and to the laws of the United States.

In *Dunham v. Lamphere*, 3 Gray, 268, it was held, (Chief Justice Shaw delivering the opinion of the court), that in the distribution of powers between the general and State governments, the right to the fisheries and the power to regulate the fisheries on the coasts and in the tidewaters of the State, were left, by the Constitution of the United States, with the States, subject only to such powers as Congress may justly exercise in the regulation of commerce, foreign and domestic. In the present case the court below was asked to reconsider that decision, mainly on the ground that the admiralty and maritime jurisdiction of the courts of the United States was not considered in the opinion, and that the recent decisions of the Supreme Court of the United States, on the power of Congress to regulate commerce, required that the decision be reconsidered; but the court stated that no recent decisions of this court had been cited which related to the regulation of fisheries within the territorial tidewaters of a State, and that the decisions of this court which related to that subject did not appear to be in conflict with the decision in *Dunham v. Lamphere*, and that it never had been decided anywhere that the regulation of the fisheries within the territorial limits of a State was a regulation of commerce.

It is further contended that by the Constitution of the United States the judicial power of the United States extends to all cases of admiralty and maritime jurisdiction, and is exclusive; that this case is within such jurisdiction; and that therefore, the courts of Massachusetts have no jurisdiction over it. In *McCready v. Virginia*, 94 U.S. 391, the question involved was whether the State of Virginia could prohibit the citizens of other States from planting oysters in Ware River, a stream, in Virginia where the tide ebbed and flowed, when her own citizens had that privilege. In that case it was said that the principle had long been settled in this court, that each State owns the beds of all tidewaters within its jurisdiction, unless they have been granted away; and that, in like manner, the States own the tidewaters themselves and the fish in them, so far as they are capable of ownership while running; and this court added, in its opinion:

The title thus held is subject to the paramount right of navigation, the regulation of which, in respect to foreign and interstate commerce, has been granted to the United States. There has been, however, no such grant of power over the fisheries. These remain under the exclusive control of the State, which has consequently the right, in its discretion, to appropriate its tidewaters and their beds to be used by its people as a common for taking and cultivating fish, so far as it may be done without obstructing navigation. Such an appropriation is in effect nothing more than a regulation of the use by the people of their common property. The right which the people of the State thus acquire comes not from their citizenship alone, but from their citizenship and property combined. It is, in fact, a property right, and not a mere privilege or immunity of citizenship.

In *Smith v. Maryland*, 18 How. 71, 74, a vessel licensed to be employed in the coasting trade and fisheries was seized by the sheriff of Anne Arundel County in Maryland, while engaged in dredging for oysters in Chesapeake Bay, in violation of a statute of Maryland enacted for the purpose of preventing the destruction of oysters in the waters of that State; and the questions presented were whether that statute was repugnant to the provisions of the Constitution of the United States which grant to Congress the power to regulate commerce, or to those which declare that the judicial power of the United States shall extend to all cases of admiralty and maritime jurisdiction, or to those which declare that the citizens of each State shall be entitled to all privileges and immunities of citizens in the several States. Mr. Justice Curtis, in delivering the opinion of this court, said:

Whatever soil below low-water mark is the subject of exclusive property and ownership belongs to the State on whose maritime border and within whose territory it lies, subject to any lawful grants of that soil by the State, or the sovereign power which governed its territory, before the declaration of independence. But this soil is held by the State, not only subject to, but in some sense in trust for, the enjoyment of certain public rights, among which is the common liberty of taking fish, as well shellfish as floating fish.

He also said that the statute of Maryland does

not touch the subject of the common liberty of taking oysters, save for the purpose of guarding it from injury, to whomsoever it may belong, and by whomsoever it may be enjoyed. Whether this liberty belongs exclusively to the citizens of the State of Maryland, or may lawfully be enjoyed in common by all citizens of the United States; whether this public use may be restricted by the State to its own citizens or a part of them, or by force of the Constitution of the United States must remain common to all citizens of the United States; whether the national government, by a treaty or act of Congress, can grant to foreigners the right to participate therein; or what, in general, are the limits of the trust upon which the

State holds this soil, or its power to define and control that trust, are matters wholly without the scope of this case, and upon which we give no opinion.

Upon the question of the admiralty jurisdiction, he said:

But we consider it to have been settled by this court, in *United States v. Bevans*, 3 Wheat. 336, that this clause in the Constitution did not affect the jurisdiction, or the legislative power of the States, over so much of their territory as lies below high-water mark, save that they parted with the power so to legislate as to conflict with the admiralty jurisdiction or laws of the United States. As this law conflicts neither with the admiralty jurisdiction of any court of the United States conferred by Congress, nor with any law of Congress whatever, we are of opinion it is not repugnant to this clause of the Constitution.

The court also held that the act was not repugnant to the clause of the Constitution which conferred upon Congress the power to regulate commerce, and that the enrollment and license of the vessel gave to the plaintiff in error no right to violate the statute of Maryland. It is said in the opinion that "no question was made in the court below whether the place in question be within the territory of the State. The law is, in terms, limited to the waters of the State"; and the question, therefore, did not arise "whether a voyage of a vessel, licensed and enrolled for the coasting trade, had been interrupted by force of a law of a State while on the high seas, and out of the territorial jurisdiction of such State." The dimensions of Chesapeake Bay do not appear in the report of the case, but it has been said that this bay is "twelve miles across at the ocean." It is a bay considerably larger than Buzzard's Bay, and is not wholly within the State of Maryland, although at the point where Anne Arundel County bounds upon it, it is wholly in that State.

Under the grant by the Constitution of judicial power to the United States in all cases of admiralty and maritime jurisdiction, and under the rightful legislation of Congress, personal suits on maritime contracts or for maritime torts can be maintained in the state courts; and the courts of the United States, merely by virtue of this grant of judicial power, and in the absence of legislation by Congress, have no criminal jurisdiction whatever. The criminal jurisdiction of the courts of the United States is wholly derived from the statutes of the United States. In each of the cases of *United States v. Bevans*, 3 Wheat. 336, and of *Commonwealth v. Peters*, 12 Met. 387, the place where the offence was committed was in Boston Harbor; and it was held to be within the jurisdiction of Massachusetts, according to the meaning of the statutes of the United States which punished certain offenses committed upon the high seas or in any river, haven, basin, or bay "out of the jurisdiction of any particular State." The test applied in *Commonwealth v. Peters*, which was decided in the year 1847, was that the place was within a bay "not so wide but that persons and objects on the one side can be discerned by the naked eye by persons on the opposite side," and was therefore within the body of a county. In *United States v. Bevans*, Marshall, C.J., said: "The jurisdiction of a State is coextensive with its territory; coextensive with its legislative power. The place described is unquestionably within the original territory of Massachusetts. It is then within the jurisdiction of Massachusetts, unless that jurisdiction has been ceded to the United States." If the place where the offence charged in this case was committed is within the general jurisdiction of Massachusetts, then, according to the principles declared in *Smith v. Maryland*, the statute in question is not repugnant to the Constitution and laws of the United States.

It is also contended that the jurisdiction of a State as between it and the United States must be confined to the body of counties; that counties must be defined according to the customary English usage at the time of the adoption of the Constitution of the United States; that by this usage counties were bounded by the margin of the open sea; and that, as to bays and arms of the sea extending into the land, only such or such parts were included in counties as were so

narrow that objects could be distinctly seen from one shore to the other by the naked eye. But there is no indication that the customary law of England in regard to the boundaries of counties was adopted by the Constitution of the United States as a measure to determine the territorial jurisdiction of Massachusetts over the sea adjacent to its coast is that of an independent nation; and, except so far as any right of control over this territory has been granted to the United States, this control remains with the State. In *United States v. Bevans*, Marshall, C. J., in the opinion, asks the following questions:

Can the cession of all cases of admiralty and maritime jurisdiction be construed into a cession of the waters on which those cases may arise? As the powers of the respective governments now stand, if two citizens of Massachusetts step into shallow water when the tide flows, and fight and duel, are they not within the jurisdiction, and punishable by the laws, of Massachusetts?

The statutes of the United States define and punish but few offenses on the high seas, and, unless other offenses when committed in the sea near the coast can be punished by the States, there is a large immunity from punishment for acts which ought to be punishable as criminal. Within what are generally recognized as the territorial limits of States by the law of nations, a State can define its boundaries on the sea and the boundaries of its countries; and by this test the Commonwealth of Massachusetts can include Buzzard's Bay within the limits of its counties.

The statutes of Massachusetts, in regard to bays at least, make definite boundaries which, before the passage of the statutes, were somewhat indefinite; and Rhode Island and some other States have passed similar statutes defining their boundaries. Public Statutes of Rhode Island, 1882, c. 1, Sections 1, 2,; c. 3, Sec. 6; Gould on Waters, Sec. 16 and note. The waters of Buzzard's Bay are, of course, navigable waters of the United States, and the jurisdiction of Massachusetts over them is necessarily limited,

Commonwealth v. King, 150 Mass. 221; but there is no occasion to consider the power of the United States to regulate or control, either by treaty or legislation, the fisheries in these waters, because there are no existing treaties or acts of Congress which relate to the menhaden fisheries within such a bay. The rights granted to British subjects by the treaties of June 5, 1854, and May 8, 1871, to take fish upon the shores of the United States had expired before the statute of Massachusetts (St. 1886, c. 192) was passed which the defendant is charged with violating. The fish Commission was instituted "for the protection and preservation of the food fishes of the coast of the United States." Title 51 of the Revised Statutes relates solely to food fisheries, and so does the act of 1887. Nor are we referred to any decision which holds that the other acts of Congress alluded to apply to fisheries for menhaden, which is found as a fact in this case not to be a food fish, and to be only valuable for the purpose of bait and of manufacture into fish oil.

The statute of Massachusetts which the defendant is charged with violating is, in terms, confined to waters "within the jurisdiction of this Commonwealth"; and it was evidently passed for the preservation of the fish, and makes no discrimination in favor of citizens of Massachusetts and against citizens of other States. If there be a liberty of fishing for swimming fish in the navigable waters of the United States common to the inhabitants or the citizens of the United States, upon which we express no opinion, the statute may well be considered as an impartial and reasonable regulation of this liberty; and the subject is one which a State may well be permitted to regulate within its territory, in the absence of any regulation by the United States. The preservation of fish, even although they are not used as food for human beings, but as food for other fish which are so used, is for the common benefit; and we are of opinion that the statute is not repugnant to the Constitution and the laws of the United States.

It may be observed that Sec. 4398 of the Revised Statutes (a reenactment of Sec. 4 of the joint resolution of February 9, 1871) provides as follows, in regard to the Commissioner of Fish and Fisheries:

The commissioner may take a cause to be taken at all times, in the waters of the seacoast of the United States, where the tide ebbs and flows, and also in the waters of the lakes, such fish or specimens thereof as may in his judgment, from time to time, be needful or proper for the conduct of his duties, any law, custom, or usage of any State to the contrary notwithstanding.

This enactment may not improperly be construed as suggesting that, as against the law of a State, the Fish Commissioner might not otherwise have the right to take fish in places covered by the state law.

The pertinent observation may be made that, as Congress does not assert, by legislation, a right to control pilots in the bays, inlets, rivers, harbors, and ports of the United States, but leaves the regulation of that matter to the States, *Cooley v. Board of Wardens*, 12 How. 299, so, if it does not assert by affirmative legislation its right or will to assume the control of menhaden fisheries in such bays, the right to control such fisheries must remain with the State which contains such bays.

We do not consider the question whether or not Congress would have the right to control the menhaden fisheries which the statute of Massachusetts assumes to control; but we mean to say only that, as the right of control exists in the State in the absence of the affirmative action of Congress taking such control, the fact that Congress has never assumed the control of such fisheries is persuasive evidence that the right to control them still remains in the State.

Judgment Affirmed.

Questions

1. How does the court support state jurisdiction over fisheries in what are admittedly navigable waters subject to admiralty jurisdiction?

2. Does the court recognize any distinction between the types of fisheries involved?

3. How does the court address the charge that this is an example of discrimination against fishermen from other states?

Bayside Fish Flour Co. v. Gentry, 297 U.S. 422 (1936)

MR. JUSTICE SUTHERLAND delivered the opinion of the Court.

This is a suit brought to enjoin appellees, officers of the State of California, from enforcing certain provisions of the State Fish and Game Code alleged to contravene the commerce clause, and the due process and equal protection clauses of the Fourteenth Amendment, of the Federal Constitution. The court below sustained a motion to dismiss the bill, on the ground that it did not state facts sufficient to constitute a cause of action or to entitle appellant to any relief by injunction or otherwise. 8 F. Supp. 67. We are of opinion that this decree must be affirmed.

Appellant is a California corporation engaged in the business of manufacturing, from the meat of sardines, fish flour for human consumption. The sardines are caught by fishermen upon the high seas beyond the three-mile limit to which the jurisdiction of the state extends, sold to appellant, and brought into the state and there reduced to fish flour at appellant's reduction plants. The fish flour is made with the expectation of selling and shipping it in interstate and foreign commerce; and it is so sold and shipped and is used as food in the United States and foreign countries. Sardines are a migratory fish found in great numbers in the Pacific Ocean beyond the three-mile limit, as well as within that limit. So far as known, they spawn upon the open seas. In the process of reducing the fish, appellant uses a portion for producing flour for human consumption, the remainder being converted into a meal used for chicken feed, and into fertilizer, fish oil, and other nonedible substances.

Sardines caught in the same way are also purchased by packers, who clean, cook, and can or preserve them for human food, using in that process only a part of the fish and utilizing the remainder for reduction into nonedible products.

The bill alleges that appellees will prevent appellant from manufacturing fish flour in its reduction plants while at the same time permitting packers to use sardines, taken from the waters of the state or those outside, in their packing plants.

First. There is nothing in the state act to suggest a purpose to interfere with interstate commerce. It in no way limits or regulates or attempts to limit or regulate the movement of the sardines from outside into the state, or the movement of the manufactured product from the state to the outside. The act regulates only the manufacture within the state. Its direct operation, intended and actual, is wholly local. Whether the product is consumed within the borders of the state or shipped outside in interstate or foreign commerce are matters with which the act is not concerned. The plain purpose of the measure simply is to conserve for food the fish found within the waters of the state. Over these fish, and over state wild game generally, the state has supreme control. Sardines taken from waters within the jurisdiction of the state and those taken from without are, of course, indistinguishable; and to the extent that the act deals with the use or treatment of fish brought into the state from the outside, its legal justification rests on the ground that it operates as a shield against the covert depletion of the local supply, and thus tends to effectuate the policy of the law by rendering evasion of it less easy.

If the enforcement of the act affects interstate or foreign commerce, that result is purely incidental, indirect, and beyond the purposes of the legislation. The provisions of the act assailed are well within the police power of the state, as frequently decided by this and other courts.

Appellant places great reliance upon *Foster-Fountain Packing Co. v. Haydel*, 278 U.S. 1. There an act of the State of Louisiana forbade exportation of shrimp from which the heads and hulls or shells had not been removed. The ostensible purpose of the act was to conserve the raw shells for local use. The bill and affidavits in support of it, however, demonstrated, we held, that this purpose was feigned, and that the real purpose was to prevent the shrimp from being moved as theretofore from Louisiana to the point in Mississippi, where they were packed or canned and sold in interstate commerce, and thus through commercial necessity to bring about the removal of the packing and canning industries from Mississippi to Louisiana. The Louisiana act authorized every part of the shrimp to be shipped and sold in interstate commerce. We held that the state might have retained the shrimp for use and consumption therein; but, having fully permitted shipment and sale outside the state, those taking the shrimp under the authority of the act became entitled to the rights of private ownership and the protection of the commerce clause. It is plain that the decision has no application to the case under review.

Second. The point that the provisions of the Fish and Game Code deprive appellant of its property without due process of law seems to be based upon the contention that appellant is denied the right to contract for the purchase of sardines taken from the high seas and brought into the state. Assuming the point to have been properly raised below, which is by no means clear, it is without merit. Undoubtedly, the right to contract, with some exceptions, is a liberty which falls within the protection of the due process clause of the Fourteenth Amendment. Plainly enough, however, that right is not directly interfered with by the legislative provisions in question. Nor, because they may operate indirectly as a deterrent, do they, in the sense of the Constitution, deprive appellant of

the liberty of contract. A statute does not become unconstitutional merely because it has created a condition of affairs which renders the making of a related contract, lawful in itself, ineffective.

These provisions have a reasonable relation to the object of their enactment—namely, the conservation of the fish supply of the state—and we cannot invalidate them because we might think, as appellant in effect urges, that they will fail or have failed of their purpose. Nor can we declare the provisions void because it might seem to us that they enforce an objectionable policy or inflict hardship in particular instances.

Third. Finally, it is said that the provisions of the state code so discriminate between the business of appellant and that of persons engaged in canning or preserving fish, as to deny appellant the equal protection of the laws. Section 1010 requires a license for each plant or place of business to engage in (a) canning, curing, preserving, or packing fish, etc., and (b) manufacturing fish scrap, fish meal, fish oil, chicken feed, or fertilizer from fish or fish offal. Section 1060 defines "reduction plant" as a plant used in the reduction of fish into fish flour, fish meal, fish scrap, fertilizer, fish oil, or other fishery products or by-products; and defines "packer" as any person canning fish or preserving fish by the common methods of drying, salting, pickling, or smoking. Section 1064 is a provision intended to prevent deterioration or waste of fish, and specifically provides that, except as allowed by the Code, it shall be unlawful to use any part of the fish except the offal in a reduction plant or by a reduction process. By Sec. 1065, sardines are allowed to be taken for use in a reduction plant or by a packer only in accordance with certain provisions set forth. By Sec. 1068, the State Fish and Game Commission is authorized to grant a revocable permit "subject to such restrictions, rules, or regulations as the commission may prescribe, to take and use fish by a reduction or extraction process. No reduction of fish shall be permitted which may tend to deplete the species, or result in waste or deterioration of fish." No similar limitation is put upon, or similar power conferred in respect of, packers; and it is the resulting classification which appellant contends contravenes the equal protection clause of the Fourteenth Amendment.

It never has been found possible to lay down any infallible or all-inclusive test by the application of which it may be determined whether a given difference between the subjects of legislation is enough to justify the subjection of one and not the other to a particular form of disadvantage. A very large number of decisions have dealt with the matter; and the nearest approach to a definite rule which can be extracted from them is that, while the difference need not be great, the classification must not be arbitrary or capricious, but must bear some just and reasonable relation to the object of the legislation. A particular classification is not invalidated by the Fourteenth Amendment merely because inequality actually results. Every classification of persons or things for regulation by law produces inequality in some degree; but the law is not thereby rendered invalid, unless the inequality produced be actually and palpably unreasonable and arbitrary.

The purpose of the legislation under consideration is to prevent unnecessary waste, and to conserve for food the fish supply subject to state jurisdiction. If the legislature was of the view— as evidently it was—that the process of packing on the whole would not interfere with the effectuation of this policy while the process of reduction would do so, unless carefully limited to prevent excessive operations, we are unable to perceive any reason for saying that such view was without reasonable basis. By the process of packing—that is, canning or preserving—fish, the original form of the edible portions of the fish is not destroyed as it is by the process of reduction, by which those portions are broken down into a loose meal or flour. In the latter case it is obvious that the product may be readily diverted to other purposes than human consumption, such as chicken feed, fertilizer, etc.

It is equally obvious that such a diversion is not likely to happen in the case of canning or preserving, where the edible portions retain their original solid form. The state also points out that the process of reduction is simple, and the quantity which can be reduced in a given period of time greatly exceeds what can be utilized by packing, which is a much slower and more complicated process. These differences are enough to bring the classification within the permissible range of state power, so far as the equal protection clause of the Fourteenth Amendment is concerned.

We have considered the arguments of appellant tending to a different conclusion than that which we have reached; but at most these arguments do no more than demonstrate that the question is debatable. And, if so, the effect of the action of the state legislature in passing the statute was to decide this debatable question against the view now advanced by appellant; and since we are unable to say that such a determination by the legislature is clearly unfounded, we are precluded from overturning it.

Decree affirmed.

Questions

1. Why should the state of California care how the fish were used? What public interest is served by this policy?

2. What was the state's rationale for asserting extraterritorial jurisdiction?

3. How did the court distinguish this case from the shrimp packing example in *Foster-Fountain Packing*?

Skiriotes v. Florida, 313 U.S. 69 (1941)

MR. CHIEF JUSTICE HUGHES delivered the opinion of the Court.

Appellant, Lambiris Skiriotes, was convicted in the county court of Pinellas County, Florida, of the use on March 8, 1938, of diving equipment in the taking of sponges from the Gulf of Mexico off the coast of Florida, in violation of a state statute. The conviction was affirmed by the Supreme Court of Florida (144 Fla. 220; 197 So. 736) and the case comes here on appeal.

The case was tried without a jury and the facts were stipulated. The statute forbids the use of diving suits, helmets, or other apparatus used by deep-sea divers, for the purpose of taking commercial sponges from the Gulf of Mexico, or the Straits of Florida, or other waters within the territorial limits of that State.

The charge was that appellant was using the forbidden apparatus "at a point approximately two marine leagues from mean low tide on the west shore line of the State of Florida and within the territorial limits of the County of Pinellas." The state court held that the western boundary of Florida was fixed by the state constitution of 1885 at three marine leagues (nine nautical miles) from the shore; that this was the same boundary which had been defined by the state constitution of 1868 to which the Act of Congress had referred in admitting the State of Florida to representation in Congress. The state court sustained the right of the State to fix its marine boundary with the approval of Congress, and concluded that the statute was valid in its application to appellant's conduct.

By motions to quash the information and in arrest of judgment, appellant contended that the constitution of Florida fixing the boundary of the State and the statute under which he was prosecuted violated the constitution and treaties of the United States; that the criminal jurisdiction of the courts of Florida could not extend beyond the international boundaries of the United States and hence could not extend "to a greater distance than one marine league from mean low tide" on the mainland of the State and adjacent islands included within its territory.

In support of this contention appellant invoked several provisions of the Constitution of the United States, to wit, Article I, Sec. 10, Clauses 1 and 3, Article II, Sec. 2, Clause 2, Article VI, and the Fourteenth Amendment. Appellant also relied upon numerous treaties of the United States, including the Treaty with Spain of February 22, 1919, and the treaties with several countries, signed between 1924 and 1930, inclusive for the prevention of smuggling of intoxicating liquors. There were also introduced in evidence diplomatic correspondence and extracts from statements of our Secretaries of State with respect to the limits of the territorial waters of the United States. These contentions were presented to the highest court of the State and were overruled.

The first point of inquiry is with respect to the status of appellant. The stipulation of facts states that appellant "is by trade and occupation a deep-sea diver engaged in sponge fishery, his residence address being at Tarpon Springs, Pinellas County, Florida," and that he "has been engaged in this business for the past several years." Appellant has not asserted or attempted to show that he is not a citizen of the United States, or that he is a citizen of any State other than Florida, or that he is a national of any foreign country. It is also significant that in his brief in this Court, replying to the State's argument that as a citizen of Florida he is not in a position to question the boundaries of the State as defined by its constitution, appellant has not challenged the statement as to his citizenship, while he does contest the legal consequences which the State insists flow from that fact.

It further appears that upon appellant's arrest for violation of the statute, he sued out a writ of habeas corpus in the District Court of the United States and was released, but this decision was reversed by the Circuit Court of Appeals. *Cunningham v. Skiriotes*, 101 F. 21d 635. That court thought that the question of the statute's validity should be determined in orderly procedure by the state court subject to appropriate review by the Court, but the court expressed doubt as to the right of the appellant to raise the question, saying: "Skiriotes states he is a citizen of the United States resident in Florida, and therefore is a citizen of Florida. His boat, from which his diving operations were conducted, we may assume was a Florida vessel, carrying Florida law with her, but of course as modified by superior federal law."

In the light of appellant's statements to the federal court, judicially recited, and upon the present record showing his long residence in Florida and the absence of a claim of any other domicile or of any foreign allegiance, we are justified in assuming that he is a citizen of the United States and of Florida. Certainly appellant has not shown himself entitled to any greater rights than those which a citizen of Florida possesses.

In these circumstances, no question of international law, or of the extent of the authority of the United States in its international relations, is presented. International law is a part of our law and as such is the law of all States of the Union, but it is a part of our law for the application of its own principles, and these are concerned with international rights and duties and not with domestic rights and duties. The argument based on the limits of the territorial waters of the United States, as these are described by this Court in *Cunard Steamship Co. v. Mellon*, 262 U.S. 100, 122, and in diplomatic correspondence and statements of the political department of our Government, is thus beside the point. For, aside from the question of the extent of control which the United States may exert in the interest of self-protection over waters near its borders, although beyond its territorial limits, the United States is not debarred by any rule of international law from governing the conduct of its own citizens upon the high seas or even in foreign countries when the rights of other nations or their nationals are not infringed. With respect to such an exercise of authority there is no question of international law, but solely of the purport of the municipal law which establishes the duty of the citizen in relation to his own government. Thus, a criminal statute dealing with acts that are directly injurious to the government, and are capable of perpetration without regard to particular locality, is to be construed as applicable to citizens of the United States upon the high seas or in a foreign country, though there be no express declaration to that effect.

For the same reason, none of the treaties which appellant cites are applicable to his case. He is not in a position to invoke the rights of other governments or of the nationals of other countries. If a statute similar to the one in question had been enacted by Congress for the protection of the sponge fishery off the coasts of the United States there would appear to be no ground upon which appellant could challenge its validity.

The question is whether such an enactment, as applied to those who are subject to the jurisdiction of Florida, is beyond the competency of that State. We have not been referred to any legislation of Congress with which the state statute conflicts. By the Act of August 15, 1914 (16 U.S.C., Sec. 781), Congress has prohibited "any citizen of the United States, or person owing duty of obedience to the laws of the United States" fr.. taking "in the waters of the Gulf of Mexico or the Straits of Florida outside of state territorial limits" any commercial sponges which are less than a given size, or to possess such sponges or offer them for sale. But that Act is limited to the particular matter of size and does not deal with the divers' apparatus which is the particular subject of the Florida statute. According to familiar principles, Congress having occupied but a limited field, the authority of the State to protect its interests by additional or supplementary legislation otherwise valid is not impaired. It is also clear that Florida has an interest in the proper maintenance of the sponge fishery and that the statute so far as applied to conduct within the territorial waters of Florida, in the absence of conflicting federal legislation, is within the police power of the State. *Manchester v. Massachusetts*, 139 U.S. 240, 266. Nor is there any repugnance in the provisions of the statute to the equal protection clause of the Fourteenth Amendment. The statute applies equally to all persons within the jurisdiction of the State.

Appellant's attack thus centers in the contention that the State has transcended its power simply because the statute has been applied to his operations inimical to its interests outside the territorial waters of Florida. The State denies this, pointing to its boundaries as defined by the state constitution of 1868, which the State insists had the approval of Congress and in which there has been acquiescence over a long period. Appellant argues that Congress by the Act of June 25, 1868, to which the state courts refers, did not specifically accept or approve any boundaries as set up in the state constitution but merely admitted Florida and the other States mentioned to representation in Congress. And, further, that if Congress can be regarded as having approved the boundaries defined by the state constitution, those have been changed by the treaties with foreign countries relating to the smuggling of intoxicating liquors, in which the principle of the three-mile limit was declared.

But putting aside the treaties, which appellant has not standing to invoke, we do not find it necessary to resolve the contentions as to the interpretation and effect of the act of Congress of 1868. Even if it were assumed that the locus of the offense was outside the territorial waters of Florida, it would not follow that the State could not prohibit its own citizens from the use of the described divers' equipment at that place. No question as to the authority of the United States over these waters, or over the sponge fishery, is here involved. No right of a citizen of any other State is here asserted. The question is solely between appellant and his own State. The present case thus differs from that of *Manchester v. Massachusetts, supra,* for there the regulation by Massachusetts of the menhaden fisheries in Buzzard's Bay was sought to be enforced as against citizens of Rhode Island, and it was in that relation that the question whether Buzzard's Bay could be included within the territorial limits of Massachusetts was presented and was decided in favor of that Commonwealth. The question as to the extent of the authority of a State over its own citizens on the high seas was not involved.

If the United States may control the conduct of its citizens upon the high seas, we see no reason why the State of Florida may not likewise govern the conduct of its citizens upon the high seas with respect to matters in which the State has a legitimate interest and where there is no conflict with acts of Congress. Save for the powers committed by the Constitution of the Union, the State of Florida has retained the status of a sovereign. Florida was admitted to the Union "on equal footing with the original States, in all respects whatsoever." And the power given to Congress by Sec. 3 of Article IV of the Constitution to admit new States relates only to such States as are equal to each other "in power, dignity, and authority, each competent to exert that residuum of sovereignty not delegated to the United States by the Constitution itself." *Coyle v. Smith,* 221 U.S. 559, 567.

There is nothing novel in the doctrine that a State may exercise its authority over its citizens on the high seas. That doctrine was expounded in the case of *The Hamilton,* 207 U.S. 398. There, a statute of Delaware giving damages for death was held to be a valid exercise of the power of the State, extending to the case of a citizen of that State wrongfully killed on the high seas in a vessel belonging to a Delaware corporation by the negligence of another vessel also being to a Delaware corporation. If it be said that the case was one of vessels and for the recognition of the formula that a vessel at sea is regarded as part of the territory of the State, that principle would also be applicable here. There is no suggestion that appellant did not conduct his operations by means of Florida boats. That he did so conduct them was assumed by the Circuit Court of Appeals in dealing with appellant's arrest in *Cunningham v. Skiriotes, supra,* and that reasonable inference has not in any way been rebutted here.

But the principle recognized in *The Hamilton, supra,* was not limited by the conception of vessels as floating territory. There was recognition of the broader principle of the power of a sovereign State to govern the conduct of its citizens on the high seas. The court observed that "apart from the subordination of the State of Delaware to the Constitution of the United States" there was no doubt of its power to make its statute applicable to the case at bar. And the basic reason was, as the court put it, that when so applied "the statute governs the reciprocal liabilities of two corporations, existing only by virtue of the laws of Delaware, and permanently within its jurisdiction, for the consequences of conduct set in motion by them there, operating outside the territory of the State, it is true, but within no other territorial jurisdiction." If confined to corporations, "the State would have power to enforce its law to the extent of their property in every case." But the court went on to say that "the same authority would exist as to citizens domiciled within the State, even when personally on the high seas, and not only could be enforced by the State in case of their return, which their domicile by its very meaning promised, but in proper cases would be recognized in other jurisdictions by the courts of other States." That is, "the bare fact of the parties being outside the territory in a place belonging to no other sovereign would not limit the authority of the State, as accepted by civilized theory." *The Hamilton, supra,* p. 403. When its action does not conflict with federal legislation, the sovereign authority of the State over the conduct of its citizens upon the high seas is analogous to the sovereign authority of the United States over its citizens in like circumstances.

We are not unmindful of the fact that the statutory prohibition refers to the "Gulf of Mexico, or the Straits of Florida, or other waters within the territorial limits of the State of Florida." But we are dealing with the question of the validity of the statute as applied to appellant from the standpoint of state power. The State has applied it to appellant at the place of his operations, and if the State had power to prohibit the described conduct of its citizen at that

place we are not concerned from the standpoint of the Federal Constitution with the ruling of the state court as to the extent of territorial waters. The question before us must be considered in the light of the total power the State possesses, and so considered we find no ground for holding that the action of the State with respect to appellant transcended the limits of that power.

The judgment of the Supreme Court of Florida is *Affirmed*.

Questions

1. Can a state validly regulate the conduct of its citizens beyond its own borders? What public interest would be served?

2. How could Florida justify a boundary claim of three marine leagues on its Gulf Coast when the United States only claims three miles?

Toomer v. Witsell, 334 U.S. 385 (1948)

MR. CHIEF JUSTICE VINSON delivered the opinion of the Court.

This is a suit to enjoin as unconstitutional the enforcement of several South Carolina statutes governing commercial shrimp fishing in the three-mile maritime belt off the coast of that State. Appellants, who initiated the action, are five individual fishermen, all citizens and residents of Georgia, and a nonprofit fish dealers' organization incorporated in Florida. Appellees are South Carolina officials charged with enforcement of the statutes.

The three-judge Federal District Court which was convened to hear the case upheld the statutes, declined an injunction and dismissed the suit. On direct appeal from that judgment we noted probable jurisdiction.

The fishery which South Carolina attempts to regulate by the statutes in question is part of a larger shrimp fishery extending from North Carolina to Florida. Most of the shrimp in this area are of a migratory type, swimming south in the late summer and fall and returning north-ward in the spring. Since there is no federal regulation of the fishery, the four States most intimately concerned have gone their separate ways in devising conservation and other regu-latory measures. While action by the States has followed somewhat parallel lines, efforts to se-cure uniformity throughout the fishery have by and large been fruitless. Because of the integral nature of the fishery, many commercial shrimp-ers, including the appellants, would like to start trawling off the Carolinas in the summer and then follow the shrimp down the coast to Flor-ida. Each State has been desirous of securing for its residents the opportunity to shrimp in this way, but some have apparently been more concerned with channeling to their own resi-dents the business derived from local waters. Restrictions on nonresident fishing in the mar-ginal sea, and even prohibitions against it, have now invited retaliation to the point that the fish-ery is effectively partitioned at the state lines; bilateral bargaining on an official level has come to be the only method whereby any one of the States can obtain for its citizens the right to shrimp in waters adjacent to the other States.

South Carolina forbids trawling for shrimp in the State's inland waters, which are the habitat of the young shrimp for the first few months of their life. It also provides for a closed season in the three-mile maritime belt during the spawn-ing season, from March 1 to July 1. The validity of these regulations is not questioned.

The statutes appellants challenge related to shrimping during the open season in the three-mile belt: Section 3300 of the South Carolina Code provides that the waters in that area shall be "a common for the people of the State for the taking of fish." Section 3374 imposes a tax of 1/8 cent a pound on green, or raw, shrimp taken in those waters. Section 3379, as amended in 1947, requires payment of a license fee of $25 for each shrimp boat owned by a resident, and of $2,500 for each one owned by a nonres-ident. Another statute, not integrated in the Code, conditions the issuance of nonresident li-censes for 1948 and the years thereafter on sub-mission of proof that the applicants have paid South Carolina income taxes on all profits from operations in that State during the preceding year. And Sec. 3414 requires that all boats li-censed to trawl for shrimp in the State's waters dock at a South Carolina port and unload, pack, and stamp their catch "before shipping or trans-porting it to another State or the waters thereof." Violation of the fishing laws entails suspension of the violators' license as well as a maximum of a $1,000 fine, imprisonment for a year, or a combination of a $500 fine and a year's imprisonment.

First. We are confronted at the outset with appellees' contention, rejected by the District Court, that injunctive relief is inappropriate in this case, regardless of the validity of the chal-lenged statutes, since appellants failed to show the imminence of irreparable injury and did not come into court with clean hands.

As to the corporate appellant, we agree with the appellees that there has been no showing that enforcement of the statutes would work an irreparable injury. The record shows only that the corporation is an association of fish dealers and that it operates no fishing boats. Indeed, neither the record nor the appellants' brief sheds any light on how the statutes affect the corporation, let alone how their enforcement will cause it irreparable injury. Under such cir-cumstances, the corporation has no standing to ask a federal court to take the extraordinary step of restraining enforcement of the state statutes. The remainder of this opinion will therefore be addressed to the individual appellants' case.

As to them, it is agreed that the appellees were attempting to enforce the statutes. It is also clear that compliance with any but the in-come tax statute would have required payment of large sums of money for which South Caro-lina provides no means of recovery, that defi-ance would have carried with it the risk of heavy fines and long imprisonment, and that withdrawal from further fishing until a test case had been taken through the South Carolina courts and perhaps to this Court would have resulted in a substantial loss of business for which no compensation could be obtained. Except as to the income tax statute, we conclude that appellants sufficiently showed the imminence of irreparable injury for which there was no plain, adequate, and complete remedy at law.

Appellants' position on the income tax statute is that it is unconstitutional for South Carolina to require Georgia residents to pay South Carolina income taxes on profits made from operations in South Carolina waters. Another South Carolina statute, however, permits any taxpayer who believes a tax to be "illegal for any cause" to pay the tax under protest and then sue in a state court to recover the amounts so paid. In the absence of any showing by appellants that they could not take advantage of this procedure to raise their constitutional objections to the tax, we cannot say that they do not have an adequate remedy at law.

Some of the individual appellants had previously been convicted of shrimping out of season and in inland waters. The District Court held that this previous misconduct, not having any relation to the constitutionality of the challenged statutes, did not call for application of the clean hands maxim. We agree.

Second. The appellants too press a contention which, if correct, would dispose of the case. They urge that South Carolina has no jurisdiction over coastal waters beyond the low-water mark. In the court below *United States v. California*, 332 U.S. 19 (1947), was relied upon for this proposition. Here appellants seem to concede, and correctly so, that such is neither the holding nor the implication of that case; for in deciding that the United States, where it asserted its claim, had paramount rights in the three-mile belt, the Court pointedly quoted and supplied emphasis to a statement in *Skiriotes v. Florida*, 313 U.S. 69, 75 (1941), that "[i]t is also clear that Florida has an interest in the proper maintenance of the sponge fishery and that the [state] statute *so far as applied to conduct within*

the territorial waters of Florida, in the absence of conflicting federal legislation, is within the police power of the State."

Since the present case evinces no conflict between South Carolina's regulatory scheme and any assertion of federal power, the District Court properly concluded that the State has sufficient interests in the shrimp fishery within three miles of its coast so that it may exercise its police power to protect and regulate that fishery.

It does not follow from the existence of power to regulate, however, that such power need not be exercised within the confines of generally applicable Constitutional limitations. In the view we take, the heart of this case is whether South Carolina's admitted power has been so exercised. We now proceed to various aspects of that problem.

Third. Appellants contend that Sec. 3374, which imposes a tax of 1/8 cent a pound on green shrimp taken in the maritime belt, taxes imports and unduly burdens interstate commerce in violation of Sections 8 and 10 of Art. I of the Constitution. We agree with the court below that there is no merit in this position.

Since South Carolina has power to regulate fishing in the three-mile belt, at least where the federal government has made no conflicting assertion of power, fish caught in that belt cannot be considered "imports" in a realistic sense of the word. Appellants urge, however, that the tax is imposed on shrimp caught outside, as well as within, the three-mile limit. On its face the statute has no such effect, and appellants call our attention to no South Carolina decision so interpreting it. Since we do not have the benefit of interpretation by the State courts and since this suit for an injunction does not present a concrete factual situation involving the application of the statute to shrimping beyond the imaginary three-mile line, it is inappropriate for us to rule in the abstract on the extent of the State's power to tax in this regard.

Nor does the statute violate the commerce clause. It does not discriminate against interstate commerce in shrimp, and the taxable event, the taking of shrimp, occurs before the shrimp can be said to have entered the flow of interstate commerce.

Fourth. Appellants' most vigorous attack is directed at Sec. 3379 which, as amended in 1947, requires nonresidents of South Carolina to pay license fees one hundred times as great as those which residents must pay. The purpose and effect of this statute, they contend, is not to conserve shrimp, but to exclude nonresidents and thereby create a commercial monopoly for South Carolina residents. As such, the statute is said to violate the privileges and immunities clause of Art. IV, Sec. 2, of the Constitution and the equal protection clause of the Fourteenth Amendment.

Article IV, Sec. 2, so far as relevant, reads as follows: "The Citizens of each State shall be entitled to all Privileges and Immunities of Citizens in the several States." The primary purpose of this clause, like the clauses between which it is located—those relating to full faith and credit and to interstate extradition of fugitives from justice—was to help fuse into one Nation a collection of independent, sovereign States. It was designed to insure to a citizen of State A who ventures into State B the same privileges which the citizens of State B enjoy. For protection of such equality the citizen of State A was not to be restricted to the uncertain remedies afforded by diplomatic processes and official retaliation. "Indeed, without some provision of the kind removing from the citizens of each State the disabilities of alienage in the other States, and giving them equality of privilege with citizens of those States, the Republic would have constituted little more than a league of States; it would not have constituted the Union which now exists." *Paul v. Virginia*, 8 Wall. 168, 180 (1868).

In line with this underlying purpose, it was long ago decided that one of the privileges which the clause guarantees to citizens of State A is that of doing business in State B on terms

of substantial equality with the citizens of that State.

Like many other constitutional provisions, the privileges and immunities clause is not an absolute. It does bar discrimination against citizens of other States where there is no substantial reason for the discrimination beyond the mere fact that they are citizens of other States. But it does not preclude disparity of treatment in the many situations where there are perfectly valid independent reasons for it. Thus the inquiry in each case must be concerned with whether such reasons do exist and whether the degree of discrimination bears a close relation to them. The inquiry must also, of course, be conducted with due regard for the principle that the States should have considerable leeway in analyzing local evils and in prescribing appropriate cures.

With these factors in mind, we turn to a consideration of the constitutionality of Sec. 3379.

By that statute South Carolina plainly and frankly discriminates against nonresidents, and the record leaves little doubt but that the discrimination is so great that its practical effect is virtually exclusionary. This the appellees do not seriously dispute. Nor do they argue that since the statute is couched in terms of residence it is outside the scope of the privileges and immunities clause, which speaks of citizens. Such an argument, we agree, would be without force in this case.

As justification for the statute, appellees urge that the State's obvious purpose was to conserve its shrimp supply, and they suggest that it was designed to head off an impending threat of excessive trawling. The record casts some doubt on these statements. But in any event, appellees' argument assumes that any means adopted to attain valid objectives necessarily squares with the privileges and immunities clause. It overlooks the purpose of that clause, which, as indicated above, is to outlaw classifications based on the fact of noncitizenship unless there is something to indicate that noncitizens constitute a peculiar source of the evil at which the statute is aimed.

In this connection appellees mention, without further elucidation, the fishing methods used by nonresidents, the size of their boats, and the allegedly greater cost of enforcing the laws against them. One statement in that appellees' brief might also be construed to mean that the State's conservation program for shrimp requires expenditure of funds beyond those collected in license fees—funds to which residents and not nonresidents contribute. Nothing in the record indicates that nonresidents use larger boats or different fishing methods than residents, that the cost of enforcing the laws against them is appreciably greater, or that any substantial amount of the State's general funds is devoted to shrimp conservation. By assuming such were the facts, they would not necessarily support a remedy so drastic as to be a near equivalent of total exclusion. The State is not without power, for example, to restrict the type of equipment used in its fisheries, to graduate license fees according to the size of the boats, or even to charge nonresidents a differential which would merely compensate the State for any added enforcement burden they may impose or for any conservation expenditures from taxes which only residents pay. We would be closing our eyes to reality, we believe, if we concluded that there was a reasonable relationship between the danger represented by noncitizens, as a class, and the severe discrimination practiced upon them. Thus, Sec. 3379 must be held unconstitutional unless commercial shrimp fishing in the maritime belt falls within some unexpressed exception to the privileges and immunities clause.

Appellees strenuously urge that there is such an exception. Their argument runs as follows: Ever since Roman times, animals ferae naturae, not having been reduced to individual possession and ownership, have been considered as res nullius or part of the "negative community of interests" and hence subject to control by the sovereign or other governmental authority.

More recently this thought has been expressed by saying that fish and game are the common property of all citizens of the governmental unit and that the government, as a sort of trustee, exercises this "ownership" for the benefit of its citizens. In the case of fish, it has also been considered that each government "owned" both the beds of its lakes, streams, and tidewaters and the waters themselves; hence it must also "own" the fish within those waters. Each government may, the argument continues, regulate the corpus of the trust in the way best suited to the interests of the beneficial owners, its citizens, and may discriminate as it sees fit against persons lacking any beneficial interest. Finally, it is said that this special property interest, which nations and similar governmental bodies have traditionally had, in this country vested in the colonial governments and passed to the individual states.

Language frequently repeated by this Court appears to lend some support to this analysis. But in only one case, *McCready v. Virginia*, 94 U.S. 391 (1876), has the Court actually upheld State action discriminating against commercial fishing or hunting by citizens of other States where there were advanced no persuasive independent reasons justifying the discrimination. In that case the Court sanctioned a Virginia statute applied so as to prohibit citizens of other States, but not Virginia citizens, from planting oysters in the tidal waters of the Ware River. The right of Virginians in Virginia waters, the Court said, was "a property right, and not a mere privilege or immunity of citizenship." And an analogy was drawn between planting oysters in a river bed and planting corn in state-owned land.

It will be noted that there are at least two factual distinctions between the present case and the *McCready* case. First, the *McCready* case related to fish which would remain in Virginia until removed by man. The present case, on the other hand, deals with free-swimming fish which migrate through the waters of several States and are off the coast of South Carolina only temporarily. Secondly, the *McCready* case involved regulation of fishing in inland waters, whereas the statute now questioned is directed at regulation of shrimping in the marginal sea.

Thus we have, on the one hand, a single precedent which might be taken as reading an exception into the privileges and immunities clause and, on the other, a case which does not fall directly within that exception. Viewed in this light, the question before us comes down to whether the reasons which evoked the exception call for its extension to a case involving the factual distinctions here presented.

However satisfactorily the ownership theory explains the *McCready* case, the very factors which make the present case distinguishable render that theory but a weak prop for the South Carolina statute. That the shrimp are migratory makes apposite Mr. Justice Holmes's statement in *Missouri v. Holland*, 252 U.S. 416, 434 (1920), that "[t]o put the claim of the State upon title is to lean upon a slender reed. Wild birds are not in the possession of anyone; and possession is the beginning of ownership." Indeed, only fifteen years after the *McCready* decision, a unanimous Court indicated that the rule of that case might not apply to free-swimming fish. *Manchester v. Massachusetts*, 139 U.S. 240, 265 (1891). The fact that it is activity in the three-mile belt which the South Carolina statute regulates is of equal relevance in considering the applicability of the ownership doctrine. While *United States v. California*, 332 U.S. 19 (1947), as indicated above, does not preclude all State regulation of activity in the marginal sea, the case does hold that neither the thirteen original colonies nor their successor States separately acquired "ownership" of the three-mile belt.

The whole ownership theory, in fact, is now generally regarded as but a fiction expressive in legal shorthand of the importance to its people that a State have power to preserve and regulate the exploitation of an important resource. And there is no necessary conflict between that vital policy consideration and the constitutional command that the State exercise that power, like its other powers, so as not to discriminate without reason against citizens of other States.

These considerations lead us to the conclusion that the *McCready* exception to the privileges and immunities clause, if such it be, should not be expanded to cover this case.

Thus we hold that commercial shrimping in the marginal sea, like other common callings, is within the purview of the privileges and immunities clause. And since we have previously concluded that the reasons advanced in support of the statute do not bear a reasonable relationship to the high degree of discrimination practiced upon citizens of other States, it follows that Sec. 3379 violates Art. IV, Sec. 2, of the Constitution.

Appellants maintain that by a parity of reasoning the statute also contravenes the equal protection clause of the Fourteenth Amendment. That may well be true, but we do not pass on this argument since it is unnecessary to disposition of the present case.

Fifth. Appellants contend that Sec. 3414, which requires that owners of shrimp boats fishing in the maritime belt off South Carolina dock at a South Carolina port and unload, pack, and stamp their catch (with a tax stamp) before "shipping or transporting it to another state" burdens interstate commerce in shrimp in violation of Art. I, Sec. 8, of the Constitution.

The record shows that a high proportion of the shrimp caught in the waters along the South Carolina coast, both by appellants and by others, is shipped in interstate commerce. There was also uncontradicted evidence that appellants' costs would be materially increased by the necessity of having their shrimp unloaded and packed in South Carolina ports rather than at their home bases in Georgia where they maintain their own docking, warehousing, refrigeration, and packing facilities. In addition, an inevitable concomitant of a statute requiring that work be done in South Carolina, even though that be economically disadvantageous to the fishermen, is to divert to South Carolina employment and business which might otherwise go to Georgia; the necessary tendency of the statute is to impose an artificial rigidity on the economic pattern of the industry.

Appellees do not contest the fact that the statute thereby burdens, to some extent at least, interstate commerce in shrimp caught in waters off the South Carolina coast. Again, however, they rely on the fact that the commerce affected is in fish rather than some other commodity. They urge that South Carolina, because of its ownership of the shrimp, could constitutionally prohibit all shipments to other States. It follows, they imply, that the State could impose lesser restrictions, such as those here at issue, on out-of-state shipments.

There is considerable authority, starting with *Geer v. Connecticut*, 161 U.S. 519 (1896), to support the contention that a State may confine the consumption of its fish and game wholly within the State's limits. We need not pause to consider whether this power extends to free-swimming fish in the three-mile belt, for even as applied to fish taken in inland waters it has been held that where a State did not exercise its full power, but on the contrary permitted shipments to other States, it could not at the same time condition such shipments so as to burden interstate commerce. In *Foster Packing Co. v. Haydel*, 278 U.S. 1 (1928), the Court held it was an abuse of discretion for a district court not to enter an order temporarily enjoining, as an unconstitutional burden on interstate commerce, enforcement of a Louisiana statute which permitted the shipment of shrimp from Louisiana to other States only if the heads and hulls had previously been removed. In distinguishing the *Geer* case, the following comment was made:

As the representative of its people, the State might have retained the shrimp for consumption and use therein. . . . But by permitting its shrimp to be taken and all the products thereof to be shipped and sold in interstate commerce, the State necessarily releases its hold and, as to the shrimp so taken, definitely terminates its control. Clearly such authorization and

the taking in pursuance thereof put an end to the trust upon which the State is deemed to own or control the shrimp for the benefit of its people. And those taking the shrimp under the authority of the Act necessarily thereby become entitled to the rights of private ownership and the protection of the commerce clause.

Similarly in the present case, South Carolina has not attempted to retain for the use of its own people the shrimp caught in the marginal sea. Indeed, the State has been eager to stimulate interstate shipments and sales as a means of increasing the employment and income of its shrimp industry. Thus even if we assume that South Carolina could retain for local consumption shrimp caught in the maritime belt to the same extent as if they were taken in inland waters, the *Geer* case would not support Sec. 3414.

In upholding this statute, the court below adduced a reason not advanced by appellees, that the requirements as to docking, unloading, packing, and affixing a tax stamp were a proper means of insuring collection of the 1/8 cent-a-pound tax. But the importance of having commerce between the forty-eight States flow unimpeded by local barriers persuades us that State restrictions inimical to the commerce clause should not be approved simply because they facilitate in some measure enforcement of a valid tax.

Thus we hold that Sec. 3414 violates the commerce clause of Art. I, Sec. 8, of the Constitution.

To sum up, we hold that the District Court had jurisdiction to entertain the attacks pressed by the individual appellants, but not the corporate appellant, on all the statutes save the one relating to income taxes; that South Carolina has power, in the absence of a conflicting federal claim to regulate fishing in the marginal sea; and that in Sec. 3374 of the South Carolina Code, though not in Sections 3379 and 3414, the State has exercised that power in a manner consistent with restraints which the Constitution imposes upon the States. The District Court's judgment refusing equitable relief is affirmed with respect to Sec. 3374 and the income tax statute and reversed with respect to Sections 3379 and 3414.

Affirmed in part and reversed in part.

Questions _____

1. May a state discriminate against nonresidents with regard to fishing licenses? Are there any limits on their powers?

2. What is the purpose of the Privileges and Immunities clause of the Constitution, and how does it relate to the regulation of fisheries?

3. How did the court distinguish the facts of this case from the apparently conflicting earlier precedent of *McCready v. Virginia*?

Washington v. Fishing Vessel Assn., 443 U.S. 658 (1979)

MR. JUSTICE STEVENS delivered the opinion of the Court.

To extinguish the last group of conflicting claims to lands lying west of the Cascade Mountains and north of the Columbia River in what is now the State of Washington, the United States entered into a series of treaties with Indian Tribes in 1854 and 1855. The Indians relinquished their interest in most of the Territory in exchange for monetary payments. In addition, certain relatively small parcels of land were reserved for their exclusive use, and they were afforded other guarantees, including protection of their "right of taking fish, at all usual and accustomed grounds and stations ... in common with all citizens of the Territory." 10 Stat. 1133.

The principal question presented by this litigation concerns the character of that treaty's right to take fish. Various other issues are presented, but their disposition depends on the answer to the principal question. Before answering any of these questions, or even stating the issues with more precision, we shall briefly describe the anadromous fisheries of the Pacific Northwest, the treaty negotiations, and the principal components of the litigation complex that led us to grant these three related petitions for certiorari.

I.

Anadromous fish hatch in fresh water, migrate to the ocean where they are reared and reach mature size, and eventually complete their life cycle by returning to the freshwater place of their origin to spawn. Different species have different life cycles, some spending several years and traveling great distances in the ocean before returning to spawn and some even returning to spawn on more than one occasion before dying. The regular habits of these fish make their "runs" predictable; this predictability in turn makes it possible for both fishermen and regulators to forecast and to control the number of fish that will be caught, or "harvested." Indeed, as the terminology associated with it suggests, the management of anadromous fisheries is in many ways more akin to the cultivation of "crops"—with its relatively high degree of predictability and productive stability, subject mainly to sudden changes in climatic patterns—than is the management of most other commercial and sport fisheries.

Regulation of the anadromous fisheries of the Northwest is nonetheless complicated by the different habits of the various species of salmon and trout involved, by the variety of methods of taking the fish, and by the fact that a run of fish may pass through a series of different jurisdictions. For example, pink and sockeye salmon hatched in Canada's Fraser River pass through the Strait of Juan de Fuca in the State of Washington, swim out into international waters on the open sea, and return through the strait to the river, passing on the way the usual and accustomed fishing grounds of the Makah Indian Tribe once again in Washington. During much of the return run during which they pass through international, state, and Canadian waters, the fish are in optimum harvestable condition. Another complexity arises from the fact that the State of Washington has attempted to reserve one species, steelhead trout, for sport fishing and therefore conferred regulatory jurisdiction over that species upon its Department of Game, where the various species of salmon are primarily harvested by commercial fishermen and are managed by the State's Department of Fisheries. Moreover, adequate regulation not only must take into account the potentially conflicting interests of sport and commercial fishermen, as well as those of Indian and non-treaty fishermen, but also must recognize that the fish runs may be harmed by harvesting either too many or too few of the fish returning to spawn.

The anadromous fish constitute a natural resource of great economic value to the State of Washington. Millions of salmon, with an average weight of from four or five to about twenty pounds, depending on the species, are harvested each year. Over 6,600 non-treaty fishermen and about 800 Indians make their livelihood by commercial fishing; moreover, some 280,000 individuals are licensed to engage in sport fishing in the State.

II.

One hundred and twenty-five years ago when the relevant treaties were signed, anadromous fish were even more important to most of the population of western Washington than they are today. At that time, about three-fourths of the approximately ten thousand inhabitants of the area were Indians. Although in some respects the cultures of the different tribes varied— some bands of Indians, for example, had little or no tribal organization while others, such as the Makah and the Yakima, were highly organized— all of them shared a vital and unifying dependence on anadromous fish.

Religious rites were intended to insure the continual return of the salmon and the trout; the seasonal and geographic variations in the runs of the different species determined the movements of the largely nomadic tribes. Fish constituted a major part of the Indian diet, was

used for commercial purposes, and indeed was traded in substantial volume. The Indians developed food-preservation techniques that enabled them to store fish throughout the year and to transport it over great distances. They used a wide variety of methods to catch fish, including the precursors of all modern netting techniques. Their usual and accustomed fishing places were numerous and were scattered throughout the area, and included marine as well as freshwater areas.

All of the treaties were negotiated by Isaac Stevens, the first Governor and first Superintendent of Indian Affairs of the Washington Territory, and a small group of advisers. Contemporaneous documents make it clear that these people recognized the vital importance of the fisheries to the Indians and wanted to protect them from the risk that non-Indian settlers might seek to monopolize their fisheries. There is no evidence of the precise understanding the Indians had of any of the specific English terms and phrases in the treaty. It is perfectly clear, however, that the Indians were vitally interested in protecting their right to take fish at usual and accustomed places, whether on or off the reservations, and that they were invited by the white negotiators to rely and in fact did rely heavily on the good faith of the United States to protect that right.

Referring to the negotiations with the Yakima Nation, by far the largest of the Indian tribes, the District Court found:

At the treaty council the United States negotiators promised, and the Indians understood, that the Yakimas would forever be able to continue the same off-reservation food gathering and fishing practices as to time, place, method, species, and extent as they had or were exercising. The Yakimas relied on these promises and they formed a material and basic part of the treaty and of the Indians' understanding of the meaning of the treaty. Id., at 381 (record citations omitted)

See also id., at 363 (similar finding regarding negotiations with the Makah Tribe).

The Indians understood that non-Indians would also have the right to fish at their off-reservation fishing sites. But this was not understood as a significant limitation on their right to take fish. Because of the great abundance of fish and the limited population of the area, it simply was not contemplated that either party would interfere with the other's fishing rights. The parties accordingly did not see the need and did not intend to regulate the taking of fish by either Indians or non-Indians, nor was future regulation foreseen.

Indeed, for several decades after the treaties were signed, Indians continued to harvest most of the fish taken from the waters of Washington, and they moved freely about the Territory and later the State in search of that resource. The size of the fishery resource continued to obviate the need during the period to regulate the taking of fish by either Indians or non-Indians. Not until major economic developments in canning and processing occurred in the last few years of the nineteenth century did a significant non-Indian fishery develop. It was as a consequence of these developments, rather than of the treaty, that non-Indians began to dominate the fisheries and eventually to exclude most Indians from participating in it—a trend that was encouraged by the onset of often discriminatory state regulation in the early decades of the twentieth century.

In sum, it is fair to conclude that when the treaties were negotiated, neither party realized or intended that their agreement would determine whether, and if so how, a resource that had always been thought inexhaustible would be allocated between the native Indians and the incoming settlers when it later became scarce.

III.

Unfortunately, that resource has now become scarce, and the meaning of the Indians' treaty right to take fish has accordingly become critical. The United States Court of Appeals for the Ninth Circuit and the Supreme Court of the State of Washington have issued conflicting decisions on its meaning. In addition, their holdings raise important ancillary questions that will appear from a brief review of this extensive litigation.

The federal litigation was commenced in the United States District Court for the Western District of Washington in 1970. The United States, on its own behalf and as trustee for seven Indian tribes, brought suit against the State of Washington seeking an interpretation of the treaties and an injunction requiring the State to protect the Indians' share of the anadromous fish runs. Additional Indian tribes, the State's Fisheries and Game Departments, and one commercial fishing group were joined as parties at various stages of the proceedings, while various other agencies and groups, including all of the commercial fishing associations that are parties here, participated as amici curiae.

During the extensive pretrial proceedings, four different interpretations of the critical treaty language were advanced. Of those, three proceeded from the assumption that the language required some allocation to the Indians of a share of the runs of fish passing through their traditional fishing areas each year. The tribes themselves contended that the treaties had reserved a preexisting right to as many fish as their commercial and subsistence needs dictated. The United States argued that the Indians were entitled either to a 50 percent share of the "harvestable" fish that originated in and returned to the "case area" and passed through their fishing places, or to their needs, whichever was less. The Department of Fisheries agreed that the Indians were entitled to "a fair and equitable share" stated in terms of a percentage of the harvestable salmon in the area; ultimately it proposed a share of "one-third."

Only the Game Department thought the treaties provided no assurance to the Indians that they could take some portion of each run of fish. That agency instead argued that the treaties gave the Indians no fishing rights not enjoyed by non-treaty fishermen except the two rights previously recognized by decisions of this Court—the right of access over private lands to their usual and accustomed fishing grounds, and an exemption from the payment of license fees.

The District Court agreed with the parties who advocated an allocation to the Indians, and it essentially agreed with the United States as to what that allocation should be. It held that the Indians were then entitled to a 45 percent to 50 percent share of the harvestable fish that will at some point pass through recognized tribal fishing grounds in the case area. The share was to be calculated on a river-by-river, run-by-run basis, subject to certain adjustments. Fish caught by Indians for ceremonial and subsistence purposes as well as fish caught within a reservation were excluded from the calculation of the tribes' share. In addition, in order to compensate for fish caught outside of the case area, i.e., beyond the State's jurisdiction, the court made an "equitable adjustment" to increase the allocation to the Indians. The court left it to the individual tribes involved to agree among themselves on how best to divide the Indian share of runs that pass through the usual and accustomed grounds of more than one tribe, and it postponed until a later date the proper accounting for hatchery-bred fish. 383 F.Supp., at 416; 459 F.Supp., at 1129. With a slight modification, the Court of Appeals for the Ninth Circuit affirmed, 520 F.2d 676, and we denied certiorari, 423 U.S. 1086.

The injunction entered by the District Court required the Department of Fisheries (Fisheries) to adopt regulations protecting the Indians' treaty rights. After the new regulations were promulgated, however, they were immediately challenged by private citizens in suits commenced in the Washington State courts. The State Supreme Court, in two cases that are here in consolidated form in No. 77-983, ultimately held that Fisheries could not comply with the federal injunction. *Puget Sound Gillnetters Assn. v. Moos,* 88 Wash. 2d 677, 565 P. 2d 1151 (1977); *Fishing Vessel Assn. v. Tollefson,* 89 Wash. 2d 276, 571 P.2d 1371 (1977).

As a matter of federal law, the state court first accepted the Game Department's and rejected the District Court's interpretation of the treaties and held that it did not give the Indians a right to a share of the fish runs, and second concluded that recognizing special rights of the Indians would violate the Equal Protection Clause of the Fourteenth Amendment. The opinions might also be read to hold, as a matter of state law, that Fisheries had no authority to issue the regulations because they had a purpose other than conservation of the resource. In this Court, however, the Attorney General of the State disclaims the adequacy and independence of the state-law ground and argues that the state-law authority of Fisheries is dependent on the answers to the two federal-law questions discussed above. We defer to that interpretation, subject, of course, to later clarification by the State Supreme Court. Because we are also satisfied that the constitutional holding is without merit, our review of the state court's judgment will be limited to the treaty issue.

When Fisheries was ordered by the state courts to abandon its attempt to promulgate and enforce regulations in compliance with the federal court's decree—and when the Game Department simply refused to comply—the District Court entered a series of orders enabling it, with the aid of the United States Attorney for the Western District of Washington and various federal law enforcement agencies, directly to supervise those aspects of the State's fisheries necessary to the preservation of treaty fishing rights. The District Court's power to take such direct action and, in doing so, to enjoin persons who were not parties to the proceedings was affirmed by the United States Court of Appeals for the Ninth Circuit. 573 F.2d 1128. That court, in a separate opinion, 573 F.2d 118, also held that regulations of the International Pacific Salmon Fisheries Commission posed no impediment to the District Court's interpretation of the treaty language and to its enforcement of that interpretation. Subsequently, the District Court entered an enforcement order regarding the salmon fisheries for the 1978 and subsequent seasons, which, prior to our issuance of a writ of certiorari to review the case, was pending on appeal in the Court of Appeals.

Because of the widespread defiance of the District Court's orders, this litigation has assumed unusual significance. We granted certiorari in the state and federal cases to interpret this important treaty provision and thereby to resolve the conflict between the state and federal courts regarding what, if any, right the Indians have to a share of the fish, to address the implications of international regulation of the fisheries in the area, and to remove any doubts about the federal court's power to enforce its orders. 439 U.S. 909.

IV.

The treaties secure a "right of taking fish." The pertinent articles provide:

> The right of taking fish, at all usual and accustomed grounds and stations, is further secured to said Indians, in common with all citizens of the Territory, and of erecting temporary houses for the purpose of curing, together with the privilege of hunting, gathering roots and berries, and pasturing their horses on open and unclaimed lands: *Provided, however*, that they shall not take shellfish from any beds staked or cultivated by citizens.

At the time the treaties were executed there was a great abundance of fish and a relative scarcity of people. No one had any doubt about the Indians' capacity to take as many fish as they might need. Their right to take fish could therefore be adequately protected by guaranteeing them access to usual and accustomed fishing sites which could be—and which for decades after the treaties were signed were—comfortably shared with the incoming settlers.

Because the sparse contemporaneous written materials refer primarily to assuring access to fishing sites "in common with all citizens of the Territory," the State of Washington and the commercial fishing associations, having all adopted the Game Department's original posi-

tion, argue that it was merely access that the negotiators guaranteed. It is equally plausible to conclude, however, that the specific provision for access was intended to secure a greater right—a right to harvest a share of the runs of anadromous fish that at the time the treaties were signed were so plentiful that no one could question the Indians' capacity to take whatever quantity they needed. Indeed, a fair appraisal of the purpose of the treaty negotiations, the language of the treaties, and this Court's prior construction of the treaties mandates that conclusion.

A treaty, including one between the United States and an Indian tribe, is essentially a contract between two sovereign nations. When the signatory nations have not been at war and neither is the vanquished, it is reasonable to assume that they negotiated as equals at arm's length. There is no reason to doubt that this assumption applies to the treaties at issue here.

Accordingly, it is the intention of the parties, and not solely that of the superior side, that must control any attempt to interpret the treaties. When Indians are involved, this Court has long given special meaning to this rule. It has held that the United States, as the party with the presumptively superior negotiating skills and superior knowledge of the language in which the treaty is recorded, has a responsibility to avoid taking advantage of the other side. "[T]he treaty must therefore be construed, not according to the technical meaning of its words to learned lawyers, but in the sense in which they would naturally be understood by the Indians." *Jones v. Meehan*, 175 U.S. 1, 11. This rule, in fact, has thrice been explicitly relied on by the Court in broadly interpreting these very treaties in the Indians' favor. *Tulee v. Washington*, 315 U.S. 681; *Seufert Bros. Co. v. United States*, 249 U.S. 194; *United States v. Winans*, 198 U.S. 371. See also *Washington v. Yakima Indian Nation*, 439 U.S. 463, 484.

Governor Stevens and his associates were well aware of the "sense" in which the Indians were likely to view assurances regarding their fishing rights. During the negotiations, the vital importance of the fish to the Indians was repeatedly emphasized by both sides, and the Governor's promises that the treaties would protect that source of food and commerce were crucial in obtaining the Indians' assent. It is absolutely clear, as Governor Stevens himself said, that neither he nor the Indians intended that the latter "should be excluded from their ancient fisheries," and it is accordingly inconceivable that either party deliberately agreed to authorize future settlers to crowd the Indians out of any meaningful use of their accustomed places to fish. That each individual Indian would have an "equal opportunity" with thousands of newly arrived individual settlers is totally foreign to the spirit of the negotiations. Such a "right," along with the $207,500 paid the Indians, would hardly have been sufficient to compensate them for the millions of acres they ceded to the Territory.

It is true that the words "in common with" may be read either as nothing more than a guarantee that individual Indians would have the same right as individual non-Indians or as securing an interest in the fish runs themselves. If we were to construe these words by reference to nineteenth-century property concepts, we might accept the former interpretation, although even "learned lawyers" of the day would probably have offered differing interpretations of the three words. But we think greater importance should be given to the Indians' likely understanding of the other words in the treaties and especially the reference to the "right of *taking* fish"—a right that had no special meaning at common law but that must have had obvious significance to the tribes relinquishing a portion of their preexisting rights to the United States in return for this promise. This language is particularly meaningful in the context of anadromous fisheries—which were not the focus of the common law—because of the relative predictability of the "harvest." In this context, it makes sense to say that a party has a right to "take"—rather than merely the "opportunity"

to try to catch—some of the large quantities of fish that will almost certainly be available at a given place at a given time.

This interpretation is confirmed by additional language in the treaties. The fishing clause speaks of "securing" certain fishing rights, a term the Court has previously interpreted as synonymous with "reserving" rights previously exercised. Because the Indians had always exercised the right to meet their subsistence and commercial needs by taking fish from treaty area waters, they would be unlikely to perceive a "reservation" of that right as merely the chance, shared with millions of other citizens, occasionally to dip their nets into the territorial waters. Moreover, the phrasing of the clause quite clearly avoids placing each individual Indian on an equal footing with each individual citizen of the State. The referent of the "said Indians" who are to share the right of taking fish with "all citizens of the Territory" is not the individual Indians but the various signatory "tribes and bands of Indians" listed in the opening article of each treaty. Because it was the tribes that were given a right in common with non-Indian citizens, it is especially likely that a class right to a share of fish, rather than a personal right to attempt to land fish, was intended.

In our view, the purpose and language of the treaties are unambiguous; they secure the Indians' right to take a share of each run of fish that passes through tribal fishing areas. But our prior decisions provide an even more persuasive reason why this interpretation is not open to question. For notwithstanding the bitterness that this litigation has engendered, the principal issue involved is virtually a "matter decided" by our previous holdings.

The Court has interpreted the fishing clause in these treaties on six prior occasions. In all of these cases the Court placed a relatively broad gloss on the Indians' fishing rights and—more or less explicitly—rejected the State's "equal opportunity" approach; in the earliest and the three most recent cases, moreover, we adopted essentially the interpretation that the United States is reiterating here.

In *United States v. Winans*, the respondent, having acquired title to property on the Columbia River and having obtained a license to use a "fish wheel"—a device capable of catching salmon by the ton and totally destroying a run of fish—asserted the right to exclude the Yakimas from one of their "usual and accustomed" places. The Circuit Court for the District of Washington sustained respondent, but this Court reversed. The Court initially rejected an argument that is analogous to the "equal opportunity" claim now made by the State:

[I]t was decided [below] that the Indians acquired no rights but what any inhabitant of the Territory or State would have. Indeed, acquired no rights but such as they would have without the treaty. This is certainly an impotent outcome to negotiations and a convention, which seemed to promise more and give the word of the Nation for more. . . . How the treaty in question was understood may be gathered from the circumstances.

The right to resort to the fishing places in controversy was a part of larger rights possessed by the Indians, upon the exercise of which there was not a shadow of impediment, and which were not much less necessary to the existence of the Indians than the atmosphere they breathed. New conditions came into existence, to which those rights had to be accommodated. Only a limitation of them, however, was necessary and intended, not a taking away. In other words, the treaty was not a grant of rights to the Indians, but a grant of rights from them—a reservation of those not granted. And the form of the instrument and its language was adapted to that purpose. . . . There was an exclusive right to fishing reserved within certain boundaries. There was a right outside of those boundaries reserved "in common with citizens of the Territory." As a mere right, it was not exclusive in the Indians. Citizens might share it, but the Indians were secured in its enjoyment by a special provision of means for its exercise. They were given "the right of taking fish at all usual and accustomed places," and the right "of erecting temporary buildings for curing them." The contingency of the future ownership of the lands, therefore, was foreseen and provided for; in other words, the Indians

were given a right in the land—the right of crossing it to the river—the right to occupy it to the extent and for the purpose mentioned. No other conclusion would give effect to the treaty. 198 U.S., at 380–81

But even more significant than the languages in *Winans* is its actual disposition. The Court not only upheld the Indians' right of access to respondent's private property but also ordered the Circuit Court on remand to devise some "adjustment and accommodation" that would protect them from total exclusion from the fishery. Although the accommodation it suggested by reference to the Solicitor General's brief in the case is subject to interpretation, it clearly included removal of enough of the fishing wheels to enable some fish to escape and be available to Indian fishermen upstream. In short, it assured the Indians a share of the fish.

In the more recent litigation over this treaty language between the Puyallup Tribe and the Washington Department of Game, the Court in the context of a dispute over rights to the run of steelhead trout on the Puyallup River reaffirmed both of the holdings that may be drawn from *Winans*—the treaty guarantees the Indians more than simply the "equal opportunity" along with all of the citizens of the State to catch fish, and it in fact assures them some portion of each relevant run. But the three *Puyallup* cases are even more explicit; they clearly establish the principle that neither party to the treaties may rely on the State's regulatory powers or on property law concepts to defeat the other's right to a "fairly apportioned" share of each covered run of harvestable anadromous fish.

In *Puyallup I*, 391 U.S. 392, the Court sustained the State's power to impose nondiscriminatory regulations on treaty fishermen so long as they were "necessary" for the conservation of the various species. In so holding, the Court again explicitly rejected the equal-opportunity theory. Although non-treaty fishermen might be subjected to any reasonable state fishing regulation serving any legitimate purpose, treaty fishermen are immune from all regulation save that required for conservation.

When the Department of Game sought to impose a total ban on commercial net fishing for steelhead, the Court held in *Puyallup II* that such regulation was not a "reasonable and necessary conservation measure" and would deny the Indians their "fairly apportioned" share of the Puyallup River run. 414 U.S., 44–45, 48. Although under the challenged regulation every individual fisherman would have had an equal opportunity to use a hook and line to land the steelhead, most of the fish would obviously have been caught by the 145,000 non-treaty licensees rather than by the handful of treaty fishermen. This Court vindicated the Indians' treaty right to "take fish" by invalidating the ban on Indian net fishing and remanding the case with instructions to the state courts to determine the portion of harvestable steelhead that should be allocated to net fishing by members of the tribe. Even if *Winans* had not already done so, this unanimous holding foreclosed the basic argument that the State is now advancing.

On remand, the Washington State courts held that 45 percent of the steelhead run was allocable to commercial net fishing by the Indians. We shall later discuss how that specific percentage was determined; what is material for present purposes is the recognition, upheld by this Court in *Puyallup III*, 433 U.S. 165, that the treaty secured the Tribe's right to a substantial portion of the run, and not merely a right to compete with non-treaty fishermen on an individual basis.

Puyallup III also made it clear that the *Indians* could not rely on their treaty right to exclude others from access to certain fishing sites to deprive other citizens of the State of a "fair apportionment" of the runs. For although it is clear that the Tribe may exclude non-Indians from access to fishing within the reservation, we unequivocally rejected the Tribe's claim to an untrammeled right to take as many of the steelhead running through its reservation as it chose. In support of our holding that the State has reg-

ulatory jurisdiction over on-reservation fishing, we reiterated Mr. Justice Douglas's statement for the Court in *Puyallup II* that the "Treaty does not give the Indians a federal right to pursue the last living steelhead until it enters their nets." 414 U.S., at 49. It is in this sense that treaty and non-treaty fishermen hold "equal" rights. For neither party may deprive the other of a "fair share" of the runs.

Not only all six of our cases interpreting the relevant treaty language but all federal courts that have interpreted the treaties in recent times have reached the foregoing conclusions, see *Sohappy v. Smith*, 302 F.Supp. 899, 908, 911 (Oreg. 1969) (citing cases), as did the Washington Supreme Court itself prior to the present litigation. *State v. Satiacum*, 50 Wash.2d 513, 523–24, 314 P.2d 400, 406 (1957). A like interpretation, moreover, has been followed by the Court with respect to hunting rights explicitly secured by treaty to Indians " 'in common with all other persons,' " *Antoine v. Washington*, 420 U.S. 194, 205–6, and to water rights that were merely implicitly secured to the Indians by treaties reserving land—treaties that the Court enforced by ordering an apportionment to the Indians of enough water to meet their subsistence and cultivation needs. *Arizona v. California*, 373 U.S., 546, following *United States v. Powers*, 305 U.S. 527; *Winters v. United States*, 207 U.S. 564.

The purport of our cases is clear. Non-treaty fishermen may not rely on property law concepts, devices such as the fish wheel, license fees, or general regulations to deprive the Indians of a fair share of the relevant runs of anadromous fish in the case area. Nor may treaty fishermen rely on their exclusive right of access to the reservations to destroy the rights of other "citizens of the Territory." Both sides have a right, secured by treaty, to take a fair share of the available fish. That, we think, is what the parties to the treaty intended when they secured to the Indians the right of taking fish in common with other citizens.

V.

We also agree with the Government that an equitable measure of the common right should initially divide the harvestable portion of each run that passes through a "usual and accustomed" place into approximately equal treaty and non-treaty shares, and should then reduce the treaty share if tribal needs may be satisfied by a lesser amount. Although this method of dividing the resource, unlike the right to some division, is not mandated by our prior cases, it is consistent with the 45 percent–55 percent division arrived at by the Washington State courts, and affirmed by this Court, in *Puyallup III* with respect to the steelhead run on the Puyallup River. The trial court in the *Puyallup* litigation reached those figures essentially by starting with a 50 percent allocation based on the Indians' reliance on the right for their livelihoods and then adjusting slightly downward due to other relevant factors. The District Court took a similar tack in this case, i.e., by starting with a 50–50 division and adjusting slightly downward on the Indians' side when it became clear that they did not need a full 50 percent.

The division arrived at by the District Court is also consistent with our earlier decisions concerning Indian treaty rights to scarce natural resources. In those cases, after determining that at the time of the treaties the resource involved was necessary to the Indians' welfare, the Court typically ordered a trial judge or special master, in his discretion, to devise some apportionment that assured that the Indians' reasonable livelihood needs would be met. This is precisely what the District Court did here, except that it realized that some ceiling should be placed on the Indians' apportionment to prevent their needs from exhausting the entire resource and thereby frustrating the treaty right of "all [other] citizens of the Territory."

Thus, it first concluded that at the time the treaties were signed, the Indians, who comprised three-fourths of the territorial population, depended heavily on anadromous fish as a source of food, commerce, and cultural cohesion. Indeed, it found that the non-Indian population depended on Indians to catch the fish that the former consumed. Only then did it determine that the Indians' present-day subsistence and commercial needs should be met, subject, of course, to the 50 percent ceiling.

It bears repeating, however, that the 50 percent figure imposes a maximum but not a minimum allocation. As in *Arizona v. California* and its predecessor cases, the central principle here must be that Indian treaty rights to a natural resource that once was thoroughly and exclusively exploited by the Indians secures so much as, but no more than, is necessary to provide the Indians with a livelihood—that is to say, a moderate living. Accordingly, while the maximum possible allocation to the Indians is fixed at 50 percent, the minimum is not; the latter will, upon proper submissions to the District Court, be modified in response to changing circumstances. If, for example, a tribe should dwindle to just a few members, or if it should find other sources of support that lead it to abandon its fisheries, a 45 percent or 50 percent allocation of an entire run that passes through its customary fishing grounds would be manifestly inappropriate because the livelihood of the tribe under those circumstances should not reasonably require an allotment of a large number of fish.

Although the District Court's exercise of its discretion, as slightly modified by the Court of Appeals, is in most respects unobjectionable, we are not satisfied that all of the adjustments it made to its division are consistent with the preceding analysis.

The District Court determined that the fish taken by the Indians on their reservations should not be counted against their share. It based this determination on the fact that Indians have the exclusive right under the treaties to fish on their reservations. But this fact seems to us to have no greater significance than the fact that some non-treaty fishermen may have exclusive access to fishing sites that are not "usual and accustomed" places. Shares in the fish runs should not be affected by the place where the fish are taken. We therefore disagree with the District Court's exclusion of the Indians' on-reservation catch from their portion of the runs.

This same rationale, however, validates the Court of Appeals–modified equitable adjustment for fish caught outside the jurisdiction of the State by non-treaty fishermen from the State of Washington. So long as they take fish from identifiable runs that are destined for traditional tribal fishing grounds, such persons may not rely on the location of their take to justify excluding it from their share. Although it is true that the fish involved are caught in waters subject to the jurisdiction of the United States, rather than of the State, see 16 U.S.C. Sections 1811, 1812, the persons catching them are nonetheless "citizens of the Territory" and as such the beneficiaries of the Indians' reciprocal grant of land in the treaties as well as the persons expressly named in the treaties as sharing fishing rights with the Indians. Accordingly, they may justifiably be treated differently from non-treaty fishermen who are not . citizens of Washington. The statutory provisions just cited are therefore important in this context only because they clearly place a responsibility on the United States, rather than a State, to police the take of fish in the relevant waters by Washington citizens insofar as is necessary to assure compliance with the treaties.

On the other hand, as long as there are enough fish to satisfy the Indians' ceremonial and subsistence needs, we see no justification for the District Court's exclusion from the treaty share of fish caught for these purposes. We need not now decide whether priority for such uses would be required in a period of short supply in order to carry out the purposes of the treaty. For present purposes, we merely hold that the total catch—rather than the commercial catch—is the measure of each party's right.

Accordingly, any fish (1) taken in Washington waters or in United States waters off the coast of Washington, (2) taken from runs of fish that pass through the Indians' usual and accustomed fishing grounds, and (3) taken by either members of the Indian tribes that are parties to this litigation, on the one hand, or by non-Indian citizens of Washington, on the other hand, shall count against that party's respective share of the fish.

VI.

Regardless of the Indians' other fishing rights under the treaties, the State argues that an agreement between Canada and the United States pre-empts their rights with respect to the sockeye and pink salmon runs on the Fraser River.

In 1930, the United States and Canada agreed that the catch of Fraser River salmon should be equally divided between Canadian and American fishermen. To implement this agreement, the two Governments established the International Pacific Salmon Fisheries Commission (IPSFC). Each year that Commission proposes regulations to govern the time, manner, and number of the catch by fishermen of the two countries; those regulations become effective upon approval of both countries.

In the United States, pursuant to statute and presidential designation, enforcement of those regulations is vested in the National Marine Fisheries Service, which, in turn, may authorize the State of Washington to act as the enforcing agent. Sockeye Salmon or Pink Salmon Fishing Act of 1947, 61 Stat. 511, as amended, 16 U.S.C. Sec. 776, et seq. (hereinafter Sockeye Act). For many years Washington has accepted this responsibility and enacted IPSFC regulations into state statutory law.

The Fraser River salmon run passes through certain "usual and accustomed" places of treaty tribes. The Indians have therefore claimed a share of these runs. Consistently with its basic interpretation of the Indian treaties, the District Court in its original decision held that the tribes are entitled to up to one-half of the American share of any run that passes through their "usual and accustomed" places. To implement that holding, the District Court also entered an order authorizing the use by Indians of certain gear prohibited by IPSFC regulations then in force. 384 F.Supp., at 392–93, 411. The Court of Appeals affirmed, 520 F.2d at 689–90, and we denied certiorari. 423 U.S. 1086.

In later proceedings commenced in 1975, the State of Washington contended in the District Court that any Indian rights to Fraser River salmon were extinguished either implicitly by the later agreement with Canada or more directly by the IPSFC regulations promulgated pursuant to those agreements insofar as they are inconsistent with the District Court's order. The State's claim was rejected by the District Court and the Court of Appeals. 459 F.Supp., at 1050–56; 573 F.2d, at 1120–21.

First, we agree with the Court of Appeals that the Convention itself does not implicitly extinguish the Indians' treaty rights. Absent explicit statutory language, we have been extremely reluctant to find congressional abrogation of treaty rights, and there is no reason to do so here. Indeed, the Canadian Government has long exempted Canadian Indians from regulations promulgated under the convention and afforded them special fishing rights.

We also agree with the United States that the conflict between the District Court's order and IPSFC does not present us with a justiciable issue. The initial conflict occasioned by the regulations for the 1975 season has been mooted by the passage of time, and there is little prospect that a similar conflict will revive and yet evade review. Since 1975, the United States, in order to protect the Indian rights, has exercised its power under Art. VI of the Convention and refused to give the necessary approval to those portions of the IPSFC regulations that affected Indian fishing rights. Those regulations have accordingly not gone into effect in the United States. The Indians' fishing rights and responsibilities have instead been the subject of separate regulations promulgated by the Interior Department, under its general Indian powers,

and enforced by the National Marine Fisheries Service directly, rather than by delegation to the State. The District Court's order is fully consistent with those regulations. To the extent that any Washington State statute imposes any conflicting obligations, the statute is without effect under the Sockeye Act and must give way to the federal treaties, regulations, and decrees.

VII.

In addition to their challenges to the District Court's basic construction of the treaties, and to the scope of its allocation of fish to treaty fishermen, the State and the commercial fishing associations have advanced two objections to various remedial orders entered by the District Court. It is claimed that the District Court has ordered a state agency to take action that it has no authority to take as a matter of state law and that its own assumption of the authority to manage the fisheries in the State after the state agencies refused or were unable to do so was unlawful.

These objections are difficult to evaluate in view of the representations to this Court by the Attorney General of the State that definitive resolution of the basic federal question of construction of the treaties will both remove any state-law impediment to enforcement of the State's obligations under the treaties, and enable the State and Fisheries to carry out those obligations. Once the state agencies comply, of course, there would be no issue relating to federal authority to order them to do so or any need for the district Court to continue its own direct supervision of enforcement efforts.

The representations of the Attorney General are not binding on the courts and legislature of the State, although we assume they are authoritative within its executive branch. Moreover, the State continues to argue that the District Court exceeded its authority when it assumed control of the fisheries in the State, and the commercial fishing groups continue to argue that the District Court may not order the state agencies to comply with its orders when they have no state-law authority to do so. Accordingly, although adherence to the Attorney General's representations by the executive, legislative, and judicial officials in the State would moot these two issues, a brief discussion should foreclose the possibility that they will not be respected. State-law prohibition against compliance with the District Court's decree cannot survive the command of the Supremacy Clause of the United States Constitution. It is also clear that Game and Fisheries, as parties to this litigation, may be ordered to prepare a set of rules that will implement the Court's interpretation of the rights of the parties even if state law withholds from them the power to do so. Once again the answer to a question raised by this litigation is largely dictated by our *Puyallup* trilogy. There, this Court mandated that state officers make precisely the same type of allocation of fish as the District Court ordered in this case.

Whether Game and Fisheries may be ordered actually to promulgate regulations having effect as a matter of state law may well be doubtful. But the District Court may rescind that problem by assuming direct supervision of the fisheries if state recalcitrance or state-law barriers should be continued. It is therefore absurd to argue, as do the fishing associations, both that the state agencies may not be ordered to implement the decree and also that the District Court may not itself issue detailed remedial orders as a substitute for state supervision. The federal court unquestionably has the power to enter the various orders that state official and private parties have chosen to ignore, and even to displace local enforcement of those orders if necessary to remedy the violations of federal law found by the court. Even if those orders may have been erroneous in some respects, all parties have an unequivocal obligation to obey them while they remain in effect.

In short, we trust that the spirit of cooperation motivating the Attorney General's representation will be confirmed by the conduct of state officials. But if it is not, the District Court

has the power to undertake the necessary remedial steps and to enlist the aid of the appropriate federal law enforcement agents in carrying out those steps. Moreover, the comments by the Court of Appeals strongly imply that it is prepared to uphold the use of stern measures to require respect for federal court orders.

The judgment of the Court of Appeals for the Ninth Circuit, and the Supreme Court of the State of Washington are vacated and the respective causes are remanded to those courts for further proceedings not inconsistent with this opinion.

So ordered.

MR. JUSTICE POWELL, with whom MR. JUSTICE STEWART and MR. JUSTICE REHNQUIST join, dissenting in part.

I join Parts I–III of the Court's opinion. I am not in agreement, however, with the Court's interpretation of the treaties negotiated in 1854 and 1855 with the Indians of the Washington Territory. The Court's opinion, as I read it, construes the treaties' provision "of taking fish . . . in common" as guaranteeing the Indians a specified percentage of the runs of the anadromous fish passing land upon which the Indians traditionally have fished. Indeed, it takes a starting point for determining fishing rights an equal division of fish between Indians and non-Indians. As I do not believe that the language and history of the treaties can be construed to support the Court's interpretation, I dissent.

· · ·

III.

In my view, the district Court below—and now this Court—has formulated an apportionment doctrine that cannot be squared with the language or history of the treaties, or indeed with the prior decisions of this Court. The application of this doctrine, and particularly the construction of the term "in common" as requiring a basic 50–50 apportionment, is likely to result in an extraordinary economic windfall to Indian fishermen in the commercial fish market by giving them a substantial position in the market wholly protected from competition from non-Indian fishermen. Indeed, non-Indian fishermen apparently will be required from time to time to stay out of fishing areas completely while Indians catch their court-decreed allotment. In sum, the District Court's decision will discriminate quite unfairly against non-Indians.

To be sure, if it were necessary to construe the treaties to produce these results, it would be our duty so to construe them. But for the reasons stated above, I think the Court's construction virtually ignores the historical setting and purposes of the treaties, considerations that bear compellingly upon a proper reading of their language. Nor do the prior decisions of this Court support or justify what seems to me to be a substantial reformation of the bargain struck with the Indians in 1854–1855.

I would hold that the treaties give to the Indians several significant rights that should be respected. As made clear in *Winans*, the purpose of the treaties was to assure to Indians the right of access over private lands so that they could continue to fish at their usual and accustomed fishing grounds. Indians also have the exclusive right to fish on their reservations, and are guaranteed enough fish to satisfy their ceremonial and subsistence needs. Moreover, as subsequently construed, the treaties exempt Indians from state regulation (including the payment of license fees) except as necessary for conservation in the interest of all fishermen. Finally, under *Puyallup II*, it is settled that even a facially neutral conservation regulation is invalid if its effect is to discriminate against Indian fishermen. These rights, privileges, and exemptions—possessed only by Indians—are quite substantial. I find no basis for according them additional advantages.

Questions

1. What basis did the court have for its division of the salmon resources?

2. Is this the standard, or must it be revisited in subsequent years or when conditions change?

3. Justice Powell, in his dissent, speaks of an "extraordinary economic windfall" to Indian fishermen in the commercial fishing business. Should the economic implications of the treaty become a factor in the interpretation of the language?

Idaho v. Oregon and Washington, 462 U.S. 1017 (1983)

JUSTICE BLACKMUN delivered the opinion of the court.

In this action invoking the Court's original jurisdiction, the State of Idaho seeks an equitable apportionment against the States of Oregon and Washington of the anadromous fish that migrate between the Pacific Ocean and spawning grounds in Idaho. The Special Master has filed his final report on the merits and recommends that the action be dismissed without prejudice. We have before us Idaho's exceptions to that report.

I.

Although somewhat repetitive of the Court's prior writings in this litigation, 44 U.S. 380 (1980), we feel it worthwhile to outline once again the facts of the case and the Court's prior rulings. The dispute concerns fish, one of the valuable natural resources of the Columbia-Snake River system in the Pacific Northwest. That system covers portions of Wyoming, Idaho, Washington, Oregon, and British Columbia. From its origin in northwest Wyoming, the Snake River flows westerly across southern Idaho until it reaches the Idaho and Oregon border. At that point, the river winds northward to form the border between those States for approximately 165 miles, and then the border between Washington and Idaho for another 30 miles. Next, it turns abruptly westward and flows through eastern Washington for approximately 100 miles, finally joining the Columbia River. The Columbia, before this rendezvous, flows southward from British Columbia through eastern Washington. After it is supplemented by the Snake, the Columbia continues westward 270 miles to the Pacific Ocean. For most of the distance, it forms the boundary between Washington and Oregon.

A.

Among the various species of fish that thrive in the Columbia-Snake River system, anadromous fish—in this case, chinook salmon and steelhead trout—lead remarkable and not completely understood lives. These fish begin life in the upstream gravel bars of the Columbia and Snake and their respective tributaries. Shortly after hatching, the fish emerge from the bars as fry and begin to forage around their hatch areas for food. They grow into fingerlings and then into smolt; the latter generally are at least six inches long and weigh no more than a tenth of a pound. The period the young fish spend in the hatching areas varies with the species and can last from six months to well over a year.

At the end of this period, the smolts swim downriver toward the Pacific. In the estuary of the Columbia, the young fish linger for a time in order to grow accustomed to the chemical cues of the water. It is believed that they pick up the river's scent so that in their twilight years they can return to their original home. Even under the best of conditions, only a small fraction of the smolts that set out from the gravel bars ever reach the ocean.

Once in the ocean the smolts grow into adults, averaging between twelve and seventeen pounds. They spend several years traveling on precise, and possibly genetically predetermined, routes. At the end of their ocean ventures, the mature fish ascend the river. They travel in groups called runs, distinguishable both by species and by the time of year. All the fish return to their original hatching area, where they spawn and then die. At issue in this case are the runs of spring chinook between Feb-

ruary and May, the runs of summer chinook in June and July, and the runs of summer steelhead trout in August and September.

B.

Since 1938, the already arduous voyages of these fish have been complicated by the construction of eight dams on the Columbia and Snake rivers. In order to produce electrical power, these dams divert a flow of water through large turbines that have a devastating effect on young smolts descending to the Pacific. Spillways have been constructed to permit the smolts to detour around the turbines. The dams also present great obstacles to the adults. Fish ladders—water-covered steps—enable the returning adults to climb over the dams; in addition, the ladders provide an opportunity for compiling statistics. Varying water conditions and the demand for power can increase the mortality of both descending smolts and ascending adults. The mortality rate for ocean-bound smolts averages approximately 95 percent. Their adult counterparts die at a rate of 15 percent at each dam. Only 25 percent to 30 percent of the adults passing over the first dam, the Bonneville, succeed in running the gauntlet to traverse the Lower Granite Dam and enter Idaho.

Another factor depleting the anadromous fish population is fishing, sometimes referred to as "harvesting." In 1918, Oregon and Washington, with the consent of Congress, formed the Oregon-Washington Columbia River Fish Compact to ensure uniformity in state regulation of Columbia River anadromous fish. Idaho has sought entry into the Compact on several occasions, but has been rebuffed. Under the Compact, Oregon and Washington have divided the lower Columbia into six commercial fishery zones: zones one through five cover the Columbia from its mouth to the Bonneville Dam; zone six stretches from the Bonneville Dam to the McNary Dam below the confluence with the Snake. Each year, authorities from both States estimate the size of the runs to determine the length of a fishing season the runs can support. The States do not permit commercial harvests of chinook salmon or steelhead trout in any of their Columbia River tributaries; they do, however, permit sport fishing in most locations.

Pursuant to treaties ratified in 1859, several Indian Tribes have "the right of taking fish at all usual and accustomed places." *Sohappy v. Smith*, 302 F.Supp. 899, 904 (Oreg. 1969). In 1977, after lengthy litigation over Indian treaty rights, Oregon and Washington agreed with the Indians to preserve zone six solely for Indian fishing. They also agreed to limit commercial harvests in zones one through five to an amount that permits sufficient numbers of fish to pass over the Bonneville Dam to provide an equitable share for the Indians and to leave enough fish to replenish the runs. Under the plan, escapement goals—the number of fish passing the Bonneville—are set for each run. When the estimated size of the run exceeds the escapement goal by a specified amount, the surplus is allocated between non-Indian fishers below the Bonneville and Indian fishers above that dam. Two Indian Tribes recently have withdrawn from the agreement, however, casting its future effectiveness into doubt.

Although the parties disagree as to the causes, runs of all the relevant species since 1973 have been significantly lower. Since that year, Oregon and Washington have not permitted commercial harvests of summer chinook; in both States, steelhead trout are now designated game fish and may not be harvested commercially. Harvests of spring chinook have been permitted only in 1974 and 1977. In the years since 1973, there has been some sport fishing of all three runs.

C.

In 1976, the Court granted Idaho leave to file its complaint requesting an equitable apportionment of anadromous fish in the Columbia-Snake River system. 429 U.S. 163. The matter was referred to a Special Master, the Honorable Jean S. Breitenstein, Senior Judge for the United States Court of Appeals for the Tenth Circuit. The Special Master initially recommended that the suit be dismissed without prejudice for failure to join an indispensable party, the United States. That recommendation was not accepted, and the case was remanded for trial. 444 U.S. 380 (1980). The Court stated that Idaho "must shoulder the burden of proving that the [non-Indian] fisheries in [Oregon and Washington] have adversely and unfairly affected the number of fish arriving in Idaho." Id., 444 U.S., at 392.

After trial and oral argument, the Special Master issued his final report on the merits. He has recommended that the action be dismissed without prejudice, apparently for two distinct reasons. First, he found that Idaho has not demonstrated that it has suffered any injury at the hands of Oregon and Washington. Second, even assuming that it has suffered such an injury, he found it impossible to fashion a decree to apportion the fish fairly among the parties. Idaho has filed exceptions to the report.

II.

A.

As an initial matter, the Special Master correctly concluded that the doctrine of equitable apportionment is applicable to this dispute. Although that doctrine has its roots in water rights litigation, the natural resource of anadromous fish is sufficiently similar to make equitable apportionment an appropriate mechanism for resolving allocative disputes. The anadromous fish at issue travel through several States during their lifetime. Much as in a water dispute, a State that overfishes a run downstream deprives an upstream State of the fish it otherwise would receive. A dispute over the water flowing through the Columbia-State River system would be resolved by the equitable apportionment doctrine; we see no reason to accord different treatment to a controversy over a similar natural resource of that system.

The doctrine of equitable apportionment is

neither dependent on nor bound by existing legal rights to the resource being apportioned. The fact that no State has a preexisting legal right of ownership in the fish does not prevent an equitable apportionment. Conversely, although existing legal entitlements are important factors in formulating an equitable decree, such legal rights must give way in some circumstances to broader equitable considerations.

At the root of the doctrine is the same principle that animates many of the Court's Commerce Clause cases: a State may not preserve solely for its own inhabitants natural resources located within its borders. Consistent with this principle, States have an affirmative duty under the doctrine of equitable apportionment to take reasonable steps to conserve and even to augment the natural resources within their borders for the benefit of other States. Even though Idaho has no legal right to the anadromous fish hatched in its waters, it has an equitable right to a fair distribution of this important resource.

B.

Because apportionment is based on broad and flexible equitable concerns rather than on precise legal entitlements, a decree is not intended to compensate for prior legal wrongs. Rather, a decree prospectively ensures that a State obtains its equitable share of a resource. A decree may not always be mathematically precise or based on definite present and future conditions. Uncertainties about the future, however, do not provide a basis for declining to fashion a decree. Reliance on reasonable predictions of future conditions is necessary to protect the equitable rights of a State.

To the extent that the Special Master found that the formulation of a workable decree is impossible, we must disagree. See *Washington v. Fishing Vessel Assn.*, 443 U.S. 658, 663 (regular habits of anadromous fish make it possible to forecast size of runs). Idaho's proposed formula for apportioning the fish is one possible basis for a decree. It relies on the number of jack-fish—reproductively precocious male fish,

which return a year ahead of other members of their age group—passing over the Bonneville and the Ice Harbor Dams to predict the size of the run the following year and the percentage of fish in the run that originate in Idaho. Although the computation is complicated and somewhat technical, that fact does not prevent the issuance of an equitable decree. Nothing in the record undermines the assumption supporting Idaho's formula that there is a definite relationship between the number of jackfish and the total number of fish in a particular run the following year. Thus, if Idaho suffers from the injury it alleges, we see no reason why that injury could not be remedied by an equitable decree.

C.

The Special Master also found, however, that Idaho has not demonstrated sufficient injury to justify an equitable decree. A State seeking equitable apportionment under our original jurisdiction must prove by clear and convincing evidence some real and substantial injury or damage. In reaching his conclusion, the Special Master stated that the determination should be based on present conditions. He therefore focused on the most recent time period, 1975 through 1980, during which all the dams and various conservation programs were in operation.

We approve this approach. The Special Master found that, due to the operation of the dams, the fish runs have been depressed since 1970. It is highly unlikely that the dams will be removed or the number of deadly turbines reduced; all parties must live with these conditions in the determinable future. Although Oregon and Washington may have harvested a disproportionate share of anadromous fish over the long run, Idaho took 58.72 percent of the total harvest in the period from 1975 through 1980. Equitable apportionment is directed at ameliorating present harm and preventing future injuries to the complaining State, not at compensating that State for prior injury. We agree with the Special Master that these figures do not demonstrate that Oregon and Washington are now injuring Idaho by overfishing the Columbia or that they will do so in the future.

Moreover, Idaho has not proven that Oregon and Washington have mismanaged the resource and will continue to mismanage. The two States in 1974 did permit some overfishing of the Columbia. Idaho, however, has produced no concrete evidence of other mismanagement, and the Special Master concluded that "[t]he record shows no repetition or threatened repetition of [prior mismanagement]." Although it is possible that Washington and Oregon will mismanage this resource in the future, Idaho has not carried its burden of demonstrating a substantial likelihood of injury.

III.

For the foregoing reasons, we adopt the Special Master's recommendation and dismiss the action without prejudice to the right of Idaho to bring new proceedings whenever it shall appear that it is being deprived of its equitable share of anadromous fish.

It is so ordered.

JUSTICE O'CONNOR with whom JUSTICE BRENNAN and JUSTICE STEVENS join, dissenting.

Questions

1. What are the roots of the doctrine of equitable apportionment?
2. How do the Indian treaty rights affect Idaho's alleged injury?

Chapter 8

FEDERAL REGULATION OF FISHERIES

Selected Provisions of the Magnuson Fishery Conservation and Management Act (16 U.S.C. 1801)

Sec. 2. Findings, Purposes, and Policy

(a) Findings—The Congress finds and declares the following:

(1) The fish off the coasts of the United States, the highly migratory species of the high seas, the species which dwell on or in the Continental Shelf appertaining to the United States, and the anadromous species which spawn in United States rivers or estuaries constitute valuable and renewable natural resources. These fishery resources contribute to the food supply, economy, and health of the Nation and provide recreational opportunities.

(2) As a consequence of increased fishing pressure and because of the inadequacy of fishery conservation and management practices and controls (A) certain stocks of such fish have been overfished to the point where their survival is threatened, and (B) other such stocks have been so substantially reduced in number that they could become similarly threatened.

(3) Commercial and recreational fishing constitutes a major source of employment and contributes significantly to the economy of the Nation. Many coastal areas are dependent upon fishing and related activities, and their economies have been badly damaged by the overfishing of fishery resources at an ever-increasing rate over the past decade. The activities of massive foreign fishing fleets in waters adjacent to such coastal areas have contributed to such damage, interfered with domestic fishing efforts, and caused destruction of the fishing gear of United States fishermen.

(4) International fishery agreements have not been effective in preventing or terminating the overfishing of these valuable fishery resources. There is danger that irreversible effects from overfishing will take place before an effective international agreement on fishery management jurisdiction can be negotiated, signed, ratified, and implemented.

(5) Fishery resources are finite but renewable. If placed under sound management before overfishing has caused irreversible effects, the fisheries can be conserved and maintained so as to provide optimum yields on a continuing basis.

(6) A national program for the conservation and management of the fishery resources of the United States is necessary to prevent overfishing, to rebuild overfished stocks, to insure conservation, and to realize the full potential of the Nation's fishery resources.

(7) A national program for the development of fisheries which are underutilized or not utilized by the United States fishing industry, including bottom fish off Alaska, is necessary to assure that our citizens benefit from the employment, food supply, and revenue which could be generated thereby.

(8) The collection of reliable data is essential to the effective conservation, management, and scientific understanding of the fishery resources of the United States.

(b) Purposes—It is therefore declared to be the purposes of the Congress in this Act—

(1) to take immediate action to conserve and manage the fishery resources found off the coasts of the United States, and the anadromous species and Continental Shelf fishery resources of the United States, by exercising (A) sovereign rights for the purposes of exploring, exploiting, conserving, and managing all fish within the exclusive economic zone established by Presidential Proclamation 5030, dated March 10, 1983, and (B) exclusive fishery management authority beyond the exclusive economic zone over such anadromous species and Continental Shelf fishery resources;

(2) to support and encourage the implementation and enforcement of international fishery agreements for the conservation and management of highly migratory species, and to encourage the negotiation and implementation of additional such agreements as necessary;

(3) to promote domestic commercial and recreational fishing under sound conservation and management principles;

(4) to provide for the preparation and implementation, in accordance with national standards, of fishery management plans which will achieve and maintain, on a continuing basis, the optimum yield from each fishery;

(5) to establish Regional Fishery Management Councils to exercise sound judgment in the stewardship of fishery resources through the preparation, monitoring, and revision of such plans under circumstances (A) which will enable the States, the fishing industry, consumer and environmental organizations, and other interested persons to participate in, and advise on, the establishment and administration of such plans, and (B) which take into account the social and economic needs of the States; and

(6) to encourage the development by the United States fishing industry of fisheries which are currently underutilized or not utilized by United States fishermen, including bottom fish off Alaska, and to that end, to ensure that optimum yield determinations promote such development.

(c) Policy—It is further declared to be the policy of the Congress in this Act—

(1) to maintain without change the existing territorial or other ocean jurisdiction of the United States for all purposes other than the conservation and management of fishery resources, as provided for in this Act;

(2) to authorize no impediment to, or interference with, recognized legitimate uses of the high seas, except as necessary for the conservation and management of fishery resources, as provided for in this Act;

(3) to assure that the national fishery conservation and management program utilizes, and is based upon, the best scientific information available; involves, and is responsive to the needs of, interested and affected States and citizens; promotes efficiency; draws upon Federal, State, and academic capabilities in carrying out research, administration, management, and en-

forcement; considers the effects of fishing on immature fish and encourages development of practical measures that avoid unnecessary waste of fish; and is workable and effective;

(4) to permit foreign fishing consistent with the provisions of this Act;

(5) to support and encourage active United States efforts to obtain internationally acceptable agreements which provide for effective conservation and management of fishery resources, and to secure agreements to regulate fishing by vessels or persons beyond the exclusive economic zones of any nation; and

(6) to foster and maintain the diversity of fisheries in the United States.

Sec. 3. Definitions
. . .

(21) The term "optimum," with respect to the yield from a fishery, means the amount of fish—

(A) which will provide the greatest overall benefit to the Nation, with particular reference to food production and recreational opportunities; and

(B) which is prescribed as such on the basis of the maximum sustainable yield from such fishery, as modified by any relevant economic, social, or ecological factor.

Title I—United States Rights and Authority Regarding Fish and Fishery Resources

Sec. 101. United States Sovereign Rights to Fish and Fishery Management Authority

(a) *In the Exclusive Economic Zone*—Except as provided in section 102, the United States claims, and will exercise in the manner provided for in this Act, sovereign rights and exclusive fishery management authority over all fish, and all Continental Shelf fishery resources, within the exclusive economic zone.

(b) *Beyond the Exclusive Economic Zone*—the United States claims, and will exercise in the manner provided for in this Act, exclusive fishery management authority over the following:

(1) All anadromous species throughout the migratory range of each such species beyond the exclusive economic zone; except that management authority does not extend to any such species during the time they are found within any waters of a foreign nation.

(2) All Continental Shelf fishery resources beyond the exclusive economic zone.

Sec. 102. Highly Migratory Species

The United States shall cooperate directly or through appropriate international organizations with those nations involved in fisheries for highly migratory species with a view to ensuring conservation and promoting the objective of optimum utilization of such species throughout their range, both within and beyond the exclusive economic zone.

Title II—Foreign Fishing and International Fishery Agreements

Sec. 201. Foreign Fishing

(a) *In General*—After February 28, 1977, no foreign fishing is authorized within the exclusive economic zone, or for anadromous species or Continental Shelf fishery resources beyond the exclusive economic zone, unless such foreign fishing . . . (complies with provisions of this law).

. . .

(d) *Total Allowable Level of Foreign Fishing*—The total allowable level of foreign fishing, if any, with respect to any fishery subject to the exclusive fishery management authority of the United States, shall be that portion of the optimum yield of such fishery which will not be harvested by vessels of the United States, as determined in accordance with this Act.

Title III—National Fishery Management Program

Sec. 301. National Standards for Fishery Conservation and Management

(a) *In General*—Any fishery management plan prepared, and any regulation promulgated to implement any such plan, pursuant to this title shall be consistent with the following national standards for fishery conservation and management:

(1) Conservation and management measures shall prevent overfishing while achieving, on a continuing basis, the optimum yield from each fishery for the United States fishing industry.

(2) Conservation and management measures shall be based upon the best scientific information available.

(3) To the extent practicable, an individual stock of fish shall be managed as a unit throughout its range, and interrelated stocks of fish shall be managed as a unit or in close coordination.

(4) Conservation and management measures shall not discriminate between residents of different States. If it becomes necessary to allocate or assign fishing privileges among various United States fishermen, such allocation shall be (A) fair and equitable to all such fishermen; (B) reasonably calculated to promote conservation; and (C) carried out in such manner that no particular individual, corporation, or other entity acquires an excessive share of such privileges.

(5) Conservation and management measures shall, where practicable, promote efficiency in the utilization of fishery resources; except that no such measure shall have economic allocation as its sole purpose.

(6) Conservation and management measures shall take into account and allow for variations among, and contingencies in, fisheries, fishery resources, and catches.

(7) Conservation and management measures

shall, where practicable, minimize costs and avoid unnecessary duplication.

(b) *Guidelines*—The Secretary shall establish advisory guidelines (which shall not have the force and effect of law), based on the national standards, to assist in the development of fishery management plans.

Sec. 302. Regional Fishery Management Councils

(a) *Establishment*—There shall be established, within 120 days after the date of the enactment of this Act, eight Regional Fishery Management Councils, as follows:

(1) New England Council

(2) Mid-Atlantic Council

(3) South Atlantic Council

(4) Caribbean Council

(5) Gulf Council

(6) Pacific Council

(7) North Pacific Council

(8) Western Pacific Council

Each Council shall reflect the expertise and interest of the several constituent States in the ocean area over which such Council is granted authority.

(b) *Voting Members*—

(1) The voting members of each Council shall be:

(A) The principal State official with marine fishery management responsibility and expertise in each constituent State, who is designated as such by the Governor of the State, so long as the official continues to hold such position, or the designee of such official.

(B) The regional director of the National Marine Fisheries Service for the geographic area concerned, or his designee, except that if two such directors are within such geographical area, the Secretary shall designate which of such directors shall be the voting member.

(C) The members required to be appointed by the Secretary in accordance with subsection (b)(2).

(2) (A) The members of each Council required to be appointed by the Secretary must be individuals who, by reason of their occupational or other experience, scientific expertise, or training, are knowledgeable regarding the conservation and management, or the commercial or recreational harvest, of the fishery resources of the geographical area concerned.

Sec. 303. Contents of Fishery Management Plans

(a) *Required Provisions*—Any fishery management plan which is prepared by any Council, or by the Secretary, with respect to any fishery, shall—

(1) contain the conservation and management measures, applicable to foreign fishing and fishing by vessels of the United States, which are—

(A) necessary and appropriate for the conservation and management of the fishery to prevent overfishing, and to protect, restore, and promote the long-term health and stability of the fishery;

(B) described in this subsection or subsection (b), or both; and

(C) consistent with the national standards, the other provisions of this Act, regulations implementing recommendations by international organizations in which the United States participates (including but not limited to closed areas, quotas, and size limits), and any other applicable law;

(2) contain a description of the fishery, including, but not limited to, the number of vessels involved, the type and quantity of fishing gear used, the species of fish involved and their location, the cost likely to be incurred in management, actual and potential revenues from the fishery, and recreational interest in the fishery, and the nature and extent of foreign fishing and Indian treaty fishing rights, if any;

(3) assess and specify the present and probable future conditions of, and the maximum sustainable yield and optimum yield from, the fishery, and include a summary of the information utilized in making such specification;

(4) assess and specify—

(A) the capacity and the extent to which fishing vessels of the United States, on an annual basis, will harvest the optimum yield specified under paragraph (3),

(B) the portion of such optimum yield which, on an annual basis, will not be harvested by fishing vessels of the United States and can be made available for foreign fishing, and

(C) the capacity and extent to which United States fish processors, on an annual basis, will process that portion of such optimum yield that will be harvested by fishing vessels of the United States;

(5) specify the pertinent data which shall be submitted to the Secretary with respect to the fishery, including, but not limited to, information regarding the type and quantity of fishing gear used, catch by species in numbers of fish or weight thereof, areas in which fishing was engaged in, time of fishing, number of hauls, and the estimated processing capacity of, and the actual processing capacity utilized by United States fish processors;

(6) consider and provide for temporary adjustments, after consultation with the Coast Guard and persons utilizing the fishery, regarding access to the fishery for vessels otherwise prevented from harvesting because of weather or other ocean conditions affecting the safe conduct of the fishery; except that the adjustment shall not adversely affect conservation efforts in other fisheries or discriminate among participants in the affected fishery;

(7) include readily available information regarding the significance of habitat to the fishery and assessment as to the effects which changes to that habitat may have upon the fishery;

(8) in the case of a fishery management plan

that, after January 1, 1991, is submitted to the Secretary for review under section 304(a) (including any plan for which an amendment is submitted to the Secretary for such review) or is prepared by the Secretary, assess and specify the nature and extent of scientific data which is needed for effective implementation of the plan; and

(9) include a fishery impact statement for the plan or amendment (in the case of a plan or amendment thereto submitted to or prepared by the Secretary after October 1, 1990) which shall assess, specify, and describe the likely effects, if any, of the conservation and management measures on—

(A) participants in the fisheries affected by the plan or amendment; and

(B) participants in the fisheries conducted in adjacent areas under the authority of another Council, after consultation with such Council and representatives of those participants.

. . .

Sec. 306. State Jurisdiction

(a) In General—

(1) Except as provided in subsection (b), nothing in this Act shall be construed as extending or diminishing the jurisdiction or authority of any State within its boundaries.

(2) For the purposes of this Act, except as provided in subsection (b), the jurisdiction and authority of a State shall extend

(A) to any pocket of waters that is adjacent to the State and totally enclosed by lines delimiting the territorial sea of the United States pursuant to the Geneva Convention on the Territorial Sea and Contiguous Zone or any successor convention to which the United States is a party; . . .

(3) Except as otherwise provided by paragraph (2), a State may not directly or indirectly regulate any fishing vessel outside its boundaries, unless the vessel is registered under the law of that State.

(b) Exception—

(1) If the Secretary finds, after notice and an opportunity for a hearing in accordance with section 554 of title 5, United States Code, that—

(A) the fishing in a fishery, which is covered by a fishery management plan implemented under this Act, is engaged in predominantly within the exclusive economic zone and beyond such zone; and

(B) any State has taken any action, or omitted to take any action, the results of which will substantially and adversely affect the carrying out of such fishery management plan;

the Secretary shall promptly notify such State and the appropriate Council of such finding and of his intention to regulate the applicable fishery within the boundaries of such State (other than its internal waters), pursuant to such fishery management plan and the regulations promulgated to implement such plan.

Sec. 307. Prohibited Acts

It is unlawful—

(1) for any person—

(A) to violate any provision of this Act or any regulation or permit issued pursuant to this Act;

(B) to use any fishing vessel to engage in fishing after the revocation, or during the period of suspension, of an applicable permit issued pursuant to this Act;

(C) to violate any provision of, or regulation under, an applicable governing international fishery agreement entered into pursuant to section 201(c);

(D) to refuse to permit any officer authorized to enforce the provisions of this Act (as provided for in section 311) to board a fishing vessel subject to such person's control for the purposes of conducting any search or inspection in connection with the enforcement of this Act or any regulation, permit, or agreement referred to in subparagraph (A) or (C);

(E) to forcibly assault, resist, oppose, impede, intimidate, or interfere with any such authorized officer in the conduct of any search or inspection described in subparagraph (D);

(F) to resist a lawful arrest for any act prohibited by this section;

(G) to ship, transport, offer for sale, sell, purchase, import, export, or have custody, control, or possession of, any fish taken or retained in violation of this Act or any regulation, permit, or agreement referred to in subparagraph (A) or (C);

(H) to interfere with, delay, or prevent, by any means, the apprehension or arrest of another person, knowing that such other person has committed any act prohibited by this section;

(I) to knowingly and willfully submit to a Council, the Secretary, or the Governor of a State false information (including, but not limited to, false information regarding the capacity and extent to which a United States fish processor, on an annual basis, will process a portion of the optimum yield of a fishery that will be harvested by fishing vessels of the United States) regarding any matter that the Council, Secretary, or Governor is considering in the course of carrying out this Act;

(J) to ship, transport, offer for sale, sell, or purchase, in interstate or foreign commerce, any whole live lobster of the species *Homarus americanus*, that—

(i) is smaller than the minimum possession size in effect at the time under the American Lobster Fishery Management Plan, as implemented by regulations published in part 649 of title 50, Code of Federal Regulations, or any successor to that plan, implemented under this title;

(ii) is bearing eggs attached to its abdominal appendages; or

(iii) bears evidence of the forcible removal of extruded eggs from its abdominal appendages;

(K) to knowingly steal, or without authorization, to remove, damage, or tamper with—

(i) fishing gear owned by another person, which is located in the exclusive economic zone, or

(ii) fish contained in such fishing gear, or to attempt to do so;

(L) to forcibly assault, resist, oppose, impede, intimidate, or interfere with any observer on a vessel under this Act;

(M) to engage in large-scale drift-net fishing that is subject to the jurisdiction of the United States, including use of a fishing vessel of the United States to engage in such fishing beyond the exclusive economic zone of any nation; or

(N) to strip pollock of its roe and discard the flesh of the pollock.

(2) for any vessel other than a vessel of the United States, and for the owner or operator of any vessel other than a vessel of the United States, to engage—

(A) in fishing within the boundaries of any State, except recreational fishing permitted under section 201(j);

(B) in fishing, except recreational fishing permitted under section 201(j), within the exclusive economic zone, or for any anadromous species or Continental Shelf fishery resources beyond such zone, unless such fishing is authorized by, and conducted in accordance with, a valid and applicable permit issued pursuant to section 204(b) or (c); or

(C) except as permitted under section 306(c), in fish processing (as defined in paragraph (4)(A) of such section) within the internal waters of a State (as defined in paragraph (4)(B) of such section);

(3) for any vessel of the United States, and for the owner or operator of any vessel of the

United States, to transfer directly or indirectly, or attempt to so transfer, any United States harvested fish to any foreign fishing vessel, while such foreign vessel is within the exclusive economic zone, unless the foreign fishing vessel has been issued a permit under section 204 which authorizes the receipt by such vessel of United States harvested fish of the species concerned; and

(4) for any fishing vessel other than a vessel of the United States to operate, and for the owner of a fishing vessel other than a vessel of the United States to operate such vessel, in the exclusive economic zone, if—

(A) all fishing gear on the vessel is not stored below deck or in an area where it is not normally used, and not readily available, for fishing; or

(B) all fishing gear on the vessel which is not so stored is not secured and covered so as to render it unusable for fishing; unless such vessel is authorized to engage in fishing in the area in which the vessel is operating.

Sec. 308. Civil Penalties and Permit Sanctions

(a) Assessment of Penalty—Any person who is found by the Secretary, after notice and an opportunity for a hearing in accordance with section 554 of title 5, United States Code, to have committed an act prohibited by section 307 shall be liable to the United States for a civil penalty. The amount of the civil penalty shall not exceed $100,000 for each violation. Each day of a continuing violation shall constitute a separate offense. The amount of such civil penalty shall be assessed by the Secretary, or his designee, by written notice. In determining the amount of such penalty, the Secretary will take into account the nature, circumstances, extent, and gravity of the prohibited acts committed and, with respect to the violator, the degree of culpability, any history of prior offenses, ability to pay, and such other matters as justice may require.

. . .

(d) In Rem Jurisdiction—A fishing vessel (including its fishing gear, furniture, appurtenances, stores, and cargo) used in the commission of an act prohibited by section 307 shall be liable in rem for any civil penalty assessed for such violation under section 308 and may be proceeded against in any district court of the United States having jurisdiction thereof. Such penalty shall constitute a maritime lien on such vessel which may be recovered in an action in rem in the district court of the United States having jurisdiction over the vessel.

. . .

(g) Permit Sanctions—

(1) In any case in which (A) a vessel has been used in the commission of an act prohibited under section 307, (B) the owner or operator of a vessel or any other person who has been issued or has applied for a permit under this Act has acted in violation of section 307, or (C) any civil penalty or criminal fine imposed on a vessel or owner or operator of a vessel or any other person who has been issued or has applied for a permit under any fishery resource law statute enforced by the Secretary has not been paid and is overdue, the Secretary may

(i) revoke any permit issued with respect to such vessel or person, with or without prejudice to the issuance of subsequent permits;

(ii) suspend such permit for a period of time considered by the Secretary to be appropriate;

(iii) deny such permit; or

(iv) impose additional conditions and restrictions on any permit issued to or applied for such vessel or person under this Act and, with respect to foreign vessels, on the approved application of the foreign nation involved and on any permit issued under that application.

Sec. 309. Criminal Offenses

(a) Offenses—A person is guilty of an offense if he commits any act prohibited by—

(1) section 307(1)(D), (E), (F), (H), (I), or (L); or

(2) section 307(2).

(b) Punishment—Any offense described in subsection (a)(1) is punishable by a fine of not more than $100,000, or imprisonment for not more than six months, or both; except that if in the commission of any such offense the person uses a dangerous weapon, engages in conduct that causes bodily injury to any observer described in section 307(1)(L) or any officer authorized to enforce the provisions of this Act (as provided for in section 311), or places any such observer or officer in fear of imminent bodily injury, the offense is punishable by a fine of not more than $200,000, or imprisonment for not more than ten years, or both. Any offense described in subsection (a)(2) is punishable by a fine of not more than $200,000.

(c) Jurisdiction—There is Federal jurisdiction over any offense described in this section.

Sec. 310. Civil Forfeitures

(a) In General—Any fishing vessel (including its fishing gear, furniture, appurtenances, stores, and cargo) used, and any fish (or the fair market value thereof) taken or retained, in any manner, in connection with or as a result of the commission of any act prohibited by section 307 (other than any act for which the issuance of a citation under section 311(c) is sufficient sanction) shall be subject to forfeiture to the United States. All or part of such vessel may, and all such fish (or the fair market value thereof) shall, be forfeited to the United States pursuant to a civil proceeding under this section.

Questions

1. Has the concept of optimum yield worked to enhance or detract from the overall goal of resource conservation?

2. Are any conflict of interest problems apparent in the statute?

3. When may the federal government assert jurisdiction over fisheries in *state* waters?

Maine v. Kreps, 563 F.2d 1052
(1st Cir. 1977)

LEVEN H. CAMPBELL, CIRCUIT JUDGE

This appeal by the State of Maine follows proceedings in the district court on remand from this court's decision in *Maine v. Kreps* 563 F.2d 1043 (August 16, 1977). Maine continues her challenge to the 1977 herring quotas set by the Secretary of Commerce on the Georges Bank under the newly enacted Fishery Conservation and Management Act 16 U.S.C. Sec. 1801 et seq. (the Act); and the question now before us is the adequacy of affidavits filed by the Secretary pursuant to this court's directions in the first *Kreps* decision. We required her to supplement the administrative record so as to reveal the basis for her determination of 33,000 metric tons (m.t.) as the 1977 optimum yield figure for the Georges Bank herring stock. The district court found the material in the affidavits sufficient to demonstrate a reasoned and legally adequate basis for the 33,000 m.t. figure which, as it exceeds estimated domestic fishing needs, has the effect of allowing foreign fishing fleets to fish on the Georges Bank during the present fishing season.

We held in our earlier *Kreps* opinion that the conservation and management aims of the Act do not necessarily preclude the selection of an optimum yield figure large enough to allow some foreign fishing where, as here, the figure is still conservative enough to allow rebuilding of a depleted stock at a reasonable if not optimum rate. But we emphasized that especially where the stock is below healthy levels, as is the case in the Georges Bank area, selection of a figure which allows leeway for any foreign fishing must reflect the Secretary's rational judgment that there is benefit to the Nation, with particular reference to its food supply. We said,

Congress plainly did not intend the cardinal aim of the Act—the development of a United States' controlled fishing conservation and management program designed to prevent overfishing and to rebuild depleted stocks—to be subordinated to the interests of foreign nations. But within a framework of progress toward this goal, the Secretary is directed and empowered within specified limits to accommodate foreign fishing, Sec. 1801(c)(4); 1821. We find no congressional purpose that she disregard the benefits to be derived from cooperating with other nations. American consumers depend not only on United States producers; they benefit from our trade with the rest of the world. United States fishermen as well as consumers benefit from international cooperation. Indeed, the continued existence of fish stocks throughout the oceans of the world may well be dependent on actions by foreign nations as well as ourselves. Management of the ocean's fish resources cannot be accomplished solely within our own coastal areas. We think Congress did not require the Secretary to set optimum yield figures entirely without regard to the effects upon this country of allowing or denying foreign fishing.

On the other hand, Congress has expressly directed the Secretary to consider the overall welfare of the United States in setting the optimum yield figure. Our nation's welfare may be considered in terms of its foreign relations as well as its purely domestic needs, but the touchstone is the benefit of this nation, not that of some other. Moreover, by "particular reference to the food supply," Congress underscored that priority was to be given to food requirements: the nation's fisheries were not, for example, to be swapped for a world banking agreement. The international considerations that are given weight must ordinarily relate to fishing, fish, and other activities and products pertaining to the food supply (apart from any recreational benefits). 563 F.2d at 1049–50

Because the record did not reveal whether the Secretary had balanced these considerations in setting the optimum yield figure, further explanation was required.

Of the three affidavits subsequently submitted by the Government, most important was that of David H. Wallace, Associate Administrator for Marine Resources of the National

Oceanic and Atmospheric Administration and the official responsible for final action by the Department of Commerce on the Georges Bank herring preliminary management plan. Wallace stated that, in considering at what level to set the optimum yield figure for this stock, he took into account the traditional fishing activities of foreign fleets in the Georges Bank herring fishery; substantial benefits to be derived by the United States from continued scientific research conducted by the foreign fleets; the need for the United States to retain a credible negotiating stance with regard to the ongoing Law of the Sea deliberations; past policy statements by the Government that the transition to United States management of the fishery resources within the two hundred-mile limit would be gradual; and the difficult position the United States would be in with regard to cooperative international fishery conservation efforts, its own distant-water fishing fleets, and foreign fishery trade, if it were to renounce commitments previously undertaken through the International Commission for the Northwest Atlantic Fisheries (ICNAF), from which the United States withdrew at the end of 1976. He observed: "It is my opinion that any abrupt termination of foreign fishing, given the historical background, could have had significant adverse impacts on our international fisheries relations." Two other affidavits from Government officials involved in the development of the herring quota in essence repeated Wallace's explanation.

We are of the opinion that the explanation advanced by the Secretary for picking the figure chosen as an optimum yield provides a sufficient basis to determine that she did not act in an arbitrary or capricious manner or contrary to law, 5 U.S.C. Sec. 702(2)(A), and we accordingly affirm the order of the district court dismissing the complaint.

The Secretary of Commerce, in the exercise of her conservation and management authority under the Act, has substantial discretion in selecting the appropriate quota for a given fishery. A reviewing court may decide only whether this discretion was exercised rationally and consistently with the standards set by Congress, *Maine v. Kreps, supra*, and may not substitute its own judgment as to values and priorities for that of the Secretary.

When this case was first presented to this court, the record was insufficient to determine whether the Secretary had so exercised her discretion, and some evidence suggested "that the Secretary may have uncritically taken ICNAF's total allowable catch figure." 563 F.2d at 1049. The representations of Wallace and the other officials now indicate that the ICNAF figure was only the starting point of analysis, and that the Government weighed the consequences of departure from the previously negotiated quota in light of its "historical background." These officials determined that repudiating the ICNAF guidelines would harm United States interests, particularly food supplies, and that adhering to them would benefit the Nation. In light of the scientific evidence at hand, the 33,000 m.t. figure appeared to allow some rebuilding of the stock to foreign fishermen who relied on the grounds. Having in mind that this is the first year since the United States has asserted jurisdiction over these offshore waters, we cannot say that the Secretary's rationale is arbitrary, capricious, or contrary to the standards of the Act. 5 U.S.C. Sec. 706(2)(A).

Maine argues that, if this court were to accept the "honoring commitments to other nations" explanation in this case, the Secretary would be provided with a loophole for circumventing the management goals of the Act whenever she chose. According to the state, the Secretary could use an international agreement into which the executive branch enters as a shield for the quota set, no matter how much the figures contravene the purposes of the Act. This argument seems to us to fall quite wide of the mark. The commitments made in this case were negotiated at least in part before Congress had passed the Act, and entirely before the Act took effect. The commitments and the Secretary's response to them reflected the special considerations of a transitional year and the inauguration of exclusive United States management of this fishery. Different considerations would apply to international agreements made at a different time under other circumstances.

Maine also contends that because historical fishing patterns and past scientific cooperation are factors to be considered in allocating a fishery surplus once an optimum yield has been determined, 16 U.S.C. Sec. 1821(e)(1), (2), they are impermissible criteria for setting the optimum yield. As a matter of statutory construction, Maine's argument is overstated: while Maine is right that determination of optimum yield rests on quite different premises from surplus allocation, there is no rule that the Secretary in determining the former must totally reject considerations that may be appropriate to both. The Government, furthermore, did not rely on the fact of historical fisheries per se, but only in relation to its prior commitments. Further, the scientific research to which Wallace referred was not that conducted in the past, but that expected in the future. These were not the same factors enumerated by Section 1821(e)(1), (2).

Finally, Maine asserts that in providing an additional explanation the Government violated the notice and comment requirements of 16 U.S.C. Sec. 1855(a). The provision referred to does not apply to the development of preliminary management plans, such as the one at issue here, and nothing in the Act suggests that such plans, in distinction to regulations attendant thereto, are subject to notice and comment requirements. 16 U.S.C. Sec. 1821(g). Further the affidavits submitted to the district court did not constitute an amendment of any agency action, but only a supplemental explanation of why the agency acted as it did. The only rebuttal rights to which Maine was entitled were those provided by this court proceeding.

Maine urges us to decide this case so as to clarify for the future the limits of the Secretary's authority in this area. To some degree we have done so: for example, in our clarification of the elements of the optimum yield standard. The Secretary is now clear, if she was ever in doubt, that the broad grant of discretionary authority in the Act is tempered by the requirement that she comply with congressionally declared standards and objectives, and that her reasoning appear with sufficient clarity in the record for a court to review such compliance. But while the Secretary's discretion is not unbridled and is subject to review for arbitrariness and lack of compliance with statutory procedures and standards, Congress obviously intends her to retain the flexibility and freedom to deal effectively with different situations as they arise. This is a transitional year. What is reasonable now may be less so later. Moreover, the preliminary plan is subject to reevaluation in the preparation of succeeding plans. We have neither the authority nor the expertise to project future policies for the Secretary to follow.

Affirmed.

Questions

1. What "federal interests" were relevant in the determination of optimum yield?

2. Shouldn't the interests of U.S. fishermen always prevail under the law?

3. Why did the U.S. government feel compelled to share our "surplus" resource in 1977?

Washington Trollers Assn. v. Kreps, 645 F.2d 684 (9th Cir. 1981)

PREGERSON, CIRCUIT JUDGE

Appellants—several associations representing commercial troll fishermen, and named individual troll fishermen—appeal from a summary judgment against them in this suit challenging the 1978 Fishery Management Plan for commercial and recreational salmon fisheries off the coasts of Washington, Oregon, and California ("the Plan"). Appellants seek a declaration that the Plan does not conform to the provisions of the Fishery Conservation and Management Act of 1976, 16 U.S.C. Sec. 1801–82 ("the FCMA"), and the guidelines established pursuant to that act, 50 C.F.R. 602.2, 602.3, and hence could not serve as a proper basis for fishery management regulations promulgated by the appellee Secretary of Commerce. Because we find that material issues of fact remain unresolved, we reverse the district court's grant of summary judgment.

Section 308(a)(3) of the FCMA, 16 U.S.C. Sec. 1853(a)(3), which provides that fishery management plans are to specify the fishery's present and likely future condition, maximum sustainable yield, and optimum yield, requires that plans "include a summary of the information utilized in making such specification." Appellants contend that the Plan violates this requirement because it relies on computerized analysis systems without describing either the computer methodology or the data used to arrive at the Plan's projections and recommendations. Appellees reply that the Plan cites documents that describe the computer methodology in sufficient detail to serve as the basis for informed criticism and that as long as such documents were publicly available, it was unnecessary to include them in the Plan itself.

The kind of "summary" section 303(a)(3) requires can be understood only in light of the purposes and policies of the FCMA. Congress clearly intended to give those members of the public interested in or affected by fishery management plans and regulations a meaningful voice in shaping those plans and regulations. Section 2(b)(5)(A) of the FCMA, 16 U.S.C. Sec. 1801(b)(5)(A), states that one purpose of the Act is to "enable the States, the fishing industry, consumer and environmental organizations, and other interested persons to participate in, and advise on, the establishment and administration of fish [fishery] plans." And section 2(c)(3) of the FCMA, 16 U.S.C. Sec. 1801(c)(33), enunciates a policy of "assur[ing] that the national fishery conservation and management program . . . involves, and is responsive to the needs of, interested and affected

States and citizens." To realize these goals, Congress stipulated that when the Secretary of Commerce approves a fishery management plan and publishes it with proposed implementing regulations, "[i]nterested persons shall be afforded a period of not less than forty-five days after such publication within which to submit in writing data, views, or comments on the plan . . . and on the proposed regulations." FCMA Sec. 305(a), 16 U.S.C. Sec. 1855(a).

This provision for public comment can effectuate Congress's goals only if the public is able to make intelligent, informed, meaningful comments. The "summary of the information utilized" in the Plan's specifications required by section 303(a)(3) must therefore provide information sufficient to enable an interested or affected party to comment intelligently on those specifications. Accordingly, although the "summary" that the Plan is required to include may incorporate by reference documents containing the necessary information, those documents must be reasonably available to the interested public.

Here, appellants and appellees disagree sharply as to how readily available the documents describing the computer methodology actually were. They disagree on whether the Plan sets out the data that was fed into the computer to obtain the Plan's specifications. They even disagree on whether only one computer model was used to obtain all of the descriptions, projections, and analyses in the Plan. All of these are issues of fact, all are highly material, and all are unresolved. Summary judgment, however, is proper *only* when "there is no genuine issue as to any material fact." Therefore, we must reverse the entry of summary judgment; further proceedings will be necessary to resolve the factual disputes in this lawsuit.

The judgment of the district court is reversed, and the case is remanded for further proceedings.

POOLE, CIRCUIT JUDGE, dissenting.

Today the majority mandates that henceforth, before promulgating fishing regulations pursuant to the Fishery Conservation and Management Act, the Secretary of Commerce must make available to every interested party every computer model, methodology, statistical study, all of the raw data, and any other information which played a role in formulating fishery yield specifications pursuant to Sec. 1853(a)(3). Thus, the public now has a right of access to all that is used to formulate such specifications and may obtain the information in the form that it came to the Secretary. I cannot agree that the statute or the public's interest in commenting on proposed regulations requires imposition of such a sweeping access requirement. Nor can I agree that summary judgment was improperly granted in this case. I respectfully dissent.

I.

The key statutory provision construed is 16 U.S.C. Sec. 1853(a)(3), which provides that in promulgating a fishery management plan, that plan must: "assess and specify the present and probable future condition of, and the maximum sustainable yield and optimum yield from the fishery, *including a summary of the information utilized in making such specification*" (emphasis added). Reading this language in conjunction with provisions of the Act requiring public opportunity for comment on fishery management plans and regulations, the majority concludes that the term "summary" must be defined to require complete access to all the information and methodologies used in formulating the specifications of a fishery management plan. As the majority makes clear in the fourth paragraph of its opinion, all of the basic data used must be available if meaningful public comment is to be possible. Moreover, in light of the conclusion that material issues of unresolved fact are whether the raw data fed into the computer was disclosed in the plan, or whether the computer model was available, the majority must necessarily conclude that disclosure of such materials is essential. Absolute access is the necessary import of today's decision. . . .

The remaining issue is whether the summary provided by the Secretary pursuant to Sec. 1853(a)(3) was sufficient for purposes of the statute. The district judge found that the plan contained information about the maximum and optimum yield calculations as required by Sec. 1853(a)(3). 466 F.Supp. at 314. Reviewing the 157-page plan in its entirety, the court concluded that a reasonable effort has been made to disclose substantial amounts of information covering every issue relevant in promulgating the plan and regulations, found that no subject had been ignored, and noted that the appellants had failed to point to any information withheld or which was essential to their right to comment. The district court's conclusions are sustained by the record.

The primary purposes served by statutory requirements of public disclosure are those of apprising the public of the action the Secretary plans to take and affording an opportunity for public participation by means of the comment process. This court has said that in reviewing disclosures required by a statute to permit public comment, regulations will not be set aside for inadequate disclosure unless the disclosures were so grossly deficient as to frustrate the public right. Nowhere in the record here does it appear that the disclosure of information was so grossly deficient as to erode the public right to comment or to withhold from the public information on regulatory action proposed by the Secretary. I would affirm the judgment.

Question

1. Under the standard upheld by the majority, won't it always be possible to challenge a management plan?

Conservation Law Foundation v. Franklin, 989 F.2d 54 (1st Cir. 1993)

TORRUELLA, CIRCUIT JUDGE

In this appeal, several fishing associations, appellants here, request that we vacate a consent decree approved and entered by the district court between the Conservation Law Foundation of New England, Inc., and the Massachusetts Audubon Society (collectively, "Conservation"), and the Secretary of Commerce ("Secretary"). For the reasons that follow, we reject this request.

Prior Proceedings

Conservation sued the Secretary alleging that the Secretary failed to prevent overfishing off the coast of New England, as required by the Magnuson Fishery Conservation and Management Act of 1976, 16 U.S.C. Secs. 1801–82 ("Magnuson Act"). Appellants sought to intervene. The district court denied the request, but we granted it in *Conservation Law Foundation, Inc. v. Mosbacher*, 966 F.2d 39 (1st Cir. 1992). While the appeal seeking intervention was pending, the district court entered a consent decree between Conservation and the Secretary. Appellants now seek to vacate the consent decree on various grounds. To fully understand the present appeal, we must briefly describe the statutory context to this suit.

Statutory Background

Congress enacted the Magnuson Act to establish a comprehensive system for fisheries management for waters within the jurisdiction of the United States. 16 U.S.C. Sec. 1801(b)(1). In particular, Congress found that certain stocks of fish had been so overfished that their survival was threatened, and mandated that overfishing be prevented.

To attain these goals, the Act creates eight regional fishery management councils. The regional councils are comprised of state and federal government officials, as well as individuals nominated by state executives and appointed by the Secretary. The Magnuson Act charges the Secretary and the Councils with developing fishery management plans ("FMPs") for stocks of fish within their jurisdictions that require conservation and management. The Act specifies the procedures by which FMPs are developed and creates a number of standards to which the plans must conform. National Standard One requires that "[c]onservation and management measures shall prevent overfishing while achieving, on a continuing basis, the optimum yield from each fishery for the United States fishing industry." The Secretary has issued guidelines to assist the development of plans by the regional councils.

The Act provides that either the councils or the Secretary can develop FMPs. If a council generates a plan, the Secretary must follow a detailed procedure for review, as specified in Sec. 1854(a), (b). The Secretary first reviews the plan for compliance with statutory mandates and publishes notice of the plan in the Federal Register, soliciting comments from interested persons. After review, the Secretary may approve, partially approve, or disapprove the plan. If the Secretary disapproves or partially disapproves of a plan she must inform the council of her reasons. The council may then submit a revised plan, which the Secretary will review.

The Act authorizes the Secretary to develop an FMP with respect to any fishery if (1) "the appropriate council fails to develop and submit to the Secretary, *after a reasonable period of time*, a fishery management plan for such fishery, or any necessary amendment to such a plan, if such fishery requires conservation and management . . . ," (emphasis added); or (2) "the Secretary disapproves or partially disapproves any such plan or amendment, or disapproves a revised plan or amendment, and the Council involved fails to submit a revised or further revised plan or amendment, as the case may be." Under either statutory authority, the Secretary must submit the FMP to the appropriate council for comments, and publish notice of the plan and regulations to implement the plan in the Federal Register. Before the Secretary implements the plan, she must consider the comments of the council and the public, and ensure compliance with the national standards.

Approved FMPs are implemented by regulations promulgated by the Secretary, which are subject to judicial review in accordance with select provisions of the Administrative Procedures Act, 5 U.S.C. Sec. 701 et seq.

History of the Northeast Multispecies Fisheries Plan

This case involves the conservation and management of groundfish off the coast of New England. In its effort to manage New England fisheries, the New England Fishery Management Council ("New England Council") first eliminated foreign fishing within its jurisdiction, 42 Fed. Reg. 13 (1977). In 1985, it developed the Northeast Multispecies Fisheries Plan, Proposed Rule, 50 Fed. Reg. 49,582 (1985), because overfishing remained a problem. The Secretary approved the plan as an interim rule in 1986, indicating that the rule improved matters, but was unsatisfactory for long-term conservation and management. Interim Rule, 51 Fed. Reg. 29,642, 29,643 (1986). In 1987, the rule became final and three amendments followed. See Final Rule, 52 Fed. Reg. 35,093 (1987) (amendment one); Final Rule, 54 Fed. Reg. 4,798 (1989) (amendment two); Final Rule, 54 Fed. Reg. 52,803 (1989) (amendment three).

The Rule and its amendments did not eliminate overfishing as required by National Standard One. Pursuant to the Secretary's guidelines on what constitutes overfishing, the Council determined that cod, haddock, and yellowtail flounder in certain fisheries off the coast of New England were overfished and drafted amendment four to redress that problem. The Secretary partially approved amendment four, 56 Fed. Reg. 24,724 (1991), but found the amendment deficient, stating that it did "not constitute a complete rebuilding strategy."

In response to amendment four, Conservation sued the Secretary, complaining that she had arbitrarily and capriciously approved the amendment and that the overall FMP failed to comply with National Standard One. Thereafter, Conservation and the Secretary began negotiations to enter a consent decree settling the suit. Appellants sought to intervene but the district court denied the request. While the appeal was pending, the district court entered a consent decree on August 28, 1991. In the appeal, we granted appellants intervenor status.

The Consent Decree

The consent decree established a timetable for an FMP or an amendment to the plan applicable to New England waters that could "eliminate the overfished condition of cod and yellowtail flounder stocks in five years after implementation and . . . eliminate the overfished condition of haddock stocks in ten years after implementation." *Conservation Law Foundation, Inc. v. Mosbacher*, C.A. No. 91-11759-MA, slip op. at 2 (D. Mass., August 28, 1991) (consent decree). The decree expressly stated that it "shall meet all requirements established by applicable statutes and regulations." It directed that the New England Council would have the first opportunity to develop the groundfish rebuilding plan, but also established a timetable for the Secretary to create and implement her own plan if the council failed to act. Appellants unsuccessfully moved to vacate the consent decree. This appeal followed.

Discussion

District courts must review a consent decree to ensure that it is "fair, adequate, and reasonable; that the proposed decree will not violate the Constitution, a statute, or other authority; [and] that it is consistent with the objectives of Congress." *Durrett v. Housing Authority of Providence*, 896 F.2d 600, 604 (1st Cir. 1990). Where an administrative agency has committed itself to a consent decree, the district court must exercise some deference to the agency's determination that settlement is appropriate, and "refrain from second-guessing the Executive Branch." *United States v. Cannons Engineering Corp.*, 899 F.2d 79, 84 (1st Cir. 1990). Moreover, "the court is not barred from entering a consent decree merely because it might lack authority under [the governing statute] to do so after a trial." *Local No. 93, Int'l Assn. of Fire-*

fighters v. Cleveland, 478 U.S. 501, 525–26 (1986).

The Supreme Court has stated that district courts may properly approve a consent decree where (1) it "spring[s] from and serve[s] to resolve a dispute within the courts' subject matter jurisdiction"; (2) it "come[s] within the general scope of the case made by the pleadings"; and (3) furthers the objectives upon which the complaint was based. Therefore, the parties enjoy wide latitude in terms of what they may agree to by consent decree and have sanctioned by a court. Furthermore, we recognize a strong and "clear policy in favor of encouraging settlements," especially in complicated regulatory settings.

We review the district court's denial of a motion to vacate a consent decree for abuse of discretion. Additionally, "[t]he doubly required deference—district court to agency and appellate court to district court—places a heavy burden on those who propose to upset the trial judge's approval of a consent decree." We turn now to appellants' challenge to the decree.

Appellants contend that the consent decree constitutes improper rule making under the statute which deprives the public of an opportunity to comment. They assert that the consent decree (1) creates a new standard requiring that the FMP "eliminate" overfishing, whereas National Standard One mandates "prevention" of overfishing while maintaining maximum sustainable yield from fisheries; (2) requires a rebuilding program and a timetable for compliance not present in the Magnuson Act; (3) establishes a "good faith" performance standard for Council action; and (4) constrains the Secretary's discretion under the Act.

Appellants essentially maintain that the Secretary's action with respect to Council-generated FMPs, or amendments thereto, must follow the statutorily prescribed course of review, as set forth in 16 U.S.C. Sec. 1854(b), which requires that the Secretary notify the council of its reasons for disapproving any portion of the plan and provide an opportunity for the council to revise the plan. Appellants also argue that the consent decree essentially is improper under Sec. 1854(c), which authorizes the Secretary to generate her own plans under certain circumstances. Appellants maintain that the Secretary may not act unless the Council has failed to issue a plan after a reasonable period, or the Secretary disapproves of some aspect of a plan and the Council fails to revise it. Because neither Sec. 1854(c) condition has occurred, appellants contend that the consent decree constitutes unlawful rule making. They allege that the Secretary is not free to bypass the dictates of Sec. 1854 through a consent decree, but rather must wait for a revised amendment before developing her own plan.

Appellants' challenge fails for three reasons. First, in instances in which the rights of third parties are the basis for blocking the entry of, or vacating, a consent decree, there must be a demonstrable injury or adverse effect upon the group not party to the decree. This threshold showing is analogous to the standing requirement. A right to intervene does not necessarily suffice to meet the test for vacating a consent decree. In this case, appellants have failed to allege any specific injury to themselves, or any other party. The district court denied appellants' motion to vacate without prejudice to renewal for precisely this reason. Furthermore, appellants' suggestion that they have been excluded from the development of the plan is simply untrue. Appellants will have ample opportunity to comment on the plan contemplated by the consent decree through their influence in the New England Council, and through the notice and comment process required before final rules and regulations are promulgated by the Secretary.

Second, the statutory argument based on Sec. 1854(c)(1)(B) is without merit. Section 1854 (c)(1)(B) grants the Secretary authority to generate her own plan, after disapproving or partially disapproving a council-generated plan, only after the council fails to submit a revision. Appellants read Sec. 1854(c)(1)(B) as circum-

scribing the Secretary's authority in this case, because Conservation sued alleging the illegality of amendment four. According to appellants, the consent decree represents an improper exercise by the Secretary because the Council has not been given a chance to revise amendment four. Thus, until the New England Council fails to propose revisions, the Secretary may not act. If we were to follow appellants' suggestion, the Secretary would not be able to exercise her statutory discretion to develop her own plan once the Council submits a plan. The practical effect would permit the Council to determine the timetable for developing and enforcing FMPs.

The language of the statute, however, does not support appellants' interpretation. The statute authorizes the Secretary to develop her own plan if the council fails to submit a plan, or amendment thereto, "within a reasonable time." Section 1854(c)(1)(B) provides that the Secretary may act if "[he] disapproves or partially disapproves any such plan or amendment, or disapproves a revised plan or amendment, and the Council involved fails to submit a revised or further revised plan or amendment, as the case may be." Thus, while the provision does not expressly include the phrase "after a reasonable time," as in Sec. 1854(c)(1)(A), such a condition is implicit. Without it, the statute fails to indicate who decides when a Council has failed to act or how much time must pass before that decision maker can conclude that the council has failed to act. Since these two subsections are part of the same statutory grant of authority, and a contrary reading would create an incomprehensible gap in the statute and hold the Secretary hostage to the Councils, we hold that the Secretary may generate her own revisions to Council-generated plans, if the council fails to revise after a reasonable time.

Our reading gives proper deference to the Secretary, who, under the Magnuson Act, is ultimately charged with preventing overfishing as mandated by National Standard One. The councils serve the Secretary by presenting FMPs. The Magnuson Act also unequivocally vests the

Secretary with the discretion to determine whether a Council's progress on conservation and management is reasonable.

Furthermore, contrary to appellants' assertions, section 1854(c)(1)(B) simply is not implicated in this case. The purpose of the consent decree was to avoid a legal determination whether amendment four complied with National Standard One, or whether the Secretary had discharged her statutory duty under the Magnuson Act. The decree sought to save limited agency resources that would have been wasted on discovery, compiling an administrative record, and protracted litigation. The decree purposefully did not admit wrongdoing on the part of the Secretary or the improper approval of amendment four. It merely mandates the creation of a new amendment, rather than the revision of an old one—amendment four. As the provisions in Sec. 1854(c)(1)(B) related to revisions do not apply here, that section cannot be used as a shield to prevent the Secretary from exercising her statutory discretion.

The third, and final, reason the appeal fails relates to the permissible scope of consent decrees. Appellants argue that because the suit challenged amendment four, the consent decree cannot resolve matters beyond the terms of the amendment. They misstate the factual scope of Conservation's complaint. While it is true that Conservation's original complaint attacked the Secretary's approval of amendment four, it also sought broader relief—more vigorous conservation and management of New England fisheries. In any event, the law governing consent decrees clearly holds that parties are not restricted to the terms of the complaint, and may enter a consent decree on other matters, provided they have the legal authority to do so. *Local No. 93*, 478 U.S. at 525–26.

In the present case, the Secretary simply has exercised her discretion to set a timetable for the development of an FMP for New England fisheries. Specifically, the Secretary has stated in advance that she will exercise her authority to create a plan pursuant to Sec. 1854(c)(1)(A),

unless the Council develops an FMP within the "reasonable time" set by the consent decree. Indeed, it specifically provides that the New England Council attempt to create an FMP before the Secretary acts.

The Secretary could have established the same schedule without explicitly notifying the New England Council, or without entering a consent decree, since what constitutes a "reasonable time" under a statute is solely within the Secretary's discretion. Instead, the Secretary chose to settle Conservation's lawsuit with a fair, adequate, and reasonable consent decree that agrees to flexible dates for the development of a much needed FMP for New England.

In addition, the district court properly entered the consent decree under the other factors of *Local No. 93*. First, the decree resolved a dispute within the subject matter jurisdiction of the court since the suit challenged the Secretary's approval of amendment four, which was reviewable pursuant to Sec. 1855(b). Second, the parties agreed to develop a fishery rebuilding program to prevent overfishing which remedy is within the general scope of the pleadings. Indeed, this is exactly the relief requested. Third, it satisfies the objectives of the complaint.

We find no merit to appellants' other arguments. Appellants rely heavily on the fact that the consent decree commits the Secretary to develop a plan to "eliminate" overfishing, rather that "prevent" overfishing as stated in the Magnuson Act, 16 U.S.C. Sec. 1851(a). This change, they assert, amounts to rule making establishing a new standard. On the contrary, the decree uses the word "eliminate" because the New England Council already has determined that overfishing of cod, haddock, and yellowtail flounder presently occurs. One cannot prevent what has already occurred. Thus, the consent decree establishes that a plan to rebuild will be developed in order to "eliminate" present overfishing, and "prevent" future overfishing.

Similarly, we are unmoved by appellants' contention that the consent decree imposes a new "good faith" requirement with respect to Council action, which is not present in the Magnuson Act. The "good faith" language of the consent decree is superfluous and does not change the relationship between the New England Council and the Secretary in any respect. As the consent decree states, the Secretary maintains sole discretion to determine whether the Council's failure to act requires that she begin developing her own conservation program. Substantively, the provisions of the consent decree mirror those of Sec. 1854. "The fact that certain provisions in the Decree track the language of the Act more closely than others is irrelevant, so long as all are consistent with it." *Citizens for a Better Environment v. Gorsuch*, 718 F.2d 1117, 1125 (D.C.Cir. 1983; holding consent decree that established similar timetable judicially enforceable).

With respect to the five- and ten-year rebuilding goals, the Secretary has discretion to establish such target periods. Section 1853(b)(10) provides that the Secretary may include "such other measures, requirements, or conditions and restrictions as are determined to be necessary and appropriate for the conservation and management of the fishery." The Secretary, thus, has broad discretion concerning the contents of an FMP. Of course, the rebuilding targets in the consent decree are not rules, but rather periods that may be incorporated into a final rebuilding program contemplated by the consent decree.

The decree expressly provides that the provisions for notice and comment by the New England Council and the public will be followed. Once the Secretary approves a plan, she will promulgate regulations to enforce the plan. The consent decree, therefore, does not violate the notice and comment requirements of the statute because it creates no rule for which notice and comment is required. Appellants will have an opportunity to voice their opinions on the plan.

Appellants' last argument contends that the district court could not enter the decree because it lacked jurisdiction under 16 U.S.C. Sec.

1855(b) of the Magnuson Act, which provides for judicial review only of regulations and certain secretarial actions. The claim is without merit. The benchmark for determining whether the court properly exercised jurisdiction is the original complaint filed by Conservation. The complaint challenged amendment four, among other things. Because the district court had jurisdiction under Sec. 1855(b) to review amendment four, the district court could enter the consent decree because it resolved the dispute within the standards established by *Local No. 93*, 478 U.S. at 525–26, 106 S.Ct. at 3077.

The district court's denial of the motion to vacate the consent decree is *affirmed*.

Questions

1. Was the consent decree agreed to by the National Marine Fisheries Service an "end run" around the New England Regional Council?

2. What points were the fishing groups trying to make in seeking a distinction between "eliminating" versus "preventing" overfishing?

United States v. Kaiyo Maru No. 53, 699 F.2d 989 (9th Cir. 1983)

SKOPIL, CIRCUIT JUDGE

Introduction

The Japanese stern trawler *Kaiyo Maru No. 53* ("Kaiyo") was seized for failing to log a large quantity of fish and for taking prohibited species in violation of the Fishery Conservation and Management Act ("FCMA" or "the Act"), 16 U.S.C. Sections 1821, 1857. The district court imposed a $450,000 penalty, rejecting the government's contention that the penalty must equal the vessel's full value. The district court also rejected the vessel owners' ("claimants") arguments that the Coast Guard's search and seizure of the vessel violated the fourth and fifth amendments. The government appeals the district court's ruling on the forfeiture issue. The vessel's owners cross-appeal, seeking review of their fourth and fifth amendment arguments.

Facts

In the spring of 1979 the *Kaiyo* began fishing in the waters off the remote western part of the Aleutian Islands of Alaska. It was fishing by permit in the Fishery Conservation Zone ("FCZ"), the 197-mile-wide band of ocean beyond the territorial waters of the states in which federal fisheries management jurisdiction prevails. Early on June 2, the vessel changed from its assigned fishing area to another area which was available to it upon notice given to the Coast Guard. The required shift message was transmitted.

Later that morning the Coast Guard cutter *Storis*, while on routine patrol, sighted the *Kaiyo* with its gear down fishing within the FCZ near Kiska Island. The *Storis* requested information regarding the *Kaiyo* from its Juneau office and was erroneously informed that the *Kaiyo* had not made the required shift message. The commanding officer of the *Storis* decided to make a routine boarding of the *Kaiyo* to inspect her documents and catch, and determine if she was fishing in the proper area.

Without a warrant or probable cause to believe that wrongdoing was or had been occurring, a party of Coast Guard officers boarded the *Kaiyo*. Examination of the vessel's radio log indicated that the requisite shift message had been sent. A comparison of the *Kaiyo*'s catch log with the amount of frozen fish in the vessel's holds, however, indicated significant underreporting. A large quantity of halibut (more than eleven tons), a species prohibited to all foreign fishermen, was also discovered.

A systematic search was undertaken. Results of the search indicated serious violations of the FCMA. The *Storis* requested permission from the Juneau office to seize the vessel. The request was transmitted to the Coast Guard Commandant in Washington, D.C., who approved the seizure. The vessel was seized and escorted to Kodiak, Alaska.

The United States' complaint for forfeiture was filed on June 11 and the vessel was arrested by the United States Marshal the following day. Following a court hearing, the catch was ordered sold by the United States Marshal, and the vessel was released on security pending the outcome of forfeiture proceedings. Shortly after release, the *Kaiyo*'s fishing permit was revoked and the vessel returned to Japan.

Trial was held in May 1980, after which the district court concluded that the *Kaiyo* had violated the FCMA and assessed a civil penalty of $450,000.

The United States appeals from the district court's assessment of a civil penalty in an amount less than the entire value of the vessel. The claimants appeal the district court's rejection of their arguments regarding statutory and constitutional infirmities of the search, seizure, and arrest of the vessel. They urge that warrants should have been obtained before the search and seizure of the vessel and that a hearing should have been held before the ship was arrested.

Issues

1. Does the FCMA authorize warrantless searches and seizures?

2. Do warrantless searches and seizures under the FCMA violate the Fourth Amendment?

3. Did the arrest of the vessel by the government pursuant to Fed.R.Civ.P. C (Supplemental Rules for Certain Admiralty and Maritime Claims) violate the due process clause of the Fifth Amendment?

4. Did the district court have discretion to impose a monetary forfeiture of less than the total value of the vessel?

Discussion

1. Statutory Authorization.

[1] The FCMA provides that:

Any officer who is authorized by the Secretary [of Commerce], the Secretary [of Transportation], or the head of any Federal or State agency which has entered in an agreement . . . to enforce the provisions of this chapter may—

(1) with or without a warrant or other process—

. . .

(B) board, and search or inspect, any fishing vessel which is subject to the provisions of this chapter,

(C) seize any fishing vessel . . . used or employed in, or with respect to which it reasonably appears that such vessel was used or employed in, the violation of any provisions of this chapter; and

(D) seize any fish . . . taken or retained in violation of any provision of this chapter; and

(E) seize any other evidence related to any violation of any provision of this chapter;

(2) execute any warrant or other process issued by any court. . . . 16 U.S.C. Sec. 1861(b)

Claimants argue that the "with or without" language of the Act contemplates the use of warrants when practicable and yet affords the authority to proceed without them if exigent or other appropriate circumstances exist. Unfortunately, the legislative history is silent on the matter. Based on a reading of the Act as a whole and considering the objectives of the Act and the circumstances under which it was enacted, we conclude that the above quoted provisions of the FCMA authorize warrantless searches and seizures whether or not obtaining a warrant is practicable or exigent circumstances exist.

The FCMA was enacted at a time when overfishing, particularly by foreign fishermen, was commonplace. Commercial and recreational fisheries for a number of species were threatened because of the inability to effectively regulate the harvest beyond the three-mile jurisdictional limits. The states exercised some control over domestic fishermen beyond three miles but foreign fishermen were essentially unregulated because of meager federal efforts. The failure of the federal attempts to manage ocean fisheries

by treaty and later by the Bartlett Act led to a resource problem of crisis proportions. It was in this crisis atmosphere that the FCMA was enacted. The circumstances of its creation support our view that Congress intended to authorize the most potent possible enforcement procedures.

Our interpretation of section 1861 is also consistent with the thrust of the FCMA as a whole. The Act requires that foreign nations and the owner or operator of a vessel fishing in the FCZ allow official United States observers aboard the vessel, and to agree to permit any authorized officer to board and search or inspect the vessel. The Act requires any permit issued be prominently displayed in the wheelhouse and requires that the permit be shown upon request to any officer authorized to enforce the Act. Moreover, it is a criminal violation to refuse to allow any authorized officer to board a fishing vessel for the purpose of conducting any search or inspection in connection with its enforcement. Regulations implementing the Act also require the keeping of extensive records and logbooks and authorize the inspection of these logbooks at any time. Regulations also require that foreign vessels keep the Coast Guard constantly apprised of their location and activities. We agree with the district court that these stringent requirements support an interpretation of the Act that authorizes warrantless searches and seizures.

Claimant's interpretation reads too much into the language of section 1861. If Congress had intended warrantless searches to proceed only when there were "exigent" or "other appropriate" circumstances, it would have said so. Congress had no difficulty in expressing limitations on warrantless arrests of persons by requiring "reasonable cause to believe such person has committed an act" prohibited by the FCMA.

Congress was aware of the physical difficulties of obtaining a warrant at sea. We agree with the district court that the FCMA contemplates routine warrantless inspections or searches and seizures as part of the enforcement scheme of the Act.

2. Fourth Amendment.

The Fourth Amendment protects individuals from "unreasonable" searches and seizures. Its purpose is to impose a standard of "reasonableness" upon the exercise of discretion by government officials in order "to safeguard the privacy and security of individuals against arbitrary invasions."

a. *Search*

The Fourth Amendment applies to administrative inspection of private commercial property. However, "unlike searches of private homes, which generally must be conducted pursuant to a warrant in order to be reasonable under the Fourth Amendment, legislative schemes authorizing warrantless administrative searches of commercial property do not necessarily violate the Fourth Amendment." The greater tolerance for warrantless inspections of commercial property reflects the different sanctity accorded an individual's expectation of privacy in commercial property compared to the privacy interest in a home.

Congress has broad authority to regulate interstate commerce, including the imposition of inspection programs on private business property. Whether a regulatory scheme that includes warrantless inspections is reasonable under the Fourth Amendment is determined in a case-by-case basis. Reasonableness depends on the specific enforcement needs and privacy guarantees of each statute. . . .

Applying this analysis to the case before us we conclude that the warrantless inspections authorized by the Fishery Conservation and Management Act do not offend the Fourth Amendment. There is strong federal interest in protecting natural resources within the FCZ. The Act was adopted upon a clear showing that the supply of food fish was dangerously depleted. Congress was aware that an important national asset was at stake and that strong measures were necessary.

Congress reasonably concluded that warrantless searches are necessary to further the reg-ulatory scheme presented under the FCMA. First, the physical difficulty of obtaining and presenting a search warrant is overwhelming. Second, the nature of the industry prevents procurement of a warrant for a specific vessel in advance. The Coast Guard cannot tell when or where they will encounter a vessel fishing in the FCZ. Fishing vessels are assigned to large areas, they are frequently authorized to move from area to area, and they move in and out of the FCZ without restriction. Even if the Coast Guard knew the location of a specific vessel on a specific date, the weather would often frustrate boarding plans. These difficulties are complicated by the fact that an enforcement vessel might be at sea for weeks. The logistical problems in establishing a successful inspection program requiring warrants are insurmountable. If there is to be a successful inspection program at all, it must be a warrantless one.

Here, the only real issue before us is "whether the statute's inspection program, in terms of the certainty and regularity of its application, provides a constitutionally adequate substitute for a warrant." Warrantless searches of commercial property are permissible when authorized by statute and reasonably necessary to protect important federal interest, where the benefits of the warrant process would be minimal because the inspection is made in "the context of a regulatory inspection system of business premises which is carefully limited in time, place, and scope." *United States v. Biswell*, 406 U.S. at 315 (1972).

We conclude that the statute and enforcement policy of the Coast Guard sufficiently limit the discretion of the inspecting officers in the field as to render warrantless FCMA inspections "reasonable" within the meaning of the Fourth Amendment. First, enforcement is limited to officers authorized by the Secretaries of Commerce and Transportation. A fishing vessel operator is subject to search by only a limited number of government officers. Second, warrantless inspections are limited to specified fishing vessels. The Coast Guard has specifically limited its boardings to foreign fishing vessels actually engaged in fishing activities or otherwise within the FCZ after notifying the Coast Guard of intent to commence fishing activities and before having "checked out." Searches are thus limited to those vessels actively involved in the harvest of fish. Third, the Coast Guard has adopted standards for frequency of contact and inspection of foreign fishing vessels. In each "major statistical area," all fishing or fish-processing vessels requiring an FCMA permit are to be boarded once every three months. For each fish-processing vessel that requires an FCMA permit and operates with assigned catcher boats, 25 percent of the catcher boats are to be boarded once every three months. The inspections are not so random or infrequent that the vessel owner has no real expectation that his property will from time to time be inspected by government officials. Finally, foreign fishing in the FCZ has become such a highly regulated enterprise that, given the other limitations of the inspection program, a warrant is unnecessary. As the Supreme Court has said, "it is the pervasiveness and regularity of the federal regulation that ultimately determines whether a warrant is necessary to render an inspection program reasonable under the Fourth Amendment." *Donovan v. Dewey*, 452 U.S. at 606. Nearly every aspect of the harvest of fish in the FCZ by foreign fishermen is controlled by the FCMA and its implementing regulations. Vessel owners and operators "cannot help but be aware that [the vessel] will be subject to periodic inspections undertaken for specific purposes." *Donovan*, 452 U.S. at 600. Accordingly, we hold that foreign fishing under the FCMA is a pervasively regulated industry and that, with the limitations on the inspection program set out in the statute and by Coast Guard policy, no warrant is necessary for periodic boardings of foreign fishing vessels to determine compliance with the Act and applicable fishing regulations.

b. *Seizures*

Because the fourth amendment protects against warrantless seizures as well as searches, we must consider the validity of the warrantless seizure of the *Kaiyo*. Seizures, as well as searches, when conducted without the protections afforded by the warrant process, are per se unreasonable under the Fourth Amendment—subject only to a few exceptions. *United States v. McCormick*, 502 F.2d 281 (9th Cir. 1974).

In *McCormick* an automobile that had been used in a counterfeiting operation was seized without a warrant under authority of a federal forfeiture statute. We recognized that, despite the forfeiture statute, the seizure could not be valid unless it fit within one of the recognized exceptions to the warrant requirement. No exception applied. The "automobile exception," first established in *Carroll v. United States*, 267 U.S. 132 (1925), did not apply because there were no exigent circumstances that justified moving quickly to seize. The automobile in *McCormick* had been sitting unused in the defendant's driveway for over two months. We held the seizure invalid.

We distinguished *McCormick* in *United States v. Kimak*, 624 F.2d 903 (9th Cir. 1980). In *Kimak* the vehicle was still actively being used in the illegal enterprise, and exigent circumstances were presented because the site of the seizure was along a public highway. We held that the "automobile exception" applied.

The *Carroll* exception extends to vessels as well as automobiles and other movable vehicles as long as there is probable cause the circumstances are present that make it impractical to require seizing officers to obtain warrants prior to search or seizure. The seizure of the *Kaiyo Maru* satisfies the requirements of the exception. The Coast Guard officers knew that the *Kaiyo* was being used in the illegal harvest and retention of fish. To require the Coast Guard officers to remain aboard a vessel among potentially hostile occupants while other officers undertake a sometimes long and always hazardous journey to the nearest judicial officer would be too much to ask. Under such circumstances a warrantless seizure under authority of the FCMA forfeiture provision is "reasonable" under the Fourth Amendment.

3. Arrest Pursuant to Fed.R.Civ.P. C.

The government initiated forfeiture proceedings while the *Kaiyo* was being held in Kodiak. In order for the court to have jurisdiction over the vessel in rem it was necessary for the United States Marshal to "arrest" the vessel pursuant to Fed.R.Civ.P. C (Supplemental Rules for Certain Admiralty and Maritime Claims), which provides:

(3) Process.

Upon the filing of the complaint the clerk shall forthwith issue a warrant for the arrest of the vessel or to her property . . . and deliver it to the marshal for service.

(4) Notice.

No notice other than the execution of the process is required. . . .

Claimants argue that this procedure, which requires no pre-arrest notice or hearing violates their Fifth Amendment rights to due process. We disagree.

In *Calero-Toledo v. Pearson Yacht Leasing Co.*, 416 U.S. 663 (1974), the Supreme Court recognized that an exception has been carved out from the general due process requirements of notice and a hearing. In limited circumstances, summary seizure of property, without an opportunity for a prior hearing and without pre-seizure judicial participation, is constitutionally permissible. Such circumstances are those in which:

First, . . . the seizure has been directly necessary to secure an important governmental or general public interest. Second, there has been a special need for very prompt action. Third, the State has kept strict control over its monopoly of legitimate force: the person initiating the seizure has been a government official responsible for determining, under the standards of a narrowly drawn statute, that it was necessary and justified in the particular instance. *Fuentes v. Shevin*, 407 U.S. 67 at 91 (1972)

Calero-Toledo involved a pleasure yacht which was seized pursuant to Puerto Rican statutes providing for forfeiture of vessels used for unlawful purposes. Appellees leased the yacht to Puerto Rican residents who used it for a drug-smuggling operation about which appellees knew nothing. The yacht was seized without notice or pre-seizure hearing and made subject to forfeiture to the Commonwealth of Puerto Rico.

The Supreme Court recognized that the seizure was necessary to foster the public interest in preventing continued illegal use of property and in enforcing sanctions for past criminal activity. The Court observed that the seizure was initiated by government officials rather than self-interested private parties. The need for very prompt action was present because the vessel could have been moved, concealed, or destroyed if advance warning of confiscation were given.

Claimants argue that the need for prompt action did not exist because the vessel was already in the custody of the government. We agree, but we hold the arrest of the *Kaiyo* under the Fed.R.Civ.P. C did not deprive claimants of due process. The deprivation of claimant's property occurred when the vessel was seized at sea and held as part of the ongoing investigation for violations of the FCMA. We have held that seizure was proper. The shoreside arrest of the vessel under Fed.R.Civ.P. C did nothing to further deprive claimants of their property. The arrest was a formality to establish jurisdiction in rem so that forfeiture could be pursued. In the limited circumstances presented by this case, where property is already properly in the government's custody, arrest of the property under Fed.R.Civ.P. C does not offend due process because no deprivation of property is occasioned by the arrest.

4. Vessel Forfeiture.

The FCMA provides that:

Any fishing vessel (including its fishing gear, furniture, appurtenances, stores, and cargo) used, and any fish taken or retained, in any manner, in connection with or as a result of the commission of any act prohibited by section 1857 . . . shall be subject to forfeiture to the United States. *All or part of such vessel may, and all such fish shall,* be forfeited to the United States pursuant to a civil proceeding under this section. 16 U.S.C. Sec. 1860(a) (emphasis added).

The district court concluded that it had discretion to order forfeiture of all or part of the vessel. The court also concluded that it had authority to impose a monetary penalty in lieu of physical forfeiture. It recognized that forfeiture of an illegal catch was mandatory. Accordingly, the district court assessed a $450,000 penalty against the vessel and ordered the entire catch forfeited to the United States.

The government contends that the district court has no discretion to impose less than a complete forfeiture of the vessel. It argues that the court, upon finding the violations occurred, should have entered judgment for forfeiture of the entire vessel or its monetary equivalent. The government maintains that claimants' recourse from any harsh aspect of the forfeiture would be a petition for remission or mitigation lodged with the Secretary of Commerce pursuant to 16 U.S.C. Sec. 1860(c) and 19 U.S.C. Sec. 1618.

The government's interpretation is based on its understanding that the FCMA was intended to carry forward the forfeiture provisions of the Bartlett Act, 16 U.S.C. Sec. 1081, 78 Stat. 194 (repealed 1976). The Bartlett Act, an early and limited attempt to control foreign fishing, had mandatory forfeiture provisions. The government contends that the Bartlett Act forfeiture provisions were intended to survive that Act's repeal when Congress enacted the FCMA. We disagree.

The FCMA forfeiture provisions are significantly different from those of the Bartlett Act. The Bartlett Act's administrative forfeiture option is absent from the FCMA. All forfeitures under the FCMA, whether for catch, vessel, or gear, now require judicial intervention. More important, the "all or part" language of the FCMA is not found in the Bartlett Act, and Congress would not have included this language if it wanted to duplicate the forfeiture provisions of the Bartlett Act.

The district court correctly concluded that it had discretion to impose forfeiture of less than the whole vessel or its monetary equivalent. The Secretary of Commerce then has the option, under section 1860(c), of mitigating the effect of the forfeiture ordered.

Our interpretation of section 1860 does not deprive the Secretary of the means to impose harsh sanctions when the circumstances warrant. The Secretary has ample authority to stiffen the consequences of illegal fishing by resort to administratively imposed permit sanctions and fines.

Conclusion

The search of the *Kaiyo Maru* falls within the exception to the warrant requirement carved out for administrative searches in pervasively regulated industries. The seizure of the vessel was justified under the *Carroll* exception to the warrant requirement. The seizure did not violate due process requirements because it was initiated by the government, was necessary to secure important government interests, and there was a need for prompt action. The arrest of the vessel under Fed.R.Civ.P. C did not violate due process because the arrest did not deprive the claimants of any property. The district court has the discretion under the FCMA to impose forfeiture of less than the whole vessel or its value.

The district court is *Affirmed.*

Questions

1. When is it permissible to conduct a search without a warrant?

2. Does the level of punishment in this case seem appropriate to the violation?

Lovgren v. Byrne, 787 F.2d 857 (3rd Cir. 1986)

STAPLETON, CIRCUIT JUDGE

Gosta Lovgren and Lovgren Enterprise ("Lovgren") were found by an administrative law judge to have violated two regulations issued pursuant to the Magnuson Fishery Conservation and Management Act, 16 U.S.C. Sec. 1801 et seq. ("The Magnuson Act") and fined $50,000. The district court denied relief and Lovgren appealed to this court. We affirm.

I.

On March 24, 1983, while the *Lydia J*, a fishing boat, was unloading its catch at a dock owned by Lovgren Enterprises, agents of the National Marine Fisheries Service arrived at Lovgren's dock for the purpose of inspecting the fish being unloaded. This was a routine inspection and the officials did not suspect violation of any federal or state law.

The officials identified themselves upon Mr. Lovgren's request. Because his view of the fish already brought ashore was obstructed, Agent Livingston requested permission to climb onto a platform approximately five feet above the dock, upon which Lovgren was already standing. The other officer remained on the dock. The following is Agent Livingston's uncontradicted testimony:

As I proceeded up the ladder, in order to get a better look as to what was coming up the conveyor belt, Mr. Lovgren came to the top rung of the ladder and stood there so I couldn't complete my climb. It was at this time I said to him, you know, I wish to inspect the catch coming off the boat. . . . He said to me you f------ guys s---. You're nothing but a pain in the a--. I don't recognize National Marine Fishery Service's authority to be on my premises, pointing to me, and then he said to Mr. Winkle, he said I have no b---- with New Jersey, but the National Marine Fishery Service has f----- up this industry and I want you off my property, pointing back to me.

I then asked him, are you prohibiting me from in-

specting this boat and its catch on these premises? He said yes, I am. I said thank you very much, have a good night.

Agent Livingston testified that he had felt physically threatened during this encounter. "I was suspended on that ladder in a physically vulnerable position. If I had in my mind proceeded to the top rung and gone that step further there would have been a physical confrontation."

Lovgren was subsequently charged with violating two regulations issued pursuant to the Magnuson Act. An administrative law judge found Lovgren liable on both counts and, despite the fact that the government had requested a total penalty of $5,000, the ALJ ordered a $50,000 fine for the two violations. However, the ALJ suspended all but $10,000 of the fine on the conditions that (1) Lovgren cooperate with the government during the pendency of any appeal, and (2) commit no other violation of the Act for three years.

Lovgren's petition to the Administrator of the National Oceanic and Atmospheric Administration was denied. Subsequently, he filed this suit in district court to review the civil penalties. The district court upheld the assessment of the civil penalties and this appeal followed. Lovgren argues that the findings that he had violated the Magnuson Act regulations are not supported by the evidence.

II.

A. *The Magnuson Act*

Congress's intent in passing the Magnuson Act was to protect our nation's coastal fish, the national fishing industry, and dependent coastal economies from the stresses caused by overfishing in the waters adjacent to territorial waters.

The Magnuson Act was enacted at a time when overfishing of coastal waters was commonplace, threatening the existence of a number of species of fish. Congress found this threat aggravated by the inability to effectively regulate fishing beyond the three mile jurisdictional limit. See *Magnuson, The Conservation and Management Act of 1976: First Step toward Improved Management of Marine Fisheries*, 52 Wash.L.Rev., 427, 431–33 (1977); see also S.Rep. No. 94-416, 94th Cong., 1st Sess. (1975), reprinted in *A Legislative History of the Fishery Conservation and Management Act*, Senate Comm. on Commerce, 94th Cong., 2d Sess., 666 (Comm. Print 1976) (hereinafter cited as "Legislative History—S.Rep.").

Congress found that a viable management scheme for the Nation's fishery resources was a necessary concomitant of an extended fishery zone. Title II of the Act established seven Regional Fishery Management Councils (one for each major ocean area) to institute programs for the management and conservation of fishery resources in a "Fishery Conservation Zone" extending two hundred nautical miles from the seaward boundary of each of the coastal states. This action was deemed necessary to "assure that a supply of food and other fish products is available on a continuing basis and so that irreversible or long-term adverse effects on fishery resources or on the marine ecosystem are rendered highly unlikely." Congress found it "absolutely vital that a national management program, properly tailored to take account of the variability of fish resources, the individuality of the fishermen, the needs of the consumer, and the obligations to the general public, be established."

In order to implement this new institutional mechanism, Congress developed national standards for fishery management and conservation. The second standard, described as "one of the most important standards," states that management and conservation measures are to be based upon the best scientific information available. This emphasis demonstrated Congress's recognition that proper information was essential to the success of its management scheme. Obtaining accurate information concerning the fish caught in the regional zones is, therefore, central to the purposes of the Act.

To accomplish this goal, Congress provided, inter alia, that authorized enforcement officers may, "with or without a warrant or other process . . . board, and search or inspect, any fishing vessel" and "seize any fish (wherever found) taken or retained in violation of any provision of this chapter." Additionally, enforcement officers are authorized to "exercise any other lawful authority."

B. Sufficiency of the Evidence

Lovgren's first argument is that, because the ALJ's findings are not supported by substantial evidence, the fines cannot stand. We agree with Lovgren as to the appropriate standard of review of the ALJ's findings, but find unassailable the district court's conclusion that the ALJ's decision was justified by substantial evidence.

The ALJ concluded that Lovgren had "purposefully and effectively foreclosed the agents from carrying out their investigatory duty" by refusing them access to the platform. This action violates 50 C.F.R. Sec. 651.7(1), which makes it unlawful to refuse to permit an authorized officer to enter an "area of custody" for purposes of conducting an inspection.

Lovgren concedes that he refused the special agents access to the platform onto which the fish from the *Lydia J* were being unloaded. Furthermore, he does not dispute that the platform was an "area of custody" under the regulations. His argument seems to be that standing on the top of a ladder is not sufficient to violate the Act. However, he is being punished not for the station he maintained, but for the passage he denied.

Lovgren also challenges the ALJ's finding of liability on the second count, based on 50 C.F.R. Sec. 651.7(m), because no actual physical confrontation occurred. However, Lovgren admits that he "was upset" and that he "tends to be a volatile person." Moreover, he agreed that his statements to the agents were "aggressive" and that it was "possible" that his intent was to prevent Agent Livingston physically from coming up the ladder.

Both agents testified that Lovgren's act and manner of standing at the top of the platform with Livingston on the ladder below him were "threatening," and Livingston testified that he believed himself to be in a physically threatened position.

This testimony supports the ALJ's conclusion that Lovgren's resistance to the inspection contained elements of force and implied threats of violence. The regulation does not require fisticuffs. Forceful resistance, intimidation, or interference suffices.

We therefore agree with the district court that substantial evidence supports the conclusion that Lovgren's lack of cooperation contained elements of forceful resistance. This is sufficient to support the findings of a violation of 50 C.F.R. Sec. 651.7(m).

. . .

D. The Validity of the Regulations

The Magnuson Act explicitly authorizes inspections of fishing vessels either with or without a warrant. 16 U.S.C. Sec. 1861(b)(1)(A)(ii). See *United States v. Kaiyo Maru No. 53*, 699 F.2d 989 (9th Cir. 1983). The regulations extend that authority beyond the vessels themselves to "areas of custody," defined as "any vessels, building, vehicles, piers, or dock facilities where groundfish may be found." Lovgren claims that the Act, when properly read in the context of the strictures of the Fourth Amendment, does not authorize this extension of the inspector's purview and that the regulations he was found to have violated are accordingly invalid. We conclude that Lovgren's reading of the Act is unduly restrictive and that no Fourth Amendment problems are created by according the Act its intended scope.

1. Scope of Inspections under the Magnuson Act

As we have earlier noted, the Act directs the Secretary of Commerce, with the assistance of Regional Fishery Management Councils, to develop regional fishery management plans and to promulgate regulations to implement those plans. A plan may "prescribe" all "measures, requirements, or conditions and restrictions as are determined to be necessary and appropriate for the conservation and management of the fishery." Moreover, the Secretary is directed to "promulgate each regulation that is necessary to carry out a plan."

Pursuant to this broad authority, Part 651 of the regulations implements the Interim Fishery Management Plan for Atlantic Groundfish (i.e., cod, haddock, and yellowtail flounder). Included in that Part are the prohibitions against denying access to areas of custody and forcibly interfering with the inspection of such areas. It seems to us that the Secretary was well within his authority in determining that inspection of dock areas where groundfish are unshipped was necessary in order to monitor compliance with the requirements of the plan and obtain necessary management data.

If inspecting officials were able only to observe fish remaining on board a vessel, the agency's efforts to gather accurate information would be substantially frustrated. Those wishing to evade inspection would be aware that once the fish have reached the dock, they are safe from inspection unless the official has previously obtained a search warrant, a difficult task where the fishermen keep to no prearranged schedule. Furthermore, access by land to the fishing vessel itself would become much more difficult were officials required to obtain a warrant before being able to cross over docks to reach the vessel. This interpretation would thus significantly hamper those officials charged with the protection of our scarce fishing resources.

Lovgren does not dispute that inspection of his dock would facilitate implementation of the Atlantic Groundfish Plan. His argument is rather that the Act, by expressly mentioning only the warrantless search of vessels, impliedly denied dock inspections to the Secretary and that such an intention should be attributed to Congress because a contrary one would create serious Fourth Amendment problems. We disagree.

The negative implication which Lovgren would have us draw is not a necessary one. Given the broad regulatory authority conferred upon the Secretary it seems to us unlikely. Moreover, we believe the legislative history of the Act counsels against accepting Lovgren's argument. The Senate bill provided only for seizure of fish found on fishing vessels. Both the House bill and the bill as enacted authorized officials to seize fish wherever found. The change from the Senate bill's language to that of the bill as enacted suggests that Congress consciously extended the authority to seize fish without a warrant beyond the confines of a vessel and, a fortiori, that Congress anticipated that agents might look for those fish without a warrant wherever they could be seized.

2. Scope of Inspections under the Fourth Amendment

The Fourth Amendment protects individuals from unreasonable searches and seizures and imposes an obligation on the government to respect the reasonable privacy and security interests of individuals. A government search of private property conducted without proper consent is infirm unless it has been authorized by a valid search warrant or comes within one of a few carefully defined exceptions to the general rule. Whether a warrantless search is nevertheless a reasonable one depends on the reasonableness of the expectation of privacy in the area searched, the importance of the governmental interest occasioning the search, and the degree to which alleged authority for the search is tailored to that interest and minimizes the intrusion. We conclude that Lovgren had little if any reasonable expectation of privacy in his dock during the unshipping of a fishing vessel, that the governmental interest which occasioned the search is a compelling one, and that the Magnuson Act and regulations do not invite unnecessary intrusion on privacy. Accordingly, we

find that the Secretary's construction of this authority raises no Fourth Amendment problem.

"[T]he expectation of privacy that the owner of commercial property enjoys in such property differs significantly from the sanctity accorded an individual's home." *Donovan v. Dewey*, 452 U.S. at 598–99. Moreover, one who is engaged in an industry that is pervasively regulated by the government or that has been historically subject to such close supervision is ordinarily held to be on notice that periodic inspections will occur and, accordingly, has no reasonable expectations of privacy in the area where he knows those inspections will occur.

The industry of which Lovgren is a part is pervasively regulated. The management plans created pursuant to the Act regulate the type, number, size, and timing of the catch that can lawfully be taken as well as the equipment that may be used in its taking. Vessels must be licensed and must account for their activities. While Lovgren himself is not the operator of a vessel, he services licensed vessels from a location where surveillance is necessary to the enforcement of the overall management scheme.

In addition, while the Magnuson Act is of relatively recent origin, the fishing industry has been the subject of pervasive governmental regulation almost since the founding of the Republic. Indeed the expectation of finding the game warden looking over one's shoulder at the catch is virtually as old as fishing itself.

Also relevant to Lovgren's expectation of privacy is the fact that his dock is located on the territorial boundary of our nation and services vessels which are returning from voyages beyond its territorial waters. Given the long history of governmental control of such border activity, as well as the government regulation of the fishing industry, one can conclude with confidence that Lovgren, when he decided to engage in his business, must have been aware that government intrusions were bound to occur in the regular course of that business.

That the federal interests at stake in the effective enforcement of the Fisheries Management programs are vital to the country has been clearly articulated by Congress. We agree that there is a strong federal interest in protecting the natural resources within the Fishery Conservation Zone. "Congress was aware that an important national asset was at stake and that strong measures were necessary." *Kaiyo Maru No. 53*, 699 F.2d at 995. The measures taken, including the allowance for warrantless inspections of dock areas for the purpose of identifying the fish being off-loaded, appear reasonable in light of this strong federal interest.

Although fishing operations in the Fishery Conservation Zone are frequently observed by aircraft and other vessels, the quantity of fish caught can only be accurately determined as the catch is unshipped after the vessel docks. As this record indicates, these landing areas are at times extremely active, particularly when the fishing vessels are discharging their catch. After the fish are transferred to shore, the various species of fish are frequently commingled with the catch from other vessels and usually are soon dispatched to market, canneries, or other processors. Although the principal activity subject to regulatory control under the Magnuson Act is the fishery operation itself, the accurate determination of the quantities, and to a significant extent the species of fish caught, depends principally upon the weighing and tallying of the vessel's catch after the vessel has docked.

Unlike *See v. City of Seattle*, 387 U.S. 541 (1967), a case involving housing code violations, and *Marshall v. Barlow's Inc.*, 436 U.S. 307 (1978), a case involving OSHA inspections, the government in this case will rarely have time to obtain a warrant before the status quo is changed. The fish are highly perishable and even in the best of circumstances are unlikely to remain on the docks for any length of time. Moreover, it would often be difficult to obtain a warrant in advance since the purpose of inspection will frequently be limited to obtaining information, not seeking out wrongdoers. The government often will not know when and

where fishing boats will dock after returning from the Fishery Conservation Zone.

Finally, the statute sufficiently limits the inspecting officers in the field as to render warrantless inspections reasonable within the meaning of the Fourth Amendment. Enforcement is limited to those officers authorized by the Secretaries of Commerce and Transportation. Furthermore, the inspection scheme is carefully tailored to the requirements of the Act and does not unnecessarily intrude on the reasonable privacy interests of those in the industry. The scope of the inspection is limited to only those times when and those places where groundfish may be found. Individuals can only be fined for refusing to permit a search "in connection with the enforcement of the Magnuson Act." Thus, the participants in the fishing industry need not fear an attempt by the government to use the warrantless search provisions of the Act to enforce other statutes or to discover other criminal activity.

E. Other Claims

Lovgren's remaining claims do not require extended discussion. Contrary to his assertions, Lovgren was punished for denying access to the agents and for forcibly interfering with the agents' inspection; he was not punished for exercising his rights of free speech. The first amendment does not insulate Lovgren's refusal to obey the law, even if motivated by a political belief. Finally, we cannot say that the ALJ abused his discretion by imposing a greater penalty on Lovgren than the government had sought. The ALJ explicitly took into account each factor required by the statute, 18 U.S.C. Sec. 1858(a), and explained why he felt justified in assessing the maximum penalty allowed. We cannot say that this penalty was unwarranted in law or without justification in fact, and therefore see no reason to overturn the ALJ's determination.

III.

For these reasons, the judgment of the district court will be affirmed.

FULLAM, DISTRICT JUDGE, dissenting in part.

I agree entirely with the excellent majority opinion, except for its conclusion that there is adequate evidentiary support for imposing separate penalties for two separate violations. It is quite clear that appellant violated 50 C.F.R. 651.7(1), in that he did "refuse to permit an authorized officer to board a fishing vessel, or to enter areas of custody, subject to such person's control, for purposes of conducting any search or inspection in connection with the enforcement of the Magnuson Act. . . ." But there is no evidence to support the separate charge of violation of 50 C.F.R. 651.7(m). Under the undisputed facts, appellant simply did not "*forcibly* assault, resist, oppose, impede, intimidate, or interfere with any authorized officer *in the conduct of any inspection or search*" (emphasis added).

Appellant was not liable to punishment for expressing negative views of the federal program and its officials. The words used, however colorful, cannot be regarded as amounting to assault or intimidation; there is simply no evidence that appellant "*forcibly*" did anything. He just made clear to the inspector that he would not permit the inspector on the dock. This was an obvious violation of 651.7(1), but it was—also obviously, I suggest,—not a violation of 651.7(m).

There was no use or actual threat of force. The officer's perception that appellant was angry, and the concomitant (alleged) apprehension that, if the officer had insisted on proceeding with the search, force might have been used against him, simply do not suffice to establish a violation of 651.7(m). Moreover, the officer was not then "in the conduct of" a search or inspection—he had been denied permission to begin one. To the extent that the majority sustains the separate penalty under 651.7(m), therefore, I respectfully dissent.

Questions

1. Does a $50,000 fine seem harsh for using some bad language and standing in the wrong place?

2. What does being "pervasively regulated" have to do with a reasonable expectation of privacy in this case?

United States v. F/V Alice Amanda, 987 F.2d 1078 (4th Cir. 1993)

WIDENER, CIRCUIT JUDGE

This case requires us to interpret the regulations that govern fishing for the Atlantic sea scallop. Between October 9, 1989, and October 12, 1989, agents of the National Marine Fisheries Service thawed, sampled, and counted ten pounds of Atlantic sea scallops from the catch of the *Alice Amanda*. Based on the count, the agents declared the entire catch illegal and demanded the proceeds from the sale of the catch. The owner, on the advice of counsel, refused to deliver the proceeds.

One month later, the *Alice Amanda* was boarded and seized by the Coast Guard. See 16 U.S.C. Sec. 1861. The United States then initiated this forfeiture proceeding against the *Alice Amanda* in the district court. The ship was released on the posting of a $300,000 bond. See 16 U.S.C. Sec. 1860(d)(1)(B). After a bench trial, the district court ordered that the United States recover $25,000 in partial forfeiture of the *Alice Amanda*.

The *Alice Amanda* appeals the order of forfeiture. The United States cross-appeals, arguing that the district court abused its discretion by setting the amount of forfeiture too low. We now reverse the order to forfeiture. Accordingly, we decide the government's cross-appeal is without merit.

I.

A. Statutory and Regulatory Background

The Magnuson Fishery Conservation and Management Act (the Act), 16 U.S.C. Sec. 1801 et seq., was enacted in 1976 to preserve the nation's fishery resources. The Act establishes an Exclusive Economic Zone in the waters off the coast of the United States, extending from the seaward boundary of each of the coastal States to two hundred nautical miles offshore. Within this zone, all fish are subject to the exclusive fishery management authority of the United States. The Act is administered by the Department of Commerce, National Oceanic and Atmospheric Administration, National Marine Fisheries Service (the Agency). The Act divides the Exclusive Economic Zone into eight regions and creates a Regional Fishery Management Council for each region. 16 U.S.C. Sec. 1852.

A Fishery Management Council's primary responsibility is the preparation and amendment of Fishery Management Plans for various fisheries. The fishery involved in this case is the Atlantic Sea Scallop Fishery, which covers the species *Placopecten magellanicus*, the Atlantic sea scallop, in the entire Atlantic Coast Exclusive Economic Zone. The New England Fishery Management Council has primary responsibility for the Atlantic Sea Scallop Plan.

After a Council has adopted a Fishery Management Plan, or an amendment to an existing Plan, it forwards the Plan and suggested regulations to the Agency. The Agency then undertakes notice and comment rule-making procedures established by the Magnuson Act if it proposes to give effect to the Council's action. The Magnuson Act also allows the Agency itself to prepare a Fishery Management Plan, or an amendment to a Plan, under certain circumstances. Regulations to implement such a Plan also must go through notice and comment rule-making procedures.

As a final method of controlling fishing practices, the Act provides for the promulgation of emergency regulations by the Secretary without regard to the existence of a Fishery Management Plan. 16 U.S.C. Sec. 1855(c). The Act requires that "[a]ny emergency regulation promulgated . . . shall be published in the Federal Register together with the reasons therefor." 16 U.S.C. Sec. 1855(c)(3)(A). Emergency regula-

tions are limited in duration to a maximum of 180 days.

The regulations governing the Atlantic Sea Scallop Fishery are codified at 50 C.F.R. Part 650. The regulations require vessel permits, control certain aspects of possession and landing, and control the minimum size of scallops permitted in possession. Only the minimum size requirements are at issue here.

The regulations use two size measures. For scallops in the shell, they specify a minimum shell height. For shucked scallop meats, the regulations specify a maximum number of meats per pound. This latter measure is known as the "meat count." All other things being the same, a higher meat count indicates smaller scallops. Because the catch of the *Alice Amanda* had been shucked at sea, meat count, rather than shell height, is the relevant measure in this case.

At the time that the *Alice Amanda* landed her catch, the maximum allowable meat count was 33 meats per pound. The Agency also allowed a 10 percent tolerance as an exercise of enforcement discretion. The net result was that no violation would be cited unless the average meat count exceeded 36.3 meats per pound. The regulations make it unlawful to "[p]ossess, at or prior to the first transaction in the United States, any nonconforming Atlantic sea scallops, including those that exceed the maximum allowable meat count."

The procedure for measuring the meat count is governed by 50 C.F.R. Sec. 650.21. This section provides in relevant part as follows:

Compliance with the specified meat-count and shell-height standards will be determined by inspection and enforcement up to and including the first transaction in the United States as follows:

(a) *Shucked meats.* The Authorized Officer will take one-pound samples at random from the total amount of scallops in possession. The person in possession of the scallops may request that as many as ten one-pound samples be examined as a sample group. A sample group fails to comply with the standard if the averaged meat count for the entire sample group exceeds the standard. The total amount of scallops in possession will be presumed in violation of this regulation if the sample group fails to comply with the standard.

As indicated, a catch is presumed to be in violation when the average meat count from samples exceeds the maximum allowable meat count.

The Magnuson Act makes it "unlawful . . . to violate . . . any regulation . . . issued pursuant to" the Act. The Act provides that violations may be punished by a civil penalty up to $25,000 per violation, or by forfeiture of the catch, its fair market value, or the fishing vessel. In this case, the government sought forfeiture of the fishing vessel, the *Alice Amanda*.

Regulations implementing the Fishery Management Plan for Atlantic Sea Scallops were first enacted in 1982. From the outset, the principal management measure for shucked scallops was a maximum meat count. With minor exceptions, the sections defining the manner in which the meat count was to be determined have not changed.

In 1982, when the regulations were adopted, Atlantic sea scallops were landed in one of two ways, in the shell, or shucked on ice. During the fishing voyage, shucked scallops were placed in cheesecloth bags and packed on ice. Because scallops could not be kept fresh on ice for longer periods, the average voyage lasted ten days.

Around 1988, a new technology, the freezer vessel, began to be used in scallop fishing. The *Alice Amanda* is a freezer vessel. By 1989, when this case began, the *Alice Amanda* still was one of only a handful of freezer vessels in the Atlantic sea scallop fleet.

The *Alice Amanda* is equipped with freezer bins below decks and a plate freezer on deck. Instead of storing scallops on ice, they are quick-frozen in the plate freezer then stored below decks in the freezer bins. On the *Alice Amanda*, scallops are shucked soon after being collected in the ship's dredges. The shucked scallops then are rinsed in a bucket and allowed to drain in a washer, a container equivalent to a large colander. The drained scallops then are packed in cheesecloth bags. Each bag holds sixteen to eighteen pounds of scallops. The bags are placed in the plate freezer, where they are kept at twenty below zero for four hours. The bags of frozen scallops then are transferred to the freezer bins below decks. Because it was able to store the scallops frozen, instead of packed in ice, the *Alice Amanda's* fishing trips averaged thirty days, twenty days longer than the average trip for a boat storing shucked scallops on ice. The longer trip allows a larger catch, the catch at issue here being 19,668 pounds.

Upon being landed frozen, a catch from the *Alice Amanda* routinely was unloaded, weighed, and then thawed for processing. The scallops were thawed by immersing the frozen mass in a mixture of water and tripolyphosphate. The scallops then were weighed a second time, sorted by size, and packaged for sale.

B. Frozen Scallop Sampling Procedure

Beginning in early 1988, Agency personnel began to consider the issues involved in sampling scallops frozen at sea on freezer vessels. In response to an inquiry from the owner of the freezer vessel *Mr. Big*, the Agency's Regional Director, Richard Roe, advised that frozen shucked scallops would be subject to the same sampling procedures as shucked scallops on ice, but that he expected the New England Council soon would address the issue. Roe then wrote the Chairman of the New England Council to urge that the frozen scallop sampling issue be placed on the Council's agenda. Roe wrote: "The scallop regulations currently in force do not address such handling. Enforcing the meat count average against these vessels will be difficult, if not impossible." The New England Council Chairman disagreed in his interpretation of the regulations, responding as follows: "I would recommend that the NMFS immediately implement an interim policy to sample frozen scallops to determine compliance with the meat count standard. . . . There is nothing here that precludes sampling frozen scallops."

On December 1, 1988, however, the Scallop Oversight Committee of the Council voted unanimously that two studies be undertaken by the Regional Director's office "before enforcement efforts on frozen product." The first of the two recommended studies would compare scallop meat weight before freezing and after thawing, the purpose being to obtain a formula that would convert the weight of thawed samples to the equivalent weight of a fresh sample, in order to compensate for dehydration during freezing and thawing. The second recommended study would be a statistical analysis of the problem associated with sampling sorted scallops. Obviously, this latter study was to be undertaken to establish the statistical validity of the sampling process. On December 15, 1988, the New England Council voted unanimously to undertake these two studies. This resolution is discussed in more detail later in this opinion.

On April 20, 1989, the National Marine Fisheries Service General Counsel in conjunction with the Chief Enforcement Officer issued a memorandum to all law enforcement agents. That memorandum set out a procedure to be used in sampling frozen shucked scallops to determine compliance with meat count limit. Agents were instructed to examine at least ten one-pound samples, chosen "from various parts of the load in a patternless manner, without definite aim and without examining the size of individual scallops." The scallops then were to be thawed "at room temperature," the thawed scallops mixed in each of the ten containers, and a sample of at least one pound scooped from each container onto a scale and weighed. The number of scallop meats in each of the ten samples then was to be counted and divided by the exact weight of the sample to obtain the number of meats per pound. The meats per pound figures for each weight category were arranged and then all the samples are analyzed to obtain an average meats per pound figure for the entire sample group.

We have noted that at the time the April 20th Enforcement Memorandum was issued, the Fisheries Management Council had adopted formal resolutions that prior to enforcement a factor had to be arrived at to equate the meat count of the scallops after freezing with that of the scallops before freezing, and indeed we suggest that any such factor which did not equate the meat count of the scallops landed after freezing to that of scallops landed after being stored on ice would be so subject to universal criticism as to be practically unattainable, even if not outright illegal, because of an unabashed discrimination in favor of the old technology and against the new.

The reasons for the council resolutions are apparent from the record. There was at hand study after study which had been made through the years with respect to weight change by scallops after they had been shucked at sea. As we have recited, those shucked at sea were stored packed on ice until they were landed. While the precise amount of weight gain is not formally found as a fact by the Agency and is not shown with precision by the record, the only reasonable conclusion which can be drawn from the studies at hand is that scallops shucked at sea and kept packed on ice for the duration of the ordinary voyage of about ten days gained some significant weight by the absorption of water. So a meat count of forty, given as one example, at sea, might well be thirty-four upon landing. And we note that the meat count upon landing was that which was enforced by the Agency, for under the regulations, the critical time is at or prior to the first transaction in the United States. Similar but related studies had also been done by the Fisheries Service, or were in hand by the Fisheries Service, with respect to any weight change of scallops which had been shucked at sea but which had been frozen, as were those on board the *Alice Amanda*, and later thawed. Again, while the precise amount of any weight loss was not formally ascertained by the Agency or is not shown with precision in the record, the only reasonable conclusion which can be reached is that when scallops are shucked at sea, quick plate frozen, stored frozen in cheesecloth bags for several weeks, and then thawed in air, there is a significant weight loss. So the meat count of such scallops will be higher after thawing than when caught.

Thus, any meat count of thawed in air but previously frozen scallops will be higher than that which existed when the scallops were caught, and even higher than a meat count for the same scallops which had been caught and stored on ice until landing.

C. *Enforcement against the Alice Amanda*

Upon completion of her maiden voyage on April 4, 1989, at Hampton, Virginia, enforcement agents attempted to sample the *Alice Amanda*'s catch. Because the catch was frozen and the Agency had not yet issued the Enforcement Memorandum, the agents left without taking samples. The memorandum was issued before the end of the *Alice Amanda*'s next voyage, and agents sampled the *Alice Amanda*'s catch at the end of each of her next four voyages. On each occasion they found no violation.

Finally, at the end of her sixth voyage, the agents obtained a meat count in excess of the legal limit. By the time the agents arrived at the pier, unloading already had begun and four hundred of a total of eleven hundred bags of scallops had been unloaded and taken to cold storage at another location. The entire catch, having been kept in the freezer bins below decks, consisted of frozen shucked scallops in cheesecloth bags weighing fifteen to seventeen pounds each. As they were being unloaded onto the pier, an enforcement agent, Passer, selected seven bags from among the seven hundred bags that had not yet been taken to cold storage. Meanwhile, a second agent, Hermann, went to the cold storage warehouse to select three bags from among the four hundred that were there. The agents had decided to select one sample bag per hundred bags, which amounted to one

bag per pallet. Agent Passer attempted to choose randomly from various points on the pallets.

Agent Passer took all ten samples to a storage area, where he placed the ten bags into two ninety-six-quart Igloo coolers. The storage area was an unheated, locked room within a storage facility. The scallops remained there from the evening of October 9 until the morning of October 11. On the morning of October 11, Passer took the partially thawed scallops to S & S Seafood, a scallop-processing plant operated by Liston Shackelford, the owner of the *Alice Amanda*. At S & S Seafood, Passer placed each of the ten samples into a large plastic container. Passer then left the ten large containers in a hallway area to finish thawing.

Throughout the day, enforcement agents kept an eye on the scallops. During the entire thawing process, Passer periodically stirred the contents of each container, endeavoring, however, not to break the individual scallop meats. Around 3:30 P.M., Passer moved the scallops into a small break room at the S & S building. In contrast to the rest of the building, which was kept cool for scallop processing, the break room was heated by an electric heater.

When the scallops had thawed enough to be counted, about an hour after moving them to the heated break room, Passer began the actual sampling procedure. He first called the *Alice Amanda*'s captain, Captain Belvin, to witness the sampling. Using a sixteen-ounce cup, Passer scooped scallops from the center of each large plastic container and placed them into a separate container. After removing all bits and pieces, Passer placed the whole scallops on the scale. Another agent recorded the number of scallop meats and the exact weight of each sample. This process was performed once for each of the ten large containers of scallops, a total of ten samples of about sixteen ounces each. Five samples were below 36.3, and five above. The resulting average meat count for all ten samples was 40.6 meats per pound which exceeded the maximum allowable meat count of 36.3.

Following the Agency's penalty guidelines, the agents told Liston Shackelford and Captain Belvin that the severity of the violation would require a seizure of the entire value of the catch. Shackelford asked to consult with his lawyer, and the agents agreed to return the next morning. The next morning, Shackelford refused to relinquish the proceeds of the catch.

A month later, on November 16, 1989, the Coast Guard seized the *Alice Amanda*. The Agency then initiated this proceeding, seeking forfeiture of the *Alice Amanda* under 16 U.S.C. Secs. 1860, 1861. Alice Amanda, Inc., a corporation controlled by Liston Shackelford, filed a claim to the *Alice Amanda*. Pending trial of the forfeiture action, the vessel was released on the personal recognizance bond of Liston Shackelford. The bond was for $300,000 and was conditioned on redelivering the ship should the court so order. After a bench trial, the district court found for the government, ordering that the United States recover $25,000 in partial forfeiture of the *Alice Amanda*. This appeal followed.

II.

A. Effect of the Enforcement Memorandum

As a preliminary matter, we must determine what effect, if any, the Enforcement Memorandum should have on our application of the regulations to the facts of this case. We find that the memorandum is, at best, only persuasive authority and we are not persuaded.

It is undisputed that the sampling procedures recited in the memorandum were not adopted after notice and comment as the Magnuson Act requires for the adoption of a regulation. Neither the memorandum nor the substance of its provisions was published in the Federal Register. Even the emergency procedures of Sec. 1855(c) were not used so it, therefore, cannot even quality as a valid emergency regulation adopted under 16 U.S.C. Sec. 1855(c)(3).

The government argues that the memoran-

dum did not constitute rule making subject to the notice and comment requirement. Rather, the argument goes that the memorandum "embodied internal Agency policies and procedures which are exempt from publication or notice and comment." This argument begs the critical question. Even assuming that the memorandum was not subject to the requirements of the Agency's opinion of what constitutes a violation of the regulations requires any deference from a court when the court is required to interpret those regulations in the course of forfeiture action initiated in court by the government.

At the outset, we note that, in this particular case, the Agency's failure to publish the memorandum in the Federal Register is not *itself* dispositive. Although the Freedom of Information Act, 5 U.S.C. Sec. 552(a)(1), provides that "a person may not in any manner be required to resort to, or be adversely affected by, a matter to be published in the Federal Register and not so published," this statute by its terms does not apply "to the extent that a person has actual and timely notice of the terms" of the unpublished matter. 5 U.S.C. Sec. 552(a)(1). In this case, the evidence shows that the Vice President of the claimant, Alice Amanda, Inc., had received a copy of the memorandum prior to the October 9 sampling. Thus the statutory defense of 5 U.S.C. Sec. 552(a)(1) is not available.

It is idle to contend, however, that the actions taken under the Enforcement Memorandum were not Agency actions, and we hold that they were. A ship was seized and forfeiture was sought.

B. Review under the Administrative Procedure Act

The Agency argues that it should be able to seize and forfeit the *Alice Amanda* or the proceeds for her whole scallop catch because its sampling procedure revealed a violation of the meat count standard. This is so, contends the Agency, even though the *Alice Amanda* is a freezer ship, with a scallop load of over nineteen thousand pounds, a type of vessel and size of catch not contemplated by the 1982 Fishery Management Plan's body of regulations. The *Alice Amanda* maintains instead that scallop fishing technology has changed, that freezer ships should be sampled differently, that the present sampling technique is inaccurate, and that the Agency was aware of all these facts yet still decided to enforce new and admittedly unproven methods on *Alice Amanda*'s catch. *Alice Amanda* argues that the Agency's enforcement and the resulting seizure of the *Alice Amanda* was arbitrary and capricious because the decision to enforce was made with full knowledge of the distinction between freezer vessel scallop fishing and the methods in vogue previously illustrated by the fact that the enforcement methods used are in contradiction to the New England Fishery Management Council's own formal resolutions.

We will "hold unlawful and set aside Agency action, findings, and conclusions found to be . . . arbitrary, capricious, an abuse of discretion, or otherwise not in accordance with the law." 5 U.S.C. Sec. 706(2)(A). Agency action is arbitrary and capricious if the Agency relies on factors that Congress did not intend for it to consider, entirely ignores important aspects of the problem, explains its decision in a manner contrary to the evidence before it, or reaches a decision that is so implausible that it cannot be ascribed to a difference in view. Although we should not venture into the area of Agency expertise, we need not "accept without question administrative pronouncements clearly at variance with established facts." *National Labor Rel. Bd. v. Morganton Full Fash. Hos. Co.*, 241 F.21d 913, 915–16 (4th Cir. 1957).

There is no substantial evidence in the record except that which reflects that the Agency was aware of the substantial difference between the new technology of freezer ship scallop fishing and the previous methods of scallop fishing contemplated by the regulations promulgated under the 1982 Fishery Management Plan. It is also beyond doubt that the Agency had actual knowledge of the problems with applying the old regulations to these new freezer ship

catches. The Regional Director of the Fisheries Service, Richard Roe, repeatedly voiced his concern over freezer ship enforcement. In a letter dated September 26, 1988, to David Borden, Chairman of the New England Fishery Council, he stated: "Enforcing the meat count average against these vessels will be difficult, if not impossible." He urged that Borden place the issue on the agenda of the next New England Fishery Council Meeting. At the next Council meeting of October 25, 1988, Roe advised the Council that "he did not know how to enforce [freezer ship scallop fishing] at the moment because the current regulations do not take into account freezing at sea." The issue was then placed on the agenda of the next meeting of the Scallop Oversight Committee.

At the Scallop Oversight Committee's meeting the Committee received a report made by an ad hoc group of government and state staff workers recommending that two studies be completed by the Regional Director of freezer ship scallop fishing before implementing an enforcement policy. The Scallop Oversight Committee unanimously voted to submit these recommendations to the New England Fishery Management Council. The New England Fishery Management Council took the matter up at its December 15, 1988, meeting and unanimously adopted the recommendations made by the Scallop Oversight Committee.

The resolution adopted was (adopting the Scallop Oversight Committee report):

1. The committee voted unanimously that the following two studies should be completed by the Regional Director prior to enforcement efforts on frozen product:

(1) A technical study must be done to compare scallop meat weight before freezing and after thawing. The results of the study will provide a factor to convert the meat count from thawed samples to fresh meat count equivalents.

(2) A statistical analysis of the sampling frame for sorted (stratified) scallops must be done. The purpose of sampling sorted sea scallops is to (a) determine that meat count categories are valid, and

(b) measure the meat count for the entire catch. The results of the study will determine the number of samples necessary from each strata, and whether secondary sampling will be necessary to measure the meat count for the entire catch.

At that meeting, Roe advised the Council that there was no enforcement for scallops frozen at sea because there was no procedure yet established. The minutes show, however, an interjection by a certain Geidt implying that there had been some enforcement and that the frozen scallops had to be defrosted. This interjection is not explained in the record.

While Part (2) of the resolution does not affect this case because the catch of the *Alice Amanda* was not sorted, Part (1) of the resolution directly affects the catch, as is at once apparent. The resolution may only be said to acknowledge the facts shown by the various studies that the meat count before freezing and after thawing is different, for it required that "a factor to convert the meat count from thawed samples to fresh meat count equivalent" be provided "prior to enforcement efforts."

Notwithstanding Roe's previously professed concerns for enforcement without factual studies upon which appropriate procedures might be based, on April 14, 1989, Roe sent a memorandum to one MacDonald, the general counsel of the Fisheries Service, urging him to begin enforcement of the scallop meat count for scallops frozen at sea and appeared before a meeting of the Scallop Oversight Committee meeting on March 23, 1989, at which he assured the committee that the Fisheries Service could start to enforce the regulations on scallops frozen at sea pending completion of the two studies being done to facilitate enforcement. How this would be accomplished Roe did not explain, and there is no explanation in the record for this about-face.

Then, without regard to any studies or discussion of policy, the Fisheries Service General Counsel, in conjunction with the Chief of Law Enforcement, one McCarthy, issued an Enforcement Memo on April 20, 1989. The memo set out a procedure for sampling and stated that freezer ship catches would be required to comply with the normal scallop meat size requirements. The *Alice Amanda*'s catch at issue here was sampled pursuant to this procedure and found to be in violation of the Magnuson Act on October 11, 1989. The Enforcement Memo was contrary to the formal resolutions of the New England Fishery Management Council, which had voted unanimously to stay enforcement until the recommended studies were made to determine an accurate method to be used by the Fisheries Service field agents for sampling freezer ship catches. The Agency gave no explanation for this memo at the time, nor does it now.

We are of the opinion the actions of the Agency in this case are arbitrary and capricious under 5 U.S.C. Sec. 706(2)(A). Because the Agency failed to consider the relevant factors that possibly distinguish between frozen scallops and iced scallops, there is an absence of substantial evidence to support its action.

While there is no contention that the Agency relied on any factor that Congress did not intend for it to consider, the Enforcement Memorandum ignored the important aspect of the problem that the meat count after thawing in air of scallops frozen at sea was different from the meat count before freezing. There is no evidence in the record that this is not so, and there is also substantial evidence in the record that the meat count of scallops, frozen at sea, which are thawed at room temperature in air, and not in water, had their meat count considerably raised above those scallops which had been counted after having been packed on ice as was the older practice. The decision reached here by the general counsel and the chief enforcement agent was so implausible that it could not be ascribed to a difference in view. We do not invade the realm of the Agency expertise when we refuse, as we do here, to accept without question the administrative pronouncement, implicit in the enforcement of the same meat count, that the meat count of scallops frozen at sea and thawed at room temperature would be the same as scallops not frozen at sea but packed on ice. Such an administrative pronouncement is clearly at variance with established facts which were even acknowledged by formal resolution of the New England Fisheries Council, the principal rule-making originator of the Agency involved.

Accordingly, the judgment of the district court is reversed and the government's cross-appeal is held to be without merit.

Questions

1. Does this case give you a sense of why the fishing industry and the National Marine Fisheries Service are frequently at odds with each other?

2. Does it also give a sense of how complex fisheries law enforcement has become?

State of La., Ex Rel. Guste v. Verity, 853 F.2d 322 (5th Cir. 1988)

JERRY E. SMITH, CIRCUIT JUDGE

Appellants, the State of Louisiana and the Concerned Shrimpers of Louisiana ("Concerned Shrimpers"), appealed the district court's entry of summary judgment in favor of the Commerce Department, upholding in all respects the Secretary's regulations requiring shrimp trawlers to install and use "turtle excluder devices," also known as "TEDs," in their nets or to limit their trawling to ninety minutes or less at a time. On July 11, 1988, six days after oral argument, we affirmed the judgment of the district court but postponed issuance of an opinion detailing the reasons for our ruling in order that we could immediately notify the parties that we were vacating the district court's order staying execution of its judgment. We now offer our reasons for affirming summary judgment below.

I.

Five species of sea turtles—the Kemp's ridley, loggerhead, leatherback, green, and hawksbill—frequent the Gulf of Mexico and the Atlantic Ocean, off the southeast coast of the United States. All of those species are listed as either "endangered" or "threatened" under the Endangered Species Act of 1973 ("ESA"), 16 U.S.C. Sec. 1531 et seq. Upon inclusion of any species on the list as endangered, section 9 of the ESA prohibits any person from "taking" any such species within the United States, or upon the high seas. In the case of sea turtles, it is equally forbidden to take threatened and endangered species. In addition to these prohibitions, the ESA permits the Secretaries of Commerce and the Interior to promulgate protective regulations.

On June 29, 1987, the Commerce Department, through its National Marine Fisheries Service ("NMFS"), promulgated final regulations requiring shrimp trawlers in the Gulf and South Atlantic to reduce the incidental catch and mortality of sea turtles in shrimp trawls. The regulations attempt to supplement ESA's prohibitions against the "taking" of protected species, and were to become effective for Louisiana on March 1, 1988. Specifically, the regulations require shrimpers operating in offshore waters *and* in vessels twenty-five feet or longer to install and use certified "turtle excluder devices," or "TEDs," in search of their trawls. If the vessel is less than twenty-five feet or is trawling in inshore waters, the shrimper may limit each towing period to ninety minutes or less as an alternative to using a TED.

The reason for the regulations is simple: Researchers have found that during shrimping operations sea turtles are caught in the large nets, or trawls, pulled behind commercial shrimping vessels. The nets drag the turtles behind the boats and thereby prevent them from surfacing for air. According to one study, once a turtle is within the mouth of a shrimp trawl, the animal's initial reaction is to attempt to outswim the device. Of course, this strenuous effort consumes oxygen but affords the turtle no opportunity to replenish the supply. Once trapped, if the exhausted turtle is not released quickly, it will drown. Research cited in the administrative record indicates that trawl times in excess of ninety minutes are highly likely to result in the death of a captured turtle.

The TED requirement thus applies without exception to large shrimping vessels that operate offshore, as these vessels frequently pull their nets for long hours prior to bringing their catches aboard. All of the presently certified TEDs are coated mesh, rope, or rigid frame devices inserted into the cone-shaped shrimp nets at an angle, at the point where the trawl begins to narrow. When a captured turtle reaches the TED, the device deflects the turtle to an escape portal in the top or bottom of the net. The alternative measure of restricting tow time to ninety-minute intervals applies both to smaller vessels, which tend to pull fewer nets at a time and for shorter durations, and to inshore areas, where TED use by either large or small vessels may be impaired by often heavier concentrations of underwater debris.

In October 1987, the State of Louisiana filed a complaint in federal district court, contending that both the TED and tow limit requirements are invalid. The State's complaint alleged that the regulations are arbitrary and capricious, unsupported by the record, and were promulgated in violation of the Administrative Procedure Act's procedural requirements and Executive Order 12291's requirement of a regulatory impact analysis. The State further argued that the regulations violate the Louisiana shrimpers' due process and equal protection rights.

In December 1987 the Environmental Defense Fund and the Center for Environmental Education were permitted to intervene as defendants. The parties filed cross-motions for summary judgment and orally argued their motions on February 10, 1988. Two days before oral argument, on February 8, Concerned Shrimpers of Louisiana was granted leave to intervene as plaintiff. Concerned Shrimpers neither filed, nor responded to, any summary judgment motion, nor participated in oral argument.

On February 29, 1988, the district court entered summary judgment for the defendants. *Louisiana ex rel. Guste v. Verity*, 681 F.Supp. 1178 (E.D.La), *aff'd*, 850 F.2d 211 (5th Cir. 1988). On April 12, 1988, a stay pending appeal was issued. In the present appeal, the appellants again argue that the regulations are arbitrary and capricious. In addition, the Concerned Shrimpers' appeal carries forward the equal protection challenge raised below.

II.

A.

The district court entered judgment for the Secretary on cross-motions for summary judgment. When reviewing a grant of summary judgment, a court of appeals applies the same legal standard as that which guided the district court. Review in the first instance of a challenge made to regulations promulgated under the Endangered Species Act is governed by standards set forth in the Administrative Procedure Act ("APA"), 5 U.S.C. Sec. 706, and it is thus to these same standards that we will look in conducting our review on appeal. Under the APA, the administrative record is reviewed to determine whether the challenged action was arbitrary and capricious, an abuse of discretion, or otherwise not in accordance with law; contrary to constitutional right; in excess of statutory jurisdiction, authority, or limitation; or without procedure required by law.

Appellants primarily charge that the regulations should be invalidated as arbitrary and capricious. Our scope of review under this standard, however, is very narrow. The court is not to weigh the evidence in the record pro and con. Rather, our role is to review the agency action to determine whether the decision "was based on a consideration of the relevant factors and whether there was a clear error of judgment."

Thus, if the agency considers the factors and articulates a rational relationship between the facts found and the choice made, its decision is not arbitrary or capricious. Indeed, the agency's decision need not be ideal, so long as it is not arbitrary or capricious, and so long as the agency gave at least minimal consideration to relevant facts contained in the record. With these principles of review in mind, we turn now to the challenges posed by the appellants.

B.

The core of appellants' challenge on appeal concerns the sufficiency of the administrative record to support the TED and trawling-period regulations. In particular, they assert that the record insufficiently demonstrates the impact of shrimp trawling on sea turtle mortality, the efficacy of the regulations as applied to inshore Louisiana waters, and the impact of the regulations on the Louisiana economy. Appellants also challenge the regulations insofar as the administrative record supporting them fails to address serious causes of sea turtle mortality other than shrimping. Based upon the limited scope of our review, we find that the record amply supports the Secretary's decision to issue the regulations in question.

1. The Impact of Shrimp Trawling on Sea Turtle Mortality

The relationship of shrimping to sea turtle mortality is strongly demonstrated by data contained in the administrative record. Since 1973, on-board observers have documented the capture and drowning of sea turtles by shrimp trawlers. Using extrapolations based upon more than 27,000 hours of shrimp trawl observation, experts have concluded that more than 47,000 endangered and threatened sea turtles are caught in shrimp trawls each year; 11,179 of these turtles drown in the shrimpers' nets. Tag returns on the Kemp's ridley also provide a fertile source of information: 84 percent of the

Kemp's ridley turtles tagged by scientists and later recovered were captured by shrimp trawlers.

The capture and mortality statistics for Louisiana waters were derived largely from the so-called Henwood-Stuntz study, a series of extrapolations based upon 16,785 hours of observer effort in the Gulf of Mexico. Of this total, 4,333 hours were spent on shrimp boats off the Louisiana shore. During the Louisiana observation period, twelve sea turtles were taken, five of which had died by the time the trawl was retrieved. This mortality rate of 42 percent is among the highest of any state, the Gulf-wide rate being 29 percent. More than one-third of the turtles that were observed to have died in Gulf shrimp trawls died off Louisiana.

Although the observers spent substantial hours on the shrimp boats, their efforts recorded the results of only a small fraction of the annual shrimping effort. Each year, commercial shrimpers are estimated to spend 2,063,074 hours trawling off Louisiana. Using a simple ratio of $5/4,333 = X/2,063,074$ and solving for X, a total of 2,381 endangered and threatened turtles would be estimated to be killed annually off Louisiana alone.

"Stranding" data further supports the conclusion that shrimping is responsible for large numbers of sea turtle deaths. Beginning in 1980, volunteers established the Sea Turtle Stranding and Salvage Network ("Network") to monitor the number and types of sea turtle carcasses stranded on beaches and in marshes and bayous. More than 8,300 dead sea turtles, including nearly 600 Kemp's ridleys, were reported to NMFS by the Network. Although determining the precise cause of a stranded sea turtle's death is difficult, a causal link to shrimping appears reasonable in light of the fact that strandings occur predominantly in areas adjacent to shrimping grounds, and that the number of sea turtle strandings increases dramatically with the advent of the shrimping season.

In addition, the administrative record established that, based upon tag returns between

1966 and 1984, 32 percent of the Kemp's ridley turtles incidentally captured are caught in Louisiana waters, by far the highest rate of any state or country. Twenty-two percent of Kemp's ridley strandings in the Gulf occur in Louisiana. In a 1984 study, twelve out of fifteen Louisiana shrimpers interviewed said they caught from one to two sea turtles each year.

In challenging the administrative fact-finding that links shrimp trawling to sea turtle mortality, appellants assert that the Secretary failed to consider the best scientific data available before using the regulations. The Henwood-Stuntz extrapolations heavily relied upon by the agency are flawed, appellants contend, because one of the field samples on which they are based is unscientifically small. Specifically, appellants point out that researchers conducting the study recorded a mere two capturings of the Kemp's ridley turtles during the entire time test trawls were pulled off Louisiana's shores. The insufficiency of this sample is borne out, they believe, by the discrepancy between the Henwood-Stuntz extrapolations and observations made by the Louisiana Department of Wildlife and Fisheries. From 1967 until 1986, the Louisiana Department conducted a total of 36,837 trawl samples, but in none of these was a single sea turtle ever reported to have been captured. At the very least, appellants conclude, the methodology of Henwood-Stuntz is prone to grossly overestimating the killing of sea turtles in shrimp trawls.

Although we believe appellants' challenge is not totally without merit, we are mindful that under the arbitrary-and-capricious standard, our deference to the agency is greatest when reviewing technical matters within its area of expertise, particularly its choice of scientific data and statistical methodology. In reviewing such technical choices, "[w]e must look at the decision not as the chemist, biologist, or statistician that we are qualified neither by training nor experience to be, but as a reviewing court exercising our narrowly defined duty of holding agencies to certain minimal standards of ration-

ality." *Avoyelles Sportsmen's League, Inc. v. Marsh*, 715 F.2d 897, 906 (5th Cir. 1983) (quoting *Ethyl Corp. v. EPA*, 541 F.2d 1, 36 (D.C.Cir.) (en banc), *cert. denied*, 426 U.S. 941 (1976)). Accordingly, where, as here, the agency presents scientifically respectable conclusions which appellants are able to dispute with rival evidence of presumably equal dignity, we will not displace the administrative choice. Nor will we remand the matter to the agency in order that the discrepant conclusions be reconciled.

From our admittedly lay perspective, the Henwood-Stuntz method of extrapolating the magnitude of sea turtle takings in shrimp trawls does not necessarily appear unreasonable. There are more than eighteen thousand domestic shrimp vessels operating in the Gulf and South Atlantic. Each of these vessels simultaneously pulls from one to four trawls, generally for two to six hours at a time. Shrimping occurs in the Gulf year-round, with most activity concentrated between June and December. Therefore, while the 16,785 hours of observer effort invested in the Henwood-Stuntz study represents the equivalent of less than one hour of fishing by the entire shrimping fleet, we recognize that the size of the industry realistically precludes statistical findings based totally upon actual observation rather than extrapolation.

We are also unpersuaded by appellants' mischaracterization of the data base from which Henwood-Stuntz extrapolations were made. Appellants' attack is accomplished by isolating a narrow range of data concerning the most endangered of the five protected species—the Kemp's ridley—and concluding that the data concerning this single species in waters off a single state was insufficient to justify the regulations. As already indicated, however, the regulations are intended to prevent the illegal taking of all of the five endangered and threatened sea turtle species, whose habitats are not confined by state boundaries but may encompass thousands of square miles of sea. Because each local area, indeed each shrimper, is responsible for catching only a few sea turtles each year, it is only by aggregating this information that the relevant statistics can be approximated.

2. The Efficacy of the Regulations as Applied to Louisiana's Inland Waters

The administrative record amply demonstrates that sea turtles are found in inshore waters. Kemp's ridleys, for example, are known to frequent the inshore waters of the Gulf, which hosts their favorite food species, the blue crab. Kemp's ridleys are most abundant in Louisiana, particularly in the near-shore white shrimp grounds. At least one expert has observed that "Kemp's ridley could logically be labeled the Louisiana turtle, because its greatest abundance is found there. . . . It is beyond doubt the commonest marine turtle in the state, concentrated in the shallow water from Marsh Island to the Mississippi Delta." Of all tag returns of nesting Kemp's ridley females, 59 percent are from Louisiana near-shore waters. Other species, including loggerheads and green turtles, also frequent inshore Louisiana waters. The Kemp's ridley is also found in nearby Texas coastal waters, as are green turtles and loggerheads.

Sea turtles not only frequent inshore waters; the record is replete with evidence to show that they are captured there as well. Most recoveries of "headstarted" Kemp's ridleys have occurred in inshore waters. Fully 12 percent of these recoveries have been off Louisiana, even though most of the releases have been off Texas. Nearly all of the Louisiana shrimpers who reported catching sea turtles (80 percent of those interviewed) caught them in shallow near-shore waters. In testimony before the National Oceanic and Atmospheric Administration, a Georgia marine fisheries expert reported that seven of the shrimpers interviewed had captured between twenty and one hundred sea turtles each, in a single shrimping season, mostly in inshore waters.

By 1976, as evidence mounted that shrimp trawling is a substantial cause of sea turtle mortality, NMFS began research into equipment modifications that would allow turtles to escape shrimp trawls without causing a significant loss of shrimp. To ensure that the new gear would accomplish the program's objectives, NMFS required its proposed TED design to be at least 97 percent effective at releasing sea turtles. After more than fifteen thousand hours of testing in the Atlantic and Gulf of Mexico, the agency concluded that the NMFS TED met this standard, without resulting in significant shrimp loss. Tests also showed that the new gear created certain savings for shrimpers. For example, the TED not only deflected turtles out of the net, but also other "by-catch"—marine animals that shrimpers normally must sort through and discard after retrieving the trawl from the water. And the reduced "by-catch" appeared to result in fuel efficiency as well, by reducing the unproductive (i.e., non-shrimp) drag on the vessel's engine.

Data concerning TED effectiveness was based primarily upon tests done in offshore waters, so although the agency had sufficient data that turtles frequent inshore waters and that shrimpers catch them there, the agency was receptive to time limitations on trawling as an alternative measure for inshore areas. During hearings on the proposed regulations, commenters urged that TEDs will not be effective inshore because the TEDs will clog with debris that reportedly lines the bottom of these waters, particularly the inshore Gulf waters. Commenters also urged that TEDs were unnecessary in inshore waters, because the debris makes it impossible for shrimpers to trawl for more than sixty to ninety minutes at a time, less time than it generally takes to drown a captured turtle. As Louisiana's Senator Breaux put it, "in all probability, shrimping in [inshore] waters will not result in any significant sea turtle mortality because it is practically impossible to tow a net for a sufficient length of time to drown a turtle." Based upon these assurances, the agency determined that tow-time restrictions offer a reasonable alternative to TED use in inshore waters.

Appellants nevertheless argue that, if the

agency had insufficient data to apply the more intrusive TED requirement to inshore shrimping, it automatically had insufficient data to support any other type of regulation. We disagree. Since the data was more than adequate to support the tow-time restriction in inland waters, it follows that the Secretary's decision to give shrimpers the option to use TEDs as an alternative is no less supportable. Inshore shrimpers who find the TED onerous need not use it. On the other hand, should shrimpers who experiment with the TED in inshore waters find the device compatible with their needs, they will be free to use it instead of having to haul aboard their nets after every ninety minutes of fishing. The shrimpers can hardly complain that the agency has given them a choice.

3. The Impact of the Regulations on Louisiana's Economy

The proposed regulations, which were to be phased in over a two-year period, will require 17,200 shrimpers using certain size nets to install TEDs and use them when fishing in offshore waters during the shrimping seasons. Shrimpers will purchase and install certified TEDs at an expected cost of $200–$400 per TED. The average annual cost to the entire industry was estimated at $5.9 million, which included the cost of expected shrimp loss during the start-up period, before gear adjustments and changes in trawling techniques overcome any initial inefficiencies. There is substantial evidence in the administrative record indicating that anticipated catch loss resulting from use of the TEDs will amount to no more than 5 percent.

Although we do not denigrate appellants' concern with the expense and inconvenience the regulations will visit on Louisiana's shrimping industry, Congress has decided that these losses cannot compare to the "incalculable" value of genetic heritage embodied in any protected living species. While we do not mean to imply that economic impact can never be considered in determining whether a particular

regulation promulgated under the ESA is arbitrary or capricious, the protections afforded by the regulations before us have not been shown to be achievable through less costly means. Thus, the costs shouldered by the industry are not arbitrary, but reasonably related to Congress's purpose.

4. The Secretary's Failure to Regulate Other Major Causes of Sea Turtle Mortality

Appellants argue that the TED regulations are arbitrary and capricious because they do not address other serious causes of sea turtle mortality. As we understand this argument, however, appellants are in fact raising two separate points. First, they appear to be urging us to adopt a novel proposition that regulations failing to address all of the causes of a problem are, for that reason, arbitrary and capricious. In doing so, they ignore the well-established rule that regulations need not remedy all evils, or none. Nor must the government "choose between attacking every aspect of a problem or not attacking the problem at all." *Dandridge v. Williams*, 397 U.S. 471 (1970). Thus, the agency's decision to attack one of the major causes of sea turtle mortality through regulation is entirely within its discretion. That dredges, commercial fishermen from other nations, and pollution also contribute to sea turtle deaths does not undermine the validity of these restrictions.

Appellants' second contention is based upon the proposition enunciated in *Connor v. Andrus*, 453 F.Supp. 1037, 1041 (W.D. Tex. 1978), that regulations issued under the ESA must halt, or even reverse, the population depletion of an endangered species. In *Connor*, the administrative record was found not to support a finding that banning all duck hunting in designated portions of New Mexico, Texas, and Arizona would increase, or tend to increase, the population of the endangered Mexican duck. The record did demonstrate, however, that the Mexican duck was threatened by other causes not targeted by the regulation, namely, the destruction of its natural habitat and its hybridization with another species, the mallard.

Having thus found that the agency had failed to consider all of the statutorily relevant factors, the *Connor* court held the challenged regulation to be arbitrary and capricious. Id. Accordingly, appellants believe the administrative record in the instant case is similarly deficient: There is no finding that the regulations will ultimately save sea turtles from extinction; nor does the record show that sea turtles saved from drowning in shrimpers' nets will ultimately survive the other causes of sea turtle mortality for such time as to replenish or increase their numbers.

An essential part of appellants' argument assumes that the ESA authorizes the Secretary to issue protective regulations only if found actually to save an endangered species from extinction. We believe, however, that this assumption finds no support in the statutory grant of regulatory authority, 16 U.S.C. Sec. 1533(d). To be sure, the statute mandates the Secretary to "issue such regulations as he deems necessary and advisable to provide for the conservation of [threatened] species." "Conservation" is elsewhere defined in the ESA as "all methods and procedures which are necessary to bring endangered species or threatened species to the point at which the measures provided pursuant to this chapter are no longer necessary." 16 U.S.C. Sec. 1532(3).

In addition to this mandatory duty, however, the ESA also provides the Secretary discretionary authority to prohibit by regulation the taking of *any* threatened species of fish and wildlife. This regulatory authority supplements the statutory prohibition against the taking of endangered species, the enforcement of which is not conditioned upon any showing that the prohibition will itself operate to restore the species to a level considered unendangered. Rather, Congress simply presumes that prohibited takings will deplete the species. We must honor that legislative determination.

In sum, therefore, regulations aimed at preventing the taking of a protected species cannot be invalidated on the ground that the record fails to demonstrate that the regulatory effort will enhance the species' chance of survival. Insofar as *Connor v. Andrus*, *supra*, requires such a showing, we disapprove its holding. Rather, the record need only show that such regulations do in fact prevent prohibited takings of protected species. Here, the record developed by the Secretary amply satisfies this burden.

III.

The Concerned Shrimpers also challenge the regulations on equal protection grounds. The basic concepts of equal protection as set forth in the Fourteenth Amendment apply to federal action through the due process clause of the Fifth Amendment. Where administrative classifications are made, absent a fundamental right or suspect classification such as race, equal protection requires only that the classification bear a rational relationship to the legislative purpose of the enabling statute.

Concerned Shrimpers argue that the regulations cannot meet the "rational basis" test because (1) they do not constrain activity north of North Carolina, even though sea turtles are believed to frequent those waters; (2) they regulate Gulf shrimpers with the same intensity as they regulate Atlantic shrimpers, even though Atlantic shrimpers catch more sea turtles per capita; and (3) they regulate based upon boat size, rather than net size. With respect to the first of these challenges, the Shrimpers themselves provide the best answer: "It is no requirement of equal protection that all evils of the same genus be eradicated or none at all." Nor, as we have already noted, must the agency "choose between attacking every aspect of a problem or not attacking the problem at all." Even assuming, as the Shrimpers assert, that Kemp's ridleys do turn up off Long Island, there is no evidence that they are caught there by shrimp trawlers. Moreover, the government's regulation of a known evil at one place does not become invalid by the discovery of a similar, as-yet-unregulated evil at another.

The Concerned Shrimpers' next argument—that the regulations violate equal protection because they regulate Gulf and Atlantic shrimpers in the same way—is similarly without merit. The agency is under no obligation to treat Atlantic and Gulf shrimpers differently, so long as its rule is reasonably related to its purpose. Here, both Gulf and Atlantic shrimpers apparently cause large numbers of sea turtle deaths. It is the agency's purpose to protect these turtles from harm; it has no interest in penalizing shrimpers for the number of turtles caught, only to prevent such captures, to the extent possible, in the future. The regulations create an even-handed regulatory scheme, rationally related to their legitimate purpose. This is all that equal protection requires.

Finally, the Shrimpers challenge the use of boat size as the trigger for the TED requirement, because, they urge, it is the size of the net, not the boat, that is critical. As originally proposed, the regulations indeed used net size as the basis for the TED requirement, but public comments persuaded the agency that this criterion could not work: It was not only difficult to enforce, but would cause significant intrusions into shrimper operations.

The compromise reached by the agency—to use boat size as a proxy for net size—was entirely reasonable. Boats below twenty-five feet in length generally do not pull the larger nets. But even if some twenty-four-foot vessels do pull larger nets, as the Shrimpers say, the government need not achieve the "mathematical nicety" the Shrimpers demand in order to meet constitutional requirements. Rather, as the Supreme Court has long recognized, "[t]he problems of government are practical ones and may justify, if they do not require rough accommodations." The "rough accommodation" attained by these regulations plainly passes constitutional muster.

IV.

For the foregoing reasons, the judgment of the district court is *affirmed*.

Questions

1. Is there an adequate scientific basis for forcing TEDs on shrimp fishermen?

2. Do TEDs have any other benefits besides saving turtles?

3. Why, as a nation, have we exerted such effort to protect turtles?

Balelo v. Baldridge, 724 F.2d 753 (9th Cir. 1984)

ALARCON, CIRCUIT JUDGE

In *Balelo v. Klutznick*, 519 F.Supp. 573 (S.D.Cal. 1981), plaintiffs-appellees, who are captains of tuna purse seiners (hereinafter the Captains), institute this action against defendants-appellants (hereinafter the Secretary) seeking declaratory and injunctive relief. The district court granted a declaratory judgment invalidating subsection (f) of regulation 50 C.F.R. Sec. 216.24 (1981) promulgated by the Secretary of Commerce pursuant to the Marine Mammal Protection Act (hereinafter MMPA), 16 U.S.C. Sec. 1371.

Under the regulation, the Captains are permitted to take porpoise during commercial fishing operations only if they comply with certain conditions. They must allow government observers to board and accompany the vessel on regular fishing trips "for the purpose of research or observing operations." 50 C.F.R. 216.24(f). The regulation further authorizes the collection of data which may be used in MMPA enforcement proceedings. The district court ruled that the regulation was unconstitutional only insofar as it permitted the use of observer-collected data in MMPA enforcement proceedings.

In *United States v. $50,178.80, the Monetary Value of 57 Tons of Tuna and Gladiator Fishing, Inc.*, Cv. No. 79-4466-LEW (MX) (C.D.Cal. April 21, 1982), a civil forfeiture proceeding, the district court denied a motion to suppress evidence of observer-collected data.

We have taken these matters en banc to consider whether the regulation is valid under the MMPA, and if so, whether it violates the Fourth Amendment. For the reasons set forth below, we have concluded that: (1) the regulation was authorized under the broad rule-making power delegated by Congress to the Secretary; (2) the regulation is consistent with the policies and objectives of the MMPA; and (3) the regulation falls within the pervasively regulated industry exception to the warrant requirement of the Fourth Amendment.

Factual and Statutory Background

The Captains utilize a method of fishing for yellowfin tuna which results in the incidental taking of certain species of porpoise. Porpoises tend to swim in association with yellowfin tuna in the eastern tropical Pacific. The porpoise is larger and more active on the ocean's surface. Thus, the Captains can locate yellowfin tuna by spotting porpoises. Purse seine nets are then set around schools of porpoises. The tuna swimming beneath them are encircled when the net is closed or "pursed" around them. During this operation, significant numbers of porpoises are injured or drowned. Their carcasses are discarded into the sea. In the two years preceding the enactment of the MMPA in 1972, the incidental taking resulted in more than 600,000 porpoise mortalities. *Committee for Humane Legislation Inc. v. Richardson*, 414 F.Supp. 297, 300 (D.D.C.), *aff'd*, 540 F.2d 1141 (D.C.Cir. 1976).

Congress's overriding purpose in enacting the MMPA was the protection of marine mammals. Congress declared the immediate goal of the MMPA to be "that the incidental kill or incidental serious injury of marine mammals permitted in the course of commercial fishing operations be reduced to insignificant levels approaching a zero mortality and serious injury rate." 16 U.S.C. Sec. 1371(a)(2) (1976–1982). To accomplish this goal, Congress imposed a moratorium on the taking and importing of marine mammals. 16 U.S.C. Sec. 1371(a) (1976–1982). A two-year exemption from the moratorium for

the taking of marine mammals incidental to commercial fishing operations was allowed. 16 U.S.C. Sec. 1371(a)(2) (1976), *amended by* 16 U.S.C. Sec. 1371(a)(2) (1982). The legislative history indicates that the exemption was provided "for the refinement of these fishing gear modifications" which industry representatives proffered as a solution to the porpoise mortality problem. *Committee for Humane Legislation*, 414 F.Supp. at 301. In addition, the Act directed the "immediate" undertaking of a research and development program to devise improved fishing methods and gear as to reduce the incidental taking of marine mammals in connection with commercial fishing. 16 U.S.C. Sec. 1381(a) (1976).

Although the commercial fishing industry was exempted for two years from the moratorium, the incidental taking of mammals during this time was conditioned on industry compliance with section 1381. Subsection (d) of section 1381 requires the industry to allow agents of the Secretary "to board and to accompany any commercial fishing vessel . . . on a regular fishing trip for the purpose of conducting research or observing operations in regard to the development of improved fishing methods and gear as authorized by this section." Since expiration of this two-year exemption in 1974, the taking of marine mammals incidental to commercial fishing must be pursuant to a permit issued by the Secretary, 16 U.S.C. Sec. 1371(a)(2), "subject to regulations prescribed by the Secretary in accordance with section 1371." 16 U.S.C. Sec. 1371(a)(2) (1976–1982).

Section 1373 requires the Secretary to consider, in promulgating the regulations, the "existing and future levels of marine mammal species and population stocks," and the "marine ecosystem and related environmental considerations." The regulations may also restrict the taking of porpoises by species, number, age, sex, or other factors. In addition to the rule-making authority conferred upon the Secretary, 16 U.S.C. Sec. 1371, the MMPA provides for the imposition of civil and criminal penalties for violations of the provisions of the Act or the regulations or permits issued thereunder.

In 1974, the Secretary promulgated a regulation, 50 C.F.R. Sec. 216.24(f) (1974), in language virtually identical to that set forth in section 1381, the statutory observer program, that required the placement of observers on vessels.

Pursuant to the powers granted under the MMPA, the Secretary promulgated the regulation at issue here. The challenged regulation, effective January 1, 1981, requires as a condition of engaging in fishing operations that vessel owners:

(1) . . . [S]hall, upon the proper notification by the [NMFS], allow an observer duly authorized by the secretary to accompany the vessel on any or all regular fishing trips for the purpose of conducting research and observing operations, *including collecting information which may be used in civil or criminal penalty proceedings, forfeiture actions, or permit or certificate sanctions.*

· · ·

(4) The Secretary shall provide for the payment of all reasonable costs directly related to the quartering and maintaining of such observers on board such vessels. A vessel certificate holder who has been notified that the vessel is required to carry an observer, via certified letter from the National Marine Fisheries Service, shall notify the office from which the letter was received at least five days in advance of the fishing voyage to facilitate observer placement. *A vessel certificate holder who has failed to comply with the provisions of this section may not engage in fishing operations for which a general permit is required.* 50 C.F.R. Sec. 216.24(f) (1981) (emphasis added).

The Captains appear to have no objection to the observers' scientific role on board ship. Their objection is directed solely at those provisions of the 1981 regulation which authorize the use of observer-collected data in enforcement proceedings. In the Captain's opening brief we are told that: "The District Court's injunction properly stripped the observer program of its unauthorized and impermissible *search* function and restored it to its pristine role of pure scientific fact-gathering." Appellees' opening brief at 9 (emphasis added).

Constitutionality of the Regulation

The Captains contend that the regulation authorizes a warrantless search in violation of the Fourth Amendment.

Whether the observer program constitutes a search is a question which is not free from doubt. The regulation does not authorize an inspection of private papers, or a search of the person, or the personal effects of the Captains or their crews. Instead, the observers must confine their observations to the fishing operations of the vessel, which occur on the open sea or on deck. Thus, the information they may gather is restricted to evidence which is in plain view. "What a person knowingly exposes to the public, even in his own home or office, is not a subject of Fourth Amendment protection." *Katz v. United States*, 389 U.S. 347 at 351 (1967). See *United States v. Whitmire*, 595 F.2d 1303, 1312 (5th Cir. 1979), (high levels of privacy might be accorded to crew's living quarters on a tanker that travels for months, but no crew member had legitimate claim of privacy on open deck of a fishing smack or in the hold of a cargo vessel available for hire), *cert. denied*, 448 U.S. 906 (1980).

It can be argued with equal force, however, that the observer's constant surveillance of the activities of the Captains and their crews, for a prolonged period of time, constituted an intrusion into liberty and privacy interests, protected by the Fourth Amendment, by exposing "what [a person] seeks to preserve as private, even in an area accessible to the public." *Katz*, 389 U.S. at 351.

We need not pause to resolve this nice question. Even if we assume that the regulation authorizes a warrantless *search* of the operations of a fishing vessel, it is our view that the regulation requiring the presence of observers on purse seiners does not violate the Fourth Amendment.

The Fourth Amendment prohibits *unreason-*

able searches and seizures. Warrantless searches may be reasonable under certain circumstances. In *Carroll v. United States*, 267 U.S. 132 (1924), the Supreme Court commented: "Under the common law and agreeably to the Constitution [a] search may in many cases be legally made without a warrant. The Constitution does not forbid search, as some parties contend, but it does forbid unreasonable search."

The Supreme Court has recognized that warrantless searches in closely regulated industries can be reasonable. The Court has held that warrantless inspections are reasonable if they are reasonably necessary to further important federal interests and the federal regulatory presence is sufficiently comprehensive and predictable that "the assurance of regularity provided by a warrant is rendered unnecessary." *Donovan v. Dewey*, 452 U.S. 594 (1981).

Since 1972, the tuna industry has been closely regulated by Congress because its fishing operations threatened the extinction of the porpoise. Congress's interest in the protection of marine mammals was made known to all commercial fishermen in 1972 when Congress expressly authorized the placing of observers on purse seiners to protect the porpoise under the MMPA. As discussed above, in the MMPA, Congress authorized the Secretary to prescribe regulations and to issue a permit restricting the taking of marine mammals. Congress also authorized the Secretary to limit the issuance of permits to those persons who can demonstrate that any taking of marine mammals will be consistent with the MMPA, 16 U.S.C. Sec. 1373. Thus, commercial fishermen have been made aware since 1972 that to take porpoises they must have a permit which is subject to conditions that will insure that marine mammals are given the protection required by Congress. The statutory observer program had been one such condition. Since 1974 commercial fishermen have also been aware of the regulation which prescribes the observer program. Any tuna boat Captain who does not wish to expose himself to

the observation of his open deck activities is free not to submit to such an intrusion by refraining from seeking a permit.

Conclusion

We hold that the requirement that observers be permitted to board purse seiners on a scheduled basis as a condition of obtaining a permit to take porpoises is reasonable under the Fourth Amendment. The regulation and field manual do not authorize the observers to conduct searches of the persons, personal effects, or living quarters of the Captains and their crews. Such a search would have to be justified independently under the Fourth Amendment.

The judgment in *Balelo* is reversed and remanded for further proceedings consistent with this opinion. The judgment in *Gladiator* is affirmed.

FERGUSON, CIRCUIT JUDGE, dissenting.

Today the majority installs a federal agent in the temporary home of fourteen to eighteen fishermen for a two- to three-month period without requiring a warrant or a showing of probable cause to believe that the law has been broken. The Fourth Amendment, assuring that the people are to be secure in their homes, mandates that warrantless government intrusion into even a temporary home is per se unreasonable. This protection is not lost because the place called home is also used for commercial purposes, i.e., as a fishing vessel, for both commercial premises and seafaring vessels are covered by the Fourth Amendment.

The National Oceanic and Atmospheric Administration (NOAA), an agency of the federal government, has by regulation placed federal agents on board tuna fishing vessels for two- to three-month fishing trips by conditioning the license to fish for tuna upon the vessel owner's consent to the presence of federal observers. 50 C.F.R. Sec. 216.24(f) (1982). The federal "observers" are authorized to conduct research and collect information "which may be used in civil or criminal penalty proceedings, forfeiture actions, or permit or certificate sanctions," id. Sec 216.24(f)(1), while they live for the extended fishing trip on a 150- to 250-foot boat with the crew of fourteen to eighteen men. M. K. Orbach, *Hunters, Seamen, and Entrepreneurs* (1977) (hereinafter "Orbach"). It has been stipulated by the parties that the observers take their meals with the fishermen, are not confined to any particular areas of the vessel, and are expected to "maintain open communication" with and question vessel operators and other personnel while recording data pertaining to the enforcement of the Marine Mammal Protection Act, 16 U.S.C. Sections 1361–1407.

Any possibility of separating the business aspects of a fishing vessel from the home aspects is belied by the realities of life on such a vessel:

[I]t is impossible to get more than about fifty feet from any of the other fifteen men with whom you are going to spend the next two months. You can draw curtains or close doors and remain out of sight a good part of the time, but you can never get away from them, and the fishing process forces you into regular interaction with them. Orbach at 25

Both Congress and the Supreme Court have acted to specially protect the rights and comforts of seamen due to this unusual characteristic of their work. *See Aguilar v. Standard Oil Co.*, 318 U.S. 724, 732, (1943) ("of necessity, during the voyage [the seaman] must eat, drink, lodge, and divert himself within the confines of the ship. In short, during the period of his tenure the vessel is not merely his place of employment; it is the framework of his existence").

The NOAA's effort to install a federal agent on board a fishing vessel without securing a warrant based on probable cause is reminiscent of the "indiscriminate searches and seizures conducted under the authority of 'general warrants' [which] were the immediate evils that motivated the framing and adoption of the Fourth Amendment." *Payton v. New York*, 445 U.S. 573 (1978). The Fourth Amendment protects "[t]he right of the people to be secure in their persons, houses, papers, and effects. . . ."

The Supreme Court has defined the scope of the Fourth Amendment to include a person's "reasonable expectation of privacy." *Katz v. United States*, 389 U.S. 347 (1967). As the Court stated over twenty years ago:

At the very core [of the Fourth Amendment] stands the right of a man to retreat into his own home and there be free from unreasonable governmental intrusion. This Court has never held that a federal officer may without warrant and without consent physically entrench into a man's office or home, there secretly observe or listen, and relate at the man's subsequent criminal trial what was seen or heard. *Silverman v. United States*, 365 U.S. 505, 511–12 (1961)

It is precisely this "right to be let alone," that is trampled when tuna fishermen are required to live, eat, sleep, lodge, and relax in the presence of a federal agent within the confines of a 150- to 250-foot boat in the middle of the ocean for two to three months at a time.

Tuna fishermen do not waive their right to be free from unreasonable search or surveillance by temporarily living on board a fishing vessel. The fishing boat is not just their place of employment, but for two to three months it is "the framework of [their] existence," *Aguilar v. Standard Oil Co.*, 318 U.S. at 732, and their home. This home cannot be entered by law enforcement officers absent a warrant based on probable cause to believe that a crime has been or is being committed. It is well established that an administrative regulation which by its terms violates the Fourth Amendment is unconstitutional and should not be enforced.

The Fourth Amendment was a response to the general warrant whereby an officer was authorized to search private premises without evidence of unlawful activity. *Marshall v. Barlow's Inc.*, 437 U.S. at 311. Today the majority holds that a federal agent cannot only search a private vessel, but collect data, question fishermen, and live on the vessel for months at a time without the need to secure a warrant based on a legitimate suspicion of unlawful activity. The regulation at issue here can subject "even the most law-abiding citizen" to unprecedented and un-justified government intrusion and surveillance. Surely the lives of porpoises cannot be more sacred to us than the right to privacy and free-dom from government intrusion protected by the Fourth Amendment.

Questions

1. After this case, what *would* be considered an unreasonable search in this "pervasively reg-ulated industry"?

2. Can you think of any other means to accom-plish the management objective in a less in-trusive manner?

Chapter 9

ADMIRALTY LAW

Foremost Insurance Co. v. Richardson,
457 U.S. 668 (1982)

JUSTICE MARSHALL delivered the opinion of the Court.

The issue presented in this case is whether the collision of two pleasure boats on navigable waters falls within the admiralty jurisdiction of the federal courts. We granted certiorari to resolve the confusion in the lower courts respecting the impact of *Executive Jet Aviation, Inc. v. City of Cleveland*, 409 U.S. 249 (1972) (*Executive Jet*), on traditional rules for determining federal admiralty jurisdiction. The United States Court of Appeals for the Fifth Circuit held that an accident between two vessels in navigable waters bears a sufficient relationship to traditional maritime activity to fall within federal admiralty jurisdiction. We affirm.

I.

Two pleasure boats collided on the Amite River in Louisiana, resulting in the death of Clyde Richardson. The wife and children of the decedent brought this action in the United States District Court for the Middle District of

Louisiana, alleging inter alia that petitioner Shirley Eliser had negligently operated the boat that collided with the vessel occupied by the decedent. Respondents also named petitioner Foremost Insurance Company, Eliser's insurer, as a defendant. Jurisdiction was claimed under 28 U.S. Code, sec. 1333(1), which gives federal district courts exclusive jurisdiction over "[a]ny civil case of admiralty or maritime jurisdiction." Petitioners moved to dismiss, arguing that the complaint did not state a cause of action within the admiralty or maritime jurisdiction of the District Court.

In ruling on petitioners' motion, the District Court found the following facts to be undisputed:

(1) One boat was used for pleasure boating, such as boat riding and water skiing, and at the time of the accident the boat was actually pulling a skier on a zip sled;

(2) The other boat was used exclusively for pleasure fishing and was described as a bass boat;

(3) Neither boat had ever been used in any "commercial maritime activity" before the accident;

(4) At the time of the accident neither boat was in-

volved in any "commercial maritime activity" of any sort;

(5) Neither of the two drivers of the boat were being paid to operate the boat nor was this activity in any way a part of their regular type of employment;

(6) None of the passengers on either boat were engaged in any kind of "traditional maritime activity" either before or at the time of the accident;

(7) Neither of the boats involved was under hire in any traditional maritime form;

(8) There is no evidence to indicate that any "commercial activity," even in the broadest admiralty sense, had ever been previously engaged in by either of the boats in question, and in fact the two boats would have to be classified as "purely pleasure craft," not in any way "involved in commerce"; and

(9) There was no other instrumentality involved in this accident that had even a minor relationship to "admiralty" or "commerce," i.e., a buoy, barge, oil-drilling apparatus, etc. *Richardson v. Foremost Insurance Co.*, 470 F.Supp. 699, 700 (MD La. 1979).

After reviewing decisions of this Court and the Fifth Circuit, as well as relevant commentary, the District Court found that there must be some relationship with traditional maritime activity for an injury sustained on navigable water to fall within federal admiralty jurisdiction. The District Court held that commercial maritime activity is necessary to satisfy this relationship, and granted petitioners' motion to dismiss the complaint for lack of subject matter jurisdiction because the collision of these two pleasure boats did not involve any commercial activity.

The Court of Appeals reversed. *Richardson v. Foremost Insurance Co.*, 641 F.2d 314 (5 Cir. 1981). The Court of Appeals agreed that *Executive Jet, supra*, and relevant Fifth Circuit decisions establish that "admiralty jurisdiction requires more than the occurrence of the tort on navigable waters—that additionally there must be a significant relationship between the wrong and traditional maritime activity." It disagreed with the District Court, however, on the application of this principle to the undisputed facts of this case. Relying on the fact that the

"Rules of the Road" govern all boats on navigable waters, and on the uncertainty that would accompany a finding of no admiralty jurisdiction in this case, the Court of Appeals held that "two boats, regardless of their intended use, purpose, size, and activity, are engaged in traditional maritime activity when a collision between them occurs on navigable waters."

II.

Prior to our opinion in *Executive Jet*, there was little question that a complaint such as the one filed here stated a cause of action within federal admiralty jurisdiction. Indeed, the *Executive Jet* Court begins its opinion by observing that, under the traditional rule of admiralty jurisdiction, "[i]f the wrong occurred on navigable waters, the action is within admiralty jurisdiction." 409 U.S. at 253. Under this rule, an action arising out of a collision between two pleasure boats on navigable waters clearly falls within the admiralty jurisdiction of the district courts. When presented with this precise situation in the past, this Court has found it unnecessary even to discuss whether the district court's admiralty jurisdiction had been properly invoked, instead assuming the propriety of such jurisdiction merely because the accident occurred on navigable waters. *Levinson v. Deupree*, 345 U.S. 648, 651 (1953). See also *Just v. Chambers*, 312 U.S. 383 (1941) (injury to guest from carbon monoxide poisoning in the cabin of a pleasure boat). In light of these decisions, we address here only the narrow question whether *Executive Jet* disapproved these earlier decisions sub silentio.

In *Executive Jet*, this Court held that a suit for property damage to a jet aircraft that struck a flock of sea gulls upon takeoff and sank in the navigable waters of Lake Erie did not state a claim within the admiralty jurisdiction of the district courts. In reaching this conclusion, the Court observed that the mechanical application of the locality rule as the sole test for determining whether there is admiralty jurisdiction had been widely criticized by commentators, and that the federal courts and Congress had been compelled to make exceptions to this approach in the interests of justice in order to include certain torts with no maritime locality. The Court determined that claims arising from airplane accidents are cognizable in admiralty only when the wrong bears a significant relationship to traditional maritime activity. Given the realities of modern-day air travel, the *Executive Jet* Court held that, "in the absence of legislation to the contrary, there is no federal admiralty jurisdiction over aviation tort claims arising from flights by land-based aircraft between points within the continental United States."

The express holding of *Executive Jet* is carefully limited to the particular facts of that case. However, the thorough discussion of the theoretical and practical problems inherent in broadly applying the traditional locality rule has prompted several courts and commentators to construe *Executive Jet* as applying to determinations of federal admiralty jurisdiction outside the context of aviation torts. See, e.g., *Kelly v. Smith*, 485 F.2d 520 (5 Cir. 1973); Calamari, *The Wake of Executive Jet—A Major Wave or a Minor Ripple*, 4 Maritime Lawyer 52 (1979). We believe that this is a fair construction. Although *Executive Jet* addressed only the unique problems associated with extending admiralty jurisdiction to aviation torts, much of the Court's rationale in rejecting a strict locality rule also applies to the maritime context. Indeed, the *Executive Jet* Court relied extensively on admiralty and maritime decisions of this Court and on congressional action extending admiralty jurisdiction to torts with a significant relationship to traditional maritime activity, but with no maritime locality.

We recognize, as did the Court of Appeals, that the *Executive Jet* requirement that the wrong have a significant connection with traditional maritime activity is not limited to the aviation context. We also agree that there is no requirement that "the maritime activity be an exclusively commercial one." Because the "wrong" here involves the negligent operation of a vessel on navigable waters, we believe that it has a sufficient nexus to traditional maritime activity to sustain admiralty jurisdiction in the District Court.

We are not persuaded by petitioners' argument that a substantial relationship with commercial maritime activity is necessary because commercial shipping is at the heart of the traditional maritime activity sought to be protected by giving the federal courts exclusive jurisdiction over all admiralty suits. This argument is premised on the faulty assumption that, absent this relationship with *commercial* activity, the need for uniform rules to govern conduct and liability disappears, and "federalism" concerns dictate that these torts be litigated in the state courts.

Although the primary focus of admiralty jurisdiction is unquestionably the protection of maritime commerce, petitioners take too narrow a view of the federal interest sought to be protected. The federal interest in protecting maritime commerce cannot be adequately served if admiralty jurisdiction is restricted to those individuals actually *engaged* in commercial maritime activity. This interest can be fully vindicated only if *all* operators of vessels on navigable waters are subject to uniform rules of conduct. The failure to recognize the breadth of this federal interest ignores the potential effect of noncommercial maritime activity on maritime commerce. For example, if these two boats collided at the mouth of the St. Lawrence Seaway, there would be a substantial effect on maritime commerce, without regard to whether either boat was actively, or had been previously, engaged in commercial activity. Furthermore, admiralty law has traditionally been concerned with the conduct alleged to have caused this collision by virtue of its "navigational rules—rules that govern the manner and direction those vessels may rightly move upon the waters." *Executive Jet*, 409 U.S., at 270. The potential disruptive impact of a collision between boats on navigable waters, when coupled with the traditional concern that admiralty law holds for navigation, compels the conclusion that this collision between two pleasure boats on navigable waters has a significant relationship with maritime commerce.

Yet, under the strict commercial rule proffered by petitioners, the status of the boats as "pleasure" boats, as opposed to "commercial" boats, would control the existence of admiralty jurisdiction. Application of this rule, however, leads to inconsistent findings or denials of admiralty jurisdiction similar to those found fatal to the locality rule in *Executive Jet*. Under the commercial rule, fortuitous circumstances such as whether the boat was, or had ever been, rented, or whether it had ever been used for commercial fishing, control the existence of federal court jurisdiction. The owner of a vessel used for both business and pleasure might be subject to radically different rules of liability depending upon whether his activity at the time of a collision is found by the court ultimately assuming jurisdiction over the controversy to have been sufficiently "commercial." We decline to inject the uncertainty inherent in such line drawing into maritime transportation. Moreover, the smooth flow of maritime commerce is promoted when all vessel operators are subject to the same duties and liabilities. Adopting the strict commercial rule would frustrate the goal of promoting the smooth flow of maritime commerce, because the duties and obligations of noncommercial navigators traversing navigable waters flowing through more than one State would differ "depending upon their precise location within the territorial jurisdiction of one state or another." *Richardson v. Foremost Insurance Co.*, 641 F.2d, at 316.

Finally, our interpretation is consistent with congressional activity in this area. First, Congress defines the term "vessel," for the purpose of determining the scope of various shipping and maritime transportation laws, to include all types of waterborne vessels, without regard to whether they engage in commercial activity. See, e.g., 1 U.S. Code, sec. 3 (" 'vessel' includes every description of watercraft or other artificial contrivance used, or capable of being used, as a means of transportation on water"). Second, the federal "Rules of the Road," designed for preventing collisions on navigable waters, apply to all vessels without regard to their commercial or noncommercial nature. Third, when it extended admiralty jurisdiction to injuries on land caused by ships on navigable waters, Congress directed that "[t]he admiralty and maritime jurisdiction of the United States shall extend to and include all cases of damage or injury . . . *caused by a vessel on navigable water*." Extension of Admiralty Jurisdiction Act, 62 Stat. 496, as set forth in 46 U.S. Code, sec. 740.

In light of the need for uniform rules governing navigation, the potential impact on maritime commerce when two vessels collide on navigable waters, and the uncertainty and confusion that would necessarily accompany a jurisdictional test tied to the commercial use of a given boat, we hold that a complaint alleging a collision between two vessels on navigable waters properly states a claim within the admiralty jurisdiction of the federal courts. Therefore, the judgment of the Court of Appeals is affirmed.

JUSTICE POWELL with whom the CHIEF JUSTICE, JUSTICE REHNQUIST, and JUSTICE O'CONNOR join, dissenting.

No trend of decisions by this Court has been stronger—for two decades or more—than that toward expanding federal jurisdiction at the expense of state interests and state court jurisdiction. Of course, Congress also has moved steadily and expansively to exercise its Commerce Clause and preemptive power to displace state and local authority. Often decisions of this Court and congressional enactments have been necessary in the national interest. The effect, nevertheless, has been the erosion of federalism—a basic principle of the Constitution and our federal union.

Today's Court decision, an example of this trend, is not necessary to further any federal interest. On its face, it is inexplicable. The issue is whether the federal law of admiralty, rather than traditional state tort law, should apply to an accident on the Amite River in Louisiana between two small boats. "One was an eighteen-foot pleasure boat powered by a 185 h.p. Johnson outboard motor that was being used for water-skiing purposes at the time of the accident. The other was a sixteen-foot 'bass boat' powered by an outboard motor that was used exclusively for pleasure boating." *Richardson v. Foremost Ins. Co.*, 470 F.Supp. 699, 700 (MD La. 1979). It also is undisputed that both boats were used "exclusively for pleasure"; that neither had ever been used in any "commercial maritime activity"; that none of the persons aboard the boats had ever been engaged in any such activity; and that neither of the boats was used for hire. The Court of Appeals conceded that "the place where the accident occurred is seldom, if ever, used for commercial activity." *Richardson v. Foremost Ins. Co.*, 641 F.2d 314, 316 (5 Cir. 1981).

The absence of "commercial activity" on this waterway was held by the Court of Appeals to be immaterial. While recognizing that there was substantial authority to the contrary, the court held that federal admiralty law applied to this accident. This Court now affirms in a decision holding that "all operators of vessels on navigable waters are subject to uniform [federal] rules of conduct," conferring federal admiralty jurisdiction over *all* accidents. In my view there is no substantial federal interest that justifies a rule extending admiralty jurisdiction to the edge of absurdity. I dissent.

I.

Executive Jet Aviation v. City of Cleveland, 409 U.S. 249 (1972), established that admiralty jurisdiction does *not* extend to every accident on navigable waters. The Court today misconstrues *Executive Jet*. We emphasized in that case that it is "consistent with the history and purpose of admiralty to require ... that the wrong bear a *significant* relationship to *traditional maritime activity*." Id., 409 U.S. at 268 (emphasis added). We acknowledged that "in a

literal sense there may be some similarities between the problems posed for a plane downed on water and those faced by a sinking ship." Id., 409 U.S. at 269. But, recalling that "[t]he law of admiralty has evolved over many centuries," we noted that admiralty was "concerned with [matters such as] maritime liens, the general average, capture and prizes, limitation of liability, cargo damage, and claims for salvage." Id., 409 U.S. at 270. "It is clear, therefore, that neither the fact that a plane goes down on navigable waters nor the fact that the negligence 'occurs' while a plane is flying over such waters is enough to create such a relationship to *traditional maritime activity* as to justify the invocation of admiralty jurisdiction." Id., 409 U.S. at 270–71 (emphasis added).

Executive Jet's recognition that "[t]he law of admiralty has evolved over many centuries" provides the appropriate understanding of that case's "traditional maritime activity" test. Admiralty is a specialized area of law that, since its ancient inception, has been concerned with the problems of seafaring *commercial* activity. As Professor Stoltz has demonstrated, "[t]here can be no doubt that historically the civil jurisdiction of admiralty was exclusively concerned with matters arising from maritime commerce." Stolz, *Pleasure Boating and Admiralty: Erie at Sea*, 51 Calif. L. Rev. 661, 669 (1963).

This case involves only pleasure craft. Neither of these boats had ever been used in any commercial activity. There is, therefore, no connection with any historic federal admiralty interest. In centuries past—long before modern means of transportation by land and air existed—rivers and oceans were the basic means of commerce, and the vessels that used the waterways were limited primarily to commercial and naval purposes. "Pleasure boating is basically a new phenomenon, the product of a technology that can produce small boats at modest cost and of an economy that puts such craft within the means of almost everyone." Stolz, *supra*, at 661. Thus, the "traditional" connection emphasized in *Executive Jet* is absent where pleasure boats are concerned. Moreover, even the Court today is hard put to identify an arguably substantial federal admiralty interest *of any kind*. I now comment briefly on the Court's reasoning.

II.

The Court's justification for extending federal admiralty jurisdiction to streams and inlets of our country is the need for "uniform rules of conduct." I agree, of course, that standard codes should govern traffic on waterways, just as it is crucial that certain uniform rules of traffic prevail on neighborhood streets as well as interstate highways. But this is no reason for admiralty jurisdiction to be extended to all boating activity. Congress has provided some rules governing water traffic, just as it has done for some land traffic. See 23 U.S. Code, sec. 154 (55 m.p.h. speed limit). Yet no one suggests that federal jurisdiction is needed to prevent chaos in automobile traffic, or that only federal courts are qualified to try accident cases.

State courts are duty bound to apply federal as well as local "uniform rules of conduct." The Court does not suggest that state courts lack competency to apply federal as well as state law to this type of water traffic. And this Court stands ready, if necessary, to review state decisions to ensure that important issues of federal law are resolved correctly.

In an effort to rescue its logic, the Court refers to the "potential disruptive impact of a collision between boats on navigable waters. . . ." Yet this reasoning is countered by *Executive Jet*—a decision that the Court acknowledges to be a key authority for this case. For if "potential disruptive impact" on traffic in navigable waters provides a sufficient connection with "traditional maritime activity," then the crash of an *airplane* "in the navigable waters of Lake Erie," necessarily would support admiralty jurisdiction. The holding of *Executive Jet* is precisely to the contrary. The Court's reasoning in essence resurrects the locality rule that *Executive Jet* rejected, for *any* accident "located" on nav-

igable waters has a "potential disruptive impact" on traffic there.

Oral argument in this case revealed the degree to which the Court's decision displaces state authority. The Court posed a hypothetical in which children, for their own amusement, used rowboats to net crawfish from a stream. Two of the boats collide and sink near the water's edge, forcing the children to wade ashore. Counsel for respondents replied that this accident *would* fall within the admiralty jurisdiction of the federal courts, provided that the waterway was navigable. Today the Court agrees.

For me, however, this example illustrates the substantial—and *purposeless*—expansion of federal authority and federal court jurisdiction accomplished by the Court's holding. In this respect I agree with Chief Judge Haynsworth:

The admiralty jurisdiction in England and in this country was born of a felt need to protect the domestic shipping industry in its competition with foreign shipping and to provide a uniform body of law for the governance of domestic and foreign shipping, engaged in the movement of commercial vehicles from state to state and to and from foreign states. The operation of small pleasure craft on inland waters which happen to be navigable has no more apparent relationship to that kind of concern than the operation of the same kind of craft on artificial inland lakes which are not navigable waters. *Crosson v. Vance*, 484 F.2d 840, 840 (4 Cir. 1973)

In the rowboat example, as in the case at bar, the Federal Government has little or no genuine interest in the resolution of a garden variety tort case. "Only the burdening of the federal courts and the frustration of the purposes of state tort law would be thereby served." *Adams v. Montana Power Co.*, 528 F.2d 437, 440–41 (9 Cir. 1975).

The Court's opinion largely ignores the fact that expansions of federal admiralty jurisdiction are accompanied by application of substantive—and *preempting*—federal admiralty law. "The chief objection to application of admiralty law to pleasure boating is that it implicitly prohibits the exercise of state legislative power in an area in which local legislatures have generally been thought competent and in which Congress cannot be expected either to be interested or to be responsive to local needs." Stolz, 51 Calif. L. Rev., at 664. For me, this federalism concern is the dominating issue in the case. I agree that "the law of pleasure boating will develop faster and more rationally if the creative capacities of the state courts and legislators are freed of an imaginary federal concern with anything that floats on navigable waters." Id., at 719.

Federal courts should not displace state responsibility and choke the federal judicial docket on the basis of federal concerns that in truth are only "imaginary." In accord with the teaching of *Executive Jet*, I would not extend federal admiralty jurisdiction beyond its traditional roots and reason for existence. I dissent from the Court's decision to sever a historic doctrine from its historic justification.

Questions

1. Where do you draw the line? How small can the boats get and still qualify for admiralty jurisdiction?

2. Does the court's holding seem consistent with its earlier ruling in *Executive Jet*?

Sisson v. Ruby, 497 U.S. 358 (1990)

JUSTICE MARSHALL delivered the opinion of the Court.

We must decide whether 28 U.S.C. Sec. 1333(1), which grants federal district courts jurisdiction over "[a]ny civil case of admiralty or maritime jurisdiction," confers federal jurisdiction over petitioner's limitation of liability suit brought in connection with a fire on his vessel. We hold that it does.

Everett Sisson was the owner of the *Ultorian*, a fifty-six-foot pleasure yacht. On September 24, 1985, while the *Ultorian* was docked at a marina on Lake Michigan, a navigable waterway, a fire erupted in the area of the vessel's

washer/dryer unit. The fire destroyed the *Ultorian* and damaged several neighboring vessels and the marina. In the wake of the fire, respondents filed claims against Sisson for over $275,000 for damages to the marina and the other vessels. Invoking the provision of the Limited Liability Act that limits the liability of an owner of a vessel for any damage done "without the privity or knowledge of such owner" to the value of the vessel and its freight, 46 U.S.C. Sec. 183(a) (1982 ed.), Sisson filed a petition for declaratory and injunctive relief in federal District Court to limit his liability to $800, the salvage value of the *Ultorian* after the fire. Sisson argued that the federal court had maritime jurisdiction over his limitation of liability action pursuant to Sec. 1333(1). The District Court disagreed, dismissing the petition for lack of subject-matter jurisdiction. In re. *Complaint of Sisson*, 663 F.Supp 858 (ND Ill. 1987). Sisson sought reconsideration on the ground that the Limited Liability Act independently conferred jurisdiction over the action. The District Court denied Sisson's motion, both on the merits and on the basis of Sisson's failure to raise the argument before the dismissal of the action. In re. *Complaint of Sisson*, 668 F.Supp. 1196 (ND Ill. 1987). The Court of Appeals for the Seventh Circuit affirmed, holding that neither Sec. 1333(1) nor the Limited Liability Act conferred jurisdiction. In re. *Complaint of Sisson*, 867 F.2d 341 (1989). We granted certiorari, 110 S.Ct. 863 (1990), and now reverse.

Until recently, Sec. 1333(1) jurisdiction over tort actions was determined largely by the application of a "locality" test. As this Court stated the test in *The Plymouth*, 3 Wall. 20, 36, (1866): "Every species of tort, however occurring, and whether on board a vessel or not, if upon the high seas or navigable waters, is of admiralty cognizance." See also *Executive Jet Aviation, Inc. v. City of Cleveland*, 409 U.S. 249, 253–54 (1972) (describing the locality test). *Executive Jet* marked this Court's first clear departure from the strict locality test. There, a jet aircraft struck a flock of sea gulls while taking off, lost power, and crashed into the navigable waters of Lake Erie, which lay just past the end of the runway. The owner of the aircraft sued the City of Cleveland, the owner of the airport, in federal court, arguing that Sec. 1333(1) conferred federal jurisdiction over the action. Noting "serious difficulties with the locality test," we refused to enter into a debate over whether the tort occurred where the plane had crashed and been destroyed (the navigable waters of Lake Erie) or where it had struck the sea gulls (over land). Rather, we held that jurisdiction was lacking because "the wrong [did not] bear a significant relationship to traditional maritime activity."

Although our holding in *Executive Jet* was limited by its terms to cases involving aviation torts, that case's "thorough discussion of the theoretical and practical problems inherent in broadly applying the traditional locality rule . . . prompted several courts and commentators to construe *Executive Jet* as applying to determinations of federal "admiralty jurisdiction outside the context of aviation torts." *Foremost Ins. Co. v. Richardson*, 457 U.S. 668 (1982). In *Foremost*, we approved this broader interpretation of *Executive Jet*. *Foremost* involved a collision, on what we assumed to be navigable waters, between an eighteen-foot pleasure boat and a sixteen-foot recreational fishing boat. Neither vessel had ever been engaged in any commercial maritime activity.

This case involves a fire that began on a non-commercial vessel at a marina located on a navigable waterway. Certainly, such a fire has a potentially disruptive impact on maritime commerce, as it can spread to nearby commercial vessels or make the marina inaccessible to such vessels. Indeed, fire is one of the most significant hazards facing commercial vessels.

Respondents' only argument to the contrary is that the potential effect on maritime commerce in this case was minimal because no commercial vessels happened to be docked at the marina when the fire occurred. This argument misunderstands the nature of our inquiry.

We determine the potential impact of a given type of incident by examining its general character. The jurisdictional inquiry does not turn on the *actual* effects on maritime commerce of the fire on Sisson's vessel; nor does it turn on the particular facts of the incident in this case, such as the source of the fire or the specific location of the yacht at the marina, that may have rendered the fire on the *Ultorian* more or less likely to disrupt commercial activity. Rather, a court must assess the general features of the type of incident involved to determine whether such an incident is likely to disrupt commercial activity. Here, the general features—a fire on a vessel docked at a marina on navigable waters—plainly satisfy the requirement of potential disruption to commercial maritime activity.

Our approach here comports with the way in which we characterize the potential disruption of the types of incidents involved in *Executive Jet* and *Foremost*. The first aspect of the jurisdictional test was satisfied in *Executive Jet* because "an aircraft sinking in the water could create a hazard for the navigation of commercial vessels in the vicinity." Likewise, in *Foremost* the Court noted "the potential[ly] disruptive impact of a collision between boats on navigable waters." Indeed, we supported our finding of potential disruption there with a description of the likely effects of a collision at the mouth of the St. Lawrence Seaway, an area heavily traveled by commercial vessels, even though the place where the collision actually had occurred apparently was "seldom, if ever, used for commercial traffic." Our cases thus lead us to eschew the fact-specific jurisdictional inquiry urged on us by respondents.

We now turn to the second half of the *Foremost* test, under which the party seeking to invoke maritime jurisdiction must show a substantial relationship between the activity giving rise to the incident and traditional maritime activity. As a first step, we must define the relevant activity in this case. Our cases have made clear that the relevant "activity" is defined not by the particular circumstances of the incident, but by the general conduct from which the incident arose. In *Executive Jet*, for example, the relevant activity was not a plane sinking in Lake Erie, but air travel generally. This focus on the general character of the activity is, indeed, suggested by the nature of the jurisdictional inquiry. Were courts required to focus more particularly on the causes of the harm, they would have to decide to some extent the merits of the causation issue to answer the legally and analytically antecedent jurisdictional question. Thus, in this case, we need not ascertain the precise cause of the fire to determine what "activity" Sisson was engaged in; rather, the relevant activity was the storage and maintenance of a vessel at a marina on navigable waters.

Our final inquiry, then, is whether the storage and maintenance of a boat on a marina on navigable waters has a substantial relationship to a "traditional maritime activity" within the meaning of *Executive Jet* and *Foremost*. Respondents would have told us that, at least in the context of noncommercial activity, only navigation can be characterized as substantially related to traditional maritime activity. We decline to do so. In *Foremost*, we identified navigation as an example, rather than as the sole instance, of conduct that is substantially related to traditional maritime activity. Indeed, had we intended to suggest that navigation is the only activity that is sufficient to confer jurisdiction, we could have stated the jurisdictional test much more clearly and economically by stating that maritime jurisdiction over torts is limited to torts in which the vessels are in "navigation." Moreover, a narrow focus on navigation would not serve the federal policies that underlie our jurisdictional test. The fundamental interest giving rise to maritime jurisdiction is "the protection of maritime commerce," and we have said that that interest cannot be fully vindicated unless "*all* operators of vessels on navigable waters are subject to uniform rules of conduct." The need for uniform rules of maritime conduct and

liability is not limited to navigation, but extends at least to any other activities traditionally undertaken by vessels, commercial or noncommercial.

Clearly, the storage and maintenance of a vessel at a marina on navigable waters is substantially related to "traditional maritime activity" given the broad perspective demanded by the second aspect of the test. Docking a vessel at a marina on a navigable waterway is a common, if not indispensable, maritime activity. At such a marina, vessels are stored for an extended period, docked to obtain fuel or supplies, and moved into and out of navigation. Indeed, most maritime voyages begin and end with the docking of the craft at a marina. We therefore conclude that, just as navigation, storing and maintaining a vessel at a marina on a navigable waterway is substantially related to traditional maritime activity.

For the foregoing reasons, we conclude that the District Court has jurisdiction over Sisson's limitation claim pursuant to Sec. 1333(1). Neither the District Court nor the Court of Appeals have addressed the merits of that claim, and we therefore intimate no view on that matter. The judgment of the Court of Appeals is reversed, and the case is remanded for further proceedings consistent with this opinion.

So ordered.

Questions

1. Explain how Justice Marshall used his two-part test from *Foremost* to find admiralty jurisdiction in this case.

2. Why did the owner of the *Ultorian* seek protection in the federal district court?

Delta Country Ventures, Inc. v. Magana, 986 F.2d 1260 (9th Cir. 1993)

FERGUSON, CIRCUIT JUDGE

Delta Country Ventures, Inc. ("Delta") appeals the district court's order dismissing its complaints in admiralty for lack of subject matter jurisdiction. We affirm.

I.

This case arises from an accident which occurred on September 3, 1989, when defendant-appellee Don Magana dove from the deck of Delta's houseboat and struck something under water, sustaining serious injuries. Delta had leased the houseboat to John Guerry for recreational use. Fifteen-year-old Magana was on the boat as a guest. At the time of the incident, the boat was anchored in the Snodgrass Slough, at the convergence of the Sacramento and Mokelumne rivers. After diving and injuring himself, Magana was pulled from the water and airlifted by a Highway Patrol helicopter to a trauma center in Sacramento. He was diagnosed as quadriplegic.

In July 1990, Delta filed a complaint in district court alleging admiralty jurisdiction and seeking exoneration or limitation of liability under 46 U.S.C. App. Sec. 183 et seq. In August 1990, Magana filed a personal injury action in state court against Delta, the Guerrys, and various public entities. In October 1990, Magana moved to dismiss Delta's complaint on the ground that the federal court lacked subject matter jurisdiction. The district court found that Delta had not met its burden of showing that the activities resulting in Magana's injuries bore a substantial relationship to traditional maritime activities, and granted the motion. Delta appeals.

II.

The district court's judgment was final, and we have jurisdiction under 28 U.S.C. Sec. 1291.

The existence of subject matter jurisdiction is a question of law which we review de novo. We must accept the district court's factual findings on jurisdictional issues unless clearly erroneous.

District courts have original and exclusive jurisdiction over any civil case of admiralty or maritime jurisdiction pursuant to 28 U.S.C. Sec. 1333(1). Admiralty jurisdiction is appropriate "when a 'potential hazard to maritime commerce arises out of activity that bears a substantial relationship to traditional maritime activity.'" *Sisson v. Ruby*, 497 U.S. 358 (1990) (quoting *Foremost Ins. Co. v. Richardson*, 457 U.S. 668 (1982)). Here, Delta seeks to invoke admiralty jurisdiction in order to limit its liability to its interest in the houseboat under 46 U.S.C. App. Sec. 183.

In *Sisson*, the Supreme Court stated that "protecting commercial shipping is at the heart of admiralty jurisdiction" and "'[n]ot every accident in navigable waters that might disrupt maritime commerce will support federal admiralty jurisdiction.'" The Court then set forth a two-step inquiry for determining whether jurisdiction exists: First, we "assess the general features of the type of incident involved to determine whether such an incident is likely to disrupt commercial activity." Second, we ask whether the party seeking to invoke maritime jurisdiction has shown "a substantial relationship between the activity giving rise to the incident and traditional maritime activity."

Here, the district court found that the "incident," a diving accident on navigable waters requiring emergency rescue operations, was the type likely to disrupt commercial activity. The court dismissed the complaint, however, because it found no substantial relationship between the activity giving rise to the incident, in this case diving from the boat, and traditional maritime activity.

Delta contends that the district court erred in its definition of the "activity giving rise to the incident." Delta contends that the relevant "activity" is not diving, but rather the mooring or anchoring of the boat in tidal waters and the examination of tidal changes. We find this argument unpersuasive in light of the Supreme Court's reasoning in *Sisson*:

Our cases have made clear that the relevant "activity" is defined not by the particular circumstances of the incident, but by the general conduct from which the incident arose.... This focus on the general character of the activity is, indeed, suggested by the nature of the jurisdictional inquiry. Were the courts required to focus more particularly on the causes of the harm, they would have to decide to some extent the merits of the causation issue to answer the legally and analytically antecedent jurisdictional question. Thus . . . we need not ascertain the precise cause of [the incident] to determine what "activity" [the party] [was] engaged in. Id.

To define the relevant "activity" as mooring of the boat and ascertainment of tidal changes would be to delve into the merits of the causation issue. We know with certainty that Magana was engaging in the activity of diving when he was injured. It is inappropriate for us to speculate on what ultimately caused his injury. Consistent with *Sisson*, we believe that aquatic recreation off a pleasure boat was the activity that gave rise to the incident here.

We conclude that Delta has not shown a substantial relationship between aquatic recreation off a pleasure boat and traditional maritime activity. Prior to *Sisson* we, like most other circuits, had established a four-part test to determine whether a substantial relationship to traditional maritime activity existed:

(1) traditional concepts of the role of admiralty law;

(2) the function and role of the parties;

(3) the types of vehicles and instrumentalities involved; and

(4) the causation and nature of the injury suffered.

Every circuit to have considered the issue has ruled the four-part test survives *Sisson*. We join our fellow circuits in holding that the four-part test is still valid, except for the fourth factor's causation inquiry, which is precluded by *Sisson*. Applying the four-factor test as modified, we conclude that the traditional concepts of admiralty law do not support the assertion of admiralty jurisdiction over the claim of a houseboat guest who sustains personal injuries as a result of his diving off the boat. We conclude that a substantial relationship with traditional maritime activity is lacking.

Delta makes a series of circular arguments in an attempt to establish that the relevant activity here was navigation, which is undoubtedly traditional maritime activity. We find the reasoning of *Foster v. Peddicord*, 826 F.2d 1837 (4th Cir. 1987), *cert. denied*, 484 U.S. 1027 (1988), to be persuasive. *Foster* also involved a guest injured after diving off a pleasure boat. The Fourth Circuit rejected an argument similar to Delta's:

The injury in this case occurred when [the plaintiff] dove from the boat and hit bottom in shallow water. To conclude that the location where [the defendant] parked his boat constituted "navigational error" and that this in turn was the cause of the injury would reflect neither a reasonable definition of navigation nor common sense. 826 F.2d at 1876

Delta goes a step further, straining not just common sense but credulity, by arguing that a diver ascertaining the depth of water before diving is engaged in navigational activity. See *Smith v. Knowles*, 642 F.Supp. 1137, 1140 (D.Md. 1986). ("the defendant's estimate of the water's depth did not affect the navigation of the boat. The defendant might as well have been estimating the depth of a swimming pool").

We agree with the district court's determination that the activity giving rise to the incident in this case bears no substantial relationship to traditional maritime activity. The district court's order dismissing Delta's complaint for lack of subject matter jurisdiction is AFFIRMED.

KOZINSKI, CIRCUIT JUDGE, dissenting.

This is our first opportunity to define and limit the breadth of admiralty jurisdiction in the wake of *Sisson v. Ruby*, 497 U.S. 358 (1990). It's difficult to imagine a more tragic setting in which to do so. Don Magana, a fifteen-year-old boy, was permanently paralyzed in an accident he suffered while engaged in the kind of carefree activity enjoyed by many teenagers; Delta Country, the owner of the boat on which he was injured, then invoked federal admiralty jurisdiction to deny him, through the Limitation of Liability Act, the full measure of his damages. But sad as this case may be, we must not forget that the test we adopt for the exercise of admiralty jurisdiction applies not just to Limitation of Liability Act cases but to all admiralty cases in the Ninth Circuit. I fear the compelling facts of this case have led my colleagues to formulate far too narrow a definition of our admiralty jurisdiction.

I.

Although the Limitation of Liability Act gives a vessel owner a cause of action to limit his liability to the value of his boat, 46 App. U.S.C. Sec. 183, it most likely does not provide an independent basis for federal jurisdiction. Rather, to invoke the Act in federal court a shipowner's claim must present a "civil case of admiralty or maritime jurisdiction." 28 U.S.C. Sec. 1333(1). According to the Supreme Court's most recent interpretation of section 1333, admiralty jurisdiction is proper "when a 'potential hazard to maritime commerce arises out of activity that bears a substantial relationship to traditional maritime activity.' " *Sisson v. Ruby*, (quoting *Foremost Ins. Co. v. Richardson* (1982)). To determine whether this requirement is satisfied in a particular case, federal courts must conduct two separate inquiries.

A. First we must "determine the potential impact of a given type of incident by examining its general character. The jurisdictional inquiry does not turn on the *actual* effects on maritime commerce. . . . Rather, a court must assess the general features of the type of incident involved to determine whether such an incident is likely to disrupt commercial activity." While the majority does not discuss this point, there can be no doubt that Delta fulfilled the first *Sisson* requirement. The emergency response to Magana's accident required the assistance of a neighboring yacht, the fire department, and a rescue helicopter. A diving accident such as this one, which occurred at the intersection of the Sacramento and Mokelumne rivers—both navigable waterways—posed an undeniable potential impediment to the passage of other boats engaged in maritime commerce.

B. The second *Sisson* inquiry calls for the "party seeking to invoke maritime jurisdiction [to] show a substantial relationship between the activity giving rise to the incident and traditional maritime activity." The majority defines the relevant activity as "aquatic recreation off a pleasure boat," rather than more generally as the anchoring and mooring of the boat at the time of the accident. It is here that my colleagues and I part company. I recognize that disputes about the appropriate level of generality always carry with them a certain degree of arbitrariness. But here we are not cast adrift without standards to inform our decision; *Sisson* provides compelling guidance in resolving this question.

Sisson involved a fire that erupted aboard the pleasure vessel *Ultorian* while she was docked at a marina on Lake Michigan. In deciding whether the relevant activity was a fire in the washer/dryer of a fifty-six-foot pleasure yacht or, alternatively, the docking and maintenance of a boat, the Court said:

[T]he relevant "activity" is defined not by the particular circumstances of the incident, but by the general conduct from which the incident arose. . . . Were courts required to focus more particularly on the causes of the harm, they would have to decide to some extent the merits of the causation issue to answer the legally and analytically antecedent jurisdictional question. 497 U.S. at 364

The majority also quotes this passage, but goes on to define the relevant activity in the most fact-specific way possible—omitting from the description only that the injured victim's initials were D. M. But by focusing on the minutiae of the incident, rather than the "general conduct from which the incident arose," the majority ignores what the Court actually did in *Sisson*: It defined the relevant activity as the "storage and maintenance of a vessel at a marina on navigable waters," not as doing the laundry or as installing and maintaining household appliances.

In addition, the Court cited with approval *Executive Jet Aviation, Inc. v. Cleveland*, 409 U.S. 249 (1972), where "the relevant activity was not a plane sinking in Lake Erie, but air travel generally." 110 S.Ct. at 2897. *Sisson* also explained that in *Foremost Ins. Co. v. Richardson*, which involved a freak collision between a ski boat and a bass boat on a river, the "relevant activity [was] navigation of vessels generally."

What we must examine under the second prong of *Sisson* is whether the injury took place on or about a vessel engaged in traditional maritime activity. The injury in *Executive Jet* did not, so admiralty jurisdiction did not attach; the injuries in *Foremost* and *Sisson* did, so admiralty jurisdiction attached. This does not, as the majority suggests, reinstate the maritime locality test. Many things that take place on or about vessels wouldn't support admiralty jurisdiction. See, e.g., *Penton v. Pomono Constr. Co., Inc.*, 976 F.2d 636 (11th Cir. 1992) (construction worker injured while building a jetty by operating a crane on a barge); *David Wright Charter Serv. v. Wright*, 925 F.2d 783, 784 (4th Cir. 1991) (explosion of boat stored in shed seventy-five feet away from water); *Myhran v. Johns-Mansville Corp.*, 741 F.2d 1119 (9th Cir. 1984) (pipe fitter's exposure to asbestos while repairing vessel); *Ozzello v. Peterson Builders, Inc.*, 743 F.Supp. 1302 (E.D.Wis. 1990) (construction employee injured by hose while working on deck).

It's possible, of course, to define any set of circumstances in a way that will appear to have little or no relationship to traditional maritime activity. Here, a dive off a boat anchored on a navigable waterway becomes "aquatic recreation off a pleasure boat"—nomenclature so stilted it could appear only in a judicial opinion. A jet-skier injured on a river might likewise be said to be involved in "aquatic recreation on a pleasure craft." But see *Wahlstrom v. Kawasaki Heavy Indus., Ltd.*, 800 F.Supp. 1061 (D.Conn. 1992). Negligence by emergency personnel in treating an injured riverboat pilot aboard the vessel could be recast

as "medical malpractice." But see *Antoine v. Zapata Haynie Corp.*, 777 F.Supp. 1360 (E.D.Tex. 1991). A passenger hurt while boarding a cruise ship could just as easily be described as "falling down the stairs." But see *Jimenez v. Peninsular & Oriental Steam Navig. Co.*, 974 F.2d 221 (1st Cir. 1992); see also *Price v. Price*, 929 F.2d 131 (4th Cir. 1991). A person injured while scuba diving off a boat might be deemed to be engaged only in "recreational underwater sports." But see *Sinclair v. Soniform, Inc.*, 935 F.2d 599 (3rd Cir. 1991). And a wiring defect in a space heater which causes a fire aboard a moored pleasure yacht might be described as an "electrical malfunction." But see *Unigard Security Ins. Co. v. Lakewood Eng'g & Mfg. Corp.*, 982 F.2d 363 (9th Cir. 1992). Had each of these post-*Sisson* cases been as creative in the use of language as the majority is here, they could all have concluded that there was no admiralty jurisdiction.

C. Even were I to accept my colleagues' formulation of the relevant activity, none of the adjectives they employ to distract from the essentially maritime aspect of what happened here makes a bit of difference. Thus, the fact that the vessel here is a "pleasure boat" makes it no less susceptible to maritime jurisdiction than any other vessel. *Sisson* itself involved a yacht docked in a marina—a pleasure craft among pleasure crafts; and *Foremost* involved a collision between two recreational boats. For purposes of admiralty jurisdiction a houseboat is no less a boat than an aircraft carrier: "The need for uniform rules of maritime conduct and liability . . . extends . . . to any other activities traditionally undertaken by vessels, *commercial or noncommercial.*" *Sisson*, 497 U.S. at 367. Nor does the fact that Magana was engaged in "aquatic recreation" matter. Passengers on vessels always have purposes unrelated to the maritime aspects of the voyage: They want to take a cruise, go fishing, or maybe just get from here to there. Few passengers, if any at all, board a boat for the purpose of engaging in maritime activities. Unless we're willing to say that injuries suffered by passengers on vessels fall outside the ambit of maritime jurisdiction—something we're not free to do under controlling case law—I don't see how we can define what happened here in terms so divorced from the maritime aspects of the incident.

The only case the majority can muster in support of its dubious position is *Foster v. Peddicord*, 826 F.2d 1370 (4th Cir. 1987), *cert. denied*, 404 U.S. 1027 (1988), which predates *Sisson* and must be considered overruled to the extent it's inconsistent therewith. No Fourth Circuit case cites or discusses the vitality of *Foster* after *Sisson*. The only case to do so is *In re. Bird*, 794 F.Supp. 575 (D.S.C. 1992), a Limitation of Liability Act case which involved a drunken partygoer aboard a pleasure yacht who knocked another passenger overboard. While the *Bird* court recognizing that *Foster* was "almost identical, factually," 794 F.Supp. at 578, *Bird* nonetheless concluded that maritime jurisdiction attached after *Sisson*. It thus appears that we are paying more heed to *Foster* than are the courts in the Fourth Circuit.

While the majority embroiders the nexus inquiry with qualifiers that make the activity *sound* less maritime, we're still confronted with the fact that Magana was injured when he took a dive from the side of a boat into shallow water. Going into the water off a vessel has a relationship to even the most traditional definition of maritime activity. The location of the vessel—how far from shore, how close to rocks or shoals—also has very much to do with maritime activity. And the fact that the boat was anchored in the middle of a navigable river is significant, as vessels drop anchor to protect themselves from wind, storms, and currents; anchoring also allows repairs and provisioning without the necessity of docking. All of this suggests that the activity here has no less a relationship to traditional maritime activity than the washer/dryer fire in *Sisson*. It's only through verbal squinting that the majority manages to reach the opposite conclusion.

II.

The Limitation of Liability Act is an anachronism, a holdover from the days when encouraging commerce by sea was considered more important than providing full redress to victims of maritime accidents. As I have said before, such a law no longer makes sense. See *Esta Later Charters, Inc. v. Ignacio*, 875 F.2d 234, 235 and n. 1 (9th Cir. 1989). One of the many unfortunate consequences of the Limitation of Liability Act is that it leads courts to contort the law to avoid unjust results: "Misshapen from the start, the subject of later incrustations, arthritic with age, the Limitation Act has 'provided the setting for judicial lawmaking seldom equalled.'"

Although Congress has acknowledged our suggestion that the Limitation of Liability Act be repealed, see S. Rep. No. 94, 101st Cong., 1st Sess. at 4 (1989) (citing *Esta Later*), the statute remains on the books, a sad reminder of the power of legislative inertia. Until Congress sees fit to decommission the Act, we're bound to apply it. Incongruous as we may find its outmoded assumptions, we will do more harm than good by gerrymandering our admiralty jurisdiction in an effort to avoid the statute's plain import. Reluctantly, I dissent.

Questions

1. Do you suspect, as the dissent argues, that the majority was swayed by the harsh result that would have resulted from a finding of admiralty jurisdiction?

2. Is there any justification left for the Limitation of Liability Act?

McDermott International v. Wilander, 498 U.S. 112 (1991)

JUSTICE O'CONNOR delivered the opinion of the Court.

The question in this case is whether one must aid in the navigation of a vessel in order to qualify as a "seaman" under the Jones Act, 46 U.S.C. App. Sec. 688.

I.

Jon Wilander worked for McDermott International as a paint foreman. His duties consisted primarily of supervising the sandblasting and painting of various fixtures and piping located on oil-drilling platforms in the Persian Gulf. On July 4, 1983, Wilander was inspecting a pipe on one such platform when a bolt serving as a plug in the pipe blew out under pressure, striking Wilander in the head. At the time, Wilander was assigned to the American-flag vessel M/V *Gates Tide*, a "paint boat" chartered to McDermott that contained equipment used in sandblasting and painting the platforms.

Wilander sued McDermott in the United States District Court for the Western District of Louisiana, seeking recovery under the Jones Act for McDermott's negligence related to the accident. McDermott moved for summary judgment, alleging that, as a matter of law, Wilander was not a "seaman" under the Jones Act, and therefore not entitled to recovery. The District Court denied the motion. In a bifurcated trial, the jury first determined Wilander's status as a seaman. By special interrogatory, the jury found that Wilander was either permanently assigned to, or performed a substantial amount of work aboard, the *Gates Tide*, and that the performance of his duties contributed to the function of the *Gates Tide* or to the accomplishment of its mission, thereby satisfying the test for seaman status established in *Offshore Co. v. Robison*, 266 F.2d 769 (5 Cir. 1959). The District Court denied McDermott's motion for judgment based on the jury findings.

The case then proceeded to trial on the issues of liability and damages. The jury found that McDermott's negligence was the primary cause of Wilander's injuries, but that Wilander had been 25 percent contributorily negligent. The jury awarded Wilander $337,500. The District Court denied McDermott's motion for judg-

ment notwithstanding the verdict, and both parties appealed.

The United States Court of Appeals for the Fifth Circuit affirmed the determination of seaman status, finding sufficient evidence to support the jury's finding under the *Robison* test. 887 F.2d 88, 90 (1989). McDermott asked the court to reject the *Robison* requirement that a seaman "contribut[e] to the function of the vessel or to the accomplishment of its mission," in favor of the more stringent requirement of *Johnson v. John F. Beasley Construction Co.*, 742 F.2d 1054 (7 Cir. 1984). In that case, the Court of Appeals for the Seventh Circuit—relying on cases from this Court requiring that a seaman aid in the navigation of a vessel—held that seaman status under the Jones Act may be conferred only on employees who make "a significant contribution to the maintenance, operation, or welfare of the *transportation* function of the vessel." Id. 742 F.2d at 1063 (emphasis added).

The Fifth Circuit here concluded that Wilander would not meet the requirements of the *Johnson* test, but reaffirmed the rule in *Robison* and held that Wilander was a "seaman" under the Jones Act. We granted certiorari to resolve the conflict between the *Robison* and *Johnson* tests on the issue of the transportation/navigation function requirement, and now affirm.

II.

A.

In 1903, in *The Osceola*, 189 U.S. 158, this Court summarized the state of seaman's remedies under general maritime law. Writing for the Court, Justice Brown reviewed the leading English and American authorities and declared the law settled on several propositions:

1. That the vessel and her owners are liable, in case a seaman falls sick, or is wounded, in the service of the ship, to the extent of his maintenance and cure, and to his wages, at least so long as the voyage is continued.

2. That the vessel and her owner are, both by En-

glish and American law, liable to an indemnity for injuries received by seamen in consequence of the unseaworthiness of the ship....

3. That all the members of the crew ... are, as between themselves, fellow servants, and hence seamen cannot recover for injuries sustained through the negligence of another member of the crew beyond the expense of their maintenance and cure.

4. That the seaman is not allowed to recover an indemnity for the negligence of the master, or any member of the crew....

The Osceola affirmed a seaman's general maritime right to maintenance and cure, wages, and to recover for unseaworthiness, but excluded seamen from the general maritime negligence remedy.

Congress twice attempted to overrule *The Osceola* and create a negligence action for seamen. The Merchant Marine Act of 1915, 38 Stat. 1164, dealt with proposition 3 of *The Osceola*, the fellow servant doctrine. Section 20 of the 1915 Act provided: [t]hat in any suit to recover damages for any injury sustained on board vessel or in its service seamen having command shall not be held to be fellow-servants with those under their authority." The change was ineffective. Petitioner in *Chelentis v. Luckenbach S.S. Co.*, 247 U.S. 372 (1918), a fireman on board the steamship *J. L. Luckenbach* attempted to recover from the ship's owner for injuries resulting from the alleged negligence of a superior officer. The Court explained that the 1915 Act was "irrelevant." The Act successfully established that the superior officer was not Chelentis's fellow servant, but Congress had overlooked *The Osceola*'s fourth proposition. The superior officer was no longer a fellow servant, but he was still a member of the crew. Under proposition four, there was no recovery for negligence.

Congress tried a different tack in 1920. It passed the Jones Act, which provides a cause of action in negligence for "any seaman" injured "in the course of his employment." 46 U.S.C. Sec. 688. The Act thereby removes the bar to negligence articulated in *The Osceola*.

The Jones Act does not define "seaman." Neither does *The Osceola*; it simply uses the term as had other admiralty courts. We assume that the Jones Act uses "seaman" in the same way. For one thing, the Jones Act provides what *The Osceola* precludes. "The only purpose of the Jones Act was to remove the bar created by *The Osceola*, so that seamen would have the same rights to recover for negligence as other tort victims." G. Gilmore and C. Black, *The Law of Admiralty*, 328–29 (2d ed., 1975). The Jones Act, responding directly to *The Osceola*, adopts without further elaboration the term used in *The Osceola*. Moreover, "seaman" is a maritime term of art. In the absence of contrary indication, we assume that when a statute uses such a term, Congress intended it to have its established meaning. Our first task, therefore, is to determine who was a seaman under the general maritime law when Congress passed the Jones Act.

B.

Since the first Judiciary Act, federal courts have determined who is eligible for various seamen's benefits under general maritime law. Prior to the Jones Act, these benefits included the tort remedies outlined in *The Osceola* and a lien against the ship for wages. Certain early cases limited seaman status to those who aided in the navigation of the ship. The narrow rule was that a seaman—sometimes referred to as a mariner—must actually navigate: "[T]he persons engaged on board of her must have been possessed of some skill in navigation. They must have been able to 'hand, reef, and steer,' the ordinary test of seamanship." *The Canton*, 5 F. Cas. 29, 30 (No. 2,388) (D.Mass. 1858).

Notwithstanding the aid in navigation doctrine, federal courts throughout the last century consistently awarded seamen's benefits to those whose work on board ship did not direct the vessel. Firemen, engineers, carpenters, and cooks all were considered seamen.

Some courts attempted to classify these seamen under a broad conception of aid in navigation that included those who aided in navigation indirectly by supporting those responsible for moving the vessel: "[T]he services rendered must be necessary, or, at least, contribute to the preservation of the vessel, or of those whose labor and skills are employed to navigate her." *Trainor v. The Superior*, 24 F. Cas. 130, 131 (No. 14,136) (ED Pa. 1834). This fiction worked for cooks and carpenters—who fed those who navigated and kept the ship in repair—but what of a cooper whose job it was to make barrels to aid in whaling? As early as 1832, Justice Story, sitting on circuit, held that "[a] 'cooper' is a seaman in contemplation of law, although he has peculiar duties on board of the ship." *United States v. Thompson*, 28 F. Cas. 102 (No. 16,492) (CCD Mass.). Justice Story made no reference to navigation in declaring it established that "[a] cook and steward are seamen in the sense of the maritime law, although they have peculiar duties assigned them. So a pilot, a surgeon, a ship carpenter, and a boatswain are deemed seamen, entitled to sue in the admiralty."

By the middle of the nineteenth century, the leading admiralty treatise noted the wide variety of those eligible for seamen's benefits: "Masters, mates, sailors, surveyors, carpenters, coopers, stewards, cooks, cabin boys, kitchen boys, engineers, pilots, firemen, deck hands, waiters,—women as well as men,—are mariners." E. Benedict, *The American Admiralty* Sec. 278, p. 159 (1850). Benedict concluded that American admiralty courts did not require that seamen have a connection to navigation. "The term mariner includes all persons employed on board ships and vessels during the voyage to assist in their navigation and preservation, *or to promote the purposes of the voyage*" (emphasis added). Moreover, Benedict explained, this was the better rule; admiralty courts throughout the world had long recognized that seamen's benefits were properly extended to all those who

worked on board vessels in furtherance of the myriad purposes for which ships set to sea:

It is universally conceded that the general principles of law must be applied to new kinds of property, as they spring into existence in the progress of society, according to their nature and incidents, and the common sense of the community. In the early periods of maritime commerce, when the oar was the great agent of propulsion, vessels were entirely unlike those of modern times—and each nation and period has had its peculiar agents of commerce and navigation adapted to its own wants and its own waters, and the names and descriptions of ships and vessels are without number. Under the class of mariners in the armed ship are embraced the officers and privates of a little army. In the whale ship, the sealing vessel—the cod fishing and herring fishing vessel—the lumber vessel—the freighting vessel—the passenger vessel—there are other functions besides these of mere navigation, and they are performed by men who know nothing of seamanship—and in the great invention of modern times, the steamboat, an entirely new set of operatives are employed, yet at all times and in all countries, all the persons who have been necessarily or properly employed in a vessel as co-laborers to the great purpose of the voyage, have, by the law, been clothed with the legal rights of mariners—no matter what might be their sex, character, station or profession. Id., Sec. 241, pp. 133–34

By the late nineteenth and early twentieth centuries, federal courts abandoned the navigation test altogether, including in the class of seamen those who worked on board and maintained allegiance to the ship, but who performed more specialized functions having no relation to navigation. The crucial element in these cases was something akin to Benedict's "great purpose of the voyage." Thus, in holding that a fisherman, a chambermaid, and a waiter were all entitled to seamen's benefits, then-Judge Brown, later the author of *The Osceola*, eschewed reference to navigation: "[A]ll hands employed upon a vessel, except the master, are entitled to a [seaman's lien for wages] if their services are in furtherance of the main object of the enterprise in which she is engaged." *The*

Minna, 11 Fed. 759, 760 (ED Mich. 1882). Judge Learned Hand rejected a navigation test explicitly in awarding seamen's benefits to a bartender: "As I can see in principle no reason why there should be an artificial limitation of rights to those engaged in the navigation of the ship, to the exclusion of others who equally further the purposes of her voyage, . . . I shall decide that the libelant has a lien for his wages as bartender."

We believe it settled at the time of *The Osceola* and the passage of the Jones Act that general maritime law did not require that a seaman aid in navigation. It was only necessary that a person be employed on board a vessel in furtherance of its purpose. We conclude therefore that, at the time of its passage, the Jones Act established no requirement that a seaman aid in navigation. Our voyage is not over, however.

· · ·

IV.

We think the time has come to jettison the aid in navigation language. That language, which had long been rejected by admiralty courts under general maritime law, and by this Court in *Warner*, a Jones Act case, slipped back in through an interpretation of the Longshoremen and Harbor Workers' Compensation Act at a time when the LHWCA had nothing to do with the Jones Act.

We now realize that the LHWCA is one of a pair of mutually exclusive remedial statutes that distinguish between land-based and sea-based maritime employees. The LHWCA restricted the definition of "seaman" in the Jones Act only to the extent that "seaman" had been taken to include land-based employees. There is no indication in the Jones Act, the LHWCA, or elsewhere that Congress has excluded from Jones Act remedies those traditional seamen who owe allegiance to a vessel at sea, but who do not aid in navigation.

We believe the better rule is to define "master or member of a crew" under the LHWCA, and therefore "seaman" under the Jones Act,

solely in terms of the employees' connection to a vessel in navigation. This rule best explains our case law, and is consistent with the pre–Jones Act interpretation of "seaman" and Congress's land-based/sea-based distinction. All who work at sea in the service of a ship face those particular perils to which the protection of maritime law, statutory as well as decisional, is directed. It is not the employee's particular job that is determinative, but the employee's connection to a vessel.

The key to seaman status is employment-related connection to a vessel in navigation. We are not called upon here to define this connection in all details, but we hold that a necessary element of the connection is that a seaman perform the work of a vessel. In this regard, we believe the requirement that an employee's duties must "contribut[e] to the function of the vessel or to the accomplishment of its mission" captures well an important requirement of seaman status. It is not necessary that a seaman aid in navigation or contribute to the transportation of the vessel, but a seaman must be doing the ship's work.

V.

Jon Wilander was injured while assigned to the *Gates Tide* as a paint foreman. He did not aid in the navigation or transportation of the vessel. The jury found, however, that Wilander contributed to the more general function or mission of the *Gates Tide*, and subsequently found that he was a "seaman" under the Jones Act. McDermott argues that the question should not have been given to the jury. The company contends that, as a matter of law, Wilander is not entitled to Jones Act protection because he did not aid in navigation by furthering the transportation of the *Gates Tide*.

It is for the court to define the statutory standard. "Member of a crew" and "seaman" are statutory terms; their interpretation is a question of law. The jury finds the facts and, in these cases, applies the legal standard, but the court must not abdicate its duty to determine if there is a reasonable basis to support the jury's conclusion. If reasonable persons, applying the proper legal standard, could differ as to whether the employee was a "member of a crew," it is a question for the jury.

The question presented here is narrow. We are not asked to determine if the jury could reasonably have found that Wilander had a sufficient connection to the *Gates Tide* to be a "seaman" under the Jones Act. We are not even asked whether the jury reasonably found that Wilander advanced the function or mission of the *Gates Tide*. We are asked only if Wilander should be precluded from seaman status because he did not perform transportation-related functions on board the *Gates Tide*. Our answer is no. Accordingly, the judgment of the Court of Appeals is affirmed.

Questions

1. Which test do you think made more sense—that of *Offshore v. Robison*, or *Johnson v. Beasley Construction*?

2. After this court's ruling, could a dance instructor aboard a cruise ship claim seamen status?

Mitchell v. Trawler Racer, Inc., 362 U.S. 539 (1960)

MR. JUSTICE STEWART delivered the opinion of the Court.

The petitioner was a member of the crew of the Boston fishing trawler *Racer*, owned and operated by the respondent. On April 1, 1957, the vessel returned to her home port from a ten-day voyage to the North Atlantic fishing grounds, loaded with a catch of fish and fish spawn. After working that morning with his fellow crew members in unloading the spawn, the petitioner changed his clothes and came on deck to go ashore. He made his way to the side of the vessel which abutted the dock, and in accord with recognized custom stepped onto the ship's rail in order to reach a ladder attached to the pier. He was injured when his foot slipped off the rail as he grasped the ladder.

To recover for his injuries he filed this action for damages in a complaint containing three counts: the first under the Jones Act, alleging negligence; the second alleging unseaworthiness; and the third for maintenance and cure. At the trial there was evidence to show that the ship's rail where the petitioner had lost his footing was covered for a distance of ten or twelve feet with slime and fish gurry, apparently remaining there from the earlier unloading operations.

The district judge instructed the jury that in order to allow recovery upon either the negligence or unseaworthiness count, they must find that the slime and gurry had been on the ship's rail for a period of time long enough for the respondent to have learned about it and to have removed it. Counsel for the petitioner requested that the trial judge distinguish between negligence and unseaworthiness in this respect, and specifically requested him to instruct the jury that notice was not a necessary element in proving liability based upon unseaworthiness of the vessel. This request was denied. The jury awarded the petitioner maintenance and cure, but found for the respondent shipowner on both the negligence and unseaworthiness counts.

An appeal was taken upon the sole ground that the district judge had been in error in instructing the jury that constructive notice was necessary to support liability for unseaworthiness. The Court of Appeals affirmed, holding that at least with respect to "an unseaworthy condition which arises only during the progress of the voyage," the shipowner's obligation "is merely to see that reasonable care is used under the circumstances . . . incident to the correcting of the newly arisen defect." 265 F. 2d 426, 432. Certiorari was granted to consider a question of maritime law upon which the Courts of Appeals have expressed differing views.

In its present posture this case thus presents the single issue whether with respect to so-called "transitory" unseaworthiness the shipowner's liability is limited by concepts of common-law negligence. There are here no problems, such as have recently engaged the Court's attention, with respect to the petitioner's status as a "seaman." The *Racer* was on active maritime operation, and the petitioner was a member of her crew.

The origin of a seaman's right to recover for injuries caused by an unseaworthy ship is far from clear. The earliest codifications of the law of the sea provided only the equivalent of maintenance and cure—medical treatment and wages to a mariner wounded or falling ill in the service of the ship. Markedly similar provisions granting relief of this nature are to be found in the Laws of Oleron, promulgated about 1150 A.D. by Eleanor, duchess of Guinenne; in the Laws of Wisbuy, published in the following century; in the Laws of the Hanse Towns, which appeared in 1597; and in the Marine Ordinances of Louis XIV, published in 1681.

For many years American courts regarded these ancient codes as establishing the limits of a shipowner's liability to a seaman injured in the service of his vessel. During this early period the maritime law was concerned with the concept of unseaworthiness only with reference to two situations quite unrelated to the right of a crew member to recover for personal injuries. The earliest mention of unseaworthiness in American judicial opinions appears in cases in which mariners were suing for their wages. They were required to prove the unseaworthiness of the vessel to excuse their desertion or misconduct which otherwise would result in a forfeiture of their right to wages. The other route through which the concept of unseaworthiness found its way into the maritime law was via the rules covering marine insurance and the carriage of goods by sea.

Not until the late nineteenth century did there develop in American admiralty courts the doctrine that seamen had a right to recover for personal injuries beyond maintenance and cure. During that period it became generally accepted that a shipowner was liable to a mariner injured in the service of a ship as a consequence of the owner's failure to exercise due diligence. The decisions of that era for the most part treated maritime injury cases on the same footing as cases involving the duty of a shoreside employer to exercise ordinary care to provide his employees with a reasonably safe place to work.

This was the historical background behind Mr. Justice Brown's much quoted second proposition in *The Osceola*, 189 U.S. 158, 175: "That the vessel and her owner are, both by English and American law, liable to an indemnity for injuries received by seamen in consequence of the unseaworthiness of the ship, or a failure to supply and keep in order the proper appliances appurtenant to the ship." In support of this proposition the Court's opinion noted that

[i]t will be observed in these cases that a departure has been made from the Continental codes in allowing an indemnity beyond the expense of maintenance and cure in cases arising from unseaworthiness. This departure originated in England in the Merchants' Shipping Act of 1876 . . . and in this country, in a general consensus of opinion among the Circuit and District Courts, that an exception should be made from the general principle before obtaining, in favor of seamen suffering injury through the unseaworthiness of the vessel. We are not disposed to disturb so wholesome a doctrine by any contrary decision of our own. 189 U.S., at 175

It is arguable that the import of the above-quoted second proposition in *The Osceola* was not to broaden the shipowner's liability, but, rather, to limit liability for negligence to those situations where his negligence resulted in the vessel's unseaworthiness. Support for such a view is to be found not only in the historic context in which *The Osceola* was decided, but in the discussion in the balance of the opinion, in the decision itself (in favor of the shipowner), and in the equation which the Court drew with the law of England, where the Merchant Shipping Act of 1876 imposed upon the owner only the duty to use "all reasonable means" to "insure the seaworthiness of the ship." This limited view of *The Osceola*'s pronouncement as to liability for unseaworthiness may be the basis for subsequent decisions of federal courts exonerating shipowners from responsibility for the negligence of their agents because that negligence had not rendered the vessel unseaworthy. In any event, with the passage of the Jones Act in 1920, 41 Stat. 1007, 46 U.S.C. Sec. 688, Congress effectively obliterated all distinctions between the kinds of negligence for which the shipowner is liable, as well as limitations imposed by the fellow-servant doctrine, by extending to seamen the remedies made available to railroad workers under the Federal Employers' Liability Act.

The first reference in this Court to the shipowner's obligation to furnish a seaworthy ship as explicitly unrelated to the standard of ordinary care in a personal injury case appears in *Carlisle Packing Co. v. Sandanger*, 259 U.S. 255. There it was said "we think the trial court might have told the jury that without regard to negligence the vessel was unseaworthy when she left the dock . . . and that if thus unseaworthy and one of the crew received damage as the direct result thereof, he was entitled to recover compensatory damages." This characterization of unseaworthiness as unrelated to negligence was probably not necessary to the decision in that case, where the respondent's injuries had clearly in fact been caused by failure to exercise ordinary care (putting gasoline in a can labeled "coal oil" and neglecting to provide the vessel with life preservers). Yet there is no reason to suppose that the Court's language was inadvertent.

During the two decades that followed the *Carlisle* decision there came to be a general acceptance of the view that *The Osceola* had enunciated a concept of absolute liability for unseaworthiness unrelated to principles of negligence law. Personal injury litigation based upon unseaworthiness was substantial. And the standard texts accepted that theory of liability without question. See Benedict, *The Law of American Admiralty* (6th ed., 1940), vol. I, sec.

83; Robinson, *Admiralty Law* (1939), p. 303 et seq. Perhaps the clearest expression appeared in Judge Augustus Hand's opinion in *The H. A. Scandrett*, 87 F.2d 708:

> In our opinion the libelant had a right of indemnity for injuries arising from an unseaworthy ship even though there was no means of anticipating trouble.
>
> The ship is not freed from liability by mere due diligence to render her seaworthy as may be the case under the Harter Act (46 U.S.C.A. Sections 190–95) where loss results from faults in navigation, but under the maritime law there is an absolute obligation to provide a seaworthy vessel and, in default thereof, liability follows for any injuries caused by breach of the obligation. 87 F.2d, at 711

In 1944 this Court decided *Mahnich v. Southern S.S. Co.*, 321 U.S. 96. While it is possible to take a narrow view of the precise holding in that case, the fact is that *Mahnich* stands as a landmark in the development of admiralty law. Chief Justice Stone's opinion in that case gave an unqualified stamp of solid authority to the view that *The Osceola* was correctly to be understood as holding that the duty to provide a seaworthy ship depends not at all upon the negligence of the shipowner or his agents. Moreover, the dissent in *Mahnich* accepted this reading of *The Osceola* and claimed no more than that the injury in *Mahnich* was not properly attributable to unseaworthiness.

In *Seas Shipping Co. v. Sieracki*, 328 U.S. 85, the court effectively scotched any doubts that might have lingered after *Mahnich* as to the nature of the shipowner's duty to provide a seaworthy vessel. The character of the duty, said the Court, is "absolute."

> It is essentially a species of liability without fault, analogous to her well-known instances in our law. Derived from and shaped to meet the hazards which performing the service imposes, the liability is neither limited by conceptions of negligence nor contractual in character. . . . It is a form of absolute duty owing to all within the range of its humanitarian policy.

From that day to this, the decisions of this Court have undeviatingly reflected an under-

standing that the owner's duty to furnish a seaworthy ship is absolute and completely
independent of this duty under the Jones Act
to exercise reasonable care.

There is no suggestion in any of the decisions
that the duty is less onerous with respect to an
unseaworthy condition arising after the vessel
leaves her home port, or that the duty is any
less with respect to an unseaworthy condition
which may be only temporary.

There is ample room for argument, in the
light of history, as to how the law of unseaworthiness should have or could have developed.
Such theories might be made to fill a volume of
logic. But, in view of the decisions in this Court
over the last fifteen years, we can find no room
for argument as to what the law is. What has
evolved is a complete divorcement of unseaworthiness liability from concepts of negligence. To hold otherwise now would be to erase
more than just a page of history.

What has been said is not to suggest that the
owner is obligated to furnish an accident-free
ship. The duty is absolute, but it is a duty only
to furnish a vessel and appurtenances reasonably fit for their intended use. The standard is
not perfection, but reasonable fitness; not a ship
that will weather every conceivable storm or
withstand every imaginable peril of the sea, but
a vessel reasonably suitable for her intended
service.

The judgment must be reversed, and the case
remanded to the District Court for a new trial
on the issue of unseaworthiness.

Reversed and remanded.

Questions

1. When can a seaman *not* recover for his injuries aboard a vessel?

2. Can a seaman be in the service of his vessel
   while working ashore?

3. Describe the three remedies available for injured seamen under admiralty law.

United States v. Reliable Transfer Co., 421 U.S. 397 (1975)

MR. JUSTICE STEWART delivered the opinion of the Court.

More than a century ago, in *The Schooner
Catharine v. Dickinson*, 17 How. 170, this Court
established in our admiralty law the rule of divided damages. That rule, most commonly applied in cases of collision between two vessels,
requires the equal division of property damage
whenever both parties are found to be guilty of
contributing fault, whatever the relative degree
of their fault may have been. The courts of
every major maritime nation except ours have
long since abandoned that rule, and now assess
damages in such cases on the basis of proportionate fault when such an allocation can reasonably be made. In the present case we are
called upon to decide whether this country's admiralty rule of divided damages should be replaced by a rule requiring, when possible, the
allocation of liability for damages in proportion
to the relative fault of each party.

I.

On a clear but windy December night in
1968, the *Mary A. Whalen*, a coastal tanker
owned by the respondent Reliable Transfer Co.,
embarked from Constable Hooks, N.J., for Island Park, N.Y., with a load of fuel oil. The voyage ended, instead, with the vessel stranded on
a sandbar off Rockaway Point outside New York
Harbor.

The *Whalen's* course led across the mouth of
Rockaway Inlet, a narrow body of water that lies
between a breakwater to the southeast and the
shoreline of Coney Island to the northwest. The
breakwater is ordinarily marked at its southern-
most point by a flashing light maintained by the
Coast Guard. As, however, the *Whalen's* captain
and a deckhand observed while the vessel was
proceeding southwardly across the inlet, the
light was not operating that night. As the
Whalen approached Rockaway Point about half
an hour later, her captain attempted to pass a

tug with a barge in tow ahead, but, after determining that he could not overtake them, decided to make a 180-degree turn to pass astern of the barge. At this time the tide was at flood, and the waves, whipped by northwest winds of gale force, were eight to ten feet high. After making the 180-degree turn and passing astern of the barge, the captain headed the *Whalen* eastwardly, believing that the vessel was then south of the breakwater and that he was heading her for the open sea. He was wrong. About a minute later the light structure on the southern point of the breakwater came into view. Turning to avoid rocks visible ahead, the *Whalen* ran aground in the sand.

The respondent brought this action against the United States in Federal District Court, under the Suits in Admiralty Act, 41 Stat. 525, 46 U.S.C. Sec. 741 et seq., seeking to recover for damages to the *Whalen* caused by the stranding. The District Court found that the vessel's grounding was caused 25 percent by the failure of the Coast Guard to maintain the breakwater light and 75 percent by the fault of the *Whalen*. In so finding on the issue of comparative fault, the court stated:

The fault of the vessel was more egregious than the fault of the Coast Guard. Attempting to negotiate a turn to the east, in the narrow space between the bell buoy No. 4 and the shoals off Rockaway Point, the captain set his course without knowing where he was. Obviously, he would not have found the breakwater light looming directly ahead of him within a minute after his change of course, if he had not been north of the point where he believed he was.

Equipped with lookout, chart, searchlight, radiotelephone, and radar, he made use of nothing except his own guesswork judgment. After . . . turning in a loop toward the north so as to pass astern of the tow, he should have made sure of his position before setting his new seventy-three-degree course. The fact that a northwest gale blowing at forty-five knots with eight to ten foot seas made it difficult to see emphasizes the need for caution rather than excusing a turn into the unknown. . . .

The court held, however, that the settled admiralty rule of divided damages required each

party to bear one-half of the damages to the vessel.

The Court of Appeals for the Second Circuit affirmed this judgment. 497 F.2d 1036. It held that the trial court "was not clearly erroneous in finding that the negligence of both parties, in the proportions stated, caused the stranding." And, although "mindful of the criticism of the equal division of damages rule and . . . recogniz[ing] the force of the argument that in this type of case division of damages in proportion to the degree of fault may be more equitable," the appellate court felt constrained to adhere to the established rule and "to leave doctrinal development to the Supreme Court or to await appropriate action by Congress."

We granted certiorari, 419 U.S. 1018, to consider the continued validity of the divided damages rule.

II.

The precise origins of the divided damages rule are shrouded in the mists of history. In any event it was not until early in the nineteenth century that the divided damages rule as we know it emerged clearly in British admiralty law. . . .

It was against this background that in 1855 this Court adopted the rule of equal division of damages in *The Schooner Catharine v. Dickinson*, 17 How. 170. The rule was adopted because it was then the prevailing rule in England, because it had become the majority rule in the lower federal courts, and because it seemed the "most just and equitable, and . . . best [tended] to induce care and vigilance on both sides, in the navigation." There can be no question that subsequent history and experience have conspicuously eroded the rule's foundations.

It was true at the time of *The Catharine* that the divided damages rule was well entrenched in English law. The rule was an ancient form of rough justice, a means of apportioning damages where it was difficult to measure which party was more at fault. But England has long since abandoned the rule and now follows the Brussels Collision Liability Convention of 1910 that provides for the apportionment of damages on the basis of "degree" of fault whenever it is possible to do so. Indeed, the United States is now virtually alone among the world's major maritime nations in not adhering to the Convention with its rule of proportional fault—a fact that encourages transoceanic forum shopping.

While the lower federal courts originally adhered to the divided damages rule, they have more recently followed it only grudgingly, terming it "unfair," "illogical," "arbitrary," "archaic and frequently unjust." Judge Learned Hand was a particularly stern critic of the rule. Dissenting in *National Bulk Carriers v. United States*, 183 F.2d 405, 410 (CA2), he wrote: "An equal division [of damages] in this case would be plainly unjust; they ought to be divided in some such proportion as five to one. And so they could be but for our obstinate cleaving to the ancient rule which has been abrogated by nearly all civilized nations."

It is no longer apparent, if it ever was, that this Solomonic division of damages serves to achieve even rough justice. An equal division of damages is a reasonably satisfactory result only where each vessel's fault is approximately equal and each vessel thus assumes a share of the collision damages in proportion to its share of the blame, or where proportionate degrees of fault cannot be measured and determined on a rational basis. The rule produces palpably unfair results in every other case. For example, where one ship's fault in causing a collision is relatively slight and her damages small, and where the second ship is grossly negligent and suffers extensive damage, the first ship must still make a substantial payment to the second.

And the potential unfairness of the division is magnified by the application of the rule of *The Pennsylvania*, 19 Wall. 125, whereby a ship's relatively minor statutory violation will require her to bear half the collision damage unless she can satisfy the heavy burden of showing "not merely that her fault might not have been one of the causes, or that it probably was not, but that it *could not have been*." Id., at 136 (emphasis added).

The Court has long implicitly recognized the patent harshness of an equal division of damages in the face of disparate blame by applying the "major-minor" fault doctrine to find a grossly negligent party solely at fault. But this escape valve, in addition to being inherently unreliable, simply replaces one unfairness with another. That a vessel is primarily negligent does not justify its shouldering all responsibility, nor excuse the slightly negligent vessel from bearing any liability at all.

The divided damages rule has been said to be justified by the difficulty of determining comparative degrees of negligence when both parties are concededly guilty of contributing fault. Although there is some force in this argument, it cannot justify an equal division of damages in every case of collision based on mutual fault. When it is impossible to fairly allocate degrees of fault, the division of damages equally between wrongdoing parties is an equitable solution. But the rule is unnecessarily crude and inequitable in a case like this one where an allocation of disparate proportional fault has been made. Potential problems of proof in some cases hardly require adherence to an archaic and unfair rule in all cases. Every other major maritime nation has evidently been able to apply a rule of comparative negligence without serious problems, and in our own admiralty law a rule of comparative negligence has long been applied with no untoward difficulties in personal injury actions.

The argument has also been made that the divided damages rule promotes out-of-court settlements, because when it becomes apparent that both vessels are at fault, both parties can readily agree to divide the damages—thus avoiding the expense and delay of prolonged litigation and the concomitant burden on the courts. It would be far more difficult, it is argued, for the parties to agree on who was more at fault and to apportion damages accordingly.

But the argument is hardly persuasive. For if the fault of the two parties is markedly disproportionate, it is in the interest of the slightly negligent party to litigate the controversy in the hope that the major-minor fault rule may eventually persuade a court to absolve it of all liability. And if, on the other hand, it appears after a realistic assessment of the situation that the fault of both parties is roughly equal, then there is no reason why a rule that apportions damages would be any less likely to induce a settlement than a rule that always divides damages equally. Experience with comparative negligence in the personal injury area teaches that a rule of fairness in court will produce fair out-of-court settlements. But even if this argument were more persuasive than it is, it could hardly be accepted. For, at bottom, it asks us to continue the operation of an archaic rule because its facile application out of court yields quick, though inequitable, settlements, and relieves the courts of some litigation. Congestion in the courts cannot justify a legal rule that produces unjust results in litigation simply to encourage speedy out-of-court accommodations.

Finally, the respondent suggests that the creation of a new rule of damages in maritime collision cases is a task for Congress and not for this Court. But the judiciary has traditionally taken the lead in formulating flexible and fair remedies in the law maritime, and "Congress has largely left to this Court the responsibility for fashioning the controlling rules of admiralty law." *Fitzgerald v. United States Lines Co.*, 374 U.S. 16, 20. No statutory or judicial precept precludes a change in the rule of divided damages, and indeed a proportional fault rule would simply bring recovery for the property damage in maritime collision cases into line with the rule of admiralty law long since established by Congress for personal injury cases.

As the authors of a leading admiralty law treatise have put the matter:

[T]here is no reason why the Supreme Court cannot at this late date "confess error" and adopt the proportional fault doctrine without Congressional action. The resolution to follow the divided damages rule, taken 120 years ago, rested not on overwhelming authority but on judgments of fact and of fairness which may have been tenable then but are hardly so today. No "vested rights," in theory or fact, have intervened. The regard for "settled expectation" which is the heart-reason of . . . stare decisis . . . can have no relevance in respect to such a rule; the concept of "settled expectation" would be reduced to an absurdity were it to be applied to a rule of damages for negligent collision. The abrogation of the rule would not, it seems, produce any disharmony with other branches of the maritime law, general or statutory. Gilmore and Black 531 (footnote omitted)

The rule of divided damages in admiralty has continued to prevail in this country by sheer inertia rather than by reason of any intrinsic merit. The reasons that originally led to the Court's adoption of the rule have long since disappeared. The rule has been repeatedly criticized by experienced federal judges who have correctly pointed out that the result it works has too often been precisely the opposite of what the Court sought to achieve in *The Schooner Catharine*—the "just and equitable" allocation of damages. And worldwide experience has taught that that goal can be more nearly realized by a standard that allocates liability for damages according to comparative fault whenever possible.

We hold that when two or more parties have contributed by their fault to cause property damage in a maritime collision or stranding, liability for such damage is to be allocated among the parties proportionately to the comparative degree of their fault, and that liability for such damages is to be allocated equally only when the parties are equally at fault or when it is not possible fairly to measure the comparative degree of their fault.

Accordingly, the judgment before us is vacated and the case is remanded for further proceedings consistent with this opinion.

It is so ordered.

Questions

1. Why did it take so long for the United States to abandon the divided damages rule? How did the "major-minor" fault rule work?

2. What is the Coast Guard's potential for liability in maintaining aids to navigation?

Columbus-America Discovery Group v. Atlantic Mutual Ins., 974 F.2d 450 (4th Cir. 1992) (cert. denied, 1993)

DONALD RUSSELL, CIRCUIT JUDGE

"When Erasmus mused that '[a] common shipwreck is a source of consolation to all,' *Adagia*, IV.iii.9 (1508), he quite likely did not foresee inconcinnate free-for-alls among self-styled salvors." *Martha's Vineyard Scuba HQ, Inc. v. The Unidentified, Wrecked and Abandoned Steam Vessel*, 833 F.2d 1059, 1061 (1st Cir. 1987). Without doubt the Dutch scholar also could not image legal brawls involving self-styled "finders" from Ohio, British and American insurance underwriters, an heir to the Miller brewing fortune, a Texas oil millionaire, an Ivy League university, and an order of Catholic monks. Yet that is what this case involves, with the prize being up to $1 billion in gold.

This gold was deposited on the ocean floor, eight thousand feet below the surface and 160 miles off the South Carolina coast, when the S.S. *Central America* sank in a hurricane on September 12, 1857. The precise whereabouts of the wreck remained unknown until 1988, when it was located by the Columbus-America Discovery Group ("Columbus-America"). This enterprise has since been recovering the gold, and last year it moved in federal district court to have itself declared the owner of the treasure. Into court to oppose this manoeuvre came British and American insurers who had originally underwritten the gold for its ocean voyage and then had to pay off over a million dollars in claims upon the disaster. Also attempting to get into the stew were three would-be inter-

venors who claimed that Columbus-America had used their computerized "treasure map" to locate the gold. The district court allowed the intervention, but it did not give the intervenors any time for discovery.

After a ten-day trial, the lower Court awarded Columbus-America the golden treasure in its entirety, 742 F.Supp. 1327. It found that the underwriters had previously abandoned their ownership interests in the gold by deliberately destroying certain documentation. As for the intervenors, the Court held that there was no evidence showing that Columbus-America used their information in any way in locating the wreck.

Upon appeal, we find that the evidence was not sufficient to show that the underwriters affirmatively abandoned their interests in the gold. We also hold that once intervention was allowed, the district court abused its discretion by not affording the intervenors sufficient time for discovery. We therefore reverse the decision below and remand the case for further proceedings.

I.

A.

The year 1857 is justly famous in American history for its many notable events. Among these was the beginning of a fairly serious financial decline, the aptly named Panic of 1857. Associated with the Panic, and another reason why the year is so famous, is one of the worst disasters in American maritime history, the sinking of the S.S. *Central America*.

The *Central America* was a black-hulled, coal-fired, three-decked, three-masted sidewheeler with a cruising speed of eleven knots. Built in 1852, and launched the following year, she carried passengers, mail, and cargo between Aspinwall, Colombia (on the Caribbean side of the Isthmus of Panama), and New York City, with a stopover in Havana. Most, if not all, of her passengers were headed to or from California, the route being one leg of the then quickest way between the west coast and the eastern seaboard—from California to the Pacific side of the Isthmus of Panama aboard a steamship, across the isthmus on the Panama Railroad, and then from Aspinwall to New York aboard another steamship. Owned by the U.S. Mail and Steamship Company and originally named the S.S. *George Law* (until June 1857), the *Central America* completed forty-three voyages between Panama and New York in her four years of operation. During this period, the California gold rush was in full swing, and it has been said that the ship carried one-third of all gold shipped at that time from California to New York.

In August of 1857, over four hundred passengers and approximately $1,600,000 (1857 value) in gold (exclusive of passenger gold) left San Francisco for Panama aboard the S.S. *Sonora*. Many of the passengers were prospectors who had become rich and were returning home, either for good or to visit. Also on board were California Judge Alonzo Castle Monson, who resigned from the bench after losing his house and all his money in a famous poker game, and Mrs. Virginia Birch, a.k.a. "the notorious Jenny French," a former dance-hall girl well known in San Francisco. As for the gold, it was being shipped by California merchants, bankers, and express companies, including Levi Strauss and Wells Fargo, to New York banks, the banks wanting specie to stave off the effects of the financial downturn.

The travelers and the cargo reached Panama without incident, and they crossed the isthmus by rail. On September 3, over six hundred people came aboard the *Central America*, as well as $1,219,189 of the gold shipped on the *Sonora*, the remainder being shipped to England aboard a different vessel. The *Central America* first headed for Havana, which was reached on September 7. There, the ship lay over for a night, and some of the passengers debarked to catch another vessel for New Orleans. On September 8, under clear skies, the *Central America* left

Havana for New York, carrying approximately 580 persons and her golden treasure.

On the second day out of Havana, the weather changed and a mighty storm came up. What the passengers and crew could not know was that they were headed directly into the teeth of a ferocious hurricane. As the storm worsened around the *Central America*, a leak developed and soon water was rushing into the boat. The water extinguished the fires in the ship's boilers, and this in turn caused the ship's pumping system to fail. All able male passengers began a systematic bailing of water out of the ship, but it was to no avail; after thirty frantic hours, the boiler fires would still not light and the water level continued to rise.

Knowing the situation was hopeless, Captain William Lewis Herndon managed to hail a passing ship, the brig *Marine*, and one hundred persons, including all but one of the women and children aboard, were safely transferred to the other ship. Time and conditions would not allow for any more transfers, however, and shortly after 8 P.M. on September 12, the *Central America* began making its quick descent to the bottom of the ocean.

After being flung into the sea, many of the men managed to come to the top and float there, desperately holding onto any buoyant material available. Six to nine hours after the sinking, fifty of these men were rescued by the Norwegian bark *Ellen*. Earlier, a small bird had thrice circled the *Ellen* and flown directly into the face of the ship's captain. Taking this as a sign, the captain changed his course to follow from whence the bird had come, and in so doing discovered the fifty floating survivors. Three other men were also rescued when, nine days later and 450 miles away, the ship spotted their lifeboat, which had been riding the Gulf Stream.

In all, 153 persons were rescued, while approximately 425 lost their lives. Thus, less than two weeks after the disaster, the underwriters began negotiating with the Boston Submarine Armor Company about possibly raising the ship and her cargo. Also, on June 28, 1858, two of the underwriters (Atlantic Mutual Insurance company and Sun Mutual Insurance Company) contracted with Brutus de Villeroi, a Frenchman then living in Pennsylvania, to salvage the gold. The contract states that de Villeroi, "by means of his Invention of a Submarine boat" and at his own expense, would raise the treasure and receive a salvage award of 75 percent. At this time, though, no one was quite sure where the boat had gone down, or in how deep of water. At first, some estimated the ship was in only twenty-eight fathoms of water (168 feet), when in fact it was over eight thousand feet below the surface. As would be expected, nothing came of the salvage attempts in the late 1850s, and the issue, and the gold, would lie dormant for over 120 years.

B.

Beginning in the 1970s, a number of individuals and groups began discussing and planning the salvage of the *Central America*, as the decade before had seen a great advance in the technology necessary for deep-sea salvage. Still, though, no one was positive where the ship had gone down or in what depth of water. At least one group thought they had found her in shallow water fifteen miles off Cape Hatteras, which in reality was at least one hundred miles from where she actually lay.

A number of those interested in salvaging the *Central America* contacted some of the various insurers who had underwritten the gold. The would-be salvors hoped to receive a relinquishment of the insurers' rights to the property, or at least form a salvage contract with the underwriters. While the underwriters negotiated with several groups about the salvage, they did not enter into any salvage contracts nor did they relinquish any of their rights to the gold.

One of the groups that contacted several of the underwriters was Plaintiff Columbus-America Discovery Group, the eventual salvor. Columbus-America asked the underwriters to convey to it any claims they might have regarding the gold, but this was not done.

Another group that was interested in salvaging the gold was Santa Fe Communications, Inc. ("Santa Fe"), whose interests are now owned by Plaintiff-Intervenors Harry G. John and Jack R. Grimm. In 1984, Santa Fe paid Plaintiff-Intervenor Columbia University $300,000 for Columbia's Dr. William B. F. Ryan to conduct a sonar search over a four hundred-square-mile area of the Atlantic Ocean. During this sonar search, Dr. Ryan identified seven "targets" on the ocean floor. Of these targets, he found only one, target #4, to be a good candidate for being the *Central America*. Dr. Ryan felt that "this target is almost certainly the scattered debris of a shipwreck," and his report mentioned that further exploration of it would have been made but for "gale force winds and seas." In conclusion, he told Santa Fe, "you [Harry John] and Mr. Jack Grimm have a likely candidate for further exploration." Santa Fe, though, did not further pursue the matter, and on December 31, 1984, it transferred to a Catholic monastic order, the Province of St. Joseph of the Capuchin Order—St. Benedict Friary of Milwaukee, Wisconsin ("The Capuchins")—any and all rights and interests arising out of its undersea salvage operations. It now appears that target #4 was indeed the *Central America*.

The contract between Santa Fe and Columbia provided that Columbia would be able to freely publish the results of the sonar survey, but only after keeping such results confidential for a year. Shortly after the survey, Columbus-America President Thomas Thompson began contacting Dr. Ryan and others at Columbia and Santa Fe in an attempt to learn the results. Over a two-year period, Thompson and Dr. Ryan had a number of conversations about the techniques for identifying sonar images on the ocean floor, but the latter only believed that Thompson, who was associated with the prestigious Battelle Memorial Institute, was interested in this information from a scientific standpoint.

On February 12, 1986, Thompson wrote Dr. Ryan and requested certain sonar photographs taken during the survey. The letter also stated, "I am submitting this order primarily out of a personal interest. I have a personal source of funds available for data collection and correlation-type work. I am also interested in the techniques for separating anomalies from their environment and in the processing of specific anomalies to determine their character." Dr. Ryan passed along Thompson's request to Columbia, which agreed to provide the information. As a condition, though, Columbia told Thompson that "since the data you requested is not in the public domain, we would require your agreement that any photocopied records or computer tapes you receive would be for your sole use and would not be reproduced for others." Thompson agreed to this condition, but went ahead and placed the information he received into Columbus-America's files.

C.

In 1987, after much effort and expense, Columbus-America believed it had found the *Central America*. Thus, on May 27, 1987, it filed, in the United States District Court for the Eastern District of Virginia, an in rem action against the wreck, alleging that, under the law of finds, it was its "finder," or, alternatively, under the law of salvage, its "salvor." Columbus- America then asked for and received, on July 17, 1987, a preliminary injunction enjoining the other would-be salvors from operating within a specified area ("injunction box #1") of the sea. Injunction box #1 covered an area which was approximately thirty miles from Dr. Ryan's target #4.

After receiving this injunction, Columbus-America spent two years attempting to salvage the wreck they thought was the *Central America*—this time was also spent battling the other would-be salvors in court. Plaintiffs recovered several artifacts, as well as a good many lumps of coal, but at some point they recognized that they were salvaging the wrong ship. They then began to look at other likely targets, and, even-

tually, they discovered the right ship. Thus, Columbus-America requested the Court to grant them, by permanent injunction, exclusive control over the area around this new find, and this was done through an Order entered on August 18, 1989 ("injunction box #2"). Within the area of injunction box #2 was Dr. Ryan's target #4.

Since 1989, Columbus-America, through its invention of a submersible robot which can pick up objects ranging from small gold coins to a ship's anchor weighing thousands of pounds, has been salvaging objects left on the ocean floor by the *Central America*. Undoubtedly, its major interest is in recovering the gold, and so far several hundred million dollars worth (present value) of gold coins, ingots, and bars have been recovered—it is estimated that the total haul may be worth up to $1 billion.

On September 29, 1989, many of the original underwriters of the gold, plus the Superintendent of Insurance of the State of New York for several insurance companies now defunct, filed claims with the district court asserting that they were the proper owners of the gold. After this, extensive discovery was had, and the case was scheduled for trial beginning April 3, 1990.

Three days before trial, John and Grimm moved to intervene, as did Columbia two days later. The intervenors claimed that Columbus-America must have used the information from Dr. Ryan's sonar survey in locating the *Central America*, and thus they wished for a percentage of the recovery. Two weeks earlier, John had bought back for $10 any claims the Capuchins would have on the *Central America*. When Santa Fe had originally donated its rights to the monks in 1984, the Capuchins recognized the gift as worthless, and John did nothing to enlighten them on the discovery of the ship or the upcoming trial. After later realizing what John was up to, though, the monks must have protested, for on April 10 both John and Grimm signed an agreement with the Capuchins giving the Order one-third of any judgment they (John or Grimm) would recover.

The district court allowed John, Grimm, and

Columbia to intervene, but it permitted them no discovery—the Court wanting the trial to begin as scheduled. Earlier, the Court had bifurcated the trial, so that the first part would concern only whether Columbus-America was entitled to finder or salvor status. If the district court found that the insurance companies had somehow abandoned the gold, Columbus-America would be considered its "finder," and thus its owner. On the other hand, if the underwriters had not abandoned the gold, they would still remain its owners and Columbus-America would be its "salvor." If the latter scenario were found to be true, a second phase of the trial would be necessary, wherein the Court would have to determine what each underwriter had insured and the amount of Columbus-America's salvage award. Because the trial had been bifurcated, the intervenors wanted their claims adjudicated after the finder/salvor issue was decided. The Court, though, would allow intervention only if the would-be intervenors agreed to have their claims adjudicated at the same time as the finder/salvor issue—that is, beginning the next day.

The trial began on schedule, lasted ten days, and received much national attention. Over its course, many witnesses appeared and hundreds of exhibits were entered into evidence. The parties then began an anxious wait for a decision.

On August 14, 1990, the Court found for Columbus-America on all the issues, dismissing the claims of the underwriters, Columbia, John, and Grimm. *Columbus-America Discovery Group v. The Unidentified, Wrecked and Abandoned Sailing Vessel*, 742 F.Supp. 1327 (E.D.Va. 1990). On the finder/salvor issue, the district court held that the underwriters had abandoned the gold, and thus Columbus-America was its finder and sole owner. The Court based this finding of abandonment primarily on the supposed fact that the underwriters had *intentionally* destroyed any documentation they had once had concerning the case. As for the intervenors, the Court found that they failed to prove that the information furnished Thompson could have as-

sisted in locating the ship, that Columbus-America used this information in any way, or "even if the information was of value and was used, that any such use would entitle them to share in any recovery."

The underwriters and the intervenors now appeal.

II.

A.

Historically, courts have applied the maritime law of salvage when ships or their cargo have been recovered from the bottom of the sea by those other than their owners. Under this law, the original owners still retain their ownership interests in such property, although the salvors are entitled to a very liberal salvage award. Such awards often exceed the value of the services rendered, and if no owner should come forward to claim the property, the salvor is normally awarded its total value. On salvage generally, see 3A M. Norris, *Benedict on Admiralty: The Law of Salvage* (7th ed. rev., 1991).

A related legal doctrine is the common law of finds, which expresses "the ancient and honorable principle of 'finders, keepers.'" *Martha's Vineyard*, 855 F.2d at 1065. Traditionally, the law of finds was applied only to maritime property which had never been owned by anybody, such as ambergris, whales, and fish. 3A *Benedict on Admiralty* Sec. 158, at 11–15. A relatively recent trend in the law, though, has seen the law of finds applied to long-lost and abandoned shipwrecks.

Courts in admiralty favor applying salvage law rather than the law of finds. As has been succinctly stated by Judge Abraham D. Sofaer:

The law of finds is disfavored in admiralty because of its aims, its assumption, and its rules. The primary concern of the law of finds is title. The law of finds defines the circumstances under which a party may be said to have acquired title to ownerless property. Its application necessarily assumes that the property involved either was never owned or was abandoned.

... To justify an award of title (albeit of one that is defensible), the law of finds requires a finder to demonstrate not only the intent to acquire the property involved, but also possession of that property, that is, a high degree of control over it.

These rules encourage certain types of conduct and discourage others. A would-be finder should be expected to act acquisitively, to express a will to own by acts designed to establish the high degree of control required for a finding of possession. The would-be finder's longing to acquire is exacerbated by the prospect of being found to have failed to establish title. If either intent or possession is found lacking, the would-be finder receives nothing; neither effort alone nor acquisition unaccompanied by the required intent is rewarded.... Furthermore, success as a finder is measured solely in terms of obtaining possession of specific property; possession of specific property can seldom be shared, and mere contribution by one party to another's successful efforts to obtain possession earns no compensation.

Would-be finders are encouraged by these rules to act secretly, and to hide their recoveries, in order to avoid claims of prior owners or other would-be finders that could entirely deprive them of the property. *Herer v. United States*, 525 F.Supp. 350, 356 (S.D.N.Y. 1981)

In sharp contrast to "the harsh, primitive, and inflexible nature of the law of finds," is the law of salvage.

Admiralty favors the law of salvage over the law of finds because salvage law's aims, assumptions, and rules are more consonant with the needs of marine activity and because salvage law encourages less competitive and secretive forms of conduct than finds law. The primary concern of salvage law is the preservation of property on oceans and waterways. Salvage law specifies the circumstances under which a party may be said to have acquired, not title, but the right to take possession of property (e.g., vessels, equipment, and cargo) for the purpose of saving it from destruction, damage, or loss, and to retain it until proper compensation has been paid.

Salvage Law assumes that the property being salvaged is owned by another, and thus that it has not been abandoned. Admiralty courts have adhered to the traditional and realistic premise that property previously owned but lost at sea has been taken in-

voluntarily out of the owner's possession and control by the forces of nature at work in oceans and waterways; in fact, property may not be "salvaged" under admiralty law unless it is in some form of peril....

Salvage law requires that to be a salvor a party must have the intention and the capacity to save the property involved, but the party need not have the intention to acquire it. Furthermore, although the law of salvage, like the law of finds, requires a salvor to establish possession over property before obtaining the right to exclude others, "possession" means something less in salvage law than in finds law. In the salvage context, only the right to compensation for service, not the right to title, usually results; "possession" is therefore more readily found than under the law of finds. ... Moreover, unlike the would-be finder, who is either a keeper or a loser, the salvor receives a payment, depending on the value of the service rendered, that may go beyond quantum merit. Admiralty's equitable power to make an award for salvage—recognized since ancient times in maritime civilizations—is a corollary to the assumption of nonabandonment and has been applied irrespective of the owner's express refusal to accept such service....

These salvage rules markedly diminish the incentive for salvors to act secretly, to hide their recoveries, or to ward off competition from other would-be salvors.... In short, although salvage law cannot alter human nature, its application enables courts to encourage open, lawful, and cooperative conduct, all in the cause of preserving property (and life). Id. at 357–58; see also *3A Benedict on Admiralty* Sec. 158, at 11–15 to 11–16

Today, finds law is applied to previously owned sunken property only when that property has been abandoned by its previous owners. Abandonment in this sense means much more than merely leaving the property, for it has long been the law that "[w]hen articles are lost at sea the title of the owner in them remains." *The Akaba*, 54 F. 197, 200 (4th Cir. 1893). Once an article has been lost at sea, "lapse of time and nonuser are not sufficient, in and of themselves, to constitute an abandonment." *Wiggins v. 1100 Tons, More or Less, of Italian Marble*, 186 F.Supp. 452, 456 (E.D.Va. 1960). In addition, there is no abandonment when one discovers sunken property and then, even after extensive efforts, is unable to locate its owner. *Weber Marine, Inc. v. One Large Cast Steel Stockless Anchor and Four Shots of Anchor Chain*, 478 F.Supp. 973, 975 (E.D.La. 1979).

While abandonment has been simply described as "the act of deserting property without hope of recovery or intention of returning to it," *Nunley v. M.V. Dauntless Colocotronis*, 863 F.2d 1190, 1198 (5th Cir. 1989), in the lost property at sea context, there is also a strong *actus* element required to prove the necessary intent. *Zych v. The Unidentified, Wrecked and Abandoned Vessel*, 755 F. Supp. 213, 214 (N.D.Ill. 1990); "Abandonment is said to be a voluntary act which must be proved by a clear and unmistakable affirmative act to indicate a purpose to repudiate ownership." *The Port Hunter*, 6 F.Supp. 1009, 1011 (D. Mass. 1934). The proof that need be shown must be "strong . . . , such as the owner's express declaration abandoning title." T. Schoenbaum, *Admiralty and Maritime Law*, Sec. 15-7, at 512 (1987).

There are only a handful of cases which have applied the law of finds, all of which fit into two categories. First, there are cases where owners have expressly and publicly abandoned their property. In the second type of case, items are recovered from ancient shipwrecks and no owner appears in court to claim them. Such circumstances may give rise to an inference of abandonment, but should an owner appear in court and there be no evidence of an express abandonment, the law of salvage must be applied. We agree with the author of *Admiralty and Maritime Law* that:

In the treasure salvage cases, often involving wrecks hundreds of years old, the inference of abandonment may arise from lapse of time and nonuse of the property, or there may even be an express disclaimer of ownership. This calls for the application of the law of finds. By contrast, parties who intend to assert a claim of ownership may be identified. In such a case the law of salvage is applied. Sec. 15–7, at 514 (footnotes omitted)

See also *Hatteras, Inc. v. The U.S.S. Hatteras*, 1097 n. 5 (S.C. Tex. 1981) ("While mere nonuse of property and lapse of time without more do not establish abandonment, they may, under circumstances where the owner has otherwise failed to act or assert any claim to property, support an inference of intent to abandon").

The case below appears to be the only reported decision involving salvaged treasure from ancient shipwrecks wherein a court has applied the law of finds despite the fact that the previous owner appeared in court. In all other finds law cases, no prior owner has appeared. One example is the *Treasure Salvors* set of cases, all of which involved the salvage of Spanish treasure ships sunk off the Florida Keys in 1622. Widely quoted is the Fifth Circuit's phrase that "[d]isposition of a wrecked vessel whose very location has been lost for centuries as though its owner were still in existence stretches a fiction to absurd lengths." *Treasure Salvors, Inc. v. The Unidentified, Wrecked and Abandoned Sailing Vessel*, 569 F.2d 330, 337 (5th Cir. 1978). Yet the Court there also took the trouble to note that it had been stipulated by all parties involved that the original owners had abandoned the wrecks, and the district court also made mention of the fact that, "The modern day government of Spain has expressed no interest in filing a claim in this litigation as a successor-owner." Id. at 336 n. 9; *Treasure Salvors, Inc. v. The Unidentified, Wrecked and Abandoned Sailing Vessel*, 556 F.Supp. 1319, 1334 n. 2 (S.D. Fla. 1983). Another Spanish wreck, this time from the 1715 Plate Fleet, was involved in *Cobb Coin Co., Inc. v. The Unidentified, Wrecked and Abandoned Sailing Vessel*, 525 F.Supp. 186 (S.D. Fla. 1981), and there the Spanish government again made no claim of ownership.

In *Martha's Vineyard, supra*, which concerned the salvage of the S.S. *Republic*, a ship that "plummeted to a watery grave in 1909," the First Circuit made it a point to state that, "After petitioner brought its action in rem in the district court, no person or firm appeared to assert any overall claim of ownership." 833 F.2d at 1065. Likewise *Massachusetts v. Maritime Underwater Surveys, Inc.*, 403 Mass. 501, 531 N.E.2d 549 (1988), which involved salvage of "the notorious pirate ship *Whydah*," a vessel that sank in a storm off Cape Cod in April of 1717. There, the Supreme Judicial Court of Massachusetts noted that "American courts have applied the law of finds, rather than the law of salvage, in cases involving ancient shipwrecks where no owner is likely to come forward," apparently after descendants of the ill-fated pirates made no attempt to rush into court and claim the booty.

An example of a treasure salvage case where the original owner, or its successor in interest, appeared and salvage law was applied is *Zych, supra*. In this case, the *Lady Elgin* sank in 1860 on Lake Michigan, and claims were paid on the vessel and its cargo by the Aetna Insurance Company. Because of the recent advances in technology necessary for deep-water salvage, an independent salvor located the ship in the late 1980s and he, claiming finder status, attempted to have the district court declare him the owner. This claim was disputed by the Lady Elgin Foundation, to which Aetna's successor, CIGNA, had transferred its ownership interests in the wreck in April of 1990. The court, after noting "the law's hesitancy to find abandonment and the concomitant requirement that abandonment be supported by strong and convincing evidence," found that the vessel had not been abandoned. Aetna's successor in interest, the Lady Elgin Foundation, still retained its ownership interest, and the law of salvage, not finds, was applied. As for the 130 years during which no salvage was attempted, the court found that "Aetna was not required to engage in efforts to recover the wreck in order to avoid abandoning its interest when such efforts would have had minimal chances for success." 755 F.Supp. at 216.

In maintaining the position that previous owners can abandon sunken vessels even without any affirmative acts, Columbus-America re-

lies especially on two state supreme court cases decided before the Civil Wars, *Eads v. Brazelton*, 22 Ark., 499 (1861) and *Wyman v. Hulburt*, 12 Ohio 81 (1843). *Eads* involved the steamboat *America* which partially sank in the Mississippi River in 1827. The boat contained much valuable property, and in the two weeks after its sinking the owners conducted salvage operations in which they rescued all of the fur and government-owned specie on board, as well as one-half of the six hundred pigs of lead and a portion of the shot. Also, all of the machinery of the ship, including the boilers, was successfully removed. After this salvage, the owners physically abandoned the wreck and two years later an island began forming about it, on which trees would eventually grow to a height of thirty or forty feet.

The actual case concerned which of two would-be finders/salvors owned the remaining pigs of lead. As for the original owners, the Court declared that the cargo had been abandoned and then, in dicta noted that "in extreme cases property wholly derelict and abandoned has been held to belong to the finder against the former owner." Id. at 509. Such was not the case here, though, for the former owners made no attempt to claim an ownership interest in the lead. Because the boat and its contents were partially salvaged shortly after the wreck, the remaining cargo was easily salvageable for at least two years thereafter, and, most importantly, the original owners made no claim to the property once the remaining lead was salvaged, we find *Eads* inappropriate.

The facts of *Wyman* are more on point, although we doubt its precedential value. There, a schooner, *The G.S. Willis*, sank in Lake Erie during the fall of 1835. The next year it was raised by another party and $865 in specie was discovered in the cabin. Truman Wyman, the original owner of this money, then filed an action of trover in Ohio state court against the finders/salvors. The case was tried before a jury in the Supreme Court of Ashtabula County, and they returned a special verdict which included the finding that "at the time the said schooner was seized by the defendants, the same was abandoned by the plaintiff, and that said schooner was, on the day and year aforesaid, derelict property, and when found in the bottom of the Lake was worth nothing." 12 Ohio at 85.

A majority of the Ohio Supreme Court held for the finders/salvors, awarding them the entire amount. The Court based this decision on the jury's finding of abandonment, which the majority supposed was intended "to be understood that all hope, expectation, and intention to recover the property were utterly and entirely relinquished." Id. at 86–87. A seventy-two-word dissenting opinion was filed, though, by Chief Justice Ebenezer Lane. Lane was "not entirely certain that [his brethren] adopt[ed] the true sense of the word 'abandoned' [as it was employed] in the special verdict." Instead, the Chief Justice was "incline[d] to think the jury meant nothing more than a want of the plaintiff's pursuing active measures to reclaim his property, and not a positive relinquishment of his right. If this be the true meaning, it would change the judgment." Id. at 88.

Because of the meager information supplied by the court, it is impossible to know which of Wyman's acts, or omissions, the jury relied on in finding an abandonment. Also, like Chief Justice Lane, we find it difficult to know exactly what the jury meant when it found the ship to have been "abandoned." What is clear, though, is that the Chief Justice was entirely correct when he stated that an abandonment of sunken cargo so as to lose possession must be shown not by the mere cessation of attempts to recover, but by the owner's positive relinquishment of his rights in the property. We find that this is the only principle of note to be gleaned from *Wyman*.

In conclusion, when sunken ships or their cargo are rescued from the bottom of the ocean by those other than the owners, courts favor applying the law of salvage over the law of finds. Finds law should be applied, however, in situations where the previous owners are found to have abandoned their property. Such abandonment must be proved by clear and convincing evidence, though, such as an owner's express declaration abandoning title. Should the property encompass an ancient and long-lost shipwreck, a court may infer an abandonment. Such an inference would be improper, though, should a previous owner appear and assert his ownership interest. In such a case the normal presumptions would apply and an abandonment would have to be proved by strong and convincing evidence.

B.

Before addressing whether the district court correctly found that the insured shipments of gold were abandoned by the underwriters, several points should be noted. First, the *Central America* herself was self-insured, and successors in interest to the U.S. Mail and Steamship Company have made no attempt to claim an ownership interest in the wreck. Also, there appears to have been a fairly significant amount of passenger gold aboard, but this case, almost surprisingly, has failed to see descendants of any of the passengers attempt to gain a share of the treasure. Thus, an abandonment may be found, and Columbus-America may be declared the finder and sole owner, as to any recovered parts of the ship, all passenger possessions, and any cargo besides the insured shipments.

As for the insured gold, to "prima facially" prove their ownership interests at trial, the underwriters produced several original documents: entries from the Atlantic Mutual's Vessel Disasters Book concerning the disaster (one of which contained the scribbled notation, "e[stimated] l[oss] $150,000"); records of Board resolutions to pay claims; minutes from an underwriters' board meeting discussing the *Central America*; a study prepared by the New York Board of Underwriters regarding the disaster; and the salvage contract between the underwriters and Brutus de Villeroi. The insurers also produced a great many period newspaper articles. These discussed the amount of treasure on board; the insurers of this treasure and the amounts they insured; the willingness of the insurers to pay off claims; the general satisfaction the insureds received from having their claims promptly settled; and the salvage negotiations between the underwriters and the Boston Submarine Armor Company.

On appeal, Columbus-America exerts much effort in asserting that there exists insufficient evidence to prove that the underwriters who are now parties in this litigation actually insured and paid off claims upon the gold. The lower court, though, found "prima facially" that the underwriters did insure the treasure and that they received ownership interests in the gold once the claims were paid. Because of the extent of the catastrophe involved, and its feared repercussions in the American economy, newspapers around the country devoted much space and attention not only to the human aspects of the tragedy, but also the financial. Articles abounded on the quantity of gold aboard, its owners, and its insurers. Some of these articles do contradict others as to the exact amount certain underwriters insured. Still, we find that the district court did not err when it held that the underwriters who are now parties, or their predecessors in interests, paid off claims upon and became the owners of the commercial shipment of gold in 1857.

Despite finding that the underwriters owned the gold in 1857, the district court applied the law of finds and awarded Columbus-America the entire treasure. This was because at some point the insurers had abandoned their interests in the gold. On appeal, Columbus-America asserts that the lower court found an abandonment because of "twenty distinct factors." It is clear, though, that the court ruled as it did because of only two: the underwriters did nothing to recover the gold after 1858, and they supposedly destroyed all documentation they had regarding payment of claims for the gold.

During trial, the underwriters did not produce any of the original insurance contracts with the insureds, statements from shippers that goods were aboard, bills of lading, or canceled checks or receipts from paying off the claims. While such documents would have existed in 1857, none could be located in 1990. Thus, because an insurance executive testified that the usual practice *today* is for insurance companies to destroy worthless documents after five years, the district court found that the above documentation concerning the *Central America* must have been intentionally destroyed in the ordinary course of business. Such destruction, coupled with 130 years of nonuse, equalled, according to the Court, an abandonment. Specifically:

The insurance carriers destroyed their records relating to the events of the Central America. Exactly when is not shown, but evidence establishes it was their custom to keep records for some five-year periods, and thereafter destroy them. However, one expert in marine insurance testified that if a company intended to assert its right to subrogation, it always maintained its documents of proof of the claim and that it had paid the claim, and the fact it disposed of such documents was an indication it abandoned its claim. It is difficult to believe that a company claiming an asset or property worth $150,000 in the 1800s or even early 1900s would destroy all evidence of its claim if it had any intention to pursue it, or any hope of recovery. How could one better demonstrate their intention to abandon a claim to or interest in property than to intentionally destroy every evidence of its claim, right, or title thereto. . . . They deliberately destroyed every document that would in any way show they had an interest in such a claim and had any intention to pursue it. Why? Their actions speak clearly. They had no hope or idea they could locate the *Central America*, and even if they could locate it, they had no hope they could recover anything from it. They destroyed the documents and intended thereby to abandon any claim they might have.

. . . A clear intention of abandonment is given when all records or memorandum of the property are deliberately destroyed and no effort is made or undertaken to locate or recover the property for over a hundred years. 742 F.Supp. at 1344–45, 1348

Contrary to the district court, we cannot find any evidence that the underwriters intentionally or deliberately destroyed any of their documents about the *Central America*. Instead, the only evidence we have is that after 134 years, such documents that may have once existed can no longer be located. With such a passing of time, it seems as, if not more, likely that the documents were lost or unintentionally destroyed, rather than being intentionally destroyed.

As has been mentioned above, a case very similar to ours is *Zych*, *supra*. There, in an opinion handed down after our case was decided below, the Northern District of Illinois held that the insurance company in question did not at any time abandon its interests in the wreck of *The Lady Elgin* prior to its 1990 contract with the foundation. In that case, the only evidence presented as to the actual insurance was six letters found in one of Aetna's letter books. Interestingly, no insurance documents, bills of lading, or claims documents were entered into evidence. The Court, though, distinguished its case from ours, as ours was related by our lower court's opinion, by explaining: "This case, of course, differs from *Columbus-America* in that there is no affirmative act, such as the destruction of document, which indicates an intent by Aetna to abandon the wreck." 755 F.Supp. at 216. The Court did not explain, nor did it seem perturbed by, the loss of all of Aetna's documents concerning *The Lady Elgin* other than the six letters.

It is undoubtedly true that in our case some of the insurance documents from 134 years ago are missing. Yet, the underwriters did present several other original documents from their files concerning this case, and in at least one instance all the documents in an insurer's file on the *Central America* were stolen by a would-be salvor. Also, most all of the evidence in the record actually seems to indicate a specific predisposition on the underwriters' part not to abandon the treasure.

Shortly after the disaster, the underwriters negotiated with a salvage company about rescuing the gold, and the next year a salvage contract was formed between two of the insurers and Brutus de Villeroi. Nothing came of these efforts, and the issue lay dormant for 120 years. Still, it appears that the gold was not totally forgotten for when the Atlantic Mutual Insurance Company ("Atlantic Mutual") wrote its official history in 1967, it devoted a couple of pages to the *Central America* tragedy and the company's salvage contract with de Villeroi.

Because of drastic advances in deep-water salvage, the late 1970s witnessed a good many would-be salvors contacting various underwriters regarding the *Central America*. Atlantic Mutual and the Insurance Company of North America ("INA") opened their archives to these salvors, and several in turn sought to form salvage arrangements with the insurers. In particular was a Norman Scott, who, in 1978, claimed to have located the *Central America*. He approached Atlantic Mutual and INA in reference to forming a salvage contract, and they in turn proceeded to hire a New York law firm to locate the other underwriters and begin salvage negotiations. Scott, though, was mistaken as to his discovery, and no contract was ever formed.

Throughout the early and mid-1980s, would-be salvors continued to contact the underwriters for information on the wreck. Salvage contracts were sporadically discussed, but at no time did the insurers ever agree to abandon their ownership interests in the gold. As late as 1987, INA was negotiating a salvage contract with Boston Salvage Consultants, Inc., whereby INA would receive 2 percent of any treasure recovered—before the parties could enter into a contract, though, the district court enjoined (through injunction box #1) these and other salvors from working in the area where it was then thought the wreck lay. In addition, not only the American insurers, but also the British, entered into various salvage negotiations, the latter through their Salvage Association.

It is ironic that one of the salvors who contacted the underwriters in the 1980s was Columbus-America itself. The eventual salvor used Atlantic Mutual's extensive library for research and then, in 1987, it, through an attorney, wrote the following enigmatic letter to many of the underwriters:

We are writing to a number of insurance companies on behalf of one of our clients. Our client is acquiring the rights to various nineteenth-century marine wrecks. If [your company] claims or asserts any interest in vessels or cargo which were wrecked in the Atlantic Ocean during the nineteenth century and would consider conveying its claim or asserted interest please get in touch with me.

Our client would also be interested in obtaining or seeing any existing records upon which [your company] might assert a claim to any nineteenth century wrecked vessel or its cargo.

Of course, none of the underwriters responded affirmatively to such a broad and mystifying request.

In conclusion, when a previous owner claims long-lost property that was involuntarily taken from his control, the law is hesitant to find an abandonment and such must be proved by clear and convincing evidence. Here, we are unable to find the requisite evidence that could lead a court to conclude that the underwriters affirmatively abandoned their interest in the gold. Thus, we hold that the lower court clearly erred when it found an abandonment and applied the law of finds. Accordingly, the case is remanded to the district court for further proceedings.

C.

On remand, the district court is to apply the law of salvage, and in so doing it must determine what percentage of the gold each underwriter insured. Equally if not more, important, the Court must also determine the proper salvage award for Columbus-America. Although this is a decision that must be left to the lower court, we are hazarding but little to say that Columbus-America should, and will, receive by far the largest share of the treasure.

In setting a salvage award, a court of admiralty becomes a court of equity. *The Boston*, 3 F.Cas. 932 (C.C.D.Mass. 1833). Such an award "is a compensation for meritorious service, [and] it may properly be increased, diminished, or wholly forfeited, according to the merit or demerit of the salvor, in his relation to the property saved." W. Marvin, *A Treatise on the Law of Wreck and Salvage*, Sec. 218, at 226 (1858). An award for salvage "generally far exceeds a mere remuneration pro opere et labore—the excess being intended, upon principles of sound public policy, not only as a reward to the particular salvor, but, also, as an inducement to others to render like services." Id., Sec. 97 at 105.

The Supreme Court has listed six "main ingredients" admiralty courts use when fixing an award for salvage:

(1) The labor expended by the salvors in rendering the salvage service. (2) The promptitude, skill, and energy displayed in rendering the service and saving the property. (3) The value of the property employed by the salvors in rendering the service, and the danger to which such property was exposed. (4) The risk incurred by the salvors in securing the property from the impending peril. (5) The value of the property saved. (6) The degree of danger from which the property was rescued. *The Blackwall*, 77 U.S. 1, 13–14 (1869)

We thoroughly agree with all six and, in cases such as this would add another: the degree to which the salvors have worked to protect the historical and archeological value of the wreck and items salved. In *MDM Salvage, Inc. v. The Unidentified, Wrecked and Abandoned Sailing Vessel*, 631 F.Supp. 308 (S.D.Fla. 1986), the Southern District of Florida held that such a factor may be heavily considered when exclusive salvage rights are sought. This same court has also stated that "there can be no suggestion that federal admiralty procedures sanction salvaging methods which fail to safeguard items and the invaluable archeological information associated with the artifacts salved." *Cobb Coin*, 525 F.Supp. at 208. We agree, and would only add that the converse to this latter statement is also true—salvors who seek to preserve and enhance the historical value of ancient shipwrecks should be justly rewarded.

From a distance, it appears that all seven of these considerations militate toward awarding Columbus-America a significant portion of the recovered gold. Of course, it will be up to the district court to determine if this is actually the case and what salvage award should be given.

As for the logistics in making a salvage award, we believe that in a case such as this, an award in specie would be proper. See, e.g, *Cobb Coin*, 525 F.Supp. at 198 (when items salvaged are "uniquely and intrinsically valuable beyond their monetary worth, an award in specie is more appropriate"). Also, because salvaging efforts have not been completed, the lower court might want to consider denominating the award as a percentage of the total recovery, rather than as a set monetary amount—should a specific monetary award be set too high, the underwriters could end up receiving nothing, while if an award is set too low, Columbus-America would have a disincentive to completely recovering the gold.

No matter what exact award is given, though, we are confident that Columbus-America will be justly rewarded for its extensive efforts in salvaging the *Central America*.

III.

The final issue on appeal concerns the claims of the intervenors, Columbia, John, and Grimm. At trial, the district court held that for the intervenors to be eligible for any recovery, they had to prove that Columbus-America made use of the information provided and that such "information lead to or assisted in locating the *Central America*." The Court then dismissed the intervenors' claim, finding that "there [was] no credible evidence in the record to establish either of these as a fact." 742 F.Supp. at 1339–40. On appeal, the intervenors claim that the reason such evidence was not in the record is that once intervention was allowed, the district court abused its discretion by not allowing any pretrial discovery.

The district court allowed Columbia, John, and Grimm to intervene, but only on the condition that they would begin trial the next day, thereby foregoing all pretrial discovery. Columbus-America now defends the Court's decision by stating that because the would-be intervenors waited until the eve of trial to attempt intervention, the Court had it within its discretion to deny the intervention, and thus, a fortiori, the Court also had the discretion to limit discovery. Whether the district court could have denied the intervention motion because of timeliness is an interesting question not before us. Even if the intervention could have been denied, though, it does not follow that once intervention was allowed the Court could effectively deny all discovery.

We thus find that the district court abused its discretion by forcing the intervenors to begin trial without an opportunity for any discovery. Accordingly, this portion of the case is reversed and remanded for discovery and a new trial. Should it be found that Columbus-America used the intervenors' information and such use contributed to the discovery of the *Central America*, a salvage award could be proper.

Reversed and Remanded.

Questions

1. What are the critical differences between the law of finds and the law of salvage?

2. Is the circuit court's standard for "abandonment" clear in this case?

3. Is traditional admiralty law appropriate for this new high-tech treasure hunting, or would legislation or perhaps a treaty be more appropriate?

Chapter 10

MARINE POLLUTION LAW

**Salaky v. The Atlas Barge No. 3 et al.,
208 F.2d 174 (2nd Cir. 1953)**

CLARK, CIRCUIT JUDGE

Libelant is the assignee of claims of some forty-four owners of small craft under an assignment executed in the State of New Jersey. He instituted his action alleging damage to these various craft moored in and about the Yacht Basin at Perth Amboy, N.J., caused by oil sludge and foreign matter discharged from the barges *Atlas Barge No. 3* and *Catherine O'Boyle* into the water of Arthur Kill and Raritan Bay in the vicinity of Perth Amboy in April 1946. The court below found for libelant by an interlocutory decree referring the issue of damages to a commissioner for computation, and respondents appeal.

The evidence discloses that at 8 o'clock in the morning in question a representative of the U.S. Coast Guard observed oil on the waters of the Yacht Basin. Later that day, some time after 1 P.M., together with a U.S. Customs inspector, he boarded the *Catherine O'Boyle*, which was docked about 1½ miles north of the Yacht Basin on the Staten Island side of Arthur Kill. She was

found with a pump still hot from recent use, its suction line leading down into the forepeak and its discharge line leading over the side. There was oil on the water all around her.

There was, however, undisputed and unimpeached testimony to the effect that the *O'Boyle* was empty; that she had carried no oil, but tar which is solid; that to liquefy tar for unloading requires certain steam equipment, not found on board, but attached up, when needed, from another vessel or shore installation; that the cargo tanks ran clear to her bottom, leaving no standard stem to stern bilge; that the forepeak was thus an isolated storage compartment whence the crew had, on the morning in question, pumped not more than thirty gallons of water. We can find no adequate reason for rejecting this testimony. Further, as we have just indicated, there is no actual evidence that the *O'Boyle* was responsible for any of the oil found in the Arthur Kill.

The *Atlas Barge No. 3* was, at the time, tied to a dock on the New Jersey side a mile and a half further up the Kill and some three miles from the Yacht Basin. For several days she had been engaged in cleaning the tanks of three vessels, and on the day in question was pumping out the bilges of the S.S. *Lahaina Victory*. The ship was first washed down with diesel fuel, then with water, and the resulting sludge was pumped out into the tanks of the *Atlas* barge. There was ample evidence that some time after 1:30 P.M. when the Customs and Coast Guard representatives arrived, the *Atlas* barge was overloaded and sludge was spilling over from her tanks into the water.

There is, however, no evidence connecting this discharge with the damage at the Yacht Basin. The Customs Inspector traced the *Atlas* oil slick a mile or more south of the *Atlas*, extending toward the basin; but as late as 4 or 5 o'clock that afternoon it was in the same spot, and though he observed the Yacht Basin in both morning and late afternoon, he at no time observed any oil therein. The Coast Guardsman, as noted, testified to the earlier presence of oil in the basin, to wit, at 8 A.M. He also saw oil around the *Atlas* barge, but it was thicker in appearance and he did not describe the condition of the water between the two points. Nor is there any evidence that the *Atlas* overflow commenced early enough to account for oil in the basin at 8 o'clock in the morning.

The area is one in which water pollution is a frequent problem. There are several oil companies in the vicinity and passage of oil-carrying barges is constant. Throughout the night preceding the damage complained of, a British tanker had been discharging cargo about a mile and a half from the basin and in the morning, oil covered the surrounding waters. It is fully as probable that the oil found in the Yacht Basin originated with this pumping operation, or some of the general traffic on the Kill, as that it was traceable to the *Atlas*.

In view, therefore, of what the record shows or suggests, we think the trial court has failed to observe properly the burden of proof which was resting upon the libelant to show by credible evidence or reasonable inference therefrom that the pollution complained of came from the barges sued, or from either one separately. We

are left with the fairly firm conviction that neither barge contributed to the injuries for which suit is brought; consequently, the findings must be held "clearly erroneous" under Fed. Rules Civ. Proc. rule 52(a), which we have often applied in admiralty.

Having reached this conclusion, we need not consider respondents' further contentions that the assignment was invalid under New Jersey law, that certain testimony was erroneously accepted, and that in any event the findings did not identify the separate boats injured or establish actual injury sufficiently to justify the reference to a commissioner to compute damages.

The decree is reversed for dismissal of the libel.

. . .

Questions

1. What practical problem in prosecuting oil spill cases does *Salaky* demonstrate?

2. Has modern technology improved our ability to identify polluters?

Huron Cement Co. v. City of Detroit, 362 U.S. 440 (1960)

MR. JUSTICE STEWART delivered the opinion of the Court.

This appeal from a judgment of the Supreme Court of Michigan draws in question the constitutional validity of certain provisions of Detroit's Smoke Abatement Code as applied to ships owned by the appellant and operated in interstate commerce.

The appellant is a Michigan corporation, engaged in the manufacture and sale of cement. It maintains a fleet of five vessels which it uses to transport cement from its mill in Alpena, Michigan, to distributing plants located in various states bordering the Great Lakes. Two of the ships, the S.S. *Crapo* and the S.S. *Boardman*, are equipped with hand-fired Scotch marine boilers. While these vessels are docked for loading and unloading it is necessary, in order to operate deck machinery, to keep the boilers fired and to clean the fires periodically. When the fires are cleaned, the ship's boiler stacks emit smoke which in density and duration exceeds the maximum standards allowable under the Detroit Smoke Abatement Code. Structural alterations would be required in order to insure compliance with the Code.

Criminal proceedings were instituted in the Detroit Recorder's Court against the appellant and its agents for violations of the city law during periods when the vessels were docked at the Port of Detroit. The appellant brought an action in the State Circuit Court to enjoin the city from further prosecuting the pending litigation in the Recorder's Court, and from otherwise enforcing the smoke ordinance against its vessels, "except where the emission of smoke is caused by the improper firing or the improper use of the equipment upon said vessels." The Circuit Court refused to grant relief, and the Supreme Court of Michigan affirmed, 355 Mich. 227, 93 N.W.2d 888. An appeal was lodged here, and we noted probable jurisdiction, 361 U.S. 806.

In support of the claim that the ordinance cannot constitutionally be applied to appellant's ships, two basic arguments are advanced. First, it is asserted that since the vessels and their equipment, including their boilers, have been inspected, approved, and licensed to operate in interstate commerce in accordance with a comprehensive system of regulation enacted by Congress, the City of Detroit may not legislate in such a way as, in effect, to impose additional or inconsistent standards. Secondly, the argument is made that even if Congress has not expressly preempted the field, the municipal ordinance "materially affects interstate commerce in matters where uniformity is necessary." We have concluded that neither of these contentions can prevail, and that the Federal Constitution does not prohibit application to the appellant's vessels of the criminal provisions of the Detroit ordinance.

The ordinance was enacted for the manifest purpose of promoting the health and welfare of the city's inhabitants. Legislation designed to free from pollution the very air that people breathe clearly falls within the exercise of even the most traditional concept of what is compendiously known as the police power. In the exercise of that power, the states and their instrumentalities may act, in many areas of interstate commerce and maritime activities, concurrently with the federal government.

The basic limitations upon local legislative power in this area are clear enough. The controlling principles have been reiterated over the years in a host of this Court's decisions. Evenhanded local regulation to effectuate a legitimate local public interest is valid unless preempted by federal action or unduly burdensome on maritime activities or interstate commerce.

In determining whether state regulation has been preempted by federal action,

the intent to supersede the exercise by the State of its police power as to matters not covered by the Federal legislation is not to be inferred from the mere fact that Congress has seen fit to circumscribe its regulation and to occupy a limited field. In other words, such intent is not to be implied unless the act of Congress fairly interpreted is in actual conflict with the law of the State.

In determining whether the state has imposed an undue burden on interstate commerce, it must be borne in mind that the Constitution when "conferring upon Congress the regulation of commerce, . . . never intended to cut the States off from legislating on all subjects relating to the health, life, and safety of their citizens, though the legislation might indirectly affect the commerce of the country. Legislation, in a great variety of ways, may affect commerce and persons engaged in it without constituting a regulation of it, within the meaning of the Constitution." But a state may not impose a burden which materially affects interstate commerce in an area where uniformity of regulation is necessary.

Although verbal generalizations do not of their own motion decide concrete cases, it is nevertheless within the framework of these basic principles that the issues in the present case must be determined.

I.

For many years Congress has maintained an extensive and comprehensive set of controls over ships and shipping. Federal inspection of steam vessels was first required in 1838, 5 Stat. 304, and the requirement has been continued ever since. Steam vessels which carry passengers must pass inspection annually, and those which do not, every two years. Failure to meet the standards invoked by law results in revocation of the inspection certificate, or refusal to issue a new one. It is unlawful for a vessel to operate without such a certificate.

These inspections are broad in nature, covering "the boilers, unfired pressure vessels, and appurtenances thereof, also the propelling and auxiliary machinery, electrical apparatus and equipment, of all vessels subject to inspection. . . ." 46 U.S.C. Sec. 392(b). The law provides that "no boiler . . . shall be allowed to be used if constructed in whole or in part of defective material or which because of its form, design, workmanship, age, use, or for any other reason is unsafe." 46 U.S.C. Sec. 392(c).

As is apparent on the face of the legislation, however, the purpose of the federal inspection statutes is to insure the seagoing safety of vessels subject to inspection. Thus 46 U.S.C. Sec. 392(c) makes clear that inspection of boilers and related equipment is for the purpose of seeing to it that the equipment "may be safely employed in the service proposed." The safety of passengers, 46 U.S.C. Sec. 391(a), and of the crew, 46 U.S.C. Sec. 391(b), is the criterion. The thrust of the federal inspection laws is clearly limited to affording protection from the perils of maritime navigation.

By contrast, the sole aim of the Detroit ordinance is the elimination of air pollution to protect the health and enhance the cleanliness of the local community. Congress recently recognized the importance and legitimacy of such a purpose, when in 1955 it provided:

[I]n recognition of the dangers to the public health and welfare, injury to agricultural crops and livestock, damage to and deterioration of property, and hazards to air and ground transportation from air pollution, it is hereby declared to be the policy of Congress to preserve and protect the primary responsibilities and rights of the States and local governments in controlling air pollution, to support and aid technical research to devise and develop methods of abating such pollution, and to provide Federal technical services and financial aid to State and local government air pollution control agencies and other public or private agencies and institutions in the formulation and execution of their air pollution abatement research programs.

Congressional recognition that the problem of air pollution is peculiarly a matter of state and local concern is manifest in this legislation.

We conclude that there is no overlap between the scope of the federal ship inspection laws and that of the municipal ordinance here involved. For this reason we cannot find that the federal inspection legislation has preempted local action. To hold otherwise would be to ignore the teaching of this Court's decisions which enjoin seeking out conflicts between state and federal regulation where none clearly exists.

An additional argument is advanced, however, based not upon the mere existence of the federal inspection standards, but upon the fact that the appellant's vessels were actually licensees, and enrolled, by the national government. It is asserted that the vessels have thus been given a dominant federal right to the use of the navigable waters of the United States, free from the local impediment that would be imposed by the Detroit ordinance.

The scope of the privilege granted by the federal licensing scheme has been well delineated. A state may not exclude from its waters a ship operating under a federal license. A state may not require a local occupation license, in addition to that federally granted, as a condition precedent to the use of its waters. While an enrolled and licensed vessel may be required to share the costs of benefits it enjoys, and to pay fair taxes imposed by its domicile, it cannot be subjected to local license imposts exacted for the use of a navigable waterway.

The mere possession of a federal license, however, does not immunize a ship from the operation of the normal incidents of local police power, not constituting a direct regulation of commerce. Thus, a federally licensed vessel is not, as such, exempt from local pilotage laws, *Cooley v. Board of Wardens of Port of Philadelphia*, 12 How. 299, or local quarantine laws, *Morgan's Steamship Co. v. Louisiana Board of Health*, 118 U.S. 455, or local safety inspections, *Kelly v. Washington*, 302 U.S. 1, or the local regulation of wharves and docks, *Packet Co. v. Catlettsburg*, 105 U.S. 559. Indeed this Court has gone so far as to hold that a state, in the exercise of its police power, may actually seize and pronounce the forfeiture of a vessel "licensed for the coasting trade, under the laws of the United States, while engaged in that trade." *Smith v. Maryland*, 18 How. 71, 74. The present case obviously does not even approach such an extreme, for the Detroit ordinance requires no more than compliance with an orderly and reasonable scheme of community regulation. The ordinance does not exclude a licensed vessel from the Port of Detroit, nor does it destroy the right of free passage. We cannot hold that the local regulation so burdens the federal license as to be constitutionally invalid.

II.

The claim that the Detroit ordinance, quite apart from the effect of federal legislation, imposes as to the appellant's ships an undue burden on interstate commerce needs no extended discussion. State regulation, based on the police power, which does not discriminate against interstate commerce or operate to disrupt its required uniformity, may constitutionally stand.

It has not been suggested that the local or-

dinance, applicable alike to "any person, firm, or corporation" within the city, discriminates against interstate commerce as such. It is a regulation of general application, designed to better the health and welfare of the community. And while the appellant argues that other local governments might impose differing requirements as to air pollution, it has pointed to none. The record contains nothing to suggest the existence of any such competing or conflicting local regulations. We conclude that no impermissible burden on commerce has been shown.

MR. JUSTICE DOUGLAS, with whom MR. JUSTICE FRANKFURTER concurs, dissenting.

The Court treats this controversy as if it were merely an inspection case with the City of Detroit supplementing a federal inspection system as the State of Washington did in *Kelly v. Washington*, 302 U.S.1. There a state inspection system touched matters "which the federal laws and regulations" left "untouched." This is not that type of case. Nor is this the rare case where state law adopts the standards and requirements of federal law and is allowed to exact a permit in addition to the one demanded by federal law. Here we have a criminal prosecution against a shipowner and officers of two of its vessels for using the very equipment on these vessels which the Federal Government says may be used. At stake are a possible fine of $100 on the owner and both a fine and a thirty-day jail sentence on the officers.

Appellant has a federal certificate for each of its vessels—S.S. *John W. Boardman*, S.S. *S. T. Crapo*, and others. The one issued on March 21, 1956, by the United States Coast Guard for S.S. *S. T. Crapo* is typical. The certificate states, "The said vessel is permitted to be navigated for one year on the Great Lakes." The certificate specifies the boilers which are and may be used—"Main Boilers Number 3, Year built 1927, Mfr. Manitowoc Boiler Wks." It also specifies the fuel which is used and is to be used in those boilers—"Fuel coal."

Appellant, operating the vessel in waters at the Detroit dock, is about to be fined criminally for using the precise equipment covered by the federal certificate because, it is said, the use of that equipment will violate a smoke ordinance of the City of Detroit.

The federal statutes give the Coast Guard the power to inspect "the boilers" of freight vessels every two years, and provide that when the Coast Guard approves the vessel and her equipment throughout, a certificate to that effect shall be made.

The requirements of the Detroit smoke ordinance are squarely in conflict with the federal statute. Section 2.2A of the ordinance prohibits the emission of the kind of smoke which cannot be at all times prevented by vessels equipped with hand-fired Scotch marine boilers such as appellant's vessels use. Section 2.16 of the ordinance makes it unlawful to use any furnace or other combustion equipment or device in the city without a certificate of operation which issues only after inspection. Section 2.17 provides for an annual inspection of every furnace or other combustion equipment used within the city. Section 2.20 provides that if an owner has been previously notified of three or more violations of the ordinance within any consecutive twelve-month period, he shall be notified to show cause before the Commissioner why the equipment should not be sealed. At the hearing, if the Commissioner finds that adequate corrective means have not been employed to remedy the situation, the equipment shall be sealed. Section 3.2 provides for a fine of not more than $100 or imprisonment for not more than thirty days or both upon conviction of any violation of any provision of the ordinance, and each day a violation is permitted to exist constitutes a separate offense.

Thus, it is plain that the ordinance requires not only the inspection and approval of equipment which has been inspected and approved by the Coast Guard but also the sealing of equipment, even though it has been approved by the Coast Guard. Under the Detroit ordi-

nance a certificate of operation would not issue for a hand-fired Scotch marine boiler, even though it had been approved by the Coast Guard. In other words, this equipment approved and licensed by the Federal Government for use on navigable waters cannot pass muster under local law.

If local law required federally licensed vessels to observe local speed laws, obey local traffic regulations, or dock at certain times or under prescribed conditions, we would have local laws not at war with the federal license, but complementary to it. In *Kelly v. Washington, supra,* at 14–15, the Court marked precisely that distinction. While it allowed state inspection of hull and machinery of tugs over and above that required by federal statutes, it noted that state rules which changed the federal standards "for the structure and equipment of vessels" would meet a different fate:

The state law is a comprehensive code. While it excepts vessels which are subject to inspection under the laws of the United States, it has provisions which may be deemed to fall within the class of regulations which Congress alone can provide. For example, Congress may establish standards and designs for the structure and equipment of vessels, and may prescribe rules for their operation, which could not properly be left to the diverse action of the States. The State of Washington might prescribe standards, designs, equipment, and rules of one sort, Oregon another, California another, and so on. But it does not follow that in all respects the state Act must fail.

This case, like *Napier v. Atlantic Coast Line R.R. Co.,* 272 U.S. 605, involves the collision between a local law and a federal law which gives a federal agency the power to specify or approve the equipment to be used by a federal licensee. In that case one State required automatic fire doors on locomotives of interstate trains and another State required cab curtains during the winter months. The Interstate Commerce Commission, though it had the power to do so under the Boiler Inspection Act, had never required a particular kind of fire door or cab curtain. The Court, speaking through Mr. Justice Brandeis, said, at 612–13:

The federal and the state statutes are directed to the same subject—the equipment of locomotives. They operate upon the same object. It is suggested that the power delegated to the Commission has been exerted only in respect to minor changes or additions. But this, if true, is not of legal significance. It is also urged that, even if the Commission has power to prescribe an automatic firebox door and a cab curtain, it has not done so; and that it has made no other requirement inconsistent with the state legislation. This, also, if true, is without legal significance. The fact that the Commission has not seen fit to exercise its authority to the full extent conferred has no bearing upon the construction of the Act delegating the power. We hold that state legislation is precluded, because the Boiler Inspection Act, as we construe it, was intended to occupy the field.

Here the Coast Guard would be entitled to insist on different equipment. But it has not done so. The boats of appellant, therefore, have credentials good for any port; and I would not allow this local smoke ordinance to work in derogation of them. The fact that the Federal Government in certifying equipment applies standards of safety for seagoing vessels, while Detroit applies standards of air pollution seems immaterial. Federal preemption occurs when the boilers and fuel to be used in the vessels are specified in the certificate. No state authority can, in my view, change those specifications. Yet that is in effect what is allowed here.

As we have seen, the Detroit ordinance contains provisions making it unlawful to operate appellant's equipment without a certificate from the city and providing for the sealing of the equipment in case of three or more violations within any twelve-month period. The Court says that those sanctions are not presently in issue, that it reserves decision as to their validity, and that it concerns itself only with "the enforcement of the criminal provisions" of the ordinance. Yet by what authority can a local government fine people or send them to jail for using in interstate commerce the precise equipment which the federal regulatory agency has certified and approved? The burden of these criminal sanctions on the owners and officers, particularly as it involves the risk of imprisonment, may indeed be far more serious than a mere sealing of the equipment. Yet whether fine or imprisonment is considered, the effect on the federal certificate will be crippling. However the issue in the present case is stated, it comes down to making criminal in the Port of Detroit the use of a certificate issued under paramount federal law. Never before, I believe, have we recognized the right of local law to make the use of an unquestionably legal federal license a criminal offense.

What we do today is in disregard of the doctrine long accepted and succinctly stated in the 1851 term in *Pennsylvania v. Wheeling & Belmont Bridge Co.*, 13 How. 518, 566, "No State law can hinder or obstruct the free use of a license granted under an act of Congress." The confusion and burden arising from the imposition by one State of requirements for equipment which the Federal Government has approved was emphasized in *Kelly v. Washington, supra,* in the passage already quoted. The requirements of Detroit may be too lax for another port. The variety of requirements for equipment which the States may provide in order to meet their air pollution needs underlines the importance of letting the Coast Guard license serve as authority for the vessel to use, in all our ports, the equipment which it certifies.

Questions

1. Compare the dissent of Justice Douglas in this case with his majority opinion in the *Askew* case which follows. Can you distinguish the two cases?

2. Is it unusual for a federally licensed activity to conflict with state or local laws?

Askew v. American Waterways Operators, 411 U.S. 325 (1973)

MR. JUSTICE DOUGLAS delivered the opinion of the Court.

This action was brought by merchant shipowners and operators, world shipping associations, members of the Florida coastal barge and towing industry, and owners and operators of oil terminal facilities and heavy industries located in Florida, to enjoin application of the Florida Oil Spill Prevention and Pollution Control Act, Fla. Laws 1970, c. 70-244, Fla. Stat. Ann. Sec. 376.011 et seq. (Suppl. 1973) (hereinafter referred to as the Florida Act). Officials responsible for enforcing the Florida Act were named as defendants, but the State of Florida intervened as a party defendant, asserting that its interests were much broader than those of the named defendants. A three-judge court was convened pursuant to 28 U.S.C. Sec. 2281.

The Florida Act imposes strict liability for any damage incurred by the State or private persons as a result of an oil spill in the State's territorial waters from any waterfront facility used for drilling for oil or handling the transfer or storage of oil (terminal facility) and from any ship destined for or leaving such facility. Each owner or operator of a terminal facility or ship subject to the Act must establish evidence of financial responsibility by insurance or a surety bond. In addition, the Florida Act provides for regulation by the State Department of Natural Resources with respect to containment gear and other equipment which must be maintained by ships and terminal facilities for the prevention of oil spills.

Several months prior to the enactment of the Florida Act, Congress enacted the Water Quality Improvement Act of 1970, 84 Stat. 91, 33 U.S.C. Sec. 1161 et seq. (hereinafter referred to as the Federal Act). This Act subjects shipowners and terminal facilities to liability without fault up to $14 million and $8 million, respectively, for cleanup costs incurred by the Federal Government as a result of oil spills. It also au-

thorizes the President to promulgate regulations requiring ships and terminal facilities to maintain equipment for the prevention of oil spills. It is around that Act . . . that the controversy turns. The District Court held that the Florida Act is an unconstitutional intrusion into the federal maritime domain. It declared the Florida Act null and void and enjoined its enforcement. 335 F. Supp. 1241.

The case is here on direct appeal. We reverse. We find no constitutional or statutory impediment to permitting Florida, in the present setting of this case, to establish any "requirement or liability" concerning the impact of oil spillages on Florida's interests or concerns. To rule as the District Court has done is to allow federal admiralty jurisdiction to swallow most of the police power of the States over oil spillage—an insidious form of pollution of vast concern to every coastal city or port and to all the estuaries on which the life of the ocean and the lives of the coastal people are greatly dependent.

I.

It is clear at the outset that the Federal Act does not preclude, but in fact allows, state regulation. Section 1161 (o) provides that:

(1) Nothing in this section shall affect or modify in any way the obligations of any owner or operator of any vessel, or of any owner or operator of any onshore facility or offshore facility to any person or agency *under any provision of law for damages to any publicly owned or privately owned property* resulting from a discharge of any oil or from the removal of any such oil.

(2) Nothing in this section shall be construed as preempting any State or political subdivision thereof from imposing *any requirement or liability* with respect to the discharge of oil into any waters within such State.

(3) Nothing in this section shall be construed . . . to affect any State or local law not in conflict with this section. (emphasis added)

According to the Conference Report, "any State would be free to provide requirements and penalties similar to those imposed by this section or *additional requirements and penalties*. These, however, would be separate and independent from those imposed by this section and would be enforced by the States through its courts" (emphasis added). The Florida Act covers a wide range of "pollutants," and a restricted definition of pollution. We have here, however, no question concerning any pollutant except oil.

The Federal Act, to be sure, contains a pervasive system of federal control over discharges of oil "into or upon the navigable waters of the United States, adjoining shorelines, or into or upon the waters of the contiguous zone." Sec. 1161 (b)(1). So far as liability is concerned, an owner or operator of a vessel is liable to the United States for actual costs incurred for the removal of oil discharged in violation of Sec. 1161 (b)(2) in an amount "not to exceed $100 per gross ton of such vessel or $14 million, whichever is lesser," Sec. 1161 (f)(1), except for discharges caused solely by an act of God, act of war, negligence of the United States, or act or omission of another party. With like exceptions the owner or operator of an onshore or offshore facility is liable to the United States for the actual costs incurred by the United States in an amount not to exceed $8 million. But in each case the owner or operator is liable to the United States for the full amount of the costs where the United States can show that the discharge of oil was "the result of willful negligence or willful misconduct within the privity and knowledge of the owner." Comparable provisions of liability spell out the obligations of a "third Party" to the United States for its actual costs incurred in the removal of the oil.

So far as vessels are concerned, the federal Limited Liability Act, 46 U.S.C. Secs. 181–89, extends to damages caused by oil spills even where the injury is to the shore. That Act limits the liabilities of the owners of vessels to the "value of such vessels and freight pending." 46 U.S.C. Sec. 189.

Section 12 of the Florida Act makes all licensees of terminal facilities "liable to the state for all costs of cleanup or other damage incurred by the state and for damages resulting from injury to others," it not being necessary for the State to plead or prove negligence. There is no conflict between Sec. 12 of the Florida Act and Sec. 1161 of the Federal Act when it comes to damages to property interests, for the Federal Act reaches only costs of cleaning up. As respects damages, Sec. 14 of the Florida Act requires evidence of financial responsibility of a terminal facility or vessel—a provision which does not conflict with the Federal Act.

The Solicitor General says that while the Limited Liability Act, *so far as vessels are concerned*, would override Sec. 12 of the Florida Act by reason of the Supremacy Clause, the Limited Liability Act has no bearing on "facilities" regulated by the Florida Act. Moreover, Sec. 12 has not yet been construed by the Florida courts and it is susceptible of an interpretation *so far as vessels are concerned* which would be in harmony with the Federal Act. Section 12 does not *in terms* provide for unlimited liability.

Moreover, while the Federal Act determines damages measured by the cost to the United States for cleaning up oil spills, the damages specified in the Florida Act relate in part to the cost to the State of Florida in cleaning up the spillage. Those two sections are harmonious parts of an integrated whole. Section 1161 (c)(2) directs the President to prepare a National Contingency Plan for the containment, dispersal, and removal of oil. The plan must provide that federal agencies "shall" act "in coordination with State and local agencies." Cooperative action with the States is also contemplated by Sec. 1161 (e), which provides that "[i]n addition to any other action taken by a State or local government" the President may, when there is an imminent and substantial threat to the public health or welfare, direct the United States Attorney of the district in question to bring suit to abate the threat. The reason for the provision in Sec. 1161 (o)(2), stating that nothing in Sec.

1161 preempts any State "from imposing any requirement or liability with respect to the discharge of oil into any waters within such State," is that the scheme of the Act is one which allows—though it does not require—cooperation of the federal regime with a state regime.

If Florida wants to take the lead in cleaning up oil spillage in her waters, she can use Sec. 12 of the Florida Act and recoup her costs from those who did the damage. Whether the amount of costs she could recover from a wrongdoer is limited to those specified in the Federal Act and whether in turn this new Federal Act removes the preexisting limitations of liability in the Limited Liability Act are questions we need not reach here. Any opinion on them is premature. It is sufficient for this day to hold that there is room for state action in cleaning up the waters of a State and recouping, at least within federal limits, so far as vessels are concerned, her costs.

Beyond that is the potential claim under Sec. 12 of the Florida Act for "other damage incurred by the state and for damages resulting from injury to others." The Federal Act in no way touches those areas. A State may have public beaches ruined by oil spills. Shrimp may be destroyed, and clam, oyster, and scallop beds ruined and the livelihood of fishermen imperiled. The Federal Act takes no cognizance of those claims but only of costs to the Federal Government, if it does the cleaning up.

We held in *Skiriotes v. Florida*, 313 U.S. 69, that while Congress had regulated the size of commercial sponges taken in Florida waters, it had not dealt with any diving apparatus that might be used. Florida had such a law and was allowed to enforce it against one of its citizens. Mr. Chief Justice Hughes, speaking for the Court, said: "It is also clear that Florida has an interest in the proper maintenance of the sponge fishery and that the statute so far as applied to conduct within the territorial waters of Florida, in the absence of conflicting federal legislation, is within the police power of the State."

Similarly, in *Manchester v. Massachusetts*, 139 U.S. 240, 266, we stated that if Congress fails to assume control of fisheries in a bay, "the right to control such fisheries must remain with the State which contains such bays."

Florida in her brief accurately states that no remedy under the Federal Act exists for state or private property owners damaged by a massive oil slick such as hit England and France in 1967 in the *Torrey Canyon* disaster. The *Torrey Canyon* carried 880,000 barrels of crude oil. Today not only is more oil being moved by sea each year, but the tankers are much larger.

The average tanker used during World War II had a capacity of 16,000 tons, but by 1965 that average had risen to 47,000 tons, and new tankers delivered in 1966 averaged about 76,000 tons. A Japanese company has launched a 276,000-ton tanker, and other Japanese yards have orders for tankers as large as 312,000 tons. More than sixty tankers of 150,000 tons or more are on order throughout the world, tankers of 500,000 to 800,000 tons are on the drawing boards, and those of more than one million tons are thought to be feasible. On the new 1,010-foot British tanker *Esso Mercia* two officers have been issued bicycles to help patrol the decks of the 166,890-ton vessel.

The size of the tanker fleet itself is growing at a rate that rivals the growth in average size of new tankers. In 1955 the world tanker fleet numbered about 2,500 vessels. By 1965 it had increased to 3,500, and in 1968 it numbered some 4,300 ships. At the present time nearly one ship out of every five in the world merchant fleet is engaged in transporting oil, and nearly the entire fleet is powered by oil. 10 Harv. Int'l L.J. at 317–318

Our Coast Guard reports that while in 1970 there were 3,711 oil spills in our waters, in 1971 there were 8,736. The damage to state interests already caused by oil spills, the increase in the number of oil spills, and the risk of ever-increasing damage by reason of the size of modern tankers underlie the concern of coastal States.

While the Federal Act is concerned only with actual cleanup costs incurred by the Federal Government, the State of Florida is concerned with its own cleanup costs. Hence, there need be no collision between the Federal Act and the Florida Act because, as noted, the Federal Act presupposes a coordinated effort with the States, and any federal limitation of liability runs to "vessels," not to shore "facilities." That is one of the reasons why Congress decided that the Federal Act does not preempt the States from establishing either *"any requirement or liability"* respecting oil spills.

Moreover, since Congress dealt only with "cleanup" costs, it left the States free to impose "liability" in damages for losses suffered both by the States and by private interests. The Florida Act imposes liability without fault. So far as liability without fault for damages to state and private interests is concerned, the police power has been held adequate for that purpose. State statutes imposing absolute liability on railroads for *all* property lost through fires caused by sparks emitted from locomotive engines have been sustained. The Federal Act, however, while restricted to cleanup costs incurred by the United States, imposes limited liability for those costs and provides certain exceptions, unless willfulness is established. Where liability is imposed by Secs. 1161 (f)–(g), previously summarized, the United States may recover the full amount of the costs where the oil spillage was the result of "willful negligence or willful misconduct." If the coordinated federal plan in actual operation leaves the State of Florida to do the cleaning work, there might be financial burdens imposed greater than would have been imposed had the Federal Government done the cleanup work. But it will be time to resolve any such conflict between federal and state regimes when it arises.

Nor can we say at this point that regulations of the Florida Department of Natural Resources requiring "containment gear" pursuant to Sec. 7 (2)(a) of the Florida Act would be per se invalid because the subject to be regulated requires uniform federal regulation. Cf. *Huron Cement Co. v. Detroit*, 362 U.S. 440. Resolution of this question, as well as the question whether such regulations will conflict with Coast Guard regulations promulgated on December 21, 1972, pursuant to Sec. 1161 (j)(1) of the Federal Act, 37 Fed. Reg. 28250, should await a concrete dispute under applicable Florida regulations. Finally, the provision of the Florida Act requiring the licensing of terminal facilities, a traditional state concern, creates no conflict per se with federal legislation. Section 1171 (b)(1) of the Federal Act provides that federal permits will not be issued to terminal facility operators or owners unless the applicant first supplies a certificate from the State that his operation "will be conducted in a manner which will not violate applicable water quality standards." And Tit. I, Sec. 102 (b), of the recently enacted Ports and Waterways Safety Act of 1972, 33 U.S.C. Sec. 1222 (b), provides that the Act does not prevent "a State or political subdivision thereof from prescribing for structures only higher safety equipment requirements or safety standards than those which may be prescribed pursuant to this title."

II.

And so, in the absence of federal preemption and any fatal conflict between the statutory schemes, the issue comes down to whether a State constitutionally may exercise its police power respecting maritime activities concurrently with the Federal Government.

Historically, damages to the shore or to shore facilities were not cognizable in admiralty. Mr. Justice Story wrote in 1813,

In regard to torts I have always understood that the jurisdiction of the admiralty is exclusively dependent upon the locality of the act. The admiralty has not, and never (I believe) deliberately claimed to have any jurisdiction over torts, except such as are maritime torts, that is, such as are committed on the high seas, or on waters within the ebb and flow of the tide. *Thomas v. Lane*, 23 F. Cas. 957, 960 (No. 13,902) (CC Me)

On June 19, 1948, Congress enacted the Admiralty Extension Act, 46 U.S.C. Sec. 740. The

Court considered the Act in *Victory Carriers, Inc. v. Law*, 404 U.S. 202. In that case, the Court held that the Admiralty Extension Act did not apply to a longshoreman performing loading and unloading services on the dock. The longshoreman was relegated to his remedy under the state workmen's compensation law. The Court said, "At least in the absence of explicit congressional authorization, we shall not extend the historic boundaries of the maritime law."

The Admiralty Extension Act has survived constitutional attack in the lower federal courts and was applied without question by this Court in *Gutierrez v. Waterman S.S. Corp.*, 373 U.S. 206. The Court recognized in *Victory Carriers*, however, that the Act may "intrude on an area that has heretofore been reserved for state law." It cautioned that under these circumstances, "we should proceed with caution in construing constitutional and statutory provisions dealing with the jurisdiction of the federal courts." While Congress has extended admiralty jurisdiction beyond the boundaries contemplated by the Framers, it hardly follows from the constitutionality of that extension that we must sanctify the federal courts with exclusive jurisdiction to the exclusion of powers traditionally within the competence of the States. One can read the history of the Admiralty Extension Act without finding any clear indication that Congress intended that sea-to-shore injuries be exclusively triable in the federal courts.

Even though Congress has acted in the admiralty area, state regulation is permissible, absent a clear conflict with the federal law. Thus, in *Kelly v. Washington*, 302 U.S. 1, it appeared that, while Congress had provided a comprehensive system of inspection of vessels on navigable waters, id., at 4, the State of Washington also had a comprehensive code of inspection. Some of those state standards conflicted with the federal requirements, id., at 14–15; but those provisions of the Washington law relating to safety and seaworthiness were not in conflict with the federal law. So the question was whether the absence of congressional attention

and the need for uniformity of regulation barred state action. Mr. Chief Justice Hughes, writing for the Court, ruled in the negative, saying:

A vessel which is actually unsafe and unseaworthy in the primary and commonly understood sense is not within the protection of that principle. The State may treat it as it may treat a diseased animal or unwholesome food. In such a matter, the State may protect its people without waiting for federal action providing the state action does not come into conflict with federal rules. If, however, the State goes further and attempts to impose particular standards as to structure, design, equipment, and operation which in the judgment of its authorities may be desirable but pass beyond what is plainly essential to safety and seaworthiness, the State will encounter the principle that such requirements, if imposed at all, must be through the action of Congress which can establish a uniform rule. Whether the State in a particular matter goes too far must be left to be determined when the precise question arises. Id., at 15

That decision was rendered before the Admiralty Extension Act was passed.

Huron Cement Co. v. Detroit, 362 U.S. 440, however, arose after that Act became effective. Ships cruising navigable waters and inspected and licensed under federal acts were charged with violating Detroit's Smoke Abatement Code. The company and its agents were, indeed, criminally charged with violating that Code. The Court in sustaining the state prosecution said:

The ordinance was enacted for the manifest purpose of promoting the health and welfare of the city's inhabitants. Legislation designed to free from pollution the very air that people breathe clearly falls within the exercise of even the most traditional concept of what is compendiously known as the police power. In the exercise of that power, the states and their instrumentalities may act, in many areas of interstate commerce and maritime activities, concurrently with the federal government. Id., at 442

The Court reasoned that there was room for local control since federal inspection was "limited to affording protection from the perils of maritime navigation," while the Detroit ordinance was aimed at "the elimination of air pollution to protect the health and enhance the cleanliness of the local community." The Court, in reviewing prior decisions, noted that a federally licensed vessel was not exempt (1) "from local pilotage laws"; (2) "local quarantine laws"; (3) "local safety inspections"; or (4) "local regulation of wharves and docks."

It follows, a fortiori, that sea-to-shore pollution—historically within the reach of the police power of the States—is not silently taken away from the States by the Admiralty Extension Act, which does not purport to supply the exclusive remedy.

As discussed above, we cannot say with certainty at this stage that the Florida Act conflicts with any federal Act. We have only the question whether the waiver of preemption by Congress at Sec. 1161 (o)(2) concerning the imposition by a State of "any requirement or liability" is valid.

The Admiralty Extension Act does not preempt state law in those situations.

The judgment below is *reversed*.

Questions

1. Doesn't the imposition of individual state requirements pose an undue hardship for the tanker industry?

2. Did you note Justice Douglas citing *Huron Cement* for support despite his own dissent in that case?

Union Oil Company v. Oppen, 501 F.2d 558 (9th Cir. 1974)

SNEED, CIRCUIT JUDGE

This is another case growing out of the Santa Barbara oil spill of 1969. The plaintiffs are commercial fishermen. Each of their complaints alleges that the cause of action has been brought under the provisions of the Outer Continental Shelf Lands Act of 1953, 43 U.S.C. Sec. 1331 et seq.; that the defendants joined in an enterprise, the day-to-day operation of which was within the control and under the management of defendant Union Oil Company, to drill for oil in the waters of the Santa Barbara Channel; that during the period commencing on or about January 28, 1969, vast quantities of raw crude oil were released and subsequently carried by wind, wave, and tidal currents over vast stretches of the coastal waters of Southern California; and that as a consequence the plaintiffs have suffered various injuries for which damages are sought. Jurisdiction rests on 28 U.S.C. Sec. 1333 and 43 U.S.C. Sec. 1333(b).

. . . As we see it, the issue is whether the defendants owed a duty to the plaintiffs, commercial fishermen, to refrain from negligent conduct in their drilling operations, which conduct reasonably and foreseeably could have been anticipated to cause a diminution of the aquatic life in the Santa Barbara Channel area and thus cause injury to the plaintiffs' business.

In finding that such a duty exists, we are influenced by the manner in which the Supreme Court of California has approached the duty issue in tort law. . . . We cannot escape the conclusion that under California law the presence of a duty on the part of the defendants in this case would turn substantially on foreseeability. That being the crucial determinant, the question must be asked whether the defendants could reasonably have foreseen that negligently conducted drilling operations might diminish aquatic life and thus injure the business of commercial fishermen. We believe the answer is yes. The dangers of pollution were and are known even by school children. The defendants understood the risks of their business and should reasonably have foreseen the scope of its responsibilities. To assert that the defendants were unable to foresee that negligent conduct resulting in a substantial oil spill could diminish aquatic life and thus injure the plaintiffs is to suppose a degree of general ignorance of the effects of oil pollution not in accord with good sense.

An examination of other factors . . . only strengthens our conclusion that the defendants in this case owed a duty to the plaintiffs. Thus, the fact that the injury flows directly from the action of escaping oil on the life in the sea, *Askew v. American Waterways Operators, Inc.*, 411 U.S. at 333 n. 5, the public's deep disapproval of injuries to the environment and the strong policy of preventing such injuries, all point to existence of a required duty.

The same conclusion is reached when the issue before us is approached from the standpoint of economics. Recently a number of scholars have suggested that liability for losses occasioned by torts should be apportioned in a manner that will best contribute to the achievement of an optimum allocation of resources. See e.g., Calabresi, *The Cost of Accidents*, 69–73 (1979) (hereinafter Calabresi); Coase, *The Problem of Social Cost*, 3 J. Law & Econ. 1 (1960). This optimum, in theory, would be that which would be achieved by a perfect market system. In determining whether the cost of an accident should be borne by the injured party or be shifted, in whole or in part, this approach requires the court to fix the identity of the party who can avoid the costs most cheaply. Once fixed, this determination then controls liability.

It turns out, however, that fixing the identity of the best or cheapest cost avoider is more difficult than might be imagined. In order to facilitate this determination, Calabresi suggests several helpful guidelines. The first of these would require a rough calculation designed to exclude as potential cost-avoiders those groups/ activities which could avoid accident costs only at an extremely high expense. While not easy to apply in any concrete sense, this guideline does suggest that the imposition of oil spill costs directly upon such groups as the consumers of staple groceries is not a sensible solution. Under this guideline, potential liability becomes resolved into a choice between, on an ultimate level, the consumers of fish and those of products derived from the defendants' total operations.

To refine this choice, Calabresi goes on to provide additional guidelines which, in this instance, have proven none too helpful. For example, he suggests an evaluation of the administrative costs which each party would be forced to bear in order to avoid the accident costs. He also states that an attempt should be made to avoid an allocation which will impose some costs on those groups or activities which neither consume fish nor utilize those products of the defendants derived from their operations in the Santa Barbara Channel. On the record before us, we have no way of evaluating the relative administrative costs involved. However, we do recognize that it is probable that by imposing liability on the defendants some portion of the accident costs in this case may be borne by those who neither eat fish nor use the petroleum products derived from the defendants' operations in Santa Barbara.

Calabresi's final guideline, however, unmistakably points to the defendants as the best cost-avoider. Under this guideline, the loss should be allocated to that party who can best correct any error in allocation, if such there be, by acquiring the activity to which the party has been made liable. The capacity "to buy out" the plaintiffs if the burden is too great is, in essence, the real focus of Calabresi's approach. On this basis there is no contest— the defendants' capacity is superior.

Our holding that the defendants are under a duty to commercial fishermen to conduct their drilling and production in a reasonably prudent manner so as to avoid the negligent diminution of aquatic life is not foreclosed by the fact that the defendants' negligence could constitute a public nuisance under California law. The right of commercial fishermen to recover for injuries to their businesses caused by pollution of public waters has been recognized on numerous occasions. The injury here asserted by the plaintiff is a pecuniary loss of a particular and special nature, limited to the class of commercial fishermen which they represent.

This injury must, of course, be established in the proceedings that will follow this appeal. To do this it must be shown that the oil spill did in fact diminish aquatic life, and that this diminution reduced the profits the plaintiffs would have realized from their commercial fishing in the absence of the spill. This reduction of profits must be established with certainty and must not be remote, speculative, or conjectural. These are not small burdens, nor can they be eased by our abhorrence of massive oil spills. All that we do here is to permit the plaintiffs to attempt to prove their case, and to reject the idea urged upon us by the defendants that a barrier to such an effort exists in the form of the rule that negligent interference with an economic advantage is not actionable.

Finally, it must be understood that our holding in this case does not open the door to claims that may be asserted by those, other than commercial fishermen, whose economic or personal affairs were discommoded by the oil spill of January 28, 1969. The general rule urged upon us by defendants has a legitimate sphere within which to operate. Nothing said in this opinion is intended to suggest, for example, that every decline in the general commercial activity of every business in the Santa Barbara area following the occurrences of 1969 constitutes a legally cognizable injury for which the defendants may be responsible. The plaintiffs in the present action lawfully and directly make use of a resource of the sea, viz its fish, in the ordinary course of their business. This type of use is entitled to protection from negligent conduct by the defendants in their drilling operations. Both the plaintiffs and defendants conduct their business operations away from land and in, on, and under the sea. Both must carry on their commercial enterprises in a reasonably prudent manner. Neither should be permitted negligently to inflict commercial injury on the other. We decide no more than this.

Affirmed.

Questions

1. Why should commercial fishermen be treated differently than other claimants?

2. How would you calculate the damages the fishermen sustained?

Commonwealth of Puerto Rico, et al., v. The S.S. Zoe Colocotroni, etc., et al., 628 F.2d 652 (1st Cir. 1980)

LEVIN H. CAMPBELL, CT. J.

In the early morning hours of March 18, 1973, the S.S. *Zoe Colocotroni*, a tramp oil tanker, ran aground on a reef 3½ miles off the south coast of Puerto Rico. To refloat the vessel, the captain ordered the dumping of more than five thousand tons of crude oil into the surrounding waters. An oil slick four miles long, and a tenth of a mile wide, floated toward the coast and came ashore at an isolated peninsula on the southwestern tip of the island—a place called Bahia Sucia. The present appeal concerns an action in admiralty brought by the Commonwealth of Puerto Rico and the local Environmental Quality Board (EQB) to recover damages for harm done to the coastal environment by the spilled oil.

Defendants have raised numerous objections to the district court's judgment awarding plaintiffs $6,164,192.09 in damages for cleanup costs and environmental harm. The primary objections are that the district court: (1) abused its discretion in striking defendant's pleadings on the issue of liability as a sanction for defendants' conduct during the discovery process; (2) erred in considering depositions of the ship's master and crew on the issue of liability and in making findings as to liability after that issue had been removed from the case; (3) lacked personal jurisdiction over the underwriters West of England-Luxembourg and West of England-London; (4) erred in finding plaintiffs had standing to sue for environmental damages; (5) applied the wrong standard in measuring damages; (6) made certain erroneous findings of fact on damages; and (7) erred in denying defendants' Rule 60 motion for relief from judgment. The facts and circumstances of the oil spill and its aftermath are set forth in detail in the district court's opinion, *Commonwealth of Puerto Rico v. S.S. Zoe Colocotroni*, 1979 AMC 21, 456 F. Supp. 1327 (DP.R. 1978). After a brief review of these facts and of the trial testimony, we will address defendants' contentions in turn.

I.

The following facts found by the district court are not in serious dispute. On March 15, 1973, the *Zoe Colocotroni* departed La Salina, Venezuela, carrying 187,670 barrels of crude oil en route to Guayanilla, Puerto Rico. For the first two days of the voyage, the vessel proceeded by celestial navigation. The last star fix, however, was taken at 1859 hours on March 17. For the next eight hours, the ship proceeded by dead reckoning. As the vessel approached the south coast of Puerto Rico, it was, the district court stated, "hopelessly lost." At 0300 hours on March 18, the ship grounded on a reef. Efforts to free the tanker by alternately running the engines in forward and reverse were unsuccessful. After ten minutes, the captain ordered the crew to lighten ship by emptying the cargo of crude oil into the sea. By the time the vessel refloated, some 1.5 million gallons of crude oil—5,170.1 tons—had poured into the surrounding waters.

The oil floated westward from the site of the spill throughout the daylight hours of March 18, and began coming ashore after nightfall. Bahia Sucia is a crescent-shaped bay facing southeastward from the Cabo Rojo peninsula, which forms the southwest tip of Puerto Rico. The oil entered Bahia Sucia, washed onto the beaches, and penetrated the mangrove forests that line the western edge of the bay. The oil was particularly thick in three areas: around the rocky tip of the peninsula, in a section of mangroves known as West Mangrove between a point called "Hermit One" and an inlet called "Dogman's Cove," and on the open beach area stretching along the northern edge of the bay. In addition, as the tide ebbed and flowed, oil entered the tidal flats behind the mangrove fringe, coating the roots of mangroves growing deeper in the forest and soaking into the sediments.

A massive cleanup operation, coordinated by the United States Coast Guard and several Commonwealth agencies, commenced on the morning of March 19. Cleanup crews, hampered to some extent by variable winds that blew oil back and forth across the bay, used booms to attempt to contain oil floating on the surface. Much of this oil was pumped out, either directly from the water or from large holes dug in the beach into which oil was channeled by the cleanup crews. By March 29, approximately 755,000 gallons of oil, or about half the amount spilled, had been recovered. On several occasions during the cleanup, oil was driven by winds and currents into the eastern edge of the bay in an area known as East Mangrove. This thin layer of oil was difficult to remove, but, according to the district court's findings, it caused little or no harm to the East Mangrove forest.

By April, cleanup activities had switched from large-scale removal of oil to small-scale activities such as manual beach cleanup and bailing of oil from tidal pockets with buckets and small boats. Large amounts of contaminated sands—totaling about 4,500 cubic yards—were removed from the beach area by bulldozer and by hand. At the end of April, the major remaining cleanup efforts were halted, and all further efforts were discontinued after September 24. Despite the cleanup, oil continued to be present in Bahia Sucia, especially in the stand of mangroves on the west side of the bay.

One of the plaintiffs' expert witnesses, Dr. Ariel Lugo Garces, a wetlands specialist, testified that the ecological functions of a mangrove forest such as that at Bahia Sucia included: (1) protecting the shoreline from erosion, storms, tides, and high winds; (2) providing a habitat for wildlife, especially birds; (3) providing a protected breeding ground for fish and shellfish; and (4) acting as a food source for aquatic creatures of all kinds. Dr. Roger D. Anderson, a marine biologist who testified for defendants, agreed with Dr. Lugo that tropical mangroves are an important link in the food chain that supports fisheries and other marine resources. The district court described the Bahia Sucia mangroves as follows:

The mangrove that borders on the ocean fringe throughout Bahia Sucia is a species referred to as red mangrove (*Rhizophoro mangle*). This mangrove has both main and prop roots, in which are located lenticels or pores for gas exchange. These lenticels facilitate root respiration. Various epibenthic species such as tree oysters, snails, crabs, sponges, and molluscs dwelled in these root systems. In the waters surrounding these roots, communities of fish, shrimp, and similar floating or swimming organisms throve. The bottom around the roots was inhabited by various benthic infauna. The bottom near the red mangrove was covered with both turtle grass . . . and manatee grass.

. . .

Further inland from the fringe, as the interstitial salinity rises, the red mangrove is supplanted by the black mangrove (*Avecennia nitida*). This mangrove inhabits a zone systematically flooded by the tide, and rather than prop roots, it has fingerlike breathing tubes (called neumatafors) which rise from the ground to above high-water level. This area provided a habitat principally for crustaceans such as crabs and barnacles, and algae grazing snails, bees, and reptiles. There were also benthic infaunal communities similar in nature to those in the bottom surrounding the red mangrove fringe. 456 F. Supp. at 1338 (footnotes omitted)

The district court noted that the configuration of Bahia Sucia, together with the prevailing winds and currents, made the bay a natural trap for floating debris, including small quantities of petroleum and tar. Nevertheless, the court found that, at the time of the *Zoe Colocotroni* oil spill, "Bahia Sucia was a healthy, functioning estuarial ecosystem, typical of those found in the Southern coast of Puerto Rico and similar tropical environments." 456 F. Supp. at 1339.

A.

The Commonwealth of Puerto Rico and the EQB instituted the present action on March 19, 1973, invoking the admiralty jurisdiction of the district court. A six-week trial, addressed solely to damages, commenced on November 7, 1977. Plaintiffs first introduced testimony by expert witnesses on the impact of the oil spill on Bahia Sucia, the toxic effects of the oil, and the extent to which oil was still present four years after the spill. Other experts then presented proposals for restoring the area and testified to the costs that would be involved. Rafael Cruz Perez, an engineer, presented a proposal to remove and replace a total of 164,600 square meters (approximately 40 acres) of oil-contaminated sediments in the West Mangrove and East Mangrove areas to a depth of one meter. While the details of the Cruz Perez plan were somewhat sketchy, the geographic areas to be affected by the plan apparently consisted of the following. Of the 40 acres of contaminated sediments to be removed, about 15 acres were on the west side of the bay in the vicinity of West Mangrove and about 25 acres were on the east side in the vicinity of East Mangrove. Of the 15 acres on the west side, about 3.5 acres contained mangroves, approximately half of which were alive notwithstanding the polluted sediments. Of the 25 acres to be removed on the east side, about 16.5 acres contained mangroves. Cruz Perez thus estimated his plan for removal of 40 acres of contaminated sediments would necessarily entail the clearing of some 20 acres of existing mangroves. Furthermore, Cruz Perez testified, three additional acres of mangroves in uncontaminated areas would have to be cleared to provide access for heavy machinery. An engineering report submitted to Gabriel Fuentes, a contractor, estimated the cost of removing the sediments and mangroves to be $7,176,363.71. Charles Pennock, a San Juan nursery man, submitted an estimate of $559,500 for the replanting of 23 acres of mangroves from container-grown plants (approximately 5,500 trees per acre) and a five-year maintenance plan.

Dr. Roger Zimmerman, a marine biologist from the University of Puerto Rico, testified concerning a study he conducted in late 1976 and early 1977 comparing the number of living organisms found at Bahia Sucia with the number found in a comparable control area. Dr. Zimmerman's study established no significant differences in number or type of organisms— either plants or animals—in the sea grass beds or on the prop roots of the mangroves. The study did, however, show a substantial disparity in the number of organisms living on or under the sediments. In particular, Dr. Zimmerman stated that the number of molluscs (e.g., clams, snails) in the Bahia Sucia area was very small in comparison to the control area. On the other hand, samples taken in Bahia Sucia found a far larger number of polychaete worms, especially a genus known as *capitella* which often proliferates in areas of acute environmental distress.

Dr. Zimmerman also testified that, subsequent to this first survey, a second study was undertaken at the behest of the Environmental Quality Board. This study, again relying on core samples taken in Bahia Sucia and at a control site, concentrated on the sediments, where the first survey had found the greatest impact from the oil. Dr. Zimmerman stated that the surveyors took their samples primarily from the vicinity of a small lagoon in the West Mangrove area where previous studies and visual observation indicated the oil was heavily concentrated. This study revealed a marked difference between the two sites in the numbers of infaunal and epibenthic creatures according to Dr. Zimmerman.

Dr. Ariel Lugo Garces, the wetlands expert, testified to studies he had made indicating the presence of oil in the mangrove sediments correlated with dead or dying mangrove trees. The mangroves would not grow back, Dr. Lugo said, as long as the oil remained in the sediments. Dr. Lugo also presented a compilation, prepared by him of the data gathered by the other Bahia Sucia surveyors, summarizing the extent of damage to twelve different components of the Bahia Sucia ecosystem. Dr. Lugo stated that he considered his figures conservative, since little data was available on many other environmental components.

Finally, Dr. Philip E. Sorenson, an economist specializing in natural resources, discussed the economic theory that shippers of oil should be required to bear such external social costs as oil spill damages in order to prevent underpricing of their product. "If the producers and consumers of oil are able to conduct their affairs in such a way as to transfer to society a large part of the real cost of producing and consuming their product," Dr. Sorenson said, "we'll be in an inefficient economic situation: one in which the market price of the commodity will be less than the full social cost of producing it." Dr. Sorenson also presented a summary of plaintiff's claims for damages, including inter alia the Commonwealth's uncontested claim for cleanup expenses of $78,108.89, the $7.5 million for sediment removal and mangrove replanting, and Dr. Sorenson's own estimate of $5,526,583 as the replacement value of the invertebrate organisms killed by the oil spill.

Dr. Sorenson testified he arrived at the latter figure by way of the following calculations. Dr. Lugo's report had compiled the results of earlier studies together with the second Zimmerman survey to provide a table of environmental harms. Concentrating only on the figures from the Zimmerman study, Dr. Sorenson extrapolated the differences in number of organisms found in the ten-centimeter core samples over a square meter area to determine the net difference in creatures per square meter. Since size samples were taken at each of the four "stations" in Bahia Sucia and in the control area, he determined this involved multiplying the results of each set of six samples by 21.22. Results from one of the four stations, where more animals were found at Bahia Sucia than at the control area, were not included. The net difference was calculated to be 1,138 creatures per square meter. This figure in turn yielded the sum of 4,605,486 creatures per acre, and a total of 92,109,720 creatures for the 20 acres of mangroves allegedly impacted by oil. Dr. Sorenson testified that he took the 20-acre figure from "the survey and the map created by Mr. Cruz Perez" and that the 20 acres included a substantial area in East Mangrove.

To arrive at an estimate of damages, Dr. Sorenson testified he consulted catalogs from biological supply houses. From these catalogs he determined that "[m]any of these species sell at prices ranging from $1 to $4.50" and "that no animal on the list sold for less than 10 cents." Dr. Sorenson assigned an average replacement value to each creature, regardless of species, of six cents. Multiplying 92,109,720 times .06 resulted in an estimate of $5,526,583 as the replacement value of the organisms "missing" from the Bahia Sucia sediments. Dr. Sorenson also estimated the cost of a ten-year scientific monitoring program at $1,393,200. His total estimate of the damages was thus $14,733,755.60, consisting of $7,176,363.71 for mangrove and sediment removal, $559,500 for mangrove replanting, $5,526,583 for the replacement value of organisms, $1,393,200 for monitoring, and $78,108.89 for cleanup costs.

B.

Plaintiffs' witnesses were thoroughly cross-examined by defendants' counsel. In addition, defendants presented considerable expert testimony of their own. The primary thrust of this testimony was that the oil originally present in Bahia Sucia had "weathered" through the action of wind, waves, sunlight, and the elements and was no longer having major toxic effects on the environment. Defendants' experts also testified that some of the damaged mangroves were victims of preexisting high salinity in West Mangrove rather than oil pollution. Further testimony indicated that, in the opinion of defendants' experts, there were substantial signs of natural regeneration among the mangroves. Dr. Edward S. Gilfillan testified, for example, that he expected the area to be restored by natural processes within ten to fifteen years, if not less. He estimated the size of the area of "continuing damage" in West Mangrove at two and a half to three acres.

Defendants also offered alternative restoration or reforestation programs of their own that were less extensive or less costly than plaintiffs' proposals. Dr. Howard Teas, a biologist, testified that, in his opinion, it would be possible, though not necessarily desirable, to remove oil from the sediments without destroying existing vegetation by using "an airlift or vacuum such as divers use in unearthing treasure ships." A preferable alternative, Dr. Teas said, would be to offset damage to the oil-impacted mangroves by replanting trees at a nearby location where the mangrove forest had existed several years before. This proposal would not carry with it the same risk of totally destroying the environment in the contaminated areas in order to save it, Dr. Teas said. He suggested that construction of a canal system to provide sufficient "flushing" action would permit reforestation of the area west of Bahia Sucia and north of the Cabo Rojo lighthouse where excess salinity had apparently killed the mangroves. Dr. Teas testified that the cost of replanting fifteen acres of mangroves through methods with which he was familiar would be approximately $75,000 ($5,000 per acre), and that the cost of a ten-year monitoring program would be about $200,000.

Dr. Roger D. Anderson, a marine biologist testifying for defendants, attacked Dr. Sorenson's theory of replacement value as the measure of damages for small, commercially value-less invertebrate animals. Dr. Anderson offered as an alternative his own methodology, based on studies conducted in Georgia. Citing work done by some of plaintiffs' experts as well as other scientists, Dr. Anderson estimated the value of an acre of tropical mangrove swamp to be $50,000, based on a complex analysis of the potential significance of such land to food supply, energy supply, fisheries, wood products, aesthetics, recreation, and similar factors. From his analysis of other evidence produced at trial, Dr. Anderson testified he considered about three acres of the West Mangrove area to be a total loss, thus producing a damage figure of $150,000. He stated, however, that his estimate of $50,000 was a "yardstick" which could be applied to any number of acres of mangroves that plaintiffs could show had been substantially damaged. Dr. Anderson pointed out that plaintiffs' expert Dr. Lugo had written a paper, on which Dr. Anderson partly relied, putting a more conservative valuation of $35,000 to $40,000 per acre on the mangroves of Bahia Sucia.

Dr. Anderson also offered to testify in behalf of defendants' proposal that, as an alternative to massive replanting in the West Mangrove area, reforestation of the Cabo Rojo peninsula could be attempted. He stated that he was familiar with this technique of alternate-site restoration, and that it had been used in several states as a condition for permitting activities that would result in destruction of certain areas of marshland. Dr. Anderson's testimony on this point was excluded on grounds of irrelevancy. "I am involved here, solely, with establishing a dollar amount of damages," the court said. "[W]hether as an alternate remedy in the settlement, the restoration of other mangroves, or of these mangroves . . . could be proposed is outside the scope of this case; unless I am shown something to the contrary."

Finally, defendants presented testimony by David R. Stith, a marine contractor with experience in oil spill cleanup operations, including the Bahia Sucia cleanup. Stith testified he had prepared an estimate of the cost of removing the oil-contaminated sediments from 2.6 to 2.9 acres of the West Mangrove area using a suction device mounted on a floating barge. His estimate for this work totaled $396,859. Stith also offered to testify he had estimated the cost of constructing a channel system as proposed by Dr. Teas for replanting at the Cabo Rojo lighthouse. This estimate was $152,310. As with Dr. Anderson's, the district court excluded this testimony as irrelevant since it did not concern the damaged area. The total of defendants' proposed remedial measures was just under $1 million.

C.

The district court made the following findings on the issue of damages:

1. Plaintiffs' proven claim of damage to marine organisms covers an approximate area of about twenty acres in and around the West Mangrove. The surveys conducted by plaintiffs reliably establish that there was a decline of approximately 4,605,486 organisms per acre as a direct result of the oil spill. This means that 92,109,720 marine animals were killed by the *Colocotroni* oil spill. The uncontradicted evidence establishes that there is a ready market with reference to biological supply laboratories, thus allowing a reliable calculation of the cost of replacing these organisms. The lowest possible replacement cost figure is $.06 per animal, with many species selling from $1 to $4.50 per individual. Accepting the lowest replacement cost, and attaching damages only to the lost marine animals in the West Mangrove area, we find the damages caused by defendants to amount to $5,526,583.20.

2. The evidence is overwhelming to the effect that the sediments in and around the West Mangrove continue to be impregnated with oil. The solutions proposed by plaintiffs to this problem are unacceptable in that they would bring about the total destruction of this environment without any real guarantee of ultimate success. Furthermore, there is substantial scientific evidence to the effect that much of the undesirable effects of the oil in the sediments will be corrected in time by the weathering processes of nature. The most affected spots in the West Mangrove cover an area of approximately twenty-three acres. It is the Court's opinion that these areas can best be reestablished by the intensive planting of mangroves and restoration of this area to its condition before the oil spill. The evidence shows that the planting of mangroves runs about $16,500 per acre, thus bringing the cost of replanting twenty-three acres to $379,500. The evidence further demonstrates that the planting will require a five-year monitoring and fertilizing program which will cost $36,000 per year or $180,000 for the five years. The total damages thus suffered by plaintiffs by reason of the pollution of the mangroves in the West Mangrove amount to $559,500.

3. Plaintiffs incurred cleanup costs in the amount of $78,108.89 which were not reimbursed from any source, and they are entitled to recover said damages from defendants. 1979 AMC 21, 35–37, 456 F. Supp. 1327, 1344–45, and n.42 (D.P.R. 1978)

. . .

V.

We now turn from procedural matters to the extremely difficult substantive issues concerning damages. Defendants challenge: (A) the so-called "standing" of Puerto Rico and the EQB to recover damages for environmental injury; (B) the district court's failure to limit damages by commercial or market value standards; and (C) the approach and data relied upon by the court in assessing damages.

A.

We turn first to the issue of plaintiffs' right to bring this lawsuit. The district court held that the Commonwealth had "standing" to recover for damages to natural resources, namely the mangrove trees and the various species of marine creatures living in and around them, on the theory that the Commonwealth was the "trustee of the public trust in these resources" and had an interest in them as parens patriae. The court also ruled that the Environmental Quality Board had standing to proceed as co-plaintiff seeking similar relief under a state statute authorizing the EQB to bring damages actions for environmental injuries.

While the parties and the district court speak in terms of "standing," we think the question is more properly whether plaintiffs have stated a cognizable cause of action. Defendants concede that Puerto Rico, as owner of the real property primarily affected by the oil spill, would, like any private landowner, have a cause of action in admiralty to recover whatever damages it could prove under conventional principles for its private economic loss as measured by diminution of market value in the coastal land. The Commonwealth made no attempt to show such damages, however. It seeks relief instead under

an asserted right to recover a governmental entity on behalf of its people for the loss of living natural resources on the land such as trees and animals.

. . . Plaintiffs argue that a state regulatory interest in wildlife and other living resources expressed metaphorically in the state's status as "public trustee" of its natural resources is sufficient in itself to support an action for damages to those resources. Defendants reply that, absent a proprietary interest in the resource actually damaged, a state's unexercised regulatory authority over wildlife will not support a proper cause of action. We see no need to decide this difficult question in the present case. Here the Commonwealth of Puerto Rico, exercising its undisputed authority to protect and conserve its natural environment, has by statute authorized one of its agencies to maintain actions of this sort. Under the statute, 12 L.P.R.A., sec. 1131(29), co-plaintiff Environmental Quality Board has, among others, the following duties, powers and functions:

(29) To bring, represented by the Secretary of Justice, by the Board's attorneys, or by a private attorney contracted for such purpose, civil actions for damages in any court of Puerto Rico or the United States of America to recover the total value of the damages caused to the environment and/or natural resources upon committing any violation of this chapter and its regulations. The amount of any judgment collected to such effect shall be covered into the Special Account of the Board on Environmental Quality.

We read this statute both as creating a cause of action of the type described by its terms and as designating the EQB as the proper party to bring such action. We see nothing . . . to prohibit such legislation. Whatever might be the case in the absence of such a local statute, we think that where the Commonwealth of Puerto Rico has thus legislatively authorized the bringing of suits for environmental damages, and has earmarked funds so recovered to a special fund, such an action must be construed as taking the place of any implied common-law action the

Commonwealth, as trustee, might have brought. Any other construction would invite the risk of double recovery and lead to confusion as to the rights of the two state plaintiffs in their identical or nearly identical actions. It is unnecessary, therefore, for us to consider whether, had the legislature of Puerto Rico not delegated to the EQB the right to maintain such suits, the Commonwealth would have an inherent right to bring them itself.

Equally unavailing would be any argument that this state statutory action is not cognizable in admiralty. An oil spill on the navigable waters is a breach of federal maritime law. Where the injury occurs in the territorial waters of a state, the general rule is that admiralty will give "broad recognition of the authority of the States to create rights and liabilities with respect to conduct within their borders, when the state action does not run counter to federal laws or the essential features of an exclusive federal jurisdiction." *Just v. Chambers*, 312 U.S. 383, 391 (1941). Defendants do not argue, nor could they, that this action runs counter to the essential feature of federal jurisdiction. See *Askew v. American Waterways Operators, Inc.*, 411 U.S. 325 (1973).

B.

Defendants next argue the district court erred in failing to apply the common-law "diminution in value" rule in calculating damages. Under the traditional rule, the measure of damages for tortious injury to real property is the difference in the commercial or market value of the property before and after the event causing injury. Where the property can be restored to its original condition for a sum less than the diminution in value, however, the cost of restoration may be substituted as a measure of damages. Defendants introduced evidence at trial tending to show that the market value of comparable property in the vicinity of Bahia Sucia was less than $5,000 per acre, based on recent sales. Thus, defendants contend, damages here could not have exceeded $5,000 per af-

fected acre even if the land were shown to have lost all value.

We believe that defendants have misconceived the character of the remedy created by section 1131. The EQB is not concerned with any loss in the market or other commercial value of the Commonwealth's land. In point of fact, the EQB concedes the land has no significant commercial or market value. The claim, rather, is for the injury—broadly conceived—that has been caused to the natural environment by the spilled oil. The question before us is not whether in a typical land damage case a claim of this sort could be successfully advanced—we assume it could not—but rather whether Puerto Rico's statute empowering the EQB to proceed in cases such as this envisions the awarding of damages on a different basis than would have been traditionally allowed.

The district court found that the once flourishing natural environment of the West Mangrove had been seriously damaged by the oil, to the point where some of the underlying sediments were no longer capable of supporting any but the most primitive forms of organic life, such as worms. The Puerto Rico statute authorizing this action specifically empowers the EQB to recover "the *total value* of the damages caused to the environment and/or natural resources" upon a violation of the antipollution provisions. 12 L.PR.A. sec. 1131(29) (emphasis added). Implicit in this choice of language, we think, is a determination not to restrict the state to ordinary market damages. Many unspoiled natural areas of considerable ecological value have little or no commercial or market value. Indeed, to the extent such areas have a commercial value, it is logical to assume they will not long remain unspoiled, absent some governmental or philanthropic protection. A strict application of the diminution in value rule would deny the state any right to recover meaningful damages for harm to such areas, and would frustrate appropriate measures to restore or rehabilitate the environment.

This perception is confirmed by the course of

recent federal legislation in the area of oil pollution. The Clean Water Art of 1972 provided that the United States could recover, up to certain preset limits, the costs it incurred in cleaning up after an oil spill, but made no explicit reference to environmental damages. The Clean Water Act Amendments of 1977 significantly expanded the scope of vessel owner's potential liability. In particular, the federal government and the states were authorized to recover "costs or expenses incurred . . . in the restoration or replacement of natural resources damaged or destroyed as a result of a discharge of oil or a hazardous substance." 33 U.S. Code, sec. 1321(f)(4). Recoverable removal costs were defined as including the expenses "of such . . . actions as may be necessary to minimize or mitigate damage to the public health or welfare, including, but not limited to, fish, shellfish, wildlife, and public and private property, shorelines, and beaches." Id., sec. 1321(a)(8). The liability provision concluded:

The President, or the authorized representative of any State, shall act on behalf of the public as trustee of the natural resources to recover for the costs of replacing or restoring such resources. Sums recovered shall be used to restore, rehabilitate, or acquire the equivalent of such natural resources by the appropriate agencies of the Federal government, or the State government. Id., sec. 1321(f)(5)

Similarly, in the Outer Continental Shelf Lands Act Amendments of 1978, Congress provided that the government could recover damages for economic loss arising out of an oil spill, including "injury to, or destruction of, natural resources," 43 U.S. Code, sec. 1813(a)(2)(C), and "loss of use of natural resources," id., sec. 1813(a)(2)(D). The Submerged Lands Act, which forms the basis for the Outer Continental Shelf Lands Act, see 43 U.S. Code, sec. 1811(9), defines "natural resources" as including, "without limiting the generality thereof, oil, gas, and other minerals, and fish, shrimp, oysters, clams, crabs, lobsters, sponges, kelp, and other marine animal and plant life." 43 U.S. Code, sec.

1301(e). While the latter acts do not, by their terms, apply to Puerto Rico, see 43 U.S. Code, sec. 1301(g), like the Clean Water Act they do give some indication that Congress has determined that it is desirable to provide for environmental damages apart from the commercial loss, ordinarily measured by a market value yardstick, suffered by landowners and/or exploiters of natural resources. This perception is reinforced by the section of the OCS Lands Act which provides that sums the state recovers "shall be available for use to restore, rehabilitate, or acquire the equivalent of such natural resources by the appropriate agencies of . . . the State, but the measure of such damages shall not be limited by the sums which can be used to restore or replace such resources." 43 U.S. Code, sec. 1813(b)(3).

Especially in light of this recent federal statutory activity, we think that limitation of recovery to those damages recoverable under the common-law "diminution in value" rule would be inconsistent with the manifest intent of Puerto Rico's environmental statute. In enacting section 1131, Puerto Rico obviously meant to sanction the difficult, but perhaps not impossible, task of putting a price tag on resources whose value cannot always be measured by rules of the marketplace. Although the diminution rule is appropriate in most contexts, and may indeed be appropriate in certain cases under section 1131, see *infra*, it does not measure the loss which the statute seeks to redress in a context such as the present. No market exists in which Puerto Rico can readily replace what it has lost. The loss is not only to certain plant and animal life but, perhaps more importantly, to the capacity of the now polluted segments of the environment to regenerate and sustain such life for some time into the future. That the Commonwealth did not intend, and perhaps was unable, to exploit these life forms, and the coastal areas which supported them, for commercial purposes should not prevent a damages remedy in the face of the clearly stated legislative intent to compensate for "the total value of the damages caused to the environment and/ or natural resources." 12 L.P.R.A., sec. 1131 (29). In recent times, mankind has become increasingly aware that the planet's resources are finite and that portions of the land and sea which at first glance seem useless, like salt marshes, barrier reefs, and other coastal areas, often contribute in subtle but critical ways to an environment capable of supporting both human life and the other forms of life on which we all depend. The Puerto Rico statute is obviously aimed at providing a damages remedy with sufficient scope to compensate for, and deter, the destruction of such resources; and while we can see many problems in fashioning such a remedy, we see no reason to try to frustrate that endeavor. We therefore do not limit damages herein to the loss of market value of the real estate affected.

C.

We turn now to whether the damages awarded by the district court were appropriate. To review the court's award, we must ascertain what a fair and equitable damages measure would be in these circumstances, and, to that end, it will be helpful to examine the remedial provisions in recent similar federal statutes. There is a strong emphasis in congressional oil pollution enactments on the concept of restoration. As discussed earlier, the 1977 Clean Water Act amendments provided that the state's representative, acting as public trustee, could "recover for the costs of replacing or restoring [natural] resources." 33 U.S. Code, sec. 1321(f)(5). In accordance with the trust analogy, the state provided: "Sums recovered shall be used to restore, rehabilitate, or acquire the equivalent of such natural resources by the appropriate agencies. . . ." Id. The legislative history further elaborates this standard:

New subsections (f)(4) and (5) make governmental expenses in connection with damage to or destruction of natural resources a cost of removal which can be recovered from the owner or operator of the dis-

charged source under section 311. For those resources which can be restored or rehabilitated, the measure of liability is the reasonable costs actually incurred by Federal or State authorities in replacing the resources or otherwise mitigating the damage. Where the damaged or destroyed resource is irreplaceable (as an endangered species or an entire fishery), the measure of liability is the reasonable cost of acquiring resources to offset the loss. House Conf. Rpt. No. 95-830, 95th Cong., 1st Sess. 92

Borrowing from the suggestion provided by this federal legislation, we think the appropriate primary standard for determining damages in a case such as this is the cost reasonably to be incurred by the sovereign or its designated agency to restore or rehabilitate the environment in the affected area to its preexisting condition, or as close thereto as is feasible without grossly disproportionate expenditures. The focus in determining such a remedy should be on the steps a reasonable and prudent sovereign or agency would take to mitigate the harm done by the pollution, with attention to such factors as technical feasibility, harmful side effects, compatibility with or duplication of such regeneration as is naturally to be expected, and the extent to which efforts beyond a certain point would become either redundant or disproportionately expensive. Admittedly, such a remedy cannot be calculated with the degree of certainty usually possible when the issue is, for example, damages on a commercial contract. On the other hand, a district court can surely calculate damages under the foregoing standard with as much or more certainty and accuracy as a jury determining damages for pain and suffering or mental anguish.

There may be circumstances where direct restoration of the affected area is either physically impossible or so disproportionately expensive that it would not be reasonable to undertake such a remedy. Some other measure of damages might be reasonable in such cases, at least where the process of natural regeneration will be too slow to ensure restoration within a reasonable period. The legislative history of the Clean Water Act amendments, quoted above, suggests as one possibility, "the reasonable cost of acquiring resources to offset the loss." Id. Alternatives might include acquisition of comparable lands for public parks or, as suggested by defendants below, reforestation of a similar proximate site where the presence of oil would not pose the same hazard to ultimate success. As with the remedy of restoration, the damages awarded for such alternative measures should be reasonable and not grossly disproportionate to the harm caused and the ecological values involved. The ultimate purpose of any such remedy should be to protect the public interest in a healthy, functioning environment, and not to provide a windfall to the public treasury. In emphasizing the above measures, we do not mean to rule out others in appropriate circumstances. There may indeed be cases where traditional commercial valuation rules will afford the best yardstick, as where there is a market in which the damaged resource could have been sold that reflects its actual value. Much must necessarily be left to the discretion of courts, especially before a body of precedent has arisen.

But while the district court's discretion is extensive, we are unable to agree with the approach taken by the court here in placing a value on the damaged resources. Plaintiffs presented two principal theories of damages to the court. The first theory was somewhat analogous to the primary standard we have enunciated above, focusing on plaintiffs' plan to remove the damaged mangrove trees and oil-impregnated sediments from a large area and replace them with clean sediment and container-grown mangrove plants. This plan was estimated to cost approximately $7 million. The district court sensibly and correctly rejected this plan as impractical, inordinately expensive, and unjustifiably dangerous to the healthy mangroves and marine animals still present in the area to be restored. We can find no fault with the district court's conclusion that this draconian plan was not a step that a reasonable trustee of the nat-

ural environment would be expected to take as a means of protecting the corpus of the trust.

Plaintiffs' second theory, which the court accepted, focused on the supposed replacement value of the living creatures—the epibenthic and infaunal animals—alleged to have been permanently destroyed or damaged by the oil spill. Plaintiffs repeatedly disavowed any connection between this theory and an actual restoration plan. In other words, plaintiffs did not represent that they proposed to purchase 92 million invertebrate animals for actual introduction into the sediments (which, being contaminated with oil, would hardly support them), but rather wishes to use the alleged replacement value of these animals as a yardstick for estimating the quantum of harm caused to the Commonwealth. This theory has no apparent analog in the standards for measuring environmental damages we have discussed above. To be sure, the federal statutes from which we have borrowed speak in places of replacement as a part of the appropriate recovery. But we believe these references, in context, should be interpreted as meaning replacement as a component in a practicable plan for actual restoration. Thus, for example, if a state were seeking to restore a damaged area of forest, a portion of the damages sought might be allocated to replacement of wild birds or game animals or such other creatures as would not be expected to regenerate naturally within a relatively finite period of time even with appropriate restoration. This is a far different matter from permitting the state to recover money damages for the loss of small, commercially valueless creatures which assertedly would perish if returned to the oil-soaked sands, yet probably would replenish themselves naturally if and when restoration—either artificial or natural—took place.

The case primarily relied upon by the district court to support its grant of damages for replacement value is not to the contrary. In *Feather River Lumber Co. v. United States*, 30 F.2d 642 (9 Cir. 1929), the United States brought an action seeking damages for a public forest allegedly destroyed when defendant negligently started a forest fire and permitted it to spread onto public land. The government's chief witness, a Forestry Service official, stated that he calculated the extent of the fire damage by counting the damaged and undamaged trees on one-tenth acre sample plots located at intervals throughout the four thousand-acre area. The official separated his estimates into two categories, merchantable timber, as to which there was a present market value based on local stumpage prices, and young timber, as to which there was only the possibility of future market value. The Ninth Circuit held that this method was proper as a means of estimating the extent of damage and that, as to the merchantable timber, "the measure of damages was the [market] value of the trees." Id., at 644. The court also held:

As to the young growth, while the measure of damages in such a case is ordinarily the difference in the value of the land before and after the fire, here, there being no law to authorize the sale of the lands injured by the fire, the trial court admitted such evidence as was available to show the damage actually sustained, that is to say, what was required to make the government whole, and this, we think, might properly include the cost of restoring the land to the condition in which it was before the fire.

We think the quoted passage makes clear that the Ninth Circuit did not contemplate a purely abstract recovery such as that proposed here, where the theoretical "loss" was worked out in terms of what it would cost to buy thousands of creatures which, as a practical matter, would never be bought in such a manner and could not be expected to survive if returned to their damaged habitat. Rather, the Ninth Circuit was simply willing to permit the government to recover its actual and reasonable expected restoration costs based on the cost of replanting, a perfectly feasible and reasonable course of action in that case. Thus, leaving aside the question whether plaintiffs' evidence was sufficient to establish that 92 million creatures were de-

stroyed and that six cents represented an appropriate replacement cost estimate, we are unable to endorse the theory of damages in support of which this evidence was advanced. We thus hold that it was error to award $5,526,583.20 for the replacement value of the destroyed organisms.

D.

We come finally to the disposition of this case. Defendants argue that, having rejected plaintiffs' damages theories, we should reverse the district court's judgment, except as to the Commonwealth's undisputed cleanup costs. While this is superficially an attractive course, we do not think the matter is quite so simple. To say that the law on this question is unsettled is vastly to understate the situation. The parties in this lawsuit, and we ourselves, have ventured far into unchartered waters. We do not think plaintiffs could reasonably have been expected to anticipate where this journey would take us. Though we have affirmed the district court's rejection of the Commonwealth's original, rather grandiose restoration plan, we believe the EQB should still have an opportunity to show, if it can, that some lesser steps are feasible that would have a beneficial effect on the West Mangrove ecosystem without excessive destruction of existing natural resources or disproportionate cost. The costs projected for the carrying out of such reasonable lesser steps would be an appropriate award of damages to the EQB. Plaintiffs may wish, at the same time, to reopen the question of alternative-site restoration, as to which the district court initially declined to take evidence, although we hasten to add that we do not now rule on whether the concept of alternative site restoration would make sense in this case as a measure of damages. We therefore remand the case to the district court with instructions to reopen the record for further evidence on the issue of damages in line with our discussion of the principles governing recovery in cases of this sort.

Defendants cannot successfully claim that

this disposition will prejudice their rights appreciably. Defendants themselves introduced evidence at the first trial on damages seeking to establish that restoration projects less extensive and less costly than plaintiffs' were possible. Had the district court accepted these proposals in lieu of plaintiffs', defendants would have had a potential liability of up to $1 million. We do not mean to suggest that plaintiffs are necessarily entitled to recover this, or any other specific amount. Nor do we put any limits on defendants' right to contest any proposals put forward by plaintiffs, or to offer counterproposals. In essence, while the court and the parties are entitled to rely on the record already developed to the extent they wish to do so, we think the record should be reopened on the issue of damages, with a renewed evidentiary hearing to be conducted in light of the standards for measuring such damages we have announced today. While we regret the necessity this will entail for further delay in this already protracted litigation, we trust that the district court, with the good faith assistance of the parties, will be able to carry out further proceedings without unreasonable delay.

To avoid any question that might be raised, we note that we can see no reason why this case should not go back to the same district judge, who already possesses considerable familiarity with it.

Affirmed in part, vacated in part, and remanded for further proceedings consistent with this opinion.

Questions

1. When you consider the choices available, what method would you choose as the most equitable means to calculate natural resource damages?

2. Would the decision have been any different if Puerto Rico actually intended to "restock" the mangrove swamp?

Exxon Valdez, in re (U.S.D.C. Alaska, 1991)

H. RUSSEL HOLLAND, D.J.

Alyeska's Motion for Judgment on the Pleadings

Alyeska's motion for judgment on the pleadings was brought, pursuant to Rule 12(c), Federal Rules of Civil Procedure, on the ground that certain identified claims for economic losses made by certain identified plaintiffs should be dismissed because those plaintiffs did not complain of any physical impact or injury from the oil on their person or property, as required by maritime law and the rule in *Robins Dry Dock & Repair Co. v. Flint*, 275 U.S. 303 (1927). The plaintiffs targeted by the motion are: (i) area businesses, such as boat charters, taxidermists, and fishing lodges; (ii) those with use and enjoyment claims, such as sport fishermen, photographers, and kayakers; and (iii) fish processors and fish tenders.

Robins Dry Dock established that in those situations where negligence does not result in any physical harm, thereby providing no basis for an independent tort, and only pecuniary loss is suffered, a plaintiff may not recover for the loss of the financial benefits of a contract or prospective trade.

The Ninth Circuit, however, has eroded the "bright-line" rule of *Robins Dry Dock* by creating a limited exception to the requirement for physical harm for commercial fishermen. See *Carbone v. Ursich*, 209 F.2d 178; 181–82 (9 Cir. 1953) (held that crew members of fishing vessel could recover lost profits from owners of another vessel that negligently fouled their nets); *Union Oil Co. v. Oppen*, 501 F.2d 558, 570 (9 Cir. 1974) (held that commercial fishermen whose harvests were depleted by an oil spill could recover lost profits from defendant oil company in negligence action); *Emerson G.M. Diesel, Inc. v. Alaskan Enterprise*, 732 F.2d 1468, 1475 (9 Cir. 1984) (held that economic losses such as lost profits and repair expenses were recoverable in manufacturer's strict liability admiralty action involving commercial fishing vessel).

Maritime Tort

Alyeska characterizes the oil spill from the *Exxon Valdez* as a classic maritime tort. Whether the court is indeed faced with a maritime tort is a determination crucial to the final resolution of the motion for judgment on the pleadings. If the oil spill is not a maritime tort, then the maritime rule in *Robins Dry Dock* will not apply.

A tort falls under admiralty jurisdiction if it meets both the "locality" and the "maritime nexus" requirements which the courts have imposed. Claims satisfy the locality requirement if the wrong occurred on the high seas or navigable waters. *East River Steamship Corp. v. Transamerica Delaval, Inc.* 476 U.S 858, 863–64 (1986). Here, the wrong was the damage which occurred on or in the navigable waters and which was caused by the oil spilling from the *Exxon Valdez*, grounded in navigable waters. The locality requirement is met.

Claims meet the maritime nexus requirement if the wrong bears "a significant relationship to traditional maritime activity." *Executive Jet Aviation, Inc. v. Cleveland*, 409 U.S. 249, 268 (1972). The *Exxon Valdez* was engaged in maritime commerce, specifically the transport of oil in a ship, when the accident occurred. Maritime commerce is the primary focus of admiralty law. Therefore, the maritime nexus test is also met.

Since both tests are met for those claims for damages which occurred in or on navigable waters, the oil spill is a maritime tort subject to admiralty jurisdiction. Factual development of the claims will probably establish that the claims of the sport fishermen, kayakers, and fish tenders, who are targeted by Alyeska's motion, are for damages which occurred in or on the navigable waters.

However, a large portion of the claims are for damages that occurred on land, such as the claims of shoreside businesses and fish processors. Historically, damages to the shore or to shore facilities were not cognizable in admiralty, *Askew v. American Waterways Operators, Inc.*, 411 U.S. 325, 340 (1973). In 1948, Congress remedied that inequity by enacting the Admiralty Extension Act, 46 U.S.C. Sec. 740, which states, in pertinent part, as follows: "The admiralty and maritime jurisdiction of the United States shall extend to and include all cases of damages or injury, to person or property, *caused by a vessel on navigable water* notwithstanding that such damage or injury be done or consummated on land" (emphasis added).

A ship or its appurtenances must proximately cause an injury on shore to invoke the Admiralty Extension Act and the application of maritime law. Factual development will probably establish that the oil spill from the *Exxon Valdez* was the proximate cause of the shore-based damage claims, thereby subjecting them to admiralty jurisdiction pursuant to the Admiralty Extension Act.

Oil spills from vessels on navigable waters have consistently been held to be maritime torts by other courts. See *In re Oil Spill by Amoco Cadiz*, 699 F.2d 909, 913 (7 Cir.), cert. denied, 464 U.S. 864 (1983) (shipwreck on the high seas is quintessentially the kind of incident for which the distinctive doctrines and remedies of admiralty law were designed; any doubt created by the fact that the damage occurred on land is removed by the Admiralty Extension Act); *Puerto Rico v. SS Zoe Colocotroni*, 628 F.2d 652, 672 (1 Cir. 1980), cert. denied, 450 U.S. 912 (1981) ("An oil spill on the navigable waters is a breach of federal maritime law"); *Burgess v. M/V Tamano*, 370 F.Supp. 247, 249 (D. Me. 1973) (an oil spill occurring in Maine's coastal waters constitutes a maritime tort and is within the admiralty jurisdiction).

The issue of whether the oil spill constitutes a maritime tort is directly raised by the amended and consolidated class action complaint which alleges the maritime torts of unseaworthiness and maritime negligence. The claims of fourteen of the plaintiffs targeted by Alyeska's motion are included in the amended and consolidated class action complaint. One other complaint filed by plaintiffs targeted by Alyeska's motion also raises the issue by alleging a claim under "maritime liability."

Basically, the oil spill caused by the *Exxon Valdez* is a maritime tort. Whether any particular claim falls under admiralty jurisdiction is a question of fact as to whether damages occurred on or off shore, and if damages were on the shore, whether those damages were proximately caused by the grounding of the *Exxon Valdez*. Subject to the necessary factual development, the specific claims targeted by Alyeska's motion were caused by a maritime tort and appear to be under admiralty jurisdiction even though none of the plaintiffs have expressly invoked admiralty jurisdiction.

Application of Maritime Law

The claims on which Alyeska presently seeks judgment in this court are generally based on state law concepts of negligence, nuisance, misrepresentation, and tortious interference with contractual expectancies, as well as strict liability under AS 46.03.822. A determination that the oil spill is a maritime tort affects the substantive law applied to the case. If a cause of action is asserted which is based on a maritime tort, the substantive law applied is maritime law. *Jansson v. Swedish American Line*, 1950 AMC 1959, 1964, 185 F.2d 212, 216 (1 Cir. 1950).

[W]hen a common-law action is brought, whether in a state or in a federal court, to enforce a cause of action cognizable in admiralty, the substantive law to be applied is the same as would be applied by an admiralty court—that is, the general maritime law, as developed and declared, in the last analysis, by the Supreme Court of the United States, or as modified from time to time by act of Congress" Id. (citing to *Chelentis v. Luckenbach Steamship Co.*, 247 U.S. 372, 382 (1918))

The "saving to suitors" clause in 28 U.S.C. Sec. 1333 does not affect the application of substantive maritime law.

[T]he "saving to suitors" clause allows state courts to entertain in personam maritime causes of action, but in such cases the extent to which state law may be used to remedy maritime injuries is constrained by a so-called "reverse- *Erie*" doctrine which requires that the substantive remedies afforded by the States conform to governing federal maritime standards. *Offshore Logistics, Inc. v. Tallentire*, 477 U.S. 207, 222–23 (1986)

Under the "saving to suitors" clause a right or claim sanctioned by maritime law may be enforced through any appropriate remedy recognized by law, but the plaintiff does not have an election to have the defendant's liability measured by common-law standards rather than those of maritime law.

At least as to the claims for damages from the *Exxon Valdez* oil spill which occurred in or on navigable waters, it does not matter that plaintiffs characterized their claims in terms of state law; federal maritime law is controlling. In order to preserve uniformity, maritime law must be applied to torts cognizable under admiralty jurisdiction regardless of how plaintiffs characterize the tort under common law. Uniformity is the justification for exclusive federal admiralty jurisdiction.

As to claims for shoreside damages caused by the oil spill from the *Exxon Valdez*, the issue of applicable law is more complex.

In straightforward fact situations involving common-law claims, other courts have applied the *Robins Dry Dock* rule to deny claims of shoreside businesses for purely economic loss. See *Global Petroleum Corp. v. Northeast Petroleum*, 405 Mass. 187, 539 N.E.2d 1022, 1024 (1989) (riverfront business which suffered purely economic losses when retaining wall collapsed into river and blocked navigation, could not recover business losses merely by recharacterizing federal maritime claims as ones arising under state nuisance law); *Palumbo v.*

Boston Tow Boat Co., 21 Mass. App. Ct. 414, 487 N.E.2d 546 (1986) (*Robins Dry Dock* applied to restaurant owner's state court claim for purely economic loss arising after vessel struck bridge, forcing restaurant to close for lack of customers while bridge was being repaired).

The court concludes that general maritime law, including the rule in *Robins Dry Dock*, applies to the tort claims pleaded in this case, except for those based on a theory of strict liability.

Both Congress and the State of Alaska have enacted legislation in the area of strict liability. Congress enacted the Trans-Alaska Pipeline Authorization Act (TAPAA), 43 U.S.C. Secs. 1651–55, which provides for strict liability for oil spills in Sec. 1653(c). The State of Alaska enacted AS 46.03.822 ("Alaska Act") which provides for strict liability for any oil spills, including spills of oil that have been transported through the Trans-Alaska Pipeline.

The Alaska Act is a valid excise of the state's police power in that it attempts to protect the safety of its citizens, their property, and the state's natural resources by regulating the release of hazardous substances. The Supreme Court ruled, in *Askew v. American Waterways Operators, Inc.*, that sea-to-shore pollution was within the reach of a state's police power, and that even though Congress may have acted in the admiralty area, state regulation was permissible absent a clear conflict with the federal law. *Askew v. American Waterways Operators, Inc.*, 411 U.S. 325, 341, 343 (1973) (Florida Oil Spill Prevention and Pollution Control Act which imposed strict liability for the benefit of the state and private individuals was held not to have invaded regulatory area preempted by federal Water Quality Improvement Act which was concerned wholly with recovery of actual cleanup costs incurred by the federal government).

In exercising their police power, the states may act in maritime areas concurrently with the federal government. *Huron Portland Cement Co. v. City of Detroit*, 362 U.S. 440, 442 (1960).

Even-handed local regulation to effectuate a legitimate local public interest is valid unless preempted by federal action or unduly burdensome on maritime activities. The issue then raised is whether the Alaska Act conflicts with the rule in *Robins Dry Dock* or with TAPAA which is not limited by *Robins Dry Dock*.

When Congress enacted TAPAA, Congress spoke directly to the issue of TAPS oil spills. TAPAA imposes strict liability "notwithstanding the provisions of any other law" to the extent of $100 million. 43 U.S.C. Sec. 1653(c). Therefore, to the extent of its coverage, TAPAA, as specific federal maritime legislation, displaces the general maritime law, including the rule of *Robins Dry Dock*, regarding strict liability.

The Alaska Act is similar to TAPAA in that it imposes strict liability for oil spills "notwithstanding any other provision or rule of law." AS 46.03.822. Unlike TAPAA, the Alaska Act provides for unlimited strict liability.

In the limited situation such as this case where the oil spill was of TAPS oil, the Alaska Act and TAPAA do not conflict to the extent of $100 million. For the first $100 million of damage resulting from a TAPS oil spill, the remedy would be uniform whether claims were brought under TAPAA or the Alaska Act. A conflict does not surface until a TAPS oil spill exceeds $100 million in damages.

Robins Dry Dock applies to the claims under the Alaska Act to the extent that damages claimed are in excess of liability imposed by TAPAA because general maritime law would be the applicable law. State law may supplement federal maritime law, such as in the exercise of a state's police power, but state law may not conflict with federal maritime law, as it would be redefining the requirements or limits of a remedy available at admiralty. ("When admiralty law speaks to a question, state law cannot override it.") The Alaska Act's "notwithstanding" clause would not be effective to avoid federal law of which the limitations of *Robins Dry Dock* are a part.

TAPAA Sec. 1653(c)(9) does not alter this result. Section 1653(c)(9) states: "This subsection shall not be interpreted to preempt the field of strict liability or to preclude any State from imposing additional requirements." Section 1653(c)(9) contains no language which could be interpreted as relieving the states from the limits imposed by maritime law. It simply states that the field of strict liability is not preempted. Thus the State of Alaska may enact laws in the area of strict liability with its police power so long as they are consistent with other applicable federal laws. See *Askew v. American Waterways Operators, Inc.*, 411 U.S. 325, 341.

Section 1653(c)(9) cannot be read as an implied grant of permission to the states to legislate in derogation of general maritime law even though the TAPAA conference report states as follows: "The States are expressly not precluded from setting higher limits or from legislating in any manner not inconsistent with the provisions of this Act." H.R. Conf. Rep. No. 624, 93d Cong., 1st Sess. Congress's power to legislate concerning rights and liabilities within the maritime jurisdiction and remedies for their enforcement arises from the Constitution and is nondelegable. *Knickerbocker Ice Co. v. Stewart*, 253 U.S. 149, 164 (1920) (amendment to "saving to suitors" clause which preserved state workmen's compensation remedies in cases under admiralty jurisdiction was held ineffective).

The subject [admiralty] was intrusted to it to be dealt with according to its discretion—not for delegation to others. To say that because Congress could have enacted a compensation act applicable to maritime injuries, it could authorize the States to do so as they might desire, is false reasoning. Moreover, such an authorization would inevitably destroy the harmony and uniformity which the Constitution not only contemplated but actually established—it would defeat the very purpose of the grant. Id.

Congress may have intended for the states to be able to simply extend the strict liability provisions of TAPAA to higher limits without subjecting those higher limits to *Robins Dry Dock*, but Congress did not specifically do so, nor did

it have the authority to grant the states permission to do so. *Robins Dry Dock* applies to limit the damages recoverable under the Alaska Act in excess of the $100 million recoverable under TAPAA.

The inroads that the Ninth Circuit has made on the application of *Robins Dry Dock* do not necessarily diminish the impact of the rule on the plaintiffs targeted by Alyeska's motion. The most recent Ninth Circuit decision on recovery of economic losses was in *Emerson G.M. Diesel, Inc. v. Alaskan Enterprise*, 732 F.2d 1468 (9 Cir. 1984), a products liability action in which the court allowed recovery for purely economic losses. That decision was essentially emasculated two years later when the Supreme Court ruled in *East River Steamship Corp. v. Transamerica Delaval, Inc.*, 476 U.S. 858, 876 (1986): "Thus whether stated in negligence or strict liability, no products-liability claim lies in admiralty when the only injury claimed is economic loss."

The next most recent Ninth Circuit decision on this subject was in *Union Oil Co. v. Oppen*, 501 F.2d 588 (9 Cir. 1974), which allowed recovery of lost profits by commercial fishermen whose harvests were depleted by the Santa Barbara oil spill. That decision was limited as follows:

Finally, it must be understood that our holding in this case does not open the door to claims that may be asserted by those, other than commercial fishermen, whose economic or personal affairs were discommoded by the oil spill of January 28, 1969. . . . Nothing said in this opinion is intended to suggest, for example, that every decline in the general commercial activity of every business in the Santa Barbara area following the occurrences of 1969 constitutes a legally cognizable injury for which the defendants may be responsible. The plaintiffs in the present action lawfully and directly make use of a resource of the area, viz. its fish, in the ordinary course of their business. Id., 501 F.2d at 570

The result in *Oppen* was criticized in the dissent to *Louisiana ex rel. Guste v. M/V Testbank*,

752 F.2d 1019 (5 Cir. 1985 en banc; 10-5 decision), cert. denied, 477 U.S. 903 (1986).

Oppen allowed the fishermen to recover . . . but the opinion fails to draw a very convincing line between the rights of fishermen and the rights of others who draw their living from the water. Certainly the injury from the oil spill to others who make their living upon the water, such as boat charterers who are unable to put to sea, is as foreseeable and as direct as the injury to the fishermen. It is therefore unclear why these parties should not also be entitled to recovery. The court did not attempt to distinguish fishermen in that they "lawfully and directly make use of a resource of the sea, viz. its fish, in the ordinary course of their business." Id. 1975 AMC at 435, 501 F.2d at 570. Yet, if those who make use of a "resource of the sea" are entitled to recovery, then it seems a fortiori that those who make use of the sea itself in their business—a boat charterer, for example—would be entitled to recovery. Nor can *Oppen's* restricted recovery be explained in terms of special property rights in the fish. No one owns a wild animal, or fish, until achieving capture, and under this rule, the fishermen had no rights to the fish superior to those of Union Oil. Id. 752 F.2d at 1044 n. 23 (Wisdom, J., dissenting)

As the dissent points out, the exception to *Robins Dry Dock* is arbitrary. Id. It offers no guidance in distinguishing which of those plaintiffs targeted by Alyeska's motion might fit within its protection.

Conclusion

The oil spill from the *Exxon Valdez* gives rise to a maritime tort. Therefore, all tort claims, except those for strict liability, must be decided under general maritime law, which includes the rule in *Robins Dry Dock*.

The Alaska Act is technically not preempted by TAPAA to the extent of TAPAA's $100 million liability because the remedy is uniform whether a claim is brought under either the Alaska Act or TAPAA. *Robins Dry Dock* will only apply to those claims under the Alaska Act which exceed TAPAA's $100 million liability. However, in practical application, it would be unworkable to allow strict liability claims for the

initial $100 million to proceed under both acts and in both this court and the Superior Court for the State of Alaska. While TAPAA provides a mechanism to gather all the claims and fairly prorate them to meet its $100 million liability limits, the Alaska Act has no such mechanism. It was in part this concern which brought the court to endeavor, to the extent it could, to require all potential TAPAA claimants to file with the Fund. In that fashion, all claimants would be before one claims-processing agency—the entity that has the $100 million to pay against all claims, inclusive of purely economic losses. It was also out of concern for such individual claims, including economic loss claims, that the court previously urged that the United States Government and the State of Alaska refrain from making claims against the Fund. These governmental entities have other remedies available to them. The inclusion of those governmental claims against the Fund would drastically draw down the fund when it is allocated on a pro rata basis amongst all claimants. 43 U.S.C. Sec. 1653(c)(3). The pro rata payment out of the Fund is particularly acute for plaintiffs whose claims are not viable because of the rule in *Robins Dry Dock* once the statutory $100 million limit for strict liability is exceeded.

It is the court's perception that Congress may very well not have perceived the possibility of the situation which has developed here. Congress may have assumed that $100 million was more than enough to cover any oil spill. It is now entirely clear that, if such were the perception of Congress, it was tragically wrong. We must all now do the best we can to accommodate the present situation to TAPAA as it was written. It is the court's conclusion that such a goal will best be achieved by the prompt submission of all private claims to the Fund for adjustment and the withholding of claims by governmental entities which have other statutory remedies available to them. In this fashion, the recovery for private claimants who have suffered economic losses will be maximized.

Since factual development regarding the individual claims of the targeted plaintiffs is necessary before judgment could be entered on any plaintiff's claim, Alyeska's motion for judgment on the pleadings cannot be granted as to any specific party; however, the foregoing shall be the law of this case as to all parties.

Certification

Interlocutory decisions such as that embodied in this order may be appealed to the Ninth Court of Appeals if the criteria set forth in 28 U.S.C. Sec. 1292(b) are met.

The status of the *Robins Dry Dock* rule, in view of the decisions of the Ninth Circuit Court of Appeals, especially *Union Oil v. Oppen*, 501 F.2d 588 (9 Cir. 1974), and the within order presents "a controlling question of law as to which there is substantial ground for difference of opinion. . . ." 28 U.S.C. Sec. 1292(b). Despite the express disclaimer in *Oppen* of any intention to disavow *Robins Dry Dock* except for commercial fishermen, this court does not understand how, as a matter of principal, the rule in *Robins Dry Dock* can have application for all claimants who suffer economic loss as a result of a marine tort except commercial fishermen. If the Court of Appeals were to have second thoughts about its decision in *Oppen* as a consequence of the United States Supreme Court decision in *East River Steamship Corp. v. Transamerica Delaval, Inc.*, 476 U.S. 858 (1986), the implications of such a change of direction in this case would be of monumental proportions. The court assumes without knowing that there are thousands of commercial fishermen's claims involved in this litigation. Even if *Oppen* remains the law of the Ninth Circuit, this court and the Superior Court for the State of Alaska are confronted with a substantial number of economic loss claims. This court and, since it is bound to follow federal admiralty law as well, the Superior Court of the State of Alaska urgently need to know whether and to what extent the rule of *Robins Dry Dock* will apply to the economic claims of those who are not commercial fishermen.

Plainly, a decision on this issue will substantially expedite disposition of a substantial segment of the multiplicity of claims brought against the defendants in this litigation. Equally important to this court, an early ruling on the foregoing issue will allow all viable claims to proceed simultaneously and therefore most efficiently.

The Ninth Circuit Court of Appeals is urged to take this matter up immediately, to order a substantially foreshortened briefing schedule, and to render a prompt decision.

Questions

1. What is the purpose of the so-called "bright-line rule" in *Robins Dry Dock*?

2. Did Congress or the State of Alaska ever contemplate damages of this enormity?

In the Matter of Oil Spill by the *Amoco Cadiz* off the Coast of France on March 16, 1978, 954 F.2d 1279 (7th Cir. 1992)

Before BAUER, CHIEF JUDGE
EASTERBROOK, CIRCUIT JUDGE, and
FAIRCHILD, SENIOR CIRCUIT JUDGE
Per curiam.

On the morning of March 16, 1978, the supertanker *Amoco Cadiz* broke apart in a severe storm, spewing most of its load of 220,000 tons of Iranian crude into the seas off Brittany. The wreck resulted in one of the largest oil spills in history, damaging approximately 180 miles of coastline in one of the most important tourist and fishing regions in France. The cleanup took more than six months and involved equipment and resources from all over the country. The disaster has had lasting effects on the environment, the economy, and the people of Brittany, and has resulted in numerous lawsuits. Thirteen years later, the matter is before us. In this consolidated appeal, we are asked to resolve a myriad of issues involving jurisdiction, liability, and damages. Before we begin, a brief history of the litigation and its cast of characters is in order.

I.

A.

The origins of the *Amoco Cadiz* are not difficult to trace. The vessel was born of discussions that began in Madrid, Spain, in May 1970 between Astilleros Españoles, S.A., the shipbuilder who constructed the fleet in which Columbus voyaged to the New World, and Standard Oil Company of Indiana ("Standard"; now called Amoco), an Indiana corporation having its principal office and place of business in Chicago, Illinois. The latter was represented by Robert S. Haddow, vice president in charge of marine operations at Amoco International Oil Company ("AIOC") and chairman of Amoco Tankers and Amoco Transport. (For simplicity's sake, we generally will refer to Amoco and its various subsidiaries—Amoco Tankers, Amoco Transport, and AIOC—as "The Amoco parties" or "Amoco.") Astilleros previously had contracted to build two megatankers for Amoco; Haddow wanted two more. The Madrid meeting covered all the essentials: technical specifications, delivery date, and price. Further negotiations took place in New York and Chicago. On May 30, Astilleros confirmed the content of the negotiations and submitted a bid to build two ships, the *Amoco Cadiz* and the *Amoco Europa*. Amoco accepted the bid by letter on June 18, and the parties signed off on the final contract and ship specifications in Chicago on July 31, 1970.

The contract required that the ship be built according to the American Bureau of Shipping's ("ABS") Rules for Building and Classing Steel Vessels. The ABS is a not-for-profit maritime classification society headquartered in New York that promulgates rules and sets standards for shipbuilding, design, and seaworthiness. The ABS's technical staff in London reviewed Astilleros's proposed plan for the *Amoco Cadiz* to ensure that it complied with the ABS's rules. The ABS examined the "general arrangement" plans—plans featuring the layout and list of components used in the various parts of the

ship—as well as drawings related to the detailed design of the ship. (By "detailed design," we mean items as small as nuts and bolts.) The ABS stamped the plans and drawings with its Maltese cross emblem to signify its approval. The Amoco-Astilleros contract incorporated the general arrangement plans and required Astilleros to submit them to Amoco for acceptance prior to construction. Astilleros did so, but did not pass along to Amoco its detailed design drawings, calculations, or fabrication drawings showing the mechanical details of the steering mechanism's component parts. Amoco reviewed the design of the steering gear system and approved it on October 19, 1971. Amoco later made two modifications to the system: it designed a low fluid level alarm for the replenishment gravity tank and increased the size of the rudder. It chose not to include an optional hand-charging pump. Astilleros's representatives came to Chicago for a two-day meeting in June 1972 to firm up technical details.

Pursuant to the contract, Astilleros built the behemoth at its shipyards in Cadiz, Spain. It took four years to complete the job. Throughout the construction process, both Amoco and the ABS had representatives on the scene at the shipyard. The Amoco representatives were concerned with deadlines and whether construction conformed to the contract specifications and general arrangement drawings. They also were present to witness tests of equipment and gear and to catch any problems that might have been missed in the plan approval process. The ABS representatives monitored the progress of the ship to ensure that construction was in conformity with the ABS's Rules. The Amoco representatives deferred to the ABS representatives' technical and engineering expertise in evaluating whether construction was proceeding as it should.

At long last, the vessel was finished. It measured 1,095 feet long and 167 feet wide—the size of three football fields—and weighed 230,000 deadweight tons. It was powered by a

30,000-horsepower diesel engine driving a single screw and was equipped with a single rudder driven by a hydraulic steering engine. It had a hydraulic steering gear with movement of the rudder controlled by two pairs of rams contained in four cylinders that were filled with hydraulic fluid. The four rams were made of rolled steel, and their heads were cast steel. Ram isolation valves controlled the flow of oil through the passages in the distribution block. These valves were a critical safety component. They could capture the remaining hydraulic fluid in the rams in the event of a rupture in the piping. The valves also could be closed to isolate the various lines from the rest of the system or to block the passage of oil to or from the cylinder.

The *Amoco Cadiz*'s steering system was supposed to work in the following manner. When the helmsman turned the steering wheel or when the ship operated on autopilot, an electronic signal was generated. In response to the signal, hydraulic fluid was moved by a series of pumps, which in turn moved the rams and, eventually, the rudder. The hydraulic fluid in the cylinders kept the rudder restrained and in the desired position by exerting pressure against the rams. There was no device aboard that could be used to steer the ship if the primary system failed. The ship was not equipped with twin screws, twin rudders, or bow thrusters that could be used to steer in an emergency. The anchor was underdesigned and could not be used as a stopping device in a crisis situation.

The ABS certified the ship—and its steering gear—as being in compliance with the ABS's Rules. Even after delivery, the ABS periodically conducted inspections of the *Amoco Cadiz* to determine if it still was in seaworthy condition. Three times—June 1975, April 1976, and May 1977—the ABS inspected the steering gear and pronounced it in working order.

B.

Amoco Tankers ("Tankers"), a Liberian corporation all of whose stock was owned by Stan-

dard through a chain of wholly owned subsidiaries, took delivery of the *Amoco Cadiz* on May 11, 1974. Two weeks later, Tankers sold the vessel to Amoco Transport ("Transport"), a Liberian corporation with its principal place of business in Bermuda. Transport was a subsidiary of AIOC. In June 1974, Transport entered into a consulting agreement with AIOC. The agreement provided that AIOC was responsible for the operation of the *Amoco Cadiz*, including maintenance, repair, and training of its crew. Transport remained the owner of the vessel. Long after delivery, in August 1975, representatives from Astilleros met with Amoco in Chicago to discuss contract guarantee terms. Similar discussions were held in New York in 1976. Just like a home appliance, the *Amoco Cadiz* came with a one-year guarantee. Astilleros agreed to repair or replace any defects in the ship or its equipment during its first year of operation, 1974–75. Consequently, during that first year, the ship always had on board an engineer from Astilleros who was attuned to any problem that arose. After the one-year guarantee period had expired, AIOC took care of maintenance problems.

In June 1974, the *Amoco Cadiz* was chartered to Shell International Petroleum. "Charter hire" is the expense charterers pay owners of vessels per long ton per day. During off-hire periods, such as when the vessel is in for repairs, charter hire payments stop. It thus is in the pecuniary interest of a chartered ship's owner to keep the vessel running. The Amoco-Shell time charter required annual drydocking of the tanker for maintenance, but for reasons of economy, Amoco unilaterally lengthened the interval between drydockings to eighteen months and made plans to extend the interval to two years. (A two-year interval would save the company $1,250,000 in shipyard costs and $200,000 per year in offshore losses.) The ABS rules required two-year intervals between drydockings unless the owner received special permission from the ABS. By January 1976, Amoco decided that time-chartered vessels would be drydocked every two and one-half years.

C.

In February 1978, the fully staffed *Amoco Cadiz* took on a load of crude oil at Kharg Island, Iran, and Ras Tanura, Saudi Arabia, destined for Rotterdam around the Cape of Good Hope. The Italian crew was experienced and the officers all were properly licensed. With regard to training, Captain Pasquale Bardari and his officers and crew participated in on-shore classes and on-board safety exercises. The latter were conducted by representatives of Marine Safety Services, a British organization. In addition, the ship's library contained a collection of films, videos, and technical information pertaining to ship operations.

As the tanker approached western Europe, it sailed into a storm. Retired Royal Navy officer Leslie Maynard, an on-board representative of Marine Safety Services, later testified that he had seen worse weather only once, during a typhoon. The *Amoco Cadiz* had the capacity to weather severe storm conditions and heavy seas if she was in seaworthy condition. Buffeted by the rough seas and high winds, the ship rolled heavily on March 15 and through the night of March 16. Despite the bad weather, the helmsman reported no difficulty with the steering mechanism. During their normal inspection rounds, the crew members reported no abnormalities in the steering room.

In the morning, while the *Amoco Cadiz* was approximately nine miles off the French island of Ushant, its steering gear completed failed. The helmsman informed Captain Bardari, who broadcast a message to nearby ships giving the *Amoco Cadiz*'s position and caution to stay clear. The crew raised "non-under-command" flags as an additional warning. Almost immediately, the ship's engineers examined the steering gear only to find that the "De" flange, which had held a pipe that carried oil from the port steering gear pump to the hydraulic oil distribution block, had come off. Oil was spurting everywhere.

The crew members discovered that five of the six steel studs holding the De flange and pipe to the distribution block had broken; no other studs had failed in the system. The failure of the studs allowed the rapid escape of hydraulic fluid out of the steering system and the immediate entry of air. One of the engineers futilely tried to stop the flow of oil by closing the port steering gear pump and the isolation valves on the distribution block. The chief engineer tried to replenish the system by adding hydraulic fluid to the steering gear gravity replacement tank, but the fluid level in the gravity tank did not drop as it should have if the steering mechanism had been functioning normally.

Because of the lack of hydraulic pressure, the rudder was unrestrained. Some of the crew unsuccessfully tried to control the swinging rudder with a block and tackle, while others tried to repair the flange connection and purge the air from the system. As the crew worked, a relief valve pipe blew off, and oil hit the ceiling of the steering compartment. With the relief valve blown, the rudder's unchecked movement became more violent until it crashed into its stops, breaking apart the steering gear and hurling metal parts in every direction. The chief engineer ordered an evacuation of the compartment after one of the crewmen was struck in the head with a piece of metal. The chief engineer then reported to Captain Bardari that the steering gear could not be repaired.

About two hours after the steering failure, Captain Bardari called for salvage tugboats. In response, the *Pacific*, a salvage tug in the fleet of Bugsier Reederei and Bergungs, A.G., a corporation organized under the laws of the then Federal Republic of Germany, arrived on the scene. Bugsier undertook salvage jobs only under a "Lloyd's Open Form" ("LOF") "No-Cure-No-Pay" salvage contract. The tug did not begin operations immediately because Bardari had to call Chicago to find out if he could enter into such a deal. While the *Amoco Cadiz* foundered,

Amoco and the tug's captain, Hartmut Weinert, haggled over the LOF. Finally, Amoco and Captain Weinert came to terms. By then, the island of Ushant was less than six miles dead ahead, the shallow Chenal du Four on the port bow, and the rocky Finistere coast on the port beam. The wind was fierce, the seas high, and the *Amoco Cadiz* pitched so wildly that her bow repeatedly plunged beneath the surface.

The *Pacific* approached and secured a fair lead on the bow of the *Amoco Cadiz* intending to turn the ship to her starboard, head her out to sea, and then tow her in to shore. In hindsight, this strategy proved unfortunate. The *Pacific* was incapable of turning a ship the size of the *Amoco Cadiz* into the wind and the towing chain broke. The *Pacific* made a second tow attempt by connecting to the stern of the tanker. By then, tidal currents and heavy winds had carried the *Amoco Cadiz* dangerously close to the rocky and irregular Finistere coastline. The tanker continued to roll on the rocks and sink into the shoals. As the *Pacific* continued its futile maneuvers, its captain received the following message from Marine Safety Services representative Leslie Maynard, "Sir, we are grounded." The *Amoco Cadiz* began tearing in two and the *Pacific* lost contact altogether. Soon, the telltale odor of oil filled the air. Fifteen million gallons spilled into the sea during the first night alone.

D.

The resulting oil slick was eighteen miles wide and eighty miles long, one-fourth of the Breton coast. Over the weeks following the grounding of the *Amoco Cadiz* 4,400 men and 50 vessels (which included ships and personnel from the British Royal Navy) were dispatched to aid in the cleanup operations at sea. France sought more than 30 million francs for the cost of the cleanup at sea (see *infra*, section V). The cleanup on land took over six months and involved the participation of the French Army. Heavy machinery and volunteers were recruited from all over France. Approximately

220,000 tons of oily waste the color and consistency of chocolate mousse were recovered from the beaches along the Côtes du Nord. The infusion of oil upset the delicate ecosystem along the coastline, destroying algae and ruining oyster and lobster beds. Especially hard hit was the Breton economy. Brittany is France's second most important tourist region after the Riviera. The claimed overall cost to France was an estimated $100 million at the 1978 rate of exchange.

II.

In the aftermath of the environmental disaster, various parties brought lawsuits. The Republic of France ("France") sued Amoco to recover for pollution damages and cleanup costs. Similar actions were brought by the French administrative departments of Côtes du Nord and Finistere ("the Côtes du Nord parties"), numerous municipalities called "communes," and various French individuals, businesses, and associations, including hoteliers and fishermen who lost business as a result of the oil spill ("the French claimants"). The Côtes du Nord parties and the French claimants charged Astilleros with negligence in designing and constructing the tanker. The lawsuits were filed in Illinois and New York. Astilleros appeared and moved to dismiss the claims against it for lack of personal and subject matter jurisdiction and for forum non conveniens. Both the Côtes du Nord parties and Amoco sued Bugsier, the owner of the tug *Pacific*, claiming that it was negligent in attempting to tow the *Amoco Cadiz*. The Bugsier suits were stayed pending arbitration in London. Bugsier filed a limitation action in the lawsuits in which the Côtes du Nord parties were claimants.

Amoco brought several actions in federal district court in Chicago. It filed a complaint for exoneration from or limitation of liability pursuant to the United States Limitation of Liability Act of 1951, 46 U.S.C. App. Secs. 181–96 ("Act"). In addition, the Amoco parties filed a third-party claim and cross-claims against Astilleros. Amoco filed for contribution from the ABS to the extent that the grounding was caused by ABS's negligence and breach of contract in approving the vessel design, inspecting it, and certifying its seaworthiness. The Côtes du Nord parties and French claimants also sued the ABS. The ABS settled these claims and sued the Amoco parties in New York, seeking reimbursement for expenses in connection with the settlement. Amoco removed the matter to federal court and counterclaimed. Petroleum Insurance Limited ("PIL"), Royal Dutch Shell's subrogee, sought to recover from Amoco for loss of the oil cargo, claiming loss occurred through Amoco's lack of due diligence in making the vessel seaworthy and through Amoco's breach of the charter contract.

The various federal actions were bifurcated and brought before Judge Frank J. McGarr of the Northern District of Illinois. After consolidating the liability issues, Judge McGarr opened the bench trial on May 4, 1982. The liability phase would not end until late November of the same year. In an April 18, 1984, opinion, the court held Amoco Corporation, Astilleros (who neither participated in discovery nor in the trial), and Amoco Production Company jointly and severally liable to France, the Côtes du Nord parties, the French claimants, and to PIL. The court denied Amoco's petition for limitation of liability. Bugsier was exonerated on the claims brought against it by the Côtes du Nord parties. (Amoco's claims against Bugsier eventually were resolved in the London arbitration.) Because of its settlement with France and the Côtes du Nord parties, the ABS did not participate in the liability trial. It still is part of a pending "tag-along" action in federal district court in Chicago in which Amoco is seeking contribution from the ABS.

The court subsequently held a second bench trial on the consolidated damages issues. That trial lasted from April 1986 to June 1987. On October 5, 1987, the court awarded PIL 11,212,349.50 pounds sterling for the loss of Shell's oil cargo. The court also awarded PIL

prejudgment interest, but denied its request for compounded interest. Subsequently, the court amended its opinion by awarding PIL statutory costs and by setting the annual prejudgment interest rate at 7.22 percent. The final award to PIL was 21,215,054.68 pounds sterling. With regard to the other plaintiffs' damages, on January 11, 1988, the district court applied French law and ordered an award to cover costs of cleanup and restoration incurred by France, the Côtes du Nord parties, and the French claimants. The court awarded statutory costs as well as compound prejudgment interest at an annual rate of 7.22 percent for a total of nearly 600 million French francs.

When Judge McGarr retired in late January 1988, the case was reassigned to Judge Charles R. Norgle, Sr., who appointed Judge McGarr as a Special Master to resolve any remaining issues. Special Master McGarr issued his Final Report and Recommendations on October 31, 1989. Pursuant to Rule 53 of the Federal Rules of Civil Procedure, the Amoco Parties, France, the Côtes du Nord parties, Astilleros, and PIL filed objections. In March 1990, a hearing was held on those objections. Following the hearing, the district court adopted all of the Special Master's Recommendations relating to liability and damages and, on July 24, 1990, issued four separate final judgments awarding claimants damages in French francs and pounds sterling against the Amoco parties and Astilleros, jointly and severally. These consolidated appeals followed.

III.

Astilleros was named as a defendant or third-party defendant by Amoco, the Republic of France, the Côtes du Nord parties, and the French claimants in cases filed in both Illinois and New York. The Illinois and New York cases were consolidated in the Northern District of Illinois by the Judicial Panel on Multidistrict Litigation. Three of the judgments now on appeal were entered in Illinois cases and one in a New York case. Astilleros contends that neither

Illinois nor New York courts had personal jurisdiction over it.

IV.

Having found that Astilleros is subject to the jurisdiction of American courts, we turn to the question of liability. What caused the steering system to fail and whose fault was it? As one can well imagine, in answering these questions, Judge McGarr braved a task akin to the seven labors of Hercules. Faced with a mountain of evidence, much of it highly technical, the district court did a remarkable job of fact finding. To summarize, it found that the failure of the steering gear system of the *Amoco Cadiz* was proximately caused by a number of factors, including Amoco's (specifically, AIOC's) negligence in failing reasonably to perform its obligations to repair and maintain the steering gear, properly train its crew, provide the vessel with a redundant steering system or other means to steer the vessel in the event of a complete failure of the hydraulic system, and fulfill its duty as the party who supervised and approved the design to ensure that the design and construction properly were carried out. *Amoco Cadiz*, 1984 A.M.C. at 2154–61. Contesting jurisdiction, Astilleros chose not to defend itself against the various lawsuits filed by the Amoco parties, the Côtes du Nord parties, and the French claimants. The district court entered default judgments against the shipbuilder. The district court found that Astilleros improperly designed and built the steering gear and pressure relief valves and that the stud and flange assembly did not conform to specification or code requirements. Id. at 2162. In particular, the court found that the flange assemblies installed by Astilleros did not meet code requirements for high-pressure systems.

Our standard of review is highly deferential. We are bound by the district court's findings of fact unless they are clearly erroneous. A finding is "clearly erroneous" when, "although there is evidence to support it, the reviewing court on the entire evidence is left with a definite and firm conviction that a mistake has been made." *United States v. United States Gypsum Co.*, 333 U.S. 364, 395 (1948). The clearly erroneous rule applies "even when the district court's findings do not rest on credibility determinations, but are based instead on physical or documentary evidence or inferences from other facts." In order for us to determine whether the district court's findings of fact are clearly erroneous, we must spend some time examining the arcane workings of the steering systems of "VLCCs"—very large crude carriers.

A.

From the beginning, there were mechanical problems with the hydraulic steering system rams and bushings on the *Amoco Cadiz* and her sister ships. The rams are pistons; the bushings are the metal linings that protect the rams. The bushings on the four Amoco supertankers were constructed of cast iron, which was much harder than the rams themselves. When dirt particles are present, metal rams become scored, meaning they are marred or scratched because of close contact with something having a "plowing" effect. Ram scoring and defective bushings are especially serious because they contribute to the loss of pump efficiency and impair the reliability of the steering system. Scoring forms projections on the ram's surface, tearing the packing around the "gland," the ram casing. When the packing is torn, its sealing effect is destroyed and oil seeps through. It is good practice to change the packing every two years during drydocking or when a problem arises.

Amoco accepted the *Amoco Cadiz* with the cast-iron bushings and acknowledged the defect upon delivery. During the *Amoco Cadiz*'s sea trials in May 1974, an Amoco representative reported to AIOC vice president Robert Haddow that there were problems with the hydraulic steering gear rams and bushings. Three of the ship's four rams were scored. Subsequent inspections of the tanker revealed that the scoring problem had worsened. Astilleros prepared a list of "Exceptions and Extras Not Completed for the *Amoco Cadiz*." One of the items on the list stated, "Present rams are scored and cause rapid packing wear and leak oil excessively, resulting in excessive cleaning and expenditure for replacement oil. Repair satisfactorily or replace." Id. at 2168–69. Astilleros offered to repair or replace the scored rams and even supplied bronze replacement bushings. At the time of the wreck, a spare set of uninstalled bronze bushings was on board. Amoco had taken a cash credit from Astilleros in lieu of repair.

After visiting the ship in Genoa in March 1975, transport marine engineer Giuseppe Ciaramaglia reported, "The rams were carefully inspected and found worse conditions since last inspection. Namely, the four rams are heavily scored in the bottom side and near the bush. Particularly the ram in the position port-fore is in really bad condition and some dressing should be carried out next drydocking." Claimants' Exhibit 424. Although Amoco immediately changed the bushings on two of the *Amoco Cadiz*'s similarly constructed sister ships, the *Amoco Milford Haven* and the *Amoco Europa*, it took no action with regard to the *Amoco Cadiz*'s bushings. Unlike the *Amoco Cadiz*, the repaired vessels were not on a time charter.

Robert J. Zimmerman, an AIOC ship superintendent, visited the ship in late January 1976 and inspected the steering gear rams. Zimmerman acknowledged the scoring problem, but recommended a polishing measure in lieu of more permanent repair, which would have required two weeks in drydock. Zimmerman wrote to company officials, "Rams are deeply scored and will continue to cut packing but oil loss cost minimal against extended time required to carry out the replacement of business. . . ." Id. at 2169.

The specifications for the 1976 drydocking of the ship in Lisnave, Portugal, included changing the ram packing material. Amoco later cancelled this item to save time during the overhaul period. No work was performed dur-

ing the 1976 drydock to polish out the scoring on the existing rams, change the bushings, or repack the glands. Over the next few months up until the grounding, the *Amoco Cadiz* suffered leakage from the steering gear rams, the main hydraulic system of the steering gear, the small packing gland at the lower part of the level gauge indicator, and the mechanical seal of the main shaft of both main steering gear pumps at a rate far in excess of that which normally would occur with a properly maintained system. The *Amoco Cadiz* was losing seven to twelve liters of hydraulic fluid per day in leakage. The acceptable quantity of leakage should have been no more than a few drops per day.

There were problems with the rudder, too. During trials in Lisbon on May 14, 1974, the rudder stuck in hard starboard position. On June 15, 1974, during maneuvering at Mina al Ahmadi, the rudder again stuck in the hard starboard position. In both cases, it was necessary to stop one of the two running pumps in order to return the rudder to normal position. There were other difficulties with the rudder as well. In port, the *Amoco Cadiz* and her sister ships experienced as much as twenty-five degrees rudder movement when the system was shut down. To prevent the unwanted movement, Amoco ordered that one steering gear pump always be kept running. Amoco hired an independent marine hydraulics expert to investigate the problem, and he recommended that, as a first step in the investigation of the source of the problem, the company should check all valves in the distribution block, including relief valves and their springs. Amoco wrote a specification for the disassembly of the distribution block relief valves and associated repairs for the *Amoco Cadiz* and her sister ships. Although the work called for in the specification was performed on the *Amoco Milford Haven* and the *Amoco Europa* in 1977, the work was not performed on either the *Amoco Cadiz* or the *Amoco Singapore*, both of which were on time charter to Shell.

Another problem was that the ship's steering

gear gravity tank, which held hydraulic fluid used to replenish fluid losses in the system, often would overflow when the starboard gear pump was activated. The overflow prevented the hydraulic steering gear pumps from being changed over every twenty-four hours, as required by the hydraulic system manufacturer in its steering gear manual (the "Manises Steering Gear Manual") and Amoco's own instructions. The system would have had to be shut down in order to locate the problem. In fall 1977, an Amoco inspector recommended that repairs concerning the overflow be deferred until the next drydocking. The repairs never were done. Also, Amoco failed to renew the leather belts used to drive the evacuation and replenishing pumps of the steering gear after they slipped on two occasions. Such slippage contributes to an imbalance in the system and has been associated with gravity tank overflow.

B.

In addition to—and perhaps contribution to—these mechanical shortcomings, Amoco failed to adhere to manufacturer recommendations regarding proper maintenance of the ship's components. The instructions required that the isolation valves— the operation of which could have stabilized or immobilized the *Amoco Cadiz*'s rudder on the night of March 16, 1978—be opened, closed, and lubricated periodically to prevent their sticking as a result of being stationary for a long time or from being covered with foreign material. When the cylinder isolation valves were recovered after the wreck, they were found to have paint on the stem threads: they had been painted over with the valves in the open position. Tests performed on the valves showed that they could not be closed completely because of the paint. Had the isolation valves been totally closed when the steering gear failed, the hydraulic fluid in the cylinders could have acted as a "brake" on the rudder.

The manufacturer also recommended that the hydraulic fluid be kept free of contamination for proper operation of the hydraulic system. The Manises Steering Gear Manual stated: "The slightest impurity can bring about great damage on account of the narrowness of the channels in the Nanauer Pittler pumps. . . . The exact fulfillment of this operating instruction is the condition for a good performance of the pumps." Contamination creates an imbalance between the rate oil is removed from the main system and the rate of replenishment. Further, impurities in the oil cause wear on the internal parts of the main pumps, clogging of the filters, failure of seals, and scoring of the rams. Particulate matter in hydraulic systems acts like a grinding compound between points with close running tolerances. The manufacturer recommended that the shipowner avoid contamination of the hydraulic fluid by using clean oil filters and by filtering the oil through muslin as it is put into the system. The function of the oil filters is to strain the oil entering the system via the replenishing pump. The oil filters must be checked periodically and changed often to make sure they are clean. Checking the filters requires shutting down the system. The Manises Steering Gear Manual suggested a complete oil change after each one thousand hours of operation for the first three oil changes and after every three thousand hours thereafter, and periodic cleaning of filters. On each oil change, the tank must be drained in order to be kept free of sludge.

Amoco failed to follow these recommendations. It neither periodically replaced the oil in the hydraulic system of the steering gear with new oil, nor removed, strained, purified, or treated the oil prior to the wreck. The hydraulic fluid in the steering system was not filtered or changed between September 1977 and March 1978, and no steps ever were taken to check for contaminants. The drums containing hydraulic fluid were stored on the open deck. They were not covered over with tarpaulins. When the drums expanded and contracted because of temperature changes, the rainwaters, dirt, soot, and sea spray that collected in the recessed drum heads was sucked in around the head of the drum.

In addition, Amoco utilized improper procedures in refilling the gravity replenishment tank, which it had to do more frequently than normal because of the leakage problem. On the *Amoco Cadiz*, the gravity tank was not filled with a hand pump-storage tank. Instead, refilling was done in a rudimentary way. Crewmen would climb a ladder and pour a plastic bucket of hydraulic fluid into the tank without filtering. The bucket used to replenish the hydraulic fluid was kept uncovered in the steering gear room, which was dirty and moist. The various steam pipes that ran through the room all leaked. Transport marine engineer Ciaramaglia wrote several memoranda decrying conditions in the steering gear room. In a report describing his visit to the ship in October 1974, he stated that inspection of the rudder carrier bearing was impossible because the steering gear room was full of sea water.

The bucket method of pouring fluid into the gravity tank produced agitation that would cause air bubbles to enter the system. The steering system never was purged to remove entrapped air, a standard "good housekeeping" measure. Also, the fluid's exposure to air, which naturally contains moisture and contaminants, allowed foreign matter to enter the system. Water contamination decreases the lubricity of hydraulic fluid, which exacerbates the wear on closely moving parts and accelerates the growth of harmful bacteria. What's worse, the gravity tank on board the *Amoco Cadiz* never was cleaned.

When one of the valves of the *Amoco Cadiz*—the #9 valve located in the P loop—was recovered from the wreck and tested by the French National Testing Laboratory, it was found to be partially blocked. A properly functioning #9 valve would have allowed the fluid level in the gravity tank to drop after rupture of the flange. The hydrocarbons removed from the valve were the sort that might be expected if significant quantities of oil or rubber oxidation residue had existed, clear physical evidence of contamination in the hydraulic fluid.

C.

The ram scoring, leakage, unwanted rudder movement, and contaminated hydraulic fluid were clear signs of trouble that foreshadowed the breakdown of the steering gear. Apart from these mechanical and maintenance problems, a significant cause of the grounding of the *Amoco Cadiz* was that its crew was trained improperly with respect to the maintenance, operation, inspection, and repair of the steering gear system. This lapse in training contributed to the failure of the steering gear system and the inability of the crew to reestablish steering control after the rupture of the De flange studs. The crew was not instructed as to the acceptable level of hydraulic fluid consumption of the steering gear. Amoco never directed the crew to clean the filters or change the hydraulic fluid in the steering gear, as required by the manufacturer's manual. Although it was critical to keep the hydraulic fluid uncontaminated, Amoco never told the crew to take samples of steering gear hydraulic fluid to test for purity. The crew was not instructed to clean out the bottom casing of the steering gear pumps or the sediment in the bottom of the gravity tank. Amoco never advised the *Amoco Cadiz* crew of emergency procedures to be followed in the event of a steering gear breakdown, a critical lapse given that such drills could have familiarized the crew with emergency procedures so that they would have acted more decisively in the face of a crisis. Emergency drills also would have provided the perfect opportunity to "dry-run" emergency equipment. The crew did not practice blocking the rudder using the cylinder isolation valve as described in the steering gear manual, or using a two-ram mode of operation.

V.

Why did these deficiencies occur? The record is replete with references to the fact that it was Amoco's deliberate policy to defer drydocking and repairs in order to minimize the loss of charter hire that would be incurred by taking the ship out of service during the charter period. Item 3 on a January 2, 1976, list of specifications for repairs of outstanding guarantee items contained an order for replacement of existing bushings for steering gear rams. Someone had written on the list the following note: "Take credit and do after charter expires." Following his January 1976 visit to the *Amoco Cadiz*, AIOC ship superintendent Robert J. Zimmerman wrote his superiors that Amoco should turn down Astilleros's offer of replacement parts, take a cash credit, and defer repair until after the time charter expired.

In a March 10, 1976, memorandum from Chester J. Bysarovich, head of marine engineering for AIOC and a director of Tankers, to Tankers director Claude D. Phillips, Bysarovich emphasized the importance of keeping the *Amoco Cadiz* out of drydock for "obvious reasons":

Realizing the importance of minimizing off-hire time, . . . we have arranged to meet with Lisnave personnel at this vessel's discharge port at Genoa to go over the entire specification item by item, for the purpose of properly scheduling and organizing each item of work; and to cancel or accomplish by riding crews these items that are not absolutely necessary so that we can keep the ship's off-hire time down to eight calendar running days.

Amoco later decided that eight running days would be the limit. Bysarovich telexed the drydocking site: "Amoco is extremely concerned over the possibility that this vessel will be delayed from sailing as scheduled and agreed. This vessel is committed to a charter and any delays could result in a severe penalty to Amoco." During the 1976 drydocking, Amoco cancelled the renewal of bushings and packings because the job would have taken more than fourteen working days of two shifts per day.

In May 1977, Bysarovich wrote Phillips: "The *Amoco Singapore* and *Amoco Cadiz* are planned for maximum allowable time without drydock-

ing because these two vessels are on time charter." In an August 23, 1977, memoranda, Bysarovich informed Phillips of their 1978 goal:

The primary goal for 1978 is to keep the *Amoco Cadiz* and the *Amoco Singapore* operating without any downtime that would put these two chartered-out vessels off-hire. These two vessels will not be scheduled for their drydockings and biennial repair period until the expiration of the charters. This will mean doing various surveys during cargo operations. The charter hire of $28,000 per day per vessel multiplied by the estimated time in the shipyard of thirty days per vessel is equal to $1,680,000 of incoming money that otherwise would not be realized.

Phillips responded in a handwritten note: "Very good! Hope we can reach this goal."

Amoco tries to confuse matters by arguing that, in finding that AIOC's negligence rendered the *Amoco Cadiz* unseaworthy and caused its grounding, the district court improperly applied the admiralty doctrine of unseaworthiness, which imposes strict liability in favor of crew and cargo owners. Amoco points out that the category of individuals protected by this doctrine does not include the plaintiffs in this case. Amoco mischaracterizes the court's holding. Specifically, the court held that "AIOC negligently performed its duty to ensure that the *Amoco Cadiz* in general and its steering gear in particular were seaworthy, adequately maintained and in proper repair." *Amoco Cadiz*, 1984 A.M.C. at 2191. Although the district court did indeed use the word "seaworthy," it was not applying the admiralty doctrine of unseaworthiness. "[L]iability based upon unseaworthiness is wholly distinct from liability based on negligence." *Usner v. Luckenbach Overseas Corp.*, 400 U.S. 494, 498, 91 S.Ct. 514, 517, 27 L.Ed.2d 562 (1971). The unmistakable basis for the district court's decision that AIOC was liable was that its *negligence* caused the unseaworthy condition of the *Amoco Cadiz*. The court stated, "The *negligence* of AIOC in failing reasonably to perform its obligations of maintenance and repair of the steering gear system was a proximate cause of the breakdown of the system on March 16, 1978, the grounding of the vessel, and the resulting pollution damage." Id. 1984 A.M.C. at 2192 (emphasis added). The ship's "unseaworthy" condition, then, was the direct result of the failure to exercise reasonable care in the maintenance and operation of the vessel.

Amoco next assails the district court's concept of negligence; specifically, the court's use of the word "ensure." The court stated, "AIOC negligently performed its duty to ensure that the *Amoco Cadiz* in general and its steering gear in particular were seaworthy, adequately maintained, and in proper repair." Id. at 2191. Contrary to Amoco's contention, the district court's use of the word "ensure" did not create a new legal standard beyond the due diligence required of shipowners to take normal and reasonable precautions to make the ship seaworthy, something that Amoco failed to do before the *Amoco Cadiz*'s last voyage. Cf. *Hercules Carriers, Inc. v. Claimant State of Fla.*, 768 F.2d 1558, 1557 (11th Cir. 1985) ("Taken in context, it is obvious that the court was not using the word insure in the sense of requiring [the shipowner] to be an absolute insurer of all acts by its crew, but in the context of 'to make sure' that [its] responsibilities as owner were fulfilled; that is, exercising due diligence to furnish a competent, trained crew, provided with necessary information").

Amoco also protests that the district court improperly expanded the due diligence requirement to include safeguarding against unknown, latent defects. Amoco contends that, in so doing, the district court overlooked a number of critical factors, such as the fact that Amoco chose a highly reputable shipbuilder and enlisted the expert services of the ABS. According to Amoco, the court also ignored the supertanker's past track record for safe trips and the unforeseeable nature of the steering gear failure. It is apparent to us (though not to Amoco) that the district court both considered and rejected

these factors. Astilleros may have been a reputable shipbuilder, but the fact remains that it built the *Amoco Cadiz* with certain defects. Fully aware of these deficiencies, Amoco failed to correct them purely for economic advantage. The fact that the ABS repeatedly vouched for the *Amoco Cadiz*'s seaworthiness does not relieve Amoco of liability either. When a shipowner has prior knowledge of its vessel's defects, certification by a classification society does not establish the seaworthiness of a ship or the lack of negligence on the part of a shipowner. Amoco's argument that the *Amoco Cadiz* performed well during its four-year history with no suggestion of any malfunction that could have led to the steering gear failure on March 16, 1978, completely ignores the scored rams, excessive oil leaks, and unexplained rudder movements—of which Amoco was well aware—that hinted of future trouble.

Faced with the overwhelming amount of evidence establishing its negligence, Amoco tries to get off the hook by spending a great deal of time and energy in this appeal challenging the district court's use of the "Free-Stroke/Torque Reversal" causation theory as an explanation for the failure of the steering mechanism. Amoco contends that the theory is but a highly imaginative by-product of inference piled upon inference as to what might have happened. Parenthetically, the district court rejected as "speculative" and not supported by the evidence Amoco's theory that the disaster was caused by improperly designed relief values oscillating under pressure, thus producing repeated loads of pressure on the system and subjecting the studs to low-cycle fatigue.

The basic idea of the "Free-Stroke/Torque Reversal" causation theory is that, as a result of Amoco's shoddy maintenance practices, void spaces were present in the steering gear hydraulic system. The presence of these voids effectively impaired the two-sided restraint of the movable parts of the steering gear. A high-pressure surge originated with unintended rudder movement induced by wave action and sea forces acting upon the unrestrained rudder. Sea forces caused the movable parts to develop momentum, thereby creating an intense surge of high pressure transmitted through the hydraulic system that generated a force sufficient to break the studs of the De flange. Adopting this theory, the district court concluded that "a wave generated a pressure peak of whatever magnitude sufficient to rupture an underdesigned, below-specification, badly maintained hydraulic steering system." Id. 1984 A.M.C. at 2165.

A significant weakness in the "Free-Stroke/Torque Reversal" theory is that the expert who proposed it believed that it could account for about 330 to 450 bars of pressure on the studs, while metallurgists testified that 800 bars (Munse) and 1,200 bars (Silkiss) would have been required to rupture them.

Assuming, however, that the evidence does not support the conclusion that Amoco negligence caused the rupture, there was adequate evidence that Amoco negligence caused the grounding and ultimate spill by making the crew unable to get the rudder back under control after the rupture occurred. Consider: the studs failed because Astilleros built them improperly—as the district court found. Amoco's part lay in its failure to correct the ensuing leak. Two principal problems led to the inability to get the rudder back under control, to the point where the *Amoco Cadiz* could use its engine to assist the *Pacific*. First, there was an inability to close the pressure isolation valve because its threads were painted. Second, there was the crud in the hydraulic oil, which a court could properly determine contributed to the failure of the #9 valve to supply essential oil to replenish the system so that after isolation the rudder would have been stable. Even this is an iffy sequence. Stabilizing the rudder would have let the tanker assist the tug, but maybe this would not have been enough. Nonetheless, given deferential review, this sequence is adequate to support the district court's judgment. Thus, even without a "Free-Stroke/Torque Reversal" theory to explain the cause of the wreck, the district court's ultimate conclusion that the grounding of the *Amoco Cadiz* was caused by the negligence of the Amoco parties and Astilleros was not clearly erroneous.

The evidence establishes that the grounding of the *Amoco Cadiz* was a disaster waiting to happen. Amoco was aware of the ship's various problems—any one of which could have led to the failure of the steering system—yet chose to do nothing. The ship's high-pressure hydraulic system needed to be kept fully charged, free of contamination, and properly maintained. Amoco ignored manufacturers' instructions and failed to maintain the system in a reasonable manner, thus creating a foreseeable risk that the disaster would occur. If that were not enough, the oil giant allowed the *Amoco Cadiz* to sail without a backup means of controlling the rudder in the event of a complete failure of the steering system. Apart from the initial failure of the steering gear system, the failure to train and instruct the crew in emergency procedures and to keep the isolation valves in working order are sufficient to hold Amoco liable for the damages caused by the oil spill. Cf. *Cerro Sales Corp. v. Atlantic Marine Enterprises, Inc.*, 403 F.Supp. 562, 567 (S.D.N.YH. 1975) (although equipment functioned properly, ship unseaworthy because crew inadequately trained to handle an emergency).

VI.

Moving beyond causation issues, we next address the district court's denial of the Amoco parties' petition asserting a right to limited liability in the event that they were found to be legally responsible for the grounding of the *Amoco Cadiz*. The Limitation of Liability Act of 1851 ("the Act") was enacted to protect the American maritime industry by severely limiting shipowners' personal liability. It provides:

The liability of the owner of any vessel, whether American or foreign, for any . . . loss . . . done, occasioned, or incurred, without the privity or knowledge of such owner or owners, shall not . . . exceed the amount of value of the interest of such owner in such vessel, and her freight then pending. 46 U.S.C.App. Sec. 183(a)

The district court dismissed the petition to limit liability as to AIOC and Standard on the ground that they were not "owners" of the *Amoco Cadiz* pursuant to the Act. See *In re Oil Spill by the Amoco Cadiz off the Coast of France on March 16, 1978,* 1979 A.M.C. 1018, 1024 (N.D.Ill. 1979). (If the petition had been granted, Amoco's liability would have been limited to $700,000, the value of the *Amoco Cadiz* after sinking.) Amoco argues that the district court incorrectly assumed that only the registered owner of the *Amoco Cadiz*, Amoco Transport, could claim ownership status under the Act. Amoco claims that the term "owner" should be interpreted more liberally. Amoco has misstated the basis of the district court's dismissal. The court interpreted the term "owner" under the Limitation of Liability Act to mean "persons whose degree of possessory, managerial, and operational control, and relationship to the title holder of the vessel justifies the inference of their being 'owners.' " *Amoco Cadiz,* 1979 A.M.C. 1017, 1021 (N.D.Ill. 1979). The court found that AIOC and Standard failed to plead sufficient facts to show that they had "the requisite possessory, managerial, and operational control of the *Amoco Cadiz* to justify even a preliminary finding that they were 'owners.' " Id. at 1024. Instead, they sought to establish ownership status based upon the allegations of the complaints filed in the civil action in which they are defendants. The court rejected this strategy for the reason that, although the complaints "contain language which avers some degree of their ownership of and control over the vessel . . . [s]uch allegations are not incontrovertible admissions of indisputable fact." Id. at 1023.

What the actual facts reveal is that, pursuant to the Consulting and Chartering Agreements between Amoco Transport and AIOC, the latter was brought in to assist and advise Transport with regard to the maintenance and operation of the ship. Ultimate authority for maintenance and operation of the *Amoco Cadiz*, however, remained with Transport alone. In addition, the Consulting Agreement expressly designated AIOC to be an agent of Transport, and not the owner itself. Only Transport had the requisite degree of "possessory, managerial, and operational control" of the *Amoco Cadiz*. Thus, dismissal of the petition to limit liability with regard to Standard and AIOC was appropriate.

Despite Amoco's protests to the contrary, it was not contradictory for the district court to deny Standard and AIOC the right to rely upon the Limitation Act on the theory that they were corporate entities legally separate from Amoco Transport and later, in the damages phase of the proceedings, refuse to recognize separateness between Standard and its subsidiaries. In dismissing the limitation petition, the district court held only that there existed "no set of facts which, if proved, would establish the right of [AIOC and Standard] to limit their liability." *Amoco Cadiz,* 1979 A.M.C. at 1021. Liability for damages is another matter completely. The district court determined liability from facts showing that AIOC—the party in charge of the operation, maintenance, and repair of the *Amoco Cadiz* and the selection of its crew— shared liability for the negligently designed, maintained, and operated steering gear. Standard—the entity that exercised control over AIOC and Transport and that initially was responsible for the design, construction, operation, and management of the *Amoco Cadiz*— was liable for its own negligence as well as that of AIOC with respect to the design, operation, maintenance, repair, and crew training of the *Amoco Cadiz*. These two liability determinations do not conflict with the court's decision to deny these parties the benefits of the Act on the ground that they were not "owners." Even if AIOC and Standard were "owners," they cannot prove their freedom from privity or knowledge of the negligence that caused the grounding. The structure of Standard was so highly integrated, each of its subdivisions was a mere instrumentality of the parent corporation.

Unlike Standard or AIOC, Amoco Transport, the registered owner of the *Amoco Cadiz*, was found to be an "owner" within the meaning of the Limitation Act. Nevertheless, the district court held that Transport was not entitled to limit its liability because it had "privity" and "knowledge," 46 U.S.C.App. Sec. 183(a), of the negligence that caused the casualty. In limitations proceedings, the ultimate burden of proving lack of privity or knowledge is on the shipowner. Amoco attempts to shift focus away from Transport by arguing that a shipowner has privity or knowledge "only when it actually knows of or participates in creating causal negligence or unseaworthiness or where, in the use of ordinary care, it should have known of such conditions." Consolidated Opening Brief of Amoco Parties at 91 (citations omitted).

Not so. Privity or knowledge is not tantamount to actual knowledge or direct causation. All that is needed to deny limitation is that the shipowner "by prior action or inaction set[s] into motion a chain of circumstances which may be a contributing cause even though not the immediate or proximate cause of a casualty." *Tug Ocean Prince, Inc. v. United States*, 584 F.2d 1151, 1158 (2d Cir. 1978), *cert. denied*, 440 U.S. 959 (1979). The recent judicial trend has been to enlarge the scope of activities within the "privity or knowledge" of the shipowner, including imputing to corporations knowledge or privity of lower-level employees, requiring shipowners to exercise an ever-increasing degree of supervision and inspection, imposing a heavy burden on shipowners to prove their lack of privity or knowledge, rendering the shipowner's duty to ensure the seaworthiness of the ship nondelegable.

Transport was not entitled to limit its liability pursuant to the Act because it did not meet its burden of proving its lack of privity or knowledge of the negligence that led to the ship's grounding. Although AIOC's employees might have been directly responsible for the negligent maintenance of the *Amoco Cadiz* and the failure to train the crew properly, their knowledge of the defects in maintenance and training was attributable to Transport, which had a nondelegable duty to ensure a seaworthy vessel and a duty to control and supervise AIOC, its agent.

Two of *Amoco Cadiz*'s inspectors were Transport employees, thus Transport was well aware of the problems with ram scoring, leakage, hydraulic fuel contamination, unwanted rudder movement, and negligent maintenance. Transport's own ship inspectors included descriptions of the *Amoco Cadiz*'s problems in written reports sent to company offices in Bermuda. Instead of seeing to it that essential repairs were made, Transport employees charged with that responsibility kept the vessel out of drydock in order to squeeze more profit out of the time charter. "Neglect to take adequate precautions after a faulty condition has been revealed by a misadventure, or made known by a warning, has been held to amount to privity, if indeed it does not amount to knowledge." *Benedict on Admiralty*, Sec. 5.19 (1990).

VII.

The trial on damages lasted longer than the trial on the merits. More than a year of trial time was spread over about three years—some before Judge McGarr left the bench, some after. Two principal damages opinions span 575 pages, and there were many supplemental opinions and orders. About a dozen issues remain in dispute. Here are the principal rulings still in contention:

- Amoco and Astilleros are jointly and severally liable for all compensable losses, without reduction for the fault attributed to other parties such as Bugsier and the ABS.

- Damages compensate for all proven physical loss but not for diversion of business to other resorts.

- Governmental bodies recover not only for the marginal costs of cleaning up the oil, but also for salaries of persons who would have been employed in any event, but they do not recover the costs of operating ships and planes to the extent these costs would have been incurred in the absence of the spill.

• Private businesses recover through trade associations.

• Prejudgment interest is awarded at the postjudgment rate.

• The shippers recover the value of the oil in pounds sterling, after allowance for shrinkage, and without compound prejudgment interest.

We begin with Amoco's principal argument: that extensive use of hearsay entitled it to a new trial.

A.

During the damages trial the district court admitted a great deal of evidence it characterized as hearsay. It did so because it thought that if the rule were to be applied the trial would be too cumbersome. Yet the hearsay rule applies in all trials—jury and bench, big and small. Fed.R.Evid. 101, 1001. A defendant faced with a single $200 million claim is no less entitled to the protection of the rule than is the person defending against two hundred claims for $1 million each, or two thousand claims for $100,000.

The district court recognized that some of the hearsay was unreliable. It compensated by reducing many claims substantially, an average of 35 percent for the French State and more for the communes. Rough and ready adjustments may be too little to protect the defendants or too great, undercompensating the plaintiffs. (None of the plaintiffs has challenged the reductions on appeal, however.) The Federal Rules of Evidence are statutes, and district judges may not disregard statutes no matter how inconvenient or cumbersome they believe the rules to be. Unless the Rules of Evidence are unconstitutional (which no one suggests), they are to be followed.

Judge McGarr stated that he admitted hearsay because "plaintiffs had no other feasible way to present a case for damages." Extensive hear-

say may be the only way to prove damages if the court must tote up claims, one meter or beach and one commune at a time. Amoco resisted every bill to the last sou, as was its right. An alternative way to proceed would have been to sample the claims of loss, to prove them with admissible evidence, and extrapolate from the sample to the Brittany coast as a whole. Apparently the parties never suggested sampling, even though the *Manual for Complex Litigation* Sec. 21.484 (2d ed., 1985), recommends it, and many opinions, including our own *UNR Industries*, 942 F.2d at 1107, and *Evans v. Evanston*, 941 F.2d 473, 476–77 (7th Cir. 1991), approve the procedure. In a case bristling with expert witnesses, it could not have been too difficult to add a few statisticians. Indeed, as experts may rely on hearsay, Fed.R.Evid. 703, the use of sampling techniques could have compressed the trial and eliminated much of the evidentiary problem at the same time. Alternatively, the court could have inquired how much it would have cost to clean up and restore the coastline using prudent methods and awarded that sum as damages, without regard to the actual cost. If the plaintiffs used inefficient methods, they would have borne the loss; if they were thrifty, they could have kept the surplus. This, too, would have shortened the trial and avoided the hearsay problem. Alas, the parties suggested none of these approaches. This condemned the judge to a morass of detail, including the documents that Amoco contends are hearsay.

Amoco's briefs identify 1,236 exhibits to which timely hearsay objections were raised and overruled. There may be more, but we address only these. Our review of the record supports Amoco's position that many of these documents were hearsay. Amoco contends, without contradiction from the plaintiffs, that the hearsay exhibits underlie approximately 300 million francs of the damages award. Here is the number of documents by the party offering the exhibit [see Table 1]. As this table shows, the communes' records are the lion's share of those objected to. France does not maintain the dis-

[Table 1]

Party Offering Exhibit	Number	Percent of Total
Côtes du Nord Parties	998	80.744
Communes' records	843	68.204
Docs. used by experts	87	7.039
Departments' records	34	2.751
Maps, postcards, photos	32	2.589
Doc. used in cross-x	1	0.081
Unknown	1	0.081
France	192	15.534
Private Businesses	36	2.913
Amoco	10	0.809

tinction among national, state, and local governments that a federal republic such as Germany or the United States recognizes. The Côtes du Nord, a *departement* of France and part of the national government, administers governmental functions in a territory equivalent to a state; communes are local subdivisions of the *departement*. We follow the practice of the parties in treating the communes, the Côtes du Nord, and the Republic of France as if they were distinct entities after the American fashion.

Each commune presented a patterned set of documents: an introduction to the commune (to which Amoco did not object), followed by expense forms dealing with the costs of communal employees, requisitioned staff, food, and other costs entailed in the cleanup. Most of the expense records appear on official forms (*Bordereau de Mandat*, or memorandum of authority to spend) bearing the communal seal and are accompanied by time sheets, bills, receipts, or similar documentation.

We picked the commune of Plougrescant for close examination because its award, approximately 2 million francs before interest, is substantial—more than most but less than seven others (Perros-Guirec, at 3.94 million france, received the largest award among the communes). A sampling of documents from other communes shows that Plougrescant is representative. The following table reports the Côtes du Nord exhibit numbers, the nature of the claim, the amount requested, and the amount awarded. Plougrescant is an agricultural area with fourteen kilometers of coastline (twenty km including adjacent islands). After the coast was cleared of oil, it had to be reconstructed to prevent erosion; moreover, the narrow roads in the area were unsuited to the huge equipment that used them to reach the coast and take away oil-bearing rocks and sand, requiring renovation. The costs of coastline reconstruction and road repair are the largest items of expense [see Table 2].

[Table 2]

Exhibit No.	Nature of Documents	Claim	Allowed
8286	Introduction to commune: Maps, before-and-after pictures of coast	—	—
8287	Overtime pay for local employees: *Bordereau de Mandat* plus explanation (see also CdN 8291)	104,908	—
8288	Payments to requisitioned staff: *Mandat* plus vouchers and explanation	12,441	10,396
8289	Statement of time spent by volunteers	—	—
8290	Food served to army and volunteers: *Mandat* plus explanation by supplier and day	33,757	33,757

8291	Services performed by local employees; official statement plus explanation (no specific monetary claim; award includes overtime from CdN 8287)	—	65,000
8292	Services performed by Mayor and deputies: official statement plus explanation	160,000	160,000
8293	Distances traveled to perform services, by employee: Three official forms, plus separate sheets bearing official seal (no specific monetary claim; summary at CdN 11024-A implies listed figure)	5,031	—
8294	Vehicle repairs: *Mandat* plus bills	23,177	23,177
8295	Equipment purchases: *Mandat* plus bill	6,050	6,050
8296	Depreciation on communal equipment attributable to saltwater corrosion: Paper with official seal showing number of days' exposure (no specific monetary claim)	—	16,897
8297	Rental value of local buildings taken over for use in cleanup: Certificates dated 1985 of ninety-four days' occupancy in 1978, bearing local seal (no specific monetary claim)	—	—
8298	Building repairs: *Mandat* plus bill	2,933	2,933
8299	Road maps	—	—
8300–8304	Road repairs: *Mandats*, bills, estimates of work still to be done as of 1984	1,337,562	650,000
8306–10	Coastline restoration: *Mandats*, official statements with seal, printouts showing vendors, and bills	6,515,193	1,000,000
8312	Lost revenue from reduction in license fees	6,402	6,402
8313	Payments to victims: *Mandats* authorizing municipal payments between Fr. 200 and Fr. 1,000 to identified recipients	17,200	—
8314	Miscellaneous expenses: *Mandats* showing telephone, travel, and other charges	16,999	12,000
Misc.	Economic losses, moral damages, and related matters (supported by expert testimony discussed later)	5,438,663	—
	Total	13,680,316	1,986,612

. . .

These documents fit the definition of hearsay (out of court statements offered for the truth of the matter stated). But Amoco was not without resource when it came to questioning their accuracy and meaning: Marcel Lavanant, a deputy mayor of Plougrescant at the time of the spill, testified to the nature and meaning of these claims and was effectively cross-examined. The district court dramatically cut down the claims for road repairs and coastline restoration after concluding that several things other than the spill from the *Amoco Cadiz* contributed to the need to make these expenses. The pattern for Plougrescant was repeated many times: one witness presented a raft of documents, and Amoco made good use of the opportunity to show that the charges were exaggerated or misattributed.

Although these documents were offered for their truth, whether they were inadmissible as hearsay depends on the many exceptions to the hearsay rule. In particular, Fed.R.Evid. 803(8) permits a court to receive "records, reports, statements, or data compilations, in any form, of public offices or agencies, setting forth (A) the activities of the office or agency, or (B) matters observed pursuant to the duty imposed by law as to which matters there was a duty to report." Most of the documents submitted by Plougresant fit Rule 803(8)(A) or (B); some come within both. The *mandats* are official expense records that commune maintained independently of the litigation. Although some supplementary documents (e.g., CdN 8293, 8297) were prepared especially for use in this litigation, they remain reports of public activities. The public-document exception to the hearsay rule does not contain the requirement of the business records exception (Rule 803(6)) that the documents be kept in the course of a regularly conducted activity. Because these documents come within both letter and spirit of Rule 803(8) (founded as it is on the belief that public employees are generally reliable), we conclude that they were admissible.

Some of the documents offered by communes other than Plougrescant are not admissible under Rule 803(8). For example, CdN 8034, offered by Le Roche Derrien, is a handwritten list of numbers. None of these inadmissible documents appears to be responsible for any substantial part of the award; all are swamped by the cuts the district court made in the claims supported by admissible evidence.

We recognize that some courts treat Rule 803(8) as avoiding only the first-level hearsay problem—that is, as excusing the presence of the documents' authors. If the statements would be hearsay even were the author present in court, then Rule 803(8) does not apply, on this view. Nothing in either the text or the history of Rule 803(8) supports an approach that would make the rule essentially useless—for the bureaucrat who fills out a governmental form usually incorporates information furnished by others. Rule 803(8) has a long common-law history behind it, including cases such as *Chesapeake & Delaware Canal Co. v. United States*, 250 U.S. 123, 39 S.Ct. 407, 63 L.Ed. 889 (1919), that allow the introduction of governmental receipt and disbursement records of the sort the communes (and other governmental parties) presented. The Advisory Committee's notes endorse cases of this kind, and this subsection of Rule 803 was enacted without change or comment by Congress. Courts that treat Rule 803(8) as limited to the first-level hearsay problem rely on a negative implication of Rule 805, which says that "[h]earsay included within hearsay is not excluded . . . if each part of the combined statements conforms with an exception to the hearsay rule provided in these rules." Rule 805 does not say (or even imply) that none of the other exceptions deals with more than a single level. Rule 803(8) is a multilevel exception, in the footsteps of its common-law precursors.

This conclusion implies that the thirty-four documents offered as records of the Côtes du Nord itself were properly admitted. The thirty-two maps, postcards, and photographs were inadmissible on this theory (and the plaintiffs offer no other for them), but Amoco does not attribute any injury to their presence. So too with the one document used in cross-examination and the one with an unknown use. Of the other documents offered by the Côtes du Nord parties, only the eighty-seven used by expert witnesses remain for discussion. These are not independently admissible—but then experts' opinions need not depend on the admissibility of the evidence they use. Fed. R.Evid. 703. The question is whether the data are "of a type reasonably relied upon by experts in the particular field." Amoco's brief does not explain why these documents fall outside Rule 703. We have examined a sample of them and find that they are the sort of documents reasonably used by these experts.

Although France itself introduced fewer documents than did the Côtes du Nord parties, many of its exhibits are summaries of hundreds, even thousands, of claims, and the award to France is more than four times the award to all of the Côtes du Nord parties combined. France offered two principal categories of documents. (1) France established a program for reimbursing persons (such as oyster farmers) injured by the oil. It furnished these persons with forms to complete. One exhibit summarizes these forms; the head of the governmental body that supervised the oyster destruction program testified about the scope of the program and the way in which these forms were completed and compiled; two oyster farmers also testified at trial to facilitate understanding of the claims. (2) France collected documents showing the number of hours its own employees devoted to cleaning up the mess and presented these through summary exhibits. Public officials testified to the manner in which these documents were created and the significance they had. There are other kinds of documents among France's exhibits (some, for example, reflect negotiations between France and the United Kingdom concerning reimbursement for British help in the cleanup, and some are intra-government memos), but none of these poses significant independent problems.

So far as we can tell, all of the French exhibits are—or, what is the same thing, summarize, see *AMPAT/Midwest, Inc. v. Illinois Tool Works, Inc.*, 896 F.2d 1035, 1045 (7th Cir. 1990)—documents generated or collected by the national government in the course of its public functions. They are admissible under Rule 803(8). Admissibility need not imply utility, and Amoco insists that the trial was unfair even if the documents were technically admissible. France established by these documents that it incurred particular obligations or paid specified claims. Whether the charges reflected in these documents are attributable to the spill from the *Amoco Cadiz* is a distinct question. France addressed that subject with live testimony from public officials (admirals, ministers, and the like), whom Amoco was free to cross-examine. Amoco had, moreover, many other ways to test the connection between the exhibits and the spill. Amoco had representatives on the scene monitoring the cleanup from the start; its insurer took part in many of the early decisions concerning the nature and scope of operations. For years after the spill, Amoco sent personnel to Brittany to assess the measures being taken and the residual harm. The assistance of these persons, coupled with Amoco's ability to cross-examine the plaintiffs' many witnesses, allowed Amoco to investigate causal questions on which the documents were not illuminating. The district court's procedure, taken as a whole, was calculated to protect Amoco's interests— indeed, the extensive percentage reductions may have done so at the expense of the legitimate interests of the plaintiffs.

Other sources also helped the district court assess the significance of the documents. France provided most of the documents underlying its exhibits to Amoco before trial. Touche Ross and Co. reviewed the documents on behalf of Amoco. It concluded that 72 percent of France's claims were actually and reasonably incurred in response to the spill and were adequately supported. Touche Ross found that France proved expenses of some 316 million francs, about 40 million francs more than the district court awarded to France in damages.

We arrive at the documents concerning the private parties' claims. Rule 803(8) does not support the admission of these documents, and neither does Rule 803(6), the business records exception to the hearsay rule. Few of these documents were prepared or maintained in the regular course of business. See *United States v. Ramsey*, 785 F.2d 184, 192–93 (7th Cir. 1986). Yet this is of no concern if the authors of the documents appeared as witnesses, providing the same information orally. The Beganton Parties, comprising many of the private claimants, filed a brief asserting that all of the private claimants in question appeared personally. Amoco's reply brief does not mention this, and we treat the subject as waived. The upshot is that the use of documentary evidence does not invalidate any portion of the damages awarded in this case.

B.

After the *Amoco Cadiz* ran aground, the French Navy served Amoco with a *mise en demeure*—official demand to remove the oil or accept responsibility for it. An *arrêt* to similar effect was served by the Maritime Prefect for the Côtes du Nord. Amoco answered through its insurance representative that it could not undertake the cleanup: "The owner will not be able to provide the personnel or equipment to clean up a spill of this size. Thus on behalf of the owner, I ask the French Government to commence the cleanup. . . . [R]easonable costs for reasonable actions agreed by owners and Government will be accepted by owners." The French State invoked PLAN POLMAR, its contingency plan for an accident of this kind. The Navy, the Army, local officials, and private parties set to work. Amoco lent no aid but did consult with the persons in charge.

Needless to say, the parties have not agreed on what "reasonable costs" for the work are. France subscribes to the International Convention on Civil Liability for Oil Pollution Damage, signed in Brussels in November 1969 and implemented by French domestic law in 1975. This Civil Liability Convention establishes a form of absolute liability but also sets a cap on recovery. At the time the *Amoco Cadiz* sank, the cap was 77 million francs (approximately $16 million at the rate of exchange in 1978). The message from Amoco's representative volunteering to pay reasonable costs also referred to the maximum set by the Civil Liability Convention. In April 1978 Amoco paid 77 million francs to create a fund under the terms of that Convention, transferring control to the Commercial Court of Brest. This fund remains unclaimed. France and the other plaintiffs disdained their remedies under the Civil Liability Convention in favor of these suits in the United States, in-

voking Article 1382 of the French Civil Code, which provides: "Every act of a man which causes injury to another obliges the one by whose fault it occurred to give redress." (The parties agreed on the accuracy of this and other translations from the French.)

Amoco denies that it was at "fault," a subject we covered in Part V. It also invokes the principle of *gratuité des services publics*, known in the United States as the "free public services doctrine." In both nations, courts decline to require tortfeasors to compensate the government for the cost of services (such as police protection or firefighting) that a public body supplies. There is at least one dissenting voice in France; recently the Tribunal de Grande Instance de Cherbourg ordered the owner of a vessel that ran aground in 1987 to compensate the French State for the costs of cleaning up oil under PLAN POLMAR. Case No. 511/88 (Sept. 3, 1990). This order may depend on a statute enacted in 1983. At all events, this judgment has not yet been reviewed, and it is prudent to assume that the principle of *gratuité des services publics* remains the law of France. The district judge asserted that French courts would not apply this principle in big cases, but we do not believe that the law of France varies with the stakes of the case or the wealth of the litigants. Here, as in every other instance, we reject categorically the proposition that rules of law do not govern cases in which injuries are large or pockets deep.

The plaintiffs offer two principal responses to the principle of *gratuité des services publics*. One is that the French State may recover damages for injury to its proprietary interests. The oil spilled in its territorial waters and fouled the coast, which is national property up to the line of the extreme highest tide. The bulk of the expenses were incurred in protecting and restoring public property. Amoco concedes that France is entitled to compensation for such costs but protests that the plaintiffs failed adequately to separate the costs of protecting proprietary interests from other expenses, and that in all events this rationale does not support an award to the Côtes du Nord parties, which do not own the water and coast. The first point is true but may not matter; the latter point is dubious. The Côtes du Nord parties spent to protect their own property inland of the high-water mark. (Recall that the award to Plougrescant, discussed in Part VII.A, was principally justified by the need to reconstruct the coastline to prevent erosion and to rebuild public roads damaged in the process.) Moreover, *departements* such as the Côtes du Nord and Finistere are part of a unitary government in France; it may not be useful to separate property of the French State from property of the Côtes du Nord parties for this purpose.

Let us suppose that the sovereign's entitlement to compensation for the costs of protecting and restoring public property is insufficient to support the entire award. This takes us to the plaintiffs' second main response to the principle of *gratuité des services publics*. This principle governs only when the legislature has been silent. The United States has reserved the rule in oil pollution cases by Sec. 311 of the Federal Water Pollution Control Act of 1972, 33 U.S.C. Sec. 1321(f)(1). The plaintiffs submit that France has done likewise by Article 16 of the Law of July 7, 1976. This national statute provides:

In the event of a failure or accident at sea occurring to any ship, aircraft, rig, or platform transporting or having on board harmful, dangerous substances or oil, and capable of causing serious and imminent danger likely to impair the coastline or allied interests as defined in article II-4 of the Brussels Convention of 29 November 1969 on intervention on the high seas in the event of an accident leading to or capable of leading to oil pollution, the owner of the said ship, aircraft, rig, or platform may be served notice to take any and all measures necessary to bring an end to such dangers.

In the event this notice has no effect or does not produce the effect expected within the deadline set forth or automatically in the event of an emergency, the State may order the necessary measures to be carried out at the expense of the owner or may collect an amount equal to the cost thereof from the said owner.

The parties disagree profoundly about the meaning of this statute. The plaintiffs maintain that if an "accident at sea"—the malfunction of the *Amoco Cadiz*'s steering gear and the grounding occurred "at sea"—releases oil, then the French State may undertake (and charge for) any "necessary measures" on both land and sea. Amoco insists that the statute authorizes only measures that themselves occur "at sea," that the statute authorizes only actions within the scope of "article II-4 of the Brussels Convention of 29 November 1969 on intervention on the high seas," and that at all events the statute authorizes collection only from the "owner," Amoco Transport.

Amoco's submission that France should have sued Amoco Transport raises a subject we considered in Part VI. For purposes of this case, Amoco Corporation and its marine subsidiaries are a single entity. Amoco's other points merge into the contention that Art. 16 of the Law of July 7, 1976, does nothing more than implement a second convention signed in Brussels in November 1969. The Civil Liability Convention, Amoco submits, covers injury caused by oil that reaches shore. The other convention, the International Convention Relating to Intervention on the High Seas in Cases of Oil Pollution Casualties, permits nations to act outside their territorial waters when they fear that oil released in international waters poses a danger to territorial waters. If Article 16 is, as Amoco contends, nothing more than domestic implementation of this second Brussels convention of November 1969, it does not authorize awards for oil that drifts ashore.

Both sides invoke the "plain meaning" of Article 16. Whatever meaning the Article has is not "plain." Meaning depends on what the phrase "as defined in article II-4 of the Brussels Convention of 29 November 1969 on intervention on the high seas in the event of an accident leading to or capable of leading to oil pollution" is doing in this statute. Amoco believes that this phrase links the scope of the statute to the Intervention on the High Seas Convention. It proffers legislative history showing, among other things, that Report No. 2374 in the French National Assembly on the pending bill (*projet de loi*) confirms that this language refers to the "Brussels Convention, of November 29, 1969 on the intervention on the high seas in the event of an accident leading to or possibly leading to oil pollution, and not to the other Brussels Convention of the same date, which deals with private law, on the civil liability of the shipowners." Plaintiffs concede that the reference in the statute to the Brussels Convention is to the Intervention on the High Seas Convention but respond that this reference is included only to define the term "allied interests." On this reading, the first paragraph of Article 16 would be punctuated:

In the event of a failure or accident at sea occurring to any ship . . . transporting or having on board . . . oil, and capable of causing serious and imminent danger likely to impair the coastline or allied interests (as defined in article II-4 of the Brussels Convention of 29 November 1969 on intervention on the high seas in the event of an accident leading to or capable of leading to oil pollution), the owner of the said ship . . . may be served notice to take any and all measures necessary to bring an end to such dangers.

Each side presented an expert of the highest skill and repute supporting its interpretation. Two considerations lead us to believe that the interpretation favored by the French State is plausible. First, Article 16 refers to Article II-4 of the Intervention on the High Seas Convention, not to the entire convention, and Article II-4 defines the term "related interests." Second, France acceded to the Intervention on the High Seas Convention by Law No. 71-1002 of December 16, 1971. *Journal Officiel de la Republique Française* 12323 (Dec. 17, 1971). The Law of July 7, 1976, is redundant if designed to serve only the function Amoco attributes to it.

If all of the litigants were private parties, we would need to decide whether this understanding of the law is correct. But the Republic of France appears in this court and assures us that

Article 16 applies to oil that reaches shore. The French State has taken this position since the moment it served the mise en demeure in 1978, and it has reiterated the view in domestic disputes. The French State sought and obtained recovery under Art. 16 (as amended in 1983) in Case No. 511/88 (Tribunal de Grande Instance de Cherbourg, Sept. 3, 1990), in which the ship that released oil was flying the French flag. A court of the United States owes substantial deference to the construction France places on its domestic law. Courts of this nation routinely accept plausible constructions of laws by the agencies charged with administering them. That the interpretation may occur in (or in anticipation of) litigation does not authorize the court to disregard the agency's conclusions. We conclude that Article 16 suffices to plug any gaps in the plaintiffs' claims as proprietors of the waters and coastline, and thus to authorize an award for the costs public agencies incurred in responding to the spill.

C.

The French military took charge of the cleanup under PLAN POLMAR. More than 40 vessels, with 4,100 sailors, devoted some 600 sea days to the task; naval aircraft spent 520 hours in the air; 40,000 men from the Army led the effort ashore. Employees of the communes and the Côtes du Nord itself devoted many days to the task. The French State and the Côtes du Nord parties requested compensation for the salaries of these personnel and the costs of operating their equipment.

The district court seems to have handled these requests inconsistently. It awarded the plaintiffs the salaries of all employees devoted to the cleanup, despite Amoco's protest that the plaintiffs would have incurred the same costs had there been no spill. The court awarded the French State only the incremental cost of operating vessels and planes; it declined to award the expenses France would have borne had the equipment been operated in a normal way. The plaintiffs received approximately 30.5 million francs for personnel and operation of equipment; the district court excluded 3.5 million francs as the operational cost that would have been borne had there been no accident. Each side appeals from the adverse portion of this decision.

Our question is one of French law, once more under Article 1382 of the Civil Code. Does that law allow the victim of a wrong to recover as damages costs of salaries for employees devoted to the cure and other expenses that the victim would have borne in any event ("committed costs")? There can be no doubt that if France had hired the British Navy to clean up the coast, it could recover from Amoco the payments to the United Kingdom—even though the United Kingdom would have maintained its ships and paid its sailors anyway. So too Britain could recover if in the future it should hire the French Navy to aid in spills on the British side of the English Channel. Any victim of a tort must decide whether to deal with the injury by hiring assistance in the market or by devoting its own resources (including the time of its employees) to the subject. The problem is no different in principle from IBM's decision to make its own memory chips rather than to buy them from Texas Instruments. Internal production is costly—the cost is the opportunity given up (such as the option to sell the chips in the market, or to release the time of its employees for other tasks).

Two cases interpret the Civil Code to allow instrumentalities of the French State to recover the costs of salaries paid to employees who repair injuries done by a negligent person. In one case the Cour de Cassation allowed the French Electricity Board to recover the wages of employees who repaired electrical lines that had been damaged by a negligent pilot. *Electricité de France v. Malfray*, No. 75-10.519 (Cour de Cassation, June 23, 1976). In another the Court of Appeal awarded the French Telecommunications Administration the salaries and equipment costs incurred in monitoring the telephone lines of a person who fraudulently

obtained service. *France Telecom v. Demange*, No. 1815/88 (Cour d'Appel de Montpellier, Dec. 5, 1988). Amoco seeks to distinguish these decisions on the ground that they involve commercial operations of the government, but it is not easy to see why this should matter. Underlying Amoco's submission is the principle, well established in French law, that a victim of a tort may not make a profit on the transaction. Compensation for committed costs, on Amoco's view, is a forbidden profit, a position that does not distinguish commercial operations of the government from any operations.

One could say—Amoco's economic expert witness did say—that there is a difference between proprietary and strictly governmental operations because the proprietary arms of the government have other things to do. If the workers of the Electricity Board were not repairing the lines damaged by the plane, they could be constructing new lines; if the staff of the phone company were not tracing a freeloader's calls, they could be hooking up new phones. But if the sailors of the French Navy were not skimming oil, what would they be doing? Invading some neighbor? On this view governmental operations are different because the opportunity costs of their employees and equipment are zero. If they were not being used in the cleanup, they would have no productive use at all.

Some of the military personnel—for example, civil engineers—had clear alternative uses. Employees of the communes presumably were delivering local services, which were interrupted to free up staff for the cleanup. Military personnel deter misconduct (terrorism as well as aggression) during peacetime, and their ability to do this is diminished if their time is consumed by other pursuits. Too, we must reckon with the possibility that the risk of oil spills induced the French State to maintain larger forces than it needed for strictly military purposes. A navy has many uses: not only offense and defense, but also clearing channels for civilian vessels, the rescue of vessels in storms, and removing oil from the waters. When deciding whether to have sixty ships or only fifty-five, France may take into account these nonmilitary uses. In the short run—given that the *Amoco Cadiz* is spilling oil—the costs of the ships and sailors are committed. Costs fixed in the short run may be variable in the longer run, and this longer run is the one that matters. Consider the parallel to Bugsier, which operated the *Pacific* and a fleet of other tugs around the world. Once the *Amoco Cadiz*'s steering failed, the *Pacific* could attempt rescue at close to zero marginal cost. It would not follow that, had the rescue succeeded, Bugsier would be entitled to no more than the cost of oil burned in running the tug's engines harder. Assets such as the *Pacific* must be purchased and maintained on station at substantial "committed" cost, and compensation in the event they prevent a wreck must cover the entire committed cost—not only the salaries and other expenses during the rescue, but also the costs of keeping the tug on station during times of calm. France and the communes requested and received only the expense of salaries and equipment during the cleanup; they did not seek the costs of holding men and material at the ready. Under French law, they are entitled to this much. On the French State's appeal, we instruct the district court to add 3.5 million francs to the award. (This addition is as of 1978, with interest to be computed according to our subsequent discussion.)

. . .

VIII.

To sum up: All decisions on jurisdiction and liability are affirmed. The computation of damages is affirmed with the following exceptions:

1. France is entitled to an additional 3.5 million francs (before interest) for the expense of the cleanup.

2. L'Union des Commerçants et Artisans de Tregastel and L'Union Pleumeuroise pour la Defense des Interets des Commerçants et Artisans lack

standing, and the awards in their favor are vacated.

3. The award in favor of PIL shall be made in dollars, and the 0.5 percent deduction for shrinkage shall be eliminated.

4. The French plaintiffs are entitled to compound prejudgment interest at a rate of 11.9 percent per annum from January 1, 1980, implying a multiplier of 3.3162.

5. PIL is entitled to simple prejudgment interest at the rate of 12.31 percent per annum from March 16, 1978.

The case is remanded for the entry of judgment in accordance with this option.

Questions

1. Why was an oil spill off the coast of France litigated in Chicago?

2. Why was Amoco unable to use the Limitation of Liability Act?

3. How was Amoco negligent in the operation of the ship?

4. Why did this case take fourteen years to resolve? Is there a better way to handle casualties like this?

Selected Provisions of the Oil Pollution Act of 1990, 33 U.S.C. 2700 et seq.

Title I—Oil Pollution Liability and Compensation

. . . (23) "oil" means oil of any kind or in any form, including, but not limited to, petroleum, fuel oil, sludge, oil refuse, and oil mixed with wastes other than dredged spoil, but does not include petroleum, including crude oil or any fraction thereof, which is specifically listed or designated as a hazardous substance under subparagraphs (A) through (F) or section 101(14) of the Comprehensive Environmental Response, Compensation, and Liability Act (42 U.S.C 9601) and which is subject to the provisions of that Act;

Sec. 1001. Elements of Liability

(a) In General—Notwithstanding any other provision or rule of law, and subject to the provisions of this Act, each responsible party for a vessel or a facility from which oil is discharged, or which poses the substantial threat of a discharge of oil, into or upon the navigable waters or adjoining shorelines, or the exclusive economic zone is liable for the removal costs and damages specified in subsection (b) that result from such incident.

(b) Covered Removal Costs and Damages—

(1) Removal Costs—The removal costs referred to in subsection (a) are:

(A) all removal costs incurred by the United States, a State, or an Indian tribe...

(B) any removal costs incurred by any person for acts taken by the person which are consistent with the National Contingency Plan.

(2) Damages—The damages referred to in subsection (a) are the following:

(A) Natural Resources—Damages for injury to, destruction of, loss of, or loss of use of, natural resources, including the reasonable costs of assessing the damage, which shall be recoverable by a United States trustee, a State trustee, an Indian tribe trustee, or a foreign trustee.

(B) Real or Personal Property—Damages for injury to, or economic losses resulting from destruction of, real of personal property, which shall be recoverable by a claimant who owns or leases that property.

(C) Subsistence Use—Damages for loss of subsistence use of natural resources, which shall be recoverable by any claimant who so uses natural resources which have been injured, destroyed, or lost, without regard to the ownership or management of the resources.

(D) Revenues—Damages equal to the net loss of taxes, royalties, rents, fees, or net profit shares due to the injury, destruction, or loss of real property, personal property, or natural resources, which shall be recoverable by the Government of the United States, a State, or a political subdivision thereof.

(E) Profits and Earning Capacity—Damages equal to the loss of profits or impairment of earning capacity due to the injury, destruction, or loss of real property, personal property, or natural resources, which shall be recoverable by any claimant.

(F) Public Services—Damages for net costs of providing increased or additional public services during or after removal activities, including protection from fire, safety, or health hazards, caused by a discharge of oil, which shall be recoverable by a State, or a political subdivision of a State.

Sec. 1003. Defenses to Liability

(a) Complete Defenses—A responsible party is not liable for removal costs or damages under section 1002 if the responsible party establishes, by a preponderance of the evidence, that the discharge or substantial threat of a discharge of oil and the resulting damages or removal costs were caused solely by:

(1) an act of God;

(2) an act of war;

(3) an act or omission of a third party.

Sec. 1004. Limits on Liability

(a) General Rule—Except as otherwise provided in this section, the total of the liability of a responsible party under section 1002 and any removal costs incurred by, or on behalf of, the responsible party, with respect to each incident shall not exceed—

(1) for a tank vessel, the greater of—

(A) $1,200 per gross ton; or

(B)(i) in the case of a vessel greater than 3,000 gross tons, $10,000,000; or (ii) in the case of a vessel of 3,000 gross tons or less, $2,000,000;

(2) for any other vessel, $600 per gross ton or $500,000, whichever is greater;

(3) for an offshore facility except a deepwater port, the total of all removal costs plus $75,000,000; and

(4) for any onshore facility and a deepwater port, $350,000,000.

(c) Exceptions

(1) Acts of Responsible Party—Subsection (a) does not apply if the incident was proximately caused by:

(A) gross negligence or willful misconduct of, or

(B) the violation of an applicable Federal safety, construction, or operating regulation by, the responsible party, an agent or employee of the responsible party, or a person acting pursuant to a contractual relationship with the responsible party.

Sec. 1006. (d) Measure of Damages—

(1) In General—The measure of natural resource damages under section 1002(b)(2)(A) is—

(A) the cost of restoring, rehabilitating, replacing, or acquiring the equivalent of, the damaged natural resources;

(B) the diminution in value of those natural resources pending restoration; plus

(C) the reasonable cost of assessing those damages.

Sec. 1016. Financial Responsibility

(a) Requirement—The responsible party for—

(1) any vessel over 300 gross tons (except a non-self-propelled vessel that does not carry oil as cargo or fuel) using any place subject to the jurisdiction of the United States; or

(2) any vessel using the waters of the exclusive economic zone to transship or lighter oil destined for a place subject to the jurisdiction of the United States; shall establish and maintain, in accordance with regulations promulgated by the Secretary, evidence of financial responsibility sufficient to meet the maximum amount of liability to which, in the case of a tank vessel, the responsible party could be subject under section 1004 (a)(1) or (d) of this Act, or to which, in the case of any other vessel, the responsible party could be subjected under section 1004 (a)(2) or (d), in a case where the responsible party would be entitled to limit liability under that section. If the responsible party owns or operates more than one vessel, evidence of financial responsibility need be established only to meet the amount of the maximum liability applicable to the vessel having the greatest maximum liability.

(b) Sanctions

(1) Withholding Clearance—The Secretary of the Treasury shall withhold or revoke the clearance required by section 4197 of the Revised Statutes of the United States of any vessel subject to this section that does not have the evidence of financial responsibility required for the vessel under this section.

(2) Denying Entry to or Detaining Vessels—The Secretary may—

(A) deny entry to any vessel to any place in the United States, or to the navigable waters, or

(B) detain at the place, any vessel that, upon request, does not produce the evidence of financial responsibility required for the vessel under this section.

(3) Seizure of Vessel—Any vessel subject to the requirements of this section which is found in the navigable waters without the necessary evidence of financial responsibility for the vessel shall be subject to seizure by and forfeiture to the United States.

TABLE OF CASES

INDEX

About the Author

DENNIS W. NIXON is Associate Professor and Graduate Program Coordinator, Department of Marine Affairs, University of Rhode Island. In addition to practicing and teaching marine law, he has served as a maritime advisor to various international, federal, and state agencies, and has lectured and published widely on maritime affairs.